SEVENTH EDITION

Teaching Science Through Discovery

Arthur A. Carin

Professor Emeritus
Queens College

Merrill, an imprint of
Macmillan Publishing Company
New York

Maxwell Macmillan Canada
Toronto

Maxwell Macmillan International
New York   Oxford   Singapore   Sydney

Macmillan Publishing Company
866 Third Avenue
New York, NY 10022

Macmillan Publishing Company is part of the Maxwell Communication Group of Companies.

Maxwell Macmillan Canada, Inc.
1200 Eglinton Avenue East, Suite 200
Don Mills, Ontario M3C 3N1

Library of Congress Cataloging-in-Publication Data

Carin, Arthur A.
    Teaching science through discovery / Arthur A. Carin. — 7th ed.
        p.   cm.
    Includes bibliographical references and index.
    ISBN 0-02-319385-9
    1. Science—Study and teaching (Elementary) I. Title.
LB1585.C28   1993
372.3'5044 —dc20   92–20706
                                            CIP

Cover photo: David Young-Wolff/PhotoEdit
Editor: Linda James Scharp
Developmental Editor: Molly Kyle
Production Editor: Mary Harlan
Art Coordinator: Peter A. Robison
Photo Editor: Anne Vega
Text Designer: Jill E. Bonar
Cover Designer: Robert Vega
Production Buyer: Pamela D. Bennett

This book was set in Souvenir by Carlisle Communications, Ltd., and was printed and bound by Arcata Graphics/Halliday. The cover was printed by Lehigh Press, Inc.

Photo credits: All photos copyrighted by the individuals or companies listed. Ben Chandler/Macmillan, 2, 193; Kevin Fitzsimons/Macmillan, 11, 27; Arthur A. Carin, 17, 131, 256; Gale Zucker 18, 190; Robin Yocum, 21; Robert Finken, 23, 46, 62, 72, 78, 104, 122, 178, 205, 216, 222, 234, 236, 275, 306; Anne Vega/Macmillan, 38, 128, 333; Charles Quinlan, 43; Exploratorium, 71; Michael Siluk, 83, 96, 112, 182, 221, 270, 313, 327, A-2; David Strickler, 92; Harvey Phillips, 100, 290; Barbara Schwartz/Macmillan, 103; Barbara C. Schwartz, 211; Russell Photography, 135; Mark Madden/Macmillan, 123, 142; Jean-Claude LeJeune, 146, 147, 246; Marcia Jones/Springfield Schools, 229; Columbus Public Schools, 240; Mark E. Gibson, 252; Center of Science and Industry, 261; Tom Tondee, 270; Bruce Johnson/Macmillan, 297; Jim Cronk, 323; Macmillan, 309.

Printing: 2 3 4 5 6 7 8 9   Year: 3 4 5 6 7

PREFACE

The seventh edition of *Teaching Science Through Discovery* has been extensively revised, while retaining the popular organizational format of the previous editions. This text is designed to introduce novice teachers to the specialized content, teaching strategies, and activities necessary to teach science and technology today. At the same time, experienced teachers will find the increased emphasis on helping children construct their own scientific and technological concepts and processes a useful framework for making effective instructional decisions.

Although several approaches to teaching and learning science/technology are described in this book, emphasis is placed on a minds-on/hands-on, activity-based approach called *guided discovery teaching/learning*. Practical, classroom-tested ideas are presented on planning, organizing, managing, and assessing an effective guided discovery science program for preschool, elementary, middle and junior high school classrooms. Included are step-by-step guidelines for creating lessons that take advantage of new ideas in science teaching and current scientific and technological research.

New to the Seventh Edition

- updated, expanded coverage of the latest research developments in cognitive psychology from constructivist theorists applied to teaching science using the guided discovery approach
- suggestions for weaving science/technology themes into activities that affect the daily lives of children to encourage development of a genuine appreciation for science
- application of innovative national science projects to specific classroom teaching and learning methods
- "Chart a New Course," a feature found in most chapters, offering ideas and strategies from successful teachers across the country that can be applied or adapted to enable children to *experience* science in a meaningful, interactive way
- extensive, practical applications of cooperative group learning strategies to science teaching

- symbols in the activities section (Part II) indicating whether an activity is most suitable for use as a teacher-directed, individual student-conducted, or cooperative group activity
- more activities involving topics that hold high interest for children, including the environment, ecology, human anatomy and physiology, and health and nutrition
- informal "Quickie Starter" activities for physical, life, and earth sciences to help children achieve early successes and build their enthusiasm for learning about science and technology
- the consistent format for the activities that allows the teacher to identify appropriate activities to match lesson concepts and instructional goals

Companion textbooks include:

- *Teaching Modern Science,* sixth edition, a paperback version of Part I of this book, and
- *Guided Discovery Activities for Elementary School Science,* third edition, a paperback version of Part II.

/// FROM THE AUTHOR

I am certain you will find this text a valuable resource as you become an even more competent, confident decision-maker. I strongly encourage you to adapt these strategies and apply these concepts in ways that are meaningful to both you and your students. It is my hope that it will empower you to teach science to your students in your unique classroom situation. I wish you much success as you experience the joy of seeing your students construct and broaden their science knowledge and grow in their appreciation of this marvelous world.

While permission is granted to reproduce any parts of the guided discovery activities that your students can use directly in the classroom, activities may not be further distributed or sold without the written authorization from the author and the publisher.

ACKNOWLEDGMENTS

Many people deserve thanks for helping bring this thoroughly revised edition to fruition. The following Macmillan Publishing Company personnel were invaluable: Jeffrey W. Johnston and Linda James Scharp, who supplied the administrative leadership and who went to bat for me on so many matters; Molly Kyle and Mary Harlan, who handled all the details from "inception to birth;" Lucinda Ann Peck and Carol Driver, excellent copy editors; Anne Vega, photo editor; and David Faherty, education marketing manager. New illustrations were prepared by Precision Graphics.

Many of my colleagues have unselfishly given information and materials that enrich this textbook: Richard W. Barnes, Bountiful, Utah; Rodger W. Bybee, Associate Director of BSCS Innovative Science Education and author of *Science for Life and Living: Integrating Science, Technology, and Health;* Frances R. Curcio, Queens College of the City University of New York; Robert M. Jones, University of Houston—Clear Lake; and Senta A. Raizen, Director of the National Center for Improving Science Education, a Project of THE NETWORK, Inc.

Special thanks are extended to Joel Bass, Sam Houston State University, who made significant contributions to chapters 1 and 2. I would also like to thank the reviewers, namely, Joel Bass, Sam Houston State University; William W. Cobern, Arizona State University West; George T. Ladd, Boston College; and K. Sylvia Livingston, University of Wisconsin, Eau Claire.

My wife, my adult children, and my son-in law have again supplied encouragement, ideas, and support during the entire research, writing, and production stages of book development. Frequent visits with my three-year-old grandson Anders increased my awareness of the need for an up-to-date, easy-to-use science methods text for his future teachers. His eager, curious mind deserves teachers who are prepared to bring him a minds-on/hands-on guided discovery experience. I hope this publication can be of some assistance in that effort.

CONTENTS

TEACHING MODERN SCIENCE   **1**

GUIDED DISCOVERY ACTIVITIES   A–1

/// SECTION 2   Life Sciences and Technology   A–89

Teaching Modern Science

Modern Science does not give us truth; it offers a way for us to interpret events of nature and to cope with the world.[1]

Finding out where mountains come from and developing a way to travel around them are pursuits of science and technology, respectively. The study of science proposes explanations for "what is" in the natural world, whereas the study of technology provides solutions to human problems of adaptation. They go together like a hand in a glove and will have a mounting impact on our social and personal environment.[2]

Building Scientific and Technological Literacy

How do modern science and technology influence science learning and teaching?

What does it mean to teach science to children? What you choose to teach in science and how you teach it will be influenced by your views of both science and children. Science is an activity that can enrich the lives of children as well as adults. Youngsters of all ages are curious and enjoy observing and exploring the natural world. The earlier we encourage this curiosity, the better.

Not only is science enjoyable for children, but scientific literacy is an essential part of modern life.[3] Various national groups have built a strong case for beginning to develop scientific and technological literacy in the earliest grades. Science, its methods of developing reliable knowledge, and its applications in technology are at the heart of modern civilization. The invention and discovery of new products and procedures are being made at an exponential rate. Yet, even as we enjoy the benefits of science and technology, science and technology are making new demands on society. Problems related to issues such as health care, energy, natural resources, environmental quality, and population dynamics, increasingly demand our

attention and our best thinking. As a teacher, you must prepare children for a world vastly different from the one in which you grew up. In the 21st century, this country will need many more citizens with special training in science and technology. Perhaps only a small percent of your children will choose to be scientists, engineers, physicians, or technicians, but all of them will need more science to understand their rapidly changing world. Your own enthusiasm and encouragement in teaching can make the difference in your students' present and future encounters with science.

This chapter will examine the spirit, structure, and beauty of science, the attitudes that characterize scientists and the processes of investigation they employ, and what it means for children to do science. We will also examine the impact of science and technology on modern society and what that suggests for elementary school science.

Scientists and science educators today believe that approaches to learning and teaching science should basically parallel the procedures and attitudes scientists use in doing science.

This implies a "minds-on/hands-on" approach to elementary school science, a phrase that we will use throughout this text to remind us that effective science education means more than simply presenting information for children to learn or science equipment for students to handle. We must provide planned activities and instructional feedback for children as they think about and interpret their science experiences.

It is obvious that human endeavors as complex, divergent, and encompassing as science and modern technology can barely be introduced in one chapter. Thus, we have limited the scope of this introductory chapter to focus on understanding science and technology from the standpoint of teaching and learning. After reading this chapter, you will have a better picture of what science involves and what it means to teach science to children.

/// WHAT IS SCIENCE?

What do you think science is? Before reading on, write down several words that describe science. Share your list of attributes of science with your professor and classmates. Do they emphasize the same things you do? Which additional attributes of science do they suggest? As you read this chapter, see how your descriptions agree with the descriptions of science presented here.

Order and Organization

We live in an orderly world.[4] The universe is not random. Matter can take billions of forms, from a crystal of salt to a galaxy, from a single-celled amoeba to a complex human being. But within all of its forms is a hidden order, unseen unless searched for, that cuts across the diverse forms of matter.

Empowered with energy, matter moves and changes in orderly ways. Earth and the other planets move in predictable orbits. The moon's changing phases and times of appearance have a detectable rhythm. There is an unfailing sequence in the germination of a seed and the growth of a plant.

Human beings, endowed with innate curiosity, are driven to grasp the patterns of the universe and to discover the basic laws that produce the observed order. The activity of questioning and exploring the universe and finding and expressing its hidden order is called *science*.

Observation

Science has many characteristics. John Rigden[5], a physicist, emphasizes two fundamental characteristics in the nature of science. The first is its *empirical* character. The pursuit of science is concerned first of all with the empirical aspects of the world, that is, those aspects that can be directly observed or experienced. Leading children to explore and describe the things that surround them is an important goal of elementary and middle school science. Children need opportunity and time to hatch eggs, keep aquariums, compare leaves, tend to hamsters, play with magnets, find out about air, study the properties of minerals, explore floating and sinking, and observe weather changes. Childhood is the time to begin to appreciate the diversity of the world we live in.

Interpretation

The observable facts of science are not simply waiting to be stumbled upon. More often, the facts of science result from a dynamic dialogue carried on between a scientist and nature. This dialogue takes the form of experimentation in which specific experimental procedures become the questions asked by scientists, and the results of these procedures are the answers provided by nature.

Countless questions can be asked of nature; yet only a few are actually ever posed. What motivates these questions? Rigden finds the answer to this query in the second essential characteristic of science: its _analytical_ nature. Scientists are not satisfied with mere observations. They seek hidden meanings, look for underlying patterns, and propose explanatory schemes to bring coherence to their observations. Conceptual frameworks and theoretical structures are the imaginative results of the analytic inquiry of scientists.

The interplay between the empirical and analytic characteristics of science provides the stimulus for most activities in the world of science. New observations can stimulate the formation of new concepts; theories and accumulated knowledge can motivate the quest for new facts. Observations are empirical experiences in search of understanding; theories are tentative understandings in search of further empirical confirmation.

Science for children should include both empirical and analytic activities. The counterpart of watching is wondering. Not only should children observe the world, they should be encouraged to wonder about what they see and led to express their "why" questions in forms that can be answered through controlled investigations.

Tentativeness

Reread the first chapter opening quotation, which is from Robert E. Yager. Yager emphasizes that science offers us ways to interpret nature's events and methods for coping with the world, but, science does _not_ give us absolute truth!

Scientists seek conceptual models that can help to explain natural phenomena and provide accurate predictions based on new data. But, scientists realize that current models are tentative and subject to change as new facts are discovered. The goal of ultimate TRUTH can only be approached in science; it cannot actually be attained. But, it is the endless quest for

this goal that is the driving force of science. For the scientist, science is the quest, and in the quest it is the human imagination that makes the difference.

Modeling

It is useful to think of science as a process of constructing models of reality. A _model_ is a representation of a thing that leaves out some details but captures the most important ones. Scientists model air and other gases as tiny hard particles moving about at high speeds. This model is neither true nor false, but it is more or less useful. This particle model of gases is useful, for instance, in accounting for gas pressure. In an air-filled balloon the particles rush about colliding with one another and with the walls of the balloon, thus exerting pressure that keeps the balloon inflated. According to this model, when the air is cooled, the tiny particles slow down. When the cooler particles hit the walls, they cause less pressure and the balloon deflates. The interacting particle model of a gas is less useful, though, in trying to account for why some gases, such as neon, will glow when an electric charge is applied to them.

In _The Search for Solutions,_ the book accompanying the PBS television series by the same name, Horace Freeland Judson[6] points out that a map is a kind of model. A little girl's map of her neighborhood may leave out many details, but it will include the most important information—the road or street she lives on and her own house. The map is not true or false; it models the child's conception of her world. The map may not be very useful to her teacher, however, in trying to find her house. Science is like that. It captures our current understandings, but, it is vastly incomplete.

Science for Children

A nontechnical description of science by Nancy Paulu and Margery Martin[7] in a guide for parents called *Helping Your Child Learn Science* provides background that should prove useful to you in discussing the nature of science with children. They describe *science* as

- observing what happens;
- trying to make sense of our observations;
- using our new knowledge to make predictions about what might happen in the future; and
- testing predictions under controlled conditions to see if they are correct.

Further, Paulu and Martin point out that science involves trial and error—trying, failing, and trying again. Science does not provide all the answers; it requires us to be skeptical so that we can modify our models of the world or change them altogether as we make new discoveries.

/// **SCIENTIFIC KNOWLEDGE**

In addition to experiencing the world in a minds-on/hands-on way consistent with the descriptions of science just given, it is important for children to acquire scientific knowledge of the world. Scientific knowledge, sometimes labeled the **products of science,** has been accumulating for centuries as the result of the empirical and analytic activities of scientists. In addition to products, elementary school science also focuses on developing **scientific processes,** and **scientific attitudes.** Figure 1−1 shows the relationships among these three important components in elementary science. Refer to Figure 1−1 occasionally as you read the following sections.

Scientific knowledge generally takes the form of facts, concepts, principles, and theo-

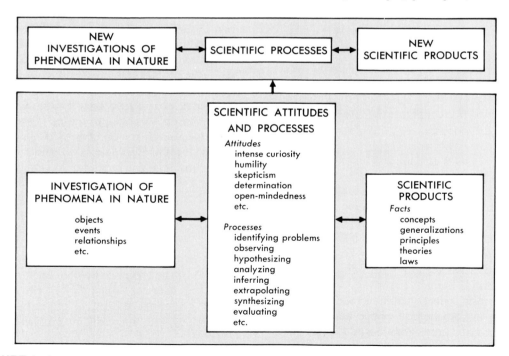

FIGURE 1−1

Interrelationships of scientific products, processes, and attitudes in investigating phenomena

ries. Facts are products of the empirical activities in science; concepts, principles, and theories are products of analytic activities.

Facts

Scientific *facts* are objectively confirmed statements about things that really exist or events that have actually occurred. It is a fact that water drops bead up on wax paper but spread out on aluminum foil. Also, water drops take a spherical shape when they fall. When water is added drop-by-drop to a small plastic medicine cup, the water tends to heap up at the rim before it starts to flow over the edges of the cup. Even then, as many as 30 paper clips can be gently slid into the cup without the water overflowing. Such facts are the empirical data or products of our observations that we organize and attempt to explain. Facts begin to make sense only as they are placed into a larger framework of concepts, principles, and theories.

Concepts

Scientific *concepts* are mental organizations about the world that are based on similarities among objects or events. They are ideas generalized from particular instances. In forming concepts, we are noting that even though items in a set may have many differences, they also have certain aspects that are similar. These similar aspects form the basis for grouping the things together into concepts. The facts about water that we just described can be accounted for through the concept of "surface tension," the skin-like effect of some liquids that is a result of the "bonding" of molecules. Another example of a concept is magnetic poles. Magnets come in an assortment of sizes, shapes, and colors. But in all magnets there are places called magnetic poles where the magnetic attraction for iron objects is greatest. All magnetic poles share the property of being the place of greatest attraction on a magnet. Some other scientific concepts encountered in elementary science include electric circuit, heat, air, air pressure, length, weight, color, texture, planets, and plant cells. What other scientific concepts can you think of that might form the basis of science activities for children?

Principles

Scientific *principles* are generalizations about the relationships among concepts. For example, "heated air expands" is a principle that relates the concepts of air, heat, and expansion in a causal way. This principle asserts that *if* air is heated *then* it will expand (unless otherwise constrained). Principles are analytic rather than empirical. They are inductive generalizations that are imaginatively based on a few examples. In forming principles, scientists (and children, too) go beyond limited observations and leap to the conclusion that what was true in a few cases will likely be true in all similar cases. Scientists refer to principles as the best descriptions of objects and events they have at any given time. It is primarily because of their inductive nature that principles are thought of as tentative and subject to change as new observations are made.

Laws

Laws are particularly well established and widely accepted scientific principles, though they are still tentative. Laws have generally undergone more rigorous testing than scientific principles and are considered to be "permanent"—at least as long as testing supports them. They are, however, still subject to change and refinement. The **law of conservation of energy** says that in an interaction, energy is neither created nor destroyed, but only changed from one form to another. In 1905, many years after the law of conservation of energy was first formulated, Einstein showed that energy could be created out of matter in special circumstances. When a little bit of matter is destroyed, a great deal of energy is created. This new discovery, which is expressed by Einstein's famous equation ($E = mc^2$), required that the law of conservation of energy be expanded.

What other scientific laws do you know about from exposure to science in your schooling?

Theories

Scientific *theories* are broader networks of related facts, concepts, and principles. A theory is a kind of *model,* a scientist's imaginative picture of how nature is put together. Like principles and laws, theories are tentative generalizations and are subject to change as new evidence accumulates. For example, the geocentric theory of the universe was dominant 500 years ago, but today it is only of historic interest. The model of the atom as a tiny solar system with electrons orbiting a nucleus is useful to us in imagining the structure of nature, but chemists today have replaced it with quantum theory, which pictures electrons as cloud-like swarms of charges swirling about a nucleus. The big bang theory of the origin of the universe, evolution as a theory of how life forms begin and change over time, and the theory of cells are some examples of scientific theories that best account for the evidence available today. Replace the word *theory* in the previous sentence with the word *model* and you may better realize the tentative nature of scientific theories.[8]

Scientific theories enable the understanding, prediction, and sometimes the control of a wide variety of natural phenomena. For example, meteorological theory enables scientists to *understand* how and why clouds and fog form. Meteorological theory helps us to determine what kinds of data to collect in order to *predict* when and where violent storms are likely to occur. Meteorological theory has already lead to the production of rain through cloud seeding. Perhaps theoretical advances will someday lead to the *control* of potentially destructive hurricanes and tornadoes.

/// SCIENTIFIC PROCESSES

In actual practice, what is known in science is inseparably linked to the methods of investigation. Knowing science is more than knowing content; it is also knowing how to gather evidence and how to relate evidence to interpretations. Figure 1–2 provides one model of a scientist's way of finding out about the universe. Scientists use a variety of empirical and analytic procedures in their efforts to clarify the marvelous mysteries of our universe; these procedures are called the **processes** of science.

Science process skills have been called **lifelong learning skills,** as they can be used for daily living and for learning in school in *any* subject area. A well-known proverb advises, "Give a man a fish and he eats for a day. Teach him how to fish and he eats for a lifetime."

Young learners do not always realize how useful science processes can be. Only 54% of seventh graders tested agreed with the statement, "Much of what you learn in science classes is useful in everyday life."[9] Help your students learn to use scientific processes or inquiry skills to confront problems, and they can learn for a lifetime.

Mechling and Oliver aptly summarized the potency of developing science process skills in our children in this way:

Competence in using process skills provides children with the ability to apply knowledge, not only to science and other subjects in the classroom, but outside the classroom in their everyday lives as well. They are the same skills

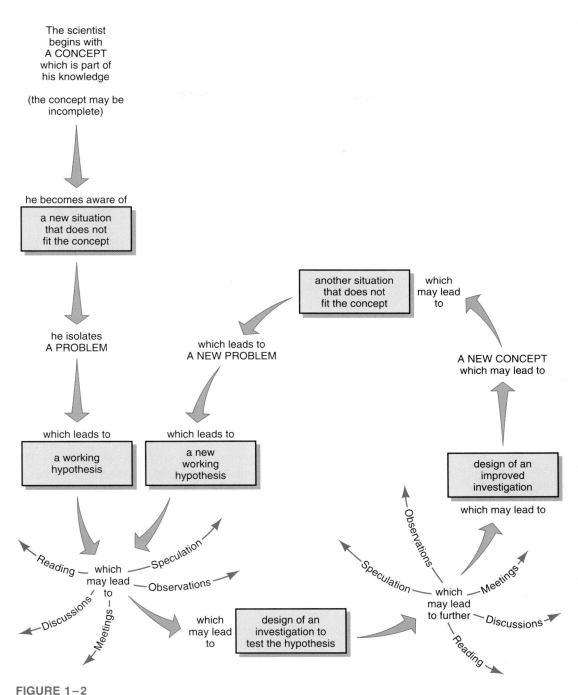

The scientist begins with A CONCEPT which is part of his knowledge

(the concept may be incomplete)

he becomes aware of

a new situation that does not fit the concept

he isolates A PROBLEM

which leads to A NEW PROBLEM

another situation that does not fit the concept

which may lead to

A NEW CONCEPT which may lead to

which leads to

a working hypothesis

which leads to

a new working hypothesis

Reading — which may lead to — Speculation
— Observations
Discussions —
Meetings

which may lead to

design of an investigation to test the hypothesis

which may lead to further

Speculation — Observations
— Meetings
Discussions
Reading

design of an improved investigation

which may lead to

FIGURE 1–2

A diagram of a scientist's way: Methods of intelligence

Source: From *Substance, Structure, and Style in the Teaching of Science,* New Edition, copyright © 1971 by Paul F. Brandwein, reprinted by permission of Harcourt Brace Jovanovich, Inc.

9

that will serve them as adults, when they measure their floor for a carpet, try to figure out why their automobile didn't start, or decide which presidential candidate to vote for. These are the thinking skills they will use when separating evidence from opinion while listening to someone's side of a story, or when looking for evidence and contradictions in written or spoken opinions. They are the science processes children will use as adults to separate inferences from evidence in a systematic way.[10]

It is very important for *all* of us to feel comfortable with and use scientific processes in our everyday lives in and out of school and not just in science; therefore, Chapter 6 (planning for teaching science) will elaborate on where and how to include specific scientific processes in the activities you prepare for your science teaching. The format suggested in that chapter for planning minds-on/hands-on guided discovery resource activities identifies specific science processes in the activity through questions that you can use to direct your students' thinking.

A broad range of science processes or inquiry skills that are particularly appropriate for elementary students to practice and learn is summarized in Table 1–1. Some of these processes are described in more detail in the following sections.

Observing

Scientific *observing* is the process of gathering information using all of the senses or using instruments that extend the senses. Observing is an empirical process of science. In one sense, science begins with observations of the natural world. However, observation always takes place from a framework of prior knowledge. What scientists or children look for in a situation and how they interpret what they see greatly depend on the relevant knowledge they bring to the situation, however naive and incomplete that knowledge might be. Observa-

tions, then, are colored by prior knowledge. Children generally have to learn to distinguish carefully between their observations and their inferences.

Learning to be a good observer is a lifelong task. Many things in children's environments can help them develop observations skills under the guidance of a sensitive teacher or parent. The following activity can be used to test your own observations skills or as an activity to help children develop their skills of observation. Obtain several seeds of at least two different kinds. Write down as many observations of the seeds as you can make. Compare your observations with those of another student. Do the activity before reading farther.

Now, use the components of good scientific observing shown in Table 1–2 as a checklist to see how comprehensive your list of observations is. Did you follow a *plan* in observing? Did you use all *appropriate senses,* and perhaps a magnifying glass to observe the seeds? What *questions* about the seeds did you raise? Did you *measure* the length or circumference of the seeds, or perhaps weigh them? Did you compare the seeds for *similarities and differences?* What *changes* did you make in the seeds? For example, did you soak one and split it apart to see what was inside it? How did you choose to *communicate* your observations? Did you include any drawings, for example?

If you made any inferences in observing the seeds, were you careful to distinguish between your inferences and your observations, showing in some way that inferences are conclusions or opinions? For example, when describing the inside of the seed, did you say ''I think'' this part is the embryonic root or ''I infer'' that this part is food storage for the developing plant?

Inferring

An *inference* is a conclusion about observations that is based on prior knowledge. Inferences,

Science starts with observations of the natural environment.

then, are made up of three interacting components: observations, prior knowledge, and conclusions. Observations, on the one hand, are statements about information that is available directly through the five senses; inferences, on the other hand, are interpretations of observations. In inferring we use knowledge that we already have or that we acquire to fill in gaps about observed information.

It is useful to think of knowledge as being organized mentally into a schema (the plural is *schemas* or *schemata*). A *schema* is a mental framework. One way schemata can be used is to guide inferences about incomplete information. All of us have many schemata available. In constructing inferences, we highlight particular cues in the observational data and search for matches between the cues and items in specific

knowledge frames. The broader our range of knowledge and the more carefully we observe and sift through our observations for relevant cues, the more powerful and accurate our inferences are likely to be. Schemata are addressed from a psychological perspective in Chapter 2.

To better understand the process of inferring, consider the following situation. Moisture is often seen collected on the outside of a glass of ice water. Before reading on, make some inferences about where the moisture came from that formed on the glass.

If you had appropriate prior knowledge, you might have inferred that the moisture on the glass came from water vapor in the air surrounding the glass. In this situation, some children will infer that the moisture came from in-

TABLE 1-1
Science processes or inquiry skills

Science Process or Inquiry Skill	Definition	Example
Classifying	Arranging or distributing objects, events, or information representing objects or events in classes according to some method or system	Taking objects such as buttons from a mixed collection and placing them in groups by color, number of holes, or shape; or arranging them in order according to size.
Creating Models	Displaying information by means of graphic illustrations or other multisensory representations	Drawing a graph or diagram; constructing a three-dimensional object; using a tape recording; constructing a chart or table; or producing a picture or photograph that illustrates information about the melting of ice cubes.
Formulating Hypotheses	Constructing a statement that is tentative and testable about what is thought likely to be true based on reasoning	Making a statement to be used as the basis for an experiment: "If one ice cube is placed in water and another placed in air at the same temperature, then the ice cube in water will melt faster."
Generalizing	Drawing general conclusions from particulars	Making a summary statement following analysis of experimental results: "Ice melts faster in water than in air when both air and water are at the same temperature."
Identifying Variables	Recognizing the characteristics of objects or factors in events that are constant or change under different conditions	Listing or describing the factors that are thought to, or would, influence the rate at which an ice cube melts in air and in water, such as: original temperature of water and air, size of the ice cube, or volume of water and air.
Inferring	Making a conclusion based on reasoning to explain an observation	Stating that heat caused the melting of an ice cube that had been placed in water.
Interpreting Data	Analyzing data that have been obtained and organized by determining apparent patterns or relationships in the data	Studying a graph, chart, or table of data collected about melting ice cubes and noting that smaller ice cubes melt faster than larger ones.
Making Decisions	Identifying alternatives and choosing a course of action from among the alternatives after basing the judgment for the selection on justifiable reasons	Identifying alternative ways to store ice cubes to avoid causing them to melt; analyzing the consequences of each alternative such as the cost, the effect on other people, or the effect on the environment; using justifiable reasons as the basis for making the choice; and choosing freely from the alternatives.

TABLE 1–1
continued

Science Process or Inquiry Skill	Definition	Example
Manipulating Materials	Handling or treating materials and equipment skillfully and effectively	Arranging equipment and materials needed to conduct an investigation of the melting rate of ice; pouring liquids from one container to another; or carrying a balance or adjusting it for use.
Measuring	Making quantitative observations by comparing to a conventional (or nonconventional) standard	Using a clock to count the number of seconds needed for an ice cube to melt; using a thermometer to determine the final temperature in degrees Celsius of the melted ice cube; or weighing ice cubes on a simple balance using paper clips as a standard.
Observing	Becoming aware of an object or event by using any of the senses (or extensions of the senses) to identify properties	Looking at a melting ice cube to determine its changing shape; feeling water from an ice cube to determine its slipperiness or coldness; or using a thermometer to determine the coldness of the water.
Predicting	Making a forecast of future events or conditions expected to exist	Stating "An ice cube whose weight is twice that of another ice cube will require twice the time to melt."
Recording Data	Collecting bits of information about objects and events that illustrate a specific situation	Taking notes; making a list or outline; recording numbers on a chart or graph; tape recording; taking photographs; or writing numbers of results of observations and measurements in an investigation, such as recording the number of cubic centimeters of water formed as an ice cube melts over time.
Replicating	Performing acts that duplicate demonstrated symbols, patterns, or procedures	Operating a balance scale or using a thermometer following procedures previously demonstrated or modeled by another person.
Using Numbers	Applying mathematical rules or formulas to calculate quantities or determine relationships from basic measurements	Computing the average time for a 10-cubic-centimeter ice cube to melt.

Source: Elementary Science Syllabus (Albany, NY: The University of the State of New York, The State Education Department, Division of Program Development, 1985), 14–15. Used by permission.

TABLE 1–2
Components of good scientific observing

1. *Plan.* Use a plan to guide observations so you do not skip important things or repeat observations unnecessarily.

2. *Senses.* Use all appropriate senses as well as instruments that extend the senses in gathering extensive and clear information.

3. *Questions.* Be curious and keep an open mind while observing; be alert to discrepancies; raise questions that can lead to new observations and new information.

4. *Measurements.* Make measurements of important variables to supplement qualitative observations when it matters.

5. *Similarities and Differences.* Identify similarities and differences between the object and other comparable objects.

6. *Changes.* Observe natural changes occurring in the objects or system of interest; whenever appropriate, make deliberate alterations in a system and observe the responding changes.

7. *Communication.* Report your observations clearly, using verbal descriptions, charts, diagrams, drawings, and other methods as appropriate.

side the glass, gradually seeping through its walls. Inferences in science need to be checked out where possible through further investigation. What kinds of investigations might be carried out to help children decide between these alternative inferences about the moisture on the glass of ice water?

To generate an inference you always need some prior knowledge. For example, the following facts, concepts, and principles are needed to support the first inference given about the moisture on the glass of ice water:

- Air often contains water vapor.
- Water vapor comes from evaporated water.
- When warm moist air is cooled to a temperature called the dew point, water vapor from the air will condense onto available cool surfaces.

Research on human cognition suggests that students are much more likely to access and use relevant prior knowledge of a phenomenon such as condensation if it is based on the analysis of many analogous experiences, for instance, considerations about clouds, fog, dew, vapor trails, eyeglasses that fog up in winter, and so forth.

Controlled Investigations

Learning to investigate and to communicate and interpret the results of investigations is an important goal of elementary school science. Investigating is a complex process, consisting of many component steps. Working with variables is one important component of investigating. A *variable* is a property of objects or events that can change and have differing amounts. The height and weight of a growing child, the time a candle can burn under a glass jar, and the amount of rainfall in a day are all examples of variables.

Three types of variables are important in scientific investigations. A *manipulated variable* (also called an independent variable) is a variable that the experimenter deliberately changes or manipulates in an investigation. A *responding variable* (also called a dependent variable) is a variable that changes in an investigation in response to changes in the manipulated variable. *Controlled variables* are variables that are deliberately kept constant or unchanged in an investigation in order not to confound the result.

An example of a simple controlled experiment for young children is germinating seeds on a wet sponge, as shown in Figure 1–3. This experiment establishes a cause-effect relationship between water and seed germination. It is very probable that seeds will germinate on the wet sponge in a few days, but not on the dry sponge. Children are helped to see some cause-effect relationship between water and seed germination, if other conditions of tem-

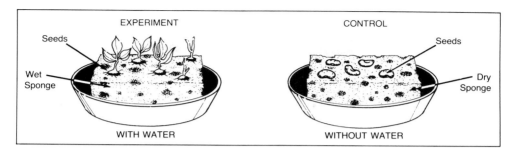

FIGURE 1–3
Controlled experiment in which the variable is water

perature and light are constant and suitable. Thus, the presence or absence of water is the **manipulated variable,** the condition that is changed to test whether it affects germination. The unchanged variables, in this case temperature and light, are the **controls.** These variables are controlled and only water is manipulated to make the investigation a "fair" test of the effects of water on germination. How would you conduct a controlled experiment to see if light is needed for seed germination?

Generalizations about relationships between responding and manipulated variables may be discovered in investigations. A *generalization* is a broad conclusion drawn from a number of particular instances. An example of a generalization would be, "Water is needed for seed germination." As we discussed earlier, generalizations about relationships are sometimes called principles.

A *hypothesis* is a guess about a possible relationship in nature that might be found through investigations. Hypotheses are used to guide experiments. They are often stated in a form such as "the greater the **manipulated variable,** the greater (or less) the **responding variable** will be." An example would be, "The heavier a pendulum weight, the slower it will swing." (Surprisingly, a controlled investigation will show this hypothesis to be false. See Chapter 2 for a discussion on children's difficulties with the pendulum and other controlled investigations.)

The notion of controlled experiments is an important tool in people's search for replicable data and valid conclusions. However, it is extremely difficult to precisely control all variables at all times. Even slight changes in conditions may yield significant differences in findings. Scientists try to account for these slight changes and build sufficient degrees of accuracy and tolerance into the standards of their work.

Problem Solving in Science. A useful model for problem solving, "The Scientific Method: A Primer," has been suggested by Don Nelson, an intermediate grade science teacher. Nelson's model incorporates 10 steps for planning and conducting investigations with elementary and middle grade students.

1. *The Question.* Teacher encourages students to ask specific testable questions of interest to them (e.g., "Do boys or girls have faster heartbeats?").
2. *The Hypothesis.* This is the statement of what you expect to find in the investigation (e.g., "I think girls have faster heartbeats.").
3, 4, 5. *The Variables.* Gender is the manipulated variable, as it is the only difference between the two experimental groups (boys and girls). Heart rate is the responding variable or the effect that can be observed and/or measured. All other boy/girl differences must be kept the same or *con-*

trolled (e.g., body size, general health, etc.). Only one difference is to be investigated per experiment.

6. *The Procedure.* How is the question to be answered? How are the boys' and girls' heart rates to be measured?

7. *Equipment and Materials.* What equipment and materials are needed to measure heart rates (clocks, stethoscopes, data sheets, etc.)?

8. *Data Collection.* How do the students accurately collect data and use charts to keep records?

9. *Hypothesis Check.* Investigators check their findings against Step 2 to answer the question, "Do the recorded data agree or disagree with the original hypothesis?"

10. *Conclusions.* What results or meanings were learned from the investigation? What further questions were raised that are still unanswered?[11]

/// SCIENTIFIC ATTITUDES

Scientists—the men and women trained in some field of science—study phenomena and events through observation, experimentation, and other empirical and analytical activities. Certain general **attitudes,** or predispositions, tend to characterize their work. Science education should promote understanding of scientific attitudes. Some important attitudes for children to learn and display in science include the following:

1. *Being Curious.* Scientists are driven by curiosity, an urge to know and understand the world.

2. *Insisting on Evidence.* Scientists insist on evidence to support conclusions and claims. Insisting on evidence means rigorous testing of ideas and respecting the facts as they are accrued.

3. *Being Skeptical.* Scientists must remain skeptical of their own conclusions and those

of others. A part of this attitude is recognition that authoritarian statements can be tested but there is an appropriate time and place to question people's conclusions. As evidence suggests different explanations of objects or events, scientists must be willing to change even their own original explanations.

4. *Accepting Ambiguity.* Scientists must be able to accept ambiguity. Scientific evidence seldom, if ever, proves something finally. Alternative viewpoints should be respected until shown to be incompatible with data.

5. *Being Cooperative.* Scientists today generally work and publish as a team. Being cooperative in raising and answering questions, analyzing data, and solving problems is another important attitude in the scientific enterprise.

6. *Taking a Positive Approach to Failure.* Wrong turns and dead ends are a natural consequence of inquiring into the unknown. Scientists must take a positive approach to failure and treat setbacks as temporary.[12]

Let us examine a few of these attitudes in more depth.

Curiosity: Fascination with the World Around Us

Human urges and needs are the forces that drive all of us to seek answers (some rational, some irrational) to questions about our world. These forces are the catalysts for the development of science. Young children enjoy discovering the texture, size, weight, color—even the taste—of sand at the seashore or in the sandbox simply because sand intrigues them. Similarly, scientists study the marvels of nature because they delight in them. This dynamic—almost compulsive—involvement of children and adults in searching for answers provides the fuel for the vehicle of investigation. Here is an example of the total absorption of scientists in their work: "When he sits down at his computer in the morning, a physicist leaves

What seems like child's play is a form of testing hypotheses.

the rest of us behind. When he comes back, he cannot explain where he has been, or what it is that he has been doing."[13]

The following description of the passion of finding something new in science says it well:

A discovery is like falling in love and reaching the top of a mountain after a hard climb all in one, an ecstasy induced not by drugs but by the revelation of a face of nature that no one has seen before and that often turns out to be more subtle and wonderful than anyone imagined.[14]

A thirst for knowing, properly nurtured in a positive learning environment, can help children become perpetual learners—constantly curious, continually seeking knowledge, and always inquiring. Your own curiosity can be the model for children to follow. "He who would kindle others, must himself glow."

Being Cooperative

We should not forget that scientific investigations are done by people, making science a human enterprise. Countless men and women combine their talents and labors to inquire into the unknown through creative activities. National boundaries often become unimportant in the free interchange of research efforts, which we called the products of science. Teams of men and women of all races and all nationalities are an essential part of modern science and technology.

Group cooperation is so effective in generating new ideas, solving problems, and helping people learn from each other that industries worldwide are adopting cooperative group procedures in manufacturing. Japanese companies adapted cooperative group learning techniques into what they call **Quality Circles (QC)**.[15] In QC's, members from all levels of the company (President and other CEO's, foremen, hourly assembly line workers, janitors, etc.) meet daily in small groups. Advantages claimed for the cooperative Quality Circles include the following:

- Improving the quality of work, products, and environment.
- Simplifying the employee's job.
- Cutting costs, eliminating product defects, and doing away with waste and expensive inventory stockpiles.

Learning to work cooperatively is an important goal for children in science and all other subjects in elementary schools.

Cooperative learning helps students generate new ideas and solve problems.

Thinking Positively About "Failure"

Scientists tell us that the more they know, the more they discover how little they actually know. Scientific findings are just temporary stopping places on the continuum of research. In the process of investigating a problem, other unanswered questions arise. At any given point scientists know that the results of their efforts are incomplete, no matter how satisfying or frustrating, because future work will doubtless reveal more about the subject. A failure in science, then, is not a dead end but a starting point.

Historical records are full of successes stemming from "failures." Dr. Paul Ehrlich, 1908 Nobel Prize winner in medicine and physiology, developed Salvarsan for the treatment of syphilis after 605 "unsuccessful" experiments. In Polaroid's search for instant color pictures, chemist Howard Rogers spent 15 years experimenting with over 5,000 different chemical compounds before synthesizing a new molecule. "Failure" was never a barrier for the prodigious inventor, Thomas Alva Edison. It is said that after more than *10,000* experiments to construct a battery had failed, Edison's response was, "I have not failed, just discovered ten thousand ways that won't work." Burnett Cross says that the picture of scientists we often give to our students does not sufficiently reveal them as persons just like us who take wrong roads, have hunches that do not pan out, make downright errors and mistakes, and experience a "sometimes hostile behavior of apparatus." How they handle these roadblocks determines their progress. Scientists succeed in the long run because of their daily, intelligent approaches to failures.[16]

In elementary science children should learn that the process of inquiry involves the challenge of trying the unknown and must necessarily result in occasional mistakes. Children often come to the inquiry process with naive conceptions about the world that lead to mistaken conclusions. The way teachers handle the mistakes and errors that come in minds-on/hands-on investigations is crucial in science teaching. On the one hand, pupils who are told that their ideas are wrong may be reluctant to participate in inquiry again. On the other hand, incorrect ideas left unchallenged can cause confusion and interfere with the construction of valid knowledge. As a teacher you will need to discover tactful ways to nurture the inquiry process while leading pupils to challenge wrong ideas and to examine their consequences through further investigations.

Acting like a scientist means using the types of attitudes and processes identified in this chapter more consciously more of the time. Developing these science attitudes and science skills is an important task of elementary education. As you will discover in chapter 7, many innovative elementary school science projects and textbook series stress the scientific attitudes and the processes of science introduced in this chapter.

/// SCIENCE TEACHING AND CONSTRUCTIVISM

Minds-on/hands-on approaches to teaching science are consistent with a philosophy of learning and instruction called **constructivism.** According to the constructivist viewpoint, order is less *discovered* than it is *invented.* Scientists imaginatively "impose" order and predictability on the phenomena and events of the world. As with many other human endeavors, scientists *construct* this order based largely on their own prior knowledge, that is, their own active organization of facts, concepts, principles, and models derived from previous studies. In the constructivist viewpoint, knowledge is considered to be a dynamic conceptual means to make sense of experience rather than a passive representation of an external world.

Constructivists stress that each person must individually construct meanings of words and ideas if they are to be truly useful. All of us—scientist and nonscientists alike—are strongly influenced by other people through social interactions. But, language *per se* cannot be the means of transferring information. Knowledge acquired from other people is useful in understanding the world only to the extent that we make it meaningful for ourselves through thoughtful processes. It is this meaningful knowledge that

scientists and nonscientists use to cope with and make sense of the environment.

The constructivist philosophy incorporates much of the work of psychologist Jean Piaget and of modern cognitive science. It implies a minds-on/hands-on discovery approach to teaching and learning science. Chapter 2 will present a fuller description of cognitive and constructivist contributions to understanding how children learn and the particular implications for teaching and learning science.

/// SEARCHING FOR ANSWERS MEANS ASKING GOOD QUESTIONS

The doing of science as well as the learning and teaching of science must be guided by thoughtful questions asked by both teachers and children. Paulu and Martin relate a story about Isidor I. Rabi, a Nobel prize winner in physics. A friend asked Rabi, "Why did you become a scientist, rather than a doctor or lawyer or businessman, like the other immigrant kids in your neighborhood?" Rabi responded:

My mother made me a scientist without ever intending it. Every other mother would ask her child after school: "Did you learn anything today?" But not my mother. She always asked me a different question. "Izzy," she would say, "did you ask a good question today?" That difference—asking good questions—made me become a scientist![17]

Young children exploring their sensory world and scientists working on deep intellectual problems ask many questions. Two types of questions are at the heart of scientific inquiry:

WHAT? "What" questions are at the empirical level. They generally ask for descriptions that lay the foundation for analytic work (e.g., "What did you see in the investigation?" "What changes took place in the plant?"

Discovery: Women in Science

I grew up in the Seventies, but even in those enlightened days, women were still being encouraged to choose nursing and teaching as careers. What else could I do? I was good in math and science.

—Lisa McCauley,
aeronautical engineer.

Strategy   Encourage female (and minority) students to choose careers in science by introducing them to role models.

The Ohio State University offers a one-day workshop each year called, "Women in Science." Female students from middle school and high school are recruited to attend. These students participate in two workshops on campus that feature women speakers who are practicing scientists or academicians.

Workshop topics come from Biological and Life Sciences (e.g., medicine, zoology, veterinary science, immunology and genetics, and nutrition and textiles); Education (science educators, science librarians); and Physical Sciences and Engineering (biomedical engineering, geology, mapping and land information, mathematics, chemistry, and physics.)

One woman who is qualified to lead a workshop is Lisa McCauley. McCauley is a special type of science teacher. She teaches space shuttle astronauts how to perform experiments in space. The experiments are set up by other scientists at Battelle Memorial Institute's Advanced Materials Center in Columbus, Ohio. Not only does McCauley teach the astronauts, she also works with NASA engineers to make sure the experiment and equipment are safe.

One recent experiment involved how to grow more perfect crystals in space. Another was designed to make polymer films that can be used in a variety of industrial applications.

On Your Own   Invite a speaker to your class, organize a school assembly featuring a panel of female and minority scientists, or ask a local university to sponsor a workshop like the one described in this article.

Locating women and people who belong to minority groups who have chosen academic or professional careers in science may be challenging, but it is not impossible. One way is to contact a speaker's bureau through the chamber of commerce of a nearby city. Local or regional industries may employ scientists who can be "loaned" to a classroom for a day. University and college campuses are also excellent resources. Newspapers and television stations often keep lists of professional resources to contact if they need a quotation from an expert.

Source: "Women Making a Difference," by Michael B. Lafferty, *The Columbus Dispatch,* Tuesday, March 3, 1992, and The Ohio State University, Columbus, Ohio. Photo of Lisa McCauley courtesy of Battelle Memorial Institute.

"What bird is on that fence?" "What are the properties of this rock?").

HOW or WHY? "How" and "why" questions are at an analytic level and require that one go beyond the information given (e.g., "Why did the balloon expand?" "How is heat or thermal energy conducted through a piece of iron?"). Answering such questions involves observing, inferring, generalizing, and using prior knowledge. Justifying answers to "why" and "how" questions may also involve identifying variables, formulating hypotheses, experimenting, and interpreting data.

"Why" questions may not have a final answer; each successive answer may lead to another, more fundamental, question. For example, a young child asks, "Daddy, why is grass green?" The father answers, "Because grass has chlorophyll," to which the child immediately asks, "Well, why is chlorophyll green?" This could go on indefinitely because each question leads back to more basic conceptional information.

Because questioning is the heart of scientific inquiry and the foundation of teaching by minds-on/hands-on guided discovery, chapter 4 is devoted to the specifics of questioning and listening techniques.

Nonscientific Answers to Questions

Sometimes in our frustration or ignorance, we respond to "why" questions with answers that are not very scientific. We may give an **anthropomorphic** response. That is, we give human form or qualities to nonhuman things (The term *anthropomorphic* comes from the Greek *anthropos,* meaning "man," and *morphos,* meaning "form"). An example of this might be how we sometimes ascribe human motives to computers with statements like, "The computer swallowed my last paragraph."

Occasionally, we may respond to questions that attribute end purpose, design, or will to nonhuman things. This is called **teleological** from the Greek word *teleos,* meaning "end." Stating that "water seeks its own level" is an example of a teleological explanation. It is the same as saying that water has the end purpose of being at some given level. Although a teleological approach may sometimes be useful as a model, it is more scientific to say that water actually moves because of the actions of forces upon it.

Scientists do not answer questions in anthropomorphic or teleological terms because these descriptions do not contribute to a better understanding of the phenomena. These answers are vague, untrue, and lead to dead ends. For example, if you are told a plant bends toward a light source because "it *likes* light", you have no need to find out how light stimulates plant hormones so cells grow more rapidly on one side of the plant, bending it toward the light source. The plant is *forced* to bend and does not *choose* to bend (as far as we know at this time). Anthropomorphic and teleological answers may discourage efforts to look deeper at cause and effect.

/// SCIENCE, TECHNOLOGY, AND SOCIETY

Science proposes explanations for observations about the natural world; **technology** proposes solutions for problems of human adaptation to the environment. Many scientists and other citizens are becoming increasingly concerned about the societal implications of science and technology. One influential group, the American Association for the Advancement of Science (AAAS), has formulated Project 2061 to propose plans for American science, mathematics, and technology education for the 21st century.[18] The long-range vision of the group is indicated by its choice of a name for the project, since the year 2061 is when Halley's comet is due to return to our part of the solar system.

A major reason for concern is that what is discovered through science and technology can be used for the benefit or detriment of society. Madame Curie, for example, did not know before her experiments the values or dangers of radioactive material. Nuclear research and development have subsequently led to cataclysmic harm for the people of Hiroshima, Nagasaki, and Chernobyl. Radiation has also been used beneficially as a treatment for cancer. (Ironically, cancer was the disease from which Marie Curie died, perhaps as a result of being overexposed to radiation in her experimental work.)

A recycling activity helps make a science-technology-society issue real to these students.

Increasingly, concerned people and scientists are trying to educate the public about problems such as population explosion, pollution, insecticide poisoning of the environment, AIDS, and drug and alcohol abuse. You must be prepared to help your students to learn both science and technology so they can see the impact of both on their everyday lives and more broadly on society. The second quotation at the beginning of this chapter highlights that science helps us explain "what is" in our world, whereas technology provides ways of dealing with complex society and modern life. In modern life, science, technology, and society are inextricably intertwined. That is why this text will use this combined form for the three: science/technology/society. **STS** is also used frequently to designate this combination. Here are some suggestions as you begin your search for ways to involve children in exploring STS problems and issues.[19]

Emphasize STS Connections

You can readily see the relationships between STS and their implications for your teaching in Figure 1–4. By linking science to technology to society, you facilitate students' learning in all three fields.

In your science teaching, *purposely* use STS themes. One excellent way to do this is to help your students identify STS issues and problems that are relevant to *their* everyday lives and society in general.

Stress Real-Life STS Problems

Paul W. Brandwein and Lynn W. Glass tell us that, "A primary purpose of science teaching is to address the most crucial problems of society. Problems . . . must become the focus of good teaching and thoughtful learning."[20] This goal of organizing learning in science around STS problems is reinforced by this recommendation

FIGURE 1–4

The relationship between science and technology and their connection to educational goals

Source: Susan Loucks-Horsley, et al., *Elementary School Science for the 90's* (Andover, MA: The NETWORK, Inc., 1989), 30. Reproduced with permission of the National Center for Improving Science Education/ The NETWORK, Inc. Copyright © 1989.

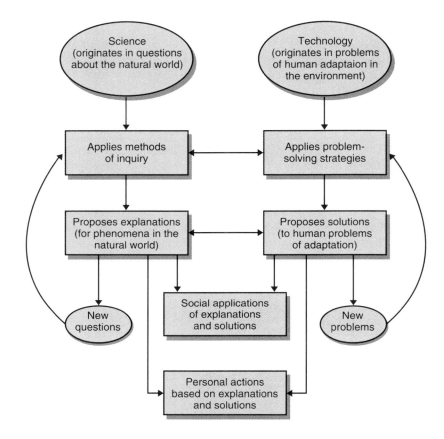

adopted by the National Science Teachers Association's Board of Directors in January 1990:

Develop curricula that provide opportunities for all students and adults to study real-life, personal, and societal science and technology problems.[21]

From your own experiences with children, your community, and the national and international situations, you know there is no shortage of real-life, personal, and societal STS problems around which your students' learnings can be focused. Our lives are influenced by science and technology in areas such as communications, transportation, medicine, farming, manufacturing, space exploration, warfare, and politics. In the early grades your students are constantly in contact with and are curious about

computers, TV, and other electronic gadgets, how schools and their homes are heated and cooled, what happens to their garbage and toilet wastes, and how their bodies are changing. The National Assessment of Educational Progress (NAEP) results presented in Figure 1–5 show that 9-year-olds wanted to help solve serious environmental problems such as pollution, energy waste, disease, and food shortages, but unfortunately, their responses showed that they had little experience with environmental issues in school and had taken few field trips related to the environment.

When your students investigate issues and problems that are real to them, they will learn not only the science and technology behind these issues and problems but will also become aware of how this science and technology ap-

	Yes
Use less electricity?	91
Spend a day helping clean up litter from a street, park, or road?	86
Use returnable bottles rather than "throw-away" bottles?	84
Walk and ride bicycles more often?	79
Separate trash (bottles, cans, paper, etc.) for recycling?	75
Use less heat in the winter to save fuel?	73
Drive or ride in a small economy car?	52

FIGURE 1–5
Percentages of 9-year-olds willing to perform various conservation activities
Source: Roger T. Johnson, "What Research Says," *Science and Children,* (February 1981): 39–41.

plies to machines, devices, and inventions. To assist you in identifying and using STS issues and problems, sources are presented in the "Self-Evaluation and Further Study" section at the end of this chapter, in Chapter 7 on innovative programs, and in the Appendices.

Guide Your Students to Become STS Decision Makers

You and your students make decisions every day about your own welfare and that of others, the environments in which you live, and directly or indirectly, the world's environment. To assist your students in making wise decisions, you must provide them with practice, skills, and guidance. Practice comes from actively involving your students in *their* real-life problem solving/decision-making situations. Guidance means helping them develop skills in solving problems and making decisions and consciously avoiding telling them what and how to decide on alternatives. This means that YOU

must become familiar with ways of approaching problem solving/decision making and then learn how to guide your students. Earlier in the chapter we presented Don Nelson's "The Scientific Method: A Primer" for solving problems. Here is another suggested model to help you.

Search, Solve, Create, Share, and Act. One model for developing STS student problem-solving skills is called "Search, Solve, Create, and Share"[22] The purpose is to conduct a search from what is known (prior knowledge) and extend that knowledge base through problem solving and application or action taking. Here's how the four phases work.

Search. Select topics for study from textbooks, demonstrations, minds-on/hands-on activities, field trips, TV exposure, or community events. After students brainstorm on an initial idea (e.g., food), they generate a list of additional ideas in question format for possible indepth investigation. One or two questions are finally selected as the search focus (e.g., "How much food is wasted in our school's hot lunch program on a typical day?"). A major characteristic of this model is that the search phase is not prepackaged or predetermined.

Solve. In the solving phase students apply previously learned information and procedures. Emphasis is on using research methodology and students can use descriptive, experimental, or correlational approaches.

Create. Collecting and analyzing information in this phase may be done through using line and bar graphs, dot charts, and other organizational methods. For example, students might explore the food waste problem by using a graph to show the amount of food wasted on different days or the amount of each kind of food that is wasted each day.

Share. Students communicate their findings and interact with their fellow students in a variety of ways in the share phase. Oral and written reports, posters, songs, videotapes, poetry, and other verbal and nonverbal projects can be used to communicate findings and recommendations.

STS problem solving is not complete until students act on their findings. A group of students might defend a point of view before the class, write a letter to a local authority, or volunteer to spend a day to help clean up litter from a park. Their new interest and level of understanding may, and frequently do, lead to new questions that provide the foundations for new explorations and subsequent actions.

Integrate Problem Solving with All Subjects

A very effective approach for your STS problem solving is to integrate or correlate it with your other subject matter, (i.e., mathematics, social studies, art, music, and oral and written expression). Many educators support this and it has the endorsement of the National Science Teachers Association Board of Directors:

Develop a K–12 curriculum framework that is integrated or correlated in terms of science, technology, humanities, mathematics, and the social studies.[23]

By making STS problem solving part of your total classroom curriculum you reinforce and enrich both science and technology and the other subject areas as well. This makes learning more meaningful for your students. Chapter 8 provides you with specific practical classroom activities and suggestions for integrating and correlating STS problem solving with all curricular areas.

Develop Scientifically and Technologically Literate Citizens

Students and citizens in general who are scientifically *and* technologically literate should (a) have an understanding of those aspects of science and technology that are meaningful to them at their present level of cognitive development, (b) find science and technology interesting and rewarding, (c) use their understanding of science and technology to enjoy the natural and social world in which they live.[24]

There is much evidence that the goals of scientific and technological literacy can be reached in the schools. Here are 10 standards that have been achieved by students in exemplary schools by seventh grade:[25]

1. Exhibit effective consumer behavior by evaluating the quality of products, the accuracy of advertising, and the personal needs for the product.
2. Use effective personal health practices.
3. Use new data and ideas in learning situations.
4. Recognize the effect of people on the environment and vice versa.
5. Recognize and accept ways in which each individual is unique.
6. Recognize that a solution to one problem often creates new problems.
7. Observe variations of individual interpretations of different data.
8. Recognize that science will provide neither magic solutions nor easy answers. Hard work and processes of science are required to resolve rather than solve many problems.
9. Develop an understanding of information and concepts from a wide variety of topics selected from the life, Earth, and physical sciences.
10. Recognize the roles of people involved in scientific pursuits and the careers available in science and technology.

/// PROBLEM SOLVING/DECISION MAKING MODEL

Problem solving and decision making are facilitated when students learn to work strategically.

Scientific literacy develops effective consumer behavior as students learn how to evaluate and compare products.

Figure 1–6 presents another model for problem solving and decision making that you might find useful. You and your students should modify or change the sequence of steps as needed. Gear it to the developmental level of your students. Avoid slavishly following the sequence.

The problem-solving/decision-making sequence begins by helping students identify a problem. To do this, use the sequence shown on the top left side of Figure 1–6. That is, assist your students to use their experiences, observations and prior knowledge to make them aware of discrepancies in phenomena and events. This should lead them to raise questions, and the questions will help them define the problem.

Once students have identified a problem by constructing a precise question, they can pro-

ceed with problem solving using the model. Since the model is organized into a sequence of steps with specific tasks for each step, you can isolate each step for instruction. Once students learn the tasks for each step, they will be able to use them, either consciously or automatically, to solve problems. Shown across the top of Figure 1–6 are the tasks at each step:

■ *Questions.* The problem solver should construct precise questions that will help clarify the problem and the steps that must be taken to solve it. Students should view each precise question as a little piece of the problem to be solved.

■ *Skills.* The problem solver can get answers to precise questions by applying appropriate skills or processes. Students should be taught

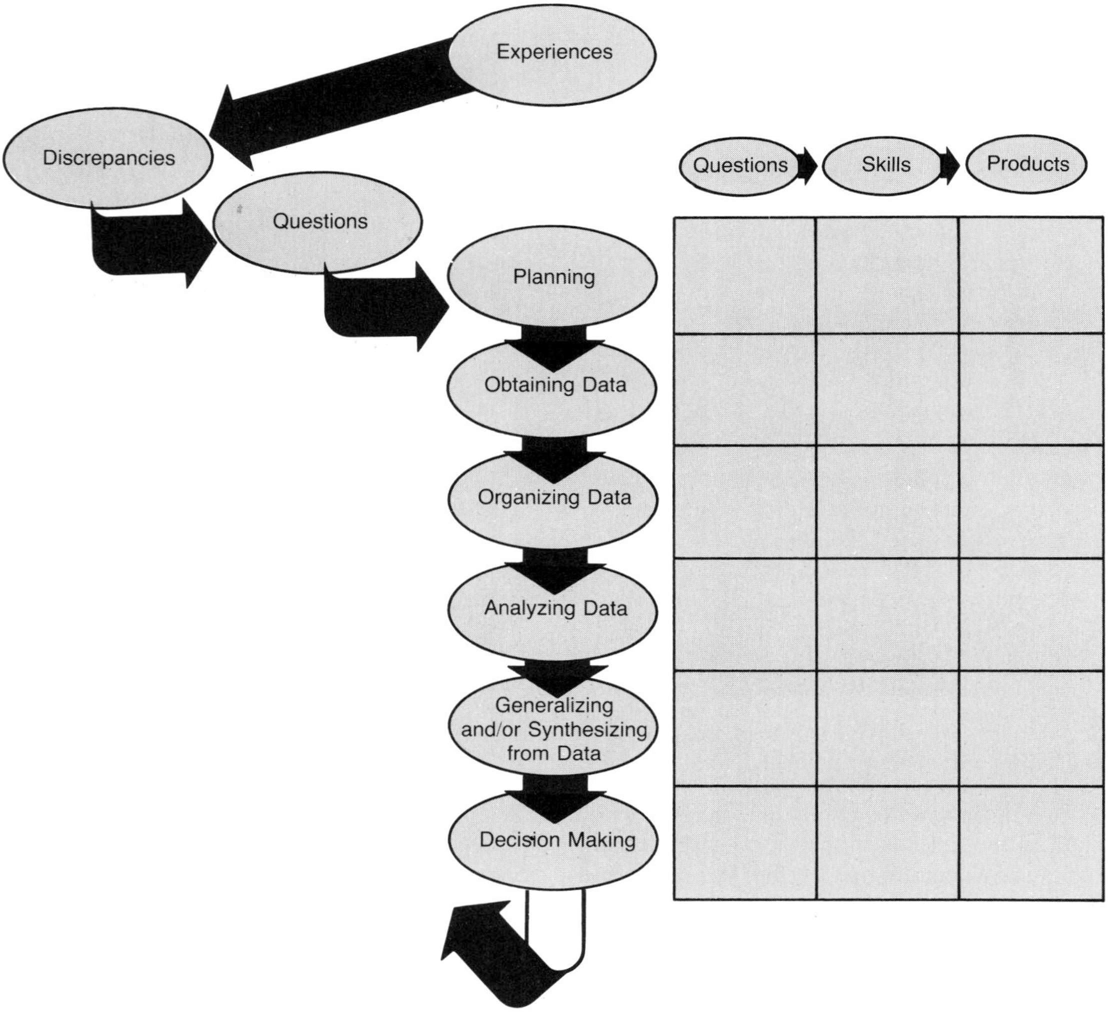

FIGURE 1–6

Model for problem solving/ decision making

Source: Elementary Science Syllabus (Albany, NY: The University of the State of New York, The State Education Department, Division of Program Development, 1985), 8. Used by permission.

to select and apply the best skills or processes for the specific task implied by the questions.

■ *Products.* The problem solver creates a tangible product by applying the appropriate skills or processes to the specific task. For example, by applying the skill of recording data, the problem solver may create the tangible product of a chart or graph. Tangible

products contain answers to questions. Let's explore the steps in the sequence.

1. *Planning.* Consider these focus questions in planning:
   a. What is the problem?
   b. What background information do I already have?

c. What new information do I need?

d. What procedure or sequence of actions do I need to follow?

e. How will I know when I have solved the problem?

Students should be taught that when they construct a plan, they must always assume that the plan may have to be revised in light of new information.

2. *Obtaining Data.* Consider this focus question: What new information do I need? Obtaining good quantitative as well as qualitative data is essential to effective problem solving.

3. *Organizing Data.* The problem solver establishes some pattern of order or form with the data obtained. Consider this focus question: In what useful way(s) can the information be organized? Finding the best way to organize the data is very important in effective problem solving.

4. *Analyzing Data.* Consider the following focus questions in analyzing data: How do the data fit together? What patterns and relationships may be here? How can the data best be analyzed? Analysis of data must be careful and reasoned in effective problem solving.

5. *Generalizing and/or Synthesizing from Data.* Here the problem solver draws conclusions or creates alternative choices (potential solutions to the problem) to use in the next

step—decision making. Consider the focus question: What can be drawn from the analyses of information? Sound alternative choices become the basis for informed decision making in effective problem solving.

6. *Decision making.* In the decision-making step, a problem solver again uses a sequence of focus questions to arrive at a decision:

a. What decision(s) need to be made?

b. What are the alternative choices and the reasons for each?

c. What are the consequences of each alternative?

d. Who will be affected by each possible choice and in what way?

e. What values are directly related to each choice, and how do they relate to it?

f. Which choice is the best?

The decision may lead directly to the solution of the problem; it may point to new directions in pursuit of the solution; or it may suggest new problems to be solved. In any case, the decision should lead to action, and the action should be freely chosen by the problem solver. In effective problem solving, the problem solver makes an informed decision by working from a rational base of data to make the best choice. Figure 1–7 shows how this is done in the middle grades.

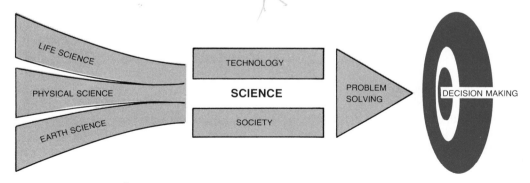

FIGURE 1–7

STS and teaching/learning science

Source: Carolyn Steele Graham, "STS in Middle/Junior High School Science: One State's Response," *Science Through Science Technology and Society Reporter,* 2, no. 5 (December 1986): 6.

Although the problem-solving model is organized into a sequence of steps that have a logical progression, it is important in practice that problem solvers often move back and forth among the steps as a problem is worked on.

As you go back over the three problem-solving models, you should note that they *all* contain elements of the questions, skills, and products approach described in this chapter.

/// FIVE DOMAINS OF SCIENCE EDUCATION

Alan J. McCormack and Robert E. Yager[26] propose five domains in a taxonomy of science education designed to help students become scientifically and technologically literate. Figure 1–8 presents the five domains with a description of what students may do or learn in each domain. McCormack and Yager say that too often science education is limited to the first two domains, knowing and understanding and exploring and discovering, which relate primarily to the products and processes of science. They contend that the other three domains must be included in these times of global environmental problems, complex social and political issues, and general concerns about the future. To address these concerns, the domain of imagining and creating emphasizes the creative dimension of using science for the benefit of people. The domain of feeling and valuing looks at human values, feelings, and decision-making skills. How to use information gained from school science studies in everyday life falls under the domain of using and applying.

A science education program, especially one that is science/technology/society oriented, must focus on all of the interrelated five domains, but it should stress the vital importance of these domains: imagining and creating, feeling and valuing, and using and applying. It is in these domains that students use their acquired science knowledge and skills to clarify and strengthen their values and then apply and act upon them as responsible citizens.

/// THE GOALS OF ELEMENTARY SCIENCE EDUCATION

The concepts of science and technology presented in this chapter provide a framework for making decisions about goals in elementary science education. Schools are social institutions; thus broad social concerns and issues should be considered when developing goals. The nature and interests of children are especially important in planning goals for elementary science. The following statements of goals for elementary science are adapted from the work of the National Center for Improving Science Education.[27] These goals are comprehensive and representative of the emphases of many different national and state organizations and local school districts.

1. *Curiosity.* Elementary science programs should nurture and sustain children's natural curiosity about the world.
   a. Allow children to explore the natural and technological world.
   b. Develop children's abilities to ask questions about the natural world.
   c. Develop children's abilities to identify problems of human adaptation.
2. *Skills for Investigating.* Elementary science programs should develop skills for investigating the natural world, solving problems, and making decisions.
   a. Enrich children's understanding of and ability to use processes of science.
   b. Advance children's understanding of and ability to use problem-solving and decision-making strategies.
3. *Knowledge.* Children's knowledge base in science and technology should be developed through elementary science programs.
   a. Guide children in acquiring relevant, useful content knowledge in science, technology, and health.

1. *Knowing and Understanding (scientific information)*
   - learns specific information (facts, concepts, theories, and laws)
   - investigates knowledge of science's history and philosophy
2. *Exploring and Discovering (scientific processes)*
   - uses processes of science to learn how real scientists think and work (observe and describe, classify and organize, measure and chart, communicate, predict and infer, hypothesize, test hypotheses, identify and control variables, interpret data, and construct instruments, simple devices, and physical models)
   - uses manipulative (psychomotor) skills, as well as cognitive skills
3. *Imagining and Creating (creative)*
   - visualizes or produces mental images
   - combines objects and ideas in new ways
   - produces alternate or unusual uses for objects
   - solves problems and puzzles
   - fantasizes
   - pretends
   - day dreams

- designs devices and machines
- produces unusual ideas
4. *Feeling and Valuing (attitudinal)*
   - develops positive attitudes toward science, school, teachers, and self
   - explores human emotions
   - develops sensitivity to and respect for the feelings of other people
   - expresses personal feelings in a constructive way
   - makes decisions about personal values and social and environmental issues
5. *Using and Applying (applications and connections)*
   - sees instances of scientific concepts in everyday life
   - applies learned science concepts and skills to real technological problems
   - understands scientific and technological principles involved in household devices
   - uses scientific processes in solving problems that occur in everyday life
   - understands and evaluates mass media reports of scientific developments
   - makes decisions related to personal health, nutrition, and lifestyles based on knowledge of scientific concepts rather than hearsay and emotions
   - integrates science with other subjects

FIGURE 1–8

The five domains of science education

Source: Modified from materials in Alan J. McCormack and Robert E. Yager, "A New Taxonomy of Science Education," *The Science Teacher,* 56, no. 2 (February 1989): 47–48.

b. Assist children in improving explanations of their world.

4. *Nature of Science, Technology, and Society.* Elementary science programs should strive to develop children's understanding of and attitudes about the nature, limits, and possibilities of science and technology.
   a. Lead children to recognize and apply scientific attitudes and habits of mind.
   b. Increase children's understanding of science and technology as major human achievements.
   c. Help children to become more aware of interactions of science and technology with society.
   d. Assist children in using scientific and technological knowledge, attitudes, and skills in decision making.

/// AN OVERVIEW OF THE TEXT

The next chapters will add flesh to the skeleton introduced here of what and how you can teach science. Chapter 2 will expand the brief introduction in this chapter to how children think and learn. Chapter 3 will look at how to combine the attributes of Chapters 1 and 2 into teaching science with an emphasis on a guided discovery, minds-on/hands-on approach. Suggestions are presented in Chapter 4 for implementing and effectively using questioning and listening skills in your science program. Chapter 5 looks at ways to use assessment to enrich and evaluate your science teaching and learning. Specifics on how to plan, arrange, and manage such a learning environment for your classroom are presented in Chapter 6. Chapter 7 will review innovative science programs and textbooks to show you newer and prom-

ising science education techniques applicable to your classroom *now*. Specifics on how to identify and use socially oriented themes and how to integrate and correlate other matter in your science teaching are the focus of Chapter 8. Chapters 9 and 10 are concerned with practical suggestions for providing for the following instructional aspects in your science classroom: arranging excellent science learning activities for *all* your students, and effectively using computers and other electronic technology. And finally, the Appendices offer you the latest resources for securing additional information and items needed to bring excellent science learning to your elementary and middle grade students.

SUMMARY

The world is replete with diversity, but also with order. Science offers all of us ways to understand, make predictions about, and adapt to our complex environment. Scientists' ways of studying the world include both empirical and analytic procedures. Science for children should model scientists' methods of investigation. This can be best achieved through a minds-on/hands-on approach. At the empirical level of investigation, scientists/students take in information and organize it for analysis. Empirical processes of science include observation, classification, and measurement. At the analytic level, scientists/students interpret their findings by using processes such as hypothesizing, controlled experimenting, inferring, and predicting. Numerous other scientific process skills are identified that can be used daily by all of us in our in-school and out-of-school problem solving. The products of empirical and analytic procedures in science are facts, concepts, principles, and theories. The products of science do not stand alone, but are connected to real-world evidence through science processes.

Both scientists and nonscientists are fascinated by the world around them. Finding nature's secrets and solving the world's problems can be an arduous task. Curiosity—the urge, even rage, to know—is the driving force behind science. Scientists attempt to overcome human tendencies to become frustrated by thinking positively about the negative or inconclusive outcomes of their investigations. Scientists insist on examining evidence offered in support of conclusions. No matter how painful, scientists must be willing to modify old ideas when new evidence surfaces. They also strive to avoid the unscientific teleological and anthropomorphic explanations we all tend to use occasionally, and they seek answers that focus on cause and effect. One important way this is done is through building in the control of relevant variables in their experiments.

Science is closely connected to technology and society. Science proposes explanations about the natural world, and technology proposes solutions for problems of human adaptation to the environment. Both science and technology must be society-oriented and must help people find answers to their problems. The following implications for an STS focus at the elementary and middle school levels were given:

■ Students must be guided to search for science/technology/society (STS) connections.
■ Students must be helped to find real-life STS issues, questions, and problems.
■ Students must be involved in STS investigations looking for answers to and making wise decisions for those problems relevant to them.

The "Taxonomy of the Five Domains of Science Education" offers a comprehensive view of STS education. Suggestions are supplied about various STS problem-solving procedures. STS problem solving in elementary and middle grades should seek to integrate or correlate STS activities with *all* curricular subjects. By doing so, you can guide your students toward becoming scientifically/technologically literate citizens.

Consistent with the descriptions of science, technology, society, and children developed in the chapter, the goals of elementary science education are:

1. to nurture and sustain children's curiosity about the world;
2. to help children develop process skills for investigating the natural world, solving problems, and making decisions;
3. to develop children's knowledge base in science and technology; and
4. to develop children's understanding of and positive attitudes about the nature, limits, and possibilities of science and technology.

SELF-ASSESSMENT AND FURTHER STUDY

1. List several facts, concepts, and principles associated with the theory of gravitation. (For example: *Fact*—all objects attract one another gravitationally; *concept*—mass; *principle*—gravitational forces are larger for large ob-

jects). Select a second theory and list facts, concepts, and principles associated with it.

2. Pick two scientific or technological discoveries or inventions that have been used to improve the earth's environment and/or to improve people and their lives. In addition, list some positive and possible negative effects of using these discoveries or inventions.

3. When working with children, listen to their scientific explanations. Identify those statements that are *anthropomorphic* and *teleological* and help students reword them so they are more scientifically accurate.

4. Using the following as a beginning source, find real, everyday issues and problems that students could use as the foci for an STS problem solving investigation:

   ■ *Science Through Science, Technology, and Society* (S-STS)
   The Pennsylvania State University
   128 Willard Building
   University Park, PA 16802
   (Publishes *S-STS REPORTER* quarterly with the latest national STS activities and reviews of STS curriculum materials.)

   ■ *The Child's World: Presenting Technology to Children in the Primary and Junior Divisions* (Willowdale, Ontario, Canada: Metropolitan Toronto School Board, 1989).

   ■ Rodger W. Bybee, et al., *Science and Technology Education for the Elementary Schools: Frameworks for Curriculum and Education for the Elementary Years* (Andover, MA: National Center for Improving Science Education, The NETWORK, Inc., 1989).

   ■ *Science for All Americans: Project 2061* (Washington, DC: American Association for the Advancement of Science, 1989).

5. Using data from #4, talk with children to identify everyday STS problems in their lives (e.g., consumer choices, health, nutrition, or local environmental issues). Write down specific questions for which they want to find answers.

6. Select one of the problem-solving approaches from this chapter and use it as a format for planning problem-solving activities in an STS study of interest to children.

7. Describe in your own words what you think Marjorie Gardner's phrase "minds-on/hands-on" science activities means.

8. With a child, interview a scientist, engineer, physician, computer expert, or other individual in your community using science and technology in their career. Help the child form interview questions about how and why the people chose their scientific or technological careers, who or what influenced them, what training they needed, what specifically they do, what are the positive and negative features of their work, and where is the field heading in the future.

9. Working with a cooperative group, research and list reasons you agree or disagree that science and technology should be connected and be society-oriented. Document your sources.

10. Pick one of these domains in the Taxonomy in Figure 1–8: imagining and creating, feeling and valuing, or using and applying. Select one of the goals within the domain you chose and develop a lesson that will help children achieve that goal.

NOTES

1. Robert E. Yager, "The Constructivist Learning Model: Toward Real Reform in Science Education," *The Science Teacher,* 58, no. 6 (September 1991): 54.

2. Susan Loucks-Horsley, et al., *Elementary School Science for the 90's* (Andover, MA: The NETWORK, Inc., 1990), Chapter 3, "Connect Science to Technology," 27. Reproduced with permission of the National Center for Improving Science Education/The NETWORK, Inc. Copyright © 1990.

3. The work of an important partnership concerned with developing scientific literacy is reported in Rodger W. Bybee, chair, et al., *Science and Technology Education for the Elementary Schools: Framework for Curriculum and Instruction* (Andover, MA and Washington, DC: A Partnership of the NETWORK, Inc. and the Biological Sciences Curriculum Study, Colorado Springs, CO, 1989).

4. See Robert M. Hazen and James Trefil, *Science Matters: Achieving Scientific Literacy* (New York: Doubleday, 1990).

5. John S. Rigden, "The Art of Great Science," *Phi Delta Kappan,* 64, no. 9 (September 1983): 613–17.

6. Horace Freeland Judson, *The Search for Solutions* (New York: Holt, Rinehart & Winston, 1980), 114.

7. Nancy Paulu with Margery Martin, *Helping Your Child Learn Science* (Washington, DC: U.S. Department of Education, Office of Educational Research and Improvement, 1991), 5.

8. Steven W. Gilbert, "Model Building and a Definition of Science," *Journal of Research in Science Teaching,* 28, 1 (February 1991): 73–79.

9. Ina V. S. Mullis and Lynn B. Jenkins, *The Science Report Card: Elements of Risk and Recovery* (Princeton, NJ: Educational Testing Service, 1988).

10. For excellent coverage on this topic, see Kenneth R. Mechling and Donna L. Oliver, *Handbook I. Science Teaches Basic Skills* (Washington, DC: National Science Teachers Association, 1983), 8–12.

11. A brief but well-written account can be found in Don Nelson, "The Scientific Method: A Primer," *Science and Children,* 25, no. 8 (May 1988), 32–33.

12. A broader list of scientific attitudes for children to develop is given in Bybee, et al., ibid., 50–52.

13. James Trefil, "Quantum Physics' World: Now You See It, Now You Don't," *Smithsonian,* (August 1987), 69.

14. M. F. Perutz, *Is Science Necessary* (New York: E. P. Dutton, 1989).

15. "What is TEI? Interview with Norman Bodek," *TEI—Total Employee Involvement,* 1, no. 1 (May 1988), 4.

16. For more anecdotal examples of the human side of such famous scientists as Hilaire Chardonnet, Alexander Fleming, and Niels Bohr, see Burnett Cross, "A Passion Within Reason: The Human Side of Process," *Science and Children,* 27, no. 4 (January 1990), 16–21.

17. Paulu and Martin, 1991, op. cit., 3.

18. For more on the work of Project 2061 see F. James Rutherford and Andrew Ahlgren, *Science for All Americans* (New York: Oxford Press, 1990).

19. The author is indebted to Susan Loucks-Horsley, et al., 1989, op. cit., especially Chapter 3, "Connect Science to Technology," 27–39.
20. Paul W. Brandwein and Lynn W. Glass, "A Permanent Agenda for Science Teachers, Part II: What Is Good Science Teaching?" *The Science Teacher,* 58, no. 4 (April 1991), 37–38.
21. "Science Teachers Speak Out: The NSTA Lead Paper on Science and Technology Education for the 21st Century Adopted by the NSTA Board of Directors January 1990," *NSTA Reports,* (April/May 1990), 42.
22. For a fuller explanation read Edward L. Pizzini, Sandra A. Bell, and Daniel S. Shepardson, "Rethinking Thinking in the Science Classroom," *The Science Teacher,* 55, no. 9 (December 1988), 22–25.
23. *NSTA Reports,* (April/May 1990), 43.
24. Bryan Nordstrum, "Advice from a Collegiate Colleague," *Science and Children,* 28, no. 8 (May 1991), 17.
25. Phyllis Huff, et al., Chapter 1, "Excellence in Elementary Education," in John E. Penick and Mitzi Bame, (Eds.). *Focus on Excellence—Elementary Science Revisited,* vol. 4, no. 3 (Washington, DC: National Science Teachers Association, 1988), 7.
26. Alan J. McCormack and Robert E. Yager, "A New Taxonomy of Science Education," *The Science Teacher,* 56, no. 2 (February 1989), 47–48.
27. Rodger Bybee, et al., 1989 op. cit., 20–27.

This emerging school of thought—which many researchers and educators call cognitive learning theory or constructivism—proposes that students actively learn and constantly construct their world view. This view of learning extends the developmental perspective of Piaget. . . . The constructivist view of learning is linked to three related ideas: prior knowledge, student learning styles, and concentration on depth and understanding, rather than on breadth of coverage and knowledge of vocabulary.[1]

CHAPTER 2

Learning Science

What is the relevance of Piagetian, constructivist, and other cognitive theories to science teaching?

As described in Chapter 1, science is an active enterprise that involves observing what's happening in the real world and trying to make sense out of it through models and theories about how the world works. Science is both content (what we know) and process (how we find out). Scientists and educators generally agree that the best way for children to learn science is through an active minds-on/hands-on approach that involves them in observing, measuring, predicting, inferring, investigating, and explaining the world in ways that parallel the methods of scientists. In teaching science to children in this active way, teachers need to have a good practical and theoretical understanding of characteristic ways that children learn and think about science, how they develop cognitively, and how such things as learning styles and common misconceptions affect their learning. This chapter provides background on these topics that will be helpful to you in teaching science. The chapter is organized around the following questions:

- What is the nature of knowledge? How is knowledge acquired and organized into memory?
- What roles do prior knowledge, information processing skills, and metacognition play in the acquisition and use of knowledge?
- What are the bottlenecks in the process of acquiring and using knowledge?
- How do students' naive theories and misconceptions affect learning?
- What are the current findings and theories on children's cognitive development and what are the implications for your classroom teaching?
- What is cooperative learning, how can it enrich your students, and what are ways for you to effectively use it in your science?
- How can the research findings about learning styles help you plan, prepare, and teach your students more effectively?

Suggestions are also offered throughout the chapter and in a special section at the end of the chapter for ways to implement the various research findings and theoretical ideas in your science teaching for greater student learning.

/// LEARNING THEORIES

Two main approaches to understanding learning—behaviorism and cognitivism—are available to teachers today. Prior to about 1975, the dominant approach to studying learning by psychologists was behaviorism. Behavioral theories focus on the external aspects of learning, including external stimuli, behavioral responses of learners, and reinforcers that follow appropriate responses. Classroom discipline systems involving rewards and punishment are usually based on behavioral theories. Behavioral theories also provide background for expository teaching approaches in which teachers present directly to children information to be learned. These approaches emphasize analyzing the material to be learned into small segments, writing behavioral objectives for each segment, presenting information to be learned very clearly and concisely, providing for a great deal of student practice, providing immediate feedback on student responses, and providing for frequent review.[2] An expository teaching model called *direct instruction* is presented in Chapter 3.

In contrast to behavioral approaches, most current theoretical approaches to learning come from a cognitive perspective. Cognitive psychologists are concerned not only with the external, observable events of learning but also with what goes on inside the learner's head—how knowledge is acquired, organized, stored in memory, and used in further learning and thinking. Look again at the chapter opening quotation, which emphasizes that in the cognitive view of learning the learner must be an active processor rather than a passive recipient of information. Some contemporary cognitive theories about how children learn and think in science and that provide background for

guided discovery models of teaching are given in the following sections.[3]

The Importance of Prior Knowledge

Cognitive approaches to learning are centered on the nature and organization of *knowledge* and how it is acquired. Chapter 1 introduced you to the vital importance of prior knowledge to both scientists and students. What they both bring to their problem solving and learning experiences critically affects how they learn and build new knowledge. The acquisition of new knowledge always occurs in the context of and is heavily influenced by pre-existing knowledge.

Look at Figure 2–1. What do you see? Study the figure before reading on. The same sensory data are available to all of us. You could probably reproduce an accurate sketch of the figure after studying it for a few seconds. The figure can be interpreted as a bear climbing up the other side of a tree. Do you see the figure differently after reading this interpretation? The bear is not inherent in the figure, but is a result of your own perception of the lines, based on the ideas you bring to the picture.[4]

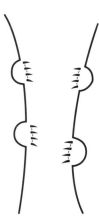

FIGURE 2–1

What do you see in the figure? What you see depends on your prior knowledge and assumptions.

In a similar way, what a student is likely to see in a science investigation also depends on prior knowledge. In a research study, Champagne and Hornig[5] note that students who observed science demonstrations reported observations more closely aligned with their *existing* viewpoints than with what actually happened. Our prior knowledge and assumptions help us to make sense of new experiences and information.

Declarative and Procedural Knowledge

Cognitive psychologists view knowledge as consisting of complex networks of information and skills. Much of the information in the knowledge base can be classified as either declarative knowledge (knowledge about something) or procedural knowledge (knowledge of how to do something). *Declarative knowledge* is knowledge about facts, concepts, and principles that can be told (declared) to others. *Procedural knowledge* is our knowledge of how to perform various physical and intellectual tasks. Procedural knowledge is learned by doing something with declarative knowledge, such as drawing inferences, constructing classifications, or making generalizations from facts available in the declarative knowledge system.

An example of declarative knowledge in science would be knowledge about light. Through science classes, children are expected to acquire factual knowledge about light, for example, that light appears to travel in straight lines; light travels very fast; the colors in the spectrum are red, orange, yellow, green, blue, indigo, and violet (ROY G BIV). Children must also know many terms related to light such as *transparent, translucent, opaque, lens, convex,* and *concave.*[6]

One criticism of elementary science teaching in the United States has been that teachers too often treat science primarily as declarative knowledge, that is, as a body of isolated facts, definitions of concepts, and statements of principles to be directly taught to the child. Although learning facts and definitions should be a part of science classes, science is much more than declarative knowledge about the world.

Procedural knowledge is knowledge that can be used in interpreting new situations, solving problems, thinking, and reasoning. In science, procedural knowledge is both needed in and constructed from such minds-on tasks as classifying minerals, inferring the cause of the morning dew, measuring the height of plants in an investigation, and predicting whether bulbs will light in a given circuit arrangement. In learning science, children should acquire both declarative knowledge (e.g., knowledge about reflection; knowledge about air pressure) and procedural knowledge (e.g., how to use knowledge about reflection to build a periscope; how to use air pressure concepts and principles to explain air pressure phenomena).

Schemata

An important property of information in memory is its organization. Cognitive psychologists believe that associated information and skills about a topic are organized in memory as networks or *schemata* (plural of *schema*). A **schema** is a cognitive framework in which we organize and store past experiences and knowledge. A schema may contain both declarative and procedural knowledge. For example, an "electricity schema" might contain such things as declarative knowledge about electrical terms, procedures for wiring a circuit, information about the function and use of electric meters, and safety rules.

According to schema theory, information is organized in such a way that the activation of one piece of information in a schema tends to activate associated information in the schema. For instance, when a problem related to electricity is encountered, the whole electricity schema might be activated and made ready for potential use.

Schemata fulfill a number of functions in learning and problem solving. They help in the assimilation of new information, provide a basis for inferences that fill in gaps in incoming information, and help to direct searches of the environment for further needed information.

Instruction must attend to the development of schemata through allowing pupils time and opportunity to construct various links among information and procedures. Students should not be left totally on their own; teachers need to provide deliberate support for students in constructing schemata. Support can be provided through questioning, supplying needed information, emphasizing connections, and suggesting alternative ways of looking at a situation.

The use of *concept maps* is one teaching technique to help children develop interrelated knowledge and understandings that make up useful schemata.[7] Figure 2–2 shows a concept map framework and an example of its use with

FIGURE 2–2

A, the concept map framework. B, a concept map for the concept of condensation

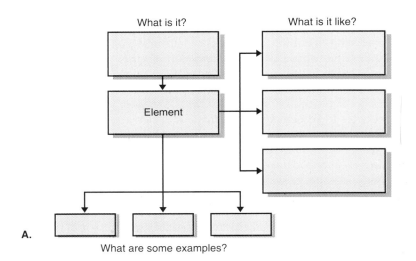

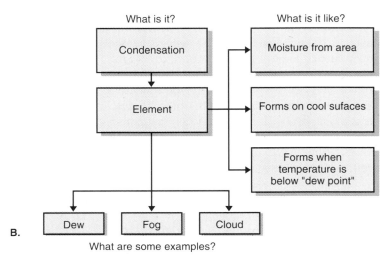

Teachers can coach students as they construct their own schemata, building on what they already know.

the concept of condensation. In using concept maps, the teacher draws the framework on the chalkboard or transparency and explains that each of the three components is necessary for a good understanding of the concept. Using information from prior experiences, hands-on investigations, texts, and other sources, the teacher and students complete as much of the framework as possible. The completed concept map is referred to often in subsequent investigations, reading, and discussion. The emphasis in instruction should be not only on understanding specific concepts but also on helping children learn how to use concept maps as a tool in developing concepts in general.

Assimilation and Accommodation

Because we are always encountering new experiences and ideas, knowledge is dynamic and in a constant state of flux. Growth of the knowledge base involves both the assimilation of new information to existing schemata and the accommodation or modification of existing schemata to better fit reality. Jean Piaget has used the term **assimilation** for the learning process in which new information is incorporated into existing schemata without the need to make major changes in the schemata. In assimilation, learners draw upon relevant schemata to assist them in organizing and making sense of new experiences. Current cognitive theorists have used the term *accretion* for the process of assimilating new knowledge into the knowledge base.

Piaget used the term **accommodation** to refer to the learning process in which existing schemata have to be altered to enable the schemata to better fit novel situations. Contemporary cognitive theorists have considerably elab-

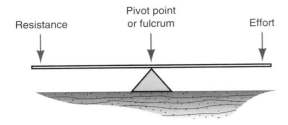

A. First-class lever

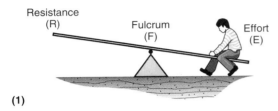

(1)

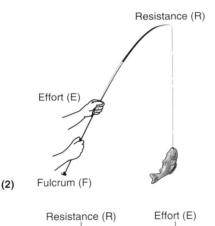

(2) Fulcrum (F)

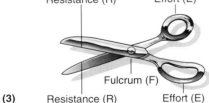

(3)

B. Which of these levers are first-class levers?

FIGURE 2–3

A, for a first-class lever, the resistance is at one end of the bar, the effort is at the other, and the fulcrum is in the middle. *B,* the tuning of a first-class lever schema.

orated Piaget's notion of accommodation, describing it in terms of creating, tuning, and restructuring schemata.[8]

Schema creation, the first type of accommodation, is the process of building new schemata to fit new information and ideas. For example, a student may have no schema to use in making sense of the term *first-class lever.* To understand the term the student would need to learn the following information:

■ A lever is a bar that is free to turn on a pivot point called a fulcrum.
■ A lever can be used to move a weight, called the resistance.
■ The force exerted to move the weight is called the effort.
■ For a first-class lever, the resistance is at one end of the bar, the effort is at the other end, and the fulcrum is in the middle, as shown in Figure 2–3A.

In creating a schema, such information would have to be practiced, elaborated on, interrelated, and organized in the mind into a useful and coherent form.

Tuning, a second process involved in accommodation, is the modification and refinement of a schema as a result of using it in different situations. Shuell outlines three learning mechanisms that are used as the basis for tuning.[9] First, a schema is broadened in its range of application through its generalization to new situations. For example, students might be shown a variety of levers and asked to determine which of them are first-class levers, as in Figure 2–2B. Students would broaden their understanding of first-class levers as they struggled to generalize their concept to new situations. Second, through a tuning process called *discrimination,* the range of applicability of a schema is refined by eliminating situations in which the knowledge would not apply. For instance, through recognizing that in some levers the fulcrum is not between the effort and the resistance, the students would further refine their schemata about first-class levers. Third, schemata are strengthened through practice, that is, through their use in many varied situations.

Restructuring, the third subprocess in accommodation, involves a more complete reorganization of an existing schema. For instance, suppose a student is required to construct a lever that can be used to move a larger weight by the use of a smaller effort. The knowledge incorporated in the first-class lever schema outlined previously is not sufficient to solve this task, which requires that the parts of a lever now be considered relationally. However, the student might restructure the schema by integrating it with knowledge gained from many playground experiences with seesaws or teeter-totters. Through playground experiences children have learned to balance heavier children by having them sit closer to the fulcrum. Thus, the students might restructure their lever schema through reorganizing it around the general rule "the greater the resistance, the closer to the fulcrum it should be placed." The teaching key in facilitating accommodation is to provide for the application of schemata in many different, challenging situations and to provide guidance and feedback to students as they work to apply and refine their existing knowledge.

In posing challenges to children teachers must consider their levels of development. Some restructuring of schemata may call for higher-order thinking abilities that elementary children have not yet developed. Carrying the lever example a step further, suppose that a student is faced with the task of predicting where an 80-gram weight would need to be placed on a balance scale to balance a 40-gram weight. Generalizing from the seesaw schema, the child would have knowledge that the heavier weight would go closer to the center, but how much closer? According to Piaget, this task requires proportional reasoning, a type of formal operational thinking that develops in adolescence and beyond. The proportionality task, then, would not be developmentally appropriate for most elementary school children.

Piaget's view of the developmental nature of knowledge is presented more extensively later in this chapter.

Information Processing

In acquiring new knowledge, information is received, encoded, transformed, and related to prior knowledge through the application of a variety of *information-processing skills.*

Attention. Processing of incoming information is strongly affected by attention. Under ordinary circumstances, learners can attend to only one information stream at a time. Competing stimuli vie for the learner's attention. In the context of learning, one function of discipline management systems is to control and direct attention. Discovery learning activities are intrinsically interesting to children and naturally engage their attention.

Encoding. Stimuli attended to must be encoded for further processing. Siegler[10] describes *encoding* as a process by which incoming information about objects and events is segmented and represented in memory. Information may be encoded in various forms: in terms of actions, images, words, and other symbols. The process of encoding plays a central role in learning. Situations that stimulate learning generally afford large amounts of information, only some of which is relevant. Learners do not usually attend to all possible features and relations within a situation, but they will likely encode a greater number of features and relations than they will use, even though they may initially fail to encode some features that are critical to learning or problem solving. How learners encode new stimuli depends on the nature and quality of their prior knowledge and whether they access that knowledge. Teachers can play an important role in facilitating encoding. The work of Siegler[11] and others shows that when children, including very young children, are helped to encode the necessary features of a situation, their problem-solving success increases dramatically.

The concept of *selective encoding* is a main feature of the new theory of intelligence proposed by psychologist Robert Sternberg.[12] Selective encoding involves sifting out relevant information from irrelevant information and representing it for further processing. Sternberg and Powell[13] have summarized the results of a number of studies on selective encoding in learning and problem solving. A major difference between better and poorer students seems to be the ability of the better students to recognize what information is important in a situation and what information to deemphasize or ignore. Successful learners also spend relatively more time encoding the terms of a problem. The longer encoding time presumably enables more effective encoding, which facilitates subsequent processing of information. Primary grade children often fail to encode all available information and jump prematurely to closure in a problem-solving or learning situation. Older children encode more exhaustively, but may fail to use all of the relevant encoded information. One way that teachers can facilitate science learning is by helping learners to focus on, take time to encode, and use more of the relevant information in learning and problem solving.

Memory. Models of memory sometimes distinguish between *short-term memory,* also called conscious thought or active memory, and *long-term memory,* which also may be referred to as stored information. Using Figure 2−4, from the work of Patricia Keig[14], follow this description of the two memory processes.

Input from the environment (or input from prior knowledge stored in long-term memory) is the stimulus for thinking. Input information is encoded and temporarily parked in short-term or active memory for further processing. Both the capacity and the duration of information in short-term memory present *bottlenecks* to the flow of information processing. Ordinarily, only a few items (about 7, plus or minus 2) can be kept at one time in the short-term store. Unless it is actively rehearsed through repetition or elaboration, information can be maintained in short-term memory for only 15 to 20 seconds (as many of us know when we forget what we went to the refrigerator to get). Also, information cannot be passed along to long-term storage for later recall or retrieval unless it is actively rehearsed.

To recall or retrieve facts and concepts, *key ideas* are activated and spread to linked concepts and details (schemata). Recognition is a part of remembering or recalling, but when it doesn't happen quickly, a memory may be salvaged by following a trail from an observed cue

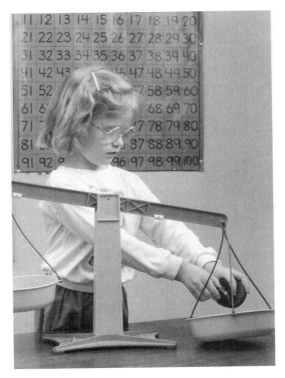

Proportional reasoning is used to balance a heavier weight with a lighter weight on an equal-arm balance.

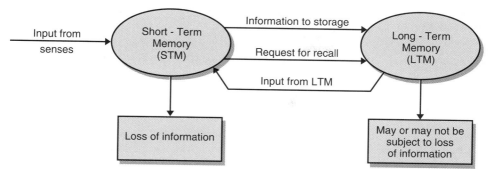

FIGURE 2–4

Simplified model of the memory system showing short-term (conscious thought) and long-term memory (stored information)

Source: Patricia F. Keig, "About Memory Facts and Concepts," *Science and Children,* 26, no. 8 (May 1989), 35.

to *linked details.* If the related details are not there, the chain of memory breaks down. Researchers tell us that memory links involved in schemata are made best when

■ information is highlighted, emphasized, made salient, or presented in other "memorable," not incidental, ways;

■ items are linked together logically or occur together in space or time; and

■ information is meaningful to the learner.

Meaning is not inherent in a learning situation. Rather, as was suggested earlier, meaning must be constructed by the learner. Information is *made* meaningful by learners through the association of the new information with their similar previous experiences and prior knowledge. The challenge for teachers, is to present information and activities that help students make memorable links with their prior experiences and knowledge. The best way to meet this challenge in science is through engaging students in situations in which they actively construct ideas through their own explorations, investigations, and analyses.

Metacognition. You may be very familiar with the notion of metacognition from your

studies of the reading process. *Metacognition* refers to the use of strategies that enable us to control and regulate our cognitive efforts. According to Linda Baker[15], a reading specialist, these strategies include planning what to do, implementing our plans, monitoring our efforts and checking the outcomes, assessing the effectiveness of our actions, remediating or adjusting any difficulties, and revising our learning and problem-solving approaches. Cognitive research indicates that learning can improve substantially when learners become more strategic in their approaches.

A goal of science instruction is that learners should develop autonomy or complete self-regulation of their own learning processes and strategies. Figure 2–5 summarizes the self-regulation process showing possible alternative routes to assimilation or accommodation.

/// NAIVE THEORIES AND MISCONCEPTIONS

When children come to science classes, they already have formed many ideas about the world from their daily experiences. Frequently

FIGURE 2–5

Self-regulation

Source: Charles R. Berman, *An Expanded View of the Learning Cycle: New Ideas About an Effective Teaching Strategy* (Washington, DC: Council for Elementary Science International, January 1990), 3.

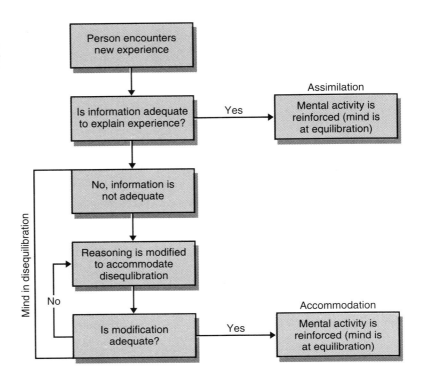

their ideas are not congruent with accepted scientific views. These misconceptions and naive theories reflect their special perspective as children. They also represent a particularly tenacious type of prior knowledge that must be dealt with in teaching elementary and middle grade science. Below are two humorous examples from Paulu and Martin's[16] collection of sixth grade students' misconceptions:

Fossils are bones that animals are through wearing.

Some people can tell what time it is by looking at the sun, but I have never been able to make out the numbers.

William C. Philips[17], an earth science teacher, compiled a list of 50 commonly held misconceptions in earth science from observations of his own students and research over a decade.

Although Philips compiled his list by age levels, he cautions us to remember that those misconceptions held by adults may also be held by children and vice versa. Here is a small sampling of misconceptions about the atmosphere:

K–9

Rain comes from holes in clouds.
Rain occurs when clouds get scrambled and melt.
God and angels cause thunder and lightning.
Clouds are made of cotton, wool, or smoke.

College

Frontal rain is caused by "cooling by contact" between fronts.

Adults

*The oxygen we breathe does not come
from plants.*

*One degree of temperature is smaller on
the Celsius and Kelvin scales than on
the Fahrenheit.*

Table 2–1 lists some additional examples of discrepancies between students' naive theories and scientific explanations.

Misconceptions and naive theories may persist even after students successfully complete traditional science courses. The problem is that naive theories are derived from prior experiences and have inherent validity. After all, stones do fall faster than leaves. Also, students may not experience things that contradict their naive theories, such as leaves and stones falling together in a vacuum. Naive theories are functional and allow students to function adequately in their everyday lives. Kathleen Roth describes an interesting example from her research and that of Charles Anderson and Edward Smith.[18] Students may not know the word *photosynthesis,* but they have a lot of ideas, some of them false, about the concept. They may have the misconception, for instance, that plants get their food from the soil through their roots. This naive explanation conflicts in critical ways with the scientific view that plants use sunlight to make food from carbon dioxide and water. But the students have arrived at their explanations through their own experience with plants (and perhaps with "plant food" that is mixed with the soil to "nourish" plants), and the explanations work for them. Personal theories are not easy to give up.

Research studies show that learners' misconceptions must be changed *before* more accurate concepts and explanations can be learned. This is difficult, as the research indicates that learners hold fast to misconceptions, even into adulthood. Further, research shows that when students' observations do not fit their predictions, they simply criticize the experiment. Also, students sometimes forget or choose not to use parts of the explanations that do not fit their own predictions. How then can you guide students into changing from their scientific misconceptions and naive beliefs to new and more sophisticated scientific notions?

Meaningful learning in science often requires students to go through a difficult process of conceptual change. Kathleen Roth[19] suggests that for conceptual change to occur, students need to recognize that their own personal the-

TABLE 2–1
Naive theories versus scientific explanations

Science Topics	Naive Theories	Scientific Explanations
Heat and temperature	Temperatures change due to flow of heat into or out of objects.	Kinetic-molecular model and heat as form of energy.
Inheritance	Individuals acquire physical characteristics (fair-skinned parents darkened in tropics having dark-skinned children).	Only genetically determined traits are inheritable.
Motion of objects	Heavier objects fall faster than light ones.	Acceleration is proportionate to force.

ories are in conflict with accepted scientific views. They need to be convinced that their own theories are inadequate, incomplete, or inconsistent with experimental evidence, and that the scientific explanations provide a more convincing and powerful alternative to their own notions. Roth believes that students need repeated opportunities to struggle with the inconsistencies between their own ideas and scientific explanations, to reorganize their ways of thinking, to abandon or modify ideas that have served them well in everyday life, and to make appropriate links between their own ideas and scientific concepts.

Additional ways of finding out about your students' misconceptions are addressed in Chapter 5, devoted to assessment. These assessment techniques can also help you discover other student factors that affect learning and teaching (e.g., student learning styles).

/// COGNITIVE DEVELOPMENT AND SCIENCE TEACHING

Through some 60 years of research with children, Jean Piaget formulated a major theory of how children develop in their ways of knowing and solving problems. Piaget dominated the field of cognitive psychology from the 1920s until the late 1970s. Science educators discovered Piaget's work around 1960. Piaget's viewpoint of knowledge as complex and hierarchically structured and of the learner as an active constructor of his or her own knowledge offered science educators a welcomed alternative to the behaviorism and associationism that was the vogue in the 1960s in American psychology. Piaget's studies of children's thinking about a wide variety of phenomena, concepts, and principles of science proved to be a rich source of ideas in the design of science programs and instructional strategies. Piagetian theory was thus influential in virtually all of the

elementary science curriculum development projects of the 1960s and has remained prominent in science education research and practice into the 1990s.

Although his findings about children have generally stood the test of time, cognitive psychologists today have challenged some of Piaget's theoretical conclusions. Nevertheless, Piaget's work on children's thinking about natural phenomena and scientific concepts has heuristic value to science teachers.

At this point in your professional preparation, you probably have considerable knowledge of children's cognitive development; this is a cumulative result of your psychology, child development, and curriculum courses, of intelligently observing children, and perhaps raising your own children. Therefore, the presentation here will focus primarily on those aspects of Piaget's theory that are particularly applicable to science teaching.

Cognitive Stages

Piaget has treated children's responses to the natural world in terms of four stages. Table 2–2 is a brief summary of research by Piaget and others of the four stages of cognitive development. In thinking about the stages, keep in mind several things:

1. Even though the stage concept has been challenged by cognitive psychologists today, it is a useful one for elementary and middle grade science teaching because it gives teachers a general idea of the thinking patterns of pupils at different ages.
2. The ages associated with each Piagetian stage are only averages. Many children in a given age group may not have developed the characteristics indicated for that age.
3. The stages are hierarchically ordered. Each successive stage incorporates and builds on the preceding one. Thus, the sequence for

TABLE 2–2

Characteristics of thinking in Piaget's four stages of intellectual development

Sensorimotor (birth to 2 years)

The child

1. adapts to the external world through actions;
2. initially has no language or other means for labeling or representing objects and actions;
3. lacks representational means and does not "think" about the world;
4. by the end of the stage has developed rudimentary schemata for coordinating actions related to substance, space, time, and causality; and
5. begins to develop language for naming familiar things and actions.

Preoperational (2 to 7 years)

The child

1. develops extensive vocabulary;
2. makes judgments on the basis of perceptions, not conceptual considerations;
3. groups things based on familiar properties;
4. begins to develop extensive physical knowledge of the properties and behaviors of objects and organisms in the world;
5. does not think "reversibly";
6. does not think about parts and wholes simultaneously; and
7. takes a subjective, egocentric view of the world.

Concrete Operational (7 to 11 years)

The child

1. takes an objective view of the world, shifts reflectively from one aspect of a situation to another, and considers elements of a whole simultaneously rather than just successively.
2. begins to think operationally (i.e., groups elements into coherent wholes and considers elements and wholes reversibly);
3. uses operational thinking to form classes and series;
4. forms and uses relationships, including one-to-one correspondences, rules, simple scientific principles, and cause and effect relationships; and
5. conserves substance, liquid volume, length, area, and weight.

Formal Operational (11 to 14+ years)

The child

1. does higher-order thinking about the knowledge formed at the previous levels;
2. forms hypotheses, carries out controlled investigations, and relates evidence to theories;
3. deals with ratios, proportions, and probabilities; and
4. constructs and understands complex explanations involving deductive chains of logic.

passing through the four stages is always the same. No person skips a stage.

4. When children reach each stage can vary considerably with differences in backgrounds and abilities. It is not unusual, for example, for children to be a year or more behind the average performance for their ages. Although they may be slower in cognitive development, this does not necessarily mean they will be cognitively inferior in later years to those who develop earlier.

The stages and their relevance to science teaching are described in more detail in the following sections.

FIGURE 2–6
Infants act on but do not represent and think about objects.

Sensorimotor Stage (Birth to 2 Years)

The child at birth can respond to specific stimuli through a few innate reflexes, but initially has virtually no knowledge useful for adapting to the environment. As a *constructivist,* Piaget emphasized that each person has to build his or her own knowledge structures. In the sensorimotor stage infants begin the long process of constructing adaptive knowledge. Children in this stage can perform only motor actions; initially lacking language and other representational functions, they cannot yet *think* about objects and events. For example, infants are fascinated with rattles (see Figure 2–6). When children in the sensorimotor stage see rattles, they try to grasp them, jangle them, throw them, and, if given the chance, put them in their mouths. But they cannot represent and think about them in the same way that adults can label and think about objects.

Many of the sensorimotor child's movements are, in a sense, experiments with the environment. Children explore the world by adapting their innate reflexes to the objects around them. Like the baby with the rattle, they grasp, push, and place things in their

mouths. They proceed to coordinate the possible actions on various objects into sensorimotor schemas.

Space at the sensorimotor level is initially limited to the area in which children can act, time is limited to the duration of their actions, and objects come and go and are not permanent. Even the most rudimentary sense of direction and purpose does not develop until later in the sensorimotor stage. For example, children at this stage are unable to detour or remove an obstacle without losing sight of where they are going.

Children progressively construct more elaborate schemas as they develop. Schemas related to causality, space, substance, and time are constructed during this period. Through adaptive actions, children at the sensorimotor stage progress from an almost total lack of knowledge to the capability of coordinating means-end relations (causality); understanding object permanence and exploring new features of objects (substance); understanding the spatial relationships among objects in the environment, which enables the child to deal with the immediate world as well as with things that are distant and out of reach (spatial schema); and coordinating hindsight and present actions to anticipate possibilities in the immediate future (time). Such schemata lay the foundation for later scientific thought.

Children at the sensorimotor stage initially have no means for representing objects or actions. At the end of the period they are becoming able to represent objects through a variety of means, including mental images, gestures, play, and most importantly, language. This enables them to call to mind (re-present) and think about people, animals, objects, and activities. By age 2, they have names for many things and activities, enabling them to elaborate their concepts in the next stage.

The reason it is important for you to consider the sensorimotor stage, even if you will not have children at this level in your classes, is that you should understand thought development as a continuous, constructive process from birth through adolescence. It begins with actions and progresses toward sensorimotor schemas that coordinate actions. This process continues toward preoperational and fully operational thought.

Preoperational Stage (2 to 7 Years)

The preoperational stage is marked especially by the child's language development. At age 18 months, the average vocabulary of children is 22 words; by age 5 it exceeds 2,200.[20] Children's very early language seems primarily concerned with naming things (balls, dogs, cars), performing social functions (saying "hi" and "bye"), and obtaining desired goals, such as food or drink. By age 5 they can use language in most of the ways that adults can. For example, they are able to request and give instructions and to give explanations of a limited form.

Largely because of the seemingly advanced verbal abilities of many young children, it is often hard for teachers to keep in mind that the thinking processes of the preoperational child

are really quite limited. Three main developments occur at this stage in the growth of a child's thought that are particularly important for science teaching.

1. Children develop from subjective, egocentric viewpoints toward objectivity. Preoperational children do not view a problem to be solved in terms of causes and effects independent of their own actions. For example, in a pendulum experiment carried out by Piaget and his colleague, Barbel Inhelder, young children constantly interfered with the swinging pendulum, grabbing hold of it or giving it an added shove. They did not give objective accounts of the experiment and failed to determine which factors might play a causal role in the pendulum's action.

In a billiard game experiment, children were able to aim a plunger to bounce a ball off of a wall and hit a target. The children focused on and were successful in achieving the goal, but they did not ask themselves why they succeeded. They did not view the physical situation objectively, from a point of view centered on the objects rather than on themselves. Thus they were unable to discover the law of reflection governing the apparatus. Viewing physical situations objectively rather than subjectively is one of the prerequisites to constructing and using lawful relationships in science. Children at the preoperational level are limited in their ability both to discover relationships in science and to understand and remember them from direct instruction.

2. Children at the preoperational level develop from successive toward simultaneous or reversible processing of information. In problem solving at the preoperational level, children tend to process information successively, step-by-step, rather than considering information together as a whole. At the preoperational level, for example, children develop the ability to group objects by common properties and, if the number is small, to count the number of objects in the group. For instance, children might put 4 nickels in one group and 2 pennies in another group. They can also combine the two groups and say there are 6 coins in all. But when asked, "Are there more nickels or more coins?" they reason that there are 4 nickels, leaving only 2 coins, so there are more nickels than coins. (See Figure 2–7.)

Success with the task, requires that the children be able to move back and forth reversibly between the class (coins) and the subclasses (nickels and pennies). In the successive thinking that is characteristic of the preoperational level, children consider the part (the nickels) or the whole (the coins), but do not consider the part and the whole simultaneously when making comparative judgments. The sequence for the development of classification abilities is shown in Table 2–3.

3. Children at the preoperational level develop from perceptual viewpoints toward conceptual viewpoints of the world. Preoperational children tend to center their attention on a striking feature of an object or problem but ignore or neglect other important features. They can shift their attention to a second feature, but when they do they tend to forget the first.

For example, in the conservation of substance experiment described in Figure 2–8, young children focus on the greater length of the transformed ball of clay, ignoring the fact that the lump is now thinner, and judge that the

rolled out clay is now "more." The children fail to conserve substance; that is, they do not realize that the amount of clay before the transformation is the same amount as afterward.

As shown in Table 2–4, young children also fail to conserve length, liquid quantity, number, area, weight, and displacement volume. Conservation of substance, length, and liquid quantity generally mark the transition from preoperational to concrete operational thought. In thinking about the transition from one stage to another, however, you should keep in mind that stages do not mean distinct, sudden changes in development. Psychologists caution us about implying that stages mean long periods of stability followed by abrupt change. Changes from one stage to another don't happen that way. Rather, most important changes happen gradually over months or years.

Preoperational children have great difficulty in carrying out meaningful measurement procedures. Consider the problems that first or second graders would have in measuring length, for example, if they did not agree that a meter stick (as well as the object measured) keeps its same length even when moved about. Or, how can they learn about pints and quarts if they do not realize that quart jars can come in many different shapes and still hold the same amount?

Concrete Operational Stage (7 to 11 Years)

The nucleus of Piaget's theory of cognitive development is a type of thinking that he called operational thinking. *Operational thinking* involves coordinating mental elements into coherent wholes or groups. A main characteristic of this special mode of thought is that it is "reversible", that is, groups that are formed by linking elements together logically can be disassembled and the individual elements returned to their starting points. Being able to

FIGURE 2–7
The concrete operational child deals reversibly with classes and subclasses.

TABLE 2–3
Classification hierarchy

Classification Task	Age Approximations
1. Grouping by a single characteristic perceptually apparent; for example, color	3–4 years
2. Grouping by abstracting common property; for example, child sees sticks and notes some are long, then collects only long ones	3–4 years
3. Multiple classification—can classify by more than one property; for example, color, size, and shape	4–5 years
4. Grouping by realizing all objects are the same in some respects but different in others; for example, fingers all grasp, but vary in shape	4–5 years
5. Class inclusion—forms subclasses and includes major classes; for example, a bird has feathers (class); some are white and some black (subclass); if asked if there are more black feathers than feathers, will say more feathers	6–10 years
6. Ascending hierarchy; for example, cat is a mammal	7–10 years
7. Descending hierarchy; for example, mammals include cats	9–10 years
8. Establishing multiple criteria for a relatively complex classification system; defines characteristics for supraordinate and subordinate classes; for example, supraordinate group (mammals) have hair, nurse their young, and so on; subordinate class (humans) stand erect, have opposite thumbs, and so on	11–14 years

Note: Remember that the ages are only approximations. A third or more of any class may not achieve the levels until a year or more later.

construct holistic groups and to shift reversibly between parts and wholes enables a person to build and use relationships in thinking about the world.

Three main types of holistic groups formed at the concrete operational level are particularly important for elementary science:

1. Classes, including concepts and hierarchical classes.
2. Series, including measurable variables used in science and mathematics, such as length, volume, weight, and temperature.
3. Relationships, including one-to-one correspondences, rules, cause and effect relationships, and simple principles or natural laws.

In addition to developing reversible thinking, at the concrete operational period children also begin to be able to take an objective rather than just a subjective viewpoint of the world and to take a conceptual orientation to a situation rather than just a perceptual view.

Concrete operational thinking can be thought of as a rudimentary type of scientific

Conservations of Substance, Interview Activity

1. Take two pieces of clay and make them into two balls, so they are approximately equal.

2. Ask, "Are these two balls equal?" If the child responds "no," ask: "Why are they not equal?" The child may say that one is bigger than the other. If this is true, pinch some clay off one, and say: "Are they equal now?" The child will probably say yes.
3. Tell the child you are going to change one of the balls of clay into a hot dog. Roll out the clay.

Ask, "Are the two pieces of clay equal now, or does one have more or less clay than the other?" The child will probably say the rolled-out clay has more.

FIGURE 2–8
Child centers on length and thinks there is more.

thinking. Both research and practical experience show that somewhere between grades one and four, most children begin to make the shift from manipulating, naming, and grouping objects (preoperational) to describing, organizing, and relating properties of things (concrete operational). Given the chance through hands-on science, concrete operational thinkers begin to organize investigations in terms of classes and variables, to measure variables meaningfully, to be able to understand and record data on charts and tables, to form and understand simple relationships, to use what they know to make direct inferences and predictions, and to do some

generalizing from common experiences. These early concrete operational years can be especially exciting times in science for children and their teachers.

Although thinking processes are considerably advanced over those of the prior level, they are still quite limited at the concrete operational stage. Children at this level must still stay quite close to concrete, immediate, practical situations. They tend to investigate unsystematically, omitting or forgetting relevant steps and information. Even though they can form relationships, they have great difficulty in transferring concepts and principles to new situa-

TABLE 2-4
Conservation hierarchy

Types of Conservation	Approximate Age	Cognition
Conservation of substance	6–7	Realizes amount of substance does not change by dividing it
Conservation of length	6–7	Realizes, for example, bending a wire does not change its length
Conservation of a continuous quantity	6–7	Realizes pouring liquid from one container to another does not change the quantity
Conservation of number	6½–7	Realizes rearranging objects does not change their number
Conservation of area	7	Realizes the area of a paper split in half covers just as much area as if it were whole
Conservation of weight	9–12	Realizes a mashed piece of clay weighs the same as when it was a sphere
Conservation of volume	11–12+	Realizes that a mashed piece of clay immersed in a liquid will occupy as much volume as when it was a sphere

tions. Thus, careful guidance and instruction by reflective teachers is especially important for concrete operational children.

Formal Operational Stage (12 Years Through Early Adulthood)

At the formal operational level, individuals begin to do thinking about thinking. That is, they begin to be able to do higher-order thinking with the classes, series, and relationships formed at the concrete operational level. The cognitive advances at the formal operational level make the following types of thinking tasks possible:

1. Searching for an underlying natural order connecting events.
2. Dealing with abstractions about concrete objects and events.
3. Dealing with hypothetical or possible arrangements, not just actual, concrete ones.
4. Formulating hypotheses.
5. Planning experiments carefully, in terms of responding (independent) and manipulated (dependent) variables and variables to be controlled.
6. Carrying out experiments (fair tests) systematically.
7. Organizing and thinking about complex data sets.
8. Expressing relationships quantitatively as well as qualitatively.
9. Dealing deductively with propositions about the world.

Types of organizations of knowledge that are formed at the formal operational level include the following:

1. Proportional relationships that coordinate several variable factors at one time.
2. Correlations and probabilities.
3. Theories and models that coordinate facts, concepts, and principles.
4. Experimental plans that involve the control of variables.
5. Explanations of complex events requiring chains of deductive logic.

Children in the formal operational stage understand the necessity of controlling variables in investigations. For example in a pendulum investigation (Figure 2–9A), they learn to control the length of the string and the release point, keeping them constant, and to manipulate only the weight to determine its effect on the rate of swing of the pendulum. Concrete operational children, on the other hand, are likely to vary two or more factors at a time and to confuse the data collected.

Formal operational youngsters can also use ratios and proportional relationships in analyzing physical situations. In working with an equal-arm balance (Figure 2–9B), they realize that the two weights and the two distances are proportionally related. Thus, they understand

that doubling the weight on one side can be compensated for by decreasing the distance of the weight from the fulcrum by one-half on that side. Children at the formal operational level can also understand that the product of the weight and distance on one side of the fulcrum must be equal to the product and distance on the other side for balance.

Formal operations enable the learner to understand the role of both the volume and the weight of an object in predicting whether it will float or sink in water. Preoperational children may say that an object floats because it is light, but when another light object sinks they will say it sank because it was heavy.

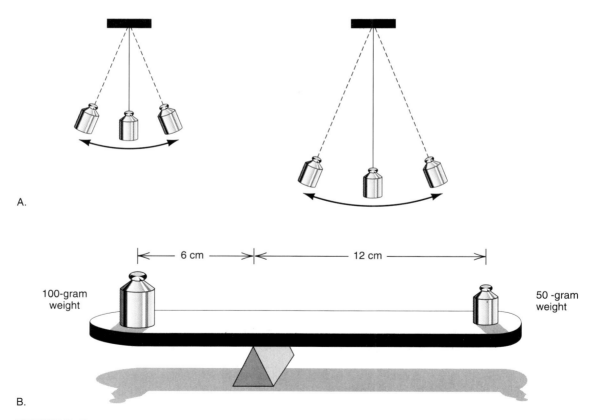

A.

6 cm
12 cm

100-gram
weight

50 -gram
weight

B.

FIGURE 2–9
Pendulum and balance Piagetian activities

Concrete operational children are more consistent in their reasoning about floating and sinking. They can order things from light to heavy and from small to large in volume. They can also place these two sets of variables in correspondence. (See Figure 2–10.) But they are still likely to confuse weight and volume. Children at the concrete operational stage think that a heavy lead cylinder will displace more water in a graduated cylinder than a lighter aluminum cylinder that is the same volume (size). They fail to realize that it is the volume of the cylinder, not its weight, that is the critical factor.

At the formal operational level, students can coordinate weight and volume, and they can reason that an object will sink if it is too heavy for its size. Further, they are able to coordinate weight and volume into the single concept of density.

Having the capability of carrying out higher-order, formal operational tasks and actually doing so independently are two very different things. Although some students at the formal operational level achieve autonomy, most students need and want *mutuality,* that is, they need the cooperation and support of other students and of a teacher in thinking formally about the world.

Factors Influencing Cognitive Development

Piaget identified four main factors that influence cognitive development:

1. *Physical Maturation.* Biological growth of the central nervous system and other body parts.

FIGURE 2–10
Examples of concrete operations with floating and sinking

Operation	Activity or Observation
Classifying	Floating versus sinking Heavy versus light Large versus small
Identifying variables and serially ordering them	Weight Volume
Placing two sets of variables in correspondence	Large and heavy Small and heavy Large and light Small and light

2. *Physical Experience.* Experiences with the physical world, including manipulation of materials objects.

3. *Social Interaction.* Interactions with other people, including formal schooling.

4. *Equilibration.* A self-regulated learning process involving recognizing discrepancies between physical reality and personal ideas, and actively and persistently working to resolve the discrepancies through assimilation and accommodation.

The first three factors contributing to development are present in most other cognitive development theories. *Equilibration* is unique to Piaget's system and emphasizes the belief that individuals must actively construct their own meanings of the world. Equilibration is a self-regulated process involving curiosity, alertness, risk, effort, and persistence. As described earlier in the chapter, assimilation involves fitting external reality to existing knowledge structures, whereas accommodation involves the modification of knowledge structures to better fit or accommodate to reality.

Physical, Social, and Logical-Mathematical Knowledge

Several different types of knowledge are recognized in Piaget's theory. *Physical knowledge* is knowledge of the properties and behaviors of objects acquired directly from experience. This is a primary type of knowledge to be acquired at every level in science, but particularly in kindergarten and the early grades. Every elementary classroom should have many things for children to explore and ample time for them to develop physical knowledge.

Social knowledge is knowledge we acquire from others through social interactions, including schooling. The names we know for things and their properties, the various conventional organizations of objects and properties into classes, and rules governing the behaviors of things are examples of social knowledge passed along to us from others.

Piaget was especially concerned with the development of *logical-mathematical knowledge,* the type of operational knowledge developed at the concrete and formal operational stages. A classification system, a statement of a relationship between physical variables, or a complex plan for controlling variables in experimenting are examples of logical-mathematical knowledge. A main assumption of constructivist approaches to teaching is that if physical knowledge and social knowledge are to be really useful in adapting to the environment through learning and thinking, they must be made operational and integrated into the existing knowledge base through constructive, problem-solving activities.

Developmentally Appropriate Science Instruction

Kindergarten Through Grade 2. Kindergarten, first, and second grade children are most likely to think about the world preoperationally. In brief, the preoperational child can be characterized primarily as an explorer and intuitive thinker. To promote the development of thinking, knowledge, and cognitive structures during the preoperational period, teachers should take the following steps:

1. Provide children many opportunities to explore objects and events in the surrounding world.

2. Help children focus on the properties of objects, that is, on the characteristics that make one object like or different from other objects.

3. Teach the meanings of words in the context of activities; allow many opportunities for students to use language to describe objects and events.

4. Understand that using correct language and understanding a concept are not the same thing.

5. Provide for considerable practice on the things to be learned.
6. Help children learn to question their own ideas and those of others, to explore systematically, and to learn how to evaluate evidence.
7. Use social interaction, including cooperative learning, to provide the child with multiple viewpoints; children should exchange ideas honestly and argue among themselves about the merits of their ideas.
8. Help children look beyond salient characteristics of a situation to possible relationships; help children to make connections between things; lead children to shift attention from one aspect of a situation to another and then to come back to the first thing; provide many opportunities for children to compare and contrast different objects and events.
9. Continually help children to see the parts of a situation or system in relation to the whole.

Grades 3 Through 5. Although learners at these grade levels are generally concrete operational, children in grade 3 often show preoperational traits of thought. Fourth graders are beginning to observe more carefully, to collect and organize data, and to ask more profound questions about the "whys" of nature. To provide cognitive support to learners at these grade levels, teachers should help students with these tasks:

1. Gather complete information from a situation in a systematic way.
2. Be alert to problems, discrepancies, and conflicts in the perceived situation.
3. Analyze situations and problems into smaller parts.
4. Label objects, properties, and actions precisely so that they can be better remembered and discussed.
5. Identify variable factors that might enter into problem solutions.

6. Collect observational data or information for problem solutions into a table, chart, or some other organized form.
7. Use diagrams, working models, charts, graphs, and pictures as well as verbal language in expressing ideas.
8. Develop generalizations, draw many inferences, and make frequent predictions using observational information and prior knowledge.

Cognitive Development and Science in Grades 5 and 6. Children in the fifth and sixth grades are not likely to be formal operational thinkers yet. But there is a world of difference between them and their younger schoolmates. Children at this level tend to search for patterns in their physical and social environments, examining their own beliefs and those of others. They are aware of cause and effect, reciprocal relationships, and the influence of events on each other. Boys in this age group are interested in technology; the interest of girls in technology increases when some sort of social involvement with technology is evident; both sexes are very interested in animals.

Consistent with these characteristics of fifth and sixth grade children, the challenge for teachers is to develop and implement a science program that will meet these criteria:

1. Introduce students to a wide variety of objects and events in the natural and man-made world.
2. Portray science to children as an unending quest to find hidden likenesses and order among the diverse objects and events in a world filled with diversity.
3. Help students become familiar with styles of scientific thinking so that, as they grow, they can participate in science, use technology wisely, and analyze important social issues related to science and technology.
4. Help children—especially girls and minority group youngsters—recognize science and

technology as cooperative human endeavors open to everyone.

/// LEARNING SCIENCE PROCESS SKILLS

Chapter 1 introduced you to the importance of children learning science process skills, such as observing, measuring, inferring, and investigating. Robert Gagné[21] emphasizes structure and sequence in the learning of science processes (as well as other intellectual skills). In devising learning sequences, he advocates beginning with the *final* behavior to be learned (usually a complex, problem-solving skill) and working backward. For example, to do task 8, you need 7; to do 7, you need 6 and 5, and so on. Prerequisite tasks are then sequentially organized into a hierarchy of tasks, from simple to complex, described as behavioral objectives. Both subject matter content and process skills are needed for mastery in science. In Gagné's approach, learning is assessed in terms of well-defined steps, moving from simple and concrete to more complex and abstract skills, concepts, and principles. Science—A Process Approach, an elementary school science program developed under the guidance of Gagné, uses this learning hierarchy theory.

/// COOPERATIVE LEARNING

Glenn T. Seaborg, the 1951 Nobel Prize winner in Chemistry and now the Principal Investigator for the Great Explorations in Math and Science (GEMS) science curriculum project, reminds us that cooperation is the norm in science. Seaborg says,

In the case of all great "discoveries" it must be remembered that science is a group process. When we devise experiments and research today, we do so on the basis of an enormous body of knowledge contributed by people from all over the world over thousands of years. . . . The modern research effort is above all a team effort.[22]

Working cooperatively is important for children also. A grandmother was taking care of

Social interaction through cooperative learning helps students try out new ideas and retain what they learn.

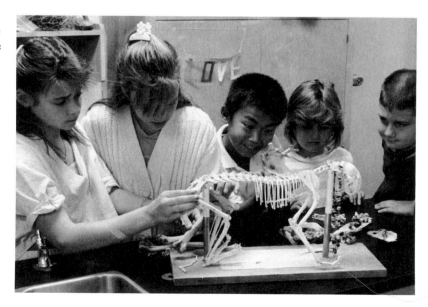

her 2-year-old twin granddaughters, when one asked for something. Not understanding what the child said, she turned to the other twin and asked, "Sarah, what is Allison saying?" Children have a special way of communicating with one another that enables them to work well together. Researchers have also found that many students learn more effectively in cooperative learning situations.

Cooperative learning usually refers to students working collaboratively in small groups, considering a problem or assignment together, verbalizing what they know, considering the multiple viewpoints of the group members, taking data together, and coming up with group solutions to problems. This is different from **competitive** learning where students compete for grades, or from **individualized** learning where students work alone. Cooperative learning has these features:

- Group members are assigned roles (e.g., principal investigator, recorder, materials manager, or reporter).
- There is face-to-face interaction among students.
- Students are responsible for their own learning as well as for that of their teammates.
- Teachers help students develop interpersonal small-group skills.
- Teachers interact with the groups as needed.

Cooperative learning activities in science and other subjects have been shown to be helpful in

1. producing greater achievement in many subject areas and in a wide age range.
2. making students more positive towards their school, teachers, subject areas, and each other (regardless of abilities, special needs, or culturally diverse backgrounds).
3. developing interaction skills in children.
4. creating positive and realistic student expectations about working with each other.
5. helping teachers manage their hands-on science programs by showing students how to take more responsibility for helping each other with assignments and problems, and distributing, using, and returning science materials.
6. improving student self-confidence.

In teaching science you should use *all* three of these types of instructional techniques. Individualized learning is best used to acquire specific declarative knowledge or to practice some new skill. Competitive learning is useful for review or practice. Cooperative learning is appropriate for problem solving, discovery or inquiry, for developing divergent thinking, or for students tutoring students.

Specifics on how to incorporate cooperative group learning in your science program are supplied in Chapter 3 in which the minds-on/hands-on guided discovery approach is detailed and in Chapter 6 on planning and managing your science program.

/// PRACTICAL APPLICATIONS OF COGNITIVE RESEARCH

Often no clear prescriptions to teaching can be drawn from cognitive research. But as suggested by John Dewey[23] in the 1929 *Kappa Delta Pi* lecture, taking a theoretical perspective can help you make observations about learners that might otherwise escape you; you will be enabled to interpret some facts that would otherwise be confused and misunderstood; and your instructional practice will be rendered more intelligent, more flexible, and better adapted to deal effectively with the concrete actions in the classroom. In short, a theoretical perspective can lead to teaching as a true profession rather than as a technical activity.

You can use your own understanding of Piagetian and other cognitive learning theories to begin to formulate your own approach to teaching. You are invited to selectively pick from the viewpoints, suggestions, and applications that follow. No single method of teaching science has been found in the research to be consistently best for the wide range of children, objectives, and classroom situations that you will encounter. Take only information and teaching/learning activities that are suited to *your* unique educational classroom needs.

Pay Attention to Students' Learning Styles

When teaching, look around the classroom and you will see that students not only look and dress differently, have different prior knowledge, misconceptions and naive theories, but they also react very differently to instruction. That is, they learn differently! Andy's answers burst out before your question is even finished. Paula reflects on possible answers for many seconds before timidly raising her hand. Jon doesn't respond at all and sits drawing pictures. Researchers call this wide array of perceiving, interacting with, and responding to the learning environment **learning styles.**

Because students have different learning styles, you must provide for a variety of learning modalities: *tactical* (involving bodily actions, manipulation of objects, hands-on), *auditory* (using the ears), *visual* (employing sight), *cerebral* (involving the mind), and even *olfactoral* (utilizing smell). Dunn and Dunn tell us that when students are taught through modalities that complement their learning styles, they learn better and achieve higher test scores.[24]

Move from the Concrete to the Abstract in Teaching

Research supports moving students' thinking from the concrete to the more abstract levels. Table 2–5 provides guidelines to help you select appropriate concrete-to-abstract experiences for your students.

Use the Learning Cycle in Teaching Science

The **learning cycle** is an approach to science teaching developed by Robert Karplus for the Science Curriculum Improvement Study (SCIS) program. The SCIS program is described in Chapter 7. Research on the learning cycle shows that students understand science better and are more likely to apply what they learn if they are not only given the opportunity and time to explore natural phenomena directly but also have the chance to interact with a knowledgeable teacher who can provide relevant instruction and feedback related to their questions. In this approach to learning, teachers act as facilitators, guides, and informers. The learning cycle has three instructional phases:

1. *Exploration.* In this phase students are allowed to explore materials freely, leading to questions and tentative ideas;
2. *Invention.* In this phase the teacher, generally through expository (e.g., direct instruction) methods invents concepts and principles that help children answer their questions and reorganize their ideas; and
3. *Application.* In this phase children try out their newly learned ideas by transferring them to new situations.

At the exploration phase, prior knowledge relevant to the problem is accessed and used in initial organization of new ideas. Chapter 3 of this text provides many examples of guided explorations in science for children. At the invention phase in the learning cycle, children are guided in forming new, powerful ideas and linking them with prior knowledge. This phase is described in more detail in Chapter 8 in connection with a discussion of science and the reading process. At the invention phase, children's incorrect notions should be squarely confronted. Students need repeated opportunities to realize that there may be problems with their spontaneous ideas and to modify

TABLE 2–5
Levels of abstraction

	Levels	Descriptions	Classroom Examples
Most Concrete	1	Active, multisensory experiences with real objects or places	Visit nursery to buy plants, plant seeds
	2	Activities that emerge from within child through art, music, and other forms of self-expression	Paint picture of garden, make up a song about seeds
	3	Use of 3-dimensional models	Sort artificial plants by size
	4	Use of pictures, diagrams, films, videotapes, teacher demonstrations	Teacher shows how to plant seeds, teacher reads books to children
	5	Complete task structured by adults	Color ditto picture of seeds, cut out teacher-drawn plants
Most Abstract	6	Require children to establish relationships between or among entities	Read the words *plant* and *seed,* count out a specific number of seeds

those ideas under the guidance of a teacher. In the application phase, the newly formed ideas are elaborated and strengthened through their application in new situations.

Use Advance Organizers

A minds-on/hands-on approach to teaching science is critically important and is the approach most emphasized in this text. However, expository methods are still useful for teaching information. The problem when teaching by direct, expository methods is how to make the new information truly meaningful. David Ausubel, an educational psychologist, emphasizes that information presented in an expository way through lecture, text, or some form of media is meaningfully learned only when it relates to prior knowledge.[25] Ausubel recommends the use of advance organizers to facilitate meaningful expository learning.

An **advance organizer** is an abstract, general introduction to a new body of information or subject matter content to be learned. The advance organizer is presented early in instruction to provide a framework for assimilating new ideas. In developing advance organizers, the new subject matter, whether from textbooks or teachers, should be assembled, organized, and sequenced in ways that can be made meaningful to children. Advance organizers should be drawn from the main principles and supporting concepts and facts to be learned. Ausubel has emphasized recently that advance organizers should incorporate both declarative and procedural knowledge.

Although the advance organizers are to be general and abstract, they can be presented in a context of examples and situations that are familiar to children using hands-on activities. The use of teacher demonstrations, diagrams, and pictures are especially recommended in the intermediate and upper elementary grades to teach advance organizers. Many textbook programs are consistent with these ideas.

Use Mastery Learning Techniques

A method for individualized learning that involves some cooperative learning features has been developed by Benjamin Bloom and his associates.[26] The teaching technique, called **mastery learning,** approximates the many positive learning effects of tutoring or "one-on-one teaching." This teaching technique has these characteristics:

1. The teacher teaches the whole class, actively involving students and reinforcing their contributions frequently.
2. At the end of a teaching unit (about two weeks), the teacher gives a "formative test" to ascertain needs for "corrective teaching." This test is not for grading, but to assess what students have not learned.
3. Common errors are identified from test results.
4. Unlearned materials are retaught in new ways.
5. Students work in groups of two or three for 20 to 30 minutes to help one another on items missed previously. If no one in the group can help, they call on the teacher.
6. Workbook exercises, text readings, films, filmstrips, or videotapes are assigned for students who need additional help.
7. An "evaluation test" is given to students as a final step.

Slower students are helped more in cooperative classroom environments when fellow students explain the content in language they understand. Teachers can help slower students in individualized instruction by giving them addi-

tional review, guided practice, and independent practice.

Use a Variety of Activities

Researchers stress that students learn best through a variety of activities, since students in any given classroom are functioning on many different cognitive levels and with diverse learning styles. Therefore, all of these activities should be used where appropriate to your students' developmental levels and learning styles: telling; showing; reading to children; using textbooks, objects, diagrams, pictures, films, filmstrips, and videotapes; minds-on/hands-on activities; computers and other electronic technology; and other teaching approaches with which you feel comfortable. This text presents a wide array of teaching activities available to you.

Providing minds-on/hands-on learning experiences that engage students in discovering science concepts for themselves is particularly important in science. This involves your careful planning and direction, so that the lessons go well and students are guided to the desired objectives and conclusions. For this reason, this text refers to this type of learning as **guided discovery,** and Chapter 3 describes it more fully. Guided discovery should be used along with other teaching/learning activities. The direct or explicit, step-by-step, or hierarchical, instruction of such psychologists as Bloom and Rosenshine should be selected when you want to teach specific skills in a sequential way.

Select Fewer Topics and Study Them Longer

Learning is an active process of construction relating new material and prior knowledge; it takes time and cannot be rushed. Therefore, your students should study fewer scientific topics, themes, or problems in depth, rather than superficially "covering" many topics. This view of topic selection has been referred to as "Less is more and longer is better." Your science topics should be studied for several weeks or longer to allow for many opportunities for your students to ask *their* questions, conduct *their* inquiries, and then construct *their* own scientific concepts from *their* observations, data collection, and tests.

This long-range exposure focuses on your students having time to construct their own meanings instead of cataloging isolated bits of information. You should emphasize *quality* and not quantity of scientific ideas and understanding, not merely memory. Your classroom should be a rich learning environment that encourages depth in exploration and concept construction related to science, technology, and societal interactions of the two.

A perennial dilemma for teachers is the decision of which concepts, topics, themes, or problems to select for your students to study in depth. Consider these variables when making those decisions. Scientific topics to be studied should

- be of interest to students and relevant to their lives;
- be organized around scientific content and processes;
- include a focus on technological applications and societal implications;
- use materials readily available in school; and
- include scientific concepts modified to your own circumstances from many different sources.

Here are a few sources for you to consider when selecting and organizing themes, problems, concepts, attitudes, and skills (from whatever sources) for your science program:

- **AAAS Project 2061**
American Association for the Advancement of Science
1333 H Street, N.W.
Washington, DC 20005

Identifies six common themes that pervade science, mathematics, and technology: systems, models (including physical conceptual, and mathematical), constancy (including stability and equilibrium, conservation, and symmetry), patterns of change including trends, cycles, and chaos), evolution (including possibilities, rates, and interaction), and scale.

- **California State Department of Education**
Publications
PO Box 271
Sacramento, CA 95802-0271

Identifies six major overarching scientific themes: energy, evolution, patterns of change, stability, systems, interactions, and scale and structure.

- **The National Center for Improving Science Education**
A Partnership of the NETWORK, Inc. and Biological Sciences
Curriculum Study (BSCS)
300 Brickstone Square, Suite 900
Andover, MA 01810
OR
1920 L. Street N.W., Suite 202
Washington, DC 20036

Identifies nine major organizing concepts with STS FOCUS: organizing, cause and effect, systems, scale, models, change, structure and function, discontinuous and continuous properties, and diversity.

- **NSTA Scope, Sequence, and Coordination (SS&C) Project**
National Science Teachers Association
1742 Connecticut Avenue N.W.
Washington, DC 20009

Although the major work of this NSTA project is currently in secondary science education, elementary and middle school scientific concepts are also being identified.

Assess Your Students' Progress Often

Assessment is a vital part of teaching with a Piagetian, cognitivist, or constructivist approach, and it shouldn't come only at the end of a study. By using a wide variety of assessment techniques at the beginning of, during, and at the conclusion of a science topic, you will get valuable information about your students that will help you plan for appropriate learning experiences. Assessment will help you determine students' prior knowledge, misconceptions, and naive theories. You will discover what your students have learned in your science lessons or what may have to be done further. Assessment can also motivate students to better attend to the assigned materials.

Because students develop meaningful conceptual understandings better in familiar contexts, assessment can aid in finding out about their interests, fears, and other relevant information. Chapter 5 presents formal and informal assessment techniques useful to you for getting a complete picture for effectively planning worthwhile science experiences for your unique students.

Use a Cognitive Instructional Model

A cognitive instructional model, adapted from the work of Daniel Neale,[27] Charles W. Anderson,[28] and others provides an instructional framework for planning the use of such things as the learning cycle, advance organizers, concept maps, and direct instruction. The model consists of nine segments:

1. *Introduction.* Make preliminary comments on lesson goals, content, or activities. This segment is intended to establish focus and to engage the learners.
2. *Review.* Discuss previous relevant lessons to help make appropriate prior knowledge ready for use.
3. *Overview.* Provide an overview of new information or problem; develop advance organizers; elicit children's ideas; brainstorm; discuss; clarify. This segment initiates the accommodation (i.e., creation, tuning, or restructuring) of schemata needed in understanding the phenomena being investigated.
4. *Investigations/Activities.* Children manipulate materials in hands-on activities to test their ideas; the teacher demonstrations that involve the children safely may also be appropriate. This segment incorporates the exploration phase of the "learning cycle" described previously in this chapter. A wide range of types of investigative activities are appropriate here. Some teacher guidance through questions in the form of suggestions, hints, and providing needed information is appropriate.
5. *Representation.* Children represent results of activities through actions, drawings, charts, tables, measurements, words, and concept maps. The key here is developing powerful means of communication; language arts methods of instruction (e.g., writing in journals and webbing) are appropriate here.
6. *Discussion.* Activity results are presented and discussed. The teacher may use questioning strategies here (What did you see or do? Why do you think it happened? What is your evidence?) The teacher particularly notes the use of naive theories and misconceptions, vague and incomplete notions, and blocks to learning that appear to be developmental in nature.
7. *Invention.* New concepts, principles, procedures, or explanations are taught at developmentally appropriate levels through brief direct instruction presentations. Task analysis and sequencing are important. Reading in the text may be useful here. Concept maps may also be used. The focus is not on memorizing but on constructing new knowl-

edge and on meaningful accommodation of existing knowledge that can be used in thinking and problem solving. In this segment children's misconceptions must be confronted with developmentally appropriate scientific knowledge.

8. *Application.* Newly constructed knowledge must be tried out in new situations. This may require a recycling through segments 4, 5, 6, and 7.

9. *Summary/Closure.* Findings, conceptualizations, explanations, and conclusions are summarized and linked to other lessons.

Be Prepared to Take on New Teaching Roles

As you become more aware of the importance of your students' cognitive development, prior knowledge, misconceptions, learning styles, need for fewer scientific concepts, and for providing minds-on/hands-on experiences, you will find that your teaching roles change. Figure 2–11 shows that change. Your primary function will no longer be that of transmitter of information, knowledge, and concepts. You'll see a need to shift away from the traditional teacher

Teachers should do less telling.

Children should do more and act on what they learn.

FIGURE 2–11
Teacher/student roles in constructivist science teaching/learning

Discovery: *The Exploratorium Science Snackbook*

Exploratorium, founded in 1969, is poised to make a major impact on the general problem of science education by providing new ideas for the teaching of science.

—*Dr. Goery Delacote, Executive Director, Exploratorium*

Strategy   Discover students' misconceptions by working alongside using hands-on materials for teaching science.

Exploratorium, a museum for hands-on science in San Francisco, is one of the first of its kind in the United States. Founded in 1969, this museum has over 650 interactive exhibits—and, in the words of Executive Director Dr. Goery Delacote, is poised to make "a major impact on the general problem of science education"—in part, by providing "new ideas for the teaching of science."

The museum has already made an impact in its training of inservice and preservice teachers. Teachers who met through the Exploratorium Teacher Institute created the *Exploratorium Science Snackbook*. The 107 "snacks" in this collection are adaptations of the Exploratorium's exhibits that teachers and students can build easily with "found" or inexpensive materials.

The contributors to the *Snackbook* were inspired by their own hands-on experiences at the Exploratorium and by the recognition that our dependence on textbooks is not the best way to teach science.

The notion behind the *Snackbook* is that today's teachers have to shake themselves free of their own misconceptions of how science should be taught—misconceptions based largely on the way science was taught to them. This resource gives them a tool for creating classroom activities and a chance to discover alongside their students. The *Snackbook* is available for purchase from the Exploratorium; call (800) 359-9899.

On Your Own   Teachers can distribute their own ideas for hands-on learning within their building or district by means of informal newsletters and by circulating copies of their own successful ideas for experiments. Inviting colleagues and students to give feedback will help establish a sense of shared discovery.

This also has potential for enhancing communication between home and school. Parents can be encouraged to contribute ideas for experiments and activities as well as materials.

Source: Exploratorium, 3601 Lyon Street, San Francisco, CA 94123. Photo courtesy of Exploratorium.

Providing a wide range of learning modalities accommodates students' different learning styles.

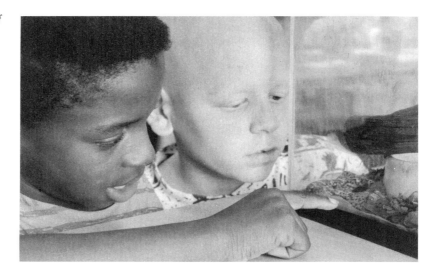

role as teller and students' roles as receivers to the teacher as facilitator and students as actors and doers.

As you move more toward an active, constructivist classroom, you will take on a newer role—facilitator of learning. As a facilitator, you will be engaged more in teaching functions that require the following roles:

1. *Manage* the classroom environment and your students' learning.
2. Be a *model* of the attitudes, skills, and values (i.e., curiosity, empathy, and sensitivity) that you wish your students to develop.
3. *Present* learning options for individual students to consider, choices of goals for groups of students to pursue, and variety in activities for students to engage in.
4. *Observe and listen* to students for information that will assist you in providing the best possible learning environment.
5. *Ask questions and pose problems* to stimulate students to want to seek information and possible solutions.
6. Be a *learning strategist* and make wise decisions concerning when and how to use individual learning, cooperative groups, and competitive activities.
7. *Assess* your students' learning to determine their prior knowledge, how to motivate them for new studies, what they learn in the studies, and how to use all of this data to enrich further learning.
8. *Document* your students' learning.
9. *Coordinate* the "public relations" of your classroom by articulating progress to students, parents, and school administrators.
10. *Build and grow* personally and professionally in *your own* scientific/technological concepts and their interrelationships to your life and society.

Don't be overwhelmed by all of these roles. Remember how terrifying it was to be separated from your mother for the first time in nursery school or kindergarten? Take one step at a time. The rest of this book will supply you with additional resources for you to build and grow professionally, step-by-step.

SUMMARY

An understanding of how children learn science is important in leading them in minds-on/hands-on science activities. Two main approaches to learning theory are available today: behaviorism and cognitivism. Behavioral approaches focus on the connections between the learning stimulus (S) and the learner's behavioral response (R). What is important in establishing S-R connections is clear presentations of stimuli, active learner responses, feedback and reinforcement to the learner from a teacher, and a great deal of practice by the learner. Direct instruction is a teaching model based on this theory.

Cognitive learning theories are concerned with describing what goes on in the learner's head during learning, that is, with how knowledge is acquired, organized, stored in memory, and used in further learning and problem solving. It is helpful to classify knowledge as declarative knowledge (knowledge *about* something) or procedural knowledge (knowledge of *how* to do something). Acquiring declarative knowledge is important in science, but science teachers must lead children to develop procedural knowledge, that is, to be able to *do* something with what they know. Some theorists suggest that knowledge begins as declarative knowledge but becomes procedural as it is used in classifying, inferring, predicting, and generalizing.

According to cognitive theories, knowledge is organized in memory as schemata, which are networks of associated information and skills. In learning, the activation of one piece of information in a schema tends to activate other information in the schema. Schemata help learners assimilate new knowledge, fill in gaps in incoming information, and search for needed information. Assimilation is the process of fitting new information into an existing schema without having to distort the schema. Accommodation is the process of creating new schemata or adjusting existing ones to better fit reality. Assimilation and accommodation are important learning processes in Piaget's theory of intellectual development. Contemporary cognitive researchers have elaborated on the notion of accommodation, describing it in terms of the creation, tuning, and restructuring of schemata. The science teaching key in provoking accommodation is to provide challenging situations for the learner to apply existing knowledge.

Various mental processes present bottlenecks to the flow of information in learning. Attention is critical in learning. What the learner encodes from a situation, how it is encoded, and how much time is allotted to encoding are important variables in the learning process. The brief duration of information in short-term memory, as well as its limited capacity, presents a bottleneck to the flow of information in learning.

Elaboration and repetition of information in short-term memory is a key to its efficient use. The use of effective strategies in metacognitive processing, that is, in planning, monitoring, and assessing the various tasks in learning, is important in knowledge acquisition and use. Part of the function of teachers is to guide young learners in controlling attention, encoding information, using memory efficiently, and developing metacognitive strategies. Self-regulation of learning is the goal, but young learners need mutuality as they progress.

The naive theories and misconceptions that learners bring to science classes must be explicitly dealt with, since they are quite tenacious, even in the face of good instruction. Students must be led to confront their own theories with evidence, to struggle to justify their ideas, and to modify them when necessary.

An important variable in learning is how the learner reacts to teaching and is called *learning styles*. These idiosyncratic learning approaches require teachers to present experiences to learners in a variety of teaching modalities, that is, tactical, auditory, visual, cerebral, and olfactoral. In addition, many students may learn more effectively from other students than from teachers. Cooperative group learning is appropriate in these instances, especially for problem-solving, discovery, or inquiry studies or for developing divergent thinking. Competitive learning is most effective for practice or review. Individualized learning is best used to learn a specific skill or acquire specific knowledge. In minds-on/hands-on science, although all three types of learning activities should be used, cooperative group learning should be stressed.

Piaget's theory has been an important part of science education since the early 1960s. Although contemporary cognitive theorists have challenged portions of Piaget's theory, including the stage notion, his work is important for teaching elementary science. According to Piaget, intellectual development is a product of four factors: physical maturation, physical experience, social interactions, and equilibration. *Equilibration* is Piaget's special term to indicate that the learner is working actively and persistently to resolve discrepancies between reality and his or her own schemata.

Piaget has described the child's thinking in terms of four stages. These four stages are useful in planning for science instruction and in teaching children.

A number of different teaching techniques and strategies are developed in the chapter, including concept maps, advance organizers, the learning cycle, and a comprehensive model of cognitive instruction. As you move more toward a constructivist classroom, the specific ideas in the "Practical Applications" section of this chapter will help you in such areas as assessment, variety of learning activities, using more concrete guided discovery minds-on/hands-on experiences, studying fewer scientific/technological concepts in depth, and becoming more comfortable with new teaching roles as facilitator of learning instead of the more traditional role of transmitter of information.

SELF-ASSESSMENT AND FURTHER STUDY

1. Read the following books and article to research students' misconceptions and naive theories using the following articles as a springboard. Try to ascertain how they are formed and how they can be modified or changed.
   - R. E. Driver, E. Guesne, and A. Tiberghien, *Children's Ideas in Science* (Philadelphia, PA: Open University Press, 1988).
   - *Proceedings of the Second International Seminar: Misconceptions and Educational Strategies in Science and Mathematics* (Ithaca, NY: Cornell University, 1987).
   - Joseph I. Stephans, et al., "Misconceptions Die Hard," *The Science Teacher*, (Sept. 1986), 65–69.
2. Interview students to discover their misconceptions or naive theories about scientific concepts in a topic of your choice.
3. Select a specific scientific/technological concept for a particular group of students and describe how you would teach it to them using concept maps, advance organizers, the learning cycle, and Gagné's learning hierarchies. What major differences would there be? Give reasons for selecting the *one* approach you favor.
4. Using the article on learning styles by Dunn and Dunn in note 24 as a beginning, list different learning styles, under which learning conditions are each most appropriate, and how they can be used successfully to guide the development of concept and skills in a science/technology area.
5. *Minds-on/hands-on* is the term coined to describe activities in which students mentally act (think) about what is being physically manipulated, such as handling, observing, or testing. How effective is this type of activity for teaching/learning science/technology? To find out, start with these references:
   - William C. Kyle, Jr., et al., "What Research Says . . . About Hands-on Science," *Science and Children*, 25, no. 7 (April 1988), 39–41.
   - Ted Bredderman, "Activity Science—The Evidence Shows It Matters," *Science and Children*, 20, no. 1 (September 1982), 39–41.
6. Prepare a plan that incorporates cooperative group, individualized, and competitive learning activities in a science/technology topic.
7. Select a science/technology topic (i.e., energy, pollution, health and nutrition) and prepare a Levels of Abstraction chart like the one in Table 2–5. Include levels of abstraction from most concrete to most abstract, descriptions of activities, and classroom examples.
8. Become more familiar with the new teacher roles in a constructivist classroom. Pick several roles and list specific ways you would incorporate them into *your* science/technology classroom.

NOTES

1. Rodger W. Bybee, chair, et al., *Science and Technology Education for the Elementary Schools: Framework for Curriculum and Instruction* (Andover,

MA and Washington, DC: A Partnership of the NETWORK, Inc. and the Biological Sciences Curriculum Study, Colorado Springs, CO, 1989), 63–64.

2. Barak V. Rosenshine, "Synthesis of Research on Explicit Teaching," *Educational Leadership*, 43, no. 7 (April 1986), 60–69.

3. A good summary of research in cognitive psychology is Thomas J. Shuell, "Cognitive Conceptions of Learning," *Review of Educational Research*, 56, no. 4 (Winter 1986), 411–436.

4. This example is adapted from Norwood Russell Hanson, *Patterns of Discovery* (Cambridge, England: Cambridge University Press, 1965), 12–13.

5. Audrey B. Champagne and Leopold E. Hornig, "Practical Applications of Theories About Learning," *Students and Science Learning* (Washington DC: American Association for the Advancement of Science, 1987).

6. Kathleen J. Roth, "Reading Science Texts for Conceptual Change," in Carol M. Santa and Donna E. Alvermann, (Eds.), *Science Learning: Processes and Applications* (Newark, DE: International Reading Association, 1991), 48–63.

7. Bonnie C. Konopak, "Teaching Vocabulary to Improve Science Learning," in *Science Learning: Processes and Applications*. (Newark, DE: International Reading Association, 1991), 134–146.

8. Shuell, op. cit., 421.

9. Shuell, ibid., 423.

10. Robert S. Siegler, *Children's Thinking* (Englewood Cliffs, NJ: Prentice-Hall, 1986).

11. Siegler, ibid., 87–93.

12. Robert J. Sternberg, *The Triarchic Mind: A New Theory of Human Intelligence* (New York: Viking Penguin Incorporated, 1988).

13. Robert J. Sternberg and J. S. Powell, "The Development of Intelligence," in P. Mussen (Series Ed.) and J. H. Flavell and E. Markman (Vol. Ed.) *Carmichael's Handbook of Child Psychology, Volume 3*. New York: Wiley, 1983.

14. Patricia F. Keig, "About Memory Facts and Concepts," *Science and Children*, 26, no. 8 (May 1989), 35.

15. Linda Baker, "Metacognition, Reading, and Science Education" in *Science Learning: Processes and Applications* (Newark, DE: International Reading Association, 1991), 2–13.

16. Nancy Paulu with Margaret Martin, *Helping Your Child Learn Science* (Washington, DC: U.S. Department of Education, Office of Educational Research and Improvement, 1991).

17. William C. Philips, "Earth Science Misconceptions," *The Science Teacher*, 58, no. 2 (February 1991), 21–22.

18. Research on children's conceptions of photosynthesis is reported in Roth, ibid. and Charles W. Anderson and Edward L. Smith, "Teaching Science," in V. Koelhler (Ed.), *The Educators Handbook: A Research Perspective* (New York: Longman, 1987).

19. Roth, ibid., 49.

20. Robert S. Siegler, "The Origins of Scientific Reasoning," in R. S. Siegler (Ed.) *Children's Thinking: What Develops?* (Hillsdale, NJ: Erlbaum, 1978).

21. Robert M. Gagné, *The Conditions of Learning* (New York: Rinehart & Winston, 1965).

22. Glenn T. Seaborg, "Some Thoughts on Discovery," *GEMS Network News* (Lawrence Hall of Science, University of California, Fall/Winter 1991), 5.
23. John Dewey, *The Sources of a Science of Education* (Kappa Delta Pi Lecture Series), New York: Liveright Publishing Corp., 1929.
24. Kenneth Dunn and Rita Dunn, "Dispelling Outmoded Beliefs About Student Learning," *Educational Leadership,* 44, no. 6 (1987), 55–62.
25. As reported in Anthony Lawson, et al., "Hypothetico-Deductive Reasoning Skill and Concept Acquisition: Testing a Constructivist Hypothesis," *Journal of Research in Science Teaching,* 28, no. 10 (1991), 953–970.
26. For greater detail about Mastery Learning review Paul Chance, "Master of Mastery," *Psychology Today,* (April 1987), 43–46.
27. Daniel C. Neale, "Primary Teachers' Current Practices and Needed Expertise in Science Lessons," presented at the annual Meeting of the National Association for Research in Science Teaching, Washington, DC, (April 1987).
28. Charles W. Anderson, "Strategic Teaching in Science," in B. F. Jones, et al. (Eds.), *Strategic Teaching and Learning: Cognitive Instruction in the Content Areas.* (Alexandria, Virginia: Association for Supervision and Curriculum Development and Elmhurst, IL: North Central Regional Educational Laboratory, 1987) 73–91.

Solid instructional models have students doing science and technology by engaging them in the acts of exploratory investigations, constructing meanings out of their findings, proposing tentative explanations and solutions, exploring concepts again, and then evaluating concepts in reference to their own lives.[1]

CHAPTER 3

Teaching Science

Why emphasize guided discovery minds-on/hands-on activities?

From previous chapters, you know about these important variables affecting your science teaching program:

- The processes and products of science.
- How children learn and think best.
- The interrelationships of science/technology/society.
- Your aims, goals, and objectives for teaching science.

Since these variables are the what and the why of science teaching, begin to consider how you will translate all you have learned into optimal science learning conditions for your students.

/// NO BEST WAY TO TEACH SCIENCE TO ALL CHILDREN

As you saw in Chapters 1 and 2, some of the other variables you must consider involve children's unique learning styles,[2] your teaching styles, physical classroom environment, com- munity and school administration priorities and pressures, and science teaching/learning resources available to you. Because of these variables, you quickly see that there is no best way to teach science to all children.

Teacher as Coach

You are well aware that you don't just "stand up front and teach science." You must constantly make decisions in your role as the professional leader of the learning environment of your classroom. Teacher decision making has been compared to that of a coach calling the plays for a football team. Just as the coach reads the opposition's defense, uses the players' strengths, and uses this information to "hypothesize" the best play, you do the same with your classroom learning variables. You must then select from the many possible teaching/learning activities available to you.

Pass, Run, or Kick? In the football analogy, coaches have two or three main options that make up their plays: pass, run, or kick. You also have options in the "plays" you run, but every action *you* initiate to guide your students "down the field of learning" is called your **teaching methods.** They are your *how* to teach, and you generally have these two broad types of teacher/student transitions, which can be called your "game plays." You can use **direct** or **indirect teaching methods.** But how do you decide which one to use in a particular situation? To answer that question, ask yourself: Would the desired outcome be better achieved through a straightforward transfer of information or by a learner-centered discovery-based method?

A Taxonomy of Common Science Teaching Methods

Some science educators have grouped direct and indirect teaching methods into a **taxonomy** (classification) of these three large groups of common teaching methods:

1. *Listening-Speaking.* Auditory learning in which students learn by hearing.
2. *Reading-Writing.* Visual learning in which students learn by seeing.
3. *Watching-Doing.* Kinesthetic learning in which students learn by doing.

Table 3–1 presents this taxonomy of common teaching methods. As you study Table 3–1, you will see that teaching methods involve several variables. Teaching methods use teaching/learning materials, but are distinct from the materials. For example, if you use a textbook, you could have your students use the text for such different tasks as reading to discover concepts, checking textbook data with what they find in a minds-on/hands-on activity, or getting directions to make a chart or build a model. Often, you might call your transaction or teaching method by the name of the material used (i.e., textbook, or chalkboard) because you are so familiar with it.

How well you use your teaching method depends on how well you have developed or perfected your teaching skills. Getting humor or excitement into your storytelling or lecturing can make these presentations fascinating or dull. But as you know, you can never predict or guarantee how effective any individual teaching method can be, because each student has a unique learning style and other classroom or environmental variables can affect the teaching and learning. That is why you should plan for as wide a variety of teaching/learning methods as you can. You will find that your teaching is enhanced when you try to combine transactions in which students use all of their senses rather than relying on only one. For example, a teacher might show a film about insect metamorphosis and then give each child a vial of fruitfly eggs to hatch. To aid you in selecting such methods, Table 3–1 has a checkmark ($\sqrt{}$) where a method is used in more than one kind of transaction.

How Much Teacher Dominance?

The second column of Table 3–1 is titled "Amount of Teacher Dominance in Method," with a scale showing high, medium, or low. The ratio of teacher dominance and student "passivity," or amount of participation, is one of the most important variables in teaching methods.

Figure 3–1 is a continuum of teacher dominance/student passivity that is based on the teaching methods in Table 3–1.

On one extreme of the continuum is direct instruction (often called explicit teaching or exposition, where the teacher lectures, gives instructions, demonstrates, or leads a field trip. Teacher dominance is high, with students relatively passive. On the other extreme, is indirect instruction (often called *exploration, inquiry, or free discovery*), in which students are most active and the teacher acts as a facilitator for developing student processing skills and building concepts; teacher dominance is low. Between

TABLE 3-1

Taxonomy of common science teaching methods

Nature of Transaction and Method	Amount of Teacher Dominance in Method			Usefulness of Method with Groups of Various Sizes (in numbers of students)				
	High	Medium	Low	1	5	10	15	30
Listening-Speaking Methods								
Lecture Method	*					*	*	*
√Giving Instructions	*			*	*	*	*	*
Recitation Method		*			*	*	*	*
√Drill Method		*		*	*	*	*	*
Review Method		*			*	*	*	*
√Questioning Method		*		*	*	*	*	*
Oral Exam Method		*		*	(Repeated with entire class)			
Discussion Method		*			*	*	*	*
Film Analysis Method			*			*	*	*
Debate Method			*				*	*
Oral Report Method			*		*	*	*	*
Brainstorming Method			*		*	*	*	*
Reading-Writing Methods								
Textbook Method	*			*	*	*	*	*
Workbook Method	*			*	*	*	*	*
Chalkboard Method	*				*	*	*	*
Bulletin Board Method	*							*
√Problem-Solving Method	*			*	*	*	*	*
Laboratory Report Method		*			*	*	*	*
√Team Learning Method			*	*				
				(Repeated with entire class)				
Peer Review Method			*	*	(Repeated with entire class)			
√Peer Tutoring Method			*	*	(Repeated with entire class)			
Programmed Instruction			*	*	*	*	*	*
√Individualized Instruction			*	*	(Repeated with entire class)			
Note-Taking Method			*	*		*	*	*
Journal-Keeping Method			*	*	*	*	*	*
Watching-Doing Methods								
Demonstration Method	*					*	*	*
Field Trip Method	*							*
√Contract Method		*		*	(Repeated with entire class)			
"Hands-On"/Lab Method		*			*	*	*	*
√Inquiry Method		*		*	*	*	*	*
√Learning Center Method			*	*	(Repeated with entire class)			
Projects Method			*	*		*		
				(Repeated with entire class)				
Stimulation Method			*			*	*	*
Games Method			*	*	*	*	*	*
√Exploration-Discovery Method			*	*	*	*	*	*

NOTE: Checkmark (√) indicates that the method is used in more than one kind of transaction: Listening-Speaking, Reading-Writing, and Watching-Doing.

Source: Rita Peterson et al., *Science and Society. A Source Book for Elementary and Junior High School Teachers* (Columbus, OH: Merrill/Macmillan, 1984), 121. Reprinted with permission of the author.

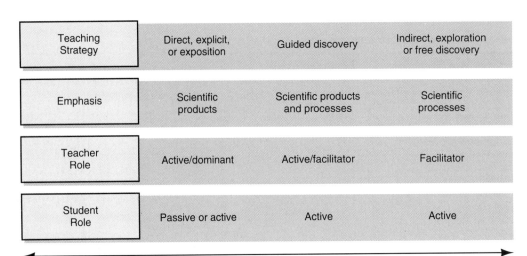

Teaching Strategy	Direct, explicit, or exposition	Guided discovery	Indirect, exploration or free discovery
Emphasis	Scientific products	Scientific products and processes	Scientific processes
Teacher Role	Active/dominant	Active/facilitator	Facilitator
Student Role	Passive or active	Active	Active

FIGURE 3–1

Dominance/passivity of science teaching methods

these two extremes of the teaching continuum is **guided discovery,** in which the teacher is an active facilitator and students are active as well.

You can apply one or all of these teaching methods in your science class as you deem appropriate. Here is a more detailed look at both direct, or explicit instruction, and the more indirect instruction of exposition, exploration, or free discovery, and guided discovery.

/// DIRECT, EXPLICIT, OR EXPOSITION INSTRUCTION

Direct instruction (also called **explicit instruction** or **exposition**), as described in chapter 2, is most effective for the transmission of **social knowledge** (scientific products). In this method, you—as teacher—are the "doer"; however, if this method of instruction is done correctly, students can be actively involved and gain the prior knowledge on which to build higher learning skills and concepts.

Direct instruction is a teaching methodology based solidly in behaviorism and association-

ism. Research findings show that it is most useful for certain types of learning, for example, the learning of facts and simple concepts in science, or the mastery of specific procedures. It emphasizes the *products* of learning more centrally than the *processes* by which students learn. More complex learnings—such as learning to apply science concepts and principles, learning to plan investigations in science, and math problem solving—do not particularly lend themselves to direct instruction techniques.

In the specific and limited situations just mentioned, when teachers explain exactly what students are expected to learn, and clearly demonstrate the steps needed to accomplish a particular task, students learn more effectively.[3] This procedure is based on the assumption that knowing how to learn does not necessarily come naturally to all students. Direct instruction systematically guides students through specific learning steps, helping them to see both the purpose and result of each step. Therefore, ideally, students learn not only the lesson's content, but also a method of learning that content, which may be applicable for other

Direct instruction is an efficient way to teach facts, simple scientific concepts, and work procedures.

content learning. Barak Rosenshine tells us that almost twenty years of research on effective teaching has firmly established the effectiveness of the systematic step-by-step direct or explicit instruction.[4]

When Is Direct Instruction Most Appropriate?

Piaget, constructivists, and other cognitive theorists say that of the three types of knowledge (social, physical, and logical-mathematical), only **social knowledge** can be taught directly by the teacher.[5] In your science teaching, social knowledge would be the body of subject matter or scientific products: facts and concepts. These scientific products are usually presented to students after they have minds-on/hands-on experiences with the science areas, or are guided to the products in books, videos, computers, or films. You readily see that direct or explicit instruction is most useful for teaching a body of content or knowledge or well-defined performance skills. It has been found to be most effective with young learners, slower learners, students with language difficulties, or all students when the content is too difficult or hierarchical.

Here is a brief summary of research on direct instruction showing the situations when its use is most effective:

1. For disseminating information to students not available in any other form.
2. To stimulate interest or motivate students.
3. To learn mastery of facts, rules, or procedures necessary for later learning.
4. To give an introduction to an indirect learning activity.

5. For efficiency or when control is vital.
6. For short-term memory.

Some of the direct instructional strategies you might pick for teaching facts and simple concepts in science are

■ telling,
■ demonstrating using scientific apparatus,
■ carrying on a discussion,
■ reading to children,
■ showing a film, filmstrip, slides, or TV presentation, and
■ having a resource person present something.

Rosenshine's Direct Teaching Strategy

Barak Rosenshine, in summarizing research studies on effective teaching divided direct or explicit instruction into these six teaching functions:

1. Daily review.
2. Presentation of new materials.
3. Conducting guided practice.
4. Providing feedback and corrections.
5. Conducting independent practice.
6. Weekly and monthly reviews.[6]

In Figure 3–2 Rosenshine outlines how to use these six direct or explicit instruction components successfully in your classroom. Further elaboration of this outline is given by Rosenshine in Figure 3–3.

Here is a condensation of Rosenshine's direct instruction steps:

■ Precisely state lesson goals for students.
■ Focus on one thought at a time before beginning another.
■ Teach in small steps, checking for understanding before going on to the next step.
■ Give step-by-step directions.
■ Organize material so one point is mastered before the next is given.
■ Avoid digressions.

1. Review
Review homework.
Review relevant previous learning.
Review prerequisite skills and knowledge for this lesson.

2. Presentation
State lesson goals and/or provide outline.
Teach in small steps.
Model procedures.
Provide concrete positive examples and negative examples.
Use clear language.
Check for student understanding.
Avoid digressions.

3. Guided practice
High frequency of questions or guided practice.
All students respond and receive feedback.
High success rate.
Continue practice until students are fluid.

4. Corrections and Feedback
Give process feedback when answers are correct but hesitant.
Give sustaining feedback, clues, or reteaching for incorrect answers.
Provide reteaching when necessary.

5. Independent practice
Students receive help during initial steps, or overview.
Practice continues until students are automatic (where relevant).
Teacher provides active supervision (where possible).
Routines are used to give help to slower students.

6. Weekly and monthly reviews

FIGURE 3–2

Rosenshine's direct or explicit teaching functions
Source: Barak V. Rosenshine, "Synthesis of Research on Explicit Teaching," *Educational Leadership,* 43, no. 7 (April 1986), 68. Reprinted with permission of the Association for Supervision and Curriculum Development. Copyright © 1985 by ASCD. All rights reserved.

Six teaching functions aid student learning of explicit, well-structured information and skills such as mathematical procedures, science facts and concepts, grammatical rules, and vocabulary.

1. Each day, start the lesson by correcting the previous night's homework and reviewing what students have recently been taught.

2. Tell students the goals of today's lesson. Then present new information a little at a time, modeling procedures, giving clear examples, and checking often to make sure students understand.

3. Allow students to practice using the new information under the teacher's direction; ask many questions that give students abundant opportunities to correctly repeat or explain the procedure or concept that has just been taught. Student participation should be active until all students are able to respond correctly.

4. During guided practice, give students a great deal of feedback. When students answer incorrectly, reteach the lesson if necessary. When students answer correctly, explain why the answer was right. It is important that feedback be immediate and thorough.

5. Next, allow students to practice using the new information on their own. The teacher should be available to give short answers to students' questions, and students should be permitted to help each other.

6. At the beginning of each week, the teacher should review the previous week's lesson and at the end of the month review what students have learned during the last four weeks. It is important that students not be allowed to forget past lessons once they have moved on to new material.

These steps may be less important and are not sufficient for less well-defined topics, such as writing a term paper, a research report, or analyzing literature.

FIGURE 3–3

Highlights of research on explicit teaching of well-defined knowledge and skills

Source: Barak V. Rosenshine, "Synthesis of Research on Explicit Teaching," *Educational Leadership*, 43, no. 7 (April 1986), 68. Reprinted with permission of the Association for Supervision and Curriculum Development. Copyright © 1985 by ASCD. All rights reserved.

Meichenbaum's Direct Teaching Problem-Solving Strategies

Donald Meichenbaum found that children who do poorly at problem solving are often impulsive. That is, they react almost without thinking, relying heavily on trial and error, and seldom check for mistakes. You have seen children who call out immediately with an answer instead of a question when they play 20 questions. Meichenbaum discovered that young children become better problem solvers if they learn to be a bit more methodical. Teachers can assist them in asking better questions and being better observers by using direct instruction that

1. helps children focus on physical properties of the object, such as "Is the object smooth or rough, round or square, light or heavy?"

2. encourages children to delay guessing or giving answers until at least 10 questions are asked; and

3. suggests categories of questions children might use, for example, directions (for locating objects) or properties (to identify objects).[7]

When using direct or explicit instruction as suggested by Rosenshine, Bloom, Meichenbaum, or others, you should know that students seem to work better when the teacher circulates around the room during instruction.

It was found that short contacts with students (averaging 30 seconds or less) are effective for monitoring and supervising their work. Students also achieve more in direct or explicit instruction when they help each other in cooperative settings during seatwork.

Slower students are also helped more in cooperative classroom environments when fellow students explain the content in language they understand. Teachers have also helped slower students in direct or explicit instruction by giving them more review, guided practice, and independent practice than faster students.

In using direct or explicit instruction, you initially take full responsibility for presenting content or a specific skill, and then gradually guide students to greater independence. The research has consistently shown that student achievement in content and skills improves when teachers instruct more systematically, along the lines recommended by Rosenshine, Bloom, and Meichenbaum.

As indicated, direct instruction has a definite, specific, but limited role in learning. To help your students with more complex learnings (i.e., applying science concepts and principles, planning science investigations, or problem solving) requires more indirect instruction strategies.

/// INDIRECT INSTRUCTION AND EXPLORATION, INQUIRY, AND DISCOVERY

Indirect instruction, on the other hand, focuses on students engaging in **exploration, inquiry, or discovery** and is based on these premises: questions and problems precede answers in the learning process, students must process information mentally to achieve meaningful understanding, and students must be actively involved in the learning. Researchers say indirect instruction has a better chance of success when

1. concepts, patterns, and abstractions are primary goals,
2. higher thinking skills are to be developed,
3. it is essential that students participate to achieve the objectives,
4. problem solving is the main goal, and
5. it is necessary to long-term retention.

On the other extreme of the continuum of Figure 3–1 are exploration or free discovery strategies that allow students to develop their abilities to manipulate and process information from a variety of sources—academic, social, and experiential. In free discovery, students identify their own problems, generate their own hypotheses or possible solutions, test these hypotheses in the light of available data, and attempt to apply their own conclusions to new data, new problems, or new situations. Free discovery or inquiry focuses on *how* students process data (processes) rather than *what* they process (products). Donald C. Orlich refers to inquiry or discovery as "a generic label for any system of questioning or knowledge seeking."[8] Educators David A. Welton and John T. Mallan have also summarized free discovery or inquiry: "In an educational context, inquiry is both a noun and a verb—both an act and a process . . . inquiry is a learning process, a way in which students and adults can go about solving problems or processing information."[9]

It is unlikely that elementary and middle school teachers will encounter many, if any, children who can engage in this very advanced mental strategy called inquiry or free discovery. Piaget's evidence about children's development (presented in Chapter 2) told us such children are rare. And yet, free discovery or inquiry processing is one of the goals of science teaching.

What you can do with your students, though, is to combine some of these free discovery or inquiry processes with direct or exposition teaching methods. This will result in a learning strategy called guided discovery, which is very appropriate for elementary and middle school children. Let's examine some strategies for guiding students' concept building along constructivist research.

Learning Cycles Built on Solid Cognitive Research

Whatever teaching methods you select to help your students construct scientific/technological concepts should parallel the same methods scientists/technologists use for learning their knowledge and solving their professional problems. Your teaching methods should be organized in a pattern that coordinates the most current cognitive development research with scientific/technological/societal (STS) teaching/learning theory. As pointed out in previous chapters, many science educators recommend instructional models congruent with constructivist learning theory. In these instructional models, teachers select activities that encourage students to construct their own understandings of concepts by

- beginning with the knowledge, skills, misconceptions, and naive theories students bring to the new classroom experience (*prior knowledge*);
- providing students with motivating experiences to test new ideas against their own previous ideas and either support them or question their thinking (*common experiences*);
- introducing students to new specific information (i.e., terms, definitions, other language) to see how they apply to students' prior knowledge (*invent language*);
- engaging students in additional experiences that challenge, refute, or extend their own ideas and new terms received (*clarifying experiences*); and
- guiding students to question, discuss, argue, conclude, and construct a new or revised concept understanding (*concept construction and understanding*).

Various instructional models have been proposed over the years to attempt to meet these learning criteria. Here is an introduction to some of them.

Karplus and Thier's SCIS Learning Cycle

Over 25 years ago, Robert Karplus and Herbert Thier, co-developers of the **Science Curriculum Improvement Study (SCIS),** devised a three-step learning cycle modeled after what Piaget and other cognitive theorists said were optimal conditions for learning and concept construction. Karplus and Thier labeled their three stages **exploration, invention, and discovery.**[10] Figure 3–4 shows the three stages of the SCIS learning cycle, but the names of the last two stages were renamed by Charles R. Barman to concept introduction and concept application to characterize more accurately what actually happens in each of these stages.[11]

As you peruse the characteristics of the three stages in Figure 3–4, you will see how they correspond to the Piagetian and other cognitive learning theories in these teacher/student roles.

1. *Exploration*
   Teacher: plays indirect role—as observer, question poser, and assistant to students
   Students: active and manipulate materials
2. *Concept Introduction*
   Teacher: more "traditional" role—gathers information about students from exploration stage, introduces terminology and additional information
   Students: participate mentally and socially
3. *Concept Application*
   Teacher: poses new situation or problem for possible solution using information from previous stages
   Students: active

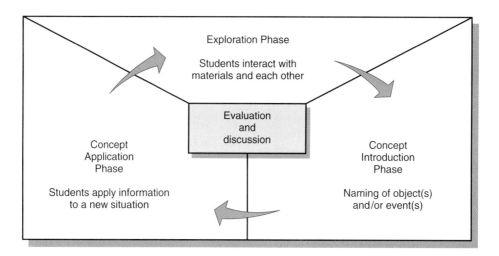

FIGURE 3-4

The learning cycle

Source: Charles R. Barman, "An Expanded View of the Learning Cycle: New Ideas About an Effective Teaching Strategy." Monograph and Occasional Paper Series, no. 4 (Washington, DC: Council for Elementary Science International, 1990), 5.

In the learning cycle three concept formation factors are involved (physical knowledge, social knowledge, and self-regulation) in this way:

Exploration — Students' physical experiences and social interaction help them build mental images (physical knowledge).

Concept Formation — Students interact with and communicate new ideas to teacher and peers to assimilate or accommodate specific ideas (social knowledge).

Concept Application — Students' physical experiences and social interactions with new ideas in new situations are applied in problem-solving situations (self-regulation).

The SCIS learning cycle has been modified and used in many science programs over the years. Several current instructional models, although differing somewhat, adhere to many of these constructivist learning conditions, and have all been built on the foundations of the SCIS model. Here are a few of these models with sources for additional information.

■ **Personal Construct Model**
L. H. T. West and A. L. Pines, Eds., *Cognitive Structure and Conceptual Change* (Orlando, FL: Academic Press, 1985).

■ **Neurologically Oriented Model**
J. Levy, "The Evidence Strongly Disputes the Idea That Students Learn with Only One Side of the Brain," *Educational Leadership,* 40, (1982) 66–71.

■ **Science, Technology, and Health Model** (Colorado Springs, CO: Biological Sciences Curriculum Study, 1991).

■ Descriptive, Empirical-Inductive, and Hypothetical-Deductive Models

A. E. Lawson, "A Better Way to Teach Biology," *American Biology Teacher,* 50, no. 5 (1988), 266–278.

■ General Learning Cycle Reference

J. W. Renner and E. A. Marek, *The Learning Cycle and Elementary School Science* (Portsmouth, NH: Heinemann, 1988).

Let's look at a specific current instructional model for more details.

Constructivist-Oriented Instructional Teaching/ Learning Model

One instructional model deserves a longer look as a promising one. It appears in the research literature under several different names, but can be recognized as either Constructivist Learning Model (CLM)[12] or Constructivist-Oriented Instructional Model to Guide Learning (The Teaching Model)[13]

This chapter's opening statement provides the philosophy underlying the constructivist teaching/learning model. This philosophy is evident in the four-step format of the National Center for Improving Science Education (NCISE) shown in Figure 3–5, in which students

1. accept an invitation to learn;
2. explore, discover, and create;
3. propose explanations and solutions; and
4. take action on what they learned.

Note that this fourth step is an STS modification of the original SCIS learning cycle.

The four-step format is based on the ways practicing science/technology professionals learn and apply new skills and information within their fields, as well as how students construct their concepts. Figure 3–5 highlights these science and technology approaches. Although the model is sequential, the arrows and loops display the complex nature of problem solving. This model is cyclical and dynamic, which means that "although single lessons or units of study may have a beginning (invitation) and an end (taking action), any new knowledge or skills will inevitably lead to new invitations, and therefore, a continuation of the cycle."[14]

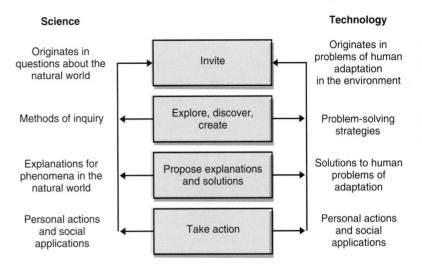

FIGURE 3–5
Constructivist-oriented instructional model to guide learning

Science		Technology
Originates in questions about the natural world	Invite	Originates in problems of human adaptation in the environment
Methods of inquiry	Explore, discover, create	Problem-solving strategies
Explanations for phenomena in the natural world	Propose explanations and solutions	Solutions to human problems of adaptation
Personal actions and social applications	Take action	Personal actions and social applications

Teaching Examples for Science	Stages in the Teaching Model	Teaching Examples for Technology
	Invitation	
Observe the natural world Ask questions about the natural world State possible hypotheses		Observe the human-made world Recognize a human problem Identify possible solutions
	Explorations, Discoveries, Creations	
Engage in focused play Look for information Observe specific phenomena Collect and organize data Select appropriate resources Design and conduct experiments Engage in debate with teachers and peers Define parameters of an investigation		Brainstorm possible alternatives Experiment with materials Design a model Employ problem-solving strategies Discuss solutions with others Identify risks and consequences Evaluate choices Analyze data
	Proposing Explanations and Solutions	
Communicate information and ideas Construct a new explanation Evaluation by peers Determine appropriate closure		Construct and explain a model Constructively review a solution Express multiple answers/solutions Integrate a solution with existing knowledge and experiences
	Taking Action	
Apply knowledge and skills Share information and ideas Ask new questions		Make decisions Transfer knowledge and skills Develop products and promote ideas
	New Invitation	

FIGURE 3–6

Detailed functions of the constructivist-oriented instructional model

Note: Although this figure has two distinct columns, a review of teaching examples clearly shows that science and technology are intertwined; many of the examples could easily be placed in both columns. Communicating information and ideas, for example, is as much a part of science as it is a part of technology.

Figure 3–6 goes into greater detail of the four stages, emphasizing examples of teaching applicable to both science and technology. By using both Figures 3–5 and 3–6, you can see how well the four stages of the teaching model correlate with constructivists' criteria for students building their own concepts. Notice also, the similarities between the SCIS Learning Cycle and the updated Constructivist-Oriented Instructional Model with its STS emphasis. The Learning Cycle and the Constructivist-Oriented Instructional model can be adapted to your current science teaching. Suggestions on how to do this follow in an adaptation of the

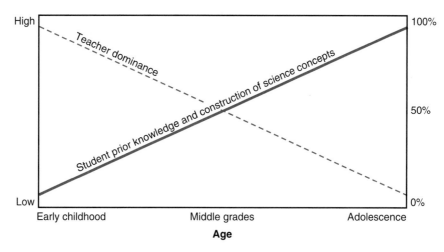

FIGURE 3–7
Teacher dominance and student learning variables

learning cycle this textbook calls Guided Discovery Teaching/Learning.

/// GUIDED DISCOVERY TEACHING/LEARNING

Guided discovery teaching/learning methods blend teacher-centered and student-centered techniques. Figure 3–7 illustrates the relationships that may exist between the amount of teacher dominance and what Piaget and other constructivists call **mental readiness** to internalize concepts, that is, students' ages or mental development, the relationships between their prior knowledge and science concepts construction, and their ability to engage in discovery learning, either free or guided. Because students can internalize only those concepts for which they are mentally "ready," the younger the students, the more you must present experiences for them to gain new information (prior knowledge) and guide them to build their own concepts. The older the student, the less you present, and the more they will initiate work with you as a facilitator, resource person, encourager, and guide.

This text emphasizes guided discovery not because it is the only way to teach but for these three important reasons:

1. More of us are familiar and comfortable with expository teaching, probably because it was used almost exclusively in our own education. However, more effective ways of using expository teaching are presented in works by Rosenshine, Bloom, and others.

2. If we want our students to be scientifically/technologically literate and able to solve problems, they must actually participate at their appropriate level in science activities with your assistance and guidance. (Expository teaching becomes even more important at this stage and was discussed earlier in this and previous chapters.) Guided discovery with young children may lead to free discovery or inquiry in adolescence and adulthood.

3. Guided discovery teaching will broaden your repertoire of teaching methods to meet the diverse backgrounds, learning styles, and levels of development of the students you teach.

Discovery teaching/learning allows students to progress at their own rate and to construct meaningful concepts.

Guiding Students to Lifetime Learning

Guided discovery teaching/learning tries to help students learn to learn and to acquire knowledge and build concepts that are uniquely their own because they discovered it themselves. Guided discovery is not restricted to finding something entirely new to the world such as an invention (television) or theory (heliocentric view of the universe). It is a matter of your students internally rearranging data so they can go beyond the mere facts to form concepts new to them. Guided discovery involves students finding their own meanings, organization, and structure of ideas.

Discovery teaching is not new. The ancient Greek philosopher Socrates, with his question-ing style, used a discovery, nontelling approach to learning. More recently, John Dewey, the main spokesman for progressive education in the 1930s, advocated that children should "learn by doing" rather than be lectured to. Jean Piaget and Jerome Bruner, former Harvard psychologists, were responsible for a sharply increased interest in learning by discovery in the middle 1960s.

Guided Discovery Advantages

Jerome Bruner, instrumental in leading the movement toward discovery teaching, outlined four reasons for using this approach:

1. Intellectual potency.
2. Intrinsic rather than extrinsic motives.

3. Learning the heuristics of discovery.
4. Conservation of memory.

By intellectual potency, Bruner means that an individual learns and develops his or her mind only by using it. He emphasizes that the only way people learn discovery techniques is by having opportunities to discover them by themselves. Through guided discovery, a student slowly learns how to organize and carry out investigations independently. One of the greatest payoffs of the guided discovery approach is that it aids better memory retention and application to new situations. Something a student discovers independently is more likely to be remembered, but concepts he or she is told can be quickly forgotten. This was reinforced more recently when Robert Glaser in summarizing research on teaching and thinking, concluded that knowledge acquired in problem-solving contexts is more likely to be applicable to new situations.[15]

Shifting Students from Extrinsic to Intrinsic Motivation

Learning may occur in response to some reward; children may also be motivated to learn to avoid failure. These two types of motivation may become a pattern in which children seek cues about how to conform to what is expected of them. The students in your class may spend the first few days finding out what it is you want, so they can please you. David Reisman, a sociologist, explained this by saying "Mental life moves from a state of outer-directedness, in which the fortuity of stimuli and reinforcement are crucial to a state of inner-directedness in which the growth and maintenance of mastery becomes central and dominant."

Reisman's term *outer-directedness* means that students are doing things for us as teachers. They want to elicit our praise and avoid our wrath. This works against our goals in science education by making the student dependent on

an authority for rewards, motivation, and constant directions.

Conversely, guided discovery helps students become more autonomous, self-directed, and responsible for their own learning. Your students will become more self-motivated when they approach learning by discovering something themselves, rather than only hearing about it. They learn to carry out their activities with the autonomy of self-reward and become *inner-directed*. More properly, you can say the reward is the discovery itself. Children learn to manipulate their environment more actively. They achieve gratification from coping with problems. Bruner believes, as a consequence of succeeding at discovery, the student receives a satisfying intellectual thrill—an intrinsic or self-satisfying reward. Teachers often give extrinsic rewards (A's, for example), but if they want students to learn for the fun of it, they have to devise instructional systems that offer students intrinsic satisfaction.

For many students, extrinsic motivation has little or no relationship to the act of learning. Intrinsic rewards are personal, vary widely from person to person, and are directly connected to obvious external incentives.

Research has shown that extrinsic motivation is more efficient in terms of the relative amount of time spent in learning the task, skill, or knowledge. However, information learned by intrinsic motivation is retained longer.[16]

J. Richard Suchman, one of the early proponents of discovery learning, believed that the very nature of discovery learning provides an environment free of extrinsic motivation. By discovery-oriented teaching, you are more likely to provide a nonpunitive, stimulating atmosphere where children engage in learning because it is fun, interesting, and self-rewarding. Your job, then, is to act as a facilitator and provide your students with an environment responsive to their needs. Try to eradicate your view of the teacher as a dispenser of information and rewards. Give your students an opportunity to try things without fear of your (external) rewards or punishment.

The Heuristics of Discovery or Metacognition

As John Dewey said, "We learn by doing and reflecting on what we do." A great deal of evidence from psychology and other sources shows that learning is not a passive process. Jerome Bruner put it this way, "The student is not a bench-bound listener, but should be actively involved in the learning process."[17]

The student must be actively involved in learning. But sometimes people misinterpret this concept and limit activity to manual or manipulative activities. Students can be actively involved by listening, speaking, reading, seeing, and thinking, if their minds are acting on what is being learned. Your job is to find ways to get the learner actively involved in whatever activities are presented. Piaget has said that no learning occurs without action. It is only through the exercise of problem solving that your students will learn the *heuristics of discovery,* that is learning how to learn. Therefore, the more they are involved in solving problems, the more likely they are to learn to generalize what they have learned into a style of discovery that serves them best.

Heuristics has similar aspects to the process of metacognition. *Meta* is derived from the Greek and means "after, amidst, and over and above." In the case of our thinking process, metacognition goes over and above thinking to *thinking about thinking.*[18] Metacognition then focuses on the mental skills and processes used within a specific problem situation. Robert Sternberg[19] describes his **metacomponential skills and processes** as metacognitive skills used in finding and delineating problems, planning what to do in seeking solution(s) to the problem, implementing the plan, and monitoring and assessing actions.

John Barell[20] relates his own mental processes as he analyzed and applied Sternberg's metacomponential skills and processes to writing his book. Barell consciously used these three knowledge classifications during his writing:

- **Declarative knowledge.** "I know that books have a system of organization."
- **Procedural knowledge.** "This is how you go about organizing a book project."
- **Conditional knowledge.** "I need to use my organizing strategies when I am working on the introduction so the rest of it will be coherent."

Knowing the *that, how,* and *when* of learning are crucial to reflective metacognition and heuristic discovery. Put another way, "Knowledge about when to use strategies is a particularly critical form of metacognition."[21] Your job as teacher is to assist students in learning how to do this. One important way is to guide them in processing new information.

Guiding Students in Their Information Processing

The human mind has often been compared to an extremely complicated computer; the biggest problem of this human computer is not the storage but the retrieval of data. Psychologists and learning researchers believe the key to retrieval is organization—knowing what information to find and how to get it. Research indicates that any organization of information that reduces the complexity of material by putting it in a pattern the *learner* has constructed will make that material easier to retrieve. Material that is organized in terms of the learner's own interests and uniqueness has the best chance of being accessible in memory. You probably can think of something you learned by setting up a system that worked for you. Do you remember high school or college science classes where your teacher tried to help you remember something by association? The best kind of system is one a person invents personally, but we should still show our students how other people remember and structure things. The very attitudes and activities that characterize figuring out or discovering things for oneself also seem to have the effect of making material readily retrievable in the learner's memory.

Psychologists call this **transfer of training.** There is little evidence that learning one subject will enhance mastery in another subject. But teachers once believed that it would, and they taught Latin to "train the mind," make the learner more logical, and improve the learning of English. However, it just did not work that way. For the transfer of training to be most effective, two factors must be at work.

1. Positive transfer of training will take place if there is a similarity between subjects. The closer the similarity of the subjects, the better the chance of a transfer of training.
2. Positive transfer of training will take place if there is a learning of knowledge, concepts, principles, or techniques in the first situation that can be usefully applied to the second situation.

Therefore, if you want your students to be problem solvers, to learn by discovery, and to do things for themselves, you must give them practice in all of these things. The more they solve problems with your guidance, the greater will be the chances that transfer of training will find its way into new situations. To find out more about transfer of learning, read David Perkins and Gavriel Salomon, "Teaching for Transfer," *Educational Leadership,* 46, no. 1 (1988), 21–31.

Research Shows Discovery Learning Is Effective

Although additional research is needed and is continuing, evidence suggests that discovery learning is effective. Students exposed to inquiry-oriented, process-approach science performed better on measures of general science achievement, process skills, analytical skills, and related skills such as language arts and mathematics.[22]

One of the best studies of discovery teaching was a three-year longitudinal investigation to see what differences (if any) this type of teaching made on the students' learning behaviors. Investigators at Carnegie-Mellon University found that a discovery-oriented social studies curriculum increased the students' abilities to inquire about human affairs significantly more than a program using nondiscovery materials. This study was important since it showed that discovery teaching over a three-year period does make individuals better learners.[23] The implications for science teaching are numerous.

In another study T. E. Allen found that "discipline problems" from "troublemakers" were significantly reduced in science classrooms where the teachers were nondirective and nonauthoritarian and where student opportunity to select and explore alternatives was increased.[24] Edmund Amidon and Ned A. Flanders also found that highly anxious children functioned better in student-centered classrooms in which there was less structure and teachers gave fewer directions.[25]

Carl Rogers further cites case studies of teachers who have used the discovery approach with much success at the elementary, high school, and college levels.[26]

The results of studies show that students preferred a discovery process approach to a more traditional textbook-oriented science program, causing them to

1. find science exciting and interesting;
2. wish they had more science;
3. feel science is useful in their everyday lives;
4. have feelings of success; and
5. have a more positive view of science and scientists than non-SCIS students.[27]

Guided Discovery Teaching Builds Positive Self-Concepts

We all have self-concepts. If our self-concepts are positive, these things happen.

We feel psychologically secure.
We are open to new experiences.

We are willing to take chances and explore.
We tolerate minor failures relatively well.
We are more creative.
We have generally good mental health.
We eventually become fully functioning
    individuals.

Part of the task of becoming a better person is building a positive self-concept. We can help students do this by actively involving them in their learning. Through active involvement, students are more likely to work up to their potential and gain insights into their "self." Guided discovery teaching provides opportunities for greater involvement, giving students more chances to gain insights and better develop their self-concepts.

Guided Discovery Teaching and Students' Expectations

Your students' self-concepts are directly related to their expectancy levels. That is, your students have certain ideas about how they can or cannot accomplish a task on their own. Many children, unfortunately, have learned (or accepted) low expectancy levels for themselves, characterized by statements like

I can't do math problems.
Boy, am I dumb.
Science is one subject I never could do.
Forget it, I couldn't do that if my life
    depended on it.

It is a vicious cycle: low expectations lead to high anxiety, and high anxiety leads to further lowering of expectations. In fact, the overwhelming weight of research has found that a high anxiety level generally accompanies poor student performance. In addition, highly anxious children tend to lack self-confidence, curiosity, and adventurousness.

It has been found, however, that students in discovery-oriented classrooms learn to think and function more autonomously. From having

Guided discovery methods help students build self-esteem and take pride in their work.

had many successful experiences in using and being encouraged to use their investigative talents, these children learn

I can work things out for myself.
Mrs. Orkand, can I try to do that, please?
Let me try doing it.
I am a valuable person.

As you know from working with students, it takes lots of time for them to learn properly and to build positive self-images.

Slow Down, You Move Too Fast!

Teachers sometimes try to rush or short-circuit learning. They think they can drastically reduce the time it takes for students to learn something. However, students need adequate time to think, reason, and gain insights into scientific concepts, principles, and skills. It takes time for students to act on things in their minds for meaningful learning. The learning process may seem meaningful to teachers, but unless it becomes meaningful to the learner, it is all for naught.

Piaget and others believed no true learning occurs unless students have time to assimilate and accommodate what they encounter in their environments. Unless this happens, you and your students are involved in what Piaget called **pseudolearning,** parroting an explanation without a real change in mental awareness about a subject. Mary Budd Rowe addresses this need for the teacher to slow down to allow student learning to adequately occur.[28]

In summary then, if you look at Figure 3–8, you can review the many advantages you will have by increasing the number of guided discovery activities in your science teaching. Although no instructional model is perfect, the shortcomings of guided discovery teaching are far outweighed by its advantages, especially for students to learn to learn and construct their own concepts and understandings.[29]

/// APPLYING GUIDED DISCOVERY TO YOUR TEACHING

This section will investigate some practical ways you can use guided discovery teaching in your classroom. How much structure to provide in guided discovery activities is probably one of your first concerns.

How Much Guidance in Guided Discovery?

Guided discovery teaching is not a laissez-faire, "Children, do what you want and you'll learn" approach. You should have enough structure to ensure that students use their minds to discover science concepts and principles. You should have some broad objectives in mind and your classroom activities should guide students toward these objectives. However, some of the time you have to refrain from telling children what you want them to learn or they will merely memorize.

Expository or Telling About Science

Teacher covers MORE

but

less is retained

Guided Discovery Science

Teacher covers less

but

MORE is retained and transferred

Teacher Orientation

View students as a reservoir of knowledge, subject-centered. Teachers have covering compulsion. The more they cover, the better they think they are.

Student Orientation

More holistic view of the learner, student-centered. Teachers more interested in cognitive and creative growth. Teach for the development of multi-talents in helping students develop their self-concepts.

FIGURE 3–8

Attributes of expository and guided discovery teaching/learning

Source: Modified from Harold H. Jaus, "Activity-Oriented Science: Is It Really Good?" Reproduced with permission by *Science and Children* (April 1977). Copyrighted by the National Science Teachers Association, 1742 Connecticut Avenue, N. W., Washington, DC 20009.

You have to present a variety of activities so students build storehouses of sensory experiences and prior knowledge from which verbal (and eventually written) words and symbols are "invented" by the teacher. For instance, here is an example of how this can easily be done at the preschool or primary level. Give your students an assortment of buttons and ask them to group them any way they want. Your purpose is to *guide* them to discover the buttons' characteristics or properties. In the SCIS Learning Cycle this stage is called *exploration*. It is called *invitation and exploration* in the Constructivist Model.

Without telling students that buttons can be grouped according to their color, shape, texture, size, or kinds of materials (all properties), you can ask, "What do all of Alice's buttons have in common?" or "What is alike in all of the buttons Harry grouped together?" Then say something like, "When you put the buttons together by their color, shape, or how they feel, scientists say you are grouping by *properties*." This is *SCIS' invention stage,* where the teacher communicates words for the sensory experience.

Now give students a variety of seeds and ask, "How can we group these seeds by their properties?" This gives students an opportunity to *apply* what they learned in the exploration and invention stages to new situations (in SCIS' terminology, the *discovery stage,* and *taking action* stage in Constructivist Model). By being involved in all these activities, students slowly build in their mind what Piaget called physical knowledge.

Here is a brief description by Ruth S. Charney of how more guidance is needed in guided discovery for very young children or children not familiar with this approach.

Guided discovery is the process that I use to structure these first introductions to materials, routines, and areas of the classroom. The guided discovery protects children from the assault of a classroom that is too full of materials and choices at first and it provides deliberate teaching of work habits and social habits, skills, and concepts. It is an opportunity to model, to role-play, and to represent a variety of outcomes. Our guided discoveries prompt and excite children to play, to explore, to communicate, and to cooperate.[30]

Importance of Minds-on/Hands-on Activities in Guided Discovery

The 1981 Board of Directors of the National Science Teachers Association unanimously endorsed the necessity of laboratory experiences for teaching and learning science. For the elementary school science program this means hands-on experiences emphasizing the science process skills of observing, measuring, recording, classifying, interpreting data, inferring, predicting, investigating, and making models. Hands- on experiences, if properly guided by the teacher, can provide practice in thinking and reasoning. Darrell Phillips summarizes the place of hands-on activities in guided discovery learning.

The individual's construction of the tools of thought (i.e., Piaget's operations and operational structures) are abstracted from actions on objects. In essence, without action on objects, there can be no abstraction, operations, or structures. Teaching science as a reading lesson, a "cookbook" lab, or an exercise in memorization inhibits the development of reasoning. . . . Teachers must offer *sciencing* (active exploration and discovery of relationships) as opposed to school *science* (passive mimicking and memorization).[31]

Elementary and middle school students are in a formative stage of mental development, which requires actions on objects for the development of reasoning. What you must supply during these vital growth years is a variety of minds-on/hands-on activities in which your students manipulate objects, are guided to see relationships, and draw conclusions. Refer to this

Hands-on/minds-on experiences provide practice in seeing relationships and drawing conclusions as students manipulate objects.

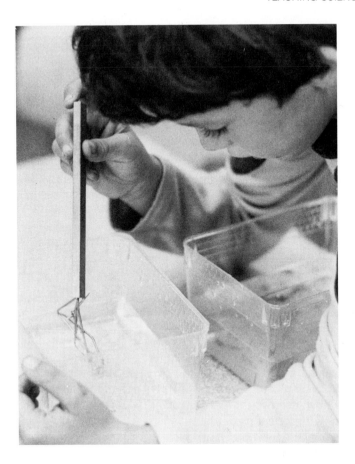

chapter and Chapter 2, on how children learn, to review the importance of laboratory or minds-on/hands-on science activities for intellectual development of elementary and middle school students. It is for these reasons that minds-on/hands-on activities are the essence of guided discovery teaching.

Format for Guided Discovery Minds-on/Hands-on Science Lessons

The format for the guided discovery minds-on/hands-on approach should address all or most of these ten major questions:

1. What age-level range might benefit from this activity?

2. What scientific/technological topics might students be exposed to in this activity?
3. What questions or problems might be investigated?
4. What science processes are involved?
5. What scientific concepts might students discover or construct?
6. What will I need for guiding this activity?
7. What will we communicate or discuss?
8. What actions will students take, individually or in groups?
9. How will students use or apply what they construct or discover?
10. What must I know? Where do I find it?

Chapter 6 on planning will give you greater details for using this activity format.

Constructivist-Oriented Model Stages	Guided Discovery Minds-On/Hands-On Format
Invitation	What scientific/technological topics might students be exposed to in this activity? What questions or problems might students investigate?
Explorations, Discoveries	What science processes are involved? What will students do individually or in groups?
Proposing Explanations and Solutions	What scientific concepts might students discover or construct? What will we communicate or discuss?
Taking Action	How will students use or apply what they construct or discover?

FIGURE 3–9

Correlation between constructivist-oriented model and the guided discovery minds-on/hands-on activity format

As you review the guided discovery minds-on/hands-on format, compare it to the Constructivist-Oriented Instructional Model in Figure 3–5 and you will see similarities. Figure 3–9 shows how the two have overlapping characteristics. This format gives you wide latitude in how they are used and allows you to gear them to your particular teaching/learning environment. But start using it as soon as possible.

Start NOW to Use Guided Discovery Activities

If you and your students have not had experience in learning through discovery, you may need more structure initially in your lessons. After you both have gained some experience in how to carry out discovery investigations, you will be able to work with less structure.

You may reach a point in your teaching where you will be more comfortable with an even freer discovery or inquiry approach. At that point you will probably want to use more of the less structured discovery activities.

As you begin teaching guided discovery science lessons, you will outline much of the planning. Your students, for example, probably will not originate the problem; you will be guiding them on how to set up and record the data. Later, however, you should have the students originate problems, determine how to resolve them, collect data, and communicate their findings.

Chapter 6 shows you how to create and give discovery minds-on/hands-on lessons. As you become more experienced with this method, you will develop your own discovery techniques and allow more freedom for your students to investigate what interests them.

Using Less Structured Guided Discovery Activities

Another way you can guide your students' discovery is through less structured activities. These differ from guided discovery in that you only motivate or initiate the problem, and then you invite your students to suggest ways they can observe, explore, or work out procedures for resolving it.

If you are a primary or lower elementary grade teacher, you will probably find this approach more useful. Upper elementary and middle school teachers may also find it useful and may, in addition, have the students outline investigative procedures for designing and carrying out their own experiments.

In less structured guided discovery, either you or your students may pose a problem. You provide the materials or the setting for resolving it. Give your students a lot of freedom to solve the problem(s). Here are some problems you might suggest to students (if they do not pose them by themselves) for involving them in less structured guided discovery activities.

Primary Level—Mainly Exploratory

What do you notice about fish in our aquarium?

What did you find out about the butterflies?

In what ways could you group these different things?

What living things do you see in the pond, on the edge of the pond, several steps back from the pond?

What did you find out about leaves?

How are these rocks different?

What things do the magnets do?

What do magnets attract?

What can you do with these objects?

Upper Elementary/Middle School— Exploratory; Devising and Carrying Out Experiments

How would you determine the effects of DDT on water snails?

What effect does temperature have on the sprouting of seeds?

What are all the ways you can get the light bulb to light using the wire and batteries?

What types of things stimulate the worms?

What affects the swing of pendulums?

What is the fastest way to get beans to sprout?

How could you determine whether this water is polluted?

Encourage your students to attack similar problems on their own or in small groups. You should set yourself up as a resource person. Give only enough aid to ensure that the children do not become overly frustrated, experience undue failure, and give up. The assistance you give should be in the form of questions to guide students' thinking about possible investigative procedures. For example, ask the children questions that help them to sense the direction for solving a problem rather than tell them what to do. In a problem where children are studying what affects the movements of earthworms, you might ask, "What effect do you think light might have on the movements of earthworms? How could you find that out?" Questions like these, asked at the right time, may stimulate the students to become more involved in their creative investigation. Contrast this approach with that of a teacher who says, "Study earthworms and find out their characteristics and what things affect them." This statement might limit your students' investigation to the physical appearance of worms. You might rob them of many more opportunities for thought and creativity in their approaches.

How does guided discovery relate to freer discovery or inquiry? Wayne W. Welch defined inquiry as "a general process by which human beings seek information or understanding. Broadly conceived, inquiry is a way of thought." Guided discovery, then, is one element of inquiry. This article discusses the difference: Wayne W. Welch, "Inquiry in School Science," in *What Research Says to the Science Teacher,* vol. 3, Norris C. Harms and Robert E. Yager, eds., (Washington, DC: National Science Teachers Association, 1981), 53–64.

Discovery: Chicago Teachers
Go Back to School

Now I get them involved with hands-on tools (blocks and magnifying glasses) first, and I use the book as a followup.

—Gladystine Butler, second-grade teacher and graduate of the Academy for Mathematics and Science Teachers.

Strategy   Take advantage of retraining opportunities throughout your teaching career.

To show teachers how to incorporate new technologies into their curricula, the Chicago school system has begun a program to retrain its 17,000 math and science teachers—the Academy for Mathematics and Science Teachers.

Nobel physicist Leon Lederman was asked to help develop the program. Lederman had previously been a driving force behind several other science programs in the Chicago area. One program, under the auspices of the Fermi National Accelerator Laboratory, was a series of ten-week Saturday sessions for high school students; another was the Illinois Math and Science Academy, a public school for gifted students.

In the course of setting up these programs, Lederman came to realize that the science teachers he encountered were hampered by out-dated notions of how children best learn about science. The special aspect of the retraining for Chicago teachers is their chance to perform with hands-on materials—to rediscover.

Now these teachers go back to their classrooms with a new appreciation for the sense of discovery. As a second-grade teacher explains, "I get them involved with hands-on tools first, and I use the book as a followup."

On Your Own   Take advantage of your local education association's in-service days; if your association doesn't offer the kind of program you think you need, get together with other area teachers to put one together.

Don't overlook the possibility of a hands-on "learning" day with your colleagues in your building. Teachers can act as students among themselves, or try out some lessons with their classes—discovering alongside their students.

Source: From USA TODAY, May 28, 1991. Copyright 1991, USA TODAY. Used by permission.

Are Your Students Ready for Free Discovery (Inquiry) Activities?

After students, over many years, have been exposed to numerous guided discovery science studies, have learned how to attack scientific problems (processes of science), have gained sufficient cognitive science knowledge (products of science), and have performed less structured discovery activities, they may be ready for free discovery, or inquiry, activities. Only you can tell if your students are ready. These free discovery activities will differ from the guided or less structured discovery activities in that your students will identify or originate what problems they would like to study. Usually this occurs in upper elementary or middle grades, but you

should be alert at the lower grades for children who are ready for free discovery activities because of their prior experiences and knowledge, abilities, interests, and skill development.

Here are some questions to ask to see if your students (and *you*) are ready to use the free discovery (inquiry) approach.

> *If you were the teacher of this class and you were going to select the most exciting things to investigate this term, what would they be?*
>
> *What are some problems related to our community that you would like to study?*
>
> *Now that you have studied, for example, salts, algae, light, heat, pollution, animal behaviors, and so on, what problems*

Mature students may be ready for free discovery or inquiry activities.

can you list that you would like to investigate individually or in teams?

After finishing this experiment, what other experiments can you think of, and which of them would you like to do?

When you see problems in the community (e.g., pollution), or when you discover some problem related to science that you would like to discuss, bring it to our attention in class.

What kind of science fiction story would you like to write?

Are *You* Ready for Constructivist-Oriented Science Teaching?

Although the question asks *if* you are ready for teaching science with a constructivist or guided discovery approach, you probably are involved in some aspects of it already. Robert Yager has devised a scale for analyzing the degree to which constructivist learning is already happening.[32] Where are you in the self-check device in Figure 3–10? Where do you want to be a week, a month, or a year from now? How will you get there? The remaining chapters will assist you in achieving your goals.

SUMMARY

No one method of teaching science is best for all students, all of the time, under all circumstances. A taxonomy of common teaching methods, including a wide range of possible teaching methods, was organized around these teacher/student transactions:

1. Listening-Speaking (auditory or hearing learning).
2. Reading-Writing (visual or sight learning).
3. Watching-Doing (kinesthetic or muscular learning).

The amount of teacher dominance in these common teaching methods varies from high, to medium, to low. The three points on a teacher dominance continuum are Direct Teaching or Expository (telling) on one extreme, Indirect Teaching or Free Discovery or Inquiry on the other extreme, and Guided Discovery between the two. Attributes of each of these teaching methods were discussed.

Teaching methods should be organized in a pattern that coordinates the most recent cognitive development research with STS teaching and learning. Various instructional models are presented to meet these learning criteria, and two were examined in detail: SCIS Learning Cycle and the Constructivist-Oriented Instructional Model.

This text advocates that you use *all* science teaching methods, but urges that you consider including more guided discovery science teaching/learning activities in your science program. Guided discovery incorporates the best of what is known about science processes and products; how children learn best at the elementary and middle school levels; the aims, goals, and objectives of science education; and the relationships between science, technology, and society.

Teacher	Identifies the Issue/Topic	Student
No	Issue is Seen as Relevant	Yes
Teacher	Asks the Questions	Student
Teacher	Identifies Written and Human Resources	Student
Teacher	Locates Written Resources	Student
Teacher	Contacts Needed Human Resources	Student
Teacher	Plans Investigation and Activities	Student
No	Varied Evaluation Techniques Used	Yes
No	Students Practice Self-Evaluation	Yes
No	Concepts and Skills Applied to New Situations	Yes
No	Students Take Action(s)	Yes
No	Science Concepts and Principles Emerge Because They Are Needed	Yes
No	Extensions of Learning Outside the School in Evidence	Yes

FIGURE 3–10

A scale for analyzing the degree to which constructivist learning is occurring

Source: Robert E. Yager, "The Constructivist Learning Model," *The Science Teacher,* 58, no. 6 (September 1991), 56.

Discovery is the process by which the learner uses the mind in logical and mathematical ways to organize and internalize concepts and principles of the world. The learner is guided to learn to learn, which is called heuristics or metacognition. John Dewey fostered the idea of learning by doing and then reflecting on what was done. The research of Jean Piaget, Jerome Bruner, and others renewed interest in discovery learning.

Some of the advantages of guided discovery learning are that the students learn how to learn; learning becomes self-rewarding, self-motivational, and is more easily transferable; it minimizes or avoids rote memory; and learners become more responsible for their own learning.

Guided discovery activities may have four elements: invitation to learn, exploration and discoveries, proposing explanations and solutions, and taking action. Minds-on/hands-on experiences are extremely important in guided discovery at the elementary and middle school levels according to Piaget's operations and operational structures; they are also important because children need to react to objects and phenomena to develop reasoning.

The amount of structure you supply depends on your students' level of development and experiences with sciencing. Guided discovery teaching has more structure than free discovery or inquiry. In guided discovery teaching you provide a great deal of guidance and direction. You provide the problems, materials, and equipment, but you encourage your students to work out the procedures for solving the problems themselves. The format for guided discovery lessons used in this text was introduced along with how it correlates with the Constructivist Instructional model stages.

In less structured discovery activities, *you* pose the problems and provide the materials or setting; students have a lot of freedom in solving the problems. You function mainly as a resource person or facilitator and give only enough aid to keep your students moving toward the solutions.

Free discovery or inquiry activities are usually for older, more experienced students in upper elementary or middle school grades. In this approach, *students* identify or originate what they would like to study, as well as how they will go about answering their questions, solving their problem(s), and taking actions.

SELF-ASSESSMENT AND FURTHER STUDY

1. Select a science study and choose science teaching activities from each of the categories of listening-speaking, reading-writing, and watching-doing teaching methods from Table 3–1. Try to vary the amount of teacher dominance in your activities.

2. How would you use guided discovery science teaching activities to help your students build (or strengthen) positive self-concepts? Give specific examples.

3. Minds-on/hands-on activities are very important in the guided discovery approach to teaching science. Read the following articles and summarize the advantages and any disadvantages of this approach to science teaching.

   ■ Harry McAnarney, "Wanted: A More Appropriate Use of Hands-on Science," *Science and Children,* 17, no. 7 (April 1980):15.

   ■ Gerald F. Consuegra, "Strategies for Teaching Elementary and Junior High Students," *Science and Children,* 17, no. 7 (April 1980): 29–30.

   ■ Kathleen M. Donnellan, "A Rationale for the Laboratory in Preschool/Elementary Programs: A Position of the NSTA Preschool and Elementary Division," in Robert E. Yager et al., "Science Activities Are Central to Science Education in the Elementary School," *Science and Children,* 19, no. 2 (October 1981): 42.

   ■ Ted Bredderman, "What Research Says: Activity Science—The Evidence Shows It Matters," *Science and Children,* 20, no. 1 (September 1982): 39–41.

4. Why is guided discovery learning more "transferable" and longer lasting than exposition or learning by rote? Use these resources and/or any others you feel document your case.

   ■ Barry Beyer, *Practical Strategies for the Teaching of Thinking* (Boston, MA: Allyn & Bacon, 1987).

   ■ Reuven Feurstein, et al., "Instrumental Enrichment: An Intervention Program for Structural Cognitive Modifiability: Theory and Practice," in S. F. Chipman, J. W. Segal, and R. Glaser, eds., *Thinking and Learning Skills: Relating Instruction to Research, Vol. I* (Hillsdale, NJ: Erlbaum, 1984).

   ■ John Hayes, *The Complete Problem Solver* (Philadelphia, PA: Franklin Institute, 1981).

   ■ David Perkins, "Selecting Fertile Themes for Integrated Learning," in Heidi Jacobs, ed., *Interdisciplinary Curriculum: Design and Implementation,* (Alexandria, VA: The Association for Supervision and Curriculum Development, 1989).

5. Describe, in your own words, what Robert Sternberg means by metacomponential skills and processes and how they affect learning.

6. Select a science problem and prepare a series of guided, less structured, or free discovery or inquiry approach activities.

7. What are some intrinsic motivational drives that you as a teacher might use to help your students move toward greater independence?

8. Learn more about different instructional models that are based on constructivist views of teaching and learning. Use references in this chapter as a beginning.

NOTES

1. Susan Loucks-Horsley, et al., "Use a Constructivist-Oriented Instructional Model to Guide Learning," in *Elementary School Science for the 90's*

(Andover, MA: The NETWORK, Inc., 1990), 59. Reproduced with permission of the National Center for Improving Science Education/The NETWORK, Inc. Copyright 1990.

2. P. Kuerbis, *Learning Styles and Elementary Science,* A paper commissioned by the Biological Sciences Curriculum Study, Colorado Springs, CO, 1986; Kenneth Dunn and Rita Dunn, "Dispelling Outmoded Beliefs about Student Learning," *Educational Leadership,* 44, no. 6 (1987), 55–62.

3. *What Works. Research About Teaching and Learning* (Washington, DC: United States Department of Education, 1986).

4. I am indebted to the following authoritative article on direct or explicit instruction, and *highly* recommend it for elaboration on the points presented in this section of the chapter: Barak V. Rosenshine, "Synthesis of Research on Explicit Teaching," *Educational Leadership,* 43, no. 7 (1986), 60–69.

5. Virginia M. Brown, "In the Area of Science, Can Constructivist Teaching, Based on Children's Own Interests and Investigations, Provide a Meaningful Environment?" *The Constructivist,* 4, no. 4 (November 1989), 1–7.

6. Information in this section can be found in Barak V. Rosenshine, "Synthesis of Research on Explicit Teaching," *Educational Leadership,* 43, no. 7 (April 1987), 64–69.

7. Donald Meichenbaum, "Teaching Thinking: A Cognitive-Behavioral Perspective", in S. F. Chipman, J. W. Segal, and R. Glaser, editors, *Thinking and Learning Skills: Research and Open Questions,* Vol. 2. (Hillsdale, NJ: Erlbaum, 1985): 407–426.

8. For specific examples of four types of inquiry, see Donald C. Orlich, "Science Inquiry in the Commonplace," *Science and Children,* 26, no. 6 (March 1989), 22–24.

9. David A. Welton and John T. Mallan, *Children and Their World: Strategies for Teaching Social Studies, 2nd ed.* (Hopewell, NJ: n.p.1981), 182.

10. For a fuller explanation of the SCIS learning cycle see Robert Karplus and Herbert Thier, *SCIS Teacher's Handbook* (Berkeley, CA: Science Curriculum Improvement Study, University of California, 1974).

11. For outstanding clarity of the history, development, and characteristics of learning cycles, you are urged to read Charles R. Barman, *An Expanded View of the Learning Cycle: New Ideas About an Effective Teaching Strategy. Monograph and Occasional Paper Series #4* (Washington, DC: Council for Elementary Science International, August 1989), 1–37.

12. Robert E. Yager, "The Constructivist Learning Model," *The Science Teacher, 58, no. 6 (September 1991), 52–57.*

13. Susan Loucks-Horsley, et al., Chapter 6. "Use a Constructivist-Oriented Instructional Model to Guide Learning," in *Elementary School Science for the 90's* (Andover, MA: The National Center for Improving Science Education, A partnership of the NETWORK, Inc. and The Biological Sciences Curriculum Study, (1990), 58–72.

14. Rodger W. Bybee, chair, et al., *Science and Technology Education for the Elementary Years: Frameworks for Curriculum and Instruction* (Colorado Springs, CO: The National Center for Improving Science Education. A partnership of the NETWORK, Inc. and The Biological Sciences Curriculum Study, 1989), 79.

15. Robert Glaser, "Education and Thinking: The Role of Knowledge," *American Psychologist,* 39, (1989), 93–104.

16. N. L. Gage and David C. Berliner, *Educational Psychology, 4th ed.* (Boston, MA: Houghton Mifflin, 1988), Chapter 15.

17. Jerome S. Bruner, "The Art of Discovery," *Harvard Educational Review,* 31, no. 1 (1961), 21-32.

18. To deepen your understanding of metacognition, these sources present the latest research: Arthur Costa and Larry Lowery, *Techniques for Teaching Thinking* (Pacific Grove, CA: Midwest Publications, 1989); Arthur Hyde and Marilyn Bizar, *Thinking in Context* (White Plains, NY: Longman, 1989); Robert Swartz and David Perkins, *Teaching Thinking—Issues and Approaches* (Pacific Grove, CA: Midwest Publications, 1989).

19. Robert J. Sternberg, *Intelligence Applied* (NY: Harcourt Brace Jovanovich, 1986).

20. Excellent treatment of how to use metacognition in the classroom by John Barell, *Teaching for Thoughtfulness. Classroom Strategies to Enhance Intellectual Development* (White Plains, NY: Longman, 1991). Chapter 11, "Empowering Through Metacognition," 206–235.

21. Michael Pressley, et al., "What Is Good Strategy Use and Why Is It Hard to Teach? An Optimistic Appraisal Associated with Strategy Instruction." Paper presented at the Annual Meeting of the American Educational Research Association, Washington, DC, April 1987.

22. James A. Shymansky, William C. Kyle, Jr., and Jennifer M. Alpert, "How Effective Were Hands-on Science Programs of Yesterday?" *Science and Children,* 20, no. 3 (1982), 14–15. James A. Shymansky, "The Effects of New Science Curricula on Student Performance," *Journal of Research in Teaching,* 20 (1983), 387-404.

23. John M. Good, John U. Forley, and Edwin Fenton, "Developing Inquiry Skills with an Experimental Social Studies Curriculum," *The Journal of Educational Research,* 63, no. 1 (September 1969), 35.

24. T. E. Allen, "A Study of the Behaviors of Two Groups of Disruptive Children When Taught with Contrasting Strategies: Directive vs. Nondirective Teaching," Ph.D. diss., The Florida State University, 1976).

25. Edmund Amidon and N. A. Flanders, "The Effects of Direct and Indirect Teacher Influence on Dependent-Prone Students Learning Geometry," in Edmund Amidon and John B. Hough, eds., *Interaction Analysis: Theory, Research, and Application* (Reading, MA: Addison-Wesley, 1967), 210–216.

26. Carl Rogers, *Freedom to Learn* (Columbus, OH: Merrill Publishing Co., 1969).

27. William C. Kyle, Jr., et al., "What Research Says: Science Through Discovery: Students Love It," *Science and Children,* 23, no. 2 (October 1985), 39-41; William C. Kyle, Jr., R. J. Bonnstetter, and T. Gadsen, Jr., "An analysis of elementary students' and teachers' attitudes toward science in process-approach vs. traditional science classes. *Journal of Research in Science Teaching,* 25 (1986) 103-120; William C. Kyle, Jr., et al., "What Research Says . . . About Hands-on Science, *Science and Children,* 25, no. 7 (April 1988), 39–40, 52.

28. Mary Budd Rowe, "Wait Time—Slowing Down May Be a Way of Speeding Up," *American Educator II,* (Spring 1987), 1.

29. For an insight into possible shortcomings of teaching science by inquiry, see Kathleen J. Roth, "Science Education: It's Not Enough to 'Do' or 'Relate'," *American Educator,* 13, no. 4 (Winter 1989), 16−22, 46−47.
30. Ruth S. Charney, "Guided Discovery: Teaching the Freedom to Explore," *A Newsletter for Teachers,* 3, no. 1 (Spring 1991), 1−3.
31. Darrell G. Phillips, "The Importance of Laboratory (Hands-On) Experiences in Science in the Elementary School: A Research Prospective," in "Science Activities Are Central to Science Education in the Elementary School," Robert E. Yager, et al., *Science and Children,* 19, no. 2 (October 1981), 43. Reproduced with permission from *Science and Children,* (October 1981). Copyright by the National Science Teachers Association, 1742 Connecticut Avenue, N.W., Washington, DC 20009.
32. Robert E. Yager, "The Constructivist Learning Model, *The Science Teacher,* 59, no. 6 (September 1991), 56.

One of the most important links between the teacher as a facilitator of knowledge and the child as experimenter is the teacher's questioning strategies. The types of questions asked and their timing can determine whether the child pursues his or her experimentation. It can also determine whether the child explores problems at a more complex level. In response to a question, the child may change his or her focus to respond to a teacher's need or perhaps even leave an activity altogether.[1]

C H A P T E R 4

Questioning and Listening

How can you make effective use of questioning and listening skills?

According to this quotation, the essence of an active, guided discovery science classroom is good questioning. Inherent in this belief is the conviction that any discussion of questioning and teaching should consider the following guidelines:

- Listening skills and strategies should always be combined with questioning. Therefore, this chapter will refer to it as **questioning/listening** or **Q/L.**
- Both teacher and student Q/L skills and strategies are important and need to be developed.

Q/L skills and strategies are analogous to batteries in cars and hearts in humans, as they are the energy and push behind any movements, or learning.

If you practice the ideas in this chapter, you will join many others in being satisfied with improvement in your Q/L skills and strategies. As an added bonus, you can even modify your own personal behavior, becoming less manip-

ulative and more sensitive and facilitative in your social and professional life.

Let's start first by looking at students and Q/L strategies and then to improving your Q/L skills and strategies by looking for answers to these questions:

1. What are the purposes of using Q/L in a constructivist-oriented or guided discovery science program?
2. How is Q/L used for guiding students to higher levels of thinking?
3. What are some Q/L strategies for making your classroom a more effective guided discovery, problem-solving learning environment?

Following the presentation of research findings and proven classroom Q/L strategies that answer these three questions, we will provide a section called "Applications for Your Classroom" to answer the question, "What can you do *now* to enrich your teaching Q/L strategies?"

/// WHAT ARE THE PURPOSES OF Q/L STRATEGIES?

Students' Own Q/L Skills Enhance Learning

When we have succeeded in a constructivist-oriented science program, our students pose their *own* questions and work together to find answers. They should spend more time asking their own questions and less on responding to ours. Beginning activities are usually planned to stimulate student questions that motivate them to want to learn the answers. We arrange the classroom learning environment to encourage student-generated questions. Many of our students' questions, then, arise from their own sensory experiences and observations during the minds-on/hands-on activities to which we expose them. The "I wonder what will happen if . . .?" questions they raise are the "sense of wonder" questions of Rachel Carson. As students collect more prior knowledge and build more concepts, they raise even more questions and search even harder for new information. Chaillé and Britain have organized these "sense of wonder" questions for young children into these organizing questions:

How can I make it move?
How can I make it change?
How does it fit or how do I fit?[2]

Nonverbal Questions. Most of the questions teachers and students ask are verbal, but sometimes words are not used or even necessary. For instance, when a student reaches for a magnet to separate iron filings from an iron filing and sand mixture, it is not necessary for her to verbalize, "I wonder if the magnet will pick up the iron filings?" The student's selection of a possible solution to the immediate problem and her testing of it is the nonverbal question the student has raised in her own mind. Many nonverbal questions are raised during sensory experiences.

Also, every time students use a nonverbal question or ask a verbal question they supply us with data about how they are thinking, processing information, and constructing concepts and schemata. Sometimes their questions ask for obvious details, showing that they may be experiencing difficulty with important concepts. At other times student questions may reveal misconceptions, naive theories, and other difficulties in relating prior knowledge and concepts.

Some upper elementary and middle school teachers use written classroom or homework assignments to challenge students' development of questions. Students are asked to write down any questions that puzzle them or they are curious about as they work with science materials or in their readings. Students are told that the questions should be ones that interest them but are still unanswered by them. If students experience difficulty with this at the beginning, the teacher might suggest the following kinds of questions to "prime the pump" for forming questions:

Who knows about . . . that I'm curious about?
What might happen if . . . ?
Does that mean . . . ?
Where do you think I could find out about . . . ?

Small-group discussions can then follow up on the students' sharing of these questions with possible ways of finding answers.

However this questioning is done, students must be motivated to identify questions of interest to them for the start of concept building.

Teachers and Q/L Strategies

Q/L strategies play a major role in your guided discovery teaching by

■ providing you with *assessment* of information about your students' prior knowledge and levels of thinking,
■ fostering student *problem-solving* skills,

■ encouraging students to *explore* further, and
■ guiding students in *discussions* and in cooperative group activities.

Here are some clues from the growing body of research on these Q/L areas as they relate to effective use in constructivist-oriented or guided discovery classrooms.

Knowing What Your Students Know (or Don't Know) Is Job #1. To help your students build and strengthen their scientific concepts and schemata, you must know at the start of any study or problem their prior knowledge, concepts, misconceptions, naive theories, and schemata. One way to assess their knowledge is to question them and then listen sensitively to their responses. Questioning that asks for information has been called a *soliciting* teaching function and is one of the easiest types of questions. Here are some ways to find out what your students know.

Ask Your Students Open or Closed Questions. One of the simplest ways to classify soliciting questions is to determine what kind of information you need by asking questions that could be classified as either closed (convergent) or open (divergent). If you are looking for specific concepts or prior knowledge of objects and cause-and-effect relations, you would pick **closed,** or **convergent,** questions. They are called closed-ended questions because they focus on a single answer (i.e., converging to one point) and may be thought of schematically as:

QUESTION ———————————ANSWER

On the other hand, **open,** or **divergent,** questions encourage a broader and deeper range of diverse responses and are often referred to as open-ended questions. They look like this:

ANSWER
QUESTION ——————— ANSWER
ANSWER

Convergent and divergent questions also differ in the type of thinking they stimulate in children. Both are legitimate and are useful in your science teaching. The "Applications for Your Classroom" section presents ways to use these questions appropriately for guiding students' concept and schemata building.

How to Use Closed or Convergent Questions. In a guided discovery science program it is generally desirable to start with convergent questions in the primary grades and move toward more divergent ones later on. Convergent questions serve many purposes. In the pictorial riddle diagram in Figure 4–1 of an insect walking on water and a needle floating on water, the student is presented with a **discrepant event,** an event in which there is an inconsistency between what can reasonably be expected to happen in a given situation and what is depicted as happening. Use convergent questions to guide the learner and to assess what he or she sees, knows, or feels about the event.

Convergent questions can direct the learner's attention to specific objects, phenomena, or events. They also sharpen the student's recall or memory faculties. In addition, these questions help you assess students' observational and recall skills and allow you to adjust your teaching to present ideas again, present new ideas, or go back to less complicated ideas. Notice how the questions accompanying Figure 4–1 do this.

Although a balance between convergent and divergent questioning is desirable, studies have shown that approximately 70 to 80% of the questions asked by teachers require only simple recall answers.[3] Convergent questions are necessary to provide children with skills and concepts to help them move to higher levels of learning where they can benefit from divergent or open-ended questioning.

Here are some divergent questions you might ask about the two dishes in Figure 4–1.

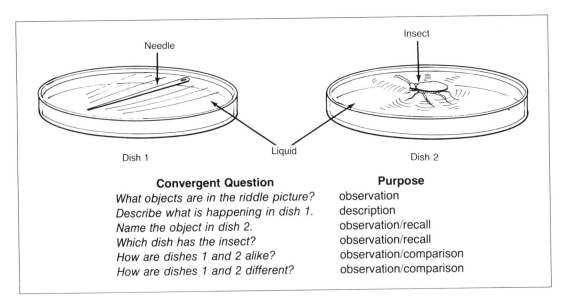

Convergent Question

	Purpose
What objects are in the riddle picture?	observation
Describe what is happening in dish 1.	description
Name the object in dish 2.	observation/recall
Which dish has the insect?	observation/recall
How are dishes 1 and 2 alike?	observation/comparison
How are dishes 1 and 2 different?	observation/comparison

FIGURE 4–1
Pictorial riddle with closed (convergent) questions

Notice that they are broader questions asking for higher levels of thinking.

Divergent Question	**Purpose**
What things can you say about these pictures?	drawing inference
Under what conditions could this be possible?	hypothesizing
How could you illustrate the scientific principles involved in this riddle?	organizing data/ experimentation
What causes the needle and the insect to "float"?	hypothesizing
Under what conditions would both the needle and the insect sink?	hypothesizing
Set up an experiment to show the above.	organizing data/ experimentation

/// HIGHER LEVEL THINKING AND Q/L STRATEGIES

Using Questioning Techniques to Stimulate Children's Thinking

The complex problems of today's science/ technology/society challenges often require more than one solution. Therefore, divergent thinking is a particularly important skill. How you question can stimulate divergent thinking. Using open or divergent questions will broaden and deepen your students' responses and spur them to think creatively and critically. Divergent questions stimulate children to become better observers and organizers of the objects and events you present. Many of these questions guide children in discovering things for themselves, help them to see interrelationships, and make hypotheses or draw conclusions.[4]

It is much more stimulating for students to start with any of the open-ended questions just suggested than it is to ask them initially, "Does surface tension affect how an object floats?" The latter question asks children to guess what is in your head, whereas the former allows them more freedom to use their minds.

It is very important for you as a science teacher (or as a teacher of social studies, reading, mathematics, or the other subjects in a self-contained elementary school curriculum) to

1. identify the differences between convergent and divergent questions,
2. quickly write good convergent and divergent questions,
3. know when it is appropriate and desirable to use both,
4. become familiar and comfortable enough with both kinds of questions to increase the number of divergent questions you are using.

Practical suggestions for increasing your use of convergent and divergent questions are presented in the "Applications for Your Classroom" section of this chapter.

In Figure 4–2 you can see that even a slight increase in the percentage of divergent questions yields a large increase in divergent productivity by students; that is, a larger number of students respond, and their responses are more thoughtful and exhibit higher levels of thinking. These types of responses, in turn, stimulate further discussion among the students.

FIGURE 4–2

Divergent teacher questions stimulate divergent student responses.

Source: Arthur Carin and Robert B. Sund, *Creative Questioning and Sensitive Listening Techniques—A Self-Concept Approach* (Columbus, Ohio: Merrill Publishing Company, 1978), 215.

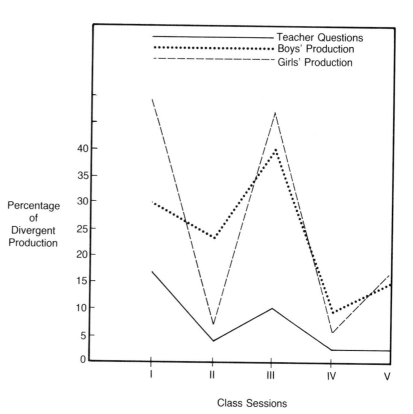

TABLE 4–1
A guided discovery discussion using both convergent and divergent questions

Teacher Asks:	Analysis
1. What can you tell us about shadows?	1. This is an excellent question because it allows for several (divergent) responses. There is no right or wrong answer, and the teacher is able to find out what the children know about the topic before introducing the rest of the lesson.
2. What ways can you make shadows?	2. This is another good question because it still allows for several answers while focusing the students' thoughts on the topic.
3. How could we find out if your ideas are correct? Determine if your idea is correct.	3. The teacher asks the children to consider some ways to proceed with an experiment and then lets them explore.
4. What did you find out about shadows?	4. This is also a relatively divergent question since it allows the children to share several of their observations and conclusions.
5. How could we make a super giant shadow here at school?	5. This again is a good divergent question that allows for a lot of creative input by the children.
6. What did you have to do to make a big shadow?	6. This is a relatively convergent question that requires the children to focus on what they have learned related to producing shadows.
7. What can you say in one sentence about how shadows are made?	7. This requires the children to construct mental concepts about what they have learned. It is a good culminating question because it helps them summarize their learning experiences.

Using Convergent and Divergent Questions in Making Shadows

Table 4–1 analyzes a guided discovery discussion about shadows as an example of convergent/divergent questioning. Notice how the teacher uses a variety of questions, both convergent and divergent, to guide students in developing higher level thinking concepts and skills. What are some other ways of using Q/L strategies to raise students' levels of thinking and problem-solving skills?

Bloom's Levels of Thinking and Q/L Strategies

Another way to use Q/L strategies is to first identify students' levels of thinking and then devise strategies to help them achieve higher levels. Benjamin Bloom devised a classification system for analyzing objectives or thinking levels in the cognitive (or knowledge or intellectual skills and abilities) domain. His classification system is referred to as **Bloom's Taxonomy of Educational Objectives: Cognitive Do-**

TABLE 4–2

Bloom's Taxonomy of Educational Objectives: Cognitive domain and possible teaching questions

	Level	Characteristic Student Behaviors	Possible Questions
Lowest	Knowledge	Recalling, recognizing, memorizing, remembering	How many states produce oil?
	Comprehension	Describing in one's own words, interpreting, translating from one medium to another	Define a lens operationally.
	Application	Problem solving, applying information to produce some result	Knowing what you know about heat, how would you get a lid off a jar that won't unscrew easily?
	Analysis	Finding underlying structure of a communication, breaking something down and showing how it is put together, identifying motives	What things do all these animals have in common?
	Synthesis	Creating unique and original products in either verbal form or physical object	Develop a plan that might avoid the negative consequences of nuclear energy electric plants.
Highest	Evaluation	Resolving differences of opinion or controversies, making value decisions about issues	How may changes in population affect life in the year 2000?

main. Table 4–2 shows Bloom's classification of cognitive behaviors or thinking levels into six categories from simple to more complex.[5] You may use Bloom's taxonomy of levels of thinking to focus on constructing levels of questions that relate to his levels of thinking. The cognitive domain could be organized this way, from the lowest level of difficulty, *knowledge,* to the highest, *evaluation.* Table 4–2 also gives some examples of possible questions for each of Bloom's six cognitive or thinking domain levels. In addition, Chapter 5 on assessment applies Bloom's taxonomy to your assessment of your students and your own science teaching.

Questions requiring responses from the higher levels of the taxonomy are more desirable, especially in the upper elementary and middle school grades, because answering them involves critical and creative thinking and indicates a deeper understanding of the concepts.[6]

Applying Your Knowledge of Bloom's Taxonomy

Return to Table 4–1 and classify the levels of the questions according to Bloom's taxonomy. Notice that convergent (closed) questions tend to cluster around Bloom's lowest thinking level, which is *knowledge.* At this level students are asked only to recall, recognize, remember, or memorize. This level requires students to draw on prior knowledge and past experiences. Convergent questions are also used to ask students to react to observations and stimuli in the *comprehension* level, where they describe events and phenomena in their own words. Divergent questions ask for higher levels of data processing like those in the *application, analysis, synthesis,* and *evaluation* levels.

Preschool and primary grade teachers may have difficulty getting their children to respond to these higher level questions. Their poor response may be caused by their lack of prior knowledge about the topic or insufficient cognitive development because they are functioning at Piaget's preoperational and lower concrete operational levels of development.

/// DEVELOPING PROBLEM-SOLVING SKILLS WITH Q/L STRATEGIES

As pointed out in previous chapters, scientific processes are the backbone of a problem-solving science program for elementary and middle school students. They are the ways in which we can help children use, on their own maturation levels and for their own relevant problems, the processes that scientists use to find answers to their problems. Developing

TABLE 4–3

Questions derived from scientific problem-solving processes

Scientific Problem-Solving Processes	Sample Questions
1. Classifying	How would you group these buttons?
2. Assuming	Using what you know about sinking and floating, what can you assume about the relationship between weight and floating?
3. Predicting, hypothesizing (making good guesses)	What do you think will happen if more salt is added to the oceans each year?
4. Inferring, interpreting data, or making conclusions	What conclusions can you make from the experiment information?
5. Measuring	How much has the plant grown?
6. Designing an investigation to solve a problem	How would you determine the effects of pollution on curb trees in our town?
7. Observing	What do you observe about these animals?
8. Graphing	How would you graph your findings?
9. Reducing experimental error	How many measurements should be made in order to report accurate data?
10. Evaluating	If you had only one heart to transplant for five patients, which type of person would you give it to and why?
11. Analyzing	Based on the things we've done with magnets, what do you think causes short circuits and fires in our electrical systems at home?

such problem-solving skills is vital and must be a part of your science program. One way you may accomplish this is to structure your questions around the critical problem-solving thinking processes described in Table 4–3.

Simple questions, when intelligently thought out and strategically used in an activity, can do much to guide students in problem-solving situations. For instance, in helping students design an investigation to solve the problem they are investigating, you could ask, "How would you determine the effects of pollution on the trees on our school grounds?" Or, to encourage students to measure and record, ask, "How much has the plant grown since we started the experiment?"

Ask Scientific Process Questions Appropriate to the Age Group

Piaget and other researchers have pointed out that significant differences exist between the thought processes of primary and upper elementary students and middle grade students. For this reason, in asking scientific process questions for the elementary and middle grades, you must adjust your questioning accordingly. Primary and lower elementary teachers should devote a great deal of attention to asking scientific process questions of the following kinds.

Primary/Lower Elementary (Ages 5 to 10)

1. Observing.
2. Grouping and simple classification; for example, multiple classification, class inclusion.
3. Measuring.
4. Using numbers; for example, counting leaves and animals.
5. Placing objects in series or ordering them; for example, from small to large, short to tall, or light to heavy.

6. Making inferences; for example, "If the animals have no eyes, how is it that they don't run into things and hurt themselves?"
7. Indicating time and space relations; for example, "Is this the same distance as this is?"
8. Conserving substance, length, number, and area.
9. Reversibility.
10. Values; for example, "How can we keep the environment clean?"
11. Interpersonal relations, such as learning to see things from other people's perspectives.
12. Predicting.
13. Making one-to-one correspondences; for example, "For every one in this row, how many are there in that row?"

Students in the upper elementary and middle grades may be asked any questions related to these areas when appropriate, plus those that follow.

Upper Elementary and Middle Grades (Beyond age 11)

1. Formulating hypotheses.
2. Learning to control a variable, such as growing one plant in light and one in the dark.
3. Designing relatively sophisticated experiments.
4. Interpreting data from experiments.
5. Understanding the conservation of weight and volume.
6. Making operational definitions.
7. Constructing models (theories about natural phenomena), such as molecules. (This probably should be limited to grades 6 to 8.)

In evaluating your questions, determine if the children in the grade level you teach are cognitively able to answer them. In many cases, this may be difficult. The way to resolve this dilemma is to test your questions in your

Probing questions guide students' thinking and encourage independent problem solving.

classroom and note your students' responses. Then, adapt your questions accordingly. But don't stop at the "right" answer!

Keep the Creative Problem-Solving Juices Flowing

When you ask questions to stimulate problem-solving process thinking in your students, do not stop the discussion when you get a correct answer; to do so prevents your students from probing even more deeply into the questions you have posed. Elicit other responses. Later you can return to the right answer and discuss it. When you do return to the correct answer, tell your students that their answers are good and indicate a lot of good thinking. Say, however, you would like to talk about one thing they said,

and then continue the discussion. Handling questions and answers in this way shows your students that you prize their *thinking* first and the content next, that you value thinking over mere memorization and recall of isolated facts.

Encourage your students to think beyond their initial responses to your questions. Use follow-up questions, or **probes,** to elicit more complete answers with questions like these:

What else do you remember about . . . ?	(recall/memory)
What other information can you give to . . . ?	(comprehension)
How else might you . . . ?	(reflection)

Probing questions stimulate greater comprehension and problem-solving processes.

Using Q/L Strategies to Encourage Problem-Solving and Further Exploration[7]

Occasions arise in a guided discovery problem-solving science program when the teacher may notice interest waning or students in need of encouragement and direction. At these times, a well-directed question at an appropriate time can stimulate students and move things along very effectively. Here are some aspects of Q/L strategies that pertain to these situations.

When to ask a question and when to refrain and remain silent is a perennial concern of teachers. Only you can decide whether your question will advance the discussion, inhibit students, or divert them from pursuing the solution to their problem. Often you are better off not asking questions and letting the students work things out. There are times, though, when a well-placed question will do the job. For instance, if the student is stuck or may be giving up in frustration, you might ask, "What might happen if you . . . ?" By asking that question, you are not telling the student what to do but are raising a possibility to be considered. If the student is still unable to see what should be done, you could ask a more limited or direct question such as, "How could you use this magnet to show . . . ?"

As you see from these examples, start with the broadest, most open-ended question before moving to a more focused or directed one. The criterion for selecting your questions should be one that answers this question: "Will my question(s) alleviate students' frustrations and move them along with a minimum of my intrusion?"

Sometimes, nonverbal questioning (asking a question without using words) is the best Q/L strategy. How can you ask a question without

"What might happen if you . . . ?"

using words? You probably have done this many times without realizing it. For instance, when my grandson, Andy, was unsuccessfully trying to reach something on the top of his bookcase, sliding a step-stool near him, non-verbally said to him, "Do you think this will assist you in getting to the top?" Andy was able to see the step-stool, consider its use, and use it, all without words. Think of all the situations where you might strategically place a helpful item within the student's grasp. The result of good questioning should be that students are encouraged to think things out independently and not always rely on the teacher for answers and solutions to their problems. Here are several other times when this independence is desirable.

Turning Questions Back to Students for Better Learning

When students ask you questions or request assistance by responding with a good question, try to challenge their thinking processes instead of giving them the answer. If students ask, "What can we use to separate iron filings from the sand/iron filings mixture?" you might respond with, "Look in the basket. Can any of those items (magnets, screening, or sandpaper) help you separate the iron filings?" Psychiatrists use this technique of turning patients' questions back to them to encourage them to reason through their problems for themselves.

When there is a classroom conflict, a safety problem, or an unusual mess as a result of an activity, questions can be used (after danger or problems are resolved) to turn the situations into learning opportunities. Your questions should help students to

- look back at the situation for an understanding by asking
What could have caused . . . ?
How did you feel when . . . was happening?

- hypothesize solutions to the problem and avoid or minimize future occurrences by asking
Next time, how can we . . . ?
What are other ways we could . . . ?

These kinds of questions can help students learn from adverse situations without casting blame or causing guilt. These and the Q/L strategies that follow can make your classroom a more supportive and better learning environment.

/// USING Q/L STRATEGIES FOR BETTER STUDENT-CENTERED DISCUSSIONS

There are two general patterns of class discussion or students, responding to questions. One pattern is called the **ping-pong pattern** or **peer interaction.** A teacher using this approach says something, a student responds, and the teacher says something else. Class discussions follow a teacher-to-student-to-teacher pattern. In this ping-pong pattern, most of the interaction takes place between the teacher and one student at a time. At best, it is a low level of thinking and responding.

Teachers of guided discovery science lead discussions that are more like a **basketball pattern.** The teacher says something and then a student-student-student-teacher-student interaction occurs. Instead of merely passing the ball back to the teacher, students are encouraged to pass the ball directly to each other.

These two teacher/student discussion patterns are illustrated in Figure 4–3.

Teachers who direct basketball type discussions pause between question-asking and answer-getting to stimulate as many different student respondents as possible. When students respond, the teacher usually says little but looks around the class to see if other students might want to respond.

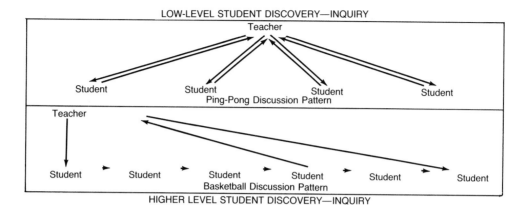

FIGURE 4–3

Patterns of teacher/student discussions

These teachers perform different roles than teachers who use ping-pong discussions. They serve as traffic directors of the discussion, pointing to whoever might speak so not more than one student is talking at a time. These teachers do not interject their thoughts until the students have finished their remarks. As a consequence, these teachers are more student-centered than ping-pong discussion instructors. Some questions teachers might ask to direct and keep discussion moving in basketball type discussions are:

Who agrees or disagrees with Terry's ideas?

What can anyone add to Selma's report?

What questions are still unanswered?

/// IMPROVING YOUR GUIDED DISCOVERY DISCUSSIONS

Wait-Time: Slow Down to Speed Up Thinking

We elementary and middle school teachers are pressured by the clock to "cover everything" in the six hours or so that we have our students in our classrooms. So it is no surprise that we try to rush through many of the things we do, even

in our question and answer times. Mary Budd Rowe found that most teachers usually wait less than a second for a response after asking a question! These very brief intervals, or **wait-times,** result in rote, verbatim memory recall, usually of textbook or teacher-made information. This is the lowest level of Bloom's taxonomy of learning. Further investigations revealed, however, that some teachers waited an average of three seconds.[8]

What differences in student responses do you think were found in the longer teacher wait-times? Dr. Rowe found that teachers who waited three seconds or longer got greater speculation, conversation, and argument than those teachers with shorter wait-times. She also found that when teachers are trained to wait an average of more than three seconds before responding, the following happens:

1. The length of student response increases 400 to 800%.
2. The number of unsolicited but appropriate responses increases.
3. Failure to respond decreases.
4. Confidence of children increases.
5. The number of questions asked by students increases.
6. Slow students contribute from 1.5 to 37% more.

7. The variety of types of responses increases. There is more reacting to each other, structuring of procedures, and soliciting.
8. Speculative thinking increases as much as 700%.
9. Discipline problems decrease.
10. Achievement improves in cognitively complex items on written tests.[9]

Dr. Rowe also found that teachers trained to prolong wait-time changed in their classroom behavior in the following ways:

1. They exhibited more flexible types of responses.
2. The number and kinds of teacher questions changed.
3. Teacher expectations for student performance were modified. Teachers were less likely to expect only the brighter students to reply and viewed their class as having fewer academically slow students.

What Are Wait-Time 1 and Wait-Time 2?

There are two types of wait-times. **Wait-time 1** is the initial wait-time when an instructor waits for the first response. **Wait-time 2** is the total time a teacher waits for a class to respond to the same questions. Wait-time 2 may involve several minutes, particularly if the question asked requires critical or creative thinking. Of the two, Rowe believes wait-time 2 is more important for a teacher to develop. She found a 500 to 700% increase in student responses when teachers used it. The responses from the poorer academic students, furthermore, increased significantly with longer wait-time 2s.

Untrained Teachers Wait Less Than 1 Second for Wait-Time 1. Teachers untrained in questioning techniques discriminate against slower academic students. They wait only 0.9 seconds for the slow students to reply, but wait at least 1.2 seconds for the "top five" academically talented students to answer. Some evidence suggests that wait-time varies in different cultures. Rowe states, for example, that Australian teachers wait only 0.5 seconds on an average before calling on a student.

Try to Have a Wait-Time of at Least 5 Seconds. Teachers who practice a wait-time of at least 3 seconds are less likely to discriminate favorably toward the academically superior students because they get more student participation. Teachers who have a wait-time average of 5 seconds or more get even greater participation and more creative responses from their students.

If students are to inquire deeper into a subject, instructors need to increase their wait-time tolerance so learners have more opportunities to think, create, and fully demonstrate their human potential.

Provide Halting Time. Halting time is related to wait-time in that an instructor halts and waits for students to think, but the students do not answer questions. When teachers explain something that is relatively complex, they present some information and then stop, so students have time to see what the teachers have done and to think about it. The teachers then continue and may repeat this behavior several times. While stopping, they visually check with the class to see whether the students are with them. If they obtain positive indications that the students are following the explanation, they continue. If the students are not following, teachers may have to ask more specific questions or retrace the work. Philosophers, when speaking, often demonstrate this technique. They make a statement, pause a few seconds for listeners to digest it, and then continue to the next point.

Avoid Reward Giving During Discussions. Teachers traditionally have thought that giving positive verbal rewards facilitates class discussion. Research findings question this procedure.[10] In fact, it indicates that rewarding students may cause *less* student involvement. When teachers change their modes of response over several weeks so as not to give positive verbal rewards, the class participation begins to change. Not only do more students interact, but a greater number of less academically able students participate. Those students, however, who are generally reward seekers may initially become somewhat disoriented because they are not receiving their usual rewards. Nevertheless, after two or three weeks, they adapt to the new teacher behavior and become more autonomous.

Students apparently perceive subtle teacher behavior that suggests favoritism and a lack of fairness in the interaction process, preventing true democratic discourse. Teachers might find it helpful to make cassette tapes of their class discussions to evaluate how their expectations interfere with the discussion process. They should count how many praise words are used and determine which students receive them the most. Praise inappropriately used, particularly with minority students, has been found to give them an unrealistic and distorted impression of their ability, which often causes problems when the students are advanced or try to enter college.[11]

Rewards Are Not Always Undesirable— We All Need Strokes! The point of not giving rewards is to spark more speculative and critical thinking among your students and to encourage more involvement during group discussions. However, it is helpful to recognize the achievement of students during individual work or for performing well certain types of basic skills, especially if you make a point to recognize each student for specific things he or she has done well.[12]

A forceful book, *Try Giving Yourself Away,*[13] documents the power of such recognition in changing the lives of individuals, making positive efforts to recognize and reward others for their kindness, humanism, and achievements. Teachers who try to look for good and value in every student and who inform them specifically and privately about these things are effective. They also are more likely to enjoy their teaching. This book documents how easy it is to look for something good to say to each individual, for example, when they come into class or in private discussions. Why don't more teachers make greater efforts to do this? Now even curriculum materials try to get teachers to do this more frequently. For example, in elementary school, writing "warm fuzzy" comments in which some psychological trait is recognized on a card for each student is a popular activity. Remember also, as Abraham Maslow, a prominent psychologist, indicated in his theory of human needs, that we all need to be recognized as valuable persons so our self-concepts continue to grow positively.

Cooperative Learning Improves Classroom Discussions

Cooperative learning, small-group learning where members are assigned roles and rotate the roles, provides students with excellent opportunities to verbalize what they know, believe, or feel and to consider the multiple viewpoints of their fellow group members. These groups offer a chance for students to test their understandings against the understandings of other group members on a face-to-face basis. How different this is from the more traditional total class discussions of the ping-pong variety (especially in college classes), where all you see are the backs of your fellow classmates' heads.

Cooperative learning is invaluable for discussions for such activities as problem solving, divergent thinking, and guided discovery. For these types of activities, cooperative learning is much more effective than total class discussions.[14] By working collaboratively on a group problem, students are able to interact positively and noncompetitively. Their discussions become more sharing of ideas and materials as

Problem solving, divergent thinking, and guided discovery discussions are enhanced through cooperative learning.

they work toward solution(s) of their problems. They support each other as they take risks and contribute to the group effort. The diversity of views of the students enriches the discussions and assists individual students in constructing their concepts.[15] Many shy or slower thinking students are encouraged to contribute and participate in the discussions in this nonthreatening and supportive group environment. Group cooperative learning offers teachers a strategy for breaking the ping-pong total class discussion pattern.

Practical suggestions for organizing and using cooperative learning in your classroom are given in Chapter 6 on managing your guided discovery science program.

Cooperative learning also helps teachers and students become better listeners. Here are some ways to accomplish that.

Open Your Ears and Close Your Mouth!

It has wisely been observed, "Nothing new ever entered the mind through an open mouth."[16] If teachers and students spent more time listening to each other, they would *both* improve their skills in questioning and would respond more intelligently to each other. Research has shown that people who listen well are able to relate to what the speaker is saying, understand the reasoning behind what is being said, and are better able to participate thoughtfully in discussions.[17] The implication of this for teachers is clear. Listening carefully and sensitively not only to the answer but to the thinking behind the answer provides you with much more information about your students. Students may have difficulty listening to fellow students and need practice in how to listen effectively. Karen Mahr, a first grade teacher, used this role-playing technique to focus on listening skills with her class.[18] She coached several fifth graders on what each of their roles would be when they acted out a *poor* small-group discussion. In the discussion that followed the role-playing, the first graders concluded that the fifth graders were not listening to each other. Because the first graders were now conscious of the importance of listening to each other's contribution, they had better small-group discussions in the future. Obviously, reinforcement is needed periodically, as humans, especially first graders, forget.

Good, sensitive listening skills must be taught as any other skill, and it is best learned by students who construct the concepts for themselves.

Be a Model of Sensitive Listening Techniques

Krishnamurti, an Indian philosopher, said that Americans do not truly listen because they are always judging, composing their thoughts, or preparing salvos for reacting during the time a speaker is discoursing. A person who truly listens in an open, accepting, nonjudgmental way probably is a rarity. Demonstrating poor listening skills is undoubtedly related to how teachers perceive their roles. If you see your function as being mainly to develop or achieve some subject matter concept or principle, you naturally will focus on its achievement. However, if you perceive your role as helping children develop cognitively and construct their own concepts, you will tend to focus on the student as a person first and on the content second. Listen intently to what children have to say, and only when they have finished formulate questions and responses to help them make discoveries and use their thought processes. There can be no substitute for a teacher who is primarily interested in people and really listens to them.

Teachers should listen—not analyze, evaluate, or judge—until the student has completed the response to a question. Unfortunately, some do not, and start to dissect what students say before they have had a chance to finish. Many students' ideas are good, but they suffer from poor verbalization. If you wait until students finish their answers before reacting, you will more likely grasp their ideas and better convey in nonverbal ways that you are sincerely interested in their ideas.

Helping Your Students Become Better Listeners

Children often do not learn and achieve as well as they could because they have not developed their listening skills. As a model of a good listener, you can help to modify this insufficiency. Listed in the following "Applications for Your Classroom" section are practical suggestions to help you improve your and your students' listening skills. At first you may have to consciously use these suggestions, but with time

and practice they will become a pattern of your normal conversational behavior. Try the suggestions for sensitive listening techniques.

/// APPLICATIONS FOR YOUR CLASSROOM

Here are practical, classroom-tested suggestions for improving your Q/L strategies that are based on research cited previously and can be put into practice immediately. Included with each suggestion are actual questions you might ask as you begin to work on improving your Q/L strategies.[19] Select those that fit your particular needs or modify them as needed. As you become more familiar and confident with them, you will be able to construct and use many of your own questions.

How Can You Write and Use Better Convergent/Divergent Questions?

Because they are the most frequently used type of questions, you should learn to write and ask better convergent/divergent questions. Here are some practical guidelines.

1. Avoid questions that can be answered by "yes" or "no."
2. Look at the words that *start* your questions because they often dictate the style of the answer.
3. Questions that begin with the words *do, did, are, is, can, will, would,* and *should* require a "yes" or "no" response.
4. If yes or no questions must be used, you should make them more divergent by adding: "Why? How do you know? How might we find out? What makes you think so? What gives you that idea?" (e.g., "Is baking powder a producer of gas? How might I set up an experiment to test my idea?")

5. Look for questions that ask children to discover conditions that could *change objects or events*, such as, "What can you do to the magnets to make them stronger?" or "What ways can you make the lights burn brighter with the wire, switch, and dry cell?"

6. Ask children questions that require them to *discover and compare* things (e.g., "In what places do we find mold in summer?" or "Using these objects and the bowl of water, which objects do you think will sink and which will float?")

7. Use *convergent* questions to focus children's attention to specifics.

8. Try to use more *divergent* questions. You will be pleased with the resultant higher level of responses.

Avoid Using Multiple Questions. Avoid using multiple questions without giving students opportunities to respond. To ask multiple questions usually is to ignore wait-time. For example, "What causes do you think might have contributed to this situation? Which of these were important?" These questions in themselves are not bad, but when teachers run them together, they hinder the thinking processes of their students.

Avoid Overreactions. Avoid overreacting to student responses. For example, "That is terrific—fantastic thinking, George. Wow, what an answer!" This type of reaction may act as a constricting force because other students may think their ideas will not be so highly valued if you respond with less enthusiasm to them.

Break Limited Thinking. Sometimes students become fixed on one aspect of a problem. Teachers then have to devise questions that will break the students out of their limited perceptual field. They might do this by asking the following questions:

What other factors might be contributing to . . . ?

What other information are we given in this . . . ?
What other interpretations are possible?
What alternatives are there?
What other things or ways are . . . ?

Ask Students to Clarify Materials. A student may present a prolonged reply on material that is not easily understood by the other members of the class. The teacher may help to clarify this reply by saying

You said it was similar. Similar in what respect?
Please give an example to show where this is occurring.
What other examples are there?
What do you mean when you say . . . ?

Guard Against Overgeneralizations. When students make overgeneralizations, focus the class's attention on these by asking questions such as

You mean that is true for all . . . ?
What in your investigations indicated that this was true for all . . . ?
Where and under what conditions would this be true?

Ask Your Students to Summarize. Asking students to summarize is particularly needed when the concepts involved are abstract or vague, when the student reply has been lengthy, or when some investigations have taken a great deal of time. The teacher might ask

Briefly, please summarize what you have just said.
Tell us in your own words what we have learned.
What were the main ideas discussed today?
What is the main point of what you are saying?

Amplify and Pursue the Thought. Often, you need to act as a stimulus to keep the discussion going. This can be done by having students refocus, summarize, and consider alternatives, other forces, and factors that might move the discussion to a higher level. This may be done in the following ways:

I see you have come up with an answer. How did you obtain it?

What evidence do you have that it is correct?

You said that this animal behaved in this manner. Why do you think that?

What effect do you think, for example, polluting the stream will have?

Always Consider the Emotional Overtones of the Materials. Because of students' diverse backgrounds, many topics may have emotional overtones. In discussions where this is the case, you must be particularly careful to phrase questions that do not inhibit the rational responses of the students. For example, in a class with a boy who was bitten by a snake, it may be difficult for him not to become emotional if you ask questions about snakes.

Paraphrase What Students Say. When you are not sure what the student has said, you can paraphrase his or her statement to make the point clearer. For example, "I hear you say that . . . Am I correct?" You can also use this strategy when you think other students may not have heard the student's comments.

Focus on What the Person Is Saying. Maintain eye contact with the speaker. Try not to evaluate what the speaker is saying until he or she has completed all statements.

Do Not Take the Discussion Away from the Students. Students are the ones who need to develop their minds. To do this, they must practice speaking, formulating their own questions, constructing their ideas and concepts,

Feelings are foundations for building science concepts.

and sharing their ideas with their classmates. There is no shortcut by teacher doing it for them.

Give Positive Nonverbal Signals. Show you are concerned and that you are listening by

1. maintaining eye contact;
2. holding a concerned posture, for example with your body turned toward the student;
3. smiling appropriately because the student is expressing himself or herself;
4. nodding to indicate understanding to the student; and
5. using gestures.

Develop Silent-Time. This is similar to wait-time except that silent-time is the time taken after a student apparently has finished speaking and before you reply. Silent-time prevents you from cutting off a student's statements and allows others to interject their ideas without your interference. Calm silence also helps to indicate to the student and the class a trust in their abilities to think and make significant statements.

Look for Indicators That Students May Want to Say Something. Be sensitive to students who may want to contribute to the discussion. Especially look for students who are

1. waving their arms;
2. rising up in their seats;
3. making eye contact with you;
4. glancing meaningfully at you or the speaker;
5. pressing their lips together as if they are going to say something; and
6. mumbling.

When these signs occur, invite participation (e.g., "Jon, is there something you would like to say?").

Do Not Interrupt. Don't interrupt, even to clarify, until you are certain the student has completed his or her message.

Other Types of Questions to Use.[20]

The following examples show other kinds of questions to use to get student reactions for various purposes.

Use Questions to Get Varied Responses. Consider these forms:

> What do you notice about . . . , for example, this picture, this equipment, the environment?
> What will happen if . . . ?
> If this is so, then . . . ?
> This is so if and only if what? (To be used only in upper elementary and middle grades)

Use Questions to Stimulate Creative Responses. Use a lot of "what if" questions:

> What if you changed the size, shape, color of . . . ?
> What if you added or took something away from . . . ?
> What if you were going to begin a better . . . what would you do?
> What if different materials were used, what would happen?

Ask future-oriented questions.

> What will you look like in the future?
> What things do you think will happen to our town in the future?
> What would happen if we were to plant more trees around our school or in our park?
> What kind of energy will you use in the future?

Use more "How-would-you" questions.

> How would you design an investigation to find out about . . . ?
> How would you, for example, improve the experiment?
> How would you make something to . . . ?
> How would you do it better?

Use Questions to Invite Students to Publicly Affirm Their Values. During the time students are in school, they develop values for life. Teachers, therefore, need to help them construct their own values without imposing or moralizing. The following questions will help students focus and clarify their values.

What valuable things have you learned today?

In what ways have you been successful today, this week, this year?

What makes you feel great about what we have been doing in science?

What makes you feel bad?

What do you think about, for example, what science does for society, pollution, or health?

How do you feel about this part of your work?

How did you come to this opinion?

What other conclusions could you have reached?

How do you think the other person sees the problem?

How do most people feel about that?

What have you done about, for example, keeping our environment clean?

A Bonus for You When You Improve Your Q/L Skills

Research indicates that teachers trained to ask better questions are able to construct them significantly better than those without training.[21] With this knowledge in mind, your task is to modify your questioning behavior, not only in teaching science but also in other areas. To help your students learn how to ask *you* good questions don't be afraid to say, "I don't know the answer."[22] Good Q/L skills will facilitate better learning and human development by you and your students.

Consider other things you need to work on to increase your Q/L skills and strategies. What are they? The other suggestions in this chapter should give you some help.

SUMMARY

The foundation of minds-on/hands-on guided discovery teaching/learning is built on good questioning and listening (Q/L) skills and strategies for *both* students and teachers. Q/L skills enhance students' concept and schemata building by improving their posing questions of interest to them and then pursuing answers to their questions. Students must be encouraged and shown ways to ask themselves questions as they engage in sensory and cognitive activities. Emphasis must shift from teacher-dominated question asking to student-centered questioning.

Teachers use Q/L strategies for many purposes; a vital one in a constructivist-oriented learning classroom is to assess what your students know and don't know, so that you can facilitate the best learning conditions. Suggestions were given for using convergent and divergent questions for this purpose and for stimulating students' thinking. Higher level questions are used for developing students' problem-solving skills. Bloom's Taxonomy of Educational Objectives: Cognitive Domain iden-

Discovery: The Science Lady

I have been amazed at how much demand there is for a person who can make science real for kids.

—Ann Piening McMahon, "The Science Lady"

Strategy   Make science special by taking advantage of local resource people or consider taking on a special persona of your own when teaching science.

For the past year, Ann Piening McMahon, a former McDonnell Douglas missile systems engineer, has performed as one of her two alter egos: The *Science Lady* in schools or *Serendipity, The Science Magician,* at weekend parties. As the Science Lady, McMahon wears the lab coat pictured. As Serendipity, she changes name tags and adds a glitter-covered black top hat. McMahon, who lives near St. Louis, Missouri, took advantage of entrepreneurial training sponsored by her former employer to learn how to run her own small business.

One of her major motivations for adapting her science background to education occurred as the result of the recent fiftieth anniversary reunion of Westinghouse National Science Talent Search winners. As McMahon spoke with other past winners, including some Nobel prize winners, she discovered a consistent theme—each had become excited about science at a very early age and had received encouragement. Many of these scientists lamented that they are seeing fewer students who share their early passion for science.

Although she has had no formal training in education, McMahon has drawn upon her 20 years experience explaining astronomy to the public to develop the science activities. The Science Lady bases her activities on the process framework of the scientific method. She has also learned from the preschool and elementary school teachers where she presents her lessons. The teachers have taught her some questioning strategies. One of the best questions for any age student is, "What words can you use to talk about this?"

On Your Own Put the scientific method to work in your classes. Play "What do we know?" about a topic. Record sensory information about the topic. After gathering information, sort it. Come up with as many different ways of sorting as possible. Then guess what would happen if the pattern was taken one step further. Test the guess. Compare what you learned from the test to the guess. Have students write or draw a picture of what was done, how it was done, and what they learned. Keep in mind the process is more important than the product.

Source: Interview with Ann Piening McMahon. Photo courtesy of Ms. McMahon.

tifies these levels of thinking, and questions were generated using these levels for developing student problem-solving skills. Scientific processes are also the basis around which questions can be structured to guide students' problem solving. Scientific process questions appropriate to a wide age range were presented as were ways to motivate and keep students' creative problem-solving "juices" flowing. Verbal and nonverbal questioning was discussed, along with how to turn questioning back to students for them to structure their own concepts and schemata.

Q/L strategies for better student-centered discussions focused on the effective uses of patterns of peer interaction (ping-pong and basketball), wait-time, rewards, and cooperative learning groups. Sensitive listening techniques for both students and teachers must be learned, and examples of how to achieve this were explored.

The "Applications for Your Classroom" section is a resource of specific Q/L strategies for immediate classroom adaptation including topics such as writing and using better convergent and divergent questions; avoiding multiple questions, overreaction, and overgeneralization; asking students how to summarize, amplify, and pursue thinking; improving listening skills of students and teachers; and asking a variety of questions for particular purposes (e.g., creative, future-oriented, "how-would-you", and values clarification).

Research indicates that teachers trained in questioning and listening techniques change their questioning and listening behavior in the classroom, asking more sensitive, creative, and science process questions.

Suggestions to Help You Develop Better Q/L Skills

Several "rules" have been presented in this chapter.

1. Talk less but ask more.
2. Use some classification system to analyze your questions as a basis for improving them.
3. Use more divergent questions.
4. Avoid asking questions that can be answered by *yes* or *no*.
5. Try to ask more questions that are higher on Bloom's taxonomy system.
6. Evaluate your questions for the scientific processes your students require.
7. Ask more questions to discover multitalents.
8. Do not stop the discussion with the right answer.
9. Increase wait-time 1 to at least 3 seconds.
10. Increase wait-time 2 to several minutes.
11. Lead more student-student-student, basketball-type discussions and cooperative learning groups.
12. Do not give rewards during a discussion.

13. Look for something good to say to individuals in private discussions.
14. Provide good halting times.
15. Avoid asking multiple questions.
16. Avoid overreaction.
17. Ask students to clarify material.
18. Guard against overgeneralizations.
19. Ask students to summarize.
20. Develop sensitive listening techniques.
21. Develop silent-time.
22. Ask questions appropriate to the Piagetian level.
23. For creativity:
    a. Ask many "what-if" questions.
    b. Ask future-oriented questions.
    c. Use more "how-would-you" questions.

SELF-ASSESSMENT AND FURTHER STUDY

Activities to Use in Microteaching or Teaching Students

1. Ask someone to make an audio- or videotape recording of a pictorial riddle or guided discovery activity-based discussion that you lead. (Check the index of this text for pictorial riddles or guided discovery activities.) When you have completed the activity, do the following evaluations.
    a. Check every time you ask a question that is a convergent (yes or no) type.
    b. Listen to or watch your tape to determine your average wait-time 1 and wait-time 2.
    c. Determine what areas of questioning you need to improve.
2. Lead a discussion in which you try to get a basketball-type interaction. Evaluate how well you did. Determine by using a cassette recorder how many students you get to interact before you respond.
3. Try to improve your nonverbal indicators of sensitive listening. For example, face the person speaking, maintain better eye contact, smile more, or nod your head.
4. Work on getting your students to listen more to each other. For example, occasionally have them paraphrase what has been said. Invite them to play "add on." (One student says something about a topic and another student adds on to it with his or her ideas.)

Other Self-Assessment Activities

5. Look at the nine questions shown in Table 4–4. Rate them according to whether you think they stimulate high or low levels of student thinking.

TABLE 4–4
Rating questions on stimulating levels of children's thinking

	Stimulates Children's Thinking	
	High Level	Low Level
1. Which tree is taller?		
2. Does the heat of the candle affect the air in the jar?		
3. What do you think will happen if you add cold coffee to the water with the brine shrimp?		
4. If you were going to design an experiment to show, for example, the effects of cigarette smoke on an animal or plant, what would you do?		
5. How would you group these objects?		
6. Can you tell which of these metals was influenced by the magnet?		
7. What did you notice about how the flies in the jar behaved when half of it was covered with black paper?		
8. Which of these things are metals and which are not?		
9. What do you conclude from the experiment?		

■ Which three questions are the *best* to ask? Why?

■ Which questions require the student to *evaluate* something?

■ Which questions allow only a *few* responses?

■ Which questions encourage *many* responses?

■ Which questions require the student to mainly *observe*?

■ Which questions require the students to formulate *operational definitions*?

■ Which questions require the student to mainly *classify*?

■ Which questions require the student to demonstrate *experimental* procedure?

■ Which questions require the student to *hypothesize*?

■ How would you group or *classify* most of the questions?

Explain why. Now answer the 10 questions about the first set of questions. Write down your answers.

6. Observe or tape a classroom conversation and classify the questions asked according to one of the classification systems suggested in this chapter.

7. Write some discussion questions and classify them according to Bloom's taxonomy and science processes.

8. List as many words as possible that would require only a yes or no answer when used as the first word of a question.

9. Lead a short discussion and have someone check your wait-time, halting time, and silent-time and how well you get students to talk to each other instead of to you.

10. After reading more about cooperative learning groups in Chapter 6, plan and organize one for a group of students. Audio- or videotape the first session and analyze it for effectiveness.

NOTES

1. Christine Chaillé and Lory Britain, *The Young Child As Scientist: A Constructivist Approach to Early Childhood Science Education* (New York: Harper Collins, 1991), 63.

2. Christine Chaillé and Lory Britain, *The Young Child As Scientist,* 26.

3. Joseph P. Riley, "The Effect of Teachers' Wait Time and Knowledge Comprehension Questioning on Science Achievement," *Journal of Research in Science Teaching,* 23, no. 45 (April 1986): 335–342.

4. For additional examples of divergent questions and the teacher's role in using them, see Mary Jo Puckett Cliatt and Jean M. Shaw, "Open Questions, Open Answers," *Science and Children,* 23, no. 3 (November/December 1985): 14–16.

5. Benjamin S. Bloom, Thomas Hastings, and George F. Madaus, *Handbook of Educational Objectives: Handbook I, The Cognitive Domain* (New York: David McKay, 1980).

6. Suggestions for evoking higher thought processes using Q/L strategies can be found in Deborah B. Strother, "Developing Thinking Skills Through Questioning," *Phi Delta Kappan,* (December 1989): 324–325.

7. For an excellent treatment of this topic for early childhood education students see Christine Chaillé and Lory Britain, *The Young Child as Scientist,* 66–67.

8. Mary Budd Rowe, "Wait-Time and Rewards as Instructional Variables, Their Influence on Language, Logic, and Fate Control: Part One—Wait-Time," *Journal of Research in Science Teaching,* 11, no. 2 (June 1974): 81–94.

9. Mary Budd Rowe, "Wait-Time: Slowing Down May Be a Way of Speeding Up," *American Educator,* 11, no. 1 (Spring 1987): 38–47.

10. K. O. McGraw, "The Detrimental Effects of Reward on Performance: A Literature Review and a Prediction Model," in M. A. Pepper and D. Green,

eds., *The Hidden Costs of Reward: New Perspectives on the Psychology of Human Motivation* (Hillsdale: NJ: Erlbaum, 1978).

11. David L. Martin, "Your Praise Can Smother Learning," *Learning,* (February 1977): 46.

12. Ibid, 48.

13. David Dunn, *Try Giving Yourself Away* (Englewood Cliffs, NJ: Prentice-Hall, 1970).

14. David W. Johnson and Roger T. Johnson, *Learning Together and Alone: Cooperation, Competition, and Individualization* (Englewood Cliffs, NJ: Prentice-Hall, 1987).

15. An excellent classroom resource based on the cooperative learning works of Johnson and Johnson is Dee Dishon and Pat W. O'Leary, *A Guidebook for Cooperative Learning* (Holmes Beach, FL: Learning Publications, 1984).

16. Andrew Wolvin and Carol Coakley, *Listening,* 2nd ed. (Dubuque, IA: Wm. C. Brown, 1985), 15.

17. J. T. Dillon, *Questioning and Teaching: A Manual of Practice* (NY: Teachers College Press, 1988).

18. Karen Mahr, "Mr. Detective, Can You Help Solve This Problem?" Unpublished manuscript, Montclair State College, NJ, 1989.

19. For a greater variety and specification of practical Q/L suggestions, you are urged to see Arthur Carin and Robert B. Sund, *Creative Questioning and Sensitive Listening Techniques: A Self-Concept Approach,* 2nd ed. (Columbus, OH: Merrill, 1978).

20. To help you select the right questions to guide your students to not only producing the "right" answers but also developing the skills to learn for themselves, see Patricia E. Blosser, *How to Ask the Right Questions* (Washington, DC: National Science Teachers Association, 1991).

21. L. R. DeTure, "Acquisition of Wait-Time: Training Techniques and Related Teaching Behaviors, Modeling Protocols" (Paper presented at the annual meeting of the National Science Teachers Association, Cincinnati, April 1985).

22. For a one-page summary of the importance of teachers admitting not knowing the answers, see Robert E. Yager, "Wanted: More Questions, Fewer Answers," *Science and Children,* 25, no. 1 (September 1987): 22.

With increased attention being given to . . . thematic science, and cooperative learning, multiple-choice tests no longer seem adequate for measuring student abilities. More often, teachers are using open-ended problems, notebooks, folders, journals, lab reports, and portfolios for student evaluation. These new assessment methods can more thoroughly reveal who students are, both in and out of school.[1]

CHAPTER 5

Assessment

How can you use assessment to guide, enrich, and evaluate teaching and learning?

As the opening statement cautions us, the roles, procedures, and techniques for assessment have gradually changed to correspond to the new directions our science teaching has taken. You now need newer and more relevant techniques for assessing your pupils' progress as they acquire science content and skills in scientific processes or STS problem solving, as well as attitudes and value clarification skills. In addition, you will need to develop self-assessment skills to evaluate your effectiveness in your classroom. This chapter, therefore, will focus on the following assessment topics and on applications to teaching science with a minds-on/hands-on guided discovery approach:

1. Assessment as a tool for planning, guiding, and enriching classroom science learning/teaching.
2. Assessment as communication of the importance of science to students, administrators, school boards, parents, and the public.
3. Assessment techniques for monitoring outcomes of science learning/teaching and program improvement.

4. Assessment as influence on science curriculum and teaching.[2]

/// ASSESSMENT—A CONTINUOUS PROCESS

Assessment does not just happen by chance. It must be well thought out, executed, and redone daily from your first to your last day of school. To do this effectively, you have to go back to your goals in teaching science, which could be organized around these three questions:

1. *What* will I teach? (content, processes, STS problem-solving skills, and values)
2. *How* will I teach it? (physical and intellectual environment, teaching methods, student activities, and science materials and equipment)
3. *How well* have I taught? (What have my students learned? What must be retaught? How will I grade them?)

143

Number 3 in this list constitutes assessing your science teaching, which is similar to teaching a good science lesson; they both require thorough planning, skillful execution, and careful, constant review and modification. To assess your science teaching well, here is a suggested format for you to follow.

1. Develop an assessment plan based on your goals and objectives for teaching science.[3]
2. Stress the skills, knowledge, and processes you will emphasize during your science teaching.
3. Choose appropriate assessment strategies (tests and other techniques).
4. Gather assessment data about your students.
5. Analyze the assessment data.
6. Study the implications of your assessment data analysis for future teaching.[4]

Measurement and Assessment in Science Teaching

Although the terms *measurement* and *evaluation* are similar, they are not synonymous. **Measurement** usually involves collecting information about your students through tests, checklists, and worksheets. Very often, measurement (as the term is used in mathematics) involves a numerical score or other reading.

On the other hand, **assessment** is a broader concept that involves your professional judgments, which are based on a variety of data such as measurement, your feelings and observations, and other information you gather from the learning environment. Assessment is not merely a device you use at the end of a science lesson or unit of study. Instead, you need to use assessment minute by minute throughout all of your teaching. You can accomplish much assessment by judicious and effective informal questioning and sensitive lis-

tening, as discussed in the previous chapter. Continuous assessment will help you quickly spot which science areas your students have been exposed to previously, their prior knowledge, misconceptions, naive theories, and how they construct concepts.

It has been said that measurement is a descriptive activity (usually in numbers), whereas assessment involves judgment.[5]

Types of Assessment

Three major types of assessment approaches will help you carry out your assessment objectives: diagnostic, formative, and summative.

Diagnostic assessment is useful *before* you start teaching material to discover what your students know and don't know about the topic to be explored, their misconceptions, and naive theories. You will use **formative assessment** *during* your teaching to discover what your students are learning and to supply you with feedback to modify your lesson plans and teaching methods, where needed. **Summative assessment** is used *after* you have taught the material to assess how much students have learned and to assign grades. You will need to use all three of these at various times in your science teaching. Table 5–1 summarizes when, why, and how each type of assessment can be used in your teaching.

Vital Role of Diagnostic Assessment in Constructivist Classrooms

Assessment procedures can supply you with much diagnostic data about individual students in your class. Such procedures can help you identify a student's science strengths, weaknesses, and interests. This information will also indicate how well students work alone or in groups, with your direct assistance or on their own, with a variety of sensory devices (film-strips, films, and audiotapes), or by reading. By using informal questioning or a paper and pencil device for assessment *before* you start your teaching, you can determine what specific experiences will best encourage students' science progress. Diagnostic data help you to adjust the learning to your students' individual differences.

Once the learning is under way, it becomes your responsibility to find out how well students are doing with the learning activities you have prescribed as a result of your diagnosis. Your teaching/learning model is very much like the physician's endless loop model.

Research has shown that you can increase science content achievement in your students by giving more diagnostic tests that correspond to your learning objectives. Studies also show that if you follow your diagnostic testing with reteaching and student restudying, you will bring about significant increases in achievement, even among students who have low aptitudes.[6]

Assessment techniques give you insights into how well your students are learning the scientific content and processes you planned for them through diagnostic devices. By skillfully using these achievement data with your students, increased interest and motivation can be provided by

1. making students *active* partners in the teaching/learning act rather than the traditional passive absorbers of information,

2. inviting students to set *realistic goals* and providing information to both you and them concerning their progress toward these goals,

3. showing students that *progress has been made,* no matter how small, to help them attain satisfaction and a desire to continue learning,

4. guiding students to become increasingly *self-directed* as they put into perspective where they were, are, and should be in the future, and

5. showing students that *an adult really cares* about their progress.[7]

There is much evidence that how you interpret assessment results to your students affects their future achievement.[8] The way you relate the results of measurement and assessment to your students affects their self-ratings and estimates of self-perceptions. Show students how well they are doing, and they will strive to do

TABLE 5–1
Types of assessment

	Diagnostic	Formative	Summative
When?	*Before* teaching	*During* teaching	*After* teaching
Why?	Assess student needs. Find out how much students know. Match 1 and 2 with teaching methods.	Provide immediate feedback to guide students to complete tasks. Modify teaching of concepts.	Use primarily for assigning grades. Assess how much students have learned before moving on to next topic.
How?	Three broad categories of evaluation techniques: Paper and pencil tests Student projects and written reports Teacher observations and student performance tasks		

Take advantage of opportunities to notice and praise students' achievements.

well on the next task. Remember that success breeds success; failure breeds more failure.

Using Assessment Data to Communicate to the Public

Assessment can provide you with the raw data you need to report to parents, school administration and boards, and the community at large. Good communication between you and your students' parents helps supply the best possible learning experiences for your students. By having good assessment procedures and solid information on which to make interpretations to your community, you are better able to handle questions and criticisms of your science program intelligently. You will be better equipped to communicate your objectives and achievements in the science program with such infor-

mation. Through adequate science assessment, administrators also will be provided with valid information to make their judgments and recommendations to school boards of education. Administrators need such data to support your efforts. With the millions of dollars and countless hours being spent on science programs, communities deserve to know the effectiveness of the programs they support. The "back-to-basics" movement in some communities means, unfortunately, an across-the-board de-emphasis of science education from kindergarten through high school. Some school systems have cut science programs to transfer additional funds into "politically acceptable" areas of education such as reading and language arts.

Our objectives, assessment techniques, and our communication of them to the public, must be specific, in concrete, unambiguous terms. Keep in mind the words of the late noted sci-

Collecting assessment data helps you communicate with parents and school administrators.

ence writer Isaac Asimov, speaking before the annual convention of the National Science Teachers Association, in Washington, DC, in 1977: "Science must fight to maintain its honor. We must reach out to the public. We must be proselytizers."

/// HOW TO USE ASSESSMENT IN YOUR SCIENCE TEACHING/ LEARNING

The rest of this chapter will provide specific practical suggestions for implementing assessment in your science teaching/learning and specific directions on how to construct and effectively use these devices. As you read these assessment suggestions, please keep these important assessment ideas in mind:

1. Many assessment techniques, instruments, and procedures are necessary to understand and display what each student has learned.

2. Materials and processes of assessment are to be so developed and used that they are integral to, not apart from, the other learning processes in a course.

3. Assessment procedures are most effective when students and teachers work together in their development and implementation. Assessment should provide students and teachers with opportunities to summarize and interpret what they have accomplished. It should not be restricted to securing data for grading.

4. Planning, judging, and revising materials and procedures for assessment is most effectively accomplished when students and teachers work together to improve their quality.

5. Quality of thinking, development of competencies in criticism and assessment, and reflection on and integration of learning will take priority over moving on to new subject areas whenever these alternatives are in contention for class time.[9]

Organizing Assessment Around Taxonomies

Benjamin Bloom organized educational objectives into these three categories or **domains:**

■ **Cognitive domain.** Intellectual skills and knowledge.
■ **Affective domain.** Interest, appreciations, attitudes, and values.
■ **Psychomotor domain.** Motor, manipulative, and physical skills.

Bloom arranged each domain in a hierarchy, so that each item in the domain is ranked by its importance. This type of classification is called a **taxonomy.**[10]

Alan McCormack and Robert Yager, in their taxonomy, added two additional domains to Bloom's three in this statement:

We feel that restricting the scope of science education to content and process alone is the most significant problem facing the science education community today. We believe there are five domains of science education: Knowledge and Understanding, Exploring and Discovering, Imagining and Creating, Feeling and Valuing, and Using and Applying.[11]

(See Chapter 1 and Figure 1–10 for a fuller description of the McCormack/Yager Taxonomy.)

You can use these five domains as a basis for your science teaching/learning assessment. Here are suggestions on how to do this.

/// ASSESSMENT IN THE COGNITIVE DOMAIN

The **cognitive domain** contains the intellectual behaviors associated with scientific processes and products in your science teaching. This area receives major emphasis in science education today, although many educators want to increase activities involving scientific

processes, Piagetian and other constructivist types of concept building, and affective objectives, as indicated in Chapter 2. Since emphasis today is still on scientific knowledge and its applications, it is imperative that you become as proficient as possible in assessment in this domain.

Bloom's cognitive domain, (and what McCormack and Yager call knowledge and understanding) beginning with the simplest, consists of six levels of intellectual objectives:

1. *Knowledge* of facts and principles (direct recall).
2. *Comprehension* (understanding facts and ideas).
3. *Application* (applying facts and ideas to new situations).
4. *Analysis* (breaking concepts down into parts and seeing their relationships).
5. *Synthesis* (putting facts and ideas together).
6. *Evaluation* (judging value of facts and ideas).

Studies have shown that most tests given by teachers require only the lowest form of the cognitive domain: recall of knowledge.[12] These low-level objectives solicit students' knowledge and comprehension of scientific facts, concepts, and principles. Bloom and many other cognitive psychologists believe that learners must know these things before they can progress to higher levels of thinking: application, analysis, synthesis, and evaluation. The following practical assessment techniques will assist you in evaluating your students' mastery of all levels of the cognitive domain.

Assessing for Scientific Products: Knowledge

Over the years, teachers and schools have concentrated (almost exclusively) on the area of knowledge and comprehension in assessing teaching/learning in their science programs. Historically, because of this emphasis, many helpful techniques for assessment of knowledge have been tried; however, many have proved to be too time-consuming for most teachers who, although highly motivated and dedicated, have difficulty fitting such techniques into their already crowded school day. Therefore, most elementary school teachers rely more on written assessment devices. For this reason then, this chapter concentrates on helping you improve your written assessment devices. Other assessment techniques are also presented in this chapter and throughout this book (especially in Chapter 4 on questioning and listening) for your use in your total assessment program.

Using Written Tests to Assess Students' Recall of Knowledge. You can devise simple tests to discover your students' knowledge of terminology and specific facts. First, determine the specific observable behavioral objective and then prepare the test. Two examples follow.

Behavioral Objective: To identify whether students can define technical terms by giving their properties, relations, or attributes.

> *A volt is a unit of:*
> a. *weight.*
> b. *force.*
> c. *distance.*
> d. *work.*
> e. *volume.*

Behavioral Objective: To identify whether students can recall terms, events, discoveries, and reactions.

> *Which of the following types of waves can travel through a vacuum?*
> a. *sound.*
> b. *light.*
> c. *electromagnetic.*
> d. *a and b*
> e. *b and c*

These assessment devices are termed **recall tests.** As the name implies, recall questions ask students to bring back into their consciousness information they explored in the past. Psychologists have found that people associate items with other items and rarely, if ever, completely isolate them. The ways in which we associate isolated items is still a mystery. Even tests of isolation, such as the inkblot designs used in the Rorschach tests, evoke widely divergent responses because of the unique backgrounds, perceptions, and formed associations of individuals. Testing recall with children thus becomes a problem of framing your questions to stimulate the remembrance of situations in which the intended information occurred. One of the best ways to do this is to use pictures, especially if you are working with younger children.

Using Pictures for Assessing Knowledge of Classification. Picture tests can be used for the more complex aspects of knowledge such as classification, methodology, principles, abstractions, generalizations, and theories. Imagine showing a series of slides on a screen and asking questions using a tape recorder. In the latter case, all the students have to do is identify the right diagram.

Researchers found that the science knowledge test showed expectedly strong dependence on reading.[13] However, when the students were given the Pictorial-Aural Inventory of Science, they showed no significant differences in mean scores between good-reading student groups and the poor-reading students. The implication of this research to science is that you must guard against overemphasizing reading-dependent tests. All teachers have students who clearly understand and contribute in class discussion, but flunk a paper-pencil test; the use of more pictorial assessment devices may remedy this. With practice, you will soon develop your skill in preparing these devices and gain better insights into whether you are truly assessing your objectives.

Figure 5–1 is an example of a pictorial test of knowledge of classification. The behavioral objective is to observe whether the student can classify objects on the basis of whether they sink or float in water.

Even though the pictorial test shown in Figure 5–1 has a minimum of words and uses pictures for reinforcement, some children may still find it too difficult. For these children, you can make **wordless** pictorial tests. Either you or your students can get pictures from magazines, or you can take a series of still pictures of some scientific event. As in Figure 5–2, you might take pictures of a melting snowman and verbally ask the children questions as you show them the pictures.

Which aspect of Bloom's cognitive domain does the wordless snowman pictorial riddle evaluate? What observable behavioral objective is being tested? The test is intended to determine the children's knowledge of trends and sequences.

Another Oral Assessment Technique. Another technique for assessing students who have difficulty reading is administering assessment devices **orally** to students.

Test items or questions are read aloud to students who silently follow along and answer orally, in writing, or by drawing pictures. Garry Hardy and his associates call this the "looking-listening" method, and found it did eliminate some of the disadvantages faced by poor-reader test takers.[14] Being able to read is only one of the many factors that teachers must consider that affect assessment measures.

What are other ways of testing your students' knowledge of scientific principles?

Test each object in the water.
Circle the word *floats* if your object floats in water.
Circle the word *sinks* if your object sinks in water.

object		object	
rock	floats / sinks	scallop shell	floats / sinks
button	floats / sinks	bean	floats / sinks
piece of metal	floats / sinks	piece of wood	floats / sinks 17
rubber band	floats / sinks	crayon	floats / sinks
plastic spaghetti	floats / sinks	paper clip	floats / sinks
sugar cube	floats / sinks	bottle cap	floats / sinks 18

FIGURE 5–1

Pictorial test of knowledge of classification

Source: Science Curriculum Improvement Study (SCIS), Material Objects Teacher's Guide (Nashua, NH: Delta Education, Inc., 1988), 73. Reprinted with permission by Delta Education, Inc., Nashua, NH.

Teacher shows pictures and says to children:

What differences do you see in these 3 pictures?
Which do you think will happen first? Second?
 Last?
Why do you think the snowman is changing?

FIGURE 5–2

Wordless pictorial test

Source: Science Curriculum Improvement Study (SCIS), Material Objects Teacher's Guide (Nashua, NH: Delta Education, Inc., 1988), 72. Reprinted with permission by Delta Education, Inc., Nashua, NH.

Using Matching Tests. Matching tests, as used by teachers, usually test only for a low level of objectives: recall. They should be used sparingly, as matching tests also present several problems:

1. Students are asked to put things into pigeonholes that might not be of the same kind of classification as their thinking.
2. The tests do not always indicate the student's ability to perceive deeper meanings or relationships.
3. If an even number of items and matching answers is presented, students will get two incorrect answers for each one answer that is wrong.

To overcome the problem described in item 1, you might have the children in the upper elementary grades make up their own matching tests following a science lesson. For item 3, you should always have more responses (answers) than premises (items to be matched).

Using Multiple-Choice Tests. Multiple-choice tests are one of the most frequently used ways to assess your students' understanding of scientific principles and concepts, and have these real practical advantages for teachers:

■ A wide range of subject matter can be tested in a short time.
■ They are easy to administer and score.
■ They can be used to assess the whole range of levels of learning from knowledge to analysis and evaluation.
■ They provide a lower probability of correct guesses than true-false tests.[15]

However, it is obvious that multiple-choice testing also has disadvantages:

■ It does not usually provide teachers with knowledge about how the student arrives at the answer (their concept constructs).
■ Good test items are difficult and time-consuming to write.
■ Generally, students are not asked to generate information in their own words.
■ Reading, concentration levels, and format may be inappropriate for younger students.
■ It may be difficult or impossible to use in some STS problem-solving situations or process skills areas.[16]

You will probably use multiple-choice testing frequently in your assessment program. To make your multiple-choice tests (your own or textbook or other commercially made ones) assess what you really want, keep these things in mind:

1. They have three parts:
   a. *Stem:* presenting task to your students
   b. *Distractors:* incorrect responses
   c. *Correct response*
2. Be sure your **stem:**
   a. asks a direct question or poses a problem in a simple and clearly worded manner.
   b. avoids use of confusing negatives.
3. Check your **distractors** to
   a. see if you have one correct response.
   b. keep your responses (both distractors and correct response) to four. More responses are unwieldy, and fewer make it almost a true or false test.
   c. avoid the phrases "all of the above" or "none of the above," because these responses may confuse some students.
   d. ensure that the relative length of alternatives does not provide a clue to the correct response.
   e. make all distractors plausible.
4. In your **correct response**

a. distribute the order randomly, so there isn't a discernable pattern, i.e., favoring the first or last answer.
b. make sure there is clearly only one correct response.
c. avoid verbal clues, i.e., absolute words (*never, all*) and repeating words used in the stem.[17]

Here is a sample of a multiple-choice test:

If you wanted to get a top to spin a long time, which of the following would you do? Why? Would you spin it:
a. under water.
b. on a syrup-covered surface.
c. on a thin, oil-covered surface.
d. on sand.

The addition of the *"why"* in this multiple-choice question can help the teacher in assessing how the student is thinking and provide additional information useful for further teaching or reteaching.

Using Crossword Puzzles to Assess Knowledge. Another technique for assessing children's knowledge of specifics and terminology is the **crossword puzzle.** Generally, children in the primary grades have limited reading vocabularies, and primary grade teachers have made simple crossword puzzles using words from primary reading lists. Words to be found in a crossword puzzle may be placed in a list below the puzzle for children who have limited reading vocabularies. Intermediate and upper grade teachers find students respond favorably to science crossword puzzles. In fact, students like to create their own puzzles at the conclusion of a science study. A student teacher wrote the puzzle in Figure 5–3 for her fourth grade class.

All of these illustrations of testing devices are limited to Bloom's simplest level of thinking—knowledge. This level is equated with scientific products. Let us examine now the higher levels of thinking.

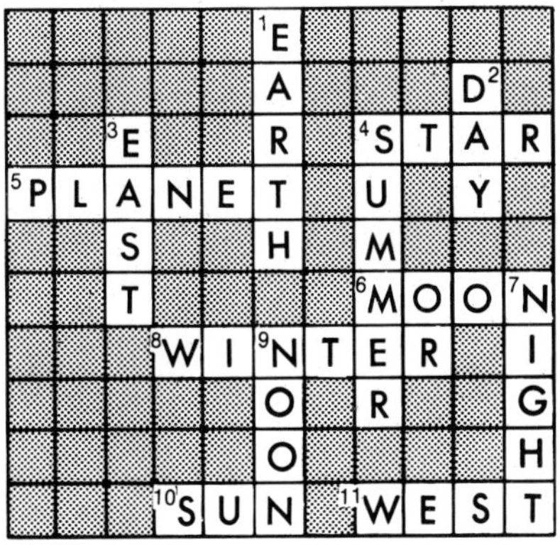

FIGURE 5–3
Crossword puzzle using science terms

DOWN

1. The planet on which we live.
2. When the sun shines.
3. The sun rises in the _____.
4. The hot time of the year.
7. When we see the stars.
9. When the sun is straight over your head.

ACROSS

4. Twinkle, twinkle little _____.
5. The earth is a _____.
6. The man in the _____.
8. The time of the year when it snows.
10. The yellow ball that shines in the daytime.
11. The sun sets in the _____.

Assessing Higher Levels of Thinking

Bloom's next five levels of thinking enter the realm of testing students' understanding of the thinking processes: comprehension, application, analysis, synthesis, and evaluation. The scientific processes we are really trying to assess are the students' abilities to

1. *Translate* major ideas into their own words.
2. *Interpret* the relationships among major ideas.
3. *Extrapolate,* or go beyond, data to implications of major ideas.
4. *Apply* their knowledge and understanding to the solutions of new problems in new situations.
5. *Analyze* or break an idea into its parts and show that they understand their relationship.
6. *Synthesize* or put elements together to form a new pattern and produce a unique communication, plan, or set of abstract relations.
7. *Evaluate* or make judgments based on evidence.

McCormack and Yager have many of these processes that real scientists use for thinking and working in their exploring and discovering domain.

Many possible testing devices are available to assess your students' level of process thinking.

Using Essay Tests to Assess Translation Skills

The use of essay tests in science is a two-headed proposition. Like all testing devices, the essay presents many serious disadvantages along with many positive assessment advantages. This brief summary gives some advantages and disadvantages of the essay test.

1. It shows how well the student is able to organize and present ideas, but scoring is very subjective due to a lack of set answers.
2. It shows varying degrees of correctness, since there is not only a right or wrong answer, but scoring requires excessive time.
3. It tests ability to analyze problems using pertinent information and to arrive at generalizations or conclusions, but scoring is influenced by spelling, handwriting, sentence structure, and other extraneous items.
4. It gets to deeper meanings, reasoning, and interrelationships rather than isolated bits of factual materials, but questions usually are either ambiguous or obvious.

To offset the disadvantages of the essay test, you must carefully consider the construction of each essay question. You should word the question so your pupil will be limited as much as possible to the concepts being tested. For instance, for junior high or middle school level, it is better to use an item like this:

If you moved to Greenland, how would the days and night differ from where you live now? How would the seasons differ?

than an item like this:

Discuss the differences between the places in the world in relation to their days and nights throughout the seasons.

The second question is much too broad and does not give your pupils direction to know what you expect.

With a fourth grade student, you might ask this question for an essay test.

How is your life affected by the shorter daylight hours in winter? How do you think animals in your area are affected?

You will be able to overcome or minimize the shortcomings of excessive subjectivity in scoring essay questions by preparing a scoring guide beforehand and by scoring each question separately. If a list of the important ideas you expect is made before scoring, there is less chance for indecision while scoring.

You should be flexible and open-minded in setting up the important ideas you will accept as answers for an essay. There may be valid student ideas that you have not considered. You should also explain to your students your scoring so they can benefit from the test and use it for a further learning experience. An example of an essay to test your students' ability to translate scientific concepts into their own words, along with an appropriate behavioral objective, might be

Behavioral Objective: To determine whether students are able to state a scientific principle in their own words.

In one paragraph, in your own words, explain how oil helps make it possible for things to move more easily.

Assessing Students' Interpretation Skills

In Bloom's interpretation category, the student discovers relationships among facts, generalizations, definitions, values, and skills. The following are two essay evaluation devices you might use to test this:

Compare how the following different happenings have the same or similar scientific explanations: In the Cartesian

Diver you made, how does the medicine dropper that went up and down as you squeezed the plastic bottle compare to a submarine submerging and surfacing?

Compare the "scientific" explanations of the universe of people who supported the heliocentric point of view as opposed to the geocentric one.

Assessing Students' Extrapolation Skills

Bloom's extrapolation category has the learner going beyond the immediate data to implications of major ideas. Collecting, organizing, and graphing data are only the beginning. We must ask our students what the collected data mean with questions like these:

We have all closely observed squids, their shapes, and their body parts. Based on your observations, what could you guess would be the ways a squid might move through the water?

We read that people tend to migrate from rural areas to urban or city areas; also, minority members tended to locate in slum areas near the central business districts of inner cities. Why do you think this happens?

Assessing Students' Applications Skills

In Bloom's application category, students use previously acquired knowledge and comprehension to solve problems in situations new or uniquely different from those to which they were previously exposed. In essence, we are asking if students understand the elements of a particular idea well enough to apply them in another context. The teacher might use the following kind of evaluation activity to test this:

Now that we have studied about heat and thermal energy for some time, see if you can apply your understandings to these new situations:
a. According to your understanding of energy source and energy sink, why is this common statement inaccurate: Close the door; you're letting in the cold.
b. How would you correct statement **a** to make it accurate?
c. Using the ideas in items **a** and **b**, how would you account for a person getting a bad burn if he or she touches dry ice?

Here is another example of a test item to assess your students' application skills:

If you were in a stalled elevator, which action(s) would be best for you to take until you were rescued? Explain your choice.
a. take deep breaths.
b. sit on the floor.
c. stand quietly.
d. move periodically from corner to corner.

Assessing Analysis Skills

Students are asked to reduce ideas into their component parts in Bloom's category analysis. They are also asked to show they understand the relationship of the component parts. Although this category appears very similar to the previous one on interpretation and application, these differences exist.

1. *Interpretation and application.* Emphasis is on using subject matter to arrive at conclusions.
2. *Analysis.* There is concern for subject matter, but students must also be conscious of the intellectual processes they are using and know the rules for reaching valid conclusions.

Cartoons, graphs, pictures, and other non-verbal forms offer the teacher an opportunity to evaluate the learners' ability to put ideas into their own words and thoughts. An example might be to ask students what the artist's purpose was for drawing the cartoon in Figure 5–4.

Assessing Analysis of Elements

Here you would be assessing to see if your students can break down ideas into their parts and show the relationships. The examples in Figure 5–5 ask your students to separate the elements of observations from inferences. A more advanced or complex example of an inference assessment device requiring good spatial relations ability, probably for ages 10 to 12, is shown in the second drawing.

Assessing Analysis of Relationships

Figure 5–6 can help you assess your students' perceptions of cause and effect relationships. From this sample, you can develop similar ones that fit into your science program. These work very nicely with minimal equipment and encourage "doing" even in testing. See the reference cited in Figure 5–6 for additional suggestions.

FIGURE 5–4

Analysis of a cartoon

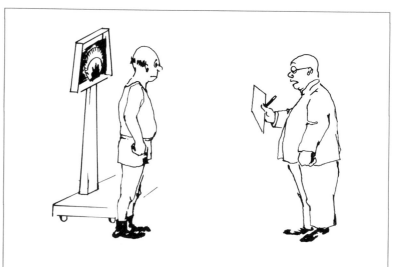

"According to the charts, George, you're going to have to lose some of that extra weight."

The cartoon illustrates that
1. People in the United States tend to be fatter than other people in the world.
2. The doctor doesn't practice what he preaches.
3. The doctor was being funny.
4. This person hasn't been watching weight charts closely enough.

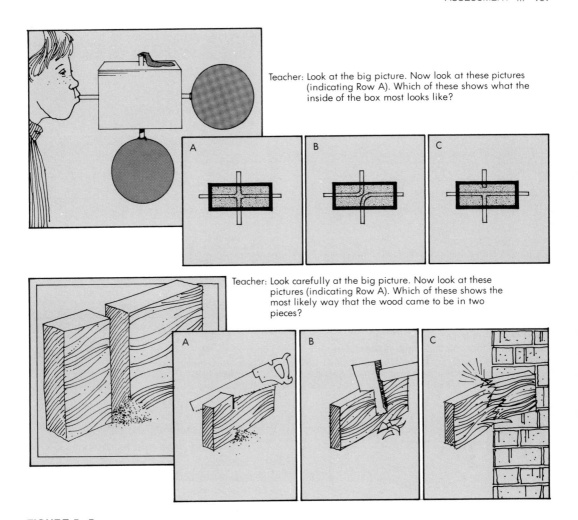

Teacher: Look at the big picture. Now look at these pictures (indicating Row A). Which of these shows what the inside of the box most looks like?

Teacher: Look carefully at the big picture. Now look at these pictures (indicating Row A). Which of these shows the most likely way that the wood came to be in two pieces?

FIGURE 5–5
Analysis of elements assessment device
Source: Loretta L. Molitor, "Why? 'Cause It's 'Sposed To!" Reproduced with permission by *Science and Children*, 13, no. 3 (November/December 1975): 18–19. Copyright 1975 by The National Science Teachers Association, 1742 Connecticut Avenue, N.W., Washington, DC 20009.

Assessing Synthesis Skills

Unlike analysis, which breaks a whole into its parts, **synthesis** asks your students to put parts together, to make patterns that are new to them. Bloom divides these higher creative thinking processes into these three subcategories:

1. Production of a unique communication.
2. Production of a plan or proposed set of operations.
3. Derivation of a set of abstract relations.

Here are some ways to find out your students' perceptions in synthesis using open-ended or

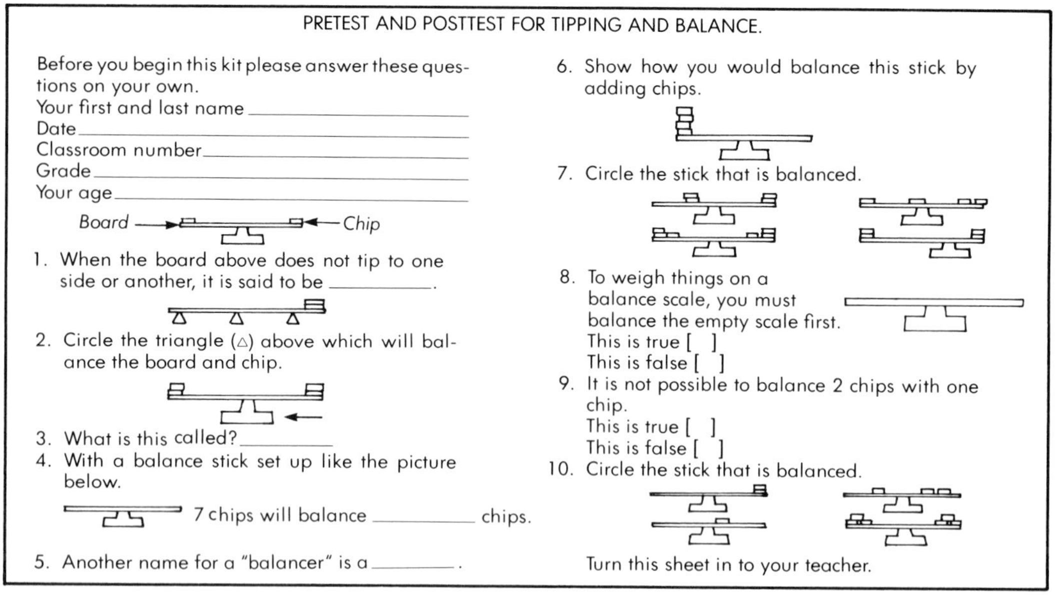

PRETEST AND POSTTEST FOR TIPPING AND BALANCE.

Before you begin this kit please answer these questions on your own.

Your first and last name _____

Date _____

Classroom number _____

Grade _____

Your age _____

Board ———→ ▭ ◁—— Chip

1. When the board above does not tip to one side or another, it is said to be _____.

2. Circle the triangle (△) above which will balance the board and chip.

3. What is this called? _____

4. With a balance stick set up like the picture below.

   7 chips will balance _____ chips.

5. Another name for a "balancer" is a _____ .

6. Show how you would balance this stick by adding chips.

7. Circle the stick that is balanced.

8. To weigh things on a balance scale, you must balance the empty scale first.
   This is true [ ]
   This is false [ ]

9. It is not possible to balance 2 chips with one chip.
   This is true [ ]
   This is false [ ]

10. Circle the stick that is balanced.

Turn this sheet in to your teacher.

FIGURE 5–6

Cause and effect relationships assessment

Source: Joseph Abruscato and Douglas Varney, "Kits for Less Than Fifty Cents." Reproduced with permission by *Science and Children*, 13, no. 1 (September 1975): 13. Copyright 1975 by The National Science Teachers Association, 1742 Connecticut Avenue, N.W., Washington, DC 20009.

divergent questions from situations common to most of your students' lives.

Production of a Unique Communication

The teacher might structure this type of question: "We have just come back from a trip to our city's water purification plant. For homework tonight, write your answers to these questions so we can discuss them tomorrow."

> I agree with the water commissioner that big industries in our town are polluting our waters because . . .
>
> I disagree with the water commissioner that little can be done to correct the pollution because . . .

Older students could address themselves to local situations such as

> High school students should have a say in deciding dress rule regulations because . . .
>
> A request to build an atomic power plant outside the city should not be granted because . . .

Production of a Plan or Proposed Set of Operations

Here we ask students to move beyond "cookbook experiences" where everything is planned out for them. They are asked to devise other ways of investigating by questions such as

> We just finished studying about static electricity and ways of producing and controlling it. Use that information to explain why you get a "shock" every time you slide across the plastic

seatcovers in your parents' car. How would you devise ways to prevent the shock?

Derivation of a Set of Abstract Relations

Learners are encouraged to formulate hypotheses to explain elements of phenomena they analyze. Help them learn how to ask the "right" kinds of questions with exercises such as

We are on a class picnic and field day. As the bus stops at the park, three volunteers go to find us a good picnic spot.
They all come back excited about their finds for the spot.
What questions would you ask them to decide which spot to pick?

Assessing Bloom's Highest Level of Thinking: Evaluation

Bloom's highest order of cognitive domain is the evaluation stage of learning. Your students are asked to blend knowledge, comprehension, analysis, and synthesis to perform two kinds of judgments:

1. Judgments in terms of **internal evidence** (set up their own standards of values)
2. Judgments in terms of **external criteria** (determine how closely ideas and phenomena meet the standards or values above)

You can use these techniques to discover your students' skills at evaluating data on internal and external criteria. But remember that your students must have the prerequisite knowledge before they can answer your evaluation questions. Do not give these kinds of questions until students are ready for them, can understand the questions, and recall the information needed to answer them.

1. *Which of these things do you think should be done if Big Foot is found? Explain your reasons for your choice.*
   a. Put it in a zoo.
   b. Put it in a cage and have a circus travel with it.
   c. Photograph and study it, but do not remove it from its environment.
   d. Kill it, stuff it, and put it into a museum.
2. *Of all the experiments we did on air pressure, which ones do you think were the best ones to show that air is real and exerts pressure? Explain.*

For older students or for gifted or talented students, here is a unique device for assessing their skills in evaluation. After your students have had experiences with measuring, reading graphs and tables, making observations, and preparing reports, ask them to define, carry out, and evaluate science experiments. The following steps can be used as a guide in doing this.

1. Have students select statements (such as those shown in Figure 5–7) that could be tested, and then categorize them according to the kind of test that would be appropriate.
2. After classifying testable questions according to which type of test would be most appropriate, have your students discuss those that could be tested with laboratory experiments.
3. Your whole class can discuss tests they might use to answer one of the questions, and then design an experimental plan.
4. Discuss with students how variables can be used in carrying out their experiments.
5. Carry out the experimental plan.
6. Using group definition of fair testing, have students evaluate each other's experiments.

FINDING TESTABLE STATEMENTS

Below are some familiar ideas. Underline the statements that you think could be tested; circle those that could be tested without causing harm to any living animal. (Some statements may be underlined *and* circled.)

1. You can catch a cold by being chilled.
2. "_____ (brand of paper towels) is the quicker pick-er up-er!"
3. "_____ (name of airlines) is ready when you are."
4. Warm water freezes faster than cold water.
5. You can't teach an old dog new tricks.
6. You catch more flies with honey than with vinegar.
7. Blood is thicker than water.
8. Sitting too close to a television can hurt your eyes.
9. Liver is good for you.
10. The grass is always greener on the other side of the fence.
11. Reading with only dim lighting can hurt your eyes.
12. Crossing your eyes will cause them to stay that way.
13. Birds of a feather flock together.
14. A stitch in time saves nine.
15. Too many cooks spoil the broth.
16. You can't stop progress.
17. A watched pot never boils.
18. A bird in the hand is worth two in the bush.
19. You can catch a bird by putting salt on its tail.
20. There is a calm before a storm.
21. An ounce of prevention is worth a pound of cure.
22. Cracking your knuckles will give you arthritis or make them larger.
23. An apple a day keeps the doctor away.
24. When the cat's away, the mice will play.
25. Rolling stones gather no moss.

FIGURE 5–7

Finding testable statements

Source: Marilyn Fowler Cain, "What Is a Fair Test? Lessons in Problem Solving." Reproduced with permission by *Science and Children,* 24, no. 3 (November/December 1986): 10. Copyright 1986 by The National Science Teachers Association, 1742 Connecticut Avenue, N.W., Washington, DC 20009.

/// ASSESSMENT IN THE AFFECTIVE DOMAIN

Cognitive domain dealt with knowledge and intellectual understandings. Bloom's **affective domain** (McCormack and Yager's feeling and valuing domain) deals with feelings, emotions, interests, attitudes, values, and appreciations. It deals with how your students are affected by their learning and how their feelings affect their learning.

Until recently, science education has done relatively little to include these objectives in its teaching and evaluation. Now more science educators are beginning to see how important it is for students to build positive social value systems while acquiring scientific knowledge and processes. Some techniques are briefly presented here. For greater detail, you are urged to read the following book and use the media pack that accompanies it, especially Chapters 7 and 8, "Questioning for Values and the Affective Domain" and "How to Write Cognitive Domain Questions" in Arthur A. Carin and Robert B. Sund's *Creative Questioning and Sensitive Listening Techniques: A Self-concept Approach,* 2nd ed. (Columbus, OH: Merrill Publishing Co., 1978).

Discovering Your Students' Scientific Attitudes

One of the best ways to evaluate your students' attitudes is to observe them directly as they work and play with other children and not only while you are teaching science.

Checklists can help you organize and record observations of your students' affective domain attitudes and behaviors. Bloom divides the affective domain into five subcategories.

1. **Receiving.** Student's sensitivity to stimuli and phenomena.
2. **Responding.** Student does something about the stimuli.
3. **Valuing.** Student develops criteria of worth for things, phenomena, and behaviors.
4. **Organizing.** Student begins formulation of a value system.
5. **Characterization by a value system.** Student internalizes value system.

These five subcategories of affective domain are described by most nonprofessionals as students' interests, appreciations, attitudes, values, and adjustments.

Leopold Klopfer prepared a grid to show how Bloom's affective domain corresponds to science phenomena. In Figure 5–8, the vertical axis lists phenomena toward which some

affective behavior by your students is sought. The phenomena are grouped into four divisions: events in the natural world, activities, science, and inquiry. The horizontal axis contains Bloom's affective domain subdivisions. By using this grid as a foundation you can develop a checklist to observe and record your students' affective behaviors.

You can develop any observable behavioral objectives that suit the purposes for your checklist.

Assessing Your Students' Feelings

Another way you might assess your students' feelings is with a **forced-choice continuum.** Figure 5–9 shows such a device using the theme, "Science is . . ." Try to make one yourself using themes such as:

Building atomic power plants is . . .
Being a vegetarian is . . .
Scientists should . . .

Make certain you have the two extremes of each idea you use. Older children could be asked to make their own forced-choice continuum, either individually or in small groups, for the other students to respond to.

Assessing Your Students' Values

The following are thought-provoking questions students may tackle either individually or in small groups of their own choosing. The questions are intended to stimulate values-related responses. Therefore, students may want to jot down or explicitly mention what beliefs or values they are protecting or holding. The questions deal with a topic that makes many people anxious and, yet, is so conscientiously avoided—death.

Have you ever seen a dead bird?
How did you feel about it?
What might have caused it to die?

PHENOMENA	A.O. Receiving			B.O. Responding			C.O. Valuing			D.O. Organization		E.O. Characterization: by a value complex	
	Awareness	Willingness to Receive	Controlled or Selected Attention	Acquiescence in Responding	Willingness to Respond	Satisfaction in Response	Acceptance of a Value	Preference for a Value	Commitment	Conceptualization of a Value	Organization of a Value System	Generalized Set	Characterization
	A1	A2	A3	B1	B2	B3	C1	C2	C3	D1	D2	E1	E2
1.0 Events in the natural world 　1.1 Biological events 　1.2 Physical events													
2.0 Activities 　2.1 Informal (generally outside of school) 　　2.11 science activities 　　2.12 science-related activities 　2.2 Formalized science learning activities in school													
3.0 Science 　3.1 Science as a source of knowledge about the natural world 　　3.11 science in general 　　3.12 any content area in science 　3.2 Science as enterprise organized to gain understanding of natural world 　3.3 Science in its interrelationships with society 　3.4 Scientists as people													
4.0 Inquiry 　4.1 Processes of scientific inquiry 　4.2 Scientific inquiry as a way of thought 　4.3 Inquiry as a way of thought 　　4.31 in association with phenomena and problems in science 　　4.32 in association with phenomena and problems not in science													

FIGURE 5–8

The affective domain and science education

Source: Leopold E. Klopfer, "A Structure for the Affective Domain in Relation to Science Education," *Science Education*, 60, (July–September 1976): 299–312. Reprinted by permission of John Wiley & Sons, Inc.

What happens to living things when they die?

What other things have you seen that died?

Many more affective domain techniques and devices are available. Easily administered and scored tests and teaching ideas for the affective domain can be found in these sources:

■ P. E. Blosser, *Attitude Research in Science Education* (Columbus, OH: ERIC/SMEAC, 1984), 1:1–18.

FIGURE 5-9

Forced-choice feelings
continuum

Source: Albert F. Eiss and Mary
Blatt Harbeck, *Behavioral Objectives in the Affective Domain*
(Washington, DC: National Science Teachers Association,
1969), 20. Reprinted with permission.

Directions
Please place a check *anywhere* along the continuum of each of the
two opposing words on a line to show how YOU feel about science.

SCIENCE IS

whee.	.yetch!
theoretical.	practical
inconvenient	convenient
complex.	simple
wide	narrow
easy	troublesome
unnecessary	basic
dull	emotional
efficient	inefficient
universal.	limited
outgoing	ingrown
broadly interpretive.	dogmatic
imaginative.	unimaginative
interesting.	uninteresting
objective	subjective
clear	fuzzy
useful.	harmful
good	bad
exciting	boring

■ D. N. Aspy and F. N. Roebuck, "Affective
Education: Sound Investment," *Educational
Leadership,* 39, no. 7 (1982).
■ Rodney L. Doran and Elizabeth A. Meng,
Evaluation in Elementary Science (Colum-
bus, OH: ERIC/SMEAC, 1989).
■ J. R. Farley, "Raising Student Achievement
Through the Affective Domain," *Educa-
tional Leadership,* 39, no. 7 (1982).

/// ASSESSMENT IN THE PSYCHOMOTOR DOMAIN

The **psychomotor domain** emphasizes muscular or motor skills or manipulation of materials
of the kind used in most "doing" or minds-on/
hands-on science programs. Bloom and his associates did not prepare for the psychomotor do-

main as they did for the cognitive and affective
domains, and McCormack and Yager included
these skills in their exploring and discovering domain. However, Table 5-2 presents a schema
for classifying educational objectives in the psychomotor domain with examples from a study
of plants in an elementary school classroom.

There are many situations in your science
program for assessing your students' manipulative skills. To make your assessment more objective, specific, and most important, observable, you can use an observational checklist
and rating scales of performance. Figure 5-10
is an example of this kind of manipulation skills
assessment device for use when your students
are engaged in using microscopes. You can
readily see that it can be adapted to many
minds-on/hands-on activities.

This structured teacher observational checklist/
rating scale assesses students' skills in using a

TABLE 5–2

Educational objectives in the psychomotor domain

Objectives	Definitions	Science Example
Perception	Sensory cues that guide action for a particular motor activity (seeing, hearing, and so on)	Recognition of different sizes of plants as a prerequisite to nonnumerical or numerical measurement
Set	Preparatory adjustment or readiness for a particular kind of action or experience (mental, physical, emotional set)	Knowledge of bigger-than, smaller-than, inches or millimeters, and so on
Guided response	Overt behavioral act under the guidance of a teacher or in response to self-evaluation (imitation, trial and error)	Imitation of procedures for using meterstick to measure plant growth presented by teacher
Mechanism	Learned response becoming habitual	Ability to measure growth of plants over a period of two weeks by himself or herself
Complex overt response	Individual performing a motor act considered complex with skill, smoothly and efficiently	Measuring and recording daily meterstick readings of plants on graph paper
Adaptation	Altering motor activities to meet the demands of new problematic situations	Adapting the measuring skills to another aspect of plant growth, that is, measuring precisely the amount of water given at set periods

Behavioral Objectives	Always	Sometimes	Never
Is careful in handling microscope.			
Cleans lenses properly.			
Focuses instrument properly.			
Prepares slides correctly.			
Arranges mirror for correct amount of light.			

FIGURE 5–10

Checklist/rating scale for use of microscope

microscope properly. Note the use of specific behavioral objectives, such as "focuses instrument properly," instead of broad, nebulous goals, such as "can use microscope effectively." After identifying the specific *observable* objectives you wish to assess in your students, this can be used as a model for you for any manipulative checklist you wish to make. This is how observable objectives were used with the microscope checklist/rating scale:

1. Handle the instrument with great care.
2. Clean the lenses only with "lens tissue" or with a soft, clean cloth.
3. Never focus the microscope downward toward the slide. Always move the objective downward while the eye is away from the eyepiece and then focus the microscope upward with the eye looking through the microscope.
4. Prepare materials for observation using the techniques most appropriate to the things being examined; comparatively large materials (minute crustacea, for example) require either depression slides or bridge arrangements so that they are not crushed; smaller items can simply be covered with a cover slip.
5. Arrange the mirror for optimum amount of light. Too much light is quite as unsatisfactory as is too little light.

/// ASSESSMENT IN THE IMAGINING/CREATING AND USING/APPLYING DOMAINS

Little has been done in science programs to stimulate and assess students' creative thinking and abilities to use and apply what they learn. McCormack and Yager include these aspects in their imagining and creating domain:

- Putting ideas and objects together in unique ways.
- Using objects in an unusual or novel manner.

- Solving problems.
- Devising and constructing models and devices.
- Producing visuals.

In their using and applying domain, they include efforts to sensitize students to use their classroom-learned scientific concepts, processes, skills and attitudes in everyday life situations.

To assess your students in these domains then, it is necessary to find or develop practical assessment techniques that go beyond paper-and-pencil testing.

Practical Assessment Techniques

Your assessment should match your teaching. If you include minds-on/hands-on activities, your imagining/creating and using/applying domain assessments must allow your students to demonstrate their proficiencies in "laboratory" and science thinking skills. Your emphasis must be on both the *approach* and the *product*—how answers are arrived at in minds-on/hands-on activities and the "correctness" of the answers, performances, and products.

Practical assessment offers teachers opportunities to assess students' practical skills and techniques on minds-on/hands-on tasks, scientific problem solving, and their "feel" for the phenomena they are investigating.[18] Practical assessment usually involves manipulative activities where directions are administered orally to either individuals or in groups. Student responses may be oral or written. These activities are most appropriate for assessing scientific processes and problem-solving skills. The disadvantages of practical tests are (a) need for minds-on/hands-on materials, (b) space to conduct them, (c) preparation and cleanup times, (d) the length of time to take them, (e) they "cover" less science content, and (f) fewer students can be tested in a prescribed time.

Here are some science areas that lend themselves to practical assessment. You will readily see that these areas also are applicable to assessment in the psychomotor domain. Consider assessing your students' minds-on/hands-on skills in these scenarios suggested by Lehman and Marianne Barnes:[19]

■ *Working with basic science equipment,* such as a thermometer, a triple beam balance, a meterstick, a graduated cylinder, and a stopwatch.

■ *Performing laboratory skills and procedures,* such as working with a magnifying glass or microscope, heating or filtering a substance, mixing a solution, or measuring rates.

■ *Observing and classifying three-dimensional objects,* such as shells, rocks, and animals (currently, most assessment tests employ visual observation in two-dimensional settings).

■ *Collecting and recording data in tables, charts, and graphs that students create themselves,* such as graphs that reflect temperature changes over times, heartbeats per minute, or a ratio of the manipulated variable to a responding variable.

■ *Designing experiments and performing investigations from a set of materials and a specific question* (Which paper towel will hold the most water? How can you make the tablet dissolve faster? Which material would keep you warmer?).

■ *Generating a set of investigative questions from a set of materials,* such as a cart, weights, and an inclined plane; a set of paper gliders; or a set of pendulums.

■ *Manipulating objects to demonstrate understanding of concepts and connections among concepts,* for example, understanding electrical circuits, or understanding the relationships between the mass, volume, and density of an object.

■ *Building models,* physical representations that demonstrate natural phenomena, such

as a cell, the solar system, or a geological structure.

■ *Communicating in the process of investigation* during small-group work, individual writing, summarizing and presenting to others, or creating a display.

An example of a practical science processes skills assessment will help you see how you might develop them yourself.

An Example of a Practical Science Process Skills Assessment

Data was collected in the United States and from sixteen other countries during the 1980s from students in grades 5 and 9 on a series of practical hands-on tests. The research was published in 1988 by the International Association for the Evaluation of Educational Achievement (IEA) and is titled "Second International Science Study" (SISS).[20] This material is based upon work supported by the National Science Foundation. Six hands-on tasks were developed to assess students' skills in three broad categories: investigating, performing, and reasoning. Table 5–3 shows the specific skills included in these three categories; notice how they are similar to those in McCormack and Yager's imagining/creating and using/applying domains.

These tests used science content and equipment common to each grade from physics, chemistry, and biology. A person (other than the teacher involved) administered specific oral directions. Equipment and materials were set out in six stations, with a different hands-on situation at each station. Students were asked to manipulate equipment and materials, observe, reason, record data in student test booklets, and interpret data. For each task, questions and pictures of equipment set up as students experience them, are presented in the student test booklets.

Figure 5–11 is a sample of the student test booklet for a hands-on task where students are

TABLE 5–3

SISS process test categories

Skill		Comments
Performing	To include:	observing, measuring, and manipulating.
Investigating (problem solving)	To include:	planning and design of experiments.
Reasoning	To include:	interpreting data, formulating generalizations, and building and revising models.

Source: Willard J. Jacobson and Rodney L. Doran, *Science Achievement in the United States and Sixteen Countries: A Report to the Public* (New York: Second International Science Study—U.S., Columbia University, 1988), 68. Reprinted with permission.

International Science Study

Lab Exercises, Set 5A, page 2

Experiment 1

Before you are two containers.
One contains a blue liquid.
Place the straw in the stopper of the container that has no liquid in it, and blow into the straw for about one minute.

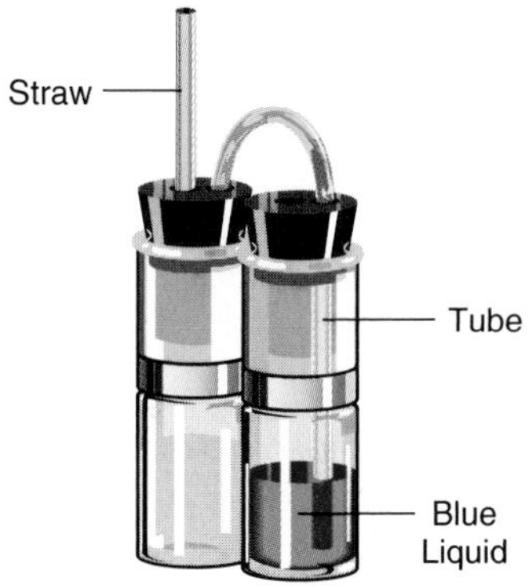

Straw

Tube

Blue Liquid

1. What change has taken place?

_____

_____

_____

2. What is an explanation for this change?

_____

_____

_____

_____

FIGURE 5–11

SISS hands-on process test

Source: "International Science Study, Grade 5A, Booklet 2," page 2 in Willard J. Jacobson and Rodney L. Doran, *Science Achievement in the United States and Sixteen Countries: A Report to the Public* (New York: Second International Science Study—U.S., Columbia University, 1988). Reprinted with permission.

asked to describe and explain color change of bromthymol blue solution after they blow through the straw. Students were given 45 minutes to perform and manipulate equipment, record their observations, and interpret their results in their student test booklets for the first three tasks. After a brief rest, they repeated the procedure for the second half of the hands-on tests. Standardized equipment and a detailed scoring guide were used to assess students.

Survey your science program to see where *you* could use these suggestions and this example of a hands-on test to develop assessment devices to suit your immediate needs. When you do, you will need methods of recording students' responses and resulting products to the situations you set up.

Recording Student Responses to Practical Assessment

Some ways you can record and keep track of student responses during practical assessment are

■ Audio- and videotape recordings of discussions and question-and-answer sessions;
■ teacher conversations;
■ anecdotal record keeping; and
■ teacher-pupil interviews.

Electronic technology today offers teachers "user friendly," almost foolproof devices to assist you in recording students' performances. Either you or students trained in their use can do the actual recording.

Using Audio- and Videotape Recorders

Excellent and easy devices to use in evaluation are audio- and videotape recorders. This is also the simplest means of assessing your students'

accuracy in observations of objects and events. The tape recordings can be used even if you teach in a nursery, preschool, or kindergarten. Cassette audio- and videotape recorders are relatively inexpensive, easy enough for even young children to operate, and are generally durable and can take some abuse. You can tape-record practical science situations and questions; students can then listen to the tape, stop where instructed, and perform the required tasks using materials you supply.

Another practical use of audiotapes is taping questions for tests for children who might have difficulty reading them. This has been found to be of exceptional value also for presenting materials to students who are blind or visually handicapped. If you have such students in your class, tape-record your questions and have the children respond to the questions either by recording their answers on the tape or by working with a classmate.

Occasionally, you may want to audiotape your class discussions so you and your class can evaluate them. Part of the audiotaped class discussion can be your self-evaluation, perhaps consisting of these questions you have about your questioning techniques (as discussed in Chapter 4).

■ What cognitive processes and operations did I try to develop?
■ How much time was involved in teacher talk compared with student talk?
■ If I were to conduct this discussion again, how would I modify my behavior?
■ How many of my questions did I answer?
■ In how many situations did I not give sufficient wait-time after a question?
■ What types of reasoning questions did I use?

Beginning with a short segment of one of your class discussions (about 15 minutes would be sufficient), you might concentrate one time on how you open or structure the lesson. In subsequent recordings, you could focus on student responses or other aspects of the class discussion.

Using Record Keeping in Your Practical Assessment

Another simple way to informally assess your students' accuracy in terms of objects and events is to keep records of their actions. This is in keeping with the emphasis you teach in science: that people should write their observations down, because humans forget things and may not remember when they need the data. Records in your classroom can be notations about events or observations that students put into some form for future use in their science studies, such as:

1. Lists and labels
2. Diagrams
3. Charts and tables
4. Simple memoranda
5. Descriptive/narrative records
6. Tape recordings
7. Symbols and pictures
8. Graphs
9. Sequential records
10. Records of raw data from observations
11. Three-dimensional reports
12. Formal experiment reports

These records can be kept in a portfolio (discussion to follow in this chapter) as evidence of students' assessment in imagining/creating domains. For instance, your students could make simple drawings (pictures and symbols) of the sun on a calendar to indicate that they have accurate observations of the day's weather. What other types of science record keeping can you add to your students' portfolios? For additional ideas on how children's drawings, record keeping, and other writings can reveal students' science knowledge, see Verne N. Rockcastle, "Nothing Succeeds Like Succession," *Science and Children,* 23, no. 7 (April 1986).

Let's investigate how these evidences of students' scientific works can be saved and used in assessment.

Using Portfolios to Assess Students' Scientific Works[21]

A device that is gaining popularity for greater teacher understanding of students' science achievement, knowledge, concept construction, and positive attitude development is the student **portfolio.** Besides being valuable for *teacher* data, portfolios can also be used by *students* to keep abreast of the history of their scientific learning development. But what is a portfolio, how is it organized, and how can it be effectively used in your science assessment?

Portfolios are containers (folders, boxes, crates, or other containers) into which students and teachers place student products or other evidences of their skills in science, such as written assignments, logs, group work, tests, homework, projects, models, drawings, and other creative expressions. The 12 items in the previous record-keeping discussion are examples of the types of work that might become part of a portfolio. You could also place students' work in the portfolio from the practical assessment situations (described previously by Lehman and Marianne Barnes). These samples could be evidences of growth in scientific content knowledge, concept construction, processes, skills, and attitudes.

Portfolio item selections should be *positive* (what students did correctly) rather than *negative* (students' mistakes). Either the teacher (for younger children) or the student can catalog items with an index or table of contents, each item dated, descriptions of assignments, and any other pertinent background.

The purpose of the portfolio usually shapes its design, construction or type of container selected, and items to be included. Students can customize their portfolios. Also, by having students pick the items *they* want to be included, there is strong learner ego involvement, leading to greater self-learning and self-assessment. Teacher benefits from portfolios are insights into students' thinking processes and products, what students value and use in the classroom learning environment, and are an important supplement to paper and pencil assessments and for areas that do not readily lend themselves to easy assessment.

Portfolios offer teachers techniques that are easy to make and use for enriching both teacher and student assessment. For assistance in setting up *your* portfolios, see references in the endnotes and Rexford Brown, "Testing and Thoughtfulness," *Educational Leadership,* 46, no. 7 (April 1989); Arthur Costa, "Re-Assessing Assessment," *Educational Leadership,* 46, no. 7 (April 1989), 2.

/// APPLICATIONS FOR YOUR CLASSROOM

Identify Your Objectives Clearly. Avoid objectives that are vague, nebulous, or too broad.

Whenever Possible, Write Your Objectives in Specific, Observable Terms. Emphasize objectives you can phrase in human behavior. Good objectives are specific, capable of being observed and therefore assessed, and varied.

Determine Content, Methods, Materials, and Type of Assessment for Achieving and Assessing Your Students' Achievement. Table 5–4 shows how to match your teaching strategies (individual, small group, and total class) to your assessment procedures. Students' oral, written, and performance tasks are

the assessment devices used to assess their science knowledge, skills, and attitudes.

Select and Use a Variety of Assessment Devices. Avoid overdependency on any one type of evaluating device. Include a wide range of tests and other assessment devices such as:

1. Essay
2. Short answer
3. Fill-in (AVOID)
4. True-false
5. Multiple-choice
6. Matching (MINIMAL USE)
7. Crossword puzzle
8. Picture tests
9. Situational tests
10. Performance or motor
11. Checklist/rating scale
12. Student self-assessment
13. Student observations
14. Students explain actions
15. Listen to student discussions
16. Others you devise and use

Make Your Tests and Other Assessment Devices Assess What You Taught and Want Learned. Assess only those things to which your students were exposed or can reasonably be expected to project into relatively similar situations.

Assess Often and Have Your Students Participate in the Results. If you assess your students continually, you can help them lessen their anxiety and fear of assessment, especially if the results are used for instruction instead of punishment. You should stress that assessment is merely one step along the path to learning and not the end of the journey.

Your Assessment Should Show What You Value in Science Teaching. Your students will follow your lead. If you stress mem-

TABLE 5–4
Assessment procedures and science teaching

	Evaluation Process		
	Oral	Written	Demonstration
Instructional Strategy: Individual	A student can be called on in class to give a brief summary of basic information discussed in class that day. A student can be asked to critique an experiment conducted by a fellow classmate or critique a published study.	A student can be asked to write a review of a science program shown on television. A student can be asked to write a brief report of research he/she conducted.	A student can take responsibility for studying an experiment and presenting a demonstration of it to the class.
Instructional Strategy: Group	Students can collaborate on presenting a summary of the key concepts studied in a unit. Students can conduct a roundtable discussion of an important topic.	Students can collaborate on producing a bibliography of important books or articles.	Students can share the responsibility for preparing and presenting an experiment or discussion on an interesting topic to the class or school.
Instructional Strategy: Class	A class might conduct an assembly on a topic of interest or concern to the entire school.	A class might keep a log of their science experiments and provide written comments and critiques of each other's work.	A class might dramatize an important event in the history of science.

orization or recall in your assessment, they will memorize. If process, problem solving, and higher cognitive levels of thinking are important to you, make certain your assessment reflects these criteria.

Continually Assess Your Assessment. Scrutinize your assessment often and revise your assessment techniques as a result of your students' responses to them. Invite your students' comments on your assessments and even have them try making up their own. Suggest that they make self-assessments, such as that shown at right.

Mark a B below for what you knew before about the science topics we studied. Mark an A for what you knew after the study.

Science Topics

volcanoes	1	② B	3	④ A	5
floods	① B	2	3	④ A	5
weather	1	2	③ B	4	⑤ A

1 = knew little
5 = knew a lot

Continue Your Own Self-Assessment. Teachers today are professionally committed to improving the learning of all students. You probably believe "children do fail to learn; they can only assimilate what their minds are ready to learn." Therefore, do not blame the students or yourself if not all of them do well on some assessment devices. Use the situation to look more closely at your students. At the same time, look more introspectively at your own teaching to examine the impact of your goals, methods of teaching, and assessment techniques. Such self-assessment will also make you more effective with students who are handicapped or who have culturally diverse backgrounds. Assessment will help you grow as a person and a teacher. It will help you see the individual differences of your students with clearer and more sensitive vision. Because learning to use assessment effectively will help you become a better teacher, it is clearly worth the effort.

SUMMARY

Newer and more relevant assessment techniques are needed for conducting guided discovery, minds-on/hands-on STS problem-solving science programs. In constructivist teaching/learning, assessment is a *continual* process for planning, guiding, and enriching students' science learning; as communication with students, school administrators, parents, and the public; for monitoring outcomes of your science program; and as an influence on science curriculum and teaching.

Assessment then, affects the *what, how,* and *how well* of your science teaching/learning. A suggested format for an effective assessment program was proposed, which included these three kinds of assessment: diagnostic (before starting teaching), formative (during teaching), and summative (after teaching). The purposes and effective uses of each kind of assessment were examined.

Assessment can be organized around Bloom's Taxonomy of Educational Objectives which contains these three domains: cognitive (knowledge and higher levels of thinking), affective (interests, feelings, attitudes, and values), and psychomotor (muscular or manipulative skills). McCormack and Yager's Taxonomy, developed to help students attain the level of scientific literacy needed in an STS society, adds the two additional domains of imagining/creating (producing unusual ideas, designing devices) and using/applying (applications to everyday life).

Individual schools and school districts want to know how good their science programs are. They must have this information to determine which programs to continue, drop, or modify, as well as to help them communicate to the public about financing the schools through taxes.

Teachers use assessment as a continuous and all-encompassing part of their science programs. It is part of diagnosing students' prior knowledge and misconceptions and learning needs, prescribing what learning activities are needed, and determining a learner's progress, so additional learning activities can be planned.

Suggestions are given for techniques for assessing scientific knowledge. Among these are multiple-choice tests, picture tests, matching tests, and crossword puzzles. You can test higher thinking with cartoon tests, pictorial-sequence tests, essays, interpretation tests, story situation analysis tests, application of knowledge tests, and evaluation of evidence tests.

Affective domain objectives are more difficult to assess. Several ways to discover your students' attitudes and interests are the teacher checklist, forced-choice continuum, and situational tests.

The psychomotor objectives have not been as extensively developed as the cognitive and affective domain objectives. They can, however, be evaluated by the teacher observational checklist, rating scales, and performance tests.

To assess students in the imagining/creating and using/applying domains, you need to go beyond paper and pencil tests. Practical assessments (minds-on/hands-on "laboratory-type" devices) involving manipulative activities are most appropriate for assessing scientific processes and problem-solving skills. Suggestions were given for areas that lend themselves to practical assessment. In addition, an example was provided of how practical assessment was used in surveying students' scientific process laboratory skills in 16 countries for the Second International Association for the Evaluation of Educational Achievement (SISS). Specific techniques were provided for recording student responses to practical assessments and include audio- and videotaping, record keeping, and making and maintaining student portfolios.

SELF-ASSESSMENT AND FURTHER STUDY

1. Organize your class for setting up and maintaining student portfolios using suggestions and references in this chapter. To begin you might ask your students to put in their portfolio two samples of their work that they feel show
   - what they are most proud of in their science learning;
   - how they learned something new;
   - where they solved a problem;
   - something they "invented" (unusual or different);
   - evidence of growth in scientific knowledge; or
   - anything *they* feel is important to include.
2. Give some reasons you think teachers generally give more attention to the development and assessment of cognitive parts of science learning.
3. Select several hands-on science activities in which children handle simple science equipment and materials. Construct devices and teacher checklists

to record and rate their psychomotor skills, using the types of devices presented in this chapter and these references: Joyce R. Blueford, "A Guide to Hands-on Science: Follow these guidelines for a custom-made science program," *Science and Children, 26*, no. 4 (January 1989): 20–21., *Learning by Doing: A Manual for Teaching and Assessing Higher Order Skills in Science and Mathematics* (Report #17-HOS-80) (Princeton, NJ: Educational Testing Service, 1987).

4. Record a test especially for children who cannot take a written one (non-readers, preschool and nursery school children, the blind or visually impaired, or non-English-speaking students) on audio- or videotape.

5. Reading level and vocabulary are vital for proper assessment devices. Select several of your assessment devices and analyze (and modify where needed) the reading level and vocabulary for appropriateness for your students. For assistance, see Steven J. Raskow and Thomas C. Gee, "Test Science, Not Reading. Use Simple Words, Clear Concepts," *The Science Teacher, 54*, no. 2 (February 1987): 28–31; and Marvin N. Tolman, et al., "Does Reading Ability Affect Science Test Scores?" *Science and Children, 29*, no. 1 (September 1991): 44–47.

6. Work with a group of students in a science area and devise ways of cooperatively assessing your teaching and their learning. Have your students prepare a variety of assessment techniques (such as the pictorial type), administer and score them, and share the results with their peers. When they have completed this work, assess the assessment with your students.

7. Prepare a practical minds-on/hands-on assessment at the conclusion of a science study. Use the SISS Science Process Laboratory Skills Test in this chapter as a starting base. Write a simply worded problem with a drawing or photo of the actual equipment that students will handle during the test. Arrange equipment and materials on tables. Give succinct directions and have students manipulate equipment and record their observations and analysis on test booklets. Review students' responses with them. For assistance see F. Blumberg, et al., *A Pilot Study of Higher Order Thinking Skills Assessment Techniques in Science and Mathematics—Final Report* (Princeton, NJ: National Assessment of Educational Progress, Educational Testing Service, 1986) and George E. Hein, ed., *The Assessment of Hands-on Elementary Science Programs: Papers from the Lesley College Science Assessment Planning Conference, November 1988* (Grand Forks, ND: North Dakota Study Group, 1989).

NOTES

1. Mary Hamm and Dennis Adams, "Portfolio Assessment. It's Not Just for Artists Anymore," *The Science Teacher, 58*, no. 5 (May 1991): 18. Reprinted by permission of NSTA.

2. Rodger W. Bybee, chair, et al., *Science and Technology Education for the Elementary Years: Frameworks for Curriculum and Instruction* (Andover,

MA: The National Center for Improving Science Education, A Partnership of the NETWORK, Inc. and the Biological Sciences Curriculum Study, Colorado Springs, CO, 1989), 75–78.

3. For specifics on how to match your assessment to your goals read Elizabeth Meng and Rodney L. Doran, "What Research Says . . . About Appropriate Methods of Assessment," *Science and Children,* 28, no. 1 (September 1990): 42–45.

4. Gail Marshall, "Evaluation of Student Progress," in David Holdzkom and Pamela B. Lutz, eds., in *Research Within Reach: A Research-Guided Response to the Concerns of Educators,* (Charleston, WV: Appalachian Educational Laboratory, Inc., 1985), 59–77.

5. For greater details on the differences between measurement and assessment see Robert E. MacDonald, *A Handbook of Basic Skills and Strategies for Beginning Teachers. Facing the Challenge of Teaching in Today's Schools* (New York: Longman, 1991), 190–193.

6. J. Hastings and J. Stewart, "An Analysis of Research Studies in Which 'Homemade' Achievement Instruments Were Utilized," *Journal of Research in Science Teaching* 20, (1983): 697–703.

7. Joan Boykoff Baron, "Evaluating Thinking Skills in the Classroom" in Joan Boykoff Baron and Robert J. Sternberg, eds., *Teaching Skills: Theory and Practice* (New York: W. H. Freeman and Co., 1987).

8. Rodney L. Doran and Elizabeth A. Meng, *Evaluation in Elementary Science* (Columbus, OH: ERIC/SMEAC, 1989).

9. Senta A. Raizen, et al., *Assessment in Elementary School Science Education* (Andover, MA: The National Center for Improving Science Education, a partnership of the NETWORK, Inc. and The Biological Sciences Curriculum Study, Colorado Springs, CO, 1989), 45–74.

10. Benjamin S. Bloom, J. T. Hastings, and G. F. Madus, *A Taxonomy of Educational Objectives: Handbook 1, The Cognitive Domain* (New York: David McKay, 1980).

11. Alan J. McCormack and Robert E. Yager, "A New Taxonomy of Science Education. Teacher's Forum: The Scope of Science," *The Science Teacher,* 56, no. 2 (February 1989): 47. Reprinted by permission of NSTA.

12. Donald W. Dorr-Bremme and Joan L. Herman, *Assessing Student Achievement: A Profile of Classroom Practices* (Los Angeles, CA: University of California, Center for the Study of Evaluation, 1986).

13. M. N. Tolman, et al. "Does Reading Ability Affect Science Test Scores?" *Science and Children,* 29, no. 1 (September 1991): 44–47.

14. Garry R. Hardy, et al., "Does Listening Ability Affect Science Test Scores?" *Science and Children,* 29, no. 2 (October 1991): 43–45.

15. For greater detail on multiple-choice testing see Janice K. Johnson, ". . . Or None of the Above. What Do Your Multiple-Choice Questions Really Measure?" *The Science Teacher,* 56, no. 4 (April 1989): 57–61.

16. For additional suggestions on multiple-choice (and other kinds) testing improvement, read Chapter 10, "Evaluating and Grading Student Performance," in Robert E. MacDonald, *A Handbook of Basic Skills and Strategies for Beginning Teachers. Facing the Challenge of Teaching in Today's Schools* (New York: Longman, 1991), 189–211.

17. See the clearly written, comprehensive coverage of multiple-choice test improvement in Jacqueline Shick, "Textbook Tests. The Right Formula?" *The Science Teacher,* 57, no. 6 (September 1990): 33–39.

18. B. E. Woolnough and T. A. Allsop, *Practical Work in Science* (Cambridge, England: Cambridge University Press, 1985).

19. The author acknowledges the valuable contribution of Lehman W. Barnes and Marianne B. Barnes, "Assessment, Practically Speaking. How can we measure hands-on science skills?" *Science and Children,* 28, no. 6 (March 1991): 14–15.

20. For an excellent summary of the SISS and other international science surveys see Rodney L. Doran, "What Research Says . . . About Assessment," *Science and Children,* 27, no. 8 (May 1990): 26–27.

21. The author is appreciative of the comprehensive description of the purposes, development, and uses of portfolio assessment in science education for and with students in Mary Hamm and Dennis Adams, "Portfolio Assessment. It's Not Just for Artists Anymore," *The Science Teacher,* 58, no. 5 (May 1991): 18–24.

The challenge for the teacher as an environment organizer is to plan carefully, observe the results of the plan, and then evaluate its effectiveness and alter the environment as necessary.[1]

CHAPTER 6

Planning and Classroom Management

How does an effective teacher convert learning goals into workable lesson plans? What must you do to become a successful classroom manager?

Previous chapters charted a logical direction for science teaching/learning in the elementary and middle schools. You learned that science is a dynamic human activity made up of products, processes, STS problem-solving skills, and attitudes that are closely interrelated. Also, you discovered that students are environmental investigators from birth (and even before birth, we are discovering), using all their senses to observe, sample, experience, and construct concepts about everything around them. In addition, you saw how science teaching is concerned with developing scientifically/technologically literate citizens who understand how science, technology, and society influence one another and are able to use this knowledge in their everyday decision making. Therefore, the *why?* and *what?* in your science teaching is concerned with these science attributes, how students develop and learn, how science/technology/society are interrelated, and how scientifically/technologically literate citizens are developed.

You investigated *how* these aspects of science education are effectively achieved by using the Learning Cycle in a guided discovery minds-on/hands-on teaching/learning approach. Taking the opening quotation as a guide, this chapter will focus on helping you put this all into action with suggestions for

- planning the best learning experiences for your students,
- arranging a rich learning classroom environment, and
- managing and guiding student learning.

Then, only *you* can supply the *when?* and *where?* To begin, let's look at the levels of planning needed to start.

/// LEVELS OF PLANNING

To select, prepare, and provide meaningful science learning activities for your students, you must be responsible for planning on a long-range and short-range basis. The eventual achievement by your students of science understandings, processes, skills, and attitudes depends on how well you spell out these long-term, daily, individual lesson expectations. To accomplish this, teacher planning usually takes place on three distinct levels:

1. *Your Aims.* Broad expectations of the science program from school district, school, textbook, or other source.
2. *Your Goals.* Unit or problem solving.
3. *Your Objectives.* Individual lessons or learning activities.

Each of these three levels of planning plays a part in successful student learning.

Let's look now at the roles that aims, goals, and objectives can play in your science teaching. You will see how to understand what they are, where you can find them, and how you can personalize their use for your particular science teaching/learning needs. This will keep you from starting from scratch or reinventing the wheel each time you plan for teaching science.

Aims: High Hopes for Teaching Science

Aims are the highest expectations or general purposes you have for yourself, your students, your school, and your community. They often are broad and philosophical and, tend to ask such broad questions as the following:

> What are the purposes of the public schools and science education?
> What do we want our students to become?
> How should the ways children develop and learn influence what and how we teach in science?

How you answer these broad questions and others like them helps to shape how you view science teaching. They are your **philosophy of science teaching,** or your **aims,** and were discussed in Chapter 1.

The aims of science programs in the elementary and middle schools should correlate with other curricular subject areas and be part of a planned and coordinated K–12 curriculum.

Generally where such a K–12 curriculum exists, a syllabus is provided to teachers for planning purposes. Is one available to you?

Because aims are so broad, some may take more time to achieve than the years you have students in your elementary or middle school. This is evidenced in Chapter 1 by the broad "ten standards" or aims that scientifically/technologically literate students should achieve in exemplary elementary/middle schools by the seventh grade.

You may find aims for your science teaching in publications from national science teacher organizations such as NSTA and AAAS, your state education department, your school or local school board, or a science textbook. They can provide you with a broad, general direction for your science teaching. After that beginning, you will need to make your planning more specifically geared to your philosophy, to the philosophy of the school and community where you teach, and especially to the needs, interests, and abilities of the students you have in your classroom. More specific goals and objectives will help you meet these criteria.

Units or Problem-Solving Goals: Can Your Students Achieve Them This Year?

Two of the criteria for identifying and using goals in your science teaching should be the answer to this question:

> What (a) attainable outcomes do I want my students to accomplish (b) by the end of the year?

In answering this question and contrasting it with the purposes of aims, you see that **goals** have these distinct characteristics:

1. Although goals are somewhat long-range, they have a shorter, definitive time frame or **target date** for being accomplished.
2. Goals are more specific than aims.

3. Students can accomplish the goals within their developmental levels.
4. Goals usually originate with local schools and teachers rather than on the national or state levels.
5. Goals may be stated as either the teacher's expectations or what is expected in the students' behaviors.
6. Because they are more specific, goals can be assessed making local schools and individual teachers more accountable for specific learnings by predetermined target times.

How Can Goals Help Me in My Science Teaching?

Since you probably teach many subjects besides science, you may well ask, "How can I use goals in my teaching?" Every time you select anything for your students to learn, you are setting goals that give direction to your teaching and help you plan to accomplish your goals. Having goals also helps you to assess or measure the extent to which your students have achieved these goals.

Goals help to articulate your science program to your students (so they know what is expected of them), to their parents, and to your colleagues and school administrators. In addition, written goals help a substitute teacher prepare good science lessons should you be absent. When someone visits your science classroom (e.g., a parent or the principal) to observe your science lessons, handing them well-planned goals shows where you are going.

Some teachers send goal statements home to parents when they seek materials or assistance:

One of the goals I have for your children this year is to plan, shop for, cook, serve, and clean up for several meals using what they've learned about good nutrition and consumer education.

Below is a schedule of times when we could use your help and also some items we may need. If you are able to help, could you please support us by signing up? Thank you.

Also, you will often be asked to give a presentation at meet-the-teacher night or open-school night. Good goal statements will enhance your performance and show parents that you have carefully considered the things to which their children will be exposed.

Where Can I Get Ideas for Science Goals?

If you are a beginning teacher, your school science curriculum or textbook teacher's manual will be a good place to start for finding "ready-made" science goals. If you are more experienced, you may write your own science goals for the year and then compare them with goals, expectations, and priorities of people in your community. You could survey your students, parents, and school colleagues and principal to get additional ideas about science education goals.

After doing some of this research, select five or six goals that seem to you to be most desirable. Pick those most applicable to your particular students and what you want for them. Only you will have enough information about your students to define the precise goals that will meet their needs, levels of maturation, interests, and cultural and social environments.

After selecting your goals, try to rank them in the order of importance to you. Now you are ready to organize these broad goals into very specific ways to help your students achieve these goals. Teaching/learning units will help you do this.

Putting Goals into Teachable Units

Because there are so many resources for science teachers, your problem will be to select

Use library resources when planning your science program.

and organize those ideas that fit *your* specific classroom setting, students, aims, goals, and objectives in science. Because your classroom is unique, you will probably have to make some of your own teaching materials because nothing exactly right exists. After you identify the aims and goals for your class (either by a school district, textbook, or commercial science curriculum), the next concern is organizing your thoughts into units of teachable sizes.

Start by Getting or Constructing Science Units

Exciting science learning for your students relates to and originates from your broader science teaching aims and goals. Planning **science units** can help you provide this kind of learning for your classes.

Science units are organized around a general science theme, questions, or central problem. They focus learning activities around large blocks of time and may take from several days to several weeks to complete. From a constructivist point of view, the topic to be studied should interest students and arise from a problem relevant to their lives. Units contain broad goals, as well as a wide range of detailed strategies and activities for students to learn the anticipated scientific content, processes, problem-solving skills, and attitudes.

Actual unit formats vary; however, Figure 6–1 shows an example of a science unit on measuring from a state science curriculum guide. It contains these common elements:

- **Title.** States a focusing question ("Which Is More?")
- **Problem Overview.** Provides the setting or context for the problem (the "Problem Overview").
- **Suggested Schedule.** Lists specific program activities in the recommended sequence for instruction. Time allotments shown are approximate amounts of weekly class time needed to complete activities.
- **Syllabus Emphasis.** Indicates the cross-reference of each activity to the skills/science attitudes/science content sections of the syllabus.
- **Suggested Approach.** Provides an overview of the procedure and activities you might use to conduct the unit.
- **Materials.** Lists materials needed for the entire unit in quantities per student and per class.
- **More Ideas.** Lists other activities that you can use at your discretion to extend the unit, enrich the unit, or reinforce learning outcomes.

Built into each science unit should be continuous **assessment** to help you monitor and modify the suggested unit plans as they unfold. This is vital if your unit plan is to respond to the unique learning pace and styles of you and your students.

PROBLEM OVERVIEW	A child is often confronted with problems that have to do with making comparisons. Determining which distance is longer or shorter, which object is heavier or lighter, or which container is larger or smaller in capacity are only a few of the many instances that occur in presenting the problem. The activities in this unit identify situations in which the student cannot easily resolve	comparisons unless measurements are made. Each situation poses a different kind of measuring problem that will expose the student to objects and events with distinctive properties, provide an opportunity for the student to develop the skill of measuring, and help the student develop scientific attitudes toward investigations.
SUGGESTED APPROACH	This unit is flexible in many aspects. The total amount of time to be devoted to the unit or to individual activities can be adjusted in accordance with the teacher's judgment of student interest and readiness. Comparison activities can be deleted or changed in sequence according to the results of the preliminary brainstorming activity. Some of the activities in the unit may provide students with new experiences to reinforce learning acquired earlier.	Some activities may serve as an introductory experience for more formal instruction at a later time. Care must be taken to keep the emphasis of each activity at the appropriate level for the students at this point in their development. The unit has a strong connection to mathematics, providing many opportunities to develop other specific skills and understandings listed in the mathematics syllabus.

MATERIALS

(per student, unless otherwise indicated)

Paper squares, approximately 5 cm square or 2 ⅛ inches square — 100

Double-pan balance materials: support pans (pie plates), balance arm, etc. (one for two to four students)

Tongue depressors or ice cream sticks

Ruler (cm scale)

String 1–2 meters

Paper tape, 1–2 meters

Thermometer (one per two students)

Medicine cup

Kitchen measuring cup

Paper cups, 8 oz.

Sponges, mops (available for class)

Pails, small (one for two to four students)

Geoboards (four per class)

Small washers (one bag per class)

Colored rubber bands (four sets per class)

Balance board and fulcrum (one for two to four students)

Large washers (one bag per class)

Ice cubes, uniform size

Paper clips (one box per class)

Plasticine (one package per class)

Objects from home such as toys

Containers of various sizes: cereal boxes, plastic cans, tubs, bottles, etc.

Wrapping paper, brown (one roll per class)

Clock (wall type with sweep second hand) — one for class

FIGURE 6–1

Sample unit format on measuring — "Which Is More?"

Source: Supplement to the Science Syllabus, Level 1 (Ages 4 through 7) (Albany, NY:The University of the State of New York, The State Education Department, 1986), 30–31. Reprinted with permission.

SUGGESTED SCHEDULE/SYLLABUS EMPHASIS

#	Activity Title	Week 1	Week 2	Week 3	Week 4	Week 5	Week 6	Emphasis
1	Brainstorming Which is More?	▨						Classifying/Communicating Information
								A-2.24 Contributions, others
								I-C Objects, events, properties
2	Measuring Distance		▨					Measuring/Manipulating Ideas
								A-1.31 Concepts, terms, techniques
								I-C-1.3 Object properties, amount of space
3	Measuring Temperature			▨				Measuring/Manipulating Ideas
								A-2.21 Safety
								I-C-1.5 Object properties, surrounding conditions
4	Measuring Capacity				▨			Measuring/Manipulating Ideas
								A-2.22 Use of resources
								I-C-1.3 Object properties, amount of space
5	Measuring Surface					▨		Measuring, Using Numbers/Manipulating Ideas
								B-1.2 Resourcefulness, innovativeness
								I-C Objects, events, properties
6	Measuring Weight					▨		Manipulating, Measuring/Communicating Information
								B-1.2 resourcefulness, innovativeness
								I-C-1 Object properties, material condition
								I-D-3.1 Uniform balance beam
7	Measuring Time						▨	Manipulating, Measuring/Communicating Information
								A-2.25 Truthful reporting
								I-C-2.2 Event, duration of time

MORE IDEAS

1. Make cutouts of hands, feet, or head profile. Use very small squares to determine the amount of surface.
2. Determine which is the shortest route from home to school.
3. Determine which is colder, warmer, or the same temperature: indoors-outdoors; one person's hand or another's hand; oral temperatures (done by nurse).
4. Determine which is heavier: one sheet of paper or a penny; one sugar cube and a glass of water or the sugar cube dissolved in the glass of water; a slice of bread or the slice of bread toasted; two slices of bread or 1 hard-boiled egg.
5. Determine volume change in popcorn when cooked. (¼ liter uncooked equals what volume cooked? Compare brands.)
6. Determine which takes longer: cold water to freeze or hot water to freeze; a large diameter candle to burn a fixed length or a small diameter candle to burn the same length.
7. Determine equals in a student's own body dimensions: handspan, distance between ears, head size (circumference), arm length (nose to fingertips), foot size, knee height, step or pace, arm span, waist, length of nose, width of smile, etc. It is important for you to take into special consideration possible differences in a student's measurements due to a handicapping condition.

FIGURE 6–1 , *Continued*

After getting samples of such science units or preparing your own, you must break the large blocks of learning activities into manageable pieces for each day's teaching. Daily lesson plans help you to do this.

/// TRANSLATING UNITS INTO DAILY LESSON PLAN OBJECTIVES

After you decide (or it has been decided for you in your syllabus or textbook) on a year's science program and select a unit for a given time block, you must organize your thoughts into teachable lesson plans. To see how lesson planning fits into this scheme, visualize lesson planning in the same way you would plan a vacation, as shown in Table 6–1. See how the short-range vacation planning uses state and local maps to plan daily trips, just as lesson planning is used for specific learning behaviors. In addition, assessment is used in both to plan next-day travel or the next teaching lesson. Daily lesson plans help you select and use specific objectives in your science program.

Suggestions for Customizing Your Minds-on/Hands-on Lesson Plans

This section focuses on how to make and use science lesson plans with an emphasis on ac-

tively (physically and mentally) involving your students in minds-on/hands-on activities. However, this does not mean that every lesson you teach in science must have children handle or manipulate science materials. Your lessons should include all of the teaching methods as mentioned in Chapter 2, such as listening-speaking, reading-writing, and watching-doing.

This text will emphasize activity-based science lesson plans because research shows that students learn science best by doing. **Activity-based science lessons** are referred to by such common names as laboratory, minds-on/hands-on, doing, or guided discovery lessons. **Guided discovery lessons,** as used in this text, designate *active* (physical and/or mental) participation by the learner. Other types of science lessons are presented in later chapters on individualizing science and encouraging creativity and critical thinking.

Putting Aims, Goals, and Objectives into Workable Lessons

Writing guided discovery science lesson plans takes practice. You cannot learn to write science lesson plans by only reading about them any easier than you could learn to play tennis by just watching. You must actually prepare several lessons to develop your creative potential to create your own brand of lesson. You

TABLE 6–1	Time Frame	Lesson Planning	Vacation Planning
Comparison of lesson planning and vacation planning	Long-range	Select aims, goals, and objectives; establish units in large time blocks	Decide on cross-country drive; select states to visit; agree upon time to spend for trip
	Short-range	Make daily lesson plan with specific behaviors; evaluation helps plan next lesson	Use state and local maps to plan daily trip; next day's destination planned from current day

must translate your aims and goals into manageable daily teachable objectives. To do this, you need to describe specific **objectives**—for your students to achieve each day or each lesson—that lead to your selected broad aims and goals.

An analogy between the field of medicine and teaching using aims, goals, and objectives is shown in Table 6–2. You can see from this table that after the broad aim (originated in both areas by *outside* authorities), physicians and teachers use their professional training and sharpened observational skills to diagnose (set goals) and prescribe actions (state objectives). For teachers, the following kinds of objectives are possible:

■ *Instructional or Teaching Objectives.* Stated in terms of *teacher* behavior, these objectives answer the question, "What will the teacher do to help students achieve the kinds of behavior the students should exhibit?"

■ *Behavioral or Performance Objectives.* Stated in terms of what *students* do to achieve the desired behavior, these objectives answer the question, "What will students be able to do after completing the learning activity?" Table 6–3 shows the differences between instructional or teaching objectives and student behavioral or performance objectives.

Sources Are Useful When You Begin Writing Science Lesson Plans

If you do not have a good science background or are unfamiliar with teaching science, you may need help in finding activities and content appropriate to the interests and learning levels and styles of your students. The following sources will help get you started in writing your own science lessons. Lists of these sources are also in the appendices and other chapters of this text.

■ Elementary school science textbooks. Each textbook comes with a teacher's guide suggesting lessons to accompany the student's textbook. If these are handled as suggestions instead of being used verbatim, they can be useful, especially to inexperienced teachers or student teachers. Other helpful sources include the following:

■ State or local science curriculum guides.

TABLE 6–2 Medicine/teaching similarities	Medicine	Teaching
	Aim: Care and cure of patients (Source: Hippocratic Oath)	**Aim:** Develop scientifically/ technologically literate citizens (Source: Project Synthesis)
	Diagnose: Identify single illness or disease (Source: doctor using training, patient symptoms, judgment)	**Goal:** Use information and values to make rational decisions and evaluate the personal consequences (Source: textbook, teacher judgment)
	Prescribe: Specific medicine or other medical protocol (Source: training, pharmaceutical company information, judgment)	**Objective:** Rank and select alternatives on basis of most positive effect for those concerned (Source: teacher-written objective based on teacher judgment)

TABLE 6–3

Differences between teacher and student objectives

TEACHER Instructional/Teaching Objectives	STUDENT Behavioral/Performance Objectives
Teach respect for plants and animals.	Students will handle, care for, and be responsible for plants and animals in the classroom under supervision.
Present concepts of magnetism.	Students, after using a variety of magnets, will state that like poles repel and unlike poles attract.
Instruct how to measure temperature.	After being instructed, students will be able to read temperature differences from hot to cold among a range of substances.

- Published science programs.
- National Science Teachers Association publications.
- Professional science textbooks for teachers.
- Successful science teachers in your school or college classes.

Modify Ready-Made Lessons to Make Them Uniquely Yours

Do not let commercially prepared or other ready-made materials prevent you from designing your own lessons. Remember, if you use something you modified or made, you probably will do a much better job of teaching than if you follow someone else's lessons. *Never* follow any lessons like recipes. Always modify each lesson and adapt it in any way that you think will make it better. By so doing, you will continually increase your understanding of, appreciation for, and commitment to guided discovery learning. For example, an idea like using a candle for an experiment may come from some publication, but the way you design the activity using the candle comes from your own creativity. Keep your creative potential alive, and write or modify all of the science lessons you use.

/// WRITING AND USING GUIDED DISCOVERY SCIENCE LESSONS

Before writing discovery lessons of your own, you may wish to look over published guided discovery lessons. If possible, teach some of them to your students. Do not use them verbatim, but modify them to suit your own creativity and teaching style. They are a valuable resource to use in constructing a science curriculum or for enriching a program. I know from working with thousands of teachers over the years that they can quickly learn to teach by discovery by microteaching (teaching short, mini-lessons about 10 minutes in length) several kinds of lessons. Once you know how to use and give guided discovery lessons of this type, it is relatively easy to construct similar lessons of your own.

A Sample Guided Discovery Science Lesson

Figure 6–2 shows a sample guided discovery science lesson. Notice that certain activities are mainly for teachers and others are essentially the concrete minds-on/hands-on sections for students. Review Figure 6–2 carefully; study

How Does the Length of the Vibrating Body Affect Sound? (3–6)

What Concepts Might Students Discover or Construct?

Bodies in vibration make a sound.
The longer the vibrating body, the lower the tone.

What Will I Need?

Balsa wood strip 12 inches long
10 straight pins
Piece of wood approximately
 6 × 6 inches × 1 inch

3 tacks or nails
Rubber band
Hammer

What Will We Discuss?

What do you think would happen if you vibrated pins set to different depths in a strip of balsa wood?
Would you get the same sound from each of the pins?
If you think that different pins will give off different tones, which one would give off the highest tone?

What Will Children Do?

PROCESSES

Part I

1. Obtain a balsa strip and set pins in it to varying depths. (See the diagram below.)

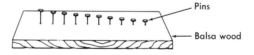

Observing
Inferring
Hypothesizing

2. Determine if each vibrating pin gives off the same tone.
What relationship is there between pin length and tone?
Would nails stuck in balsa wood give the same results as pins?

FIGURE 6–2
Sample guided discovery science activity

the format and the nature of the questions to gain a good understanding of how to make your own guided discovery science lessons.

How to Write Your Own Guided Discovery Lessons

The following list gives you steps for creating your own guided discovery science lessons. In

following these procedures, you will not only be able to make better lessons but will also be able to modify and improve almost any science activities. In writing your own lessons, be sure to refer to the chapter on questioning, particularly those questions stressing a divergent nature.

1. Decide what scientific/technological concepts or principles you want to teach and

Part II

Hypothesizing

1. Look at the diagram below.
   Where would you pluck the rubber band to get the highest note?

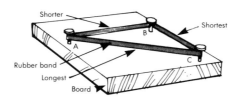

Hypothesizing

Where would you pluck the rubber band to get the lowest note?

2. Obtain three tacks or nails, a rubber band, and a piece of wood. Pound the tacks or nails into the wood block as shown in the diagram. Place the rubber band around the tacks or nails.

3. Pluck the rubber band to see if your hypothesis was correct.

Comparing

4. *How do the results of Part I compare with the results of Part II?*

How Will Children Use or Apply What They Discover?

1. *What would happen if you plucked rubber bands having the same length but different thicknesses?*

2. *What would happen to a tone if the vibrating length of the rubber band were kept the same, but different amounts of tension were applied?*

3. *How does sound travel from the rubber band to your ears?*

Where Do I Find It?

1. Melvin Berger, *The Science of Music* (NY: Crowell, 1989).

2. Etta Kaner, *Sound Science* (Menlo Park, CA: Addison-Wesley, 1989).

state the problem in the form of a question.

2. In determining an appropriate grade level, indicate a range of grades for each lesson.

3. List the specific scientific/technological content concepts and principles that are related to the problem and that you want your students to discover.

4. Leave space for a list of materials but do not fill in this section until you have completed writing the activity section.

5. Write questions (especially divergent) that will set the stage of the lesson.

6. Consult science source books, science curriculums, or elementary science texts, or look around you for ideas to use. This part of the lesson is given to the students in writing if they are able to read or orally if they cannot.

a. Design the activities so the students will be involved in minds-on/hands-on activities and science processes.

b. After roughly outlining the activity, write the first step of the activity sheet in which you tell the students to collect the materials they will need.

c. Ask how they would use the equipment to find an answer to the problem.

d. Write a question asking what they think will happen if a certain proce-

Students may be guided in their discoveries by data collection recorded on minds-on/hands-on lab sheets or in personal journals.

dure of investigation is used (hypothesize).

e. Tell the students to perform the procedure and observe what happens to test their hypotheses.

f. Ask the students to record what they observe. Strive to have them use mathematics in measuring and graphing where possible.

g. Ask them to interpret or make inferences about the data they collected.

7. Reread your statements and compare them with these thinking processes: comparing, summarizing, criticizing, assuming, imagining, making decisions (evaluation of what to do), and applying. (See Chapter 2.) List one of these appropriate processes in the left margin by each of the questions you have asked. Compare your lesson with the list of processes and determine how it can be modified to include more processes. Comparing your lesson questions with the critical thinking science processes described in Chapter 4 further assists you in evaluating how sophisticated your lesson is and what it requires students to do cognitively. (Review the Piagetian and constructivist operations described in Chapter 2.)

8. Ask divergent, open-ended questions to determine how students can use and apply what they discovered.

9. Finish listing the materials you will need for the lesson.

10. Include any source content you need to know.

How To Write Open-Ended Questions in Your Science Lesson Plans

Experimental Factors or Variables. In any experimental situation, **variables,** or factors, are being tested. The question, "What effect does water have on the sprouting of seeds?" is asking: What does the variable—water—have to do with the sprouting of seeds?

Look at the problem of sprouting seeds again and think of three open-ended questions that suggest further investigation. You should have little difficulty in doing this. All you have to do is to ask yourself what might influence the sprouting of seeds. You may think of factors such as light, temperature, pH (acidity), and seed population (the number of seeds present). The following list shows some examples of factors or variables that may be involved in experimental conditions. You probably will think of many others. Use this list or prepare one yourself to guide you in writing open-ended questions:

■ Temperature.
■ Light.
■ Sound.

■ Water or humidity.
■ Food or presence of minerals.
■ pH—alkalinity or acidity.
■ Air or other gases or lack of them (space flight conditioning).
■ Pressure.
■ Type of motion.
■ Fields—gravitational, magnetic, electrical.
■ Friction.
■ Force.
■ Population density.

Qualitative Questions. Several of the factors or variables listed here may vary in **qualitative** ways. For example, a student may have done an activity to find out whether light is needed for photosynthesis in leaves. The student does not know, however, whether all wave lengths of light are necessary. The teacher may then ask the following qualitative questions about light in the open-ended questions section of the lesson:

> *What colors of light do you think are necessary for photosynthesis to take place?*
> *How will different colors of light speed up or slow down photosynthesis?*

The students may then cover plants with different colored cellophane to find answers to these questions.

Quantitative Metrical Questions. All of the factors in this list may also involve **quantitative** questions. For example, "How much light is necessary for photosynthesis to take place?" "How do different intensities of light affect photosynthesis?"

Look at the list of factors again and design qualitative and quantitative questions for the various factors that affect the sprouting of seeds. If you can accomplish this task, you will have little difficulty writing open-ended questions to accompany your own activity exercises.

/// LESS STRUCTURED GUIDED DISCOVERY ACTIVITIES

Less structured discovery science activities offer a higher degree of exploratory lessons where students are encouraged to find out through their own ingenuity as much as possible about some phenomenon. The teacher may provide the problem and materials and then allow time and freedom for the students to "mess about." For example, the teacher may give students many different things that roll on inclined planes or ask them to observe as many things as possible. The teacher may also provide metric sticks, hand lenses, flashlights, lemon juice, forceps, and jars to serve as aquaria for the students to use in studying organisms. After allowing the students to investigate for some time, the teacher will collect the animals or equipment and discuss what was discovered. This activity may be followed by more structured assignments, such as writing and reading about their discoveries or doing experiments related to them.

Less structured, minds-on/hands-on guided discovery experiences with physical objects are particularly important for students because these activities allow them to develop physical and logical knowledge such as the realization that things can be classified, conserved, and ordered in different ways. Less structured lessons then have relevance for *all* grades. The sophistication of student involvement depends largely on experience, cognitive development, and the motivations of the children. An example of a less structured guided discovery lesson is shown in Figure 6–3.

Helping Your Students Develop Greater Autonomy in Their Learning

The purpose of less structured discovery activities is not merely to teach science concepts. More importantly, such activities provide experiences where students can work alone or in

What Do Feathers Do? (K–4)

Materials

Bring several different feathers into class. Give them to the students; also provide trays of water.

Opening Questions

What can you find out about these feathers?
What can you do with feathers?

Allow a lot of time for the children to "mess around" with the feathers. Later ask questions such as

What did you find out about your feathers?
What did you do with them?
What do they do?
How do they do it?
How do they vary in shape?
In what other ways are they different?
Which feathers would be the best to have for flying? Why?
Which would be the best to keep a bird warm? Why?
Which would act as a raincoat?
How could we make a wing from feathers?

Some Possible Activities

You might suggest, if the students don't think of it themselves, what would happen if they poured water over wing feathers. Do the same with the down feathers and note what happens.

You might also bring to class a down-filled parka or gloves and let the children place their hands inside to feel how warm they become. Invite the children to drop various types of feathers and note how they float and how lightweight they are. Discuss how birds need strong wings but how they must be lightweight so they don't have to work so hard in flying. Set up a place in your room where children can pin feathers they collect. Talk about how Indians (Native Americans) used feathers. Talk about how the children's grandparents or great-grandparents used feathers.

FIGURE 6–3
Less structured guided discovery activity

Less structured activities encourage ingenuity and promote careful observation.

groups to gain physical, social, and logical-mathematical knowledge. They are designed to allow students a great deal of **autonomy** so they may become more self-directed and creative persons. Piaget and other constructivists believed that students construct knowledge only through their *own* physical and mental actions on objects. The purpose of less structured discovery activities is not necessarily to advance students from one cognitive level to another. However, the activities undoubtedly will contribute to this to some extent. Their main objective, however, is to have students, on their individual cognitive levels, learn to generate questions and solve problems relative to objects without the teacher imposing objectives and directions. If teachers always tell students what to do, the students never learn to be responsible for their own learning, nor do they develop well their own creativity and social competence.

Less structured activities often focus the learner on performing various types of actions on objects: pushing, sliding, rolling, floating, swinging, dropping, attaching-gluing-clipping, listening to sounds, mashing, or stirring. The role of the teacher is to present the materials to the learner and ask divergent questions, for example, "What can you do or make with these objects?" and then allow a lot of time for the learner to investigate. Teachers should withdraw and interject with questions only when they see the children are losing interest. When they do ask a question, they might have the students focus on some action. For example, "What do you think would happen if you were to (state some action here) mash it, place it in water, and so on?"

Look over the lesson illustrated in Figure 6–3 once more and create some activities of your own. All you need to do is collect some objects—for example, clothespins, cloth, juice cans, toothpicks, rubber bands—and think of different actions your students might perform using these things. You might use the following criteria for selecting and using less structured guided discovery activities:

1. The child must be able to produce the movement by his or her own action.
2. The child must be able to vary the action.
3. The reaction of the object must be observable.
4. The reaction of the object must be immediate.

Some movements of objects fascinate children and others do not. The reason this difference occurs can be at least partially explained in how well the movements meet the criteria just listed. Although these criteria may appear at first to apply only to preschool children, the criteria nonetheless appear to have relevance for other levels as well. For example, witness the acceptance of Pac-Man, Asteroids, Space Wars, and other video games that can be played on television sets—games that older children and adults also enjoy playing. How well do they meet the previous criteria? If physical knowledge activities should relate not to observation of objects in their static state, but involve active transformation, do electronic games allow for this? For a fuller explanation of electronic and/or computer-assisted instruction, see Chapter 10.

/// HOW CAN YOU START TEACHING YOUR SCIENCE LESSON PLANS?

Successful elementary and middle school teachers do a great deal of **planning** and are better **classroom managers.**[2] To summarize how your planning can help you join the ranks of good science teachers, you should

- decide on your broad goals for the whole year,
- find out what your students know and how they learn,
- decide on a science program suitable for your specific class, and
- write your unit and lesson plans down on paper.

Now you are ready to put your plans into action by becoming the best classroom manager you can.

How Do You Become a Successful Classroom Manager?

To put your planning into effect, you must be a good classroom manager. This means you

must become as proficient as possible in ordering science materials, setting realistic schedules for learning activities, organizing (with your students) the physical arrangements of your classroom, providing adequate student interaction, and handling and controlling the total learning environment. The latter point includes an element sometimes called **discipline.** Here are some suggestions for these classroom management concerns.

Survey and Order Science Teaching Materials

Carefully examine the science materials in your school, including supplies, equipment, "hands-on" materials, films, and reading matter such as textbooks, encyclopedias, magazines, tradebooks, and other "research" publications. Evaluate what's on hand and decide what new materials to order, based on your total year's goals and your unit plans. Wherever possible try to use common everyday materials such as drinking straws, buttons, or paper cups. You can add more "exotic" ones later. You will find the following appendices in the back of this textbook very helpful in ordering science teaching materials:

A—National elementary science curriculum projects.

B—Supplies, equipment, and materials obtainable from community sources.

C—Free and inexpensive materials for use in elementary science classroom.

D—Sources of commercial scientific equipment, supplies, models, living things, kits, and collections.

E—Noncommercial sources and containers for living organisms.

F—Food requirements for animals.

H—Professional science books and periodicals for teachers.

I—Professional science societies.

In addition, obtain catalogs from your district office or through advertisements in science journals, such as *Science and Children* and *The Science Teacher.* Become familiar with your school's purchasing processes and start collecting science materials *now.* See the section later in this chapter about how to store them once they arrive.

Plan Specific Times for Science Learning in Your Weekly Schedule

John Goodlad said, "The amount of time spent on a given subject is a powerful factor in learning."[3] It is recommended that the *minimum* time as noted in Table 6–4 be scheduled for science instruction.[4]

Instead of trying to integrate STS-oriented science into the traditional 25- to 40-minute daily segments, you will find the following advantages for scheduling two or three 60- to 90-minute time slots weekly:

1. It usually takes 5 minutes or more to organize, get supplies and materials, and distribute them to start your students on the science activity.
2. The same time is spent at the end of the lesson for clean-up, returning supplies, and concluding the activity.
3. Because preparation time and clean-up remain constant, cutting to two or three 60- to 90-minute lessons saves you a great deal of time.
4. You have fewer preparations.
5. You have more flexibility needed for different levels and interests of your students so that some students can manipulate materials while others read, think, or interact with you and other students.

/// ORGANIZE YOUR CLASSROOM ENVIRONMENT FOR MAXIMUM SCIENCE LEARNING

Your self-contained elementary classroom must encompass the entire elementary curriculum of math, social studies, reading and language arts, music, art, and other fields. Therefore, the physical arrangement of facilities, equipment, supplies, and other teaching materials must be flexible, and, in most cases, serve more than one purpose or subject area. Guided discovery science teaching necessitates that the following science areas be established in your self-contained classroom:

1. Activity area.
2. Temporary or portable science areas.
3. Material storage areas.
4. Equipment storage areas.
5. Student work storage.
6. Small item storage (e.g., shoe boxes).
7. Space and suitable containers for living things.
8. Discovery learning centers.
9. Research and reading materials center.
10. Total class teaching area—teacher directed learning.
11. Audiovisual equipment area.

Figure 6–4 shows how these science areas might be arranged in a self-contained classroom for primary or lower elementary grades. Teachers of more mature students in upper elementary or middle school (or in schools that departmentalize organization for science) can modify this classroom setup. You will find an invaluable source for this purpose in Jo-

TABLE 6–4 Weekly schedule for classroom science instruction	Grades	% Weekly Teaching Schedule	Actual Teaching Schedule (in Hours)
	K–2	5	1.5
	3–4	5–10	1.5–3
	5–6	10	3

hanna Kasin Lemlech, *Classroom Management* (New York: Harper & Row, 1979).

Figure 6–4 also shows some of the benefits of organizing classroom space in this way. Note the following areas:

- Provision for total class or large-group teacher-directed learning.
- Skills reinforcement areas.
- Student choice areas (e.g., art, library, and individual activities).
- Subject matter centers (science, social studies, math, etc.).
- "Special" areas (e.g., listening and writing areas).
- Way the classroom appeals to students' interests.
- Flexible areas that can change as needs change.
- Way each area serves learning needs.

The following sections discuss some of the specific areas shown in Figure 6–4.

Science Activity Area

Your elementary school classroom probably contains movable furniture. In Figure 6–4, the center of the room houses the movable desks, tables, and chairs. The wall space areas provide storage areas for more stationary science equipment and facilities. Science facilities should be grouped as much as possible in one general area of your room. The science equipment, supplies, and other materials you need should be readily available for making, assembling, experimenting, and demonstrating.

For active pupil participation in the guided discovery minds-on/hands-on science program, you must supply adequate space for all students

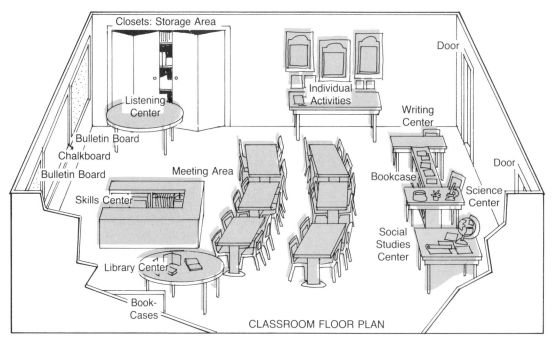

FIGURE 6–4

Primary grades self-contained classroom stressing active involvement of children

Source: Based on ideas from Johanna Kasin Lemlech, *Classroom Management* (New York: Harper & Row, 1979).

to work. Even if your classroom is small and crowded, the experiments, demonstrations, construction, and other active parts of your science program can still be performed. For instance, the space next to and beneath window sills and countertops can be used for work areas.

If your classroom has flat-top desks, you can move them together to make larger work areas. You will find it helpful to get at least one large table in your classroom for doing minds-on/hands-on activities. Try to get tables that are water- and acid-resistant. Otherwise, use fiberboard or laminated plastic to cover your desks and tables. If burners will be used, the best tops are stone or composition stone. If you do not have permanent science work areas, you can cover desks and tables with (or use pads of) tempered fiberboard.

When you plan your work areas, you should also plan for storage of certain equipment and materials:

1. Science supplies.
2. Science apparatus and equipment.
3. Consumable science items.
4. Chemicals.
5. Charts.
6. Models.
7. Audiovisual equipment and supplies.
8. Handtools.
9. Living things (plants and animals).
10. Unfinished student work.

Sources of science cabinets, shelving, and other laboratory storage furniture are listed in Appendix D.

Activity Area Storage

Your classroom has unused space that you can use for storage. Consider using the spaces beneath window ledges, countertops, sinks, above and around heating units (radiators), and even under student desks.

You can purchase excellent commercially made cabinets that fit any of these spaces, or

your students or your custodian and you can construct them. With some creativity, you and your students can arrange these cabinets in a variety of ways.

Small Items Storage. With a guided discovery activities science program, you will constantly need to store many small items. Small boxes provide space for collecting, organizing, and storing small, readily available materials for particular science areas. Appendix L illustrates how to construct and store shoe boxes for small science items.

Living Things Storage

Encourage your students to bring small animals (including insects) and plants into your classroom. To be well prepared, have these kinds of containers always available.

■ Insect cages.
■ Small animal cages.
■ Aquariums.
■ Terrariums.

See Appendix L for constructing and using these houses for living things.

Suggestions for caring for plants and animals and for setting up different kinds of terrariums can be obtained from Biological Supply House, Inc., 8200 South Hoyne Avenue, Chicago, IL 60620. Free by writing on school stationery for Turtox Service Leaflets, especially No. 10 — *The School Terrarium* and No. 25 — *Feeding Aquarium and Terrarium Animals.* NSTA Publications, 1742 Connecticut Avenue, N.W., Washington, DC 20009. Send $1.50 for How-to-Do-It Pamphlets, especially: *How to Care for Living Things in the Classroom,* by Grace K. Pratt (Stock No. PB 38/4).

Food and other requirements for a variety of water and land animals are presented in Appendix F.

Keeping Animals in Classroom for 24 Hours. Occasionally students bring animals into your classroom for an overnight stay. Here are some directions to help the students adopt a humane attitude toward the living things they are observing. Although it is recommended that animals be studied and not removed from their natural habitat, students' curiosity occasionally motivates them to remove them. John J. Dommers of the Humane Society of the United States recommends we adopt the "24-Hour Rule" to serve the best interests of the animals and children: Small animals, such as insects, turtles, frogs, and salamanders, may be kept for a period not exceeding 24 hours, if the habitat in which they were found is simulated as closely as possible in captivity. Students should observe the animals but not handle them. They should research information about identification, characteristics, feeding habits, and values. The animals should then be released unharmed in the same area they were found so they can carry on their environmental activities.

Discovery Science Learning Centers

In classrooms where students are actively engaged in hands-on activities, learning centers are essential. Learning centers are created and directed by the teacher. They motivate, support, guide, and reinforce students' learning. By having learning centers, you will have broader opportunities to meet individual needs, provide children with self-directed learning, as well as encourage their responsibility. There should be learning centers for all content areas.

Set aside at least one area of your classroom as a discovery science learning center. This center should contain collections, direction or activity sheets, activities, and materials that meet these criteria:

1. Present new science materials.
2. Reinforce previously learned science materials.
3. Develop a scientific skill.
4. Drill on specific science information.

5. Develop other science interests and creativity.
6. Make efficient use of limited class time.
7. Encourage students to work independently.[5]

Donald Orlich and his associates add these attributes of science learning centers: "Science learning centers allow teachers to design supplemental science curricula which closely match the developmental levels of their students. Tasks at the center can range from hands-on activities to written and research assignments."[6] Learning centers are places where one or more students may work apart from your regular, ongoing science activities. Students are relatively free to explore, discover, experiment, or just plain tinker.

Figure 6–5 offers a view of a typical elementary or middle school classroom using learning centers. The different learning centers are separated by dividers such as movable screens, workbenches, display or bulletin board space, bookcases, planters, tables, or shelves. There should be enough tables, chairs, and appropriate, easily obtainable materials for all of your students. See Appendix G for directions on how to construct a learning center.

Types of Science Learning Centers

There are many types of science learning centers, including (a) directed discovery science learning, (b) science processes, and (c) open learning centers.

The **directed discovery learning center** focuses on specific science concepts. For this type of center, place materials in shoe boxes with a series of guiding discovery questions, such as, "Using the materials in this box, how would you show that light appears to travel in a straight line?" Directed learning centers may be set up with one theme or separate problems.

Another kind of learning center focuses on developing **science processes,** such as ob-

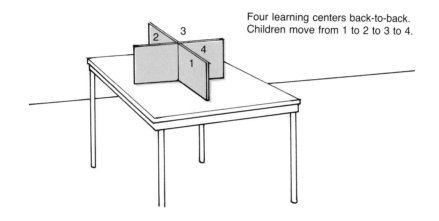

Four learning centers back-to-back.
Children move from 1 to 2 to 3 to 4.

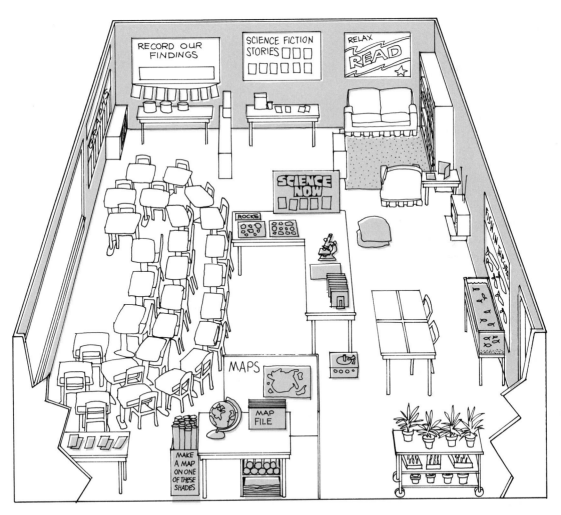

FIGURE 6–5
Integrated self-contained classroom with a variety of learning centers for
25 to 35 children

serving, predicting, and measuring. Using collections of materials and discovery guidance questions, you could ask your students to measure the items in a box in both metric and standard measurements.

The last and most creative type of center is an **open learning center.** You supply many random materials, not according to any one theme or science area. Use minimum direction for your class. For example, use the direction, "Invent something with the materials in this box."

All three types of learning centers should be based on the following format for planning a learning center.

Format for Planning Your Learning Centers

State Purpose. The purpose of a learning center should be clear, both to the teacher and student and stated as a part of the center (e.g., "At this center you will examine some seeds. You will compare sizes, weights, volumes, and shapes of the seeds.").

Consider Student Maturation Levels. The center must be appropriate for the students who will be using it. The backgrounds and experiences, the cognitive level of operation, the socioeconomic level, the maturity level and level of independence, and the psychomotor level must be defined and used as the basis for planning the activities and expected learning outcomes from the center.

Define Scientific Concepts and Skills to Be Developed. A clear statement of the scientific concepts and skills to be developed by the students using the center is necessary if the center is to be a true teaching/learning situation. If these criteria are not met, centers break down into "busy work."

Outline the Expected Learning Outcomes. These statements can be in the form of perfor-

mance or behavioral objectives. Here, a concise statement of what the student is expected to learn as a result of using the center can also serve as a guideline for assessing student success.

Select Appropriate Activities and Methods. Activities and methods must be carefully selected to harmonize with the criteria mentioned above. The activities must serve the purpose of the center and be appropriate to the students using it. They must be so designed that they will assist the student to reach the expected learnings. The directions must be clearly within the ability of the student and presented so that the student can follow them independently. The materials must be readily available.

Make Assessments. Use the objectives for the center as a base to determine whether the student has attained the expected learning, concepts, and skills stated.

Implement Changes as Needed. Student performance will provide insight into how each center can be improved to meet the needs of the students it serves, the curriculum, and the objectives and goals stated for the center. The center and its materials may also need periodic servicing.

/// IMPORTANCE OF STUDENT INTERACTION IN GUIDED DISCOVERY SCIENCE

Your bright, well-decorated classroom is enhanced by interest centers, attractive and informative bulletin boards, posters, and other visual displays. However, it is just as important for your students to have guided opportunities in their science programs to interact by drawing on each other's discoveries and communicating their ideas to each other. Science is a **participation activity,** and if its social aspects are to be fully realized, students must have guided activities involving interaction with each other.

The **physical arrangements** of the classroom can advance or hinder this interaction. Reexamine Figures 6–4 and 6–5 to see how furniture is wisely used. Rows are not straight, and desks do not face in one direction (usually toward you) where children see only the backs of the heads of the children in front of them. This enforced order impedes the development of active, involved students.

Traffic flow patterns allow students to quickly and quietly move about the room to interact. Easy access to sufficient materials facilitates cooperation rather than competition. A flexible furniture arrangement sets the atmosphere that changes will be made by students and teacher as needed to maximize interaction. Attention to such "trivial" things as providing clean up items and trash receptacles around the room where students work, rather than in one corner, improves opportunities for cooperation with minimum conflict.

Classroom Management and Discipline in Guided Discovery Minds-on/Hands-on Science

Physical arrangement of your classroom is very important, but the heart and soul of your sci-ence teaching is **classroom management.** Even if you have a well-thought out science program, a carefully prepared physical classroom, and adequate supplies, the one thing that can wreck your teaching is faulty classroom management, sometimes called discipline. Table 6–5 presents a comparison of classroom management or discipline to medicine with these three similarities: prevention, first-aid treatment, and long-term treatment.

Prevention: Anticipating Problems Before They Occur

An ounce of prevention is worth more than a pound of cure in your science teaching. Thinking and planning can help you spot many, though never all, potential trouble areas. Here are some things to keep in mind (for *preventing* classroom management or discipline problems) as you begin planning your science teaching.[7]

Phase 1 Teacher/Student Preparations

■ Identify what you want students to learn and relate it to the cognitive level of your students.

■ Pick appropriate activities for your students to learn (how).

TABLE 6–5

Comparison of classroom management and medicine

Category	Medicine	Science Classroom Management
Prevention	check-ups, good nutrition, exercise, sleep, etc.	preassessment/diagnosis; teacher/student preparation; teacher observation; student grouping; preactivity discussion; material distribution; teacher/student interactions
First-aid treatment	stopping bleeding, bandaging, etc.	separating and quieting problem students; halting disruptive activity
Long-term treatment	vitamin supplements, chemotherapy, limb in cast	individual skills improvement; teacher/student/parent conferences; student removal

■ Collect supplies and equipment you and the students will need.

■ Plan the physical room arrangement and logistics needed for the activity.

■ Organize the class into working teams.

This aspect of planning needs elaboration, especially for those who are new to teaching or who have not had groups of students working together in science instead of the total class working together. Therefore, the "Long-Term Treatment" section of this chapter presents a fuller description of an innovative strategy—**cooperative group learning**—that is very effective for managing materials and students in minds-on/hands-on activities.

■ Organize science materials before starting your activity at stations in your self-contained classroom. Team members share responsibilities for obtaining and returning science materials, eliminating confusion and expediting movement of materials. Give this considerable planning, because the distribution of materials can make or break your science lesson.

Phase 2   Pre-Activity Discussion

■ Use verbal and visual directions—pointing, using arrows, and asking questions—to help direct and focus students' attention on what will be done when they are working in their groups. Be very specific.

■ Guide students to identify the problem being investigated, design the experiment, determine data-collecting and record-keeping techniques, and decide what and how equipment and supplies will be used.

■ Give students time during this phase to discuss, to explain what will be done, and to exchange ideas. This is important for students to internalize what will be done and to form working relationships with other children.

Research has shown that (a) highly anxious students do better if the teacher is less directive; (b) students with low anxiety levels respond better to stronger direction from the teacher; (c) average and low ability students benefit more from greater structure in teacher presentations and materials; and (d) above average students learn better when they have more latitude to imagine, interpret, and rapidly manipulate symbols. Gear your pre-activity discussion to the individual needs of the specific groups with which you are working.[8]

■ By effectively using open-ended questions, you can guide students toward the goals you have for the activity.

■ Establish a reason in students' minds for doing the activity. List on the board the reasons for conducting the activity, and write down as you discuss how supplies and equipment will be distributed and collected.

■ Remember that science supplies and materials should be assembled at the distribution and collection stations *before* the lesson begins.

Phase 3   Distribution and Collection of Science Materials

■ Assign one group at a time to go to the supply stations and get the needed items. Make certain each group knows exactly what it is to get. Review with the groups what they will do, what they need, and how they will proceed before having them go for supplies.

■ Establish a realistic time limit for supply gathering and collection.

■ Always check to see that each group has all necessary science supplies.

Phase 4   Doing the Activity

■ With all the groups in their places with their supplies, review once more what each group will be doing. Sometimes it helps to check by asking the students who have the most difficulty, so that you can be sure all children understand the directions.

■ For students unaccustomed to group work, try assigning a number to each task. Giving each student a numbered task assures total group participation.

First-Aid Treatment for Classroom Management and Discipline

As the students begin their group work, you take many roles. Here's how to keep the groups working effectively.

- Move about the room. Do not plant yourself in the front of the room, but move quietly to each group.
- If students are bogged down, ask questions to guide them and move them back on the tasks to be done.
- Encourage communication among the students in each group.
- Assess the noise level and see if it's appropriate for the specific activity. If it's too noisy, you might try these solutions:

  1. Establish beforehand a signal calling for quiet (e.g., putting lights out for a moment, ringing a bell, raising a hand in the air). When everyone quiets down, remind the class that it is too loud. Ask the students to quiet down.
  2. Move to the offenders and quietly remind them to lower their noise.
  3. Conclude the lesson if you are unable to quiet the class. Do this only as a last resort.

- Praise students who are working well instead of criticizing those who are not working well. Be specific with your praise so children know exactly the behavior you are praising, such as, "Notice how quietly Ann's group is discussing what effect the length of the pendulum cord has on its swings," or "Class, Jon's so helpful by going around and showing each group how to wire the bell."
- Temporarily remove from their groups students who cause problems and ask them to watch groups that are working well together. In a few minutes you might say, "Jason, I know you want to work with your group, so when you're ready, quietly go back to them and see if you can now work quietly and share your materials properly."

- Be enthusiastic.
- Show respect for students by speaking politely and listening to each student in an unhurried manner.
- Do not add to class noise by shouting above students' voices. Calm and quiet the students with a firm but soft voice.

Long-Term Treatment in Classroom Management and Discipline

Evaluate your group lessons to see if you need to address any of these problems.

- Some students may be too immature for group work. You may have to work with them individually while the rest of the class works in groups.
- Additional total class or small-group instruction may be necessary for those students who need science concepts/skills improvement before they are able to fully benefit from group work.
- Review, sharing of information, and discussions are necessary to follow up students' work.
- Make sure that all students understand the conclusions and generalizations.
- Build time into each lesson for students to clean, disassemble, and return to collection stations all supplies and equipment used. This also places some responsibility on students and teaches them that teachers are not servants or maintenance people.
- After each lesson, abstract a minimum set of working rules from the students to be used for future work, such as, "Make certain you know what you must do," or "Find out what materials you will have to use in the lesson."
- If there is a chronic offender in your class, you might (a) talk with the student; (b) try to determine her or his interests; (c) ask for the student's perceptions of the problem and schedule a student-parent-teacher conference to see what can cooperatively be done;

and if needed, (d) invite the principal to attend with the aid of information from the school psychologist, social worker, or other professional.

A classroom management approach that incorporates many of these group considerations is the Cooperative Group Learning Model presented in the following section.

/// COOPERATIVE LEARNING GROUPS

In the 1960s, Martha Piper developed a **Cooperative Learning Group (CLG) Model** to assist teachers in effectively guiding minds-on/hands-on science activities.[9] She and others (Roger and David Johnson, Robert Jones, and the Biological Science Curriculum Study Group) built on the original and developed variations that are widely used today.[10]

But what are CLGs? Basically, CLGs are classroom group techniques for facilitating and guiding minds-on/hands-on science activities. They are especially useful in classrooms where science materials and equipment are limited, cooperative group processes and skill development are desired, and an orderly and controlled classroom system is necessary.

CLG Advantages

CLGs offer minds-on/hands-on science teachers many advantages, among which are the following:

1. They are very effective as problem-solving/divergent thinking activities.[11]
2. They provide for group sharing of limited science equipment and supplies.
3. There is "positive interdependence"—that is, students concern themselves with the performance and learning of *all* team members.

4. Students have a vested interest in each other's success, so all students tend to be more successful.
5. Success builds success!
6. Students develop both cognitive and group participation skills.
7. The teacher is assisted in classroom management by students who
   a. manage science materials,
   b. take responsibility for helping team members with assignments and problems, and
   c. alleviate some of teacher stress by maintaining order and keeping students working.
8. Teachers can use CLGs outdoors as well as in classrooms.
9. Students become more positive about contributing in groups, as well as about their schools, teachers, and subject areas.

To make full use of these advantages, teachers must learn how to set up CLGs, assign roles to student members, and guide the teams in their activities.

CLG Team Formation

Initially, it is best for you to assign students to a team, because they tend to gravitate to friends only. For primary grades, or older students who have not worked previously in CLGs, it is best to start with two students. As they acquire basic cooperative group skills, combine two groups of two as a working team. Generally, CLG teams of three to five are recommended to cooperate to conduct minds-on/hands-on science activities. Include both girls and boys with a variety of abilities and cultural diversity. Keep teams together for at least three to six weeks so teammates have time to learn to work with each other. As a team builder, let each team choose its own name. Then, change team membership, so students get to work with other classmates.

Develop a way of fairly rotating jobs and post it prominently so all students can see it. All students should have experiences in all CLG jobs to develop the skills involved.

CLG Job Assignments and Functions

A specific job is assigned to each CLG team member. The names and functions are quite similar in all CLGs. The following are from Robert Jones' Inquiry Task Group Management System (ITGMS):[12]

■ **Principal Investigator.** In charge of all team operations (i.e., checking assignments, communicating activity directions, asking teacher informational questions, assisting group members, conducting group discussions about activity results, and either directing activity or assigning it to other team members).

■ **Materials Manager.** Gets and distributes materials to each team, sets up and operates any activity equipment, and is usually the only student moving around the room without special permission during activity.

■ **Recorder/Reporter.** Collects, records, and certifies data on team work or lab sheets, reports results to total class orally or written on Class Summary Chart posted on chalkboard.

■ **Maintenance Director.** Responsible (with team members he assigns) for clean-up and return of materials and equipment, directs used materials disposal, and is responsible for team members' safety.

■ **Technical Advisor.** (Special role for "dependable" students who finish work fast and accurately). Moves to teams having difficulties and assists, may prepare activity materials for teacher or inspect equipment.

■ **Observer.** (Teacher's administrative assistant). May use form to record and share team problems.

Cooperative learning groups foster creative problem solving and team effort.

CLG Job Badges

To supply easy identification of team members' jobs and responsibilities, **badges** are usually recommended. These badges might look like those in Figure 6–6, used by the ITGMS.

Badges help both teachers and team members keep track of job responsibilities and resolve conflict. They also help team members remember what they are supposed to do. Teachers can also spot a difficulty (or impending problem) and by referring to a team member's badge, guide the person to proper actions. This is a very positive and effective discipline management.

You can make up badges or allow students to design and make their own. Try to include pictures for easy job identification, laminate for durability and strength, and punch holes for stringing around the neck. Encourage CLG team members to refer to job descriptions and badge pictures to resolve disputes regarding who does what.

CLG Job Description Cards

Job description cards may be left at each science activity station for student use for performing their assigned part of the activity. Users have found it is best to write direct "you" statements on each card. The cards spell out the job responsibilities and limits. Figure 6–7 is a sample of an ITGROUP job description card for a four-member team. Note the low reading level of the statements.

Job description cards should be modified according to team size (2, 3, 4, or 5 members), students' age, maturation, learning levels and styles, and any other variables that affect their

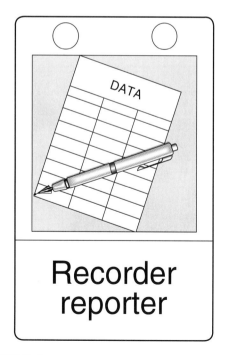

FIGURE 6–6

Cooperative Learning Group job badges[13]

> **Materials Manager**
>
> 1. You pick up the materials.
> 2. You operate the equipment.
> 3. You return the materials.

FIGURE 6–7
Cooperative job description cards[14]

usage. Often, teachers color code CLG description cards according to job description.

Using CLGs in Your Classroom

So how do I get started using CLGs in my classroom? Although each classroom situation is unique, several CLG models adhere to the following prototype developed by Martha Piper. The specific sequence is recommended initially, but sequence and steps themselves should be modified as teachers and students gain experience and confidence with CLG techniques.[15]

Step 1 —Introduction. Minds-on/hands-on guided discovery activity is introduced to the *whole class* by these tasks before a small group begins work:

■ *Arranging* (or rearranging) *furniture* to facilitate minds-on/hands-on activities and to avoid excessive noise, movement, or confusion. Consider the furniture configuration in Figure 6–8.

■ *Writing activity objective* on chalkboard or chart.

■ *Introducing or Reviewing* pertinent activity information, safety precautions, vocabulary, and such CLG skills as

When we begin, move quietly and quickly into your team.
Stay with your team at all times.
Speak softly when working and take turns.
Do only your assigned job.

■ Solicit and answer all students' questions now.

Step 2 —Distributing Science Materials. Do *not* begin distributing materials until all Step 1 items are completed. Then, have the *Materials Manager* collect science materials from the central materials station and deliver to each team station.

Step 3 —Team Investigation. *Principal Investigators* in each team review directions with team members so that they all understand the

FIGURE 6–8
Cooperative learning group classroom furniture arrangement

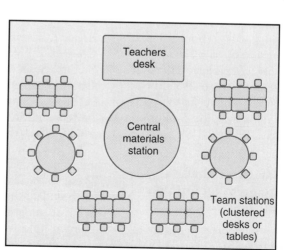

procedures to be used. *Materials Manager* directs materials setup while *teacher* moves from team to team to ensure proper use of materials, procedures, safety, and results. *Principal Investigators* may signal teacher if assistance is needed. *Recorders/Reporters* collect data on data sheets, check with other team results, and post results.

Step 4 — Discussion of Activity Results.

The *teacher* conducts a discussion of the results posted on Class Summary Chart, clarifies concepts and skills, similarities and discrepancies of team data, and may assign follow-up activities involving readings, duplicated worksheets, and other individualized reinforcements.

Step 5 — Team Cleanup. *Maintenance Directors* (and any assigned team members) make sure work areas are clean, inspect all materials and equipment, and return them to designated areas.

Step 6 — Team Member Assessment.

Teacher (cooperatively with students) uses a variety of devices to assess team members' demonstrated mastery of CLG processes and skills objectives. See Assessment chapter for appropriate devices.

CLGs are valuable techniques for minds-on/hands-on science programs with possibilities for all elementary and middle school subject areas. For an excellent step-by-step account of how to set up and use cooperative learning groups in your classroom, read Robert M. Jones, *TEAMING UP! The Inquiry Task Group Management System, User's Guide* (LaPorte, Texas: Robert M. Jones, 1990).

Application of CLG and Other Classroom Management Techniques to Your Classroom

Although no classroom management system is foolproof or a substitute for an alert and intelligent teacher, Figure 6–9 summarizes techniques that can help in your minds-on/hands-on guided discovery science teaching.

Simple, Clear Rules and Work Directions

1. Establish with students a minimum set of rules and working directions that contain primarily fairness and courtesy behaviors. Wherever possible, give students a reason for the rule, e.g., "We will ask that only one team come up at a time to the science supply station so we can avoid bumping into each other and spilling things. Understand?" Post the rules on a chart.
2. Determine an appropriate "attention and quieting signal" to which students can automatically respond.
3. Set up and review often the system for distributing and collecting science supplies and equipment, as well as your clean up procedures.

Classroom Management Maintenance and Reinforcement

4. Develop a repertoire of praise and reinforcement for students working cooperatively. These articles give specifics in this area: Donald B. Neumann, "Elementary Science for All Children — An Impossible Dream or a Reachable Goal?" *Science and Children,* 18, no. 6 (March 1981): 4–6; Roger T. Johnson and David W. Johnson, Chapter 2 "What Research Says About Student-Student Interaction in Science Classrooms" and James R. Okey and David P. Butts, Chapter 3 "Linking Teaching Behaviors and Student Behaviors in Science," in Mary Budd Rowe, ed., *Education in the 80's: Science* (Washington, DC: National Education Association, 1982), 25–52.
5. Present concise directions for each activity that each student can understand. Assess often to see if all students know exactly what to do.
6. Demonstrate what is expected, as well as any new idea or procedure.

Environmental Factor	Whole-class I Students Listen to Teacher	Whole-class II Students Work Independently	Small Groups	Individual
Example teaching methods	Giving class directions; discussion; demonstrations; science review drills	Worksheets; short quizzes; reinforcement sheets; problem-solving puzzles	Role-playing; lab activity groups; manipulative investigations; field trips; simulations and games	Learning centers; science/math fair projects; individualized homework or task cards
Cooperative vs competitive instruction	Competitive	Mostly competitive unless using peer teaching strategy	Most cooperative class arrangement	Neither
Use of manipulative materials	Most difficult arrangement to use manipulatives. Students are most passive in their learning	Can be done in this arrangement, but is limited to simple exercises such as mystery boxes or puzzle pieces	Easy to use manipulatives. Students are highly active in their learning	Easiest to use manipulative materials. Most active learning takes place
Content coverage, selection, and individualization	The most content can be covered and is selected by the teacher. Retention is generally low	Good content coverage, but opportunity to individualize is limited	Less content covered because more time is needed in small group activities. More individualized instruction can take place	Less content covered in traditional "textbook sense," but students' content selection is high and so is retention level
Student values and decision making	Student preferences not explored or considered to a high degree	More student choice is permitted	Best opportunity to conduct affective activities such as simulations on topics like the environment	Best opportunity to encourage student decision-making skills
Creativity and problem solving	Not conducive to actual problem-solving process other than as an excellent way to present problems to be solved by the class in other arrangements	Can be conducive through the use of "brainteaser" types of problems. It is hard to determine, however, the difficulty level of problems presented to the whole class	Best opportunity for problem solving and creative activity, since students benefit from listening to the solutions of others in the group	Very good arrangement to encourage problem solving and creativity, especially for those students who work well alone.

FIGURE 6–9

Types of classroom arrangements

Source: Modified from Stan Rachelson, "Rethink and Regroup." Reproduced with permission by *Science Scope*, 14, no. 2 (October 1990): 39. Copyright 1990 by The National Science Teachers Association, 1742 Connecticut Avenue, N.W., Washington, DC 20009.

Discovery: Take-Home Science

Many teachers say they are frustrated because they lack facilities and class time to allow students to try hands-on experiments. Two hints about "take-home" science: Always allow class time for both introductory and follow-up discussions; for larger projects, allow sufficient time to gather materials and perform the experiment (at least a weekend).

Strategy   Prepare "take-home" science experiments with simple written instructions to involve the entire family in "real science."

Sometimes teachers want children to be able to do a science experiment that doesn't lend itself to the resources available in the classroom. One sixth-grade teacher, for example, has no running water in the room where she teaches science. Rather than have students miss the opportunity to see a chemical process at work, she has them perform the experiment at home.

This teacher sends students home with the directions for the investigation. Students make their own "laboratory" in their kitchens, using two drinking glasses, two eggs, and vinegar. Each child puts one egg in a drinking glass and covers it with vinegar. The other goes into a second drinking class and is covered with water.

Students prepare for the experiment in class by discussing the procedure and formulating hypotheses. They perform the experiment at home and record their observations independently. Then, they come back to class and discuss their independent observations and reach conclusions.

On Your Own   Overcome classroom deficiencies of space and resources and translate them into purposeful use of "at-home" experimentation.

Have your students perform experiments at home to give them a chance to demonstrate to their families how scientists work. Parent involvement is nearly unavoidable, and explaining the procedures to younger siblings will give them excellent peer teaching practice.

Assign intermediate and middle school students an experiment to do at home as preparation for the larger-scale science fair projects they will be expected to perform independently—and as practice for parents who will be called on to "consult."

Source: This feature was prepared with the collaboration of Susan Winer, a teacher at Cassingham Elementary School, Bexley, Ohio.

Handling Problems and Emergencies

7. Prepare contingency plans for disruptive situations, e.g., spilling of science supplies, "explosive" student behavior (fighting and pushing), or unexpected science occurrence (hamster gives birth). Remember—if anything can go wrong, it will!

8. Consider beforehand the pro's and con's of discipline, such as removing a student from the situation or physically restraining, so you can effectively use it if necessary.

9. If you feel the lesson is getting away from you, don't hesitate to end it. Assess what went wrong and plan the next lesson to eliminate the problem.

For additional help in preparing to teach science through guided discovery, see Chapter 9 on individualizing a guided discovery program.

SUMMARY

To put a minds-on/hands-on guided science discovery teaching program into effect in your classroom, you must adequately provide for four aspects of your teaching:

1. Long- and short-range planning
2. Physical classroom environment
3. Student interaction
4. Classroom management or discipline

Exciting science lessons do not happen by chance. Begin your planning by deciding on your long-range goals for the whole year. Find out what your students know and then select a science program that fits you and your students. Then, start putting your broad goals into a science unit format. An example of a unit format was presented to assist you. This will help you in preparing to write individual guided discovery lesson plans.

In writing lesson plans, include all types of teaching and learning methods including listening-speaking, reading-writing, and watching-doing. Emphasis is placed on minds-on/hands-on guided discovery activity-based lessons because research shows that students learn science best this way. Resources help teachers use this approach. However, you still need to know how to construct guided discovery lessons on your own. Lessons tailored to your own class are more appropriate than commercially prepared ones.

Discovery activities vary in how experimental they are in the structure they provide for the student. If you follow the guided discovery lesson planning formats in this chapter, you will learn to write good guided discovery lessons.

Once you learn how to construct guided discovery science lessons, you will feel confident to write these, as well as less structured ones, because you will know the nature of the process.

Most science in the elementary school is taught in self-contained classrooms. This chapter suggests various physical arrangements of the classroom, including sample floor plans and storage for materials, small items, and living things.

Discovery learning centers in a classroom allow your students to explore, discover, and experiment in less structured situations. This chapter describes how to construct and use learning centers.

Not only the physical arrangement of the room, but also student interaction is critical, since science is a participation activity. Teachers must arrange furniture in flexible and creative ways.

Classroom management, or discipline, can make or break your science teaching. Classroom management is compared to medicine; both feature prevention, first-aid, and long-term treatment. Cooperative learning groups offer many advantages for teachers of minds-on/hands-on science programs, and ideas of how to set one up in your classroom was presented.

SELF-ASSESSMENT AND FURTHER STUDY

1. Draw a floor plan on graph paper for your classroom. Arrange the room to include these science areas: activity, equipment and supplies storage, living things storage, discovery learning center, research and library center, conference center, and audiovisual center.
2. You and your students can obtain free materials from a local grocery, fast-food chain, or other source and construct several of the storage areas or shoe box collections.
3. Using the information in this chapter, construct with your students several containers to house insects, small animals, or birds.
4. Cooperatively with students, set up and maintain an aquarium or terrarium. Once established, add a small animal(s) or fish, as appropriate.
5. With your class, plan and develop a discovery science learning center around a single topic of science.
6. Select a guided discovery science activity and write a plan for classroom management using prevention, first-aid, and long-term treatment. Be specific.
7. Using text readings and others you can find, prepare a list of positive reinforcement statements to encourage and reinforce cooperation among your students. Start your research with Ann Jensen, "Classroom Rewards: Do They Work?" *American Educator,* 7, no. 1 (Spring 1983).
8. Take a textbook science unit and modify the lessons to meet the uniqueness of your students, your classroom environment, and a minds-on/hands-on guided discovery approach.

9. The following terms are used almost interchangeably by some teachers. Define each one in your own words and indicate any differences that might exist:
   a. Experiment.
   b. Observational, classificational, and experimental investigations.
   c. Structured discovery lesson.
   d. Less structured discovery lesson.
   e. Minds-on/hands-on science activity.
   f. Activity-based science activity.
   g. Guided discovery science activity.
10. Using references in this chapter as a beginning, select a cooperative learning group model, become familiar with the approach, and arrange to teach several minds-on/hands-on guided discovery lessons using that approach. Include such items as job descriptions and badges, procedures you will follow, and materials and assessments you will use.

NOTES

1. Christine Chaillé and Lory Britain, *The Young Child as Scientist: A Constructivist Approach to Early Childhood Education* (New York: HarperCollins, 1991), 68.
2. Specifics on exemplary science teacher attributes are found in R. J. Bonnstetter, J. E. Penick, and R. E. Yager, *Teachers in Exemplary Programs: How Do They Compare?* (Washington, DC: National Science Teachers Association, 1984) and J. E. Penick, ed., *Focus on Excellence: Science as Inquiry, vol. 1, nos. 1 and 2* (Washington, DC: National Science Teachers Association, 1983).
3. John I. Goodlad, *A Place Called School: Prospects for the Future* (New York: McGraw-Hill Book Co., 1983).
4. *Elementary Science Syllabus* (Albany, NY: The University of the State of New York, State Education Department, Division of Program Development, 1986), 3.
5. For additional specifics on Science Learning Centers see Leon L. Ukens, "Learning Stations and Science Teaching," *Science and Children,* 14, no. 3 (November/December 1976): 13 and Kathleen A. O'Sullivan, "Creating a Learning Center," *Science and Children,* 24, no. 6 (March 1984): 15–17.
6. Donald C. Orlich et al., "Science Learning Centers—An Aid to Instruction," *Science and Children,* 20, no. 1 (September 1982): 18–19.
7. The following book provides excellent ideas on classroom management and discipline in minds-on/hands-on science: Robert E. MacDonald, *A Handbook of Basic Skills and Strategies for Beginning Teachers: Facing the Challenge of Teaching in Today's Schools,* Chapter 9, "Staying on Top of Classroom Management," (NY: Longman Publishing Group, 1991), 168–185; Ray Petty, "Discipline in Your Classroom. Teachers Forum: Immediate,

Firm, and Consistent," *The Science Teacher,* 55, no. 2 (February 1988): 34–35; Susan O. Spellman, "Mission Possible: Teaching Hands-on Science to Disruptive Students," *Science and Children,* 26, no. 4 (January 1989): 15.

8. Structure in learning is discussed in John J. Koram, Jr. and Jeffrey R. Lehman, "What Research Says: Teaching Children Science Concepts: The Role of Attention," *Science and Children,* 18, no. 4 (January 1981): 31–32.

9. Martha K. Piper, "A Science Activity Teaching Plan," *School Science and Mathematics,* 80, no. 5 (1980): 390–406.

10. The author acknowledges these comprehensive descriptions of CLG models and highly recommends you read Roger T. Johnson, David W. Johnson, and Edythe Johnson Holubec, *Structuring Cooperative Learning: Lesson Plans for Teachers* (Edina, MN: Interaction Book Co., 1987); Robert M. Jones, *Teaming Up! The Inquiry Task Group Management System, User's Guide* (LaPorte, TX: ITGROUP, December 1990); *Science for Life and Living: Integrating Science, Technology, and Health: Sneak Preview* (Colorado Springs, CO: Biological Sciences Curriculum Study, 1990); and *any* edition of *Cooperative Learning (The Magazine for Cooperation in Education),* 136 Liberty Street, Santa Cruz, CA 95060.

11. Robert M. Jones and John E. Steinbrink, "Home Teams: Cooperative Learning in Elementary Science," *School Science and Mathematics,* 91, no. 4 (April 1991): 139–143.

12. For a fuller explanation of the CLG job assignments and functions see Robert M. Jones, *Teaming Up!,* 10–12.

13. Robert M. Jones, *Teaming Up!,* 55.

14. Robert M. Jones, *Teaming Up!,* 43.

15. The author found this source very valuable: Robert M. Jones, *Teaming Up!,* 13–19.

The history of recent science curriculum development may hold valuable lessons for future programs. . . . The research indicates that the innovative programs of the sixties and seventies were more effective in raising student performance and attitudes than the traditional reading-based programs.[1]

ESS, SAPA, and SCIS should be examined in great detail to identify the successful parts and the parts where trouble was encountered. These programs and the hundreds of studies of these programs represent one of the greatest resources of information on what actually works in the elementary science classroom.[2]

CHAPTER 7

Using Science Programs and Textbooks

What programs and textbooks are available for teaching science? How can you use these tools to accomplish your teaching goals?

As seen in these two opening quotations, you can find useful applications for your science classroom by looking at the history of science education. Table 7−1 provides a summary of the evolution of science in the elementary school.

This chapter will only introduce you to a few of the many "next generation" innovative science programs that could positively and directly affect your classroom science teaching. Should you wish to further pursue them, sources are provided.

But first, let's see how the "alphabet science programs" (ESS, SCIS, and SAPA) contributed to where we are today.

/// THE LEGACY OF EARLIER FUNDED SCIENCE PROJECTS

As you see from Table 7−1, funded, experimental science projects were developed in the late 1950s, 1960s, and 1970s to try to reform science education. Some of the major projects were

- ESS—Elementary Science Study.
- SAPA—Science—A Process Approach.
- SCIS—Science Curriculum Improvement Study.

These projects had the following similarities, which set the pattern for today's science innovations:

1. Distinguished professional scientists initiated many of these innovations in science teaching rather than professional science educators, state departments of education, or teacher education institutions.
2. For the first time, funds were made available to do curriculum research and development *before* inclusion or exclusion in schools.
3. Each project had a team of psychologists and other learning specialists, science educators, scientists, and elementary school teachers. Although each member brought expertise to the project, the give-and-take

TABLE 7-1

Summary of evolution of science education in the elementary schools

Period	Educational Priorities	Period	Educational Priorities
1850s	Memorization of facts for religious explanations Descriptions and memorizations in object teaching Structured curriculum based upon formal scientific classification and terminology Methodology and utilitarianism of science curriculums based upon sequence of major science principles and their applications	1960s	Curriculums influenced by funded national science projects Expanded teacher training in science
		1970s	Teaching science as processes and products: discovery and inquiry approach; conceptual schemes
		1980s	Individualized science for all children: handicapped, gifted, normal More emphasis on human values, ecology, and the government Science, technology and society emphasis
1950s	Textbook series and state adoptions Textbook series scope and sequence School's science content and methods of teaching	1990s	Integration of STS science activities with mathematics and all other subject areas

Stress on problem solving of relevant everyday, real-life personal, society, and STS issues
Encouraging students to seek alternative solutions in problem solving and to take action
Concern for environmental and ecological problems and solutions
Emphasis on fewer, broader thematic science topics in depth, rather than more areas superficially
Using cooperative learning groups to enhance science concept and group skills learning

of working relationships resulted in a blending of the best.

4. Projects were experimental. They were tested, rewritten as a result, and retested until the teams were more sure of the procedures and materials. The projects generally wed good teaching and learning practices with the latest in science disciplines.

5. Great emphasis was placed on the active participation of the learner in all of the new projects. Most of the projects claimed that all students could participate, not just select groups. In effect, each of these projects emphasized the open-ended laboratory or hands-on approach where students use simple equipment in the elementary classroom.

6. Departure from the standard textbook was evident in all projects having a total pro-

gram. Where printed materials were available for students, they were for purposes of recording what had been observed, planning future activities, and answering questions.

7. There was a definite trend away from teaching *many* science content areas to teaching a relatively *few* content areas.

8. More abstract content was generally introduced earlier in these projects than in former science curricula.

9. Most of the projects did *not* follow the typical science unit, which consciously integrates science with social studies, reading, written expression, and other areas.

10. These projects were much more quantitative than descriptive, unlike previous science curriculums. Mathematical skills and understandings were highly stressed and an integral part of the projects, which used

techniques such as measurement, graphing, and recording data.

11. There was a trend toward open-ended, relatively unstructured methods of discovery rather than teaching one method of problem solving. Knowledge was viewed as part of a creative process of finding out rather than as something to be accumulated.

12. The emphasis shifted away from technology and application of science to abstractions, theories, and basic ideas of science.

13. "Packaged programs," including hardware and software, were constructed to give a whole program to teachers. These aided teachers in adapting new programs to their particular situations. These packages also contained many new curricular innovations that provided the teacher with flexibility to handle a wide range of student abilities and varying teaching conditions.

14. The change in the teacher's role in the science program was one of the most dramatic breaks with the past. The teacher was the guide to, not the teller of, science. Most projects had extensive provisions for training (and retraining) teachers for this role through implementation programs and dissemination of materials. (*Note:* For more details of earlier innovative science programs including ESS, SCIS, SAPA, and HAP, see the previous edition of this textbook. Specific suggestions for teachers interested in implementing an experimental science project are presented later in this chapter.)

How Do I Benefit from Earlier Funded Science Projects?

According to the research, students in the "new" programs outperformed those in traditional, textbook-based classrooms on every criterion measured, as indicated by the following:

- Process skills measures were 19 percentile points better for students in innovative projects over their counterparts in traditional classrooms.
- Attitudes toward the science program were 17 percentile points better.
- The average student in an ESS, SCIS, or SAPA classroom performed better than 62 percent of the students in traditional classrooms across all performance criteria measured—a 12 percentile-point gain.
- Students in SCIS and SAPA scored higher than students in comparable textbook-based classrooms on tests of reading and arithmetic skills.

Regardless of what kind of science program you have, you could benefit from looking at the programs developed through funded science projects to see what you could adapt for your particular classroom and students.

Also, the earlier innovative science projects greatly influenced state and local science programs, science textbooks, and the direction and procedures used by present-day projects. Here are a few ways they impacted.

New Generation Science Textbooks

The National Science Teachers Association, with funding from the National Institute of Education of the Department of Education, reviewed science textbooks and funded science projects. NSTA compared "Frequently Used Science Textbooks," "NSF Texts" (SCIS, ESS, SAPA), and what they called "New Generation Texts," on the characteristics in Table 7–2. NSTA concluded, "There is a marked contrast between the first group of texts and the other two. The influence of the NSF programs is very evident in the program characteristics of the third group."[3]

Textbook authors and publishers have been influenced by funded science projects. They have incorporated many of the better points of

TABLE 7–2
Congruence of existing program characteristics to desired states

Characteristics	Frequently Used Texts	NSF Texts	New Generation Texts
1. Interdisciplinary	Low to None	High to Good	High
2. Alternatives	None	High	High to Low
3. Firsthand Experience	Low	High to Good	Good
4. Involved in Data-Gathering	Easily Avoided	High	High
5. Alternative Modes	Single-Mode Text	Single-Mode Text Hands-On	Combination
6. Reflects How Children Learn	Low	High	High

Source: Harold Pratt et al., "Science Education in the Elementary School," in Norris C. Harms and Robert E. Yager, eds., *What Research Says to the Science Teacher, Volume 3,* (Washington, DC: National Science Teachers Association, 1981): 84. Reprinted with permission.

these projects into their textbooks, resulting in high-quality textbooks for the elementary schools. Among the more visible science textbook improvements are the following:

1. Publishers have made a greater effort to improve the accuracy of scientific information.
2. A discovery, or laboratory-centered, approach is apparent in more recent textbooks because of the greater emphasis on question-and-answer techniques rather than the dialogue or telling techniques so popular in some previous elementary science textbooks.
3. Authors are beginning to develop styles of writing that convey the fascination and intellectual excitement inherent in science disciplines.
4. An emphasis on science processes is appearing more frequently in current textbooks, including manipulative activities.
5. Several of the publishers are including (very often as optional) kits of materials to carry out the experimental activities included in their texts.

6. Limited opportunities are beginning to appear in texts for developing scientific attitudes as well as skills for creative and critical thinking.
7. The format of modern textbooks is much more inviting than that of previous texts; there is more extensive use of pictures and other illustrations and sequential photos of scientific phenomena. Film loops and films are also available to supplement the books.
8. Publishers are offering fewer comprehensive science units, which are explored in greater depth, rather than providing the numerous isolated lessons of the past.

Trends in Today's Programs from Former Innovative Projects

What trends are seen in science education in the 1990s and into the 21st century? The revised versions of SCIS and SAPA, as well as newer projects show some of the following observable trends in science education:

Studying science builds awareness of the need for action on environmental and ecological problems.

1. Science programs employ a more humanistic approach in which examples from the student's life are used to emphasize and correlate to the science concepts introduced.
2. Science programs increasingly show the direct relationships of people's lives and conditions to the processes and concepts of scientific investigations.
3. More emphasis is placed on relating the science programs to environmental and ecological issues.
4. Values and social aspects of science and technology are integrated into the science curriculum.
5. Science is being more broadly integrated with the other curricular areas of language arts, social studies, and mathematics.
6. The programs make wider use of more flexible techniques and individualization of instruction because more special needs and gifted students are mainstreamed in the elementary school classroom.
7. The programs use cooperative learning groups to develop group process skills for problem solving.

These trends can be observed in the increased number of today's funded projects with these emphases. An example of a funded project that incorporates these humanistic trends follows.

Science and Children's Lives

Increasing numbers of funded science projects are employing a more humanistic approach in which children's lives are used to highlight and correlate the science concepts. An exemplary program of this type is the **Health Activities Project (HAP)** developed by the Lawrence Hall of Science of the University of California at Berkeley, supported by a grant from the Robert Wood Johnson Foundation, and published by Hubbard Publishers of Northbrook, Illinois. HAP is a series of scientifically formulated activities designed to develop concepts of "self" and health care such as

how the body works and changes,
how the body can be controlled to increase
  performance, improve skills, develop
  strength, and make decisions that result in
  healthier, more efficient living,

Learning about science includes learning about maintaining or improving healthy bodies and about the importance of exercise.

how technological devices are used to evaluate health, and

how the preventative aspects of health can be learned.

Notice that HAP is also concerned with helping children raise their consciousness so they can control their bodies and improve their personal performance. HAP currently has four modules: "Breathing and Fitness," "Sight and Sound," "Heart Fitness," and "Action." Each module has activity folios for students to use in their activities, activity sheets to fill out, teacher's guides and charts, and labeling supplies. Additional information about HAP can be obtained from Hubbard Publishers, P.O. Box 104, Northbrook, Illinois 60062.

Summaries follow of current projects that have applications to your classroom science program. Some of the projects are funded and some commercial. Often, funded projects have a dissemination component to publicize their work. Sometimes, commercial projects were originally funded by governmental or private sources.

/// CURRENT FUNDED SCIENCE PROGRAMS

At any given time, hundreds of funded programs are under way. Here are some of the more widely known projects.

Activities for Integrating Mathematics and Science Project (AIMS)

Developer: Pacific College, Fresno, California, (National Science Foundation Funded).

Initially, AIMS was to train teachers in grades 5 to 8 in how to integrate science and mathematics into their classrooms. The project was so successful that it was expanded to include grades K through 8.

Fifteen teaching booklets were produced using these underlying principles:

1. Because mathematics and science are integrated in real life, they should be integrated in school.
2. Mathematics skills and science processes should be closely combined in all teaching/ learning activities.
3. All learning materials should raise questions relevant to the learners' lives and environment for greater motivation and interest.
4. The emphasis is on making students active participants in the learning process.
5. Activities are purposely designed to appeal to students, because the developers want the learning to be as positive as possible.

Additional information is available from AIMS Education Foundation, PO Box 7766, Fresno, CA 93747.

Science for Life and Living: Integrating Science, Technology, and Health

Developer: Biological Science Curriculum Study (BSCS). (This is a nonprofit educational research and development organization affiliated with The Colorado College.) 830 North Tejon Street, Colorado Springs, CO 80903. *Phone:* (719) 578-1136.

The goal of the project is to have students learn about science, technology, and health, because they need to understand and use them in making informed choices in their daily lives and as future citizens.

The program has some of the following features:

1. Science, technology, and health are introduced at each level of the program with one major concept and one major skill integrating those disciplines to help students make meaningful connections between the three study areas.

2. Cooperative learning is built into each lesson to promote student learning and help teachers with classroom management.

3. An instructional model that frames the learning experiences is based on constructivist learning theory with these five *Es:*

a. **E**ngage the learner with an event or question.
b. **E**xplore the concept, skill, or behavior through hands-on activities for students to acquire a common set of experiences.
c. **E**xplain the concept, skill, or behavior and define terms.
d. **E**laborate the concept, skill, or behavior by applying what has been learned in unique situations.
e. **E**valuate students' understanding of the concept and their intention to use the skills or behaviors.

4. Major concepts and skills that connect the hands-on activities in science, technology, and health include the following:

Level	Major Concept	Major Skills
1	Order	Organization
2	Change	Measurement
3	Patterns	Prediction
4	Systems	Analysis
5	Energy	Investigation
6	Balance	Decisions

5. Active learning encourages students to actively participate physically and mentally and share responsibility for their learning and improvement in problem solving, critical thinking, decision making, and taking actions.

6. Kits of hands-on materials not readily available in classroom or students' homes are part of the program.

7. An implementation guide assists teachers and other school personnel to use the project successfully.

Science for Life and Living: Integrating Science, Technology, and Health is commercially available from Kendall/Hunt Publishing Company, 2460 Kerper Blvd., PO Box 539, Dubuque, Iowa 52004-0539. *Phone:* 1-800-258-5622.

Insights: A Hands-On Elementary Science Curriculum Improving Urban Elementary Science (IUES) Project

Developer: Educational Development Center, (Nonprofit research and development organization), 55 Chapel Street, Newton, MA 02160. *Phone:* (617) 969-7100. Over 60 projects are currently in progress.

The goal of the IUES Project is to develop a new inquiry-based science program consisting of 17 thematic modules that can be used together as a complete curriculum or as individual modules in conjunction with existing programs. The five major organizing themes for these modules are systems, change, structure and function, diversity, cause and effect, and energy. IUES science modules are organized around a teaching/learning framework that guides teaching through four phases: getting started, exploring and discovering, processing for learning, and extending ideas.

Hands-on, open-ended activities and the urban environment are the focus of this project to interest and motivate children living in the city. To accomplish this, playground equipment, materials from construction sites, and children themselves are the backdrop for science concept construction. To keep the quality of these activities relevant to urban students, schools in the following eight major urban areas are development sites with teachers continually providing EDC with feedback: Baltimore, Boston, Cleveland, Los Angeles, Montgomery County, San Francisco, Yonkers, and New York City. An extensive field test of the curriculum is being conducted by the Boston Center for the Study of Testing, Evaluation, and Educational Policy.

EDC is seeking a new publisher for IUES.

Improving Urban Middle School Science: A Collaborative Approach Project (IUMSS)

IUMSS, a new project developed by EDC for the middle school science curriculum, targets the needs of all early adolescents while specifically addressing urban students. The curriculum and materials packages are being co-developed by a coalition of EDC science curriculum specialists and teams of innovative middle school teachers from urban areas such as Boston; Cleveland; Haverhill, Massachusetts; Los Angeles; Montgomery County, Maryland; and Providence, Rhode Island. The same thorough field testing and evaluation will be conducted as was done for (IUES).

The National Science Foundation (NSF) funded the project, which builds on IUES's conceptual framework and pedagogical strategies, and school district partnerships, and is the grades 7 and 8 extension of IUES's K through 6 curriculum. The IUMSS Project will produce the following materials:

■ Eight STS thematic problem-solving science modules for grades 7 and 8 with a multi-science perspective integrating the physical, human and health, life, and earth sciences. A hands-on, inquiry approach will be used to develop scientific thinking and process skills.

- Module-specific software packages and a technological tools package for gathering, analyzing, and graphically displaying data.
- Full assessment strategies (diagnostic, prescriptive, and performance).
- Staff development package—approaches, activities, resources, and management plans.
- Guidelines and suggestions for program adopters to introduce and implement the program.
- Printed matter—Teacher's Guide, Student Journal, Student Data Recording Book (record and analyze activities and data), and a book of Student Resource Readings.

IUMSS will be commercially available once a publisher is selected.

Lawrence Hall of Science Projects

Developer: Lawrence Hall of Science, University of California, Berkeley, CA 94720. *Phone:* (510) 642-8941.

The Lawrence Hall of Science has been a prodigious developer of funded science projects since the 1960's original SCIS project. Here are only a few of the many on-going projects.

Chemicals, Health, Environment, and Me (CHEM).

This societal, issue-oriented science project uses experience-based activities. Ten units were developed by CEPUP at the Lawrence Hall of Science to help fifth and sixth graders understand the nature of chemicals and how they interact with the environment and affect their own lives.

Each unit comes with a CHEM Teacher's Guide, and a materials kit accompanies the project. CHEM and the National Science Teachers Association are part of a national cooperative effort to implement the program through a training program. If you are interested, contact CHEM at the Lawrence Hall of Science.

Full Option Science System (FOSS).

FOSS is an upper elementary science program (grades 3 through 6). It is a collection of 16 modules (four to each grade) of thought-provoking, easy-to-use, hands-on activities in life science, physical science, earth science, and scientific reasoning. The FOSS activities use multisensory materials and methods to meet the needs of all students, including regular and special education.

FOSS grew out of two earlier Lawrence Hall of Science projects that later combined into one project called Science Activities for the Visually Impaired (SAVI)/Science Enrichment for Learners With Physical Handicaps (SELPH) or SAVI/SELPH. Nine of the FOSS modules are from the SAVI/SELPH project. Several optical laboratory equipment kits accompany the modules. A Teacher's Guide explains how to implement FOSS and integrate it with textbooks and other science programs.

To receive further information, contact the Center for Multisensory Learning at the Lawrence Hall of Science or FOSS's commercial publisher, Encyclopedia Britannica Educational Corp., Chicago, IL. *Phone:* (800) 554-9862.

Great Explorations in Math and Science (GEMS).

GEMS is a publication series from the Lawrence Hall of Science that makes available some of their best activities in a teacher's guide format.

After nationwide field testing with hundreds of teachers, units were developed for both novice and experienced teachers of science and mathematics. GEMS units are available for prekindergarten through 10th grade. All of the activities are geared for high student interest, use the hands-on approach to science and math, present important concepts, and stress cooperative learning and critical thinking skills. Only inexpensive and readily available materials are required to conduct the activities.

Outdoor Biology Instructional Strategies (OBIS). OBIS is *not* a science curriculum, but is a series of outdoor "instructional strategies" that offer young people fun and educational opportunities to investigate ecological relationships in their local environments. The instructional strategies include games, simulations, craft activities, experiments, role-playing, data collection, and analysis.

These activities are designed for children 10 to 15 years old, but may be modified for older or younger people. The activities may be presented by nonprofessional groups (e.g., scouts and 4-H) or teachers as a supplement to classroom, outdoor education, and environmental education. The theme of OBIS revolves around ecosystems.

Each of the 97 individual OBIS activities is on a heavy laminated 8½″ × 11″ card and contains all of the information needed to conduct it with children: science and other teaching background information for the leader, simple or homemade materials needed, required preparation, a lesson guide, and several suggestions for followup. The activities in the OBIS Modules may be done independently, in a sequence, or as a lead-in to or culmination of other activities. Most activities take less than an hour, but many are open-ended. The commercial distributor of OBIS is Delta Education, Inc., PO Box 915, Hudson, NH 03051-0915. *Phone:* 1-800-258-1302.

Science and Technology for Children (STC)

Developer: National Science Resources Center (NSRC), Smithsonian Institution, Arts & Industries Building, Washington, DC 20560. *Phone:* (202) 357-2555.

Science and Technology for Children (STC) is one of the projects of the National Science Resources Center (NSRC), which was established by the Smithsonian Institution and the National Academy of Sciences to improve the teaching of science in the nation's schools. To accomplish this, NSRC maintains a collection and database of teaching resources, disseminates information about effective science teaching resources, develops science curriculum materials, and sponsors outreach activities to help school districts improve their science programs.

STC is a four-year elementary science curriculum for grades 1 through 6 and is based on the principle that students learn best by *doing* science. NSRC's goal is to assist as many schools as possible to offer hands-on science programs to all students, with special concern for interesting more minority and female students in science.

Twenty-four STC units (four for each grade level) are being developed by NSRC in cooperation with school districts throughout the country. The units are topics in physical science, life science, earth science, and technology and are field-tested in inner city, suburban, and rural classrooms, and reviewed by prominent scientists and educators. STC units are built around four central themes that correlate the teaching of science with developing students' skills in mathematics, language arts, and social studies. Each unit contains a teacher's guide with 16 lessons (8 weeks of instruction), 30 reusable student activity books, and a classroom kit of inexpensive, easily maintained materials.

The *commercial distributor* for STC units is Carolina Biological Supply Company, 2700 York Road, Burlington, NC 27215. *Phone:* (919) 584-0381.

/// APPLICATIONS OF FUNDED SCIENCE PROJECTS FOR YOUR SCIENCE CLASSROOM

You may be asking, "All of this research, innovation, and experimentation is great, but what does it have to do with me? I'm only a classroom teacher, not a science education researcher." It has a lot to do with *any* elementary school teacher who must include science in the curriculum.

More educational ideas and materials are being produced today than ever before. What used to take 30 years to accomplish—from the development of a new educational idea to actual classroom implementation—now occurs very rapidly. Because of the rapid pace of current scientific and technological advances, we must all be more involved in professional growth activities through self-improvement and pre-service and in-service training than ever before in our professional history.

Teacher education courses must present the new programs in science education to all prospective teachers. If this is done *before* teachers enter the profession, it is less expensive and more effective than "retraining" teachers through in-service education. Those responsible for pre-service science education courses must be committed to including factual materials about and hands-on activities for the most recent science education projects.

Elementary school teachers (and administrators) currently in service will have to study these projects in depth before committing themselves to any specific *total* program or the incorporation of *parts* of innovative science programs into their existing science curriculum or textbook program. How can this be done?

Reaching Out for Information About Innovative Science Projects

If you will use parts or all of innovative science projects in your classroom, you must first become knowledgeable about what projects are out there. Here are some ways to accomplish that.

Build a Science Innovative Projects Resources File. Build these files in your school with assistance from the school or community librarian. To begin, you *must* get and read these excellent resources cover-to-cover:

■ *Science for Children: Resources for Teachers,* 1988. This guide (developed by the National Science Resources Center) lists hundreds of recommended materials and resources for teaching science to children. It includes information on curriculum materials, science activity and teaching books, children's and teacher magazines, past and present elementary science projects, professional organizations and associations, science publishers, and materials suppliers. The publisher is National Academy Press, 2101 Constitution Ave, NW, Washington, DC 20418.

■ *Science Education Programs That Work: A Collection of Proven Exemplary Educational Programs and Practices in the National Diffusion Network,* October 1990. This inexpensive ($1.75), short (24 pages) booklet is produced by the National Diffusion Network (NDN), a federally funded system that makes exemplary educational programs available for adoption by schools. NDN provides dissemination funds to exemplary programs, called Developer Demonstrator Projects or Dissemination Process Projects. These are very valuable for you because NDN helps local schools *(at little or no cost)* improve their science teaching by (a) providing teacher in-service training, (b) in-school follow-up assistance, and (c) arranging a regional sharing network of adopters of similar projects.

Besides giving data on 15 innovative science programs available for you now, this booklet lists State and Private School Facilitators for every state who can arrange for your school to start improving your science teaching. State facilitators are supported by NDN grants so there is no cost to you for their services. For more information contact your State Facilitator or U.S. Department of Education, Recognition Division, 555 New Jersey Avenue, NW, Washington, DC 20208-5645. *Phone:* (202) 219-2134.

Discovery: Modular Approach to Teaching Science (MATS)

How do you ensure that your students are learning science in an active, involved way? Here's how one school system engages students in science activities without using textbooks.

Strategy Avoid overreliance on textbooks by circulating boxes that contain materials and supplies for process-oriented, age appropriate, hands-on science activities.

Concerned that science teachers were relying too heavily on textbooks, the Springfield City Schools looked around for a better technique. Springfield liked what it saw going on in Schaumberg, Illinois, and in Mesa, Arizona: experimental science programs without textbooks where teachers and peers helped children construct their own knowledge of science. The Springfield schools, like their pioneering counterparts, are determined to give their 7,000 students a science education appropriate to the complex world they will face in the twenty-first century.

Four science units circulate to all the city's K through 5 grades each year—in boxes. Each box contains everything necessary for the science module, including materials and supplies for each student to employ hands-on. Because there is no textbook, instructional materials do not rely on a child's reading level. Instructional goals are based on process skills appropriate to the grade level, and the units are developed accordingly.

Science Supervisor Marcia Jones sees results when the Springfield students take field trips that include children from other school districts. The Springfield students, she says, "are the first to answer questions about what's going on and can tell other students about what they've all done" following group activities or demonstrations because "they know from doing it themselves."

On Your Own The boxed units can be developed at inservice workshops or as part of an university-sponsored independent study project in summer school. Individual parents or parent groups can provide money or materials to stretch limited school funds. A teacher packet could be developed to accompany each box that would suggest ways to integrate the science unit with other subjects. Jones also suggests that networking is an important link for teachers. Sharing ideas helps reduce anxiety about trying new approaches and helps teachers break away from the tendency to teach the same way they were taught.

Source: This feature was prepared with the assistance of Marcia A. Jones, Curriculum Supervisor, Springfield City Schools, Springfield, OH.

Send for *Science Education Programs That Work* PIP 90-846 from the U.S. Government Printing Office, Superintendent of Documents, Washington, DC 20402-9329.

Request that Local Colleges Teach About Innovative Science Projects. If you are teaching, take a course in innovative science programs for the elementary schools. If one is not currently offered by your local college, request that one be given. The course you take should involve a hands-on approach that has you doing the science activities in the same way children will experience them; merely talking about the projects is not enough.

Send for Additional Information. A group of teachers in your school or school district could send for information about science projects from the sources listed in this chapter. List the things you want to investigate, among which might be the following questions:

1. How do the units cover the elements of science/technology and learning espoused by your school or school district?
2. Are there many varied activities for students to obtain information, attitudes, and so on?
3. How are the concepts appropriate for the interests and abilities of your particular students?
4. In what ways do the concepts challenge the students?
5. How does the project provide for systematic development of concepts, skills, and attitudes?
6. How do the teacher's guides provide you with sufficient science and pedagogical information for you to guide the students to discover the goals of the program?

Contact the Distributor of the Program. The distributor will usually arrange for a consultant to speak to you about your interests and concerns about the program without any com-

mitment. Prepare a list of questions for him or her ahead of time. The same can be done with many state education departments eager to improve science in the local schools.

Contact the Distributor Again When Your School or School District Chooses a Specific Program. The distributor will usually set up a series of free in-service workshops for all the teachers using the program. Consultants giving workshops are often former classroom teachers or college professors especially trained in the new science project.

Try the Materials Yourself. Become familiar with the materials, science concepts, and teaching strategies during the workshops. Try the activities yourself! When you feel comfortable with the activities, you can then be a good guide for your students.

Make Certain You Have All the Materials Needed. New science programs depend on materials, student record sheets, and assessment sheets where appropriate. Be sure the program offers the materials you will need.

Share Your Success and Failures. Communicate with your fellow teachers and the consultant or distributor about which programs are effective and which are not. Constant self-evaluation and sharing of ideas will help you achieve the goals of the project.

If you become involved in teaching any of the new science programs you will be part of a new and exciting venture. You have a new role in developing the science curriculum. Part of this role is being the *only* member of the educational team (professional scientist, child psychologist, curriculum writer, classroom teacher, and so on) setting up a new science program who knows a great deal about the actual teaching relationships with your students. In addition, you are on the "firing line" of testing the value of any new science program *with students.*

Many of the decisions on new science programs will eventually rest with you. Therefore, you must be well informed about the current science projects and texts, so you can help select, carry out, and evaluate innovation in science education in the elementary and middle schools. The unique contribution and potential power of elementary and middle school teach-ers are summarized by this statement of Hubert H. Humphrey, former school teacher and vice-president of the United States:

What you really need is a little teaching power. Who knows better what ought to go in a classroom? Who knows better about the kind of teaching tools that work? Who knows better about young people than those who work with them and live with them? Who knows better what the purposes of education are than a trained teacher?

SUMMARY

The past 100 years have seen radical changes in elementary school science programs, reflecting the century's unprecedented social, economic, scientific, and technological transformations. Each change in science programs was born out of the needs and interests of its time. Programs of the 1950s to the 1980s showed intense interest in science as both processes and products using the discovery approach and conceptual schemes.

The 1990s added these aspects to science education as a result of our changing world and greater knowledge of how students learn: Science/Technology/Society approach, problem solving of STS real-life situations, encouraging student actions, studying in depth fewer thematic science topics, and using cooperative learning groups in science.

Experimentation, innovation, and reform in elementary school science were accelerated by massive grants of money from federal, state, and local governments, as well as private foundations such as the Ford Foundation and the National Science Foundation. These funded science projects share common elements such as a trend toward open-ended methods of discovery rather than one method of problem solving, and they view knowledge as part of a creative process of finding out, rather than the mere accumulation of information.

This chapter summarized some of the highlights of a few recent science projects. Innovative science projects have had and continue to provide a substantial impact on many aspects of science in the elementary schools. Science textbooks reflect the discovery activity orientation of these projects. Teachers in those districts that have adopted new science programs must become familiar with them, and this chapter suggests how to do this. You are the key to whether the new science programs succeed or fail.

A key trend in science for the 1990s is the wider use of teaching activities for all students, especially the mainstreaming of special needs students, inner city students, and students with diverse cultural backgrounds. Chapter 9 will investigate methods and resources for helping these students to learn science/technology concepts and skills and use them in their lives.

SELF-ASSESSMENT AND FURTHER STUDY

1. Select an innovative science project (AIMS, FOSS, IUESS, OBIS, or STC) and contrast it either to a local or state school science curriculum or a major science textbook series approach. How are they different? Similar? Which do you prefer? Why?
2. Imagine that you have been asked by your principal or supervisor to pick one of the new elementary school science programs to use in teaching your students. React to these items.
   a. What criteria would you use to pick one?
   b. How would you collect data to make your choice?
   c. Which innovative science project would you pick? Why?
   d. How would you evaluate your teaching?
3. Which of the science projects fits most easily into schools with a "conventional" science program? Why? With open classroom science? Why?
4. Pick any innovative science project and give examples of how it attempts or does not attempt to present these trends in science education:
   a. Humanistic approach relating concepts to students' lives
   b. Environmental and ecological orientation
   c. Values and social aspects of science
   d. Integration of other subject areas with science
   e. Individualization of teaching strategies
   f. Science/Technology/Society approach
   g. Cooperative learning groups
   h. Fewer, thematic science topics
   i. Problem solving of real-life situations leading to action
5. Select a unit from any science project that fits into what you are currently teaching in science and integrate it into your teaching. If not currently teaching your own class, prepare to teach such a unit to a group of students.

NOTES

1. James A. Shymansky, "What Research Says . . . About ESS, SCIS, and SAPA," *Science and Children,* 26, no. 7 (April 1989):33–34.

2. Thomas Richardson, "SCIS, ESS and SAPA—18-Year Sales History Preliminary," *Proceedings of the National Science Foundation Stony Brook Conference on Elementary School Science Education, SUNY at Stony Brook* (Stony Brook, NY: State University of New York, 1985), 33.

3. Harold Pratt, et al., "Science Education in the Elementary School," in Norris C. Harms and Robert E. Yager, eds. *What Research Says to the Science Teacher, Vol. 3,* (Washington, DC: National Science Teachers Association, 1981), 84.

Theme studies are successful with all children because they help them become responsible, independent learners who cooperate with classmates at the same time that they become self-disciplined. One of the most important outcomes is that students gain self-confidence and self-esteem as they become successful and motivated to learn and apply what they are learning.[1]

CHAPTER 8

Integrating Science Across the Curriculum

In what ways can you integrate science with other subjects?

You have more pressures on you today as a teacher than ever before. More things are being added to the curriculum with too little time to do them all. There is a movement to "back-to-the-basics" and a diminished emphasis on science teaching in elementary schools by both the public and the funding agencies.

Because of these pressures, you must be efficient and judicious in planning your limited class time to "fit science in" and still help your students develop skills in all the other self-contained classroom subjects. One excellent way to do this is to integrate science with other subjects around a central STS theme.

/// INTEGRATION OF SCIENCE AND OTHER SUBJECTS AROUND STS THEMES

Research shows that when science is integrated with other subjects, especially around a central STS theme, both science and the other subjects are learned more effectively.[2] Also, the integration of science with other disciplines (e.g., language arts, social sciences, fine arts, and mathematics) has potential for improving both the quantity and quality of science instruction and learning.[3]

Weave Science and Other Subjects Around a Central STS Theme

As discussed in previous chapters, integration of science and other subjects is best achieved by clustering all subjects around a central STS theme. To review, the benefits of this are that students

understand and remember better when they listen, talk, read, write, and "do" to explore what they are learning,
get their language learning reinforced, and
learn best by active involvement, collaborative projects, and interaction with classmates, teachers, and their world.[4]

Therefore, as you select a science area for your students to investigate, select an STS

All subjects can be taught around science-technology-society themes.

theme-centered study and plan for other subjects to be woven into your unit. To help you do this, Figure 8–1 shows how a middle grade teacher integrated learning science and other subject matter areas in a unit study of insects.[5] All of the activities extend students' learning about insects, while giving a rich exposure to and direct experiences with a wide variety of subject matter and skills for the broad range of learning levels and styles of your students. You can easily use this model in your own classroom.

To help you integrate science with other subjects in your STS thematic units, let's investigate each subject with its potential for integration.

/// HOW ARE MINDS-ON/HANDS-ON SCIENCE AND READING SIMILAR?

Reading and minds-on/hands-on science emphasize the same intellectual skills, and both are concerned with thinking processes:

Other skills appear to be "built in" for use in the discovery process being stressed by most new science materials. The scientific experiences are designed so that the student will be asked to define problems, locate information, organize information into graphic form, evaluate findings, and draw conclusions. . . . It becomes obvious that this type of science curriculum demands a myriad of skills concomitant with those of a well-developed reading program.[6]

In the context of this quotation, you are currently teaching reading in your science program whether or not you realize it. For instance, when you help your students develop scientific processes, you are also helping them develop reading processes.[7]

Table 8–1 gives you examples of problem-solving skills in science and the corresponding reading skills. Notice the correspondences. For instance, when you are working on "observing" in science, students are also learning to discriminate shapes, sounds, syllables, and accents for reading. The skills of predicting, classifying, and interpreting are essential to logical thinking and to forming the basic skills for learning to read and decode.

Both science and reading are concerned with processes and content. Content can be thought of as subject matter. The reading/

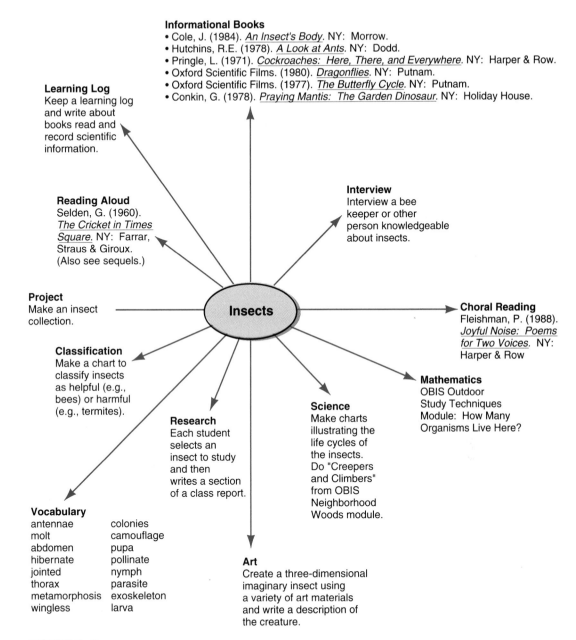

Informational Books
- Cole, J. (1984). *An Insect's Body*. NY: Morrow.
- Hutchins, R.E. (1978). *A Look at Ants*. NY: Dodd.
- Pringle, L. (1971). *Cockroaches: Here, There, and Everywhere*. NY: Harper & Row.
- Oxford Scientific Films. (1980). *Dragonflies*. NY: Putnam.
- Oxford Scientific Films. (1977). *The Butterfly Cycle*. NY: Putnam.
- Conkin, G. (1978). *Praying Mantis: The Garden Dinosaur*. NY: Holiday House.

Learning Log
Keep a learning log and write about books read and record scientific information.

Reading Aloud
Selden, G. (1960). *The Cricket in Times Square*. NY: Farrar, Straus & Giroux. (Also see sequels.)

Interview
Interview a bee keeper or other person knowledgeable about insects.

Project
Make an insect collection.

Insects

Choral Reading
Fleishman, P. (1988). *Joyful Noise: Poems for Two Voices*. NY: Harper & Row

Classification
Make a chart to classify insects as helpful (e.g., bees) or harmful (e.g., termites).

Mathematics
OBIS Outdoor Study Techniques Module: How Many Organisms Live Here?

Research
Each student selects an insect to study and then writes a section of a class report.

Science
Make charts illustrating the life cycles of the insects. Do "Creepers and Climbers" from OBIS Neighborhood Woods module.

Vocabulary
antennae
molt
abdomen
hibernate
jointed
thorax
metamorphosis
wingless

colonies
camouflage
pupa
pollinate
nymph
parasite
exoskeleton
larva

Art
Create a three-dimensional imaginary insect using a variety of art materials and write a description of the creature.

FIGURE 8–1

Thematic cluster of subject matter on insects

Source: Modified from Gail E. Tompkins and Kenneth Hoskisson, *Language Arts: Content and Teaching Strategies,* 2nd ed. (New York: Macmillan Publishing Co., 1991), 545. Used by permission.

TABLE 8–1

Skills important to both minds-on/hands-on science and reading

Source: Glenda S. Carter and Ronald D. Simpson, "Science and Reading: A Basic Duo." Reprinted with permission by *The Science Teacher,* 45, no. 3 (March 1978): 20. Copyright 1978 by The National Science Teachers Association, 1742 Connecticut Avenue, N.W., Washington, DC 20009.

Examples of Problem-Solving Skills in Science	Corresponding Reading Skills
Observing	Discriminating shapes Discriminating sounds Discriminating syllables and accents
Identifying	Recognizing letters Recognizing words Recognizing common prefixes Recognizing common suffixes Recognizing common base words Naming objects, events, and people
Describing	Isolating important characteristics Enumerating characteristics Using appropriate terminology Using synonyms
Classifying	Comparing characteristics Contrasting characteristics Ordering, sequencing Arranging ideas Considering multiple factors
Designing investigations	Asking questions Looking for potential relationships Following organized procedures Reviewing prior studies Developing outlines
Collecting data	Taking notes Surveying reference materials Using several parts of a book Recording data in an orderly fashion Developing precision and accuracy
Interpreting data	Recognizing cause and effect relationships Organizing facts Summarizing new information Varying rate of reading Inductive and deductive thinking
Communicating results	Using graphic aids Logically arranging information Sequencing ideas Knowledge of technical vocabulary Illuminating significant factors Describing with clarity
Formulating conclusions	Generalizing Analyzing critically Evaluating information Recognizing main ideas and concepts Establishing relationships Applying information to other situations

scientific process relationship has been described as the accumulation of details, concepts, and generalizations of a particular curriculum. Process consists of the reading and scientific skills necessary to acquire and apply content. This is very consistent with constructivist learning theory.

Remember, your students started to talk before they could read. They first had to be able to recognize relationships between sounds and symbols. They used processes to distinguish between vowels and consonants, learning the sounds of letters, letter blends, and syllables. Then they began to build a reserve of frequently used "sight words," (prior knowledge) words not easily sounded out (for example, *mustache*). Once students master basic vocabulary, they are exposed to many comprehension skills: reading for the main idea, following directions, and solving problems. Again, you can see the parallel between reading and science skills.

Does Your Science Teaching Teach Reading?

Evidence suggests that early experience with science helps students with language and logic development regardless of their socioeconomic status. Several studies found that young children's experiences with natural phenomena in active science programs improved reading readiness and reading skills.[8]

/// A NATURAL COMBINATION— SCIENCE AND READING

What are the things you can do *today* in your science program that will enhance your students' reading abilities and at the same time enrich your science teaching? What can you do to wed your science program and your reading program? What are you currently doing with reading in your science program that should be enlarged and expanded?

Using Printed Science Materials with Nonreaders

One of the best techniques for working with nonreaders is to read *to* them. Investigations of the effects of reading aloud to students regularly showed significant increases in vocabulary growth, knowledge of word meanings, visual decoding, motor decoding, and reading comprehension achievement. Two important elements in improving reading performance are the regularity of reading to children and the length of time the reading aloud is done. It was found that *daily* reading aloud was the most effective frequency and 10 minutes per session was the most effective length. Younger children may benefit more from being read to than older children. Reading aloud to young children also affects their reading interests. After being read to, young children are more eager to read for themselves the books that had been read aloud to them. Librarians found science was the second most popular category of books. The first was fiction, some of which were in science fields or science fiction.

Reading aloud to your students need not be limited to younger children. Reading aloud to children who are in the lowest range of reading achievement in any grade produces reading growth. When fourth graders heard taped readings of stories, those at the lower extremes of reading achievement showed the greatest growth in comprehension and total reading scores.

Many companies (e.g., Listening Library) produce audiocassettes packaged with print books. This helps today's "bred on television" generation, who have not developed "inner-picture-making skills", use the books together with the audiocassette to visualize stories in their own mind. Many children's TV shows (e.g., Sesame Street) read to children while simultaneously showing them the printed book.[9]

We all can find times in our discovery science programs when it would be useful and appropriate to read aloud to our students. Which times are best for you in your discovery science program? How can you interject more reading aloud in your science activities?

Give your students many opportunities to listen to how science sounds. Besides providing students with experience using another sense (hearing), giving them the chance to listen also helps them see that words in books are merely spoken words put down in written form. This in turn helps children begin to see a relationship between spoken and written language.

"Inventing" New Words for Students' Concepts

Words are the **verbal labels** you must choose to focus your students' attention clearly and explicitly on the conceptual ideas they have been investigating. In your discovery science program, you have supplied multisensory, minds-on/hands-on activities for your students. After they have experienced exploratory manipulative activities, you "invent" words and terms for what they have been doing. Constructivists say teachers "invent" words to assist learners to construct and understand scientific concepts and principles. To do so, follow these guidelines:

1. Group your students near you so they can all see anything you demonstrate, can

Listening and reading simultaneously stimulate deeper sensory learning.

hear your questions, and are able to communicate with each other.

2. Carefully plan and interestingly introduce an activity the students have done themselves before this lesson.

3. During the activity, introduce the label (word) for the concept you want to develop. For instance, if you show a large magnet lifting a toy truck you could say: "When the magnet lifts the truck, we can say it is evidence of interaction (new "invented" word) between the magnet and the truck." Write the word *interaction* on the chalkboard at this point. (This gives visual as well as oral introduction of the new word to students.) This repeats an activity your students have already done, but adds a new word for the concept. (See Figure 8–2.)

4. Now perform a new activity using interaction. For instance, pour vinegar over baking soda and ask, "What do we call what is happening to the vinegar and baking soda?" (The bubbles are *evidence of interaction*.)

5. Ask your students about the similarities and differences in the two demonstrations. You are trying to stress that something happens between the objects—magnet and truck, vinegar and soda.

6. Ask your students to focus on the changes in both demonstrations and show them how we interpret this evidence of interaction between objects.

7. To reinforce and to see which students understand the concept of evidence of interaction, ask, "Give us an example where you have seen evidence of interaction between objects."

8. Focus the students' attention on examples given to clarify objects and evidences of interaction.

9. As a followup, have students cut pictures out of magazines at home of evidences of interaction.

10. The next day make a bulletin board of evidences of interaction from students' magazine pictures using the words *evidence of interaction* often as reinforcement, as shown in Figure 8–3.

FIGURE 8–2

"Inventing" the word *interaction*

FIGURE 8–3
Evidences of interaction bulletin board

Using Operational Definitions to Invent Science Words

Science educators also use the term **operational definition** to describe the inventing of science words growing out of your students' activities. Operational definitions use *actions* to describe what is happening, such as evidences of interaction. Note, however, as Piaget suggested, that the invention of terms must come after the learners have actually handled various materials. Otherwise you will be teaching by rote. Numerous follow-up activities are then needed to reinforce the concept presented with a variety of new situations containing the same concept, that is, evidence of interaction in the environment.

Science Dictionaries

As students are exposed to sensory experiences and the subsequent inventing by you of words and terms for science concepts, you can help them make and keep up-to-date **science dictionaries.** As a science topic is investigated and new terms are introduced, a "class science dictionary" can be displayed in your science center or on a corner of the bulletin board. Using large primer paper, you can keep a running list of science words and their meanings for the area studied. For younger children, include a picture instead of (or in addition to) the definition, as in Figure 8–4.

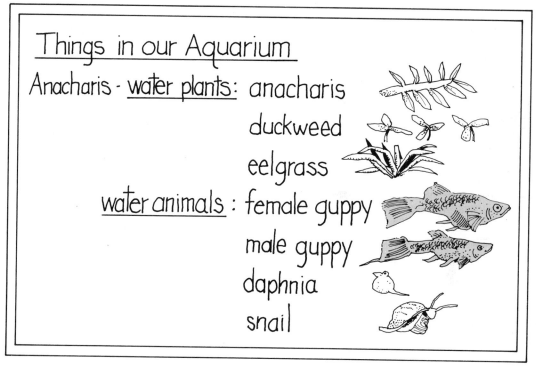

Things in our Aquarium
Anacharis · <u>water plants</u>: anacharis
                              duckweed
                              eelgrass
        <u>water animals</u> : female guppy
                              male guppy
                              daphnia
                              snail

FIGURE 8–4
Science dictionary with pictures

Try to interest older students in looking up and researching the origins of interesting words. You can "invent" the term *etymology*—the origin and development of words. You can also read to students about interesting words such as *sandwich* and, in this case, tell how the word was named for a gambler (the Earl of Sandwich) too busy to leave his gaming table to eat his roast.

To become familiar with the etymology of words, see Wilfred John Funk's *Word Origins and Their Romantic Stories* for general words. For scientific word origins and development, see one of Isaac Asimov's specialized dictionaries, such as *Words of Science and the History Behind Them.* Have your students keep a "science words etymology dictionary" and have them share it with each other and other classes.

Use Record Keeping to Expand Science Vocabulary

Keeping records is as important to science as breathing is to people. It is through records that we compare and analyze scientific experimentation. Students need to do this, too. Through their own record keeping, your students will expand their scientific vocabulary.

Collecting, recording, and reading their science record books, science logs, and science lab reports (or any other name given by you) give students much practice in learning and constantly using new science words. The first records your students keep may contain a minimum of words but lots of pictures. For example, one record may be an "experience chart" made by the total class or a small group, in which you record on primer chart paper things your students observed and shared with the class after a field trip walk around the park near your school. The experience chart may look like the one shown in Figure 8–5.

Record keeping for older students can include brief descriptions of what they did, in addition to specific evidences of the number of objects they observed and counted. At first, you may want to use a group activity such as the experience chart. As your students learn how to give brief descriptions of what they did in groups, they are ready to start their own individual record keeping. You can make a page such as the one shown in Figure 8–6, on which your students record their "sink or float experimentation." Another record-keeping experience for your students is the science log (see the discussion in this chapter of science minibooks or logs made by teachers and students).

/// USING TEXTBOOKS IN MINDS-ON/HANDS-ON SCIENCE

Even though your science program is discovery- or process-oriented, do not overlook the po-

tential value of science textbooks, especially if you use them judiciously. Your students can be helped to see reading as a process to enrich their firsthand experimentation. Textbooks are a resource of science's products of reliable and tested facts, concepts, and principles. Instead of "reinventing the wheel" for every step of our investigations about the wonders of the universe, you can use reading as one of science's processes to find and share other people's information and to check our own findings for validity.

Here are some ways you can use your science textbooks to enrich and expand your students' scientific explorations.[10]

Select Appropriate Reading Levels

Using the cloze and Piagetian measures for cognitive levels or other methods, select textbooks that your students can read. Try to get a variety of levels of texts, so you may individualize assignments. When investigating a science topic, list pages in each of the levels where your students can find information about that topic. Allow your students to select the level of their

Our Trip to the Park

Things We Saw	Things We Heard	Things We Smelled
Sally: Branches moving in wind	Birds singing	
Greg: Little bugs crawling		Fresh air
Tom: A bird's nest	An airplane	Flowers
Amy: Yellow flowers in grass	Dog barking	
Jon: Squirrel running	Twigs snapping	Dirt (soil)
Jill: Water drops on grass	Our class laughing	Wet grass

FIGURE 8–5
Experience chart of field trip observations

You have been working with things that sink or float. What did you do to find out which objects sink or float? Draw a picture.

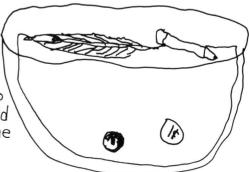

We put objects in the bowl of water. If the object floated, we put it in box with label Float. If it sank, we put it in box Sink. Then we tried all the objects in the Float box to check if they all floated. We did the same with the objects in the Sink box.

What did you find about which objects sink or float? Record your observations on the chart below.

OBJECT	MADE OF	SINK	FLOAT
PENNY	METAL	X	
PENCIL	MOSTLY WOOD		X

FIGURE 8–6
Combination experience chart and review exercise

choice or suggest particular pages to specific students. Most science textbook series have a wide range of reading levels for each science topic from one grade to the next.

Organize Your Class for Science Reading

Group your students in any way that facilitates using books to find information, to check the validity of experimentation, or for any other purpose you intend. Sometimes it is practical to group students homogeneously if you are working on skills and only a small group of your students needs help. At other times you may find that you can use heterogeneous groupings.

1. Form a "buddy system" by pairing students having trouble reading with better readers who are more cognitively advanced.
2. Form groups of four to six students who have varying levels of reading abilities. Let them read and discuss your assignments cooperatively.

Individualize Textbook Assignments

So each of your students will get the maximum benefit from using science textbooks, incorpo-

"Buddy system" reading can benefit both good and poor readers.

rate some of these individualization techniques into your classroom.

1. If you have poor readers or immature or disadvantaged children in your class, reading to them may be useful. By listening to you as they follow their textbook, they hear words at the same time they are learning to decode and thus learn to read independently. To be most effective, try reading to and with your students under the following conditions:
   a. Have students put other work away.
   b. Pick a special "listening place" such as on a rug or the lawn under a tree in warm weather, so your students can sit or lie down.
   c. Read with expression and enthusiasm, so the students can see the relationships between written and spoken language.
   d. Stop occasionally and ask questions. Invite questions, too. Be careful, though, that the kind of questions and their frequency do not detract from the reading, but whet your students' interest.
   e. Stop occasionally and ask the children to read the next portion to themselves to find a particular answer to your question or to prepare to read to the class if they want to.
   f. Ask for a volunteer to read to the class only after the students have had an opportunity to read and prepare first. Avoid asking poor readers to read to a group anything they are seeing for the first time and have not prepared. Sometimes it is valuable to put sections of your textbook on audiocassettes for poor readers to use either with or in place of the text. Commercially prepared cassette and picture science programs for the elementary level, such as those by Coronet Films, are also available. They provide oral reinforcement and assistance and help with word recognition and concept development. Your better readers can get practice with oral reading by making the cassettes for you. Supplement reading assignments for poor readers with other

learning activities such as films, film-strips, tradebooks, and field trips.

2. You can enrich the textbook assignments for your better readers by trying these approaches:

   a. Improve your reading assignments. All your reading assignments should include these three elements: (1) *Content.* Specifically indicate what you expect your students to get from reading the text: finding facts, interpreting, or drawing conclusions. (2) *Motivation.* Relate the assignment to ongoing work and to previous materials; demonstrate its relevance. (3) *Skills.* Indicate how an assignment should be read, such as what type of recall is expected.

   b. Guide your students to learn to locate and organize information from their textbooks. Teach them reading skills and enhance comprehension and retention of science concepts in written materials. Become familiar with techniques for teaching your students reading/study skills in science, such as those listed in Figure 8–7.[11]

/// USING NON-TEXTBOOK SCIENCE READING MATERIALS

You will have many opportunities to use other non-textbook reading materials in your minds-on/hands-on science program to enrich both your science and reading processes and content. Some of the ways include the following:

1. Children's literature.
   a. Tradebooks or informational books.
   b. Science minibooks and logs.
   c. Fiction/science fiction.
2. Student/teacher-made reading materials.
   a. Creative writing.
   b. Data collections (surveys and so on).
   c. Other written communications.

All kinds of literature supply enrichment science learning experiences. Your students' literature and science programs complement each other. You will find excellent resources for using children's literature in your activity-based science in the following science reading materials.

Science Tradebooks or Informational Books

Library books, tradebooks, or **informational books** are books that are *not* basic textbooks. Tradebooks got their name because they are sold through trade outlets such as bookstores. They offer many enrichment opportunities for adding science information to your science program. Usually, tradebooks limit themselves to one topic, such as weather, rocks, or trees.

Used in conjunction with your minds-on/hands-on science program and/or your science textbook series, tradebooks provide these important aspects of learning for your students:

1. Because some students learn best through reading or reinforcement of what they have previously learned, tradebooks help meet the individual learning styles of your students.
2. Students learn to "research" and to cross-check data from many different sources.
3. Students are given opportunities to work independently and at their own pace in reading materials geared to their individual reading levels.
4. Tradebooks give students in-depth information on the subject being investigated.
5. For students who have difficulty with reading, tradebooks can be especially helpful by increasing motivation and involvement.
6. Many recently published books contain information on timely subjects students hear and see on radio or TV or in newspapers.
7. Informational books provide students with opportunities to experience the excitement of new discoveries.

Locating Information in Text
1. Tables of contents
2. Indexes
3. Appendices
4. Glossaries
5. Footnotes
6. Bibliographies
7. Chapter headings
8. Unit titles
9. Keys
10. Cross-references

Using Reference Books
1. Encyclopedia
2. Dictionaries
3. Atlases
4. Almanacs
5. Periodical indexes
6. Library card catalogs

Selecting Information
1. Recognizing main ideas
2. Differentiating between relevant and irrelevant ideas
3. Differentiating between supporting and nonsupporting ideas
4. Noting important details

Organizing Information
1. Note-taking
2. Outlining
3. Summarizing information

Using Graphic Aids
1. Maps
2. Illustrations
3. Graphs
4. Tables
5. Cartoons
6. Charts

Following Directions

Developing Reading Flexibility
1. Scanning for specific information
2. Skimming for general ideas
3. Slow, careful reading and rereading for detailed mastery

FIGURE 8–7
Reading/study skills in science

8. Tradebooks encourage self-reliance, because one enjoyable discovery can motivate students to make further investigations.
9. Critical reading and thinking skills can be developed by students comparing books on the same subject to evaluate objectivity, qualifications, and accuracy of authors.
10. Informational books stretch students' minds by informing them about values, beliefs, and lifestyles of others, as well as introducing them to new words and technical terms.[12]

Ask your school or local librarian to suggest tradebooks for the topics you will investigate. Many outstanding science tradebooks have been published in the last ten years. Book lists and book reviews abound to help you select. Here are a few from an extensive compilation by Robert Karlin, in *Teaching Elementary Reading*, 3rd ed. (New York: Harcourt Brace Jovanovich, Inc., 1980), 429–433.

■ *Appraisal. Children's Science Books.* Children's Science Book Review Committee, Harvard Graduate School of Education, Cambridge, Massachusetts. Issued three times a year.
■ *Bulletin of the Center for Children's Books.* University of Chicago Press, Chicago, Illinois. Issued monthly.
■ *Outstanding Science Tradebooks for Children. Science and Children Magazine* (jointly with Children's Book Council), National Science Teachers Association, 1742 Connecticut Avenue, N.W., Washington, DC 20009. Issued annually in the March issue of *Science and Children*.

■ *Science Books: A Quarterly Review.* American Association for the Advancement of Science, 1776 Massachusetts Ave., N.W., Washington, DC 20036. Issued quarterly.

Here are some considerations that were specifically tailored to help you select effective science informational books. Such books should

1. have accurate facts,
2. eliminate stereotypes,
3. have illustrations that clarify the text,
4. encourage analytical thinking,
5. organize material to help understanding, and
6. stimulate interest by the writing style.[13]

Science Minibooks

Would you like to increase the number of printed science materials available to your students by 25 or even 100? Would you like to make the printed science materials you currently have more attractive to your students? Would you like to recycle old science textbooks ready to be destroyed by your school district or school to enhance your discovery science program? If the answer to any or all of these questions is positive, you should become familiar with the construction and use of "minibooks."

Minibooks are small books that are either commercially made, teacher-made, or student-made. Commercial minibooks are made by assembling as many and as wide a variety of reading-level science books as you can get. The books you pick for making minibooks should be those that can be separated into parts and can be cut up. Using a single-edged razor blade, slit the paper glued near the binding within the front and back covers. (*CAUTION:* You are the only one that should carefully do this, and never students!) Separate each chapter (or part of a chapter) into specific science topics. You or your students can make cardboard or oaktag front and back covers. Staple them together and have the students illustrate the covers with drawings, magazine pictures, or other illustrative materials.

If your original science textbook had 8 units of approximately 50 pages each, you will now have 8 separate books of 50 pages each! A 50-page unit on "Plants and Food for the World" can be further divided into separate minibooks on topics such as kinds of leaves, plants that "eat" animals, how leaves make sugar, and how leaves change color.

Science Minibooks or Logs Made by Teachers and Students. In addition to securing commercially prepared books for reassembly into minibooks, you and your students can make your own minibooks or logs. They can be class collections of student reports, logs, or other written works and are illustrated with students' drawings or instant-type photos; or individuals or small groups of students could make their own minibooks.

To begin, select a size that appeals to you and the students. The size may be dictated by the materials you have available to you, for example, the size of paper (8 ½" × 11") used in most schools. Have the children put in their minibooks things they have studied and found for a particular science topic, a field trip, and so on. These might include experiments or other activities, observational records, drawings, magazine pictures, and handwritten or typed science content.

Have your students add front and back covers, illustrate them, laminate and bind them together or put in a three-ring, loose-leaf binder. They can share their minibooks with each other, and some schools have even set up a special "Our Own Minibook" section in their libraries. This is an excellent opportunity to integrate science with reading, writing, art, mathematics, and other subjects. Figure 8–8 shows how minibook or log covers can be made attractive.[14]

Other Science and Language Activities

There are many opportunities in your activity-based science program to enrich and enlarge

FIGURE 8–8
Attractive minibooks or science logs

your students' science and communication skills through written and oral activities, such as creative writing, science fiction writing, data-collection activities, and teacher/pupil communication.

Creative Writing and Science

Combining science and creative writing can benefit your science program and encourage students' imaginations to soar. One of your goals in science education is to get students to think not only vertically (logically, analytically, precisely), but also laterally and more holistically. **Lateral thinking,** according to Edward deBono of Cambridge University in England, moves sideways from established or ingrained ways of looking at problems to novel and unusual approaches. Lateral thinking is not look-

ing for the best answer, only for a variety of alternatives. From this perspective, you can see that what deBono calls lateral thinking is what we are most familiar with as **creativity.**

Creative writing can stimulate lateral thinking or creative, holistic thinking using science language. Encourage your students to write their own fiction, implementing the science concepts learned in your discovery science program. Combining scientific knowledge with their creative writing allows the students to reinforce concepts and also to develop their creative and critical thinking skills. They also

■ are motivated to check scientific facts,
■ look for additional data if needed,
■ develop research skills,
■ practice science vocabulary in meaningful new situations, and
■ increase their oral and written language skills.

H. Kay Reid and Glenn McGlathery have suggested 33 science creative writing themes that are adjustable to any grade level in an elementary or middle school. Here are three of these science themes:

■ *"Just-So."* (Rudyard Kipling's stories). Explain how the monkey got a long tail or the leopard its spots; any other animal characteristic basic to protection, motion, or eating can be used.
■ *Trash Machine.* Collect pieces of litter and design your machine. How does it work and how does it help us?
■ *Haiku.* Write a poem about nature. The haiku form has three lines. Five syllables are in the first and third lines. Seven syllables are in the second. The following poem is a haiku:

> *Fall brings new colors*
> *Bright orange, yellow, and brown*
> *Marking summer's end*
> *—Laurie McGlathery*[15]

Don't forget to stimulate your students' creative thinking abilities by asking (as suggested in Chapter 4) divergent, thought-provoking questions like these:

Why do you think a particular character behaved in a certain way?
What are some other ways the character could have handled the problem?
What might happen if . . . ?
Suppose you substitute a different animal (or anything with different attributes). How would this alter the situation?

/// SCIENCE AND SOCIAL STUDIES

As discussed in Chapter 1, many decisions concerning societal problems require a basic understanding of science, technology, and society (STS). Therefore, science and social studies are clearly related, and have a mutual, specific mandate: the development of an informed citizenry of scientifically/technologically literate citizens. What then are some ways you can incorporate into your science program the best of science and social studies, without diminishing either the science or the social studies?

Integrating Science and Social Studies

Integrating social studies with science is a "natural" way your students learn. It is the life learning we all usually do that is multidisciplinary, and not the usual elementary school separation of subject areas into reading, social studies, mathematics, and science. Social studies/science integration can also have these advantages to the teacher and learner:

■ Students can use concepts and processes learned in science in other curricular areas, especially the social studies.
■ Other subject areas can be used to reinforce science skills.
■ Both science and social studies are often taught through a problem-solving approach.
■ Science and social studies share two common categories of learning, namely concepts and processes.

Process skills for science were elaborated on in previous chapters and include classifying, formulating hypotheses, generalizing, identifying variables, inferring, interpreting data, making decisions, measuring, observing, predicting, and recording data. Social studies process skills include problem solving, communicating, map and globe reading and interpretation, time and chronology usage, data evaluation, and chart/graph/table interpretation. In reviewing the social studies process skills, notice the similarities to the science process skills. So, you can find common ground for science and social studies where science and technology affect human concerns and issues. Where this happens, you can identify central societal themes for your science studies.

Build Science Around Societal/Technological Themes. As discussed earlier in this chapter, another technique for integrating science skills and processes with social studies involves planning your science around societal/technological themes instead of narrow or specific isolated science topics. Some of these STS themes might be the following:

- Energy and its interrelationships to everyday applications, such as heating/cooling, transportation, sources (for instance, oil and its geopolitical ramifications), alternative sources (solar, wind, and geothermal).
- Industrial production and its adverse effects on communities (air, water, and noise pollution).
- Physical environmental influences on the settlement and development of cities.
- Weather/climate influences on people, their histories, and agriculture.

Here are some ways that STS theme studies can be conducted together to enhance students' learning of both:

- In studying heat and heat transmittal, students could investigate how their school is heated, insulated, and cooled by having the custodian show them the heating/cooling systems and trace the movement of heat in the building.
- Children's bicycles, roller skates, and other toys could be examined when you are studying machines, gears, and mechanical advantage, and it all can be tied to manufacturing.
- Radio, television, and electronic games could be used to study light and sound in communication.
- As students study plants or animals, you might introduce them to population concepts and the problems associated with over-population.
- In a science unit on weather and climate, you might help children see the interrelationship between geographical areas and how pollution in one area could cause acid rain or other pollutants to fall on people thousands of miles away.
- Insect studies lend themselves to exploring ways of avoiding or ridding urban areas of rodents, roaches, and other disease-carrying animals.

An energy STS theme relates science to everyday life.

FIGURE 8–9
Puppets used to stimu-
late creative science
thinking

/// SCIENCE AND ART EXPERIENCES

Many suggestions for using art in science are scattered throughout this book in bulletin boards, use of visual aids and projected objects, posters, and drawings. Here are some ways to get students involved with aesthetic or artistic appreciation and skills through integration with science.

■ While studying light, cover the ends of flashlights with different colored cellophane, using several layers to produce strong colors. Darken the room and have students experiment with various colors.

■ In discussions about the properties of matter, give each student several different kinds of textured papers, such as sandpaper, watercolor paper, or oatmeal paper. Have students draw or scribble on papers with crayons to discover the different textures.

■ Mobiles are excellent ways to show graphically such things as the solar system or weather elements.

■ Puppets of all kinds (paperbag, hand, or tennis ball) allow children to engage in artistic and fantasy extensions of science (see Figure 8–9).

■ Making objects with clay or other malleable substances permits children to produce three-dimensional representations of mental images.

■ Working with wood and tools (saws, hammers, drills, or screwdrivers) shows students how people use knowledge of machines to make work easier.

/// SCIENCE AND PHYSICAL ACTIVITIES

Often, it is difficult to approach theoretical concepts with elementary or middle school students, especially those in the primary grades. We have difficulty helping these students see the how and why of physical occurrences; activities like games, dances, and role-playing can help us explain physical occurrences. Story-dances about familiar physical phenomena, in which students role-play invisible entities, have these advantages for science learning:

1. Dances that tell a story have an ancient and universal appeal that helps to motivate students.
2. Students involved in physical activity are not as easily bored as those listening passively.
3. Sufficient roles are required so that the whole class can have a part. Nobody has to sit and watch; handicapped students can also participate.
4. Each dance is short, usually less than five minutes. Time is available for two or three repetitions with a chance for trading roles.
5. No stage equipment is required—only a roll of masking tape or some chalk to outline objects on the floor.[16]

Dances that help children "see" invisible particles are possible in such areas as matter,

FIGURE 8–10

Physical activity involving molecule concepts

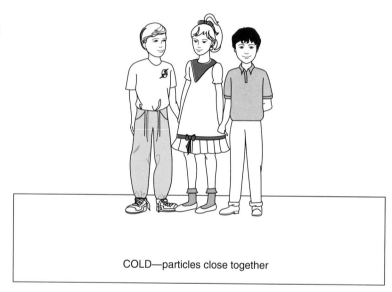

COLD—particles close together

HOT—particles further apart

energy, and motion in melting ice, boiling water, electricity, atoms, and subatomic particles. By acting as the microscopic particles, children can act out such concepts as molecules slowing down or speeding up or the movement of electrons. They can visualize what happens in expansion and contraction of metals due to heat or cold by moving closer together or farther apart as metal molecules, as shown in Figure 8–10.

Help students to conceptualize invisible particle theories by using more physical movement. However, in relating physical activities to science, consider the appropriateness of the cognitive level. For example, the concept of particles and their relationships seems to be too abstract for preoperational or early concrete operational students.

/// SCIENCE AND MUSIC

Investigating vibrating bodies presents opportunities to show that science and music are interrelated. Your students can make simple musical instruments from drinking straws, rubber bands, and soda bottles. Then, these science concepts can be used to observe how "real" musical instruments work. Have the students discover how the length and thickness of piano strings determine the pitch (high or low) of the

sounds produced. Ask your students or band members from upper grades to bring to class and share the musical instruments they play. Encourage them to

- demonstrate how the musical instrument works,
- classify the instruments on how the sound is produced (You may have to introduce *sustained* vibration through continuous excitation and *damped* vibration through single excitation), and
- point out the *excitor* (what causes the vibration).

Then the students could complete a table such as the one shown in Table 8–2. Your students can be helped to see that *plucked* instruments produce damped vibrations, while *bowed* and *wind* instruments produce sustained vibrations. As students demonstrate their musical instruments, your class will be fascinated by the roles valves, air column lengths, strings, and reeds play in producing sound.

Use folk music and popular songs as often as they fit naturally into your science studies. Many popular musical groups sing about people, the environment, pollution, and other societal issues. Many music videos of groups may also appeal to students on environmental issues. Analyze the lyrics and see how they relate to science, technology, and society. Do the

TABLE 8–2

Characteristics of vibrations from five instruments

Instrument	Type of Vibration	How Vibration Is Initiated	Excitor
Guitar	Damped	Plucking	Finger or pick
Violin	Sustained	Bowing	Bow
Clarinet	Sustained	Blowing	Wind
Flute	Sustained	Blowing	Wind
Piano	Damped	Striking	Hammer

Source: Kenneth D. Willems, Arnold L. Willems, and William B. Stacy, "Physical and Musical Vibrating Systems: Basic Concepts." Reprinted with permission by *Science and Children*, 18, no. 4 (January 1981): 11. Copyright 1981 by The National Science Teachers Association, 1742 Connecticut Avenue, N.W., Washington, DC 20009.

Take advantage of students' natural interest in music to teach and reinforce science concepts.

same with folk songs, and you will see that the words of "Home on the Range," for instance, can be used as you discuss variables of weather changes. Contrast this to "Dakota Land," about drought in the West, and discuss with your students the different effects of weather on people.

Encourage older students to bring records or audiotapes and videotapes to class for the science topics you investigate, such as whales (recordings of their sounds), birds, or insects. In addition to helping students learn science concepts, music offers students emotional experiences that are not limited to the cerebral or intellectual levels only. Truly, music is an international and cross-cultural experience. Use more of it in your science classroom, and you and your students will enjoy learning a great deal.[17]

/// SCIENCE, HEALTH, PHYSIOLOGY, AND NUTRITION

Your elementary or middle school students are very interested in their bodies, as well as other aspects of their health, including food and nutrition, height and weight, disease, body parts

and systems, and genetics. In the past, elementary and middle grade teachers lectured, scolded, scared, and preached about science and health to their students. They used to put long lists on the board of *don'ts,* such as the following:

1. Don't drink coffee.
2. Don't eat sugar.
3. Don't use drugs.
4. Don't drink alcohol.

Although these statements do have some positive effects on health, this teaching approach has not succeeded in improving children's health.

Teaching Science/Health/Nutrition Positively to Make an Impact

The content of science/health/nutrition should include topics that interest children. However, your most important concern should be to teach science/health/nutrition concepts in such ways that they *positively* affect your students' health and health habits. To do this, educators agree that science/health/nutrition should be taught by involving students with science processes and teaching them to think and use decision-making skills applicable to their own health. Your teaching should focus on students' developing responsibility for their own health through discovery activities. They can learn how their bodies function, what they can do, and how they can improve or change the way their bodies perform. Two programs can give you specifics on how to do this. See Chapter 7 of this text for information about Science for Life and Living: Integrating Science, Technology, and Health from the Biological Sciences Curriculum Study (BSCS), and Health Activities Project (HAP).

Here are some science/health/nutrition activities that can involve your students in activities that use science processes to make health a "get-up-and-find-out-about-yourself" subject. Students can use a minds-on/hands-on approach to these activities:

- Count and record pulse rates before and after exercise.
- Compare reaction times to sight, sound, and touch stimuli.
- Formulate and test hypotheses concerning factors that affect lung volume.
- Predict, measure, and record external body temperatures at various locations on their bodies.
- Design investigations to observe the effects of exercise regimens on muscular strength.
- Simulate nutritional choices and predict effects on their bodies.
- Design experiments to test peripheral vision.
- Collect and analyze data on local and regional sources of environmental pollution.[18]

Teaching science/health/nutrition in a minds-on/hands-on activity-oriented way can make it interesting, relevant, and more likely to be absorbed into students' lifestyles. Positive attitudes and health habits grow out of relating science/health/nutrition to students' everyday lives. Try it, and it may even impact positively on *your* health habits.

/// SCIENCE AND MATHEMATICS

Science and mathematics are so integrally related that many elementary and middle school science activities have a number of mathematical implications. Let's investigate some now.

Science/Mathematics Develop Cognitive Skills

Piagetian or constructivist operations are required for learners to achieve well in the basic skills and content, and this is especially so in science and mathematics. Some of the operations basic to these disciplines are

- conservation of substance,
- conservation of length,
- conservation of number,
- one-to-one correspondence,
- ordering,
- seriating, and
- classifying.

Students who do not do these operations well, and this includes many children aged 7 to 8, have trouble reading and solving mathematical and scientific problems. They are still **prelogical** (unable to do logic) and **prenumerical** (unable to do things with numbers) in their development. Science and mathematical curricula that involve students in the operational tasks just described help them overcome such inadequacies. Thus, many science and mathematical curricula include Piagetian and constructivist activities.

Research on Science Projects and Mathematical Learnings. Science and mathematical curricula (particularly in the primary grades) have some necessary duplication, because students on the preoperational level need many similar operational experiences, such as conservation, to develop their cognitive abilities. Curricula, therefore, include Piagetian and constructivist activities in developing operational competencies. These competencies are not only fundamental to science and mathematics but to all subjects that require thinking. For example, Donald Strafford and John Renner found that the Science Curriculum Improvement Study (SCIS) caused significant gains in conservation of length, number, and other abilities in the first grade.[19]

Science/Mathematics and Problem Solving. Research has also shown that science can be useful to enlarge how you teach students to solve problems. Instead of using contrived or made-up problems, research shows that real-world science/mathematical problems can enrich and expand the problem-solving skills of your students.[20]

Because of such research studies, Mary Budd Rowe concluded that science is especially important because it helps students develop not only mental operations but also a greater willingness to solve problems. This willingness to solve problems is critical for children learning both science and mathematics. Rowe, furthermore, showed this was especially important for disadvantaged children. "Without science experiences, disadvantaged children tend to be frightened and frustrated by simple problems. Their problem-coping skills simply do not develop satisfactorily. With it, they usually learn strategies for attacking problems."[21]

Elementary science teachers who integrate science and mathematics agree that the primary value of this integration lies in helping their students solve real-life problems. The carry-over of these problem-solving skills to your students' everyday lives is high.[22]

Science/Mathematics and the Metric System (SI)

Although the movement to adopt the metric system in our country seems to have its momentum, the country is becoming more metric.

The metric system, now termed the International System of Measurement (SI), is used by all other English-speaking countries in the world. It is used exclusively in all scientific work. The pressure to change to SI has already affected machine tools, packaging (especially liquor), and temperature. Competition with the rest of the world may continue to accelerate the use of SI in business, science, and government. Students in school will have to know both systems during this transition period. You will have to teach both. The Metric Information Office of the National Bureau of Standards has published a paper to help individuals compare the two systems. (See Figure 8–11.)

Making Conversions to Metric Measures. The metric system is convenient because conversion factors within the system are powers of ten. For example, in measuring and adding the length of objects together, the metric system is often easier to use than the English system. It is easier to add 4.5 cm and 2.4 cm than to add 1 ¾ and 1 ⅛ inches. Also, because the metric system has smaller units (millimeters), it is easier to measure exactly.

With the national concern about changing to the SI system, many states are insisting that greater attention be given to using metric measures. Many science curriculum projects and texts use only metric units.

Teachers often think the SI system is difficult; they are familiar with the English system and have problems converting from it to the metric form. However, students do not have difficulty learning the metric measures. Since they do not yet have good concepts of the English system, the SI system seems as easy to learn as the English system. You should *not* stress converting from the metric to the English system. When a student measures something 2.54 cm long, accept that as a description of its length. Do not ask how many inches long it is. Students' concepts of a unit of length will be just as good without knowing the equivalent in the English system.

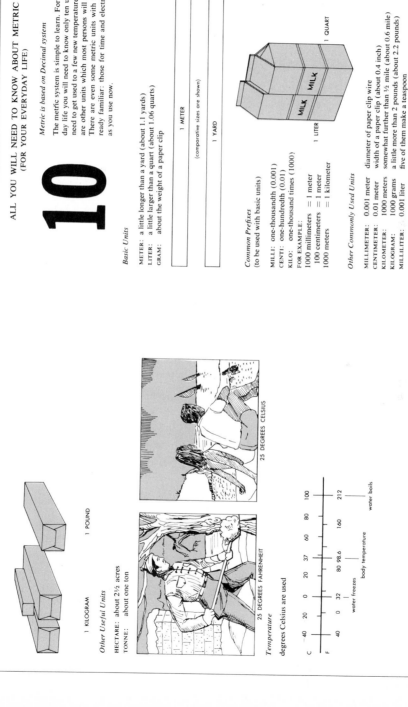

ALL YOU WILL NEED TO KNOW ABOUT METRIC
(FOR YOUR EVERYDAY LIFE)

10

Metric is based on Decimal system

The metric system is simple to learn. For use in your everyday life you will need to know only ten units. You will also need to get used to a few new temperatures. Of course, there are other units which most persons will not need to learn. There are even some metric units with which you are already familiar: those for time and electricity are the same as you use now.

Basic Units

METER: a little longer than a yard (about 1.1 yards)
LITER: a little larger than a quart (about 1.06 quarts)
GRAM: about the weight of a paper clip

1 METER

(comparative sizes are shown)

1 YARD

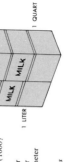

1 LITER   1 QUART

Common Prefixes
(to be used with basic units)

MILLI: one-thousandth (0.001)
CENTI: one-hundredth (0.01)
KILO: one-thousand times (1000)
FOR EXAMPLE:
1000 millimeters = 1 meter
100 centimeters = 1 meter
1000 meters = 1 kilometer

Other Commonly Used Units

MILLIMETER: 0.001 meter — diameter of paper clip wire
CENTIMETER: 0.01 meter — width of a paper clip (about 0.4 inch)
KILOMETER: 1000 meters — somewhat further than ½ mile (about 0.6 mile)
KILOGRAM: 1000 grams — a little more than 2 pounds (about 2.2 pounds)
MILLILITER: 0.001 liter — five of them make a teaspoon

1 KILOGRAM   1 POUND

Other Useful Units

HECTARE: about 2½ acres
TONNE: about one ton

Temperature

degrees Celsius are used

25 DEGREES FAHRENHEIT   25 DEGREES CELSIUS

C -40 -20   0   20 37   60   80 100
F -40   0   32 80 98.6 160   212
       water freezes body temperature water boils

FIGURE 8–11

Comparing measurement systems

Source: From the Metric Information Office of the National Bureau of Standards.

Discovery: Young Experimental Scientist (Y.E.S.)

If your school can't afford field trips, perhaps a parent group can send a smaller group of students to a state-sponsored internship program. The students can return to school as resources and they can lead their own science team.

Strategy   Utilize programs available through state or national organizations.

At Ohio's Center of Science and Industry (COSI), the Young Experimental Scientist is a unique program designed for elementary and middle school teachers to have meaningful, sharing experiences with their students. Teachers throughout the state bring students with them to the Center for a one-day conference in which they participate in hands-on science learning. A typical "team" is composed of one teacher and five students, although larger delegations can be accommodated. The teams participate in two workshops, aimed at stimulating enthusiasm "for applying thinking skills and fostering discovery learning." Topics for the 1991 Y.E.S. program included genetics, optical illusions, topology, and whales.

An important facet of the Y.E.S. program is that it gives teachers an opportunity to collaborate with their students in science discovery activities. The workshops include materials for "hands-on, make-it-and-take-it" activities.

In addition to the kit materials, this program also offers teachers these resources: ideas for obtaining materials, ideas for integrating science activities into other subject areas, innovative ways to implement hands-on activities in the classroom, motivation to try new things, and a new appreciation of the processes of learning and discovery.

One of the most important aspects of the program is that it trains the student participants, who can go back to their schools as team leaders for their classmates.

On Your Own   If you don't have access to a program such as Y.E.S., you could create your own. You might consider group tutorials after school or on Saturday. Then have the students who participate go back to their own classrooms to peer teach.

Teachers in elementary schools that are in close proximity to a high school might work out a program with the high school teachers to have elementary students visit chemistry, biology, and physics classes. The younger students can then go back to their classes to show their peers what the "big kids" do in science class.

Source: This feature was prepared with the help of Marge Ball, Ohio's Center of Science and Industry, Columbus, OH.

Using Graphs and Tables in Science/Mathematics

Graphs and tables are vital in your science/mathematics teaching. When you teach students how to make and interpret graphs and tables, they benefit by learning to use mathematical data collected in finding answers to their science problem solving and by communicating their ideas by

1. putting data obtained from their science observations into a form that other people can understand and
2. understanding their own data when they reexamine it. Students also benefit from using graphs and tables to make predictions from collected data, to see relationships between variables in the science/mathematical activities performed, to hypothesize about possible changes in their obtained data, and to draw conclusions and inferences from data.[23]

The following are some ways to introduce graphs and tables in your science/mathematics teaching.

Histograms or Line Plots. A **histogram,** also called **line plot,** is one of the simplest types of graphs and can be used as an introduction to graphs. You can construct a histogram by having your students place on the graph a gummed, colored dot that corresponds to or stands for the color of leaves collected in autumn, for example. For a line plot, an X may be used to represent each leaf. The left side, or **vertical axis,** shows the number of leaves. The bottom line, or **horizontal axis,** shows the leaf color (see Figure 8–12). Students put their gummed color dots at the appropriate color and stack them above each other at the appropriate number. For instance, in Figure 8–12, there were four orange, six red, three yellow, and two purple leaves collected.

Histograms or line plots introduce students to graphing and using symbols (gummed colored dots or an X) to represent the actual item (leaf) and show a pictorial, color, or symbolic representation of the data collected. It also helps students classify data. Then you can help them think about and discuss data differences.[24]

Variations of histograms or line plots will be referred to in the literature as **picture graphs, pictographs, pictograms,** or **pictorial graphs.** Pictures are also used with respect to labeled axes, which is most advantageous for younger children or for introducing graphs to some older students.

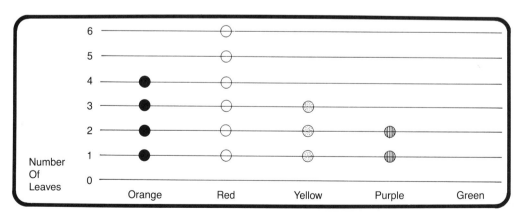

FIGURE 8–12
Histogram of fall leaves

Bar Graphs. **Bar graphs** (also referred to as **bar charts**) vividly show differences in data collected. Either horizontal or vertical bar graphs can be used. These are relatively easy to understand and can be introduced to children in grades K through 12 because the graphs can be nonnumerical. Data presented in picture graphs easily lend themselves to bar graphs. Converting a picture graph to a bar graph is a logical progression for students to move from semiconcrete representations of data to a more abstract form.

In using bar graphs for recording and analyzing plant growth, for instance, your students could cut strips of paper to use for measuring the height of the plant. Strips collected each day can be organized in a bar graph in this manner, each strip representing one day's growth with a number under it representing each day.[25] After five days of strip collecting, help your students develop prediction skills by guiding them and asking, "How tall do you think your plant will be in two days? Mark your strip (or your bar graph) to represent your prediction. In two days, we will compare your prediction strip with your measurement strip to see how accurate your prediction is."

A good extension of this activity would be for all of your students to record their own growth and to predict how tall they will be next year.

Line-Segment Graphs. **Line-segment graphs** (also called **broken-line graphs**) are more advanced than bar graphs, and children in grades 3 to 6 could learn to make and interpret them. In line-segment graphs, your students graphically show numerical data that tend to be continuous or fluctuate.

Two perpendicular lines, the horizontal and the vertical axes, serve as the reference lines. If students were line graphing plant growth as in Figure 8–13, the vertical axis is *Plant Height* (in millimeters), and the horizontal axis is *Days After Planting*. Directions for students would be, "Each day measure your plant from the soil to the top. Place an X on the graph to show the height each day."

You will have to show the students on the chalkboard how to put an X where the vertical and horizontal axes intersect, as well as how to connect points with lines. After a few days of measuring and posting on the line graph, have students predict where they think their plant height will be after 10 or 15 days by placing a red X at the point where the 10 or 15 days line intersects.

Frances Curcio has aptly summarized why elementary and middle school teachers must include graphing in their science teaching:

Elementary school children should be actively involved in collecting "real-world" data to construct their own simple graphs. They should be encouraged to verbalize the relationships and patterns observed among the collected data (e.g., larger than, twice as big as, continuously increasing). In this way, the application of mathematics to the real world might enhance students' concept development and build and expand the relevant mathematics schemata they need to comprehend the implicit mathematical relationships expressed in graphs.[26]

For additional ideas on graphing and science/mathematics (including other graphing techniques such as **circle graphs, line plots, stem-and-leaf plots,** and **box-plots**), see Antonia Stone, "When Is a Graph Worth Ten Thousand Words?" *Hands-On!* (TERC, 1969

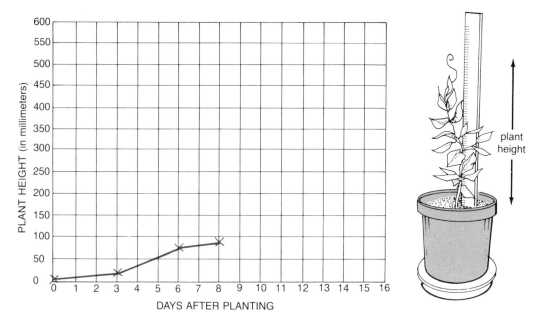

FIGURE 8–13
Line graph of plant growth

Massachusetts Ave., Cambridge, MA 02138, Spring 1988): 16–18; Susan Jo Russell, "Who Found the Most Shells? (Who Cares?)" *Elementary Mathematician,* (1988): 4, 9; Kristine L. Eng, "Real Graphs, Real Fun, Real Learning," *Learning,* 88, no. 17 (October 1988): 58–62; and Susan Jo Russell and Susan N. Friel, "Collecting and Analyzing Real Data in the Elementary School Classroom," in Paul R. Trafton, ed., *New Directions for Elementary School Mathematics, 1989 Yearbook of the National Council of Teachers of Mathematics* (Reston, VA: The Council, 1989), 134–148.

Examples of Science/ Mathematics Integration

Many opportunities exist in your science teaching for integrating mathematics. Here are a few:[27]

■ *Mathematics through science experiences.* Students explore the variable of water needed for seed germination: how much wa-

ter is needed? Quantitative evidence requires mathematics. Students plant seeds, decide on various amounts of water needed, and measure water each time plants are watered.

■ *Mathematics with science to show relationships.* Students measure their height and arm span to see if there are any relationships.

■ *Mathematics with science in interpolation.* Here are data that students collect in weighing a hamster 7 and 14 days after its birth: 7th day, 10 grams; 14th day, 20 grams. Students are asked to interpolate the point at which the hamster weighed 15 grams. Line or bar graphs could be introduced also. Usually hamsters come in multiple births, so students will need help in calculating average weight gain.

■ *Mathematics with science in extrapolation.* While investigating effects of plant hormone on pea seed growth, students dip some seeds in water and some in hormone solution. Every 24 hours for 5 days they measure seed growth and plot points on a graph to show growth. After examining the data, students are asked to extrapolate (go beyond) and predict the plant heights on the 7th day.

- *Mathematics with science in problem solving.* Students investigate a variety of materials to see which are better insulators. The problem-solving processes (the same ones in mathematics and science) introduced could be (a) the kind of investigation selected, (b) procedural steps, (c) measurement tools, (d) data recording, or (e) conclusions reached.
- *Mathematics with scientific objectivity.* In investigating reaction times of first, second, and third graders, children researchers discover that they need a "language" to communicate what they are doing. They use exact numbers instead of *some* or *group* for the number of children tested, and reaction times. Exact data allow the children to duplicate their tests to check their accuracy.
- *Mathematics with science and the metric system.* Students measure temperature each morning in Celsius and place data on a large class graph.

There are many more opportunities for you to integrate mathematics into your science program; the possibilities are limited only by your imagination.

SUMMARY

Students' learning in both science and other subjects is enhanced when science is properly integrated around STS themes in an unforced and natural way.

Minds-on/hands-on activity science programs expand and enrich the language development of students. Reading and activity science require the same intellectual skills. Through active involvement with physical objects, students learn the cognitive processes (such as class inclusion, conservation, and ordering) required to improve reading in science better than they learn them through reading alone. One of the best techniques is for you to frequently read to nonreaders to encourage the development of reading skills and positive attitudes toward reading.

Specific techniques for developing vocabulary for science reading have been presented, such as the teacher "inventing" new science words for students, using science dictionaries, keeping records of science investigations and data, effectively using science textbooks, and making and using science experience charts.

Techniques were explored for effectively using other non-textbook reading in your science program such as children's literature (tradebooks, minibooks, science logs), creative writing, and other written data collection.

Practical activities were also given for integrating science with social studies around science/technology/society themes, physical activities, music, and health.

Mathematics and science have been integrally related and have contributed to each other's advancements through the ages. Because mathematics and science are wedded in the investigation of natural phenomena, many of the educational objectives of these two disciplines overlap. When scientists collect data, they often do so in quantitative ways. Mathematics aids the scientist in collecting objective data, revealing relationships, suggesting problem-solving techniques, and replicating experiments. As a scientist works, mathematics and science are often both involved in the inquiry process, requiring many mental inductive and deductive operations.

Science curriculum projects and the more recently published elementary science texts have also included more investigations using quantitative approaches. All of these curriculums emphasize the use of the metric (SI) system since scientists use the metric system in their work. Ways to use the metric system were presented.

Using graphs and tables is also vital in the teaching of science. Examples were given of how to construct and use histograms, bar, and line-segment graphs.

This chapter cautions that science is a legitimate subject and should not be diluted or diminished when combined with any other subject matter. If the full impact of your science program cannot be realized by integration, then don't integrate it.

SELF-ASSESSMENT AND FURTHER STUDY

1. If you are using a science textbook as all or part of your science program, select several minds-on/hands-on activities that supplement what is in the text. Plan and introduce these to your students.
2. The selection of tradebooks or informational books must be given considerable thought. Use the following as beginning articles to help you pick some for your class: In *Science and Children,* see "Resource Reviews" and "Outstanding Science Trade Books for Children." (An annotated bibliography is prepared annually in the March edition.)
3. After completing a field trip, help your class write an experience chart of the experience on large primer chart paper. Illustrate it with your or your students' drawings or photos. Use the exact students' words whenever possible.
4. Identify the parts of a book that are necessary if your students are to use informational books. Choose one part (i.e., table of contents, index, glossary, or bibliography of additional readings) and prepare an activity that increases your students' understanding of that part of the book.
5. Select an informational book that encourages students to perform an experiment to understand a scientific principle. Perform the activity and evaluate it with such questions as, "Are the directions clear and appropriate for

the level for which it is intended?'' ''What modifications (if any) would you recommend?'' ''As a result of doing this activity, did you (and will students) better understand the scientific principles involved?''

6. Gather old or discarded science textbooks and tradebooks and help your students make minibooks.

7. Working with a group of students, help them make science logs following a science study.

8. Help your students make a science pictorial dictionary using drawings or magazine photos on large primer chart paper.

9. Develop activities in expository and descriptive writing for your elementary science program using these references:

   ■ Jeffrey Lehman and Jane Harper Yarbrough, ''25 (Scientific) Writing Activities,'' *The Science Teacher*, 50, no. 2 (February 1983): 27–30.

   ■ Shirley Koeller, ''Expository Writing: A Vital Skill in Science,'' *Science and Children*, 20, no. 1 (September 1982): 12–16.

   ■ Marylu Shore Simon and Judith Moss Zimmerman, ''Science and Writing,'' *Science and Children*, 18, no. 3 (November/December 1980): 7–10.

10. Devise art activities that naturally lend themselves to science topics.

11. Plan a dance-play to help students visualize invisible particles in the science theory you are studying.

12. Prepare some metric activities for the grade level you teach. Use examples from this chapter to get ideas.

13. How are Piagetian operations integrated in science and mathematics?

14. Construct with your students a histogram, bar graph, or line-segment graph for one of your science studies.

15. Select a science/technology/society theme for a science study and plan integrating activities using social studies.

16. Have your students bring in their musical instruments and plan to integrate them into your science program.

17. Plan an activity-based health study in your science program.

NOTES

1. Gail E. Tompkins and Kenneth Hoskisson, *Language Arts: Content and Teaching Strategies, 2nd ed.* New York: Macmillan Publishing Co., 1991), 521.

2. R. Gamberg, et al., *Learning and Loving it: Theme Studies in the Classroom* (Portsmouth, NH: Heinemann, 1988) and C. C. Pappas, B. Z. Kiefer, and L. S. Levstik, *An Integrated Language Perspective in the Elementary School: Theory into Action* (New York: Longman, 1990).

3. Thomas R. Koballa, Jr. and Lowell J. Bethel, ''Integration of Science and Other Subjects,'' in David Holdzkom and Pamela B. Lutz, eds., *Research Within Reach: Science Education. A Research-Guided Response to the Concerns of Educators,* (Charleston, WV: Appalachia Educational Laboratory, Inc., 1985).

4. C. Thaiss, *Language Across the Curriculum in the Elementary Grades* (Urbana, IL: ERIC Clearinghouse on Reading and Communication Skills and the National Council of Teachers of English, 1986).

5. The author is indebted to and highly recommends the coverage of themes and integration of subject matter in Tompkins and Hoskisson, *Language Arts: Content and Teaching Strategies.*

6. Stephen B. Lucas and Andrew B. Burlando, "The New Science Methods and Reading," *Language Arts,* 52, (September 1975): 769–770.

7. Kenneth R. Mechling and Donna L. Oliver, *Handbook I: Science Teaches Basic Skills* (Washington, DC: National Science Teachers Association, 1983).

8. For an excellent review of research in science teaching and reading, read Ruth T. Wellman, "Science: A Basic for Language and Reading Development," in Mary Budd Rowe, ed., *What Research Says to the Science Teacher,* vol. 1, (Washington, DC: National Science Teachers Association, 1978), 1–12.

9. For additional information on listening to books see "Audiocassettes for Kids," *EPIEgram,* 16, no. 4 (1989): 4–5.

10. The following sources were used, and you are urged to refer to them for elaboration on the brief introduction offered here: Roach Van Allen, *Language Experiences in Communication* (New York: Houghton Mifflin Co., 1986); James Moffett and Betty Jane Wagner, *Student-Centered Language Arts and Reading, K–13: A Handbook for Teachers,* 3rd ed. (New York: Houghton Mifflin Co., 1986) and K. Goodman, *What's Whole in Whole Language?* (Portsmouth, NH: Heinemann, 1986).

11. Excellent sources for effectively using science textbooks are Marie M. Scruggs, "What Research Says . . . About Textbooks," *Science and Children,* 25, no. 4 (January 1988): 24–25 and Sandra Styer, "Books That Ask the Right Questions," *Science and Children,* 21, no.6 (March 1984): 40–42.

12. To see how to put tradebooks or informational books to work for you, see Donna E. Norton, *Through the Eyes of a Child: An Introduction to Children's Literature,* 3rd Ed. Chapter 12, "Nonfiction: Biographies and Informational Books" (New York: Macmillan Publishing Co., 1991), 607–665; Seymour Simon, "Behold the World! Using Science Tradebooks in the Classroom," *Science and Children,* 19, no.6 (March 1982): 5–7; and Patricia R. Crook and Barbara A. Lehman, "On Track With Trade Books: Try Direct Instruction With Trade Books for Teaching Science Content With Flair," *Science and Children,* 27, no.6 (March 1990): 22–23.

13. National Science Teachers Association, "Outstanding Science Tradebooks for Children in 1985." *Science and Children,* 23, no.6 (March 1986):26.

14. For assistance with making minibooks see Charlotte King, "Making First-Class Books," *Science and Children,* 28, no.3 (November/December 1990): 40–41 and J. Baskwill and P. Whitman, *A Guide to Classroom Publishing* (New York: Scholastic, 1986).

15. H. Kay Reid and Glenn McGlathery, "Science and Creative Writing." Reproduced with permission by *Science and Children,* 14, no.4 (January 1977): 19–20. Copyright 1977 by the National Science Teachers Association, 1742 Connecticut Ave., N.W., Washington, D.C. 20009.

16. For an expanded discussion on the use of physical activity in elementary and middle school science see James H. Humphrey and Joy N. Humphrey, *Developing Elementary School Science Concepts Through Active*

Games (Springfield, IL: Charles C. Thomas Publisher, 1991) and Lloyd D. Remington, "Let's Get Physical in Science," *Science and Children,* 19, no. 7 (April 1982): 13–15.

17. For excellent examples of how to use science and music, you are urged to read Kathleen M. Bayless and Marjorie E. Ramsey, *Music: A Way of Life for the Young Child,* 4th ed. (New York: Macmillan Publishing Co., 1991) and Kenneth Willems, Arnold L. Willems, and William B. Stacy, "Physical and Musical Vibrating Systems: Basic Concepts," *Science and Children,* 18, no. 4 (January 1981): 9–11.

18. For additional information see David J. Anspaugh and Gene Ezell, *Teaching Today's Health,* 3rd ed. (New York: Macmillan Publishing Co., 1990) and Kenneth R. Mechling and Donna L. Oliver, *Handbook I, Science Teaches Basic Skills* (Washington, DC: National Science Teachers Association, 1983).

19. Donald G. Strafford and John W. Renner, "Development of Conservation Reasoning Through Experience" in *Research and Learning with the Piaget Model,* John W. Renner et al. (Norman, OK: University of Oklahoma Press, 1976), 34–55.

20. Howard Goldberg and Philip Wagreich, "Focus on Integrating Science and Math. For a real lesson in science, students should conduct an experiment involving quantitative variables," *Science and Children,* 26, no.5 (February 1989): 22–24; and M. H. Shann, "Evaluation of an Interdisciplinary Problem-Solving Curriculum in Elementary Science and Mathematics," *Science Education,* 61, (1977): 491–502.

21. Mary Budd Rowe, "Help Is Denied to Those in Need," *Science and Children,* (March 1975): 25.

22. D. A. Grouws and W. E. Thomas, "Problem Solving: A Panoramic Approach," *School Science and Mathematics,* 81, (1981): 307–314; National Council of Teachers of Mathematics, *Curriculum and Evaluation Standards for School Mathematics* (Reston, VA: The Council, 1989); and Douglas Cruikshank and Linda Jensen Sheffield, *Teaching Mathematics to Elementary School Children: A Foundation For the Future* (New York: Macmillan Publishing Co., 1988).

23. For outstanding coverage of graphing and its uses in elementary and middle school curricula, especially science and mathematics, you must add this source to your professional library: Frances R. Curcio, *Developing Graph Comprehension: Elementary and Middle School Activities* (Reston, VA: The National Council of Teachers of Mathematics, Inc., 1989).

24. For further elaboration on this technique see James M. Landwehr and Ann E. Watkins, *Exploring Data. Quantitative Literacy Series* (Palo Alto, CA: Dale Seymour Publications, 1986).

25. For a fuller description of this activity, see *Supplement to the Elementary Science Syllabus, Level I (ages 4 through 7)* (Albany, NY: The University of the State of New York, State Education Department, 1986), 65–66.

26. Frances R. Curcio, "Comprehension of Mathematical Relationships Expressed in Graphs," *Journal for Research in Mathematics Education,* 18, no. 5 (November 1987): 382–393.

27. The author acknowledges ideas in Kenneth R. Mechling and Donna L. Oliver, *Handbook I, Science Teaches Basic Skills* (Washington, DC: National Science Teachers Association, 1983), 24–26.

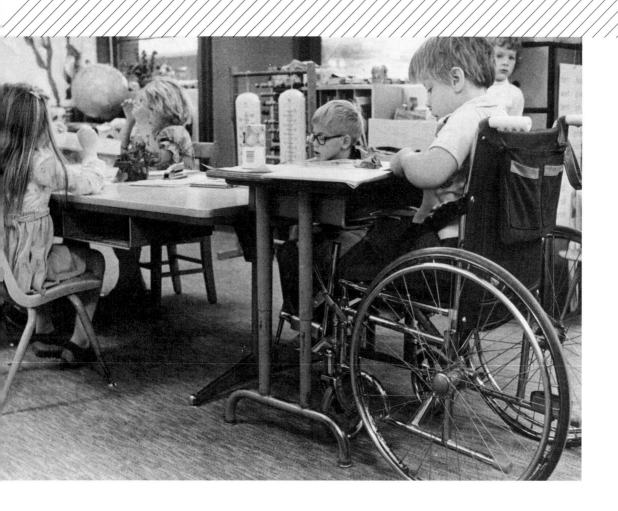

Educators and the public are very much involved in providing all children with an education appropriate to their physical, mental, social, and emotional abilities. In particular, there is a great emphasis on educating children who have needs that other children do not. There are special needs children in every classroom of every school. These children are handicapped, gifted, and children with multicultural heritages. They require teaching strategies and approaches designed to meet their individual special needs.[1]

CHAPTER 9

Reaching Students with Special Needs

How can you provide for a wide range of learning abilities and diverse cultural backgrounds?

This book has tried to show that students are alike and different in many ways. Students' differences are what make them all so unique, and we noticed they vary in

1. the levels of learning operations at which they perform,
2. their learning styles (oral, visual, and kinesthetic), and
3. their readiness to process information in new, cognitive ways.

What implications does this knowledge of students' uniqueness have for how you teach science to your students? For one thing, it shows that you and the students you teach are special individuals. You have unique potential. It is this discovery of your uniqueness that will help you (a) establish your identity as a person, and (b) see your students all as unique individuals. After all, no other person is exactly like you; nor are any two students in your class alike.

Recognizing these phenomena, this chapter emphasizes the need for individualizing your science teaching. This is especially appropriate

as we review George Morrison's opening statement as he observes that *all* students require teaching strategies and approaches designed to meet their individual special needs. In addition, suggestions are given for making you more multiculturally aware so that you may provide science experiences compatible with your students' backgrounds. This will also provide you with ways to promote multicultural understanding in your students. Let's look first at students who have a variety of special needs.

/// SPECIAL NEEDS STUDENTS IN YOUR SCIENCE CLASS

Two federal laws were passed that directly affect to whom, what, and how you teach science in your classroom. They are

1. Public Law (PL) 94-142, The Education for All Handicapped Children's Act of 1975, considers the various classes of handicapped children, and says that all schools must place

students with handicaps or learning disabilities in the "least restrictive environment."

2. The Jacob K. Javits Gifted and Talented Students Education Act of 1988 tries to define "gifted and talented" and attempts to distinguish the differences between the two.

These two laws emphasize that an "appropriate education for *all* children" must be provided within the framework of the public schools. This has resulted in the concept of **mainstreaming** instead of the previous idea of isolating "special children" from their "average peers" because of their "special needs."

The Conference on Science Education for the Handicapped Students conducted by the National Science Teachers Association emphasized the need to increase the "sensitivity to awareness of the unique needs of the physically handicapped students, as well as the needs of students with other special learning needs in science classes, while emphasizing the similarities to nonhandicapped students."[2] In doing so, not only would the education of handicapped students be improved, but the education of *all* students would be greatly enhanced. Educators would recognize that all students do not learn science in the same way. Viewed in that perspective, they would then think of PL 94-142 as "Education for *all* Children" and not "Education for All *Handicapped* Children." This was recently reinforced by the NSTA Position Statement on Laboratory Science for Preschool/Elementary Level with this suggestion:

Children at all developmental levels benefit from science experiences. Appropriate hands-on experiences must be provided for children with special needs who are unable to participate in classroom activities.[3]

How Does Mainstreaming Affect Your Science Teaching?

Students with special needs are often placed in regular public school classrooms on the as-

sumption that the regular classroom is the best place for special needs students to learn. You may have students with wide ranges of needs in your class. Here are some ways you may need to modify your science teaching to mainstream students with special needs into your class.

■ Include special needs students in regular class activities.

■ Set a wide range of competence goals for your class, which can include special needs children.

■ Assess the abilities of *all* your students, including special needs students, and realistically consider how each student's abilities affect his or her capacity to do science.

■ Locate and/or adapt science materials for the particular needs of your students.

■ Secure a broad range of science experiences to meet the needs of all your special children.[4]

What Kinds of Special Students Might Be in Your Classroom?

You may have students in your class who are identified as "special" by federal law. If so, you have unique teaching challenges. Therefore, this chapter emphasizes the need for individualizing your science teaching for all your students. Included in this individualization will be students with these special needs:

1. Physical Difference
   a. Limited or impaired hearing. Deaf, both with and without speech; hard-of-hearing.
   b. Limited or impaired vision. Braille readers; partially sighted readers, using large-print.
   c. Impaired health. Allergies.
   d. Orthopedically impaired. Limited mobility (e.g., wheelchair-bound); limited coordination (e.g., cerebral palsy, causing inability to voluntarily control movement); or seizures (e.g., epilepsy).

2. Social Differences
   a. Behavior disorders. Emotional disturbances or impairments.
   b. Culturally different. Students for whom English is a second language. *Note.* Not considered handicapped under PL 94-142.
3. Intellectual Differences
   a. Mentally retarded, slow learners, learning disabled.
   b. Gifted. *Note.* Not considered handicapped under PL 94-142.

Don't be overwhelmed; humanity's beauty is in the diversity of its skills, abilities, and talents. Your students have the potential for manifesting their talents. The beauty of teaching is the satisfaction you will receive from helping *all* your students develop their talents. Together, let's explore how you can successfully develop your skills to accomplish this.

/// WHAT IS INDIVIDUALIZED SCIENCE TEACHING?

Individualized science teaching is more than methods of teaching. It is a *philosophy* of teaching in which all students' education is matched to their unique needs or special circumstances. All of the uniquenesses described in the first paragraph of this chapter are accommodated in individualized science teaching. You capitalize on the unique manner in which each of your students learns, and modify your teaching to recognize their differences and needs.

The fact is that you probably have more individualization in your classroom right now than you realize. To see where you stand on individualization of instruction, respond to these questions.

1. Do you structure your science teaching/learning on one textbook or activity manual?

2. In your class today, were different students learning through different teaching/learning strategies?
3. Do students in your class work on different topics or activities from the total class?
4. Did your students or you design the activities on which your students work?
5. Do you spend more time with individual students, small groups (fewer than six students), large groups, or the total class?
6. On which of these two did you spend more time today:
   a. checking on materials, making and checking assignments, or grading work?
   b. working with your students on science activities individually, in small groups, or total class?[5]

How you responded to these questions says much about your current efforts at individualization. Here are some ways to expand your uses of individualization in your science classroom.

Six Elements of Individualized Science Teaching

You can immediately use the following six elements of individualization with all your students:

1. Present a wide variety of instructional materials and activities.
2. Select different media for different students.
3. Give your students the option of working on different topics or activities.
4. Have students design their own activities.
5. Increase your interaction with individuals or small groups.
6. Spend more time on working with individuals and small group activities rather than on checking materials, assignments, or grading.

These six elements of individualization can be easily incorporated into your science program. Most elementary science programs and textbooks can be adapted for individualizing. You will find many suggestions in the teachers' guides that accompany your science programs and textbooks. Some curricula, however, have been specifically designed with the purpose of individualization in mind.

If your school system does not have sufficient funds to purchase kits, such as the ESS (Elementary Science Study) units, obtain some of that program's teacher's guides. You can select individual science units or lessons and find the materials locally at little expense. These ESS units have been particularly popular with teachers for use by individuals or small groups:

Tangrams	Drops, Streams,
Mirror Cards	and Containers
Mystery Powders	Behavior of
Bones	Mealworms
Batteries and Bulbs	Tracks
Attribute Games	

See Chapter 7 for the distributor of ESS units and other resources for individualization ideas and materials.

The suggestions that follow offer specific, practical, and either free or very inexpensive ideas for incorporating the six elements of individualization into your science teaching for all your students. Following these suggestions will be additional teaching ideas for individualizing your science teaching for your students with special needs.

Practical Suggestions for Individualizing Your Science Teaching

You can use these suggestions to extend individualization of your science teaching for all your students, regardless of your teaching situation—self-contained classroom, team teaching, departmental, or systems approach. This list

is not exhaustive; alert teachers will adapt and vary these ideas for their unique classrooms, as well as discover and invent new ones. Do not be afraid to try any procedure that you consider will provide broader and richer science experiences for your students. Also, encourage your students to be constantly alert to other things *they* could be doing in science.

Set Up an Enrichment Center for Your Science-Oriented Students. This center will offer optional, free-time recreational science activities similar to the kinds of activities students get in intramural sports, band, art or photography club, and dramatics. Ideally, an entire room will be provided for the enrichment center, but it can function in a corner of a classroom, library, multimedia or audiovisual room, or any other room. See Chapter 6 for practical suggestions on physically setting up such a center.

These enrichment centers can be stocked with challenging ideas and materials for conducting simple and safe self-directed activities. Alan McCormack, while working at the Lawrence Hall of Science at the University of California, prepared materials of that kind to be used in enrichment centers. He suggested that in the enrichment center 100 or more challenges should be available on posters or "challenge cards." Students should be free to choose any one that interests them and try to solve it. Usually they have two options once a challenge is selected.

1. Solve it completely on their own with simple equipment and science supplies in the center, from home, or from the teacher.
2. Request a "solution card" and a corresponding box of materials specifically designed to go with it.

The solution cards have instructions for doing an experiment or using a method to solve the challenge, but, of course, not a specific answer. Divergent questions are used on the so-

Students should take active roles in improving their school environment.

lution cards to stimulate the student's thinking without giving cookbook answers. By having two options presented to the students, they can choose the amount of structure suitable for them at that particular time. Next time it may be a different selection.

To provide the easy-to-be-found-and-used materials that should accompany each challenge card, see Chapter 6 and Appendix L for ideas on shoebox collections of science materials.

Have Students Take an Active Role in Changing Their School Grounds Environment. Some ways they can do this are by

- organizing and participating in a general cleanup of grounds;
- making a survey of needed improvements and possible remedies for playground and school ground problems, such as worn paths where students cut across grass, eroding slopes, "dust-bowl" play areas, and so on;
- taking responsibility for improving one of the problem areas given in the previous item.

They might plant small trees or bushes around the perimeter of the school grounds with money they raise;
- writing letters to agencies for help, such as ecology groups and county agricultural agents; and
- reclaiming eroded areas by planting bushes, trees, or ground cover.

Encourage Students to Conduct a Survey of People and Places in Their Community as Possible Resources for Your Science Program. A file can be made of the kinds of science topics you teach and the places and persons who might contribute in each, like those in Table 9–1.

Encourage Students to Set Up a Rock Garden, Birdhouse, Bird Feeder, Birdbath, or Other Outdoor Projects on the School Grounds. Assist students in collecting information about what is needed and why for setting up, maintaining, and continuing their selected project.

TABLE 9–1

Community resources for science programs

Biological Sciences	Chemistry	Earth Science	Physics
Biology department (local college)	All kinds of factories	Abandoned quarry	Airport
Farm	Chemistry department (local college)	Field	Astronomical observatory
Fish hatchery	Drugstore	Geology department (local college)	Electronics factory
Food processing plant	Electroplating shop	Museum	Gas station
Greenhouse	Oil refinery	Seashore	Physics department (local college)
Hospital	Plastic industry	Stream	Power dam or electricity generator plant
House excavation	Water purification plant	Weather station	Radio station
Park	Chemical engineer	Astronomer	Television station
Pharmaceutical lab	Chemist	Geologist	Telephone exchange
Vacant lot	Druggist	Mining engineer	Newspaper printing plant
Dentist	Photographer	Pilot or navigator	Architect
Druggist		Weather forecaster	Builder
Farmer			Automobile mechanic
Florist			Electrician
Laboratory technician			Electronics engineers
Nurse			
Pet shop owner			
Physician			

Suggest that Students Visit Museums, Planetariums, Observatories, Parks, Botanical Gardens, or Other Out-of-School Places. Parents should be included in the planning by meetings or by notes sent home to them. They could accompany their children and guide their learning if requested or necessary.

Have Volunteer Students Visit the Classrooms of Younger Children to Explain Science Projects. Students might bring in and discuss raising their pets, give slide talks of recent trips, show how their musical instruments work, and so on. Some schools have a cadre of "cadet teachers" of older students to teach younger children.

Accumulate or Make Your Own Science Kits or Teacher's Guide. Encourage individuals or small groups of students to explore and use science kits (such as those from ESS) during "leisure or free time," "science time," or at home, if you think they are mature enough. Refer to Chapter 7 for more information on securing and using ESS and other innovative science program kits. Students can also be encouraged to make their own shoebox collections of science materials with challenge cards to accompany them.

Secure a Copy of Television Program Listings and Teacher's Guides. You or your students can get television listings and teacher's guides from your local commercial and educational television stations or by writing directly to one of the following major national television networks:

- American Broadcasting Company, Inc. (ABC), 1330 Avenue of the Americas, New York, NY 10019.
- Columbia Broadcasting System, Inc. (CBS), 51 East 52nd Street, New York, NY 10019.
- National Broadcasting Company (NBC), RCA Building, 30 Rockefeller Plaza, New York, NY 10020.

Make a list of science shows pertinent to what you are studying under these headings: program, TV channel, local date and time, and science topic covered.

Suggest that your students view programs of interest to them, or you might assign specific ones to them and ask them to report to the class. If you think it is needed or desirable, prepare a worksheet with specific questions to guide your students' viewing.

Set Up Surprise Science Boxes and Encourage Your Students to Work with Them. The surprise science box is an activity that is popular with students, especially with "slow" learners. Periodically you can display a labeled box. On the front of the box you can print a statement of its content in riddle form such as

I am hard.
I can push some things without your
*   seeing me push them.*
I can pull some things without your seeing
*   me pull them.*
I am made of iron and nickel.
What is my name?

One use of the surprise box is to introduce and motivate your students to a new science area of study. Some teachers put a different sur-

prise science box out each day on a table for use by individual students when they complete all their assigned work. It is also very valuable for students to make their own surprise science boxes and share them with their classmates. For excellent suggestions on additional surprise science boxes see Eddie L. Whitfield and Eva D. Samples, "Small Box Science: Independent Learning Exercises for Younger Children," *Science and Children,* 18, no.7 (April 1981): 9.

Your Students Can Pick a Scientific Topic, Collect Science Materials from Magazines and Newspapers, and Set Up a Bulletin Board. By keeping your bulletin board up no longer than one week, you can give all your students an opportunity to participate in making one. This also increases your students' interests in looking at the bulletin boards, because they participated in the planning and construction. The boards also are not up long enough to get "stale."

Have Several Students Form a Panel Discussion on a Science Topic Such as the Problems of Scientific Exploration. Students can organize the panel discussion themselves or you can suggest questions like the following as the focus:

> *What provisions would you need to take*
> *   to the moon? Mars? Antarctica?*
> *   Mohave Desert?*
> *What types of research or studies do you*
> *   think should be carried out when you*
> *   get there?*

If you tape the panel discussion, ask your students to conduct self-assessments of their own contributions and those of their classmates.

Help Students in the Upper Elementary and Middle School Grades Prepare Personal Progress Files or Portfolios. Each of these students should be given a file or portfolio into which she or he places summaries and samples of all types of science activities that she or he has completed. Refer to Chapter 5 for more details on portfolio or file construction.

Contact Your Local Museum to See What Special Science Programs Are Scheduled. Your students might attend these out-of-school programs individually, in small groups, or with their parents. Work cooperatively with your students and the museums to prepare a self-directed guide so your students do not wander aimlessly in the museum. Some museums even prepare an audiotaped presentation that highlights aspects of the exhibit as a person moves from exhibit to exhibit. A letter home to parents may get their cooperation in the project and extend school/home/community ties.

Introduce the Science Discovery Chart to Your Class. The science discovery chart is a bulletin board or chart that has pieces of string going from the board to objects near it. Students print what they think the object is on small cards, along with their names. They pin the cards to the end of the string. After several students have had a chance to pin their cards on the board, the teacher then discusses their answers. A typical chart might show some simple machines: inclined plane, pulley, lever, screw, and wheel and axle. The science discovery chart can be used to introduce or review an area of science.

Secure Many Different Science Tradebooks on a Variety of Reading Levels. Ask students to read a book of their choice and report about it to their peers in any way they want—orally, by a tape recording, with a drawing, in writing, using a video camcorder, and so on. There are many high-interest, low vocabulary science books, so all students (including very young children or those with reading difficulties) can benefit from such books as

- *What Is It? Series* (Chicago: Benefic Press),
- *All About Books* (New York: Random House, Inc.),
- *Webster Classroom Science Series—Let's Read About Series* (St. Louis: Webster Publishing, Co.), and
- *About Book Series* (Chicago: Melmont Publishing Co.).

Help Your Students See the Human Orientation of Science by Providing Them with Many Biographies of Scientists. Select books on as wide a reading level as possible. Several students may work together and put on a play or other dramatic presentation showing particular parts of their scientist's life. Make sure to include biographies of minority group scientists such as women, blacks, Hispanics, and Orientals.

Provide a Table or Bookcase for your Students to Display Their Collections of Rocks, Leaves, Bird Nests, Insects, and Coins. Your students can explain their collections with signs, reports, or an audio- or videotape for classmates to play, listen to, and watch by themselves.

Make Up a Series of Pictorial Riddles. Pictorial riddles are similar to challenge cards, use a picture format, and are usually mounted on 5″ × 8″ index cards or on larger oaktag. Here's how you or your students can make their own pictorial riddles.

1. Select some scientific concept or principle to be learned or discussed.
2. Draw a picture, use an illustration, or use a photograph that shows a scientific concept, process, or situation.
3. An alternative procedure is to present a **discrepant event,** an event that is atypical or unusual, and ask your students to find out what is wrong with it. An example might be

a picture of a big man being held up on a seesaw by a small child. Ask, "How is this possible?" (see Figure 9–1).

4. Devise a series of divergent process-oriented questions related to the picture which will help students gain insights into what principles are involved.

Make Other Activity and Task Cards. You or your students can design activity and task cards such as in Figure 9–2. These can be placed in a learning center or other place where they are available to your students. Encourage them to make as many as possible for their learning experiences and for you to build up a repertoire for your class to use.

Organize a Science/Technology/Society Club. The club can meet before or after school, during free time during the day, or on Saturdays. Perhaps a parent can serve as a guide or adult leader. Students from this club may also function as science cadet teachers or science helpers. Many schools find these students are excellent resources for teachers throughout the school.

Extend the Science/Technology/Society Club with a Weekly or Monthly School Science Newspaper. Students from kindergarten on up love to contribute art, pictorial riddles, brain teasers, book or TV reviews. News of which class has the rock collections, pets, insects, plays, or dioramas can be inserted so all may share the science activities throughout the entire school.

Use Computers and Microcomputers in Your Science Classroom. For practical applications of computers and other electronic

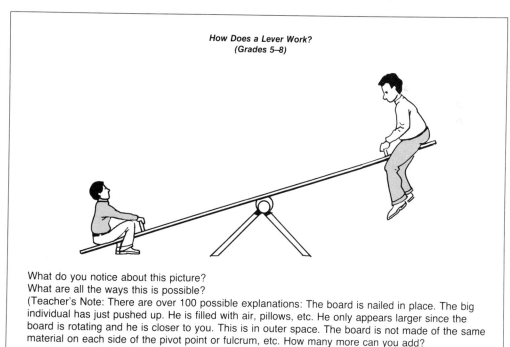

How Does a Lever Work?
(Grades 5–8)

What do you notice about this picture?
What are all the ways this is possible?
(Teacher's Note: There are over 100 possible explanations: The board is nailed in place. The big individual has just pushed up. He is filled with air, pillows, etc. He only appears larger since the board is rotating and he is closer to you. This is in outer space. The board is not made of the same material on each side of the pivot point or fulcrum, etc. How many more can you add?

FIGURE 9–1

Pictorial riddle

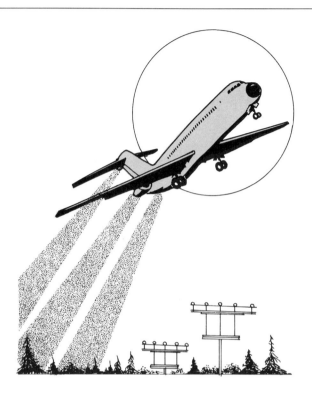

For an Activity Card
Write a short story about what you see happening in this picture. Then share your story with the rest of the class.

For a Test Card
Write a short story about what you see happening in this picture. After you're finished, go back and underline what you *observed* with a *red* pen. Then underline what you *inferred* with a *black* pen. Then share your story with the rest of the class.

FIGURE 9–2
Activity and task card for upper elementary and middle school grades

technology in your science program, see Chapter 10.

/// SCIENCE FOR CHILDREN WITH PHYSICAL DIFFERENCES[6]

The previous teaching ideas can be used by all of your students, but some of them need modification for students with special needs to use them. Also, you will need to modify your physical classroom environment, methods and materials of teaching, concepts, and evaluation for these students. In some cases, you may have to provide alternative activities entirely.

To assist you with general suggestions for your science teaching for all the variety of students with differences (physical, social and intellectual), see Table 9–2. Sandra Cain and Jack Evans developed this chart of adaptations for teaching science to students with physical, social, and intellectual differences using these headings: Disability, Physical Environment, Materials Modification, Methods Modification, Content Modification, and Evaluation. Under each of the three large classifications of differences are specific disabilities, such as visual impairment, learning disabilities, and others.

As you study Table 9–2, you will see ways you can adapt your science teaching to meet the needs of your students with differences. What follows now are elaborations of some of these suggestions which you can use in your classroom relatively easily and with moderate expenses.

Science Experience for Students with Visual Impairments

You will probably have visually impaired students in your classroom at some time. These include "any students who need special aids and/or instruction to read ordinary print as well as the student who must read Braille. This includes both totally blind students and partially sighted students."[7]

Elva R. Gough suggests that it is very important for the visually impaired to be well oriented with the laboratory or classroom activity arrangements and the equipment. When appropriate, students should prepare Braille labels and affix them to the scientific equipment; Braille grades can be affixed to papers and quizzes.

The Lawrence Hall of Science of the University of California at Berkeley produced a program for mainstreaming special needs students—**SAVI/SELPH.** Two separate programs SAVI—which stands for Science Activities for the Visually Impaired, and SELPH—which stands for Science Enrichment for Learners with Physical Handicaps, were combined and reworked into a single program, mostly for upper elementary school and be-

yond, with several of its nine modules adapted for primary grade students.

SAVI/SELPH consists of sets of activity folios, with sections on overview, background, purpose, materials, anticipating (what to do before starting), doing the activity, and followup. Figure 9–3 is an example of how the program developers provided metric measurement activities for visually impaired students. For information about SAVI/SELPH, Adapting Science Materials for the Blind (ASMB), Full Option Science System (FOSS), and other science programs for special needs students, contact the Center for Multisensory Learning, Lawrence Hall of Science, University of California, Berkeley, CA 94720.

To modify your present science program for visually impaired students, try these ideas.

■ Pair a sighted student with a visually impaired student as partners in such science activities as safety in handling equipment, fire, and chemicals; observing chemical changes; and reading thermometers.

■ Use tactile clues when student uses materials, such as different-textured sandpaper on rulers or other measuring devices or knotted string for measuring.

■ Use verbal directions, including recorded instructions, to tell the student what you are doing as you explain the procedures to be used.

■ Expect the student to use his or her remaining sight often, unless directed otherwise.

■ Be patient and encouraging about any spills and broken equipment.

■ Give as wide a range of multisensory, concrete activities as possible.

To find additional science activities for the visually impaired, see the following sources:

■ Gilbert W. Billings, E. Cuphone, and L. Nober, "Lighting Up Science for the Visually Impaired," *The Science Teacher* (March 1980).

■ Susan Kaschner, "Viewing the Earth with Closed Eyes," *Science Activities* (Fall 1978).

TABLE 9–2
Science teaching adaptations for students with differences

Disability	Physical Environment	Materials Modification	Methods Modification	Content Modification	Evaluation
Visual Impairment	Materials kept in predictable place Students seated near activity Sighted guide to aid in giving directions Well-lighted work area	Large-print or Braille reading materials Taped lessons Sighted tutor to read directions or guide movements Training with equipment prior to use Braille writer, slate & stylus, Braille typewriter, or largeprint typewriter	Hands-on activities—use of other senses to observe More verbal description and use of touch Contact with real objects	None	More verbal evaluation, or Braille or large-print materials Aid in writing responses Assistance with manipulation of materials
Hearing Impairment	Students seated near activity so they can hear better and lip-read if necessary Students seated away from distracting noises	Captioned films, film-strips Visual text to accompany tapes Model or repetition of directions	Hands-on experience to develop concept Visual aids to accompany lectures List of new vocabulary before verbal presentation Eye contact before speaking Clear enunciation Contact with real objects Repetition of instructions and verbal presentation as necessary	None	None

Health Impairment	Removal of things that could aggravate health condition (e.g., no sugar for diabetics; no plant pollen for allergic child)	None	None	None	None
Physical Impairment	Adequate space for movement Desk and table height adjusted for wheelchairs Seats near exits whenever possible for safety Barrier-free access	Training with equipment prior to use Peer to help with manipulation of materials Mechanical aids for manipulation of materials as necessary	Contact with real objects	None	Assistance with manipulation of materials Aid in writing responses
Behavior Disorders	Students seated away from distracting noises	Training with equipment prior to use	Motivation Immediate reinforcement Cueing of relevant details Short activities Eye contact and priority seating for discussions Social praise	None	None

TABLE 9–2, *continued*

Disability	Physical Environment	Materials Modification	Methods Modification	Content Modification	Evaluation
Cultural Differences	None	Concrete, relevant materials	Contact with real objects Cooperative learning	None	None
Limited English Proficiency	None	Modified reading material	Cooperative learning Concrete activities	None	Oral tests or modified for language
Gifted	None	More advanced reading material	Less repetition More emphasis on problem solving	More advanced concepts, such as universals & abstractions Emphasis on processes and synthesis & evaluation levels	More emphasis on organization and application of information
Learning Disabilities	Students seated away from distracting noises	Concrete, relevant materials	Immediate feedback Short activities Cueing of relevant details Social praise Pairing of an object and its symbol Eye contact and priority seating for discussion Multisensory activities	None	Oral tests or modified reading level Aid in writing responses Structure and frequent progress checks on projects

Mental Retardation (and slow learners)	Students seated away from distracting noises	Low reading level materials	Social praise	Emphasis on knowledge of specifics	Structure and frequent progress checks on projects
		Training with equipment prior to use	Eye contact and priority seating for discussions	Emphasis on concrete and relevant experiences	Oral tests or modified reading level materials
		Concrete, relevant, tangible materials	Short activities		Aid in writing responses
			Repetition		More objective format
			Active involvement		
			Practice in a variety of settings		
			Contact with real objects		
			Immediate feedback		
			Pairing of an object with its symbol		
			Adaptations of reading material		
			Cueing of relevant details		
			Mastery learning		
			Cooperative learning		

Source: Sandra E. Cain and Jack M. Evans, *Sciencing: An Involvement Approach to Elementary Science Methods*, 3rd. ed. (New York: Merrill/Macmillan, 1990), 244–247.

SCIENCE EDUCATION IN THE BALANCE

During the past spring and fall, SAVI answered the cry for metric measurement activities for visually impaired students with the SAVI **Measurement Module.** The six hands-on activities contained in this module introduce youngsters to standard units of metric measurement.

To develop the concept of *mass,* we needed a measuring tool that would be suitable for use by the visually impaired. We finally decided to use a balance instead of a spring scale or other device and this decision resulted in some unexpected dividends for the project.

We looked at a lot of balances before we made the decision and even built a few of our own. Finally, we chose a simple, vacuum-formed model that is commercially available at a reasonable price. Then, we went to work on it!

First, we cut the bottoms of the two balance pans so that a paper or plastic cup could be dropped securely into the hole and then removed easily. Then, we added a tactile balance indicator. These slight modifications made it possible for blind students to determine weight to an accuracy of one gram!

The removable cup was the breakthrough we needed to make accurate weighing easy for visually impaired students. Both the weights (20g, 10g, 5g, 1g plastic pieces) and the objects or substances to be weighed automatically center in the cups, thus eliminating discrepancies due to the position of objects in the cups. An object, substance, or liquid can be removed from the balance cup and *all;* a new cup can then be inserted and a new material weighed. There's no more trouble "getting all the powder out," or "transferring the beans"; the objects stay in the cups.

The students use the balances to verify that 50 ml of water (measured with a modified SAVI syringe) weigh 50g, thereby establishing the relationship between volume and mass.

Since its introduction, the SAVI balance has crept into other modules. The forthcoming **Kitchen Interactions** Module will feature an activity that focuses on the concept of *density.* Density is defined operationally using the SAVI balance: equal volumes of two different liquids are compared on the balance and the heavier one is identified as the denser liquid.

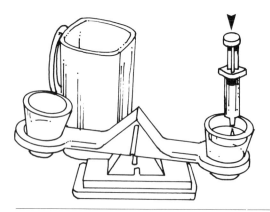

FIGURE 9–3
Science activity for the visually impaired
Source: Reprinted by permission of The Center for Multisensory Learning, Lawrence Hall of Science, University of California, Berkeley, CA 94720.

■ E. C. Keller, Jr., "A Marine Science Program with the Visually Impaired," *Journal of Visual Impairment and Blindness* (November 1981): 379.

■ Larry Malone and Linda DeLucchi, "Life Science for Visually Impaired Students," *Science and Children* (February 1979): 29–31.

■ Kenneth S. Ricker, "Writing Audio Scripts for Use with Blind Persons," *Journal of Visual Impairment and Blindness* (September 1981): 279–299.

■ Kenneth S. Ricker and Nancy Rodgers, "Modifying Instructional Materials for Use with Visually Impaired Students," *American*

Biology Teacher, 43, no. 9 (December 1981): 490–492, 501.

■ Dorothy Tombaugh "Aids in Teaching Laboratory Science to the Visually Impaired," *Science Education News* (Fall 1978/Winter 1979): 6–7.

These associations can provide you with suggestions on how to mainstream students with visual impairments into your science program:

■ The Lighthouse for the Blind and Visually Impaired, 1155 Mission Street, San Francisco, CA 94103.
■ American Printing House for the Blind, PO Box 6085, Louisville, KY 40206.
■ Science for the Blind Products, Box 888, Southeastern, PA 19399.
■ Telesensory Systems, Inc., 3408 Hillview Avenue, Mountain View, CA.

Science Teaching and Students with Hearing Impairments

Students with hearing impairments range in their hearing ability from partial hearing (hearing aid used) to total deafness. Sign language, lipreading, and reading facial movements help these students with oral communication. However, one of the major problems of the hearing impaired is language development. As hearing impaired students mature, there are increasing gaps in vocabulary, concept formation, and the ability to understand and produce complex sentences. Both language and intellectual development may be neglected for the hearing impaired.

As stated in previous chapters, minds-on/hands-on science activities can provide a variety of learning experiences that may enhance both language and cognitive growth. Therefore, here are some science teaching suggestions for implementing these types of activities for the hearing impaired in your classroom.

Use Science Minds-on/Hands-on Activities to Develop Vocabulary. The materials and experiences of minds-on/hands-on activities operationally show students differences in the meanings of words. Begin with "shape" words (such as *circle, square, triangle*) and provide cutouts of the shapes for students to identify. Introduce other words related to objects, such as color, size, and texture. Also, use objects in the students' environment to enhance concept and language development. Stress handling the objects during language/concept development. This process follows the constructivist learning cycle where the learner manipulates materials and then the teacher introduces or invents words for the scientific concepts.

Introduce or Explain Concepts Using Pictures, Drawings, Models, Films, Filmstrips, or Videotapes. Screen all materials first to see if they are appropriate for your hearing impaired students, or decide what modifications you must make. Give older students (who can read) written materials before viewing the film for orientation to new concepts. Keep written language a grade or more below that of your average class level, because the reading skills of many hearing impaired may develop slower.

Help Students with Hearing Impairments with Language Development.

1. Encourage them to participate in all verbal activities using whatever speech they have.
2. If they are working with a professional to develop speech, give your science vocabulary to the professional, so the words can be worked on for proper pronunciation and understanding.
3. Assist them with using mime, drawings, written communication, and demonstrations when communicating with their nonhandicapped classmates.

4. During oral work, always check the student's hearing aid for proper functioning, volume, and battery operation.
5. When you speak, always position yourself so that your face is well lit and that the student is not looking into a bright light. Also, try to maintain direct eye contact with the student.
6. Speak at a normal volume, speed, and tone when addressing the hearing impaired. They will understand you better than if you shout or use exaggerated speech patterns.
7. Avoid speaking *for* hearing impaired students, so that they may practice their own speech.
8. Seat hearing impaired students as close to the activity as practical and away from distracting noises, so they can hear better and lip-read if necessary.

Encourage Students with Hearing Impairments to Participate in the Same Activities as Their Classmates. However, use the following modifications when hearing is the primary sense used to learn the concepts, and change auditory observations to visual ones:

1. Use a light in a circuit instead of a buzzer.
2. Substitute a "probe box" for a "mystery box."
3. Have students feel vibrations rather than listen to pitch.
4. Show vibrations of strings and tuning forks in water waves and sand movements.
5. Make "language cards" to be used as the hearing impaired engage in the activities. These help students identify with and relate to the activity and concepts. Use diagrams and pictures to enrich the cards.
6. Encourage hearing impaired students to verbalize as much as possible to practice relating their experiences, language cards, observations, discoveries, and interpretations.
7. Whenever practical, pair impaired and nonimpaired students.[8]

Use Current Technology to Help Students with Hearing Impairments. You or someone in your school could investigate the use of the teletypewriter (TTY) in which a message is printed for the deaf person as the person on the other end of the line speaks. The hearing impaired "hears" by reading a printout. For information, see Cheryl Davis, ed., "Teletypewriter for the Deaf," *Access to Science,* 1, no. 2 (September 1977).

Computer technology for simulation experiments has great potential for teaching science to all children, with special applications for the hearing impaired. Wicat Company of Orem, Utah, has developed a computer Integrated Learning System (ILS) to assist hearing impaired students. The ILS's program consists of a file server with 28 learning stations that have substituted "phonic ears" for the regular headphones or small speakers. These phonic ears provide controls for volume, tone, and filtering that can be adjusted for each student. Each station has an extra headphone jack to allow teachers to listen in and sign to students who need help. For additional information see "Hearing Impaired Kids to Benefit from ILS," *Technological Horizons in Education (T-H-E) Journal,* 10, no. 2, (February 1991): 14.

Chapter 10 has more on technology and education for all students.

Be Aware of Research About Teaching Students with Hearing Impairments. These resources are available to you, should you want practical applications of modifications for hearing impaired in your science classroom:

■ Roberta A. Barron, "Modifying Science Instruction to Meet the Needs of the Hearing Impaired," *Journal of Research in Science Teaching,* 15, no. 4 (1978): 257–262.
■ P. J. Cunningham and H. G. Lang, "Aids in Teaching Laboratory Science to Deaf Students," *Science Education News* (Fall 1978/ Winter 1979).

- Judy E. Dodd and Harry Lang, "Science Teaching Strategies for Deaf Students," *The Science Teacher Bulletin,* XLV, no. 2 (1981).
- Harry Lang and G. Poppe, "Science Education for Hearing Impaired Students: State-of-the-Art," *Science Education* (December 1982): 860–869.
- H. Levitt et al., *Sensory Aids for the Hearing Impaired* (New York: Institute of Electrical and Electronics Engineers, 1980).
- "Hearing Impaired Students," *American Annals of the Deaf,* 127, no. 4 (August 1982): 411–417.

In addition, here are associations that can supply suggestions for maximizing learning for the hearing impaired:

- National Technical Institute for the Deaf (NTID), One Lomb Memorial Drive, Rochester, New York 14623.
- Gallaudet College, 7th and Florida Avenue, NE, Washington, DC 20002.

Science Teaching and Students with Orthopedic Impairments

Students with orthopedic impairments can have a variety of physical differences, such as large muscle dysfunctions (causing mobility or balance problems) and/or small muscle malfunctions (causing loss of coordination, dexterity, hand strength, or erratic muscular spasms; e.g., cerebral palsy and other such problems). Students with these handicaps may need crutches, braces, wheelchairs, walkers, or other devices.

For many physically impaired students, their greatest obstacles are **attitudinal and architectural barriers.** Generally, these students do not have intellectual handicaps. If you are to be effective in helping them learn as well as they can, you must understand the nature of their handicapping conditions and the parameters of their physical capabilities. Often, a little

ingenuity on your part will enable your orthopedically impaired students to be active learners in your science class. Here are some ways to begin that.

Be Aware of the Ways You Can Modify Your Architectural or Physical Classroom Environment. Meet the needs of your students with orthopedic impairments by providing:

1. Adequate space for movement by wheelchair, walker, crutches, and other devices.
2. Barrier-free movement by clearing aisles and keeping traffic lanes uncluttered.
3. Safety by placing seats or wheelchairs near exits wherever possible.
4. Appropriate desk and table heights adapted for wheelchairs and trays to hold materials needed for science activities.
5. Plastic bags or buckets for simple science materials that can be carried over the shoulder for students who use canes or walkers.
6. For outdoor activities, areas accessible to wheelchairs or canes, or make them accessible by wheeling impaired student in a wagon or by carrying.
7. Book holders or book scanners if students cannot hold books or turn pages; (Hand coordination impaired students may need pencil holders, tape recorders, or electric typewriters).

Modify Your Teaching Methods to Accommodate Students with Physical Impairments. Some suggestions include the following:

1. At the beginning of the school year, send a letter home to all parents about your science teaching goals. Mention the impairments of the students in your classroom, and refer to your pairing of impaired and nonimpaired students. Explain the experiences you plan for all your individual difference students.

Students with special physical needs may require modifications in the classroom environment to be certain they have access to a full range of science experiences.

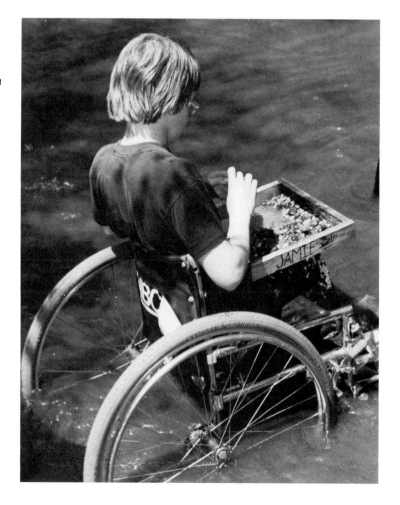

2. Plan to pair students as often as possible, stressing to your class that we all have some type or degree of impairment.

3. In pairing students, expect impaired students to do as much for themselves as they can.

4. Try to capitalize on physically impaired students' well-developed sensory channels when you present science lessons.

5. Look for adaptations and modifications for manipulations in minds-on/hands-on science activities, such as the following:

a. In a lesson on interaction of materials with a magnet, tape a magnet to the arm or hand of a student with no or limited limb control. This will enable the student to feel and see which objects interact and which do not.

b. Students can be wheeled around in a circle by their nonimpaired classmates to take the paths of planets in a lesson on the revolution of Earth around the sun.

6. Position yourself so your demonstrations and other teaching methods are visible, especially for students unable to move their heads. Avoid pacing or moving around the room while teaching if it could hinder students' abilities to learn.

Encourage Students with Physical Impairments to Participate as Fully as They Can. Encourage them to think of ways for you to modify your teaching so they will be able to engage in the activities.

Help Your Class Accept the Impaired. Plan lessons on individual differences. Have your nonimpaired students, as well as you, try to get through a day "impaired" by tying your fingers together or by staying in a chair.

Encourage All Your Students to Roll and Slide to Feel the Forces of Nature That Affect Us in Our Environment. Do this outdoors in the grass or on sand, or in the gym on mats. With parental permission and assistance, take physically impaired students out of wheelchairs or remove or unlock their braces, so they can do this also. Multisensory experiences of this type are much more meaningful for the physically impaired than reading about environmental forces.

Make Computers Available to Students with Physical Impairments. Computers can be excellent learning devices for the physically impaired, depending on how much of a physical and communication problem they have. If physically impaired learners can type on a computer keyboard, they can use the computer with special software. A control switch device can be installed so that students with muscular problems can operate the computer. See Chapter 10 for additional information on the use of computers with the physically impaired student.

Check the Literature for Other Ideas for Working with Students with Physical Impairments. These references will supply many practical suggestions for modifying your classroom and for teaching science to physically impaired students.

■ *Individually Prescribed Program of Instruction for Pupils Who Are Orthopedically Handicapped,* 1981. Available from Carol B. Busco, Consultant, Orthopedically Handicapped, South Carolina Department of Education, 1429 Senate Street, Columbia, SC.

■ E. C. Keller, Jr., ed., *Mainstreaming Teaching of the Physically Handicapped in Science—A Resource Book* (Morgantown, WV: Printech, 1983).

■ E. C. Keller, Jr., M. R. Redden, and C. A. Davis, "Science Education and the Physically Handicapped," *Science Education News* (Fall 1978/Winter 1979).

■ E. C. Keller, Jr., "Strategies for Teaching Science to the Physically Handicapped," *AAAS Abstracts,* (Washington, DC: American Association for the Advancement of Science, 1982).

■ Harry G. Lang, ed., *Testing Physically Handicapped Students in Science: A Resource Book for Teachers* (Morgantown, WV: Printech, 1983).

■ Herbert D. Thier, "Independence for the Physically Disabled Through Science and Technology," *Education Horizons* 62 (Fall 1983): 28–29.

Several sources that offer assistance with ideas for your students with impairments include the following organizations:

■ Science for the Handicapped Association, Science Center, Moorhead State University, Moorhead, MN 56563.

■ National Science Teachers Association, 1742 Connecticut Avenue, NW, Washington, DC 20009.

■ ERIC Clearinghouse on Handicapped and Gifted Children, 1920 Association Drive, Reston, VA 22091.

/// SCIENCE FOR INTELLECTUALLY DIFFERENT STUDENTS

Students with intellectual impairments are classified in many ways. Educationally, they are often grouped according to the particular area of learning disabilities:

1. Reading problems (the most frequent type of learning disorder).
2. Cerebral communication or difficulties with comprehension or expression of spoken language.
3. Visual/motor integration problems (e.g., dyslexia, which causes reading problems).

Students with learning impairments are a very heterogeneous group, since they often have overlapping problems. This makes it very difficult to classify their learning impairments and prescribe learning activities for them.

One group of students with intellectual impairments in our schools is labeled **mentally retarded.** Definitions vary widely for the severity of mental retardation. The American Association on Mental Deficiency (AAMD) uses this definition: "Mental retardation refers to subaverage general intellectual functioning which originates during the developmental period and is associated with impairment in adaptive behavior."

Many noted persons in the field, however, propose that the term *mental retardation* be abandoned because it has negative connotations and because it does not relate to education. They generally suggest the alternative term **general learning impairments.** While the latter term helps us develop a more positive and/or restrictive definition of mental retardation, the major professional organizations actively serving the retarded advocate the use of the AAMD definition.

Educators often classify retardation according to these levels of severity: **mildly retarded** (referred to as **"educable mentally retarded"**), **moderately retarded** ("trainable mentally retarded"), and **severely retarded.** Research at Colorado State College and Florida State University has found that moderately retarded students can learn some basic concepts. Mildly retarded students, in ad-

dition, can learn to predict, compare, group or classify, control a variable (with help), outline a simple investigation, measure, observe, communicate, and interpret simple data.

Mildly retarded students can be effectively educated in the regular self-contained elementary school classroom with individualized instruction and the help of specialists such as a resource teacher. This is called **mainstreaming.** Moderately retarded students generally need a highly specialized program and are commonly placed in self-contained classes with students with the same learning disabilities.

Most likely you will at some time have students who are mildly retarded. These students often have difficulty centering on one aspect of an activity at a time. Therefore, it is best to limit your goals for each lesson. If you want to discuss the students' findings at the conclusion of a lesson, collect all the materials from the students *before* starting the discussion, since these students are easily distracted by the materials before them and will not pay attention to the discussion.

Meeting the Science Needs of Students with Mild Retardation

Here are some practical suggestions for meeting special needs of these students in your regular classroom science program.

Emphasize Concrete, Meaningful Content. It is vital for these students that you use examples from the students' environment, such as colors of a school bus, grass, or their clothing when talking about colors.

Reinforce Mastery of New Materials Through Repetition and Use of Multimedia. For instance, after working with students on germinating seeds, reinforce their new learning by reading a story, showing a filmstrip, or listening to a tape.

Teach Sequenced Information from the Easy to the Difficult. If these students are to learn to cut paper strips to measure non-numerically the growth of their plants, start them cutting short straight lines, then move into cutting longer straight lines, and then to two-dimensional cuts.

Increase Attention Initially by Highlighting Relevant Dimensions and by Minimizing Unnecessary Stimuli. For example, darken the room and present materials about magnets on an overhead or opaque projector.

Secure Commercially Prepared Materials. The Biological Sciences Curriculum Study (BSCS), Boulder, Colorado, designed and field tested activity-centered science curricula for mildly retarded children. They presently have two available from commercial companies: *Me Now,* for elementary-age children, and *Me and My Environment,* for older children. Materials include filmstrips, models, film loops, teacher's guides, 35 mm daylight projection slides, test booklets, student worksheets, charts and picture cards, and scientific equipment. Presently BSCS is planning a similar type of curriculum for the primary level.

Use ESS Units for Special Education. Thirty-one ESS units have been identified as appropriate for students who have learning difficulties. A guide has been designed primarily for use by teachers of mildly retarded students, but other teachers will find it valuable. If interested, you may send for a copy through the distribution center nearest you. Ask for David W. Ball, *ESS Special Education Teacher's Guide* (St. Louis, MO: Webster/McGraw-Hill, 1978).

Units selected for special education are divided into three categories: perceptual, psychomotor, and other appropriate units. They follow the same sequence:

1. Description of audience (that is, type of child, grade range, and so on).
2. Overview of unit description and what it can do for the child.
3. Specification of objectives.
4. "Ways of getting started" for unit initiation.
5. "Keeping it going."
6. "Other classroom tips."
7. Evaluation checklist.
8. Time required.
9. Ordering information.

If you work with exceptional children, you will find this new guide extremely helpful.

When Using Films or Videotapes, Point Out the Important Parts Before the Showing. Also show small segments of the films and conduct only brief discussions afterwards because of the short attention spans of intellectually impaired students.

Help to Make Science Contribute to the Intellectually Impaired Student's Ability to Function in Everyday Society. Therefore, consider such science topics as health (including drugs, tobacco, and alcohol), human body, plants and animals, and high-interest topics such as space travel and dinosaurs.

Use Positive Reinforcement. Offer praise *immediately following* successful learning by intellectually impaired students.

Review the Literature for More Ideas for the Intellectually Impaired Student. Here are resources for additional ideas for the intellectually impaired student:

■ Janet Mansfield Davies and Daniel W. Ball, "Utilization of the Elementary Science Study with Educable Mentally Retarded Students," *Journal of Research in Science Teaching,* 15, no. 4 (1978): 281–286.
■ G. H. Ferth et al., "Values of Science Education for the Mildly Retarded: Empirical

Data Are Lacking," *Science Education, 64,* no. 5 (October 1980): 735–739.
■ E. A. Polloway et al., *Strategies for Teaching Learners with Special Needs,* 4th ed. (Columbus, OH: Merrill Publishing Co., 1989).
■ J. R. Rice, "A Special Science Fair: LD Children Learn What They Can Do," *Science and Children,* 20, no. 4 (January 1983): 15–17.

Science for Gifted/Talented Students

So far, this chapter has focused on enrichment for all students, including the physically and intellectually impaired. Although not impaired, some other students also provide challenges to teachers. They may have unusual skills, interests, talents, attitudes, and motivations. Often these students are identified as **gifted or talented.**

Defining gifted/talented usually shows what we as teachers (as purveyors of our society/culture) value. In that context, we observe, identify, and value those students who stand out from the others, because of the high degree or speed with which they usually, but not always,

■ speak well and have large and varied vocabularies,
■ display longer attention spans,
■ are extremely curious,
■ possess excellent academic skills, especially reading,
■ comprehend and follow directions very well,
■ seek out activities and hobbies in science areas,
■ enjoy puzzles and games of an open-ended type (e.g., Rubik's Cube or electronic games and computers), and
■ are more interested in broad concepts and issues than other students.[9]

These students love to participate in many activities previously mentioned in this chapter. In addition, you can challenge their intellects in many ways by providing them with meaningful enrichment activities. If you have students with the attributes listed above, the following suggestions may prove useful.

Fear Not: Learn with and from Your Gifted/Talented Students. Most elementary and middle school teachers have not majored in science and, therefore, may find that some of their gifted/talented students know more about certain areas of science than they do. Not feeling totally competent with science should not stop you from having gifted/talented students do more advanced work than the rest of the class.

Students enjoy seeing their teachers get excited about the results of students' work. In addition, this approach tends to break down the traditional view of teacher as giver of knowledge. You can truly become a teacher/ facilitator/ arranger of the learning environment, an adult questioner, and a constant positive critic. It may help you to keep a perspective when you feel inadequate in science by remembering that for all their knowledge, gifted/talented students are still elementary or middle school students socially, emotionally, and physically. They need your mature adult guidance and professional training in education and psychology.

Encourage Gifted/Talented Students to Engage in More Open-Ended Minds-on/ Hands-on Activities. Gifted/talented students should be challenged to do simple, *unstructured* experiments to find answers that are not easily available from texts or encyclopedias. These experiments differ from the cookbook kind because they do not have predetermined results or step-by-step procedures worked out in advance.

Keep these things in mind while guiding gifted/talented students through unstructured experimentation:

■ Start by using the combined talents of the class or group. Later, when routines are established, individuals may explore on their own.

■ Keep the experimentation within the limits of time, talents, and easily available apparatus. Explore these limitations before suggesting problems.

■ Be alert to the open-endedness of this type of experimentation. Frequently, questions will arise such as, "Suppose we varied the experiment in this way, what will happen?"

■ Do not assume that the gifted/talented student will continue to have a sustained interest in the problem. You must continually check on progress.

Gifted/Talented Students Should Be Encouraged to Use an Integrated Approach to Science Using All Subject Areas. Mathematics is the language of science, and gifted/talented students should be encouraged to use it as much as possible. They should be as much involved with "how much" or "what relationships exist between" as they are in answering the "how," "what," and "why." Whenever possible, ask students to quantify their findings, and encourage them to use graphing in their communications to other students and you.

With the increased availability of microcomputers, television, and videorecorders, gifted students especially are drawn to these challenging electronic learning devices. See Chapter 10 for ways to use electronic learning devices in your science teaching. Art, music, physical movement, language arts, social studies are all areas that gifted/talented students should be encouraged to integrate with their science activities. For ideas of how to do this see Joy Kataoka and James R. Patton, "Teaching Exceptional Learners: An Integrated Approach," *Science and Children,* 27, no.1 (September 1989): 48–50 and C. M. Callahan, "Science" in R. H. Swassing, editor, *Teaching Gifted Children and Adolescents* (Columbus, OH: Merrill/Macmillan, 1985).

Coordinate Home/School Learning with Gifted/Talented Students' Parents. Encourage parents of gifted/talented students to obtain books, magazines, and science kits and materials and to discuss science with their children. Often, desirable scientific learning situations arise when a family takes a vacation. Stress the importance of the parents buying or taking from the library supplemental booklets such as *How and Why Wonder Books* and the *Golden Books.* Explain the desirability of motivating and supplying "intellectual fuel" for the gifted/talented child. Encourage the parents of gifted/talented students to give their children many opportunities to take on leadership roles as they mature.

As most homes now have televisions, videocassette recorders, and even personal computers, encourage parents of your gifted/talented students to seek out television programs that stimulate and enrich children's science interests ("Nova," "Jacques Cousteau," "3-2-1 Contact"). Much interesting programming is shown on Public Broadcasting System channels. Videorecordings dealing with science can be borrowed from many public libraries or rented to be viewed and discussed at home. Gifted/talented students can share these with you and their classmates in school through written or oral presentations guided by you.

Provide Leadership Experiences for Gifted/Talented Students. Ask gifted/talented students to be science assistants to help with preparing materials, dispensing and collecting equipment and supplies, collecting information about experiments, and assisting less able classmates with some aspect of their science work. Often, peer teaching/learning is more effective than learning from teacher-pupil exchanges.

As mentioned in previous chapters, cooperative learning groups are excellent ways for gifted/talented students to work collaboratively with their classmates. They can share their abilities and talents as well as developing group skills. This can help overcome a possible concern that gifted/talented students may become elitists or loners.

Students gifted/talented in science may also create teaching models related to the science units being studied. These models may be weather instruments, electrical devices, atomic or solar systems, or scale models of local environmental or ecological systems.

Encourage Gifted/Talented Students in Your Mainstream Classroom. Previously, gifted/talented students were accelerated to higher or special, separated classes. Currently, greater emphasis has been placed on main-streaming, incorporating changes in science content to introduce higher levels of abstract thinking and independent thinking and problem-solving skills. Your challenge is to help your gifted/talented students modify, adapt, and learn how to discover new skills and concepts for themselves.

Most highly motivated, bright students need little encouragement. For those who do, try these suggestions.

1. Provide recognition for their efforts.
2. Provide extra credit for novel ideas or products.
3. Stress positive comments in all teacher-pupil exchanges.
4. Offer special privileges for specified performances.
5. Permit high-achieving students to be "teacher."
6. Encourage student-initiated projects and activities for those who have completed assignments.
7. Make special arrangements for high-achieving students to take selected subjects in higher grades.
8. Introduce elementary and middle grade students to research methods.
9. Teach debating skills and encourage students to sponsor and participate in debates on topics of their choice.
10. Have high-achieving math students create mathematical puzzles.

11. Encourage students to write scripts for TV and radio programs and "participate in" the programs.
12. Have students present a synopsis of a magazine or newspaper article to the class in a way that is interesting and understandable.
13. Have a "crazy idea" session where only unusual notions can be discussed.
14. Let them conduct a brainstorming session.
15. Let them express themselves in art forms such as drawings, creative writing, and role playing.
16. Have them dramatize their readings.
17. Have a great books seminar to introduce students to the classics.[10]

Provide Out-of-Classroom Opportunities for Gifted/Talented Students. It is very difficult, if not impossible, to provide information and activities to your gifted students in all their areas of interests in the classroom. These out-of-classroom ideas may be helpful to you.

1. Make library services available to them. If the school library is inadequate, take them on regular trips, if possible, to a public library. Arrange to secure hard-to-get materials from state or university libraries.
2. Try to guide the students to the research sources they need. Refer them to encyclopedias, dictionaries, and other reference sources.
3. Develop a catalog of other resources that students can use, possibly containing addresses of agencies providing free and inexpensive materials or local community resources.
4. Form science interest clubs with gifted/talented students as officers.
5. Identify community people who are available to work with individual gifted/talented students in a Mentor Program. Help those who are knowledgeable in their fields but do not know how to manage or teach students.

People in the community can be mentors and resources for gifted or talented students.

Your Teaching Methods Can Encourage Gifted/Talented Students. In our society, students' thinking is often trained to focus on the right answer, which sometimes discourages gifted/talented students from taking risks in academic situations. They may be confused or feel threatened with failure when they are faced with tasks in which there are no clear answers, or in which there may be a variety of correct answers. Try some of these techniques to encourage them:

1. Use a questioning technique rather than giving information.
2. Use hypothetical questions beginning with "What if . . . ?"
3. Ask students to develop open-ended situations where no one answer is correct.
4. In subjects such as arithmetic, where specific answers are required, encourage students to estimate their answers.
5. Have students check your written work for errors; let them see that all adults are fallible.
6. Instead of information only, emphasize concepts, principles, relationships, and generalizations.
7. Provide opportunities and assignments which rely on independent reading and research.
8. Have students give reports on their individual research and experimentation; this helps them acquire a sense of sharing their knowledge.
9. Provide foreign language materials—books, periodicals, recordings, newspapers—for young gifted/talented students.

Discovery: "Please Touch!" Science

Discovery Place is a hands-on, touch and feel museum. Is there such a resource near you?

Strategy   Visit a nearby "hands-on" museum or utilize its outreach program.

The Discovery Place of Birmingham, Inc., in Birmingham, Alabama, is a "hands-on, touch and feel museum." The outreach program offers "science is fun" classroom presentations as well as science assembly programs. Traveling exhibits and objects are available for loan, including nature objects and skeletons—unusual items you won't find in most classrooms! The museum also offers "hands-on" teacher workshops, where both new and experienced teachers can discover exciting ways to help children discover.

The Birmingham outreach program is available over a two-county area, with curriculum-based topics grouped for five grade levels—4-year-olds, kindergarten and first grade, second and third grades, fourth and fifth grades, and sixth through eighth grades.

Discovery Place's outreach topics are described in a way to provoke student interest. For second and third graders, a program to explore the properties of air is called "Look Out! You're Surrounded!" For fourth and fifth graders, "Stash It, Don't Trash It!" presents the effects of litter on animals and compares two mini-environments—one that has been cared for and one that has been abused.

Discovery Place has teacher workshops called "Get S.M.Art . . . Get Science with Math and Art!" Each of the 30 lessons has a math and/or art component to enhance science learning.

The workshops model the methods teachers will use to manage their own discovery classes

On Your Own   Try a Color Explosion.

MATERIALS

Shallow dish (pie pan) free of grease
Cup of whole milk at room temperature
Eyedropper
Dishwashing liquid (Dawn or Joy work well)
Food coloring—4 colors

PROCEDURE

Pour milk into the pan. Put 5 drops each of red, blue, green, and yellow food coloring at separate areas in the milk. (Don't put the drops too close to the sides of the pan.) With the eyedropper, add single drops of detergent near the colors. Observe. The colors will continue to move and blend.

Vary this science/art experiment by changing the type of milk (skimmed, whole, powdered, evaporated); temperature of the milk; type of detergent; and color combinations. Predict what will happen when the variables are changed. Record and compare results.

Why does the initial reaction occur? Surface tension is broken. Why does the reaction continue to occur? The detergent is working to break down the fat in the milk. As the detergent causes the milk to move around, the colors will mix together.

Adaptation for small groups: Put the materials for this experiment in a learning center—perhaps the art rather than the science center. Then you might ask the children:

What new colors are formed during the experiment? Watch the designs and patterns that form and change. Does this remind you of other patterns you've seen?

Source: This feature was prepared with the assistance of Pam Lovelady, Director of Education, Discovery Place of Birmingham, Inc., 1320 South 22nd Street, Birmingham, Alabama 35205.

Search the Literature for Other Ideas. Use these resources for additional ideas for gifted/talented.

- "Giftedness" in James R. Patton, et al., *Exceptional Children in Focus,* 5th ed.(New York: Merrill/Macmillan, 1991).
- Gary A. Davis and Silvia B. Rimm, *Education of the Gifted and Talented,* 2nd ed.(Englewood Cliffs, NJ: Prentice-Hall, 1989).
- Michael L. Hardman, M. Winston Egan, and Elliott D. Landau, *What Will We Do in the Morning?* (Dubuque, IA: Wm. C. Brown, 1981).
- T. Stephens, A. E. Blackhurst, and L. Magliocca, *Teaching Mainstreamed Students* (New York: Wiley, 1982).
- J. R. Whitmore, *Giftedness, Conflict, and Underachievement* (Boston: Allyn and Bacon, 1980).

/// SCIENCE FOR STUDENTS WITH CULTURALLY DIVERSE BACKGROUNDS

Gifted/talented students offer a special kind of challenge to the elementary and middle school teacher. Another kind of challenge is meeting the needs and interests of students who have cultural backgrounds that may be different from yours and the majority of students in your classroom and community. For want of a better description of students from different ethnic groups, let's refer to them as **culturally different** or **diverse.** Culturally diverse students come from home environments that may be very different from society's mainstream. Differences may revolve around economic level, ethnic background, religion, race, or language. However, their backgrounds offer rich heritages from which we all can and do benefit. Our nation has grown strong as a result of the contributions of all of our diverse cultural backgrounds.

The National Science Teachers Association recognized and appreciated the strength and beauty of cultural pluralism in its 1991 Position Statement on Multicultural Science Education.

NSTA must work with other professional organizations, institutions, and agencies to seek the resources required to ensure effective science teaching for culturally diverse learners if our nation is to achieve a position of international leadership in science education:

- Culturally diverse children must have access to quality science education experiences that enhance success and provide the knowledge and opportunities required for them to become successful participants in our democratic society;
- Curricular content and instructional strategies selected for use with culturally diverse children must reflect, as well as incorporate, this diversity;
- Science teachers must be knowledgeable about children's learning styles and instructional preferences, which may be culturally related;
- Science teachers have the responsibility to expose culturally diverse children to career opportunities in science, technology, and engineering.[11]

What Does the NSTA Position Paper Mean for You?

As you reread the NSTA Position Paper on Multicultural Science Education, consider these implications for your science classroom:

1. You must employ as wide a range of content and teaching strategies as possible to meet the learning needs and interests of students with diverse cultural backgrounds.
2. You must become knowledgeable about the learning styles of your diverse cultural students and how their cultures aid or hinder their science learning.
3. You must build on and broaden the prior knowledge your culturally diverse students bring to your classroom.

You are very aware that cultural differences can inhibit students' learning. While not all culturally diverse students have special learning needs, some may have limited experiences with the materials and concepts in your science classroom. This is particularly true where the student's home environment or language is drastically different from the one in school.

Effects of Minds-on/Hands-on Science on Culturally Diverse Students

When you study the needs, interests, and expectations of culturally diverse students, you are struck with how relevant and pertinent minds-on/hands-on science programs are, with their emphasis on actual manipulation of concrete materials. You will find these kinds of activities are excellent ways to meet the needs of all your students, but they are especially valuable for culturally diverse students who probably are wrestling with the development of a new language, customs, friendships, and living environment. Remember the constructivist learning cycle that builds on sensory experiences, introduction of vocabulary based on those concrete experiences, followed by application of this new vocabulary to other situations. This cycle is a natural for culturally diverse students.

Your job is to provide appropriate constructivist learning cycle activities that will help your students feel comfortable with two cultures. Your modified minds-on/hands-on science activities will help the students span the gap from their past experiences and language to their current immediate environment.

Here are other suggestions for helping culturally diverse students bridge the gap between their native language and English by using minds-on/hands-on science activities.

Learning English Through Minds-on/ Hands-on Science Activities

Many culturally diverse students (currently predominantly Hispanics, blacks, and Asians) have difficulties with learning mainstream English,

even though they may not always be first generation Americans. Here are some general strategies you can use in your science teaching to help improve English for culturally diverse students who are limited English proficient (LEP), even when all your teaching is conducted in English.

1. Because many LEP students learn to read English before they learn to speak it, use the chalkboard more than you otherwise might.
2. Save class time by preparing, on large sheets of paper, lists of vocabulary you will introduce during the lesson or assign for homework. Tape these sheets to the wall in full view of all students. Point to each word when you say it and talk about it.
3. Always print (upper- and lowercase) legibly. Most writing that newcomers encounter out of school is in print.
4. Display prominently in the classroom any written regulations or procedures that students are to follow every day. Each time you remind students of one of these regulations, point to the chart and read the words aloud.
5. When you give directions, give them one at a time, step-by-step: "Do A first. Next, do B. Then C."
6. When students do not understand what you have said, rephrase using different words and simpler sentences.
7. Let an English-speaking student repeat instructions for the class when repetition is necessary. This will be useful for all students, and LEP students will benefit from hearing the sentences spoken in a different voice and accent.
8. Review important points from previous lessons and list them on the chalkboard as you do so.
9. At frequent intervals, summarize what has been taught in the lesson so far. Print the key points on the board, or refer to a wall chart.
10. Beginning with the upper elementary grades, require all class members to keep notebooks written in English.

Further sources for teaching English and science to culturally diverse students through minds-on/hands-on science are

- Donna M. Gollnick and Phillip C. Chinn, *Multicultural Education in a Pluralistic Society,* 3rd ed. (New York: Merrill/Macmillan, 1990).
- Cynthia Bilotta, ed., *Delivering Academic Excellence to Culturally Diverse Populations: Language Development Through Math/Science Activities.* Proceedings from a Conference at the Peter Sammartino College of Education (Rutherford, NJ: Fairleigh Dickinson University, 1985).
- Leslie Olsen and Thomas Huckin, *English for Science and Technology* (New York: McGraw-Hill, 1983).
- Hilda Hernandez, *Multicultural Education: A Teacher's Guide to Content and Process* (New York: Merrill/Macmillan, 1989).
- James M. O'Malley, *Children's English and Service Study: Language of Minority Children with Limited English Proficiency in the U.S.* (Roslyn, VA: InterAmerica Research Associates, 1984).

Becoming a Multicultural Science Teacher

From one vantage point, *all* of your students are culturally diverse because each family is unique and has its own cultural identity. Many other groups could have been presented, but it was impractical to include students from the inner city, rural areas, "at risk," girls, and other minority groups. *At risk* is a popular description of students who are in danger of dropping out of school or otherwise failing to achieve their educational potential due to their disadvantaged status, constant underachievement, drug involvement, or other problem.

Here are some ways you can adapt your science teaching to maximize the learning of all these diverse students, while fostering a multicultural atmosphere in your science classroom.

- Find techniques for fostering collaboration and working together of all your students, such as cooperative learning groups.
- Capitalize on the broad cultural diversity within your classroom and have your students share their heritages through luncheons of their native foods (and compare to see the similarities in nutritional components), dances, or songs.
- Provide a reasonable and caring interpersonal environment for all students.
- Work to improve home/school relations with cooperation and collaboration of parents.
- Foster a classroom atmosphere that has success as its expected norm.

SUMMARY

Individualized instruction is not new; it was the main system in the one-room schoolhouse. Research has shown that learning achievement in individualized science teaching is as high as, or higher than, in traditional classes, especially for underachieving youngsters. However, there is also greater interest, better attendance, more enjoyment by students, and a more positive attitude toward teaching and schools by teachers and parents.

Most elementary and middle school science teaching can be adapted for individualized instruction. To modify your current science teaching to include more individualization consider the following practical suggestions:

1. Enrichment centers.
2. Challenge and solution cards.
3. Student school ground activities.
4. Out-of-doors activities.
5. Visits to museums, parks, and other cultural centers.
6. Students teaching students.
7. Cooperative Learning Groups.
8. Science kits.
9. Creative use of television.
10. Surprise science boxes.
11. Student bulletin boards.
12. Student panel talks.
13. Student progress files.
14. Use of museums.
15. Science discovery charts.
16. Science tradebook reports.
17. Scientist biographies.
18. Student displays.
19. Pictorial riddles.
20. Science clubs.
21. School or classroom newspapers.

Public Laws 94-142 and 95-561 have given added dimensions to our working definition of individualized science teaching, because they mandate mainstreaming students with a wide range of differences, such as physical, social, and intellectual. Practical suggestions were presented for providing for the needs of these students in addition to all our other students in your science class: visually, hearing, and intellectually impaired. Special science curricula and teaching methods have been designed for the mildly retarded and the visually impaired. Resources are also available for the hearing impaired.

Gifted/talented students present different kinds of challenges for teachers. Ideas were given on how to enrich your science teaching to meet their needs. These students have unusual talents and motivations in science, and can benefit from doing relatively unstructured experiments, exploring enrichment activities with their parents, and being given leadership roles in class.

Culturally diverse students present varying kinds of challenges. They gain a great deal from individualized minds-on/hands-on science teaching, especially in language and through investigations with real problems in their immediate environments.

SELF-ASSESSMENT AND FURTHER STUDY

1. Blindfold yourself and try to move around a laboratory. Have someone lead you through the laboratory first. Try to enumerate the things the guide should point out to you. Keep this list and use it when you have a visually impaired student in your class.
2. Put ear plugs in your ears and have another student teach you a science lesson. What problems did you encounter? What can you do to overcome some of these problems?
3. Construct some challenge cards of your own. Look at science resource books or texts to get ideas.
4. Make some discovery science charts.
5. Working with some of your students, collaboratively make some surprise science boxes.
6. Using several related pictures or pictorial riddles, make a story board. Mount these on cardboard and cover them with plastic for protection.
7. Outline how you'd invite and use student-produced display science material.
8. Investigate in depth some of the science curriculum materials mentioned in this chapter.
9. Select one or more gifted/talented students. Prescribe a series of activities for these students that will enrich the science topics you are studying with your class.
10. Select science topics to explore with culturally diverse students using real-life problems from their immediate environments and relevant to their lives.

NOTES

1. George S. Morrison, *Early Childhood Education Today,* 5th ed. (New York: Merrill/Macmillan, 1991), 354.
2. Kenneth S. Ricker, ''Science Education and the Physically Handicapped: Implications for the Future'' in Helenmarie H. Hofman and Kenneth S. Ricker, eds. *Science Education and Physically Handicapped,* (Washington, DC: National Science Teachers Association, 1979), 277.
3. An NSTA Position Statement. Laboratory Science, Adopted by the NSTA Board of Directors in January, 1990, *NSTA Reports!,* (October/November 1991): 15.
4. For additional information for individualizing teaching see Bonnie Baran Strickland and Ann Turnbull, *Developing and Implementing Individualized Education Program* (New York: Merrill/Macmillan, 1990) and Maynard C. Reynolds and Jack W. Birch, *Adaptive Mainstreaming: A Primer for Teachers and Principals,* 3rd ed. (White Plains, NY: Longman, 1988).
5. The author acknowledges James A. Shymansky, ''Rating Your Individualized Program,'' *Science and Children,* 17, no. 5 (February 1980): 33.
6. The author is indebted to these references for assistance with the content for children with differences: Rena B. Lewis and Donald H. Doorlag,

Teaching Special Students in the Mainstream, 3rd ed. (New York: Merrill/ Macmillan, 1991); Donna M. Wolfinger, *Teaching Science in the Elementary School. Content, Process, and Attitude* (Boston: Little, Brown & Co., 1984), 271–290; and Dean R. Brown, "Helping Handicapped Youngsters Learn Science By 'Doing'," in Mary Budd Rowe, ed. *What Research Says to the Science Teachers, vol. 2* (Washington, DC: National Science Teachers Association, 1979), 80–100.

7. Elva R. Gough, "Common Sense and Sensitivity in Teaching the Blind," *The Science Teacher,* 45. no. 9 (December 1978): 34–35.

8. For additional suggestions see Doris Hadary and Susan Hadary Cohen, *Laboratory Science and Art for Blind, Deaf, and Emotionally Disturbed Children: Mainstreaming Approach* (Baltimore: University Park Press, 1978).

9. Barbara Clark, *Growing Up Gifted: Developing the Potential of Children at Home and at School,* 4th ed. (New York: Merrill/Macmillan, 1992).

10. Joan S. Wolf, "The Gifted and Talented," in Norris G. Haring and Linda McCormick, eds. *Exceptional Children and Youth,* 5th ed. (New York: Merrill/Macmillan, 1990).

11. "An NSTA Position Statement. Multicultural Science Education," *NSTA Reports!* (October/November 1991): 7. Reprinted with permission of the NSTA.

The agricultural age was based on plows and the animals that pulled them; the industrial age, on engines and the fuels that fed them. The information age we are now creating will be based on computers and the networks that interconnect them . . . a hopeful vision of a future built on an information infrastructure that will enrich our lives by relieving us of mundane tasks, by improving the ways we live, learn, and work and by unlocking new personal and social freedoms.[1]

C H A P T E R   1 0

Putting Technology to Work

How do you develop computer literacy for yourself and your students? In what ways can technology enrich your classroom?

The opening quotation tries to put computers and networks into perspective for us to see where we have been and project possibilities for the future. This chapter will help you see where we currently are in using computers and other technology in science education and how you can learn what is needed for you to incorporate them effectively into a minds-on/hands-on science program in your classroom.

/// YOU ARE ALREADY IMMERSED IN A TECHNOLOGY AND COMPUTER-ORIENTED SOCIETY

Your life is permeated with computers and you use or come in contact with them everyday in these three forms:

1. **Mainframe computers.** Giants that probably prepare your phone bill, handle your transactions at the 24-hour banking stations, or process your college registration.

2. **Minicomputers.** Intermediate size generally found in offices and businesses. They read bar codes and charge you for groceries at the automatic checkout, with each item printed on the register tape automatically with prices, the accurate date, and time. Your paycheck may be produced on one.

3. **Microcomputer.** Smallest version (but becoming so powerful they are replacing minicomputers for many applications) used most frequently at home or school for personal use, such as word processing, record keeping, playing computer games, learning activities, and collecting and analyzing data. That is why microcomputers are frequently called Personal Computers or **PCs.**

In this chapter, the word **computer** refers primarily to the microcomputers that are used in the schools.

Consider your typical day and you can think of many additional activities that involve computers. Also consider these statistics of computer and other electronic technology use in elementary schools.[2]

- Of U.S. schools, 98% own at least one computer, 93% own videocassette recorders, 20% have interactive video equipment, 21% own videodisc players, and 18% have satellite dishes.
- By December of 1991 it was estimated that schools were using almost 4 million computers in some fashion in their teaching/learning environments.
- The typical elementary school has six computers.
- One-half of all elementary schools use computers in school; however, many of these computer uses are casual (such as games) and of short duration.
- Typical elementary school students using computers have access to them for 35 minutes per week, but not every week, because schools usually rotate computer use.
- More than 50% of computer time in elementary schools involves computer-assisted instruction (CAI) with drill-and-practice or tutorial programs.
- Boys usually use school computers more than girls, but not everywhere and not in all respects.
- Higher ability students are much more likely to use computers.
- Although schools are well stocked with computers, only 22% of elementary school teachers use computers in their classrooms.

What does all this mean to you? Either you have, or shortly will have, computers in your elementary school. If you are to use this new technology effectively in your science teaching, you must become computer literate.

How to Develop Your Computing Literacy Skills

You probably have heard the term *computer literacy,* which generally refers to knowledge of computers and their components and how to use them for particular purposes. Some have expanded this definition beyond just machines and use the term **computing literacy**[3] to include using computers as machines, tools, and creative instruments. Under this definition, you as a teacher using computers must learn

- *about* computers. Teaching the operation, use, and programing of computers in classroom settings;
- *with* computers. Uses of computers as tools to gather and analyze laboratory data;
- *from* computers. Computer dispenses or tests information through tutorial and drill-and-practice programs;
- about *thinking with* computers. Using problem-solving programs; and
- *managing* learning with computers. Using word processors, school schedulers, and test makers.[4]

As an intelligent adult and a citizen in a technological society, you should become literate about computers. Teachers have always adjusted to learning about and using technological changes in their teaching, such as the advent of pencils, printed books, films, filmstrips, radio, and television. You will do the same with computers if you learn the essentials:

1. Knowledge of computer components and terminology.
2. Programing computers to carry out your wishes.
3. Evaluating software and hardware.
4. Teaching/learning the uses of computers in your science teaching.

You and Your Students Can Learn the Basics of Computers. There's good news for you. You don't have to be an electronic or computer expert to use computers in your science teaching any more than you need to know how your TV, VCR, or CD player works electronically. What you will need to know is (a) what computer parts (hardware components) are necessary, (b) how to select the right computer program (software) to meet your

Teachers not only must become computer literate, but must help students become aware that they will encounter computers everywhere in the world around them.

teaching and your students' learning needs, and (c) proper procedures for loading the programs (diskettes or tape), turning on, and running the computer. The following are basics about computers that you should know and teach to your students.

What Are Some Major Components of a Computer?[5] Computers are made of electronic circuits that receive, store, process, and transmit information. Thousands or even hundreds of thousands of these circuits can be put on silicon devices called **chips,** smaller than your fingernail. The most important chip, called the **central processing unit (CPU),** controls all other parts of the computer and can be thought of as its "brain." Other chips perform the following functions:

- **ROM (Read Only Memory).** Computer's special operating instructions that cannot be erased, even when the computer is turned off.
- **RAM (Random Access Memory).** Memory that stores and holds instructions only

while the computer is on. This memory is erased when it is turned off. It is designated by the number of characters or individual letters, called **bytes,** that it can store, i.e., 16K (16,000 bytes or K = 1,000 bytes × 16). The higher the number, the more information the computer can store.

The computer you use in your elementary or middle school will probably have four or five components, as seen in Figure 10–1. A glossary of necessary computer terms appears at the end of this text.

What Are Hardware and Software? A term used for any physical parts of computers is **hardware.** Keyboards, monitors, disk drives, and printers are all hardware.

Another important part of computers is called **software.** Software are programs that when loaded into a computer at the disk drive instruct the computer what to do. These programs are usually on diskettes of 3½″ or 5½″, depending on the kind of disk drive device. Software is written in a language that the CPU

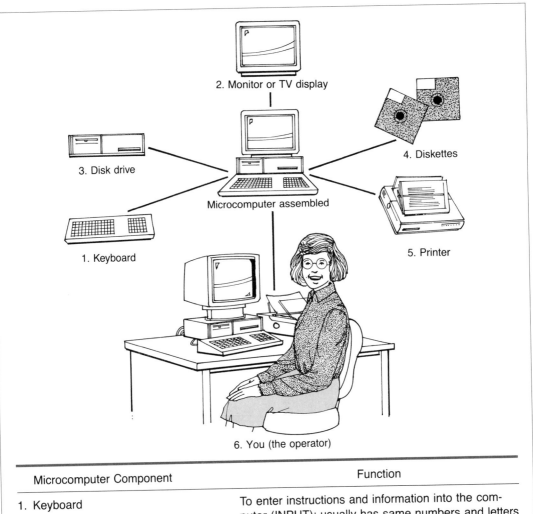

2. Monitor or TV display

4. Diskettes

3. Disk drive

Microcomputer assembled

1. Keyboard

5. Printer

6. You (the operator)

Microcomputer Component	Function
1. Keyboard	To enter instructions and information into the computer (INPUT); usually has same numbers and letters as standard typewriter plus extra keys
2. TV Screen or Monitor	To view a program or see what is being typed on the keyboard
3. Disk Drive or Playback Device	To detect and "read" information stored on a diskette; may be a cassette recorder and/or a disk drive
4. Diskette	Magnetic disk goes into disk drive and programs can be loaded and stored on them; information source
5. Printer	Makes paper copy of electronic listings in computer (OUTPUT)
6. You	Unless you do something to the microcomputer, nothing happens. They do not run by themselves. So turn it on and learn to use it while using it.

FIGURE 10–1
Microcomputer components

can understand. In your classroom computer, the language may be BASIC or LOGO. These languages give a series of instructions that allow a computer to do a particular task. This is called **programing** the computer. Programs may be written by you and your students, or you may use programs written by others. Probably, you and your students will begin with programs written by others until you are more proficient and feel confident with your computer.

Computer hardware and software vary considerably in their capacities to perform tasks; therefore, their prices also vary. Prices will be explored later in this chapter.

Now that you have a rudimentary knowledge of a computer—its hardware and software and how it functions—let's look at how it can be used in your classroom for science teaching.

/// HOW CAN COMPUTERS CONTRIBUTE TO YOUR SCIENCE TEACHING?

Computers and other classroom technology are effective because they are consistent with your visually oriented, video-based students. It is staggering to consider that the students in your classroom have probably logged about 8,000 hours in front of a TV screen! Many of them also have spent many hours playing computer and video games.[6] They come eager to use technology in their classrooms as well.

With this high motivation then, computers can enrich your science teaching in many ways, especially in these areas:

1. Computing literacy.
2. Computer-assisted instruction (CAI).
3. Computer problem solving.
4. Computer-managed instruction (CMI).

Each of these areas can have a significant impact on your science teaching. However, most elementary or middle school teachers at this time do little direct application of computer problem solving and computer-managed instruction. Therefore, the rest of this discussion will concentrate on the two readily adaptable computer fields that you may be using now in your elementary or middle school classroom: computing literacy and computer-assisted instruction.

Computing Literacy and Science Teaching/Learning

All of the material just presented to you about computing should also be taught to your students. Here are those **computing literacy concepts** in the framework of how they fit into your classroom science teaching:

1. Explain what computers are, how they work, and the basic computer vocabulary or language needed.
2. Give the meaning of and show examples of computer programing.
3. Tie in computers and science/technology/ society by showing
   a. How computers affect people's lives now and in the future;
   b. How scientists use computers in their work;
   c. What career opportunities are available for people with computer skills and information.
4. Present opportunities for students to develop skills in using computers as tools to learn, write and calculate, and then to save, display, and print this information.
5. Help students to do simple computer programing.[7]

Once your students understand how the computers work and can apply some basic computer language, you can move to other aspects of using computers in your science program.

Using Computer-Assisted Learning in Your Science Teaching

In previous chapters you have seen a variety of aids to assist you in teaching science: minds-on/hands-on activities, books, films, field trips, and other materials. Think of the computer as another aid that you may use creatively to enrich the science learning of your students. Computer-assisted instruction (CAI) may be used in five main ways to enrich your science teaching:

1. Drill and practice.
2. Dialog and tutorial.
3. Simulation and modeling.
4. "Lab" data gathering/analysis/processing.
5. Teacher utility (word processing and record keeping).

To envision the interrelationships among these five CAI learning activities and science teaching, see Figure 10–2. The pyramid is founded on four bases: drill and practice, dialog and tutorial, simulating and modeling, and teacher utility. "Lab" data gathering/analysis/processing is the pinnacle or highest point of the pyramid because it draws on all of the other four aspects and requires the highest level of thinking, participation, and learning. In effect, this ties together Bloom's taxonomy of cognitive domain levels of thinking, types and uses of computer programs, and your science teaching.

Must CAI Drill and Practice in Science Be Boring?

The most common use of CAI is **drill and practice** activities, probably because they are easy programs to write, although this is a very limited use of computers. However, if used ef-

fectively, CAI drill and practice activities are useful for

1. individualizing work for all students so they may progress at their own learning levels and pace;
2. identifying specific areas of weaknesses for students to work on;
3. reteaching vocabulary or scientific terminology;
4. presenting science content usually used by teachers from workbooks, textbooks, games, and other teaching materials;
5. showing questions, diagrams, or models in color, and even in animation;
6. alerting students immediately as to whether their responses are right or wrong;
7. showing the right answer immediately if incorrect answers are given; and
8. providing immediate positive reinforcement for all right answers.[8]

CAI drill and practice is usually used for review and not to present new science concepts. Therefore, you need to look for CAI drill and practice science programs that reinforce what you have taught, that entertain and do not bore, and that are on a learning level suitable for your particular students.

Using CAI Tutorial Software in Your Science Teaching

Another use of CAI for science teaching is **interactive tutorial or dialog.** Generally, CAI tutorials involve students in active dialog, which

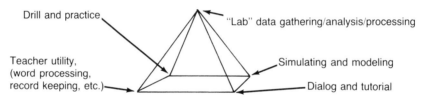

FIGURE 10–2
Uses of computer-assisted instruction (CAI) in science teaching

requires them to answer correctly before going to the next step. A topic is introduced, and various concepts are "taught" by presenting principles from step A, to step B, to step C, and so on to the conclusion of the lesson. If students answer questions incorrectly, they are returned to a lower level "reteaching step." A review is given to see if they have mastered the lesson. Some examples of science materials appropriate for CAI tutorial programs are the circulatory system, the names of the organs in the respiratory system of a fish, the parts and functioning of a microscope, and star constellation name drill. These types of computer activities are consistent with constructivist learning and reinforcing prior knowledge.

Using CAI Simulation and Modeling in Science Teaching

You would get little argument if you said the best way for your elementary or middle school students to learn something was through firsthand experiences. However, this is not always practical, cost-effective, or safe. Therefore, simulation and modeling are the next best methods. If the learner is active and not merely an observer or passive, the computer activity is called **simulation.** Simulation follows the constructivist idea that learners construct their own unique concepts through active participation.

Although difficult to program because of complex computer graphics, simulation has great potential as a CAI teaching tool. The computer can simulate activities that are difficult or impossible to do in your classroom, such as wave properties of oceans, organism population growth, introduction of new organisms into a food chain, and compass directions and measurements. Students enjoy their active and direct involvement in the graphic animated displays; witness the popularity of electronic video games. Students are placed in a situation where they control an environment by interacting with the computer. In this CAI situational simulation, they collect data, correlate results, and learn skills, attitudes, and concepts as a result of this active experience. Your job is to help your students understand the relationship of the CAI simulation and reality. You must plan activities to help them develop the logical skills needed to make these connections.

Another advantage of simulations is the fact that slower students may type in as many repetitive questions for assistance as needed without embarrassment. A computer never gets angry or impatient; its pace adapts to the student using it. Conversely, advanced students may skip parts of a program that they already understand and proceed at their pace. CAI simulation programs move students to higher or lower levels as needed.

An important aspect of CAI simulations is that students must constantly be creating ideas to drive or keep the simulation going. Your students must construct sentences, solve problems, and make decisions. By being active par-

CAI simulations are effective for developing problem-solving processes.

ticipants in the CAI simulation, students get practice in problem-solving skills in animated situations with which they can easily identify.

Many good commercial CAI simulation programs are currently available to you for your science teaching. A sample of one follows.

Odell Lake—Simulating Real Life. An example of an environmental CAI simulation software program is Odell Lake, produced by the Minnesota Educational Computing Consortium (MECC). Odell Lake is entertaining, educational, and highly interactive. It provides a discovery-based learning experience about the food web in a lake in the Cascade Mountains. Here is an outline of the CAI simulation software, Odell Lake, for grades 4 to 6:

Content	Food web among six lake fish
Skills	Simple decision making; drawing conclusions about the food web from the data collected and analyzed
Curriculum	Introduces ecological concepts in the food web
Integration values	Interdependence of all organisms
Emphasized comments	Additional pictures could enrich the program since existing illustrations are not detailed

In this simulation, the student chooses to be one of six different fish: whitefish, blueback salmon, mackinaw trout, chub, rainbow trout, or Dolly Varden trout. After selecting a fish, the student sees a frame that shows what the fish will look like.

As a particular fish, students will meet the other organisms in the lake and have to make decisions based on previous experiences. As a fish meeting another fish, they can choose op-

tions to escape deeper, escape shallow, ignore it, eat the fish, or chase it.

A student who makes the right decision is rewarded—he or she survives and/or eats the other fish. A student making the wrong decision learns a valuable experimental lesson and is eaten or loses a meal. As other encounters with other fish occur, situations may have the student chose correctly or incorrectly. As a result, students begin to see underlying relationships in the lake as they progress through the program. They eventually meet otters, water insects, and more. Interest runs high, and students carry their excitement back into classroom discussions and further study.

This type of simulation computer program provides an exciting, active learning experience that allows students to enjoy a discovery lesson, while absorbing valuable ecological concepts. You must provide closure and analysis and encourage expressions of the concepts learned through such activities as drawing posters of the food web and role-playing various participants in the interactions.

The Use of Simulations for Developing Observational Skills. Another type of CAI software is called **modeling.** Modeling differs from simulation in that the learner is an observer of a phenomenon but not an active participant. Some CAI modeling software programs might investigate the following:

■ Tracing blood flow from the heart to body parts and its return to the heart.
■ Observing the germination of seeds and the phototropism of evolving plants.
■ Following the steps in the working of an automobile or steam engine.
■ Following the pathway of electrons in a flashlight circuit.
■ Observing the movement of magma underground, through a volcano, and climaxing with the eruption of lava.

You can use CAI simulations and modeling as enrichments to your minds-on/hands-on activities and discussions, but do not use them as substitutes for "real" experiences.

CAI "Lab" Activities Develop Higher Thinking Skills

As pointed out in previous chapters, the highest level of thinking/learning/acting in science teaching is problem solving/decision making. Computer CAI software is available for developing problem-solving/decision-making skills through "lab" data gathering/analyzing/processing programs. You should become familiar with "lab" programs for these very important reasons:

1. It is so easy for you to emphasize drill and practice applications because this is what many elementary teachers know, feel comfortable with, and do themselves.
2. "Lab" data gathering/analysis/processing uses the computer as a tool to aid discovery, not merely as mechanical flash cards.
3. Computers may be new to you, and you should emphasize the most creative and innovative uses of them, rather than the least imaginative and repetitive uses.

Many student-participation "lab" software programs exist, and these two types will be investigated: **computer/sensor** and **computer/printed text/video.** Reviewing these two types of approaches to CAI use with "lab" activities will introduce you to the next level of electronic teaching aids.

Computer/Sensor Software Programs— Simulated "Lab" Activities.
Simple devices that are easy for computer users to add to their components—referred to as **user friendly**—are readily available. Among these devices, called **peripherals,** are **sensors** or **probes** that allow the computer to monitor experimental variables, such as temperature, sound, light, and heart rate, and feed the data into the computer for analysis and processing.[9] Using these peripherals with computers, your students become active participants in science

experiments. To reiterate, this technology need not replace the minds-on/hands-on aspects of your classroom science program; it can enrich and reinforce it.

These sources can help you in making or buying sensor or probe devices, connecting them to your computer, and finding ways to help your students use them for continuous measurement of environmental variables with only one computer.

- *Laboratory Catalog* (Waltham, MA: Cambridge Development), free.
- Kenneth Fuller, "Beyond Drill and Practice," a three-article series in *Science and Children.* "Using Computers to Teach Classification," 23, no. 6 (March 1986): 20–22; "Using Computers to Build Hypotheses and Design and Conduct Experiments," 23, no. 7 (April 1986): 9–12; and "Using Computers to Teach Quantitative Thinking," 23, no. 8 (May 1986): 16–19.
- *Hands-on! Magazine,* 1696 Massachusetts Ave., Cambridge, MA 02138.
- Nancy Kraft, "Lab Assistant: Elementary Science Experiments for the Apple," *Classroom Computer News* (September/October 1980): 18–19.
- Richard McLeod and Beverly Hunter, "The Data Base in the Laboratory," *Science and Children,* 24, no. 4 (January 1987): 28–30.

Any minds-on/hands-on experimental activities where a computer and sensor gather, process, and display data directly from the environment has been called **microcomputer-based laboratory** or **MBL.**[10] Much science can be done with very simple and inexpensive MBL systems.[11] In addition, MBLs turn the focus away from mere trivial mechanical processes in laboratory activities to higher and more creative levels of scientific processes, that is, analysis, hypothesizing, and evaluating.[12] With MBLs, data gathering/analyzing/processing is so easy that it motivates explorations and discovery. Students focus on thinking about data and not merely on gathering it.

The MBL programs listed in Table 10–1 are available to you. The kits supply everything you need—sensor and/or probe devices, connection hardware, simple directions, and software. Each uses a game paddle or control stick and are the simplest and least expensive programs to connect to your computer.

Using Combinations of MBLs and Multimedia Learning. Innovative MBLs are becoming more available to schools so that "traditional" print materials may be combined with the latest electronic technology—television, videodiscs, computer software, and probe and sensor devices. One such exciting approach to learning is *The Voyage of the Mimi,* jointly prepared by the Bank Street College of Education and Holt, Rinehart & Winston Publishers. Geared primarily for grades 4 through 8 (and also applicable above and below these grades), the goals of the *Mimi* are to increase students' understanding of science/mathematics and technology and society; convey that science is an exciting and rewarding human enterprise; and present activities for performing complete experiments in sound, light, and temperature.

The total *The Voyage of the Mimi* program consists of four main teaching/learning components:

1. Television series—twenty-six 15-minute dramatic documentary episodes.
2. *The Voyage of the Mimi* student's and teacher's guides.
3. Wall charts.

TABLE 10–1
Computer-based laboratory programs (MBL)

MBL Program Vendor	Sensor/Probes Used	Type Lab Activities
Comp Trol Lab EduTech 303 Lamartine St. Jamaica Plains, MA 02130	photo gate	pendulum and acceleration
Experiments in Science HRM 175 Tompkins Ave. Pleasantville, NY 10570 (800) 431-2050	light, temperature, timer, plugs, and probes	optics, heart rate, evaporation, humidity
Heat, Light, and Sound Experiments Cross Educational Software 1802 N. Trenton St. PO Box 156 Reston, VA 71270	temperature and light sensors and sound intensity meter	thermal radiation, solar, and heat gain
Atarilab Starter Kit Atari PO Box 61657 Sunnyvale, CA 94086	temperature probe	dewpoint, evaporation, melting point, temperature measurement

4. Four Software Learning Modules CAI Simulations: "Introduction to Computing," "Maps and Navigation," "Whales and Their Environments," and "Ecosystems."[13]

Figure 10–3 presents the components of the *Mimi*.

The total *Mimi* program is not inexpensive, but it is possible to start the program for several hundred dollars by carefully selecting specific components to meet your particular teaching/ learning needs. If several grades and classes use the materials, it can be cost effective for student users. Also, many schools have access to computer literacy materials and may not need the module, "Introduction to Computing." In the same vein, although the "Maps and Navigation" module is entertaining, it is not essential. You could use more traditional materials (i.e., maps, globes, or compasses) to teach these skills. However, you would probably need the two CAI simulation software programs "Whales and Their Environment" (with the Bank Street Laboratory) and "Ecosystems" (with "Land Survivors").

Reviews have indicated that *The Voyage of the Mimi* is an excellent addition to the minds-on/hands-on science program for elementary and middle school students. Other multimedia electronic programs of this type should proliferate because the technology has already arrived to augment and enrich active learning experiences for your students. As they do, you will witness a drastic reduction of prices.

/// NEW ELECTRONIC TECHNOLOGY FOR YOUR SCIENCE CLASSROOM

The "next generation" of technology for the classroom includes interactive videodiscs, LCD projection systems, and telecommunications. Brief descriptions of these promising electronic teaching aids follow.

Interactive Videodiscs—Adding Challenging Realism to Your Science Teaching

Imagine that you are teaching about volcanic action with your elementary or middle school students. Besides learning cognitive aspects, you would love to have them experience the affective domain learnings through sights, sounds, and other sensory reactions to these dramatic forces of nature. But how? Take them to a volcano? Not very practical for most of us, and it could be a potentially dangerous field trip.

Now, however, an electronic device called **interactive videodisc** is available to you to give some of these sensory impacts. These discs are plastic and look like silvery phonograph records or compact discs. They can hold any combination of 54,000 individual pictures, printed text, diagrams, films, and animations on one side of the disc, for a total of 108,000 on both sides! Videodiscs are also called **laser discs,** because they are recorded and play back by a laser or light beam. This makes them almost indestructible, because unlike phonograph records, there is no needle (or anything else) that touches, scratches, or wears down the surface of the discs. A beam of light "reads" and passes the stored electronic data from the disc to the videodisc player. The same principle is used in the compact discs used for recording music.

CD ROM, The New Videodisc on the Block

An updated optical technology storage/retrieval system similar to that of the videodisc is the **Compact Disc Read Only Memory** or **CD ROM.** CD ROMs are smaller than videodiscs and the same size (5″) as the popular CD audio discs. The major advantage of the CD ROM is the *enormous* amount of information that can be stored on one disc. One CD ROM can store

The complete program consists of:

"The Voyage of the Mimi" Television Series

Thirteen 15-minute episodes of dramatic adventure and thirteen 15-minute documentary "Expeditions" capture student interest right from the start...present a wide variety of scientific/mathematical concepts in real-world settings...form a lively basis for further study.

"The Voyage of the Mimi": The Book

Features richly illustrated summaries of each television episode...plus additional illustrations, science and math activities, and a comprehensive glossary.

Overview Teacher's Guide

Offers you detailed strategies for turning the television series and Student Guide into powerful classroom tools with additional background information for the teacher, plus a description and rationale for all components.

Learning Modules

Four "learning modules" use print materials and exciting microcomputer activities to develop specific knowledge and concepts introduced in the television series. The software games and activities extend concepts, and model real-world applications of computers and problem-solving tools.

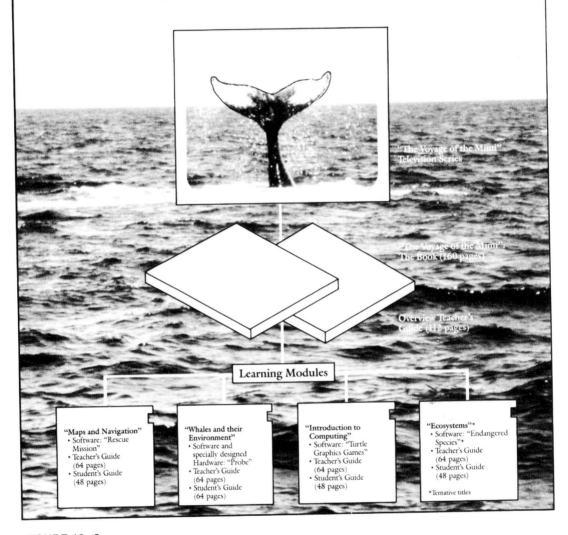

FIGURE 10–3

The Voyage of the Mimi components

Source: The Voyage of the Mimi (New York: Holt, Rinehart & Winston, 1984). Reprinted with permission by Holt, Rinehart & Winston, Inc.

whole encyclopedias (Grolier's *Electronic Encyclopedia*) or the data from 380 floppy discs that are 3½" size! Libraries are using CD ROMs for ERIC information. The National Science Foundation and the Carnegie Corporation funded and tested one CD ROM, called *Helper K–8,* that contains 1,000 hands-on science lessons that are easily retrievable and that may be freely copied and distributed. The single 5" CD ROM disc contains as much information as 250 books! You may receive a demonstration version on two floppy diskettes for use on IBM-PC or compatible computer from PC-SIG, 1030 East Duane Avenue, Sunnyvale CA 94086.

Because the process of videodiscs and CD ROMs is similar to videotape recordings with which you are familiar, Table 10–2 shows some of the advantages of videodiscs and CD ROMs over videotapes.

Videodiscs and CD ROMs are really catching on in science education. It is important to note, that *Windows on Science,* the first videodisc-based science program approved for state adoption as a "textbook" has been chosen by 65% of elementary schools in Texas. For more information contact Windows on Science, Optical Data Corp., 30 Technology Dr., Warren, NJ 07059 or (800) 248-8478.

How to Use Videodiscs or CD ROMs in Your Science Teaching[14]

You can use videodiscs and CD ROMs in your science teaching in many ways, based on the level of student interaction you want for your teaching/learning activities, the hardware and software you have, and the ways you want the interaction to take place. Table 10–3 shows these levels of interaction and the components that are needed.

Getting Started with Videodiscs and CD ROMs in Your Science Teaching. At what level you use videodiscs and CD ROMs in

TABLE 10–2
Advantages of videodiscs and CD ROMs over videotapes

Videodiscs (Laser Discs)	Videotapes
Any combination of text, diagrams, slides, maps, films, animations, and computer commands	Motion sequences only
Two sound tracks containing any combination of recorded voice, music, sound effects; can have one track in English and another in Spanish	One sound track
Store 108,000 frames or one hour of motion video	Four hours of motion video only
Play forward and backward at variable speeds and freeze single frames indefinitely without harming disc or player	Most limited to forward and rewind; if freezing frame is possible, it could damage the tape
Random access medium—locate any frame or sequence on disc by keying the frame number	Linear medium—have to wind through tape until desired spot is reached
Excellent quality audio and video production and playback	Average to good production and playback
Extremely durable, data stored under protective plastic surface; cleaned by damp cloth and even scratches do not affect reproduction	Fragile, easily harmed; wear out with frequent use

TABLE 10-3

Levels of interaction using videodiscs and CD ROMs in science teaching[15]

Interaction Levels	Type of Interaction	Components Needed
0	**Stored Data Only** (not interactive)—collections of slides, photos, animations, films, printed text	Videodiscs and player monitor
I	**Electronic Index of Stored Data**—each single frame described and categorized with a number for rapid retrieval by punching number into remote control device; example: Questions are raised about volcanoes; teacher brings up appropriate slides, films, photos that enrich discussion.	Same as above, plus remote control device
II	**Electronic Scanning of Stored Data**—students use videodisc's index to find data by: a. *Keywords* (volcano, eruption, Mount Saint Helens) b. *Topical names, chapters, outline headings* (earth's changing face) c. *Graphics* (maps of active volcanic areas, magma diagrams)	Same as above, plus micro-processor
III	**Higher Thinking Skills Tools**—all of the above functions plus these videodisc tools: a. *Simulations* with audio/visual materials for students to interact, collect, analyze, etc. b. *Tutorials* to teach at child's learning level and select appropriate data mode (slides, films, print materials, etc.) c. *Textbooks* and videodisc materials correlated with science curriculum d. *You* can create lessons using frames and films from videodiscs in any sequence you want (called authoring videodisc system).	Same plus laserdisc player, computer interface software

your science teaching will probably depend on these practical considerations and possible approaches to their solutions.

1. Budget. Prices are rapidly dropping in electronic equipment, but you will need money for a videodisc player ($500–$1,000); interactive videodisc or CD ROM packages that correlate with your school curriculum, including appropriate software and student response books ($400 and up); a computer and color monitor ($700 and up); and individual videodiscs and CD ROMs ($15 and up). You can start with basic hardware/software and add as money becomes available. If teachers share materials by grade or school, costs per child can be reduced. Teachers, students, schools, parent-teacher groups, and local business people have raised money by a variety of approaches for such purposes.

2. Becoming videodisc and CD ROM/ computing literate. Start by talking to any teacher in your school or district who has a videodisc or CD ROM, and actually work with her or him on a step-by-step orientation. If no teachers or machines are available to you, contact commercial publishers of interactive video packages specifically developed for education. Here are a few for starters. Most of them also sell the hardware components you will need to set up an interactive videodisc system.

■ The Information Laboratory Software
Addison-Wesley
2725 Sand Hill Rd.
Menlo Park, CA 94025
(800) 227-1936
■ Health EduTech
EduTech
7801 East Bush Lake Rd.
Minneapolis, MN 55435
■ The Living Textbook
Optical Data Corp.
30 Technology Dr.
Warren, NJ 07059
(800) 524-2481
■ Mammals: A Multimedia Encyclopedia
National Geographic Society
Educational Media Division
17th and M Streets, NW
Washington, DC 20036
(800) 368-2728
■ MIST
Evergreen Laser Disc, Inc.
St. Paul, MN 55100
■ Teaching Technologies
PO Box 3808
San Luis Obispo, CA 93403

■ Videodiscovery, Inc.
PO Box 85878
Seattle, WA 98145

Select a videodisc or CD ROM system that correlates with your science curriculum or your science textbook. When you feel more comfortable with commercial videodiscs or CD ROMs, prepare a videodisc of your own slides, printed text, maps, or films. Organize your own "menu" or indexing system for you and your students to use.

Examples of How to Use Videodiscs and CD ROMs in Your Science Teaching. You can use your commercial or self-made videodiscs and CD ROMs in your science classroom in many ways:

1. Creating an almost instant access storage system for volumes of information. Using a computer and an automatic videodisc or CD ROM changer, you can cross-reference materials from up to 72 separate videodiscs or CD ROMs and retrieve the required information.

2. Illustrating materials for your science lessons. Connected to a laserdisc player and video monitor, your computer becomes a powerful "teleprompter" combining your lesson plan with appropriate audiovisual aids. Using a **barcode reader,** you can incorporate bar codes (like the UPC codes on retail packaging) into your lesson plans, and at appropriate places activate them into your videodisc showing.

3. Presenting science lessons to small groups of your total class. For example, to explain the concept of phototropism, select time-lapse shots and slides of plants growing toward the light to make the learning more dramatic and meaningful. You can pause at critical points, show entire sequences in slow motion, and review important concepts quickly and easily.

4. Reinforcing minds-on/hands-on science activities. If your students are engaging in activities involving variables that affect seed germination, seeing films and animation of the same processes on videodisc or CD ROMs strengthens and clarifies students' conceptual development.

5. Helping your students research, study, and present reports. Your students can use the materials stored on videodiscs or CD ROMs when doing reports just as they would use an encyclopedia. Then, when they are ready to present their reports, they can use the indexing or menu in conjunction with the remote control device to bring up, sequence, and show pertinent segments of the videodisc. Some teachers have trained a corps of students to be "videodisc helpers," assisting others who need help using videodiscs.

6. Doing desktop publishing. You can develop your own teaching materials that range from simple handouts and overhead transparencies to student science "lab" or workbooks.

7. Assisting students in their science projects. Students use videodiscs and CD ROMs to develop their own reports, video term papers, or other project reports by selecting pictures from one disc or slides from another.

8. Evaluating students. To supplement your science classroom written tests, videodiscs and CD ROMs lend themselves to presenting slides or sequences on the TV screen for the whole class to view and respond to your related questions. This may be most appropriate and practical when showing animation and films to test your students on items such as microscopic slide identification (onion skin, etc.), plant and animal physiology processes and development, aspects of the outdoor environment (especially in inclement weather), or aspects of Earth as seen from space capsules.[16]

You and Your Students Can Produce Videotapes!

Fully automatic camcorders and simple-to-operate videocassette recorders (VCRs) make it very easy for you and your students to produce science videotapes. These videocassettes could be culminating activities for student projects, instructional for teacher presentations, or for challenges for individuals or small groups similar to the challenge cards described in Chapter 9.

Here are some ideas on how you and/or your students can produce science video challenges.[17]

1. Prepare a script for a 10 to 20 minute videocassette tape that has these elements:
   - *Grabbing the Audience.* Get a discrepant event, a funny story, unusual happening, or a unique natural occurrence to stimulate the viewer to want to participate in the challenge.
   - *Setting up the Challenge.* Ask viewers to duplicate what they just saw presented. A shoe box of science materials is provided for viewers to perform minds-on/hands-on activities relating to the challenge. Viewers are urged to stop the videocassette before they manipulate the science materials.
   - *Trying to Solve the Challenge.* Viewers are encouraged to use whatever problem-solving techniques they can (e.g., brainstorming or trial-and-error) to solve the problem presented. They may resume the tape when they have solved the challenge or need additional information.
   - *Assessing Findings.* Viewers can check their findings against the demonstrations on the videocassettes for alternative solutions, scientific principles involved, further information, and everyday scientific/technological applications.
2. Videotape your challenge, try it out with groups of students or adults, request evaluations from viewers, and modify (re-record) any sections requiring it.
3. Solicit ideas for additional videocassette challenges from viewers.

Students can plan and shoot their own videotapes.

With a camcorder, VCR, some inexpensive videocassettes, and 25 students, you can soon have quite a collection of challenges.

Making Your Presentations Bigger and Better with LCDs[18]

If you are lucky enough to have a computer or videodisc set up in your science classroom, you probably have wrestled with this problem: You want to show something to your total class from the computer or videodisc player, and you have the students crowd around your one TV monitor. There's usually shoving, other discipline problems, and complaints: "Miss Orkand, I can't see." Until now, the only solution was a $5,000 large-screen video projector. However, now an electronic breakthrough can solve this problem—a new type of **liquid crystal display (LCD)** projection system is available, simple to operate,

practically indestructible, and relatively inexpensive ($600 and up).

An LCD projection system is an electronic device that attaches to your computer or videodisc player. It looks like a plastic briefcase (without handles) with a window, and is usually no larger than 12×18 inches and a couple of inches thick. Instead of showing your computer videodisc program on your monitor, the device projects it on the system's transparent LCD screen. You then put the LCD screen on your overhead projector the same way you would for a regular transparency. Your image is lit up, projected, and enlarged to whatever size is practical to see on any size white screen. Imagine the impact microbes will have on your students if they are projected on a 9-foot screen, instead of your 15-inch monitor! Any computer or videodisc software can be shown using an LCD projection system, including films, animation, graphics, and print text. Numbers, graphics, and print text stand out more clearly than when crowded on small TV screens. (See Figure 10–4.)

Nothing Is Perfect. Although the LCD projection system is simple to operate and relatively inexpensive, be aware of these technological trade-offs:

1. You must use an overhead projector that has a light projection from the *base* and not from the top.
2. Brightly lit overhead projectors work best for LCD projection.
3. Most LCD projection systems are designed to work only with an Apple or an IBM PC or compatible microcomputer. Any other system may require additional adapters.
4. You can display your computer or videodisc simulations on a TV monitor and LCD projection system at the same time by using a **"Y" adapter** or similar electronic coupler that comes with some LCD systems, but some clarity may be sacrificed.

5. Clarity (resolution) of graphics suffers on some LCD screens. Look for faster megahertz rates (the time it takes the liquid crystals to fade and reappear on your screen) or "refresh times" for greater clarity.
6. Make sure the LCD projector system has a fan (to remove heat from the overhead projector), a remote control device, and special software for editing and saving.

Before you buy, test any LCD projector system under your own conditions: light, distance from screen to projector, and overhead projector you will use. Vendors are willing to demonstrate their products in schools. Some LCD projector system companies you might contact are the following:

- Apollo Audio Visual
  60 Trade Zone Court
  Ronkonkoma, NY 11779
  (800) 777-3750

FIGURE 10–4
Liquid crystal display (LCD) projection system

- Proxima Corporation
  6610 Nancy Ridge Dr.
  San Diego, CA 92121
  (800) 447-7694
- Dukane Corporation
  2900 Dukane Dr.
  St. Charles, IL 60174
- Elki International, Inc.
  27882 Camino Capistano
  Laguna Niguel, CA 92677
- Sharp Electronics Corporation
  Sharp Plaza
  Mahwah, NJ 07430
- Sayett Technology, Inc.
  17 Tobey Village Office Park
  Pittsford, NY 14534
  (800) 678-7469
- Telex Communications, Inc.
  9600 Aldrich Ave., South
  Minneapolis, MN 55420
  (800) 328-3771

Large screen LCD projectors add new dimensions and make a wide range of teaching/learning options for you in science teaching with computers.

Bringing the Outside World into Your Science Classroom

Another promising electronic/technology technique now available to you is **telecomputing.** Telecomputing is the communicating with computers in remote locations over phone lines. To understand telecomputing or electronic networking, visualize your personal computer not as a computational machine but as a communication device. Just as the many national and international phone systems magnify the usefulness of your individual telephone, electronic networks magnify the utility of your computer, which allows you, fellow teachers, and your students to share data and peripheral devices and send files and electronic mail.[19]

You can telecompute from your computer in two ways:

1. To an electronic **bulletin board system (BBS).** The National Science Teachers Association's *Science Line* is an example.
2. Within a **network.** *Electronic Information Exchange System (EIES), Educators' Electronic Exchange (EEE)* is an example.[20]

Your science classroom computer can be used to search through database materials from throughout the United States and other parts of the world, and instantly retrieve this information. **Databases** (electronically stored information) exist in all the curricular areas, including science. For instance, if your students are studying the interrelationships between wind direction and speed and weather conditions, they can instantly gather information from a variety of geographic locations without leaving your classroom. This not only motivates students and encourages them to use higher thinking processes, but it also helps students effectively learn how to select and secure information, a process that is vital in our information-laden society. Also, telecomputing allows your students to send and receive **"electronic mail"** anywhere in the world. It is a kind of "electronic data pen pal" for the sharing of computer information.

What's Needed for Telecomputing?

To accomplish telecomputing in your classroom, all you need is a computer and a **modem,** which works this way:

1. A modem (electronic device) connects your computer to a standard telephone line by a connector wire, or some just have the telephone receiver face down on the modem.
2. The modem translates or "modulates" electronic impulses from your computer into audible tones that can be transmitted through the telephone receiver, and also "demodu-

lates" or translates incoming audible signals back into electronic impulses that your computer can interpret. That's how we get the name *modem*: MOdulate—DEModulate.

Modems cost about $50 and up and require special communication computer software, which may or may not come with the modem. You pay for telephone charges used, and many regions of the country charge only local charges for national communications databases and networks. Some information services charge hourly fees in addition to subscription fees.

Local Area Networks (LANs)

Many areas are developing **local area networks (LANs),** which electronically link computers. In this way, software from a "host" computer is shared electronically with all the others in the LAN. This eliminates the expense of having to buy many software packages or disk drives for each machine; LANs also reduce the illegal copying of software. You will gain substantial dollar savings by participating in a LAN, as well as teaching advantages from a time and convenience standpoint. LANs can cost from $200 and up per terminal, but they more than pay for themselves in teaching/learning benefits.

Here are some curriculum-based online network projects:

- AT&T Long Distance Learning Network
  PO Box 4012
  Bridgewater, NJ 08807
  (800) 367-7225
- Global Lab
  TERC—Communications Dept.
  2067 Massachusetts Ave.
  Cambridge, MA 02140
  (617) 547-0430
- National Geographic Kids Network
  National Geographic Society
  17th and M Sts., NW
  Washington, DC 20036
  (800) 368-2728

- World Classroom
  GTE Education Services
  8505 Freeport Parkway, Suite 600
  Irving, TX 75063
  (800) 927-3000

In summarizing how telecomputing can be used in your science teaching with a computer, modem, communications software, and a telephone line, you and your students can

- access commercial databases and information services,
- do collaborative research with other teachers and students locally or around the world,
- get up-to-the-minute weather data,
- communicate using electronic mail, and
- join discussions on bulletin boards and computer conferences about science topics.[21]

/// APPLICATIONS OF ELECTRONIC TECHNOLOGY TO YOUR SCIENCE CLASSROOM

Here are some practical suggestions for using computers and other electronic technology to teach science to your students.

1. Become familiar with the relatively inexpensive computers available by asking these critical questions:
   a. Is science software available and suitable for the particular computer in your classroom? (See computer software evaluation later in this chapter.)
   b. Is the electronic equipment easily portable?
   c. Does the computer contain a true typewriter-style keyboard?
   d. Is there a minimum of 64K random access memory (RAM)?
   e. Is the electronic equipment vendor reliable? Can the vendor readily supply maintenance and repairs when needed?

2. Find out what each system looks like and how the parts work.

3. Master basic computer vocabulary such as input devices—typewriter, joy stick, touch panel, and graphics tablet; output devices—printer, loudspeaker, and television screen; memory means for storing information electronically; central processing unit—the "heart" or "brain" of the computer that carries out logical operations according to a program or a set of very precise instructions. Vocabulary is essential. One teacher has remarked, "I want to ask a question, but I don't even know the words for the things I want to ask about." (See the "Computer and Telecommunications" Glossary.)

4. Learn the procedure for starting up a computer lesson on some common computers.

5. Find out what kinds of lessons are available in your field.

6. Gain hands-on experience with a variety of lessons, simulations, and computer games.

7. Be able to describe and explain the capabilities and languages of various computer systems (e.g., IBM, Radio Shack TRS-80, Apple, Commodore Pet, and others).

8. Build up a file of articles, books, information sources, and bibliographic resources.

Setting Up and Managing Your Science/Technology-Oriented Classroom

Some elementary and middle schools are setting up computer or technology centers, group-

Computers can promote cooperative learning in addition to providing motivation for individuals and groups.

ing all their electronic equipment in one room. Classes of students are scheduled into the computer center, and either a "computer specialist teacher" conducts computer lessons, or individual teachers work with their own classes there. For a detailed plan for setting up a classroom computer system, including every aspect of implementation and possible sources of funding see Robert V. Bullough, Sr., and La-Mond F. Beatty, *Classroom Applications of Microcomputers, 2nd ed.* (New York: Merrill/Macmillan, 1991).

It is more likely that now or in the near future you will have one or more computers in your self-contained classroom. Here are some guidelines to set up and manage a computer (and possibly other electronic technology such as MBL, videodiscs, and telecommunication equipment) for a class of 30 to 35 students.

1. A variety of educational technologies should be used to accommodate a range of learning styles and backgrounds of your students (e.g., texts, videos, minds-on/hands-on materials, computers, and an MBL).
2. Tables should be strategically grouped for students to work in cooperative learning groups.
3. The following learning stations should be set up for groups of five students: listening station, video station, minds-on/hands-on materials station, a word processing station, an MBL station, and a writing station. See Figure 10–5 for a suggested floor plan for a science/technology-oriented classroom incorporating these stations.
4. The teacher's work station should have a computer (as the central server for students' computers and connected to other computers in school and outside), an LCD projection system and large-screen monitor so that everyone in your class can read the words and numbers printed by the computer, a printer, and a modem.

5. Your classroom should contain the three types of computer stations:
   - Student computer work station to run activities.
   - Microcomputer-based laboratory (MBL) for student-conducted activities.
   - An interactive videodisc/CD ROM station for viewing videos and software.
6. To begin a computer literacy program with elementary or middle school students, it is probably best to follow these steps:
   a. Obtain one of the many simple computer textbooks/software programs.
   b. Go through each section of the textbook with the whole class.
   c. For the hands-on sessions, call one student at a time to the keyboard of the computer at the teacher work station. While the student does the activity on the computer, the rest of the class follows in their textbooks and watches what is actually happening on the TV screen. Your job during this phase is to point out what the student at the computer is doing.
   d. After five minutes, call on another student to go to the computer to give as many students as possible hands-on experience. You may need to have pairs or groups of threes doing the hands-on part of the activity.
7. Normal overhead room lighting should be used, but avoid glare off the TV screen from windows. Also avoid setting up the TV screen so that it is silhouetted against a bright window.
8. Arrange to lock the computer when it is not used. Many schools engrave the name of the school on each component and bolt them to tables or portable carts.
9. Arrange your classroom schedule so that students who are responsible can use the computer(s) at any of the appropriate stations on a sign-up basis when they have completed their other classroom responsi-

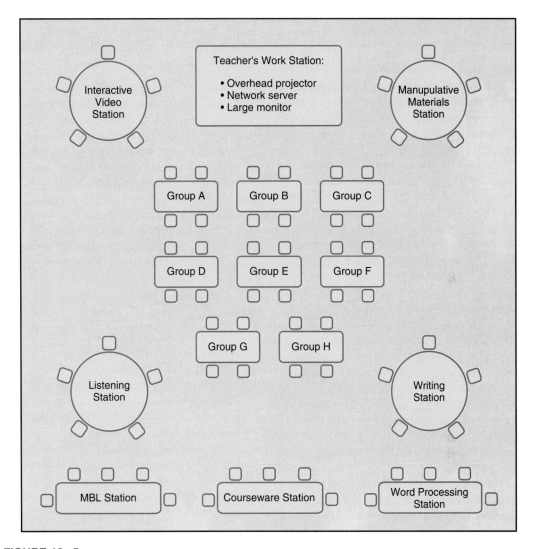

FIGURE 10–5

Science/technology-oriented classroom

Source: *New Designs for Elementary School Science and Health. A Cooperative Project of Biological Sciences Curriculum Study (BSCS) and International Business Machines (IBM)* Dubuque, IA: Kendall/Hunt Publishing Co., 1989):50. Reprinted by permission.

bilities. You will find computer experience is very popular and can positively motivate students to complete assignments. Encourage this.

10. Also encourage your students to share with their classmates any of their own software that is compatible with your computer.

11. Periodically review the computer content and skills with simple tests and introduce your students to new software as it becomes available.

Student Personal Computer Learning Stations

Besides having a computer centrally located at the teacher work station in your classroom for total class demonstrations or having it on a portable cart, you should set up student computer learning stations where up to five students can work on learning software and word processing. These would be similar to the learning centers described in Chapter 6, where collections of materials are arranged for students to work on individually or in small groups. For example, you might set up a science computer learning station in a corner of your classroom and include activity or task cards and materials and supplies for students to work on their own. You can do the same with your computers in these ways:

1. Place your computer, software, and other pertinent materials in your computer learning station, and locate it so you can see it from any place in the classroom.
2. Instruct your total class on the basics of turning on, programing or loading (booting) your computer, and any other necessary simple directions for beginning computer literacy.
3. Select two or three students who know about and have used computers, give them training before or after school, and have them become your "peer computer experts." They will have to know the hardware and software in your room, how to operate the computer, and how to positively help their classmates.
4. Set up a schedule so students can sign up for computer time at the computer station, but include some "open" or free times. Your schedule should have a sign-up sheet with time spent on the computer, so you can ensure that all students get computer time.

Your Most Important Computer Decision—Selecting Software and Courseware

Computer programs, generally referred to as **software,** vary greatly in suitability for use with your elementary and middle school students. Publishers are starting to produce software that is designed to supplement or be an integral part of science programs and textbooks, and they are calling them **courseware.** Much software and courseware will be purchased in the coming years, and you may be called on to suggest which ones your school should buy. It will take time to develop the skills to do this. Here are some guideline questions for selecting and evaluating software and courseware for your elementary and middle school science program:

1. Is the program easy to use?
2. Is the program design flexible?
3. Is the "menu" complete?
4. Is the program content accurate and well designed?
5. Does the program offer a complete learning package?
6. Is the reading level what you need?
7. Are the graphics direct and appropriate?
8. Is there a program purchase warranty?
9. Has the software been reviewed or recommended?[22]

Also consider these additional software and courseware guideline questions designed specifically for you as a science teacher:

1. Is the software and courseware program correlated with science curriculums or textbooks you use?
2. Does the software manual give a list of science vocabulary used in the software?
3. How are the software content or teaching techniques correlated with science content and processes that are your goals?

4. Are follow-up or student and teacher enrichment science activities or demonstrations offered?

For additional assistance with software and courseware assessment see

■ *Microsoft Courseware Evaluation*
Northwest Regional Evaluation Laboratory
300 S.W. 6th Avenue
Portland, OR 97204
■ *PRO/FILES*
EPIE Institute
Box 839
Water Mill, NY 11976
■ *The Educational Software Selector (T.E.S.S.)*
Teachers College Press
1234 Amsterdam Avenue
New York, NY 10027

The following sources also supply evaluations of computer software and courseware.

/// COMPUTER AND OTHER ELECTRONIC TECHNOLOGY RESOURCES

This list will help you start to collect information on computers and other electronic technologies and their uses in your science classroom.

Computer and Other Classroom Electronic Technology Journals or Magazines

■ *Byte,* PO Box 590, Martinsville, NJ 08836.
■ *Classroom Computer News,* PO Box 266, Cambridge, MA 02138.
■ *Compute,* PO Box 789-M, Morristown, NJ 07960.
■ *Computing Teacher,* Department of Computer and Information Science, University of Oregon, Eugene, OR 97403.

■ *Creative Computing,* 39 East Hanover Avenue, Englewood Cliffs, NJ 07950.
■ *Electric Learning,* 902 Sylvan Avenue, Englewood Cliffs, NJ 07632.
■ *Microgram,* PO Box 620, Stony Brook, NY 11790.
■ *Personal Computing,* 4 Disk Drive, Box 13916, Philadelphia, PA 19101.
■ *Popular Computing,* PO Box 307, Martinsville, NJ 08836.
■ *Science and Children, The Science Teacher,* and *Science Scope,* 1742 Connecticut Avenue, NW, Washington, DC 20009.
■ *Teaching and Computers,* Scholastic Inc., 730 Broadway, New York, NY 10003.

Computer Books for Teachers

■ Joseph Abruscato, *Children, Computers, and Science Teaching. Butterflies and Bytes* (Englewood Cliffs, NJ: Prentice-Hall, 1986).
■ Patricia F. Campbell and Greta G. Fein, eds., *Young Children and Microcomputers: Conceptualizing the Issues* (Englewood Cliffs, NJ: Prentice-Hall, 1986).
■ Eleanor Criswell, *The Design of Computer-Based Instruction* (New York: Macmillan, 1989).
■ Jane I. Davidson, *Children and Computers Together in the Early Childhood Classroom* (Albany, NY: Delmar, 1989).
■ Peter J. Favero, *Educator's Guide to Microcomputers and Learning* (Englewood Cliffs, NJ: Prentice-Hall, 1986).
■ Seymour Papert, *Mindstorms: Children, Computers, and Powerful Ideas* (New York: Basic Books, 1981).
■ Charles S. White and Guy Hubbard, *Computers and Education* (New York: Macmillan, 1988).
■ F. Williams and J. Williams, *Microcomputers in Elementary Education* (Belmont, CA: Wadsworth, 1984).

Discovery: Chemistry in Motion

The goal I had was to have high school chemistry reflect what scientists do.

—Donald J. Mitchell, Project Director

Strategy Maximize resources by using a well-equipped, mobile "laboratory" or learning center.

Two Pennsylvania high school teachers have identified and implemented a way to bring science teachers what their schools may not provide—the equipment to help students work as scientists do.

The innovative idea of Jan Hildenbrandt and Guy Anderson, this support program for rural high school teachers revolves around Juniata College in Huntingdon, Pennsylvania. From there, the van driver heads out to schools within a 50-mile radius, carrying the equipment and supplies that many schools cannot afford. The driver, Tom Spicher, is a former public school teacher.

For teachers who were previously limited to having to demonstrate a science experiment in front of a class, this support program is a boon. The van provides enough supplies for all the students in a class to perform the experiments themselves. Now the students at these rural schools can learn by doing rather than only watching.

How teachers use the program and the van (labeled "Chemistry in Motion") is up to them. Spicher is flexible in his approach. He conducts the class for teachers who want him to, or team teaches with those who prefer to be more involved. Some teachers just want to borrow the equipment and teach the class by themselves.

The Juniata chemistry professor who directs this support program, Donald Mitchell, sees it as a way to bring science learning into step with the

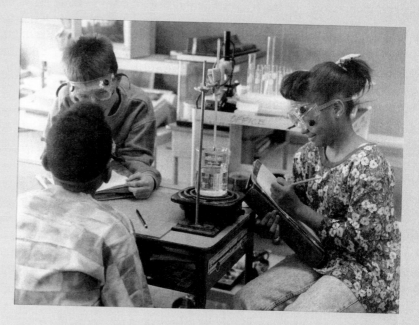

most current teaching theories. Students learn best when they discover their own answers, and the students at the schools served by "Chemistry in Motion" now have the same opportunities as their peers in larger, better-equipped schools in wealthier districts.

On Your Own   You can adapt the concept of "Chemistry in Motion" at different levels and for different purposes.

"In motion" might be inside the school building. Elementary teachers can stock a cart or wagon with materials for simple experiments and move it from one classroom to another, creating a mobile learning center. Three second-grade teachers planning a similar science unit, for example, can combine resources to save time and money by sharing this portable science lab.

Source: Reprinted with permission of Associated Press

■ ■ ■ ✔

Computers and other electronic technology open many vistas for teaching science in the elementary and middle schools, and you can avail yourself of them now. Consider them another tool in your teaching arsenal. Be curious, but critical. Attend computer workshops, conferences, and exhibitions. Most importantly, find out why students are so enthusiastic about computers and other electronic technology and learn to share their enthusiasm. For computers and other electronic technologies to serve you in your science teaching, experiment with them to see how you can find effective ways to incorporate them into your own minds-on/hands-on guided discovery-oriented classroom.

SUMMARY

Computers and other electronic technologies are available to elementary and middle school classrooms and can be as valuable as your other teaching aids in your science teaching. Just as you learned how to teach and use all kinds of teaching tools, you will have to become computer literate if you are to use computers effectively. This means not only learning computer language and how to run a computer, but also how to evaluate and select hardware and software. After you become familiar with the workings of the computer, you can find a variety of ways to use them in your science teaching. Five ways of using computer-assisted instruction (CAI) in your science teaching are drill and practice, dialog and tutorial, simulation and modeling, "lab" data gathering/analysis/processing, and teacher utility. Samples of each were presented, along with suggestions about how to use them in your science teaching.

A "doing" or minds-on/hands-on science program can be enriched by computer programs that involve students in interactive science experiences called microcomputer-based laboratories or MBLs. Other electronic resources available now for developing higher level science thinking in your students are videodiscs, CD ROMs, liquid crystal display (LCD) projection systems, and telecomputing.

Suggestions were given about how to work directly with computer-assisted instruction. Guidelines were suggested for evaluating software for your elementary science computer, along with computer data collection resources, such as computer journals, magazines, and books.

SELF-ASSESSMENT AND FURTHER STUDY

1. Using 800 numbers wherever possible, call or write to vendors listed in this chapter for catalogs on videodiscs and CD ROMs for elementary and middle schools. After reading the catalogs, if any videodisc or CD ROM pro-

grams meet your needs for your science teaching, call the vendor for a demonstration in your school.

2. Visit a local computer store and ask for a computer demonstration using a tutorial or other computer-assisted instruction program, preferably in science for elementary and middle school students. Make a simple evaluation sheet beforehand to evaluate the program for these items:
   - ■ Program name and grade level(s) applicability.
   - ■ Program description.
   - ■ Explanation of the ease of loading and using for students and how you feel students would react to it.
   - ■ *Your* reaction to using it.
   - ■ How it would fit into your science.

3. Take a stand on whether computers can be used effectively by 5- and 6-year-old children in a science program. Consult references, starting with Sandra Anselmo and R. Ann Zinck, "Computers for Young Children? Perhaps," *Young Children,* 42, no.3 (March 1987): 22–27; Douglas H. Clements, "Computers and Young Children: A Review of Research," *Young Children,* 43, no.1 (November 1987): 34–44; and Judith M. Lipinski, et al., "The Effects of Microcomputers on Young Children: An Examination of Free-Play Choices, Sex Differences, and Social Interactions," *Journal of Educational Computing Research,* 2 (1986): 147–168.

4. Using the list of computer journals and magazines in this chapter, see which ones are available in your school or local library. Select and read several that contain articles for using a computer in your classroom. List practical suggestions that you can easily implement in your classroom.

5. Draw a floor plan for making your science classroom technology-oriented. Use the information and Figure 10–5 of this chapter as your starting point. Be sure to include stations for teacher work, interactive videos, manipulative materials, MBL, word processing, courseware, listening, and writing.

6. Discuss the procedures you need to take to start, select, and train a cadre of students to serve as "peer computer helpers." How will you avoid and handle the possible "elitism" problems that could develop?

7. Locate classroom teachers in your school or district who are successfully using a computer with their science teaching. Ask them about hardware, software, and classroom usage, costs, and problems. Evaluate how you could use these ideas in your own classroom.

8. Devise a form for evaluating hardware and software for your unique science program's goals. Use these resources as starters: Ted Krause, "Finding Helpful Software Reviews," *Classroom Computer Learning,* 8, no. 3 (November/December 1987): 44–48 and Karen E. Reynolds, "How to Use the Software Evaluation Form" (with Software Evaluation Form), *Science and Children,* 23, no. 1 (September 1985): 18–20.

9. List five science topics that could be successfully enriched by using computer/videodisc/CD ROM programs. Research videodisc/CD ROM vendors to find specific videodiscs and CD ROMs to meet your teaching/learning needs in these science topics. Then, review them (with vendors demonstrating them for possible purchase) in your classroom with your students to see if they are effective.

10. Plan and make a videocassette challenge with a group of your students on a science topic of interest to them. Include a box of simple materials for conducting the minds-on/hands-on activities that accompany the challenge.

NOTES

1. Michael L. Dertouzos, "Communications, Computers and Networks," *Scientific American,* 265, no.3 (September 1991):62. You are strongly urged to read this Special Issue devoted entirely to computers with articles on Computers, Networks, and Education; The Computer for the 21st Century; Computers, Networks, and Work; and Products and Services for Computer Networks.
2. "U.S. Schools Have More Computers, Survey Reveals." *NSTA Reports!* (September 1991):90.
3. See expanded definition of computing literacy in L. The, "Squaring Off Over Computer Literacy," *Personal Computing,* 6, no.9 (1982).
4. Charles Kinzer, Robert Sherwood, and John Bransford, *Computer Strategies for Education: Foundations and Content-Area Applications* (New York: Merrill/Macmillan, 1986).
5. For an easy-to-understand introduction to computers, read Michael A. DiSpezio, "Everything You Always Wanted to Know About Computers But Were Afraid to Ask. A little explanation goes a long way when it comes to computers," *Science and Children,* 26, no.8 (May 1989):26–28.
6. For an expanded discussion of this topic, see James E. Dezell, Jr., "Restructing Tomorrow's Schools Today," *IBM Supplement to T.H.E. Journal,* (Winter 1990/91):2–3.
7. For great specificity and examples see Jane I. Davidson, *Children and Computers Together in the Early Childhood Classroom* (Albany, NY: Delmar Publishers, 1989), and Mark R. Lepper and Jean-Luc Gurtner, "Children and Computers," *American Psychologist,* 44, no.2 (February 1989):170–178.
8. For the proper place and use of CAI drill and practice activities, see M. Mackey, "Drill, Games, and Programming," *Learning,* 11, no.3 (1982).
9. To visualize how MBL equipment places the computer in the role of "lab partner" see these excellent articles: Larry Frick, "Computers in the Sciences: 'Probing' Temperature and Heat," *The Computing Teacher Conference Issue,* (1990–91):14–16, and M. C. Linn, "Computer as Lab Partner," *Teaching Thinking and Problem Solving,* 18, no.3 (Hillsdale, NJ: Lawrence Erlbaum Associates, 1986).
10. This term and many of the ideas on MBLs can be found in: George E. O'Brien, "Computer-Based Laboratory Learning," *Science and Children,* 28, no.6 (March 1991):40–41, and Tom Lam, "Probing Microcomputer-Based Laboratories," *Hands-On!* 8, no.1 (Winter 1984–85):1–7.
11. R. Nachmias and M. C. Linn, "Evaluations of Science Laboratory Data: The Role of Computer Presented Information," *Journal of Research in Science Teaching,* 24, no.5 (1987):491–506.

12. C. L. Price, "Microcomputer Applications in Science," *Journal of Science Education,* 1, no.2 (1989): 30–33.

13. For a fuller description of the total *Voyage of the Mimi Program,* see Linda Rathje, ed., in "Software Reviews," *The Computing Teacher,* (August/ September 1986):55–57.

14. The following video experts provided information and ideas for this section: Robert D. Sherwood, "Optical Technologies: Current Status and Possible Directions for Science Instruction," in James D. Ellis, ed., *1988 AETS Yearbook. Information Technology and Science Education* (Columbus, OH: Association for the Education of Teachers in Science and ERIC Clearinghouse for Science, Mathematics, and Environmental Education, 1989):35–57); *Should Schools Use Videodiscs?* (Alexandria, VA: The Institute for the Transfer of Technology to Education (ITTE), 1987); *The Educator's Handbook to Interactive Videodiscs, 2nd ed.* (Washington, DC: Association for Educational Communications and Technology, 1987); and *Videodiscs for Education: A Directory, 2nd ed.* (Minnesota Educational Computing Corp., 1987).

15. For further details see Richard Alan Smith, "Videodiscs—The Next Temptation," *Computing Teacher Conference Issue,* (1990–91):8–9.

16. For great specification see "Ten Uses of Interactive Videodisc Systems in the Educational Environment," in *Interactive Laser Disc Technology for Interactive Teaching and Learning Supplement to T.H.E. Journal* (Spring 1990):6.

17. For greater specifics see Alan J. McCormack, "The Family Channel," *Science and Children.* 28, no.2 (October 1990):24–26.

18. For specifics on LCD's see "A Look at the Big Picture," *EPIEgram,* 16, no.3 (1988):10–12.

19. Peter H. Lewis, "Plugging into The Network," in Section 4A Education Life, *The New York Times,* (November 3, 1991):38–41.

20. To learn more about telecommunication see John Kenderdine, Mary Ann Hull, and Ronald Sirianni, "Your Computer, My Computer, Let's Network. We're all "EIES," *The Science Teacher,* 55, no.3 (March 1988):40–42.

21. To see how this technology is being used in schools today, see Therese Mageau, "Teaching and Learning Online," *Electronic Learning,* 10, no.3 (November/December 1990):26–30.

22. Ted Kruse, "Finding Helpful Software Reviews," *Classroom Computer Learning,* 8, no.3 (November/December 1987):44–48.

Guided Discovery Activities

S*cience experiences and activities for young children can be designed to encourage scientific awareness by building on children's natural abilities and thought processes. We, as teachers, can zero in on and use the instinctive curiosity of children, encouraging their explorations and experimentations. To help children develop and increase their expertise in "critical thinking," we can plan activities that incorporate creative problem-solving skills into the existing curriculum.*[1]

[1]Bernice Hauser, "Developing the Skills of Observation," *Teachers Clearinghouse for Science and Society Education Newsletter* 10, no.3, Fall 1991: 15.

Using Guided Discovery Activities

This text contains guided discovery minds-on/hands-on activities for science/technology programs in nursery or preschools, elementary schools (K–6), and middle or junior high schools (6–8). As discussed in the opening paragraph, these activities are intended to assist you in incorporating creative problem-solving skills into your existing curriculum. An important advantage of the guided discovery approach is that both teachers and students become more interested in science when the learner is able to participate, on his or her own level, in physical and mental activities similar to those of scientists. This type of participation actively engages students in scientific/technological processes.

All of the science/technology activities included here have been tested by teachers and students in preschools, elementary schools, and middle or junior high schools. The teachers did not have any special preparation or training in science. In fact, science had not been part of their curricula until these activities were introduced into their classrooms. Several teachers evaluated each activity; the activities were re-

written to incorporate any suggestions, and then these revised activities were retested. Although the activities were originally written for teacher demonstration, in most cases they have been modified to be used as guided discovery minds-on/hands-on activities.

The prime objective of these activities is to have students discover, and/or self-construct, the scientific/technological concepts embedded in the activities as students do the activities. Do not tell your class the purpose of an activity or what can be expected to happen. However, before you go into your classroom to present a particular activity, read it thoroughly and go through its steps. Pay particular attention to the questions, which are meant as guide questions only. *Remember:* Although these activities have been tested in actual classroom situations, no teacher can be certain that a class will respond "according to plan" throughout an activity, so be flexible in your expectations. Also be aware that you do not have to follow the activities exactly. The ideas presented here are intended only as a resource. You must modify these activities to meet the diverse needs, interests, backgrounds, learning styles, and abilities of your individual class.

These guided discovery activities also need not be taught in the order presented since they are meant as sample activities only. It is best to supplement and integrate guided discovery activities with many other curricular activities. After you have had experience with the sample activities, you will gain competence and confidence in designing your own.

/// ORGANIZING, PLANNING, AND CONDUCTING MINDS-ON/ HANDS-ON GUIDED DISCOVERY SCIENCE/TECHNOLOGY ACTIVITIES

Making your science/technology teaching activity-centered means that a major part of it must involve guided discovery minds-on/ hands-on experiences for your students. A great deal of thoughtful planning and organization is needed to convert a well-designed idea into an enriching first-hand science/technology experience.

Planning and Organizing Guided Discovery Minds-On/ Hands-on Science/Technology Activities

The following ideas are some guidelines for preparing enriching science experiences for your students.

1. Decide what you specifically want your students to learn.

2. Select a method by which you will introduce, orient, and structure your minds-on/ hands-on activity.

3. Decide whether or not you should prepare a data collection sheet for students to use.

4. Work out the details of distribution and collection of science equipment and materials. Generally, it is much safer if students stay at their "laboratory" or activity stations (desks pushed together in a non-laboratory room). Take supplies and materials to the stations rather than having students come up for them. The same holds true for collection of materials at the conclusion of the lab activity. This can be done effectively in a Cooperative Learning Group (CLG) arrangement and appropriate tasks can be assigned to students for these purposes.

5. Will your students work individually or in cooperative learning groups? The following symbols will be used in the margin of each guided discovery minds-on/hands-on activity to suggest possible grouping arrangements for you to use at various times during the activity. If more than one symbol appears, choose the arrangement you prefer for your class.

T   *Teacher directing discussion or demonstration with total class.*

I   *Student working individually on task.*

G   *Students working in groups of two, three, or four members.*

6. You should perform the lab activity yourself *before* presenting it to your class to see what is involved, to spot any possible difficulties, and to modify it as necessary to suit your particular class.

Preparation and Safety for Minds-on/Hands-on Science/Technology Activities

1. Make certain you have the necessary science equipment and supplies in sufficient amounts to allow all your students to participate in the lab activity. Whenever possible, have work stations already set up with science materials and equipment before students come into the room or to the work stations.

2. Initial steps like boiling water, heating or cooling materials, and double checking supplies also should be done *before* an activity begins.

3. If any chemicals are used, even diluted vinegar, make sure washing materials are available for students to use.

4. Whenever possible, substitute plastics for all glassware. However, be certain when using heat that the plastics are able to withstand the temperatures. Whenever students use plastic bags, make sure the bags are too small to fit over their heads.

5. Have a fire extinguisher available if open flame is to be used, and give specific instruction on how to use the fire extinguisher properly and what to do if clothing catches fire, such as drop and roll on the ground.

6. Avoid the use of electrical house current (110 volts) for students' activities. Instead, use dry cells when students are handling electrical equipment directly.

7. Assemble glass tubing and stoppers before class, but try to substitute plastic tubing whenever possible. It is convenient to store the assembled stoppers and tubing for later use, rather than disassembling and reassembling them for each activity. (See the discussion in the following section for further suggestions on tubing and stoppers.)

8. Many elementary schools do not allow the use of open flames, or limit their use to teacher-conducted activities only. Be sure to check your school's policy before using open flames.

Conducting Guided Discovery Minds-on/Hands-on Activities

Carefully planned minds-on/hands-on science/technology activities may end in chaos and frustration on your part and your students' unless the activities are carefully conducted as well. The following are some suggestions to help your activities run smoothly.

1. Help your students see the purpose of the activity.

2. Check to see that all your students understand the procedures to be followed. Write the steps on the board and/or have students refer to their minds-on/hands-on data collection sheets. If you use CLGs, go over procedures and cooperative job assignments with individual students.

3. Introduce safety precautions *before* students begin any work. Some general safety precautions to follow are:

a. Familiarize yourself with federal, state, and local school safety regulations, especially your own school district's policies.

b. Stress the serious nature of lab work by being a role model who practices safe behavior and uses necessary protective equipment, such as wearing safety goggles.

c. All accidents, regardless of how slight, should be reported to you and the CLG leader immediately.

d. Directions for using chemicals and heat sources should be followed *exactly*. If students are not certain about something, they should ask you or the appropriate cooperative group leader.

e. Instruct students always to cut materials *away* from them, being careful to stay far enough away from other students to avoid cutting them. You may want to precut materials for those students you judge unable to safely do it themselves.

f. Children in grades K–6 should not insert glass tubing into stoppers. Teachers should follow these safety precautions when inserting glass tubing into stoppers:

(1) Use only glass tubing that is fire polished at both ends.

(2) With glycerine, liberally lubricate the end of the tubing to be inserted in the stopper as well as the stopper hole.

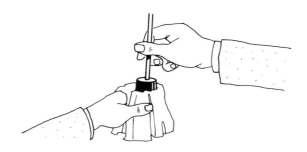

(3) After lubricating, start twisting the tubing into the stopper. Hold the tubing close to the end being inserted. This reduces chances of snapping off tubing.

(4) Glass thermometers should be inserted in stoppers in the same way.

(5) Wrapping a cloth around your hand will give greater protection in case the tubing should snap.

g. Avoid using strong acids. Whenever possible, use substitutes such as vinegar. If acids come in contact with skin, flush the area liberally with water, use a baking soda solution to counteract the acid or vinegar, and take the student to a nurse or doctor.

h. Caution students not to smell or taste *anything* unless they know exactly what it is and that it is safe. Tell them to read all labels carefully.

i. Make provisions for all broken glass, *excess* chemicals, and other waste materials to be placed in proper containers. Avoid pouring chemicals into sinks.

j. Check to see that there is adequate ventilation in the room.

k. When heating a solution in a test tube, always point the test tube away from any individuals.

l. Tell students never to mix chemicals unless they are specifically instructed to do so. Have students wash their hands and nails immediately after each activity.

m. Keep all aisles clear and wipe all spills immediately so the floors do not get slippery.

n. Purchase only safety goggles marked "Z87" on their faces, since they meet the standards set by the American National Standards Institute. Demonstrate the proper way to wear and sanitize goggles when students use sharp objects (knives), chemicals (vinegar), or materials that could fly into their faces (rubber bands).

o. Constantly be alert to any student allergies or sensitivities to foods, plants, chemicals, or other substances used in the activities.

p. Remind students never to put any objects in their mouths; be alert to the choking hazards of pennies, paper clips, marbles, etc.[2]

4. During minds-on/hands-on activities, supervise students at all times! Move about the room throughout the activity to help, answer questions, spot and prevent possible discipline problems, and guide or demonstrate anything that is needed.

5. Always build in sufficient time at the conclusion of each activity for students to clean up and put materials and equipment in their assigned places.

6. Hold a discussion at the conclusion of every activity. Review what was learned and apply students' findings toward tentative conclusions or toward further study. Develop key concepts through artful questioning. Once these concepts are developed, identify them by name. For example, if students engage in an activity where they observe a chameleon eating crickets, tell students that animals that eat other animals are called **predators** and those that are eaten are called **prey.**

/// WRITING AND USING GUIDED DISCOVERY MINDS-ON/HANDS-ON RESOURCE ACTIVITIES

Each guided discovery lesson plan in this text includes most or all of these ten major parts, which are described in the following sections.

1. Age-Level Range or Group
2. Science/Technology Topics

3. Statement of Problem/Questions
4. What Concepts Might Students Discover?
5. Scientific/Technological Processes
6. What Will We Need?
7. What Will We Discuss?
8. What Will Students Do Individually or in CLGs?
9. How Will Students Use or Apply What They Discover?
10. What Must I Know?/Where Do I Find It?

Some of the information in this list is to be used by you and other parts by your students. Some will be used with the total class, in small cooperative groupings, or by individual students. Which ones are to be used, when, and how can be determined only by you, the teacher. Some teachers—mostly in the upper elementary or middle/junior high school grades—who use the guided discovery activities have duplicated these sections for students to use as "lab" or data collection sheets:

■ Statement of Questions or Problem.
■ Student Activities.
■ Science Content, Processes, and Problem-Solving Skills.
■ Student Application of Science Processes and Content.

If you wish to use them for this purpose, you have permission to reproduce those parts of the discovery activities that your students can use directly in your classroom. (*Caution:* They may not be further distributed or sold.) The rest of the preceding format items you will find useful for your own background. In using discovery activities with students who do not read well, you can read the appropriate sections aloud to the students. Some teachers have even put the directions on cassette audiotapes for students to use by themselves.

The most important element in these discovery activities is that students can discover and construct their own concepts through actual physical and mental participation in the activities. Do not tell the students beforehand what

---

[2]For additional information on safety during minds-on/hands-on activities, see Appendix J, "Some Safety Suggestions"; *Elementary Science Syllabus* (Albany, NY: The State Education Department, 1986), 49; and J. Gerlovich and K. Hartman, *Science Safety: A Diskette for Elementary Educators.* JaKel, Inc., 6400 Robin Dr., Des Moines, IA 50322, 1990.

they should expect to find. This robs them of the joy of discovery.

Guided Discovery Minds-on/ Hands-on Lesson Format

What Age Range Might Benefit from This Activity? To help you quickly and easily select guided discovery activities that are most appropriate for your group, the activities are organized by these age ranges and groups:

Preschool.
Primary or lower elementary grades (kindergarten to third grade).
Upper elementary grades (fourth to sixth grades).
Middle or junior high school (sixth to eighth grades).

Grade levels are usually written as *ranges* because many of the guided discovery activities have been tested in several grades and found to work reasonably well in all of them. The difficulty level depends on how deeply you want to probe and the level at which your students are working.

These are age ranges only. Because of the uniqueness of each class, only you can judge the suitability of any particular guided discovery activity and how it has to be modified to fit your class.

What Scientific/Technological Topics Might Students Investigate? Students could delve into a wide variety of topics selected from the life, earth, and physical sciences. There is no set of basic topics for elementary science instruction. One criterion for selection could be student interest and the relevance of the topic to students' lives.

No effort has been made to cover all of the concepts and principles embodied in an elementary science curriculum, since such a project would require an entire book for the activities alone. The guided discovery activities

are organized along these three main sciences only as an aid for teachers in locating a particular science topic quickly:

■ Physical sciences.
■ Life sciences.
■ Earth and environmental sciences.

What Questions or STS Problems Might Students Investigate? The problem of each guided discovery activity within the three topic areas just listed is stated as a divergent question or questions, such as, "What Causes the Seasons?" This helps you quickly select the specific area within one of the three sciences to present to your class.

What Scientific/Technological Concepts Might Students Discover or Construct? This question concerns the scientific principles and concepts students might discover in doing the guided discovery activities outlined in each lesson. They are not exhaustive and others may be discovered by your students as a result of their backgrounds, your skill in guiding them, and other factors. Scientific/technological content presented here can also supply information for you to strengthen your own science content background.

What Scientific Processes Are Involved? Scientific processes are listed at the *left side* of each lesson to show you the types of mental operations your students will be required to perform in each part of the guided discovery lesson.

What Will I Need to Guide This Activity? The science supplies and equipment needed to perform the guided discovery activities are noted. Whenever possible, easily obtainable and nontechnical materials are suggested. For instance, instead of using a beaker (costly) for a nonheating activity, a plastic tumbler may be suggested, or a pyrex baby nursing bottle may be suggested for a beaker that will be heated.

Materials easily found in the immediate environment are stressed for two reasons:

- Most elementary schools do not have extensive science supplies or money to purchase them.
- It is important for children to see that the activities can be done with things easily available to them; hopefully, the children will replicate the activities at home. However, please make it very clear that students should *never* use open flame or dangerous or unknown substances without adult supervision!

Enlist your students' help in getting supplies and items needed for your guided discovery activities from their homes or environment. In addition to saving you time, it will provide for greater involvement of the students in their guided discovery science activity. Often a note sent home to parents telling them what will be studied and needed brings excellent results.

What Will We Communicate or Discuss?

Suggested discussion questions are given for you to ask *before* your students start the guided discovery activities. The purpose of this section is to motivate students and set the learning environment for the guided discovery activities that follow.

What Will Students Do Individually or in Cooperative Working Groups?

This question refers to the guided discovery activities or investigations the students actively participate in, leading to their discovery of the concepts and principles listed under "What Scientific/ Technological Concepts Might Students Discover or Construct?"

How Will Students Use or Apply What They Construct or Discover?

Open-ended questions suggest to students additional investigations they might do to apply what they discover to other real-life situations; for example, "On a cold day, why do you feel warm in the sunlight but very cold in the shade?" You should encourage interested students to attempt to answer these open-ended questions through further investigations. Many of the activities suggested by these questions can be done at home and need not take additional class time. These open-ended questions will also help children probe the *values* level of science as well as integrate other curricular subjects such as mathematics, social studies, and language arts.

What Must I Know?/Where Do I Find It?

Suggestions are given for guiding the students in their discoveries, and these are things *you* must know to make the discoveries as meaningful as possible:

- *Teaching tips* explain more complicated or involved parts of the guided discovery activity.
- *Science content* (facts, concepts, principles, or theories) relevant to the guided discovery activity.
- *Variables* in the guided discovery activity that can affect the outcome.

In addition, you should become as knowledgeable as possible about the science/ technology content, so that you can respond to your students' questions and guide them in finding answers, but not necessarily to "lecture" them on the content. Science/technology content is also presented in "What Might Students Discover?" However, because of limitations in any one textbook, you should also look for science/technology content in your classroom science textbook, children's trade books, and libraries. To assist you, several children's and/or adult science content books are listed in each activity as resources for building your science/technology content background.

Other Less Structured Guided Discovery Activities

In addition to the successful guided discovery minds-on/hands-on activities of previous editions of this text, this edition includes samples of the following:

■ Less structured, or "quickie," guided discovery activities for preschool, primary grades, open classrooms, and other classes to provide enrichment and encourage enjoyment of science.
■ Guided discovery science activities for special needs students, such as the blind or visually impaired, the deaf, and the physically, mentally, and emotionally challenged.
■ Piagetian operations guided discovery activities (i.e., classification, conservation, etc.) and suggestions on how to involve students in these processes.

The less structured, "quickie" guided discovery science activities are not meant to be exhaustive, but are simply sample activities that

■ can be done informally with minimum planning and materials.
■ motivate and stimulate ideas that can lead to deeper investigations into a problem.
■ give students science/technology enrichment opportunities.
■ provide fun and success in science and technology.
■ supply enthusiasm for "doing more science."
■ offer a wide range of opportunities for individualizing science/technology for your students.

Less structured guided activities contain fewer lesson plan details than do guided discovery activities, and may use this simple format:

Materials
Opening Questions
Some Possible Activities

You may want to develop detailed lesson plans for these less structured activities using the guided discovery minds-on/hands-on activity format. In doing so, explore other creative ways of using the "quickie" activities, or where appropriate, use guided discovery science activities in the less structured format.

As with guided discovery science activities, less structured activities also start with opening questions to elicit students' interest and motivation in the activity. Less structured activities are more open-ended and students are freer to wander and explore. For these reasons, the "quickie" activities will be presented before the more structured guided discovery activities, so you may use them as motivators and introductions to the more structured scientific investigations.

/// ORGANIZATION OF GUIDED DISCOVERY SCIENCE/TECHNOLOGY RESOURCE ACTIVITIES

It is impossible to know what specific science activities will be useful for all elementary and middle school teachers in extremely varied teaching/learning environments. Therefore, the following guided discovery science/technology activities are presented to you as possible resources only. As resources, they are ready for use or to be drawn upon and modified for your particular classroom teaching/learning needs. They are not intended to be a science curriculum. Grade levels are given in a range, since it is impossible to say categorically, "This is a first-grade activity," and because different teachers may use all or part of the activity as presented. YOU are the only one who can determine which activity will fill your teaching needs. To assist you in making these decisions, guided discovery resource activities are organized in the following way.

1. Activities are arranged in three general science/technology groups:

Sections	Guided Discovery Activities
1	Physical Sciences/Technology
2	Life Sciences/Technology
3	Earth, Ecology, and Environmental Sciences/Technology

2. Within the three general science/technology groups, activities are clustered around subgroups. (For example, under physical sciences, the subgroups are matter and energy, air pressure, etc.)

3. Activities are arranged within subgroups by age ranges (i.e., K–3, 4–6, 6–8, etc.).

4. Each activity is identified by a question, such as "What Are Water Molecules and How Do They Affect Each Other?"

5. Each subgroup of science/technology activities will start with several "quickie starter" activities, followed by the more structured guided discovery activities.

In summary then, throughout each section, you will follow an overall outline using the following format:

- General science/technology group
- Science/technology subgroup
- Quickie starters
- Guided discovery activities with suggested age ranges

May you have enjoyable and productive science/technology guided discovery minds-on/hands-on activities with your students!

SECTION 1

Physical Sciences
and Technology

MATTER AND ENERGY

QUICKIE STARTERS

Where Did the Water Go?

Materials
: Sponges, paint brushes, dish cloths (This activity should be done on a sunny day, outside the classroom.)

Opening Questions
: *What will happen to water if you brush it on different things outside? How can you find out?*
From where do you think the water will disappear first? Why?

Some Possible Activities
: Invite students to take a paint brush, dip it in water, and brush it over several places to see what happens. Have them play a game to see whose water disappears first. Have students feel the places from which the water disappeared rapidly and compare them with places from which the water did not seem to disappear as fast. For example, students could compare the feel of sidewalks in the sun and sidewalks in the shade. Have students repeat the activity, but this time have them use sponges and washcloths instead of brushes. Have them place wet sponges or cloths on different places and determine which ones dry first.

How Can We Dry Clothes Faster?

Materials

Paper towels, different pieces of cloth (some that are thin and some that are thick like a towel), sponges, twine to hold the cloth, clothespins

Opening Questions

How can we make these things wet?
How can we dry them?
How can we use the twine and clothespins to help them dry?
Where is the best place to put the clothesline? Why?
Which things do you think will dry first?

Some Possible
Activities

Have students make the clothesline; then have students dip various things in water, drain them, and place them on the clothesline with clothespins.

Why Does Water Roll Off Some Things?

Materials

Waxed paper, paper towels, napkins, typing paper, plastic wrap, eye droppers, food coloring

Opening Questions

What will happen when you drop droplets of water on these different kinds of paper and plastic?
How can you find out?
What kind of paper will hold the water the best?
What kinds of paper or plastic will water run off of the easiest?

Some Possible
Activities

Have students discover which materials soak up **(absorb)** water the best and which absorb the least. Which materials do not absorb, or **repel,** water droplets? Use red and blue food coloring to make different colored water drops. Have students use the eye droppers to place one red drop and several blue drops of water, at a distance from each other, on wax paper or plastic wrap. Invite the students to capture all the blue drops, one at a time, with the red drop.

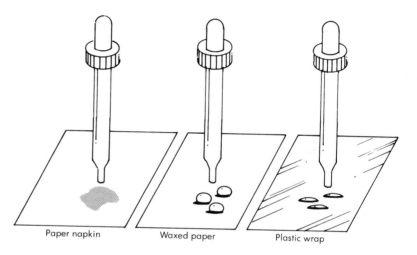

Paper napkin   Waxed paper   Plastic wrap

Have students play Water Droplet Race. Show them how to make drop slides of the same lengths and inclinations, as shown in the art. Students can vary the material they use for each slide. Have three students compete with each other to see on which slides the drops move down the fastest.

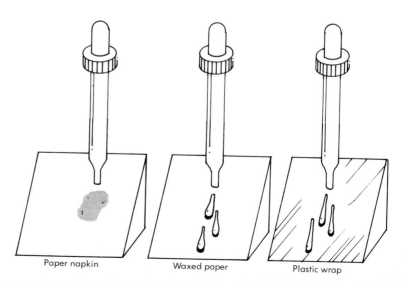

Paper napkin   Waxed paper   Plastic wrap

Applications to
Everyday Life

How might the previous information be used to choose your clothes for these days?

Headband

Wristlets

GUIDED DISCOVERY MINDS-ON/HANDS-ON ACTIVITIES

Why Does Water Appear to Disappear? (K–8)

What Concepts
Might Students
Discover or
Construct?

A liquid appears to disappear when it changes to an invisible gas when heated. The term to describe this process is **evaporation.**

What Will We Need?

An aquarium, paint jars, and containers of water
Measuring cup
Meter- or yardstick and/or a wire coat hanger
Paper clips
$3'' \times 3'' \times 1''$ sponge
Masking tape and/or marking pens

What Will We
Discuss?

Where does the water level in the uncovered aquarium go down?
What caused the water level to change?

Why do wet things take longer to dry on wet days?
How can we measure how much water a sponge holds?
What are some ways to speed up how fast wet objects dry?

PROCESSES*

What Will Students
Do?   *Measuring*

Observing
Measuring

G

Recording

Hypothesizing

Constructing

G

Part I

1. Using masking tape or marking pens, mark the beginning water levels of some uncovered water containers, such as an aquarium, a paint jar, a water jar used for plant cuttings, etc.
2. Check the water levels each morning and, using a measuring cup, add enough water to the containers to bring the water levels back up to original water level marks you made.
3. Keep a record of how much water was added to your containers each week.
   Where did the water go?

Part II

1. Using the meterstick or yardstick, wire coat hanger, and paper clips, build either of the balances shown.

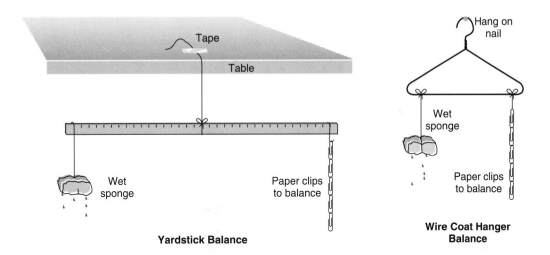

Yardstick Balance

Wire Coat Hanger Balance

2. Soak your piece of sponge until it is dripping water, then hang it with an "S"-shaped paper clip to one end of your balance. Add paper clips to the other end until the balance is level.

Measuring   *How many clips did it take?*

3. Every 15 minutes, check to see if the balance is level.

Observing   *What do you see happening after several observations?*

*Note: Processes in all minds-on/hands-on guided discovery activities refer to the italicized words that appear in the left-hand column.

Hypothesizing   *Why do you think the paper clip end of the balance is lower?*
Keep a written record of what happens.
4. At each 15-minute observation, take off and record how many paper clips must be removed to keep the balance level.

Graphing   5. When the sponge is dry, take your written observations and plot a
line graph with the data. Set up your graph like the one shown.

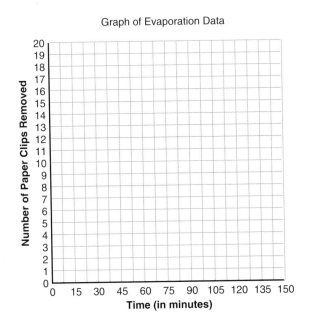

Graph of Evaporation Data

Hypothesizing   6. *What are some variables that might affect how quickly the water in
the sponge evaporates?*

*Designing an
Investigation*   *How could you set up an experiment to test these variables?*

**What Must I
Know?/Where Do
I Find It?**   Some of the variables that affect the rate of evaporation are type of
liquid, evaporation temperature of the liquid, air temperature, wind
velocity, relative humidity, etc. Guide students in gathering data and in
recording and graphing the results in the same way as was done in this
activity.

**How Will Students
Use or Apply
What They
Discover?**   *Why does water evaporate faster from your hands when you vigorously
rub them together?*
Why does your hair dry faster on a dry day than on a wet one?
*Why will a wet towel dry faster if it is spread out rather than crumpled
in a ball?*

What Are Water Molecules and How Do They Affect Each Other? (K–8)

What Concepts Might Students Discover or Construct?	The deeper the water, the greater the pressure. A **force** is defined as a push or pull on an object. Molecules of the same substance tend to "stick to" each other because they are attracted by an invisible force. Each molecule of the substance pulls other atoms to it. The force of attraction between molecules of the same kind is called **cohesive force.** Water has cohesive force.
What Will We Need?	Two one-gallon plastic milk jugs Water (enough to fill containers as desired) Pencil or nail Ruler Glass or plastic tumbler Medicine dropper Pan or bowl 12-inch squares of waxed paper Large basin or tub
What Will We Discuss?	*Why does a drop of water hold together as it runs down a windowpane?* *Why are beads of water hemispherical, especially on a well-waxed automobile?* *Why can some bugs walk on the top of water?* *Why do you think drops of water from a medicine dropper are hemispherical?*

PROCESSES

What Will Students Do?

Observing

Part I

1. Obtain a 12-inch square of waxed paper. Using a medicine dropper, place three or four drops of clean tap water on your waxed paper. *How would you describe the shape of the water droplets? What is their color?*

Observing   2. Push the drops of water around with a pencil point.
What happens to the water when you push the pencil point into a water droplet?

Observing
Hypothesizing   *What happens when you push several droplets near each other?*
Why do you think this happens?

Part II

Hypothesizing
Designing an Investigation
1. Obtain a glass or plastic tumbler and place it in a bowl or dish. Fill the tumbler completely full of water, until some water overflows.
Do you think you can add any more water to the tumbler?
Can you think of how you might test your hypothesis or guess what will happen?

2. Test your hypothesis or try this test. Holding a medicine dropper no more than ½ inch above the water level of the glass, slowly drop water into the glass. (See diagram.)

Measuring   *How many drops of water can you add until the water runs over the rim of the glass?*

Observing   *How would you describe the shape of the water above the rim of the glass? (Hint: Bend down so that you are on eye-level with the rim of the glass.)*

Inferring   *Why does the water rise above the rim of the glass?*
Observing   *At what point does the water run over the rim of the glass?*
Inferring   *Why do you think the water finally runs over the rim of the glass?*
Hypothesizing   *What do you think would happen if you added these things to the glass of water instead of water drops: pennies, paper clips, marbles, etc.?*
Try it.

Part III

Hypothesizing

If the side of a plastic milk jug were punctured with very small holes (one above another) and the jug were then filled with water, what do you think would happen to the water?
How would the water pour out of the holes?

1. Obtain a clean one-gallon milk jug that has the top cut out of it.
2. About 1 ½ in or 4 cm from the bottom of the milk jug, puncture a *very small hole* with a pencil or nail. Puncture three additional small holes ½ in apart, vertically, above the first hole. Put masking tape over the holes. *Caution:* Do not make the holes too large.
3. Fill the container with water to within an inch of the top. Hold the plastic jug over a sink, large basin, or tub and remove the masking tape as shown.

Observing　*What do you notice about the way the water comes out of the holes?*
Inferring　*Why do you think the water comes out of the holes like this?*
Hypothesizing　*If the jug were filled closer to the top with water, do you think there would be a difference in the way the water comes out?*

4. Fill the jug until the water is closer to the top.

Observing　*What do you notice about the way the water comes out of the holes?*

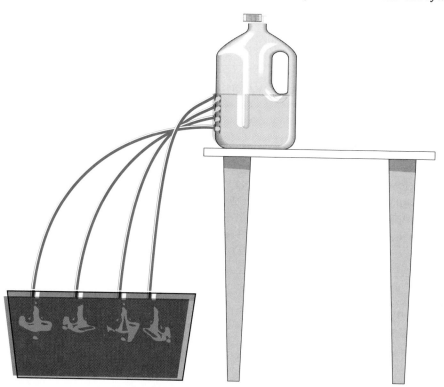

Comparing	*What difference did you notice in the way the water came from the holes of the jug when there was less water and when there was more water in it?*
Inferring	*What can you say about how water pressure varies with depth?*
Hypothesizing	*What results do you think you would get if you used a quart, half-gallon, or two-gallon container? Try it and record your findings.*

Part IV

1. About 2 cm or ½ in apart as shown in the diagram, puncture 4 very small holes in a horizontal line about ½″ from the bottom of the second one-gallon plastic jug. Put masking tape over the holes. *Caution:* Do not make the holes too large and make the holes very close together.

Hypothesizing	*What do you think will happen when water is poured into this container and the masking tape is removed?*
Hypothesizing	*How many jets of water will you get coming out of the holes in the bottom of the plastic jug?*

2. Hold the jug over a sink or large tub, pour water into the jug, and remove the tape.

Observing	*How many jets of water come out?*
Designing an Investigation	*What should you do to the water pouring out of the bottom of the jug, without plugging any holes, so that you get only one jet of water?*

3. Test your hypothesis.
4. Try this activity using quart or half-gallon milk cartons.

What Must I Know?/Where Do I Find It?	Students should pour water into the plastic jug and pinch the jets of water together with their fingers just as though they were going to pinch someone. The jets will form one stream. If the water comes out in one jet, there must be some kind of force holding the water together. The force that holds similar molecules to each other is called **cohesive force**. Each molecule of water has cohesive force that pulls and holds other molecules of water to it. The diagram represents how molecules

of water are held together to form a water droplet due to cohesive force. The pinching of the water brings the jets of water in contact, allowing cohesive force to hold them together. This is true because the cohesive force between two substances increases as the distance between them decreases.

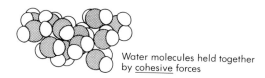

Water molecules held together by <u>cohesive</u> forces

How Will Students Use or Apply What They Discover?

1. *Why do you think a dam is built with very thick walls at the bottom and thinner walls at the top?*
2. *Why do your ears sometimes hurt when you dive deep into a swimming pool? What pushes in on your ears as you go deeper?*
3. *Why are the walls of a submarine so thick and strong?*
4. *What would happen to water escaping from two holes of a can if you plugged one hole?*
5. *What will happen to the water coming out of the bottom hole of the can as the water level gets lower in the can?*
6. *Why do many towns have water storage tanks towering high above the city or built on a hill?*

Reference Books—Water
Teacher: Jack E. Gartell, Jr., Jane Crowder, and Jeffrey C. Callister, *Earth the Water Planet* (Washington, D.C.: National Science Teachers Association, 1989).
Older Students: Brenda Walpole, *Water* (New York: Watts, 1987).

THERMAL ENERGY (HEAT)

QUICKIE STARTERS

What Makes Things Get Hotter?

1. Bend a 6-in piece of wire hanger back and forth 10 times as shown. Quickly touch the wire at the point where you bent it.
   What do you feel? (Heat)
   What do you think will happen if you bend the wire more times, i.e., 20, 25, 30, 35 times? (Each time the wire gets hotter.)
   Caution: The teacher should try this activity out first to find out how many bends will make the wire too hot for students to touch.

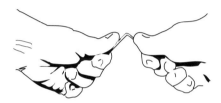

2. Rub your hands together very fast and hard.
   What do you feel?
   Try this again but put a few drops of oil or water on your hands first.
   How do you think the second rubbing will feel different from the first rubbing?
   Try it.

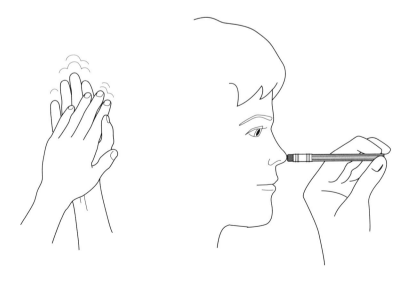

Now rub different things together and quickly touch them to your upper lip or the tip of your nose (sensitive parts of your body): brass button on a piece of wool, metal on paper, pencil eraser on paper, etc.

I

3. *Note:* It is recommended that young students go to the bathroom before and after the following activity!

Hold an ice cube in your hand over newspapers or paper towels.
How does your hand feel with the ice cube in it? (Cold)
What is happening to the ice cube?

Leave an ice cube in a nearby dish and notice the difference between this ice cube and the one in your hand.
Why the difference? (Heat from your hand melts the ice cube faster than heat from the room melts the ice cube in the dish.)

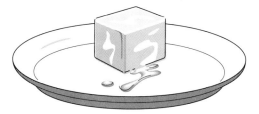

Which became warmer—your hand or the ice cube you held? (Ice cube; heat moved from hand to ice)
How is this the same as when you pour a warm soft drink over ice cubes? (The warm drink gets cooler as heat moves to the ice.)

G

4. Go on a "Heat Hunt" in school and at home. List places where heat is produced, i.e., school or home furnace, oven and stove, toaster, microwave oven, sunshine through windows, etc. Make a booklet or chart and illustrate it with magazine pictures, then use these three categories to organize your list of heat producers:

■ Where did you see it?
■ What was heated?
■ How was it heated?

GUIDED DISCOVERY MINDS-ON/HANDS-ON ACTIVITIES

What Is Thermal Energy or Heat? (K–8)

What Do I Want Students to Discover?

When an object is heated, its molecules move faster or vibrate more. When an object is cooled, its molecules move more slowly.
Heat is the total energy an object has because of the motion of its molecules.

What Will I Need?

Baby-food jar with screw top	Tea bags
Sand	Pencils
Thick towel	Sugar cubes
Thermometer	2 Pyrex™ or tin pans
12 baby-food jars or clear plastic tumblers	Colored cinnamon candies

What Concepts Might Students Discover or Construct?

Motion (shaking, stirring, rubbing, etc.) can be a source of heat.
The molecules in liquids are in continuous motion. This is called **Brownian motion.**
Scientists use controlled experiments to test their ideas.
Solids break into smaller pieces (**dissolve**) faster in hot water than in cold water.

PROCESSES

Part I

What Will Students Do?

What do you think will happen to the sand in a baby-food jar if you shake it many times?

Hypothesizing

1. Fill a baby-food jar ¾ full of sand, screw the top on the jar, and then wrap it with a thick towel.

Collecting Data

2. Each person should take a turn doing the following:
   A. Shake the sand vigorously for 5 minutes.

Measuring
Recording

   B. Measure the temperature of the sand.
   C. Write your findings on this chart.

Number of Shakes	Temperature in °F or °C

D. Pass the jar to the next person.

Comparing

E. When everyone has had a turn, compare the temperature of the sand from the first to the last reading.

Analyzing

How were they different? (The temperature rose higher after shaking.)

Communicating results

F. Set up a graph like the one shown, then graph the data from the record sheets.

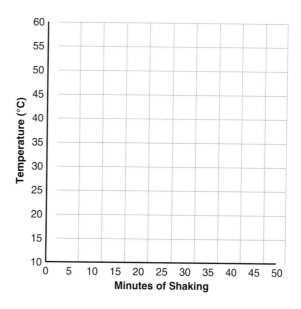

Part II

Hypothesizing

What caused the molecules to move?

Designing an investigation

How could we set up an experiment to test the effect of heat on molecule movement in a liquid?

1. Fill three baby-food jars or plastic tumblers with water to within ½ in (1 cm) of the top and let them stand until the water is room temperature.
2. Slowly lower a sugar cube into one jar, a handful of cinnamon candies into the second jar, and a tea bag into the third jar or tumbler. (See diagram.)

CONTROL: Substances dissolving without stirring

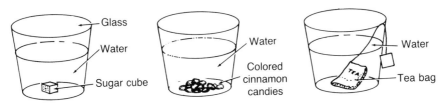

Make certain that the jars are in a spot where they will not be moved or jostled.

3. Set up three more jars and materials the same as in step 2, but this time stir the water in the jars until the materials dissolve, as shown in the diagram.

EXPERIMENT: Substances dissolving with stirring

Hypothesizing

The way this experiment was set up is called a **controlled experiment** in science. *Why do you think it is called this?*

4. Taking observations every ½ hour, record how long it takes for the control jars to look like the experimental jars.

Hypothesizing

Which materials do you think will dissolve first? Why?

Inferring

Would the results be different if hot water were used? If cold water were used? Why?

Designing an Investigation

How could we test this?

Part III

1. Set up two more sets of jars with sugar, cinnamon candies, and tea bags.
2. Place one set of jars in ice-cold water in a pan and the other set in a pan of very hot water.

 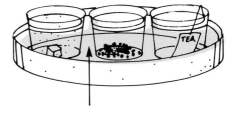

Hot water   Cold water

Hypothesizing	*In which jars—in pans of hot or cold water—will the materials dissolve first?*
Inferring	*What does the hot water in the pan do to the molecules in the baby-food jars?*

What Must I Know?

This is a review of **Brownian motion,** the continuous movement of particles suspended in a liquid. This activity also introduces several new concepts. Students will be helped to see that increasing the motion of molecules generates considerable heat. Therefore, matter that displays greater heat has greater movement of its molecules. In addition, the concept of a control is used as a standard against which scientists check their experimental work. If you think your students are ready, you can introduce the concept of variables. For instance, in Part III, the variable being tested is heat and its effect upon dissolving.

How Will Students Use or Apply What They Discover?

1. *Why do you rub a match against the side of a match box?*
2. *Why do matches not catch fire while sitting in a match box?*
3. *When you bend a wire back and forth several times, why does it get warm?*
4. *When you put two pencils together and rub them back and forth several times, what happens to your hands?*
5. *A person tried to strike a match against a piece of glass to light it. The match would not light. Why?*
6. *If you feel the tires of your car before you take a trip and then just after you get out of the car, they will not feel the same. How do you think they will differ? How would you explain the difference?*
7. *A person was chopping wood with an axe. After chopping very hard for about 10 minutes, she felt the axe. How do you think the axe felt and why?*

How Is Heat Transmitted by Conduction and Radiation? (4–8)

What Concepts Might Students Discover or Construct?

The sun or light bulbs give off radiant heat.
Heat can be transmitted from one body to another by conduction and radiation.
Light objects reflect radiant energy more than do dark objects.

Dark objects absorb more radiant energy than do light objects. Some objects conduct heat better than others.

What Will We Need?

3 tin cans of same size
Small can of shiny white paint
Candle
4 × 4-in square of aluminum foil
Styrofoam covers for cans
4-in length of copper

Lamp with 150 to 300 watts
Small can of dull black paint
Silver or steel knife
9 thumb tacks
Tripod stand
3 thermometers
2 small paint brushes

What Must I Know?

These activities may be done in groups. For immature or unruly children, the teacher should demonstrate these activities.

PROCESSES

Part I Radiation

What Will Students Do?

Hypothesizing

What do you think will happen to the three thermometers in the three different cans after being in the sun or near light bulbs for a while? (See diagram.)

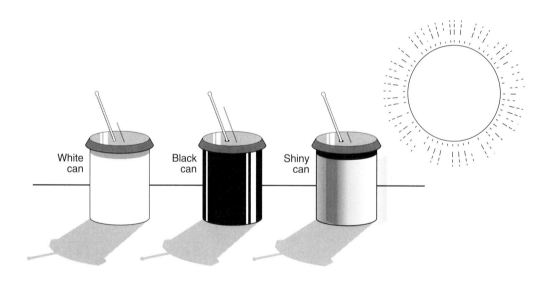

White can   Black can   Shiny can

1. Obtain three identically sized cans and remove all labels. Paint one can dull black and another can shiny whzite; leave the third can unpainted, shiny metal.
2. Fill each can with regular tap water.
3. Put a styrofoam cover on each can and insert a thermometer through each cover.
4. Set the cans in direct sunlight or at equal distances from a 150- to 300-watt light bulb.

Measuring
Observing

5. Prepare a table for data collection and record the temperature of the water in each can at one-minute intervals.

Hypothesizing   *What do you think will happen to the water temperature in the different cans?*

If there are different temperatures, how would you explain that?

Inferring   *How would you relate the result of the unequal absorption of heat in the tin cans to different land and water surfaces of the earth?*

Inferring   *Knowing what you do about how* **radiant** *(light) energy reacts on different surfaces, how would you explain the differences in the three thermometers?*

Hypothesizing   *How might this be related to the microclimates of certain geographic areas?*

What Must I Know?/Where Do I Find It?

The shiny aluminum of the unpainted can and the shiny white paint of the second can reflect radiant energy, whereas the dull black paint absorbs most of the radiant energy. Dark patches of ground absorb more radiant energy faster than do shiny water surfaces or lighter colored land surfaces.

Part II   Conduction

Hypothesizing

What do you think will happen to tacks that have been attached with wax to a strip of aluminum foil, to a silver or steel knife, and to a copper tube when the tips of these metals are heated?

1. Obtain a 4 × 4-in square of aluminum foil, a candle, a match, and nine tacks.
2. Roll the aluminum foil tightly.
3. Light the candle. Drip some wax onto three tacks and the aluminum foil rod so the tacks stick to the foil.
4. Obtain a tripod stand, silver knife, and a 4-in length of copper tubing.
5. Stick three tacks each to the knife and to the copper tubing as you did with the foil.
6. Place the foil, knife, and copper tubing on a tripod stand as shown in the diagram. Heat the tips of each of these with a candle flame.

Observing   Observe and record what happens.

Inferring   *Why did the tacks not all fall at the same time?*

Inferring   *From observing this activity, how do you think the heat affected the three metals?*

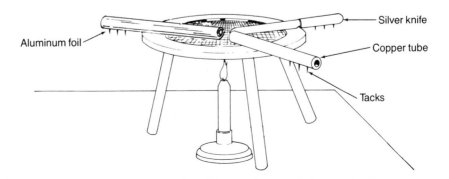

Silver knife

Aluminum foil

Copper tube

Tacks

How Will Students
Use or Apply
What They
Discover?

1. *When you stand in front of a fireplace and the front of you only is warmed by the fire, how is the heat transferred?*
2. *How does heat or thermal energy come from the sun?*
3. *What colors are more likely to absorb heat?*
4. *Why do people generally wear lighter colored clothes in the summer?*
5. *In the can experiment, what kind of energy did the black surface absorb?*
6. *How was the heat transferred from the black surface to the thermometer?*
7. *Why is it desirable to have a copper-bottomed tea kettle?*
8. *Why would you not want a copper handle on a frying pan?*
9. *What metals conduct heat well?*
10. *What advantage would there be in having a car with a white top rather than a black top?*
11. *Why do many people in warmer climates paint their houses white?*
12. *Why would you prefer to put a hot dog on a stick rather than on a wire to cook the hot dog over a camp fire?*
13. *Why do astronauts wear shiny space suits?*

Part III Convection

Hypothesizing

Where do you think the warmest and coolest spots are in your classroom? Try this activity to see if you can find the answer.

What Will Students
Do?

1. As far away as possible from the room's source of heat, tape three thermometers to a wall at these places: near the ceiling, half-way up the wall, and one near the floor. (See diagram.)

Observation

2. Make a chart of the thermometer readings once an hour for one day.

G *Communicating*
Analyzing

Using the data collected, graph the results.
From your data and graph, answer these questions:
Which thermometer had the highest temperature? The middle temperature? The lowest temperature?

Inferring

Why do you think the temperatures were different?

What Must I Know?

Convection is the transfer of heat by either a gas (air) or a liquid (water). When the air in the room is heated, it expands and becomes lighter per given volume. It then rises because it is lighter. This rising and falling is called a **convection current.**

How Will Students
Use or Apply
What They
Discover?

When you see "wiggly lines" rising from the blacktop of a parking lot on a sunny day, how is this the same as the convection current in our classroom?
Why does a "cloud" fall down from a freezer that is above a refrigerator when you open the freezer door?
Why does smoke usually rise up a chimney? Under what conditions would smoke come into the house through the fireplace opening?
Why would a pinwheel start to spin if put over a lit light bulb?

What Effect Does Heat Have on the States of Matter? (K–6)

What Concepts Might Students Discover or Construct?

There are many forms of sugar.
It is possible to obtain carbon from burning sugar.
Sugar may be broken down chemically.

What Will We Need?

Bunsen or alcohol burner or hot plate
Aluminum pie pan
Ring stand and ring
Sugar cube or teaspoon of sugar
Empty, tall glass tumbler
Pot holder

What Will We Discuss?

Hold up a piece of sugar and ask:
What are some of the properties or characteristics of this piece of sugar?

What Must I Know?

Students might say the sugar is white, cubical in shape, small, made up of crystalline material, sweet, and so on. In its present form, sugar is a white solid. There are, however, ways of changing its appearance. One of the easiest ways is simply to crush the cube, producing sugar in a smaller crystal form. These crystals can be crushed further to make a powdered sugar. Another way to change the cube's appearance is to dissolve it in a cup of water. Once the sugar is dissolved, it cannot be seen, yet the solution will taste sweet. This means that sugar is still present, because some of its characteristics are identifiable. In what ways can sugar be changed so it cannot be identified?

PROCESSES

What Will Students Do?

1. Obtain an aluminum pie pan and place it on top of an electric hot plate or ring stand. Regulate the burner so the pan is heated slowly. Because of the use of heat, you may decide to perform this as a teacher demonstration.

2. Place one teaspoon or cube of sugar in the middle of the pan. (See diagram.)

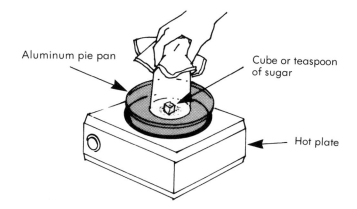

Aluminum pie pan

Cube or teaspoon of sugar

Hot plate

Hypothesizing   *What do you think will happen to the sugar when it is heated?*

Observing   3. Watch what happens to the sugar.

Observing   *What happens as the sugar begins to melt?*

4. Hold a tall, empty glass cup upside down over the bubbling sugar. Use a pot holder to do this.

Hypothesizing   *What do you think will appear on the inside of the glass?*

Observing   5. Observe the inside of the glass very carefully.

6. Lift the glass, wait 10 seconds, then touch the inside of the glass with your fingers.

Observing   *What do you feel?*

Inferring   *What do you think it is?* (Water vapor)

7. After the sugar stops bubbling, describe what you see in the pan.

Inferring   *What do you think this material could be?*

Comparing   *What does it look like?*

Taste this material. (Take this opportunity to remind students that they should *never* taste anything unless you say it is all right.)

Observing   *How does it taste?*

Does it have the properties of sugar?

What Must I Know?   It is probably carbon. Sugar has carbon combined in its molecular structure.

How Will Students Use or Apply What They Discover?

1. *From what you have learned about sugar, can you explain why a marshmallow turns black when roasted over a fire?*

2. *Why does sugar turn brown as it slowly heats up and melts?* (This brown liquid is caramel flavor.)

Reference Books—Thermal Energy (Heat)

Teacher: Barbara R. Fogel, *Energy Choices for the Future* (New York: Watts, 1985).

Students: Kathryn Whyman, *Heat and Energy* (New York: Watts, 1987).

AIR PRESSURE

QUICKIE STARTERS

What Makes Balloons Grow Bigger and Move Farther?

Materials   Balloons, metric tape or meterstick

Opening Question   *Which team can get their balloons to go the farthest?*

Some Possible
Activities

Go outside and divide the class into groups of five. Students should blow their balloons up as much as they can. Have one student in each group release his or her balloon. *Caution:* Make sure students do not release balloons into the faces of their classmates. Have the second student in each group go to where the first balloon landed, then have him or her release his or her balloon. This continues until all the students in the team have had a turn. The distance is then measured metrically to determine how far their balloons went from the starting point. The team whose balloons went the greatest distance wins.

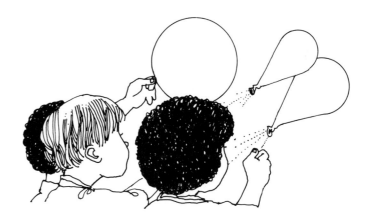

What's in Your Baggies? How Do You Know?

Materials

Plastic sandwich bags with plastic ties, sand, buttons, water

Opening Questions

How do you know if something is real?
What are some properties of matter?
How do you find out about properties of matter?
How is sand different from buttons?
How is water different from sand?
Can things be real that we cannot see?

Some Possible
Activities

Take three plastic sandwich bags and half fill them separately with sand, buttons, and water. Twist the top of each bag and tie it with a plastic tie. Take a fourth bag, swish it through the air, quickly close the mouth, twist it tightly, and tie it with a plastic tie.

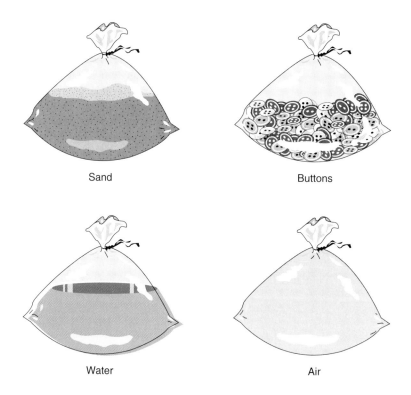

Sand

Buttons

Water

Air

Ask students to respond to these questions by looking at and carefully handling the bags. How are the properties of the objects in the bags the *same?* (They occupy space, have weight, exert pressure on the sides of the bags, can support a weight put on them, etc.) We call these things **properties of matter** and they show us that the things in the bags are all real—even the air that we cannot see.

How are the properties of the objects in the bags *different?* (They do not all weigh the same, some change shape when you squeeze them, some are solid (buttons and sand), one is a liquid (water), and one is a gas (air) that looks invisible.

You found out about properties of matter by observation. *How could you find out if*

■*the objects in your bags could be moved from one bag to another?*
■*the objects have a smell?*

How Can You Make a Kite and Get It to Fly?

Materials

Plastic such as that used by dry cleaners, paper to cover the kite, small pieces of wood to form the supports, string, transparent tape or glue, cloth for the tail

Opening Questions

How can we make kites?
What will we need?
How should they be constructed?
What shape should they be? Why?

Some Possible
Activities

Encourage students to plan in small groups how they are going to make their kites before they construct them. Guide them in discussing the properties of air and how it affects kite building and flying. After they have done this, you might bring in some books on kites. Discuss the role of the tail and how it helps to stabilize the kite. Have students experiment with how long the tail should be by flying their kites on windy and calm days. If there is a local kite store, invite students to visit it or invite the owner to your classroom. Discuss some of the dangers of flying kites near power lines. *Caution:* Point out that they should *never* use wire instead of string to fly a kite because of the danger involved if the wire hits a power line. Invite students to make several kinds of kites and find out how different cultures use them; for example, have students find out how the Japanese use kites to celebrate certain holidays.

GUIDED DISCOVERY ACTIVITIES

What Is Air? (K–3)

What Concepts
Might Students
Discover or
Construct?

Air is real.
Air is around us all the time.
Air is found inside solids and liquids.
Air takes up space and has weight.
Air exerts pressure.

What Will We Need?

Piece of cardboard
Commercial-sized mayonnaise jar or aquarium
Drinking glass or plastic tumbler
Food coloring

What Will We
Discuss?

How do you know something is real?
What could you do to find out whether air is real?

PROCESSES

What Will Students
Do?

Observing

1. Swing your hands back and forth.

What can you feel?

Observing

Inferring

2. Swing a piece of cardboard back and forth.
What do you feel now?
What is the cardboard pushing against?

Observing What do you feel pushing against you when you ride your bicycle down a hill?

Hypothesizing What do you think will happen to a glass if it is turned upside down and pushed straight down under water?

3. Turn a glass upside down and push it straight down in a large jar of water or an aquarium as shown. (Use food coloring to make the water more visible.)

4. Now turn the glass sideways as shown.

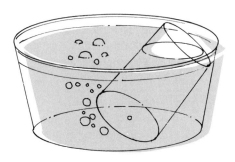

Observing What happens to the inside of the glass?
What are the bubbles that escape from the glass?
Where did the bubbles come from?

How Will Students Use or Apply What They Discover?

1. *How can you keep water in a straw by closing the top end with your finger as shown?*

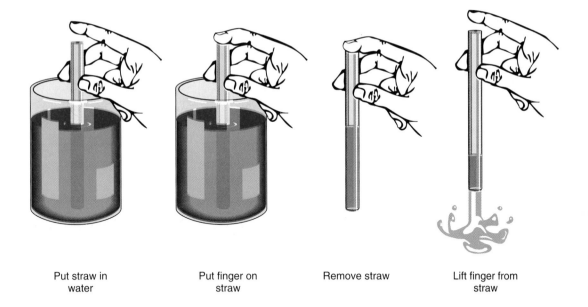

Put straw in   Put finger on   Remove straw   Lift finger from
   water   straw   straw

2. *If you fill a paper bag with air and then crush it, what happens and why?*
3. *Why does juice flow better from a tin can if you punch two holes instead of one?*

How Do the Effects of Moving Air Differ From the Effects of Nonmoving Air? (K–8)

What Concepts Might Students Discover or Construct?

The pressure of liquids or gases will be low if they are moving quickly and will be high if they are moving slowly. This principle is called **Bernoulli's principle.**

What Will We Need?

3 pieces of notebook paper
Drinking straw
Pop bottle
Thread spool
Small index card (3 × 5 in)
Pin with a head
Ping-Pong ball
Thistle tube or funnel

What Must I Know?

Before doing this student inquiry activity, potential energy and kinetic energy should be explained.

PROCESSES

What Will Students Do?

Hypothesizing

Part I

1. Obtain a piece of notebook paper.
2. Make a fold 1 inch wide along the long end of the paper. Make another 1-inch fold at the opposite end as indicated in the diagram.
3. Place the paper on a flat surface.

What do you think will happen if you blow under this folded paper?

4. Using the drinking straw, blow a stream of air under the paper.

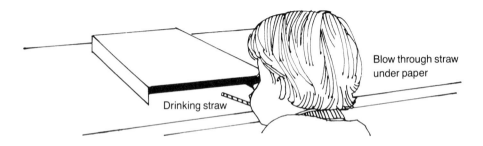

Blow through straw under paper

Drinking straw

Observing

What do you notice about the way the paper moves?
Describe how the air was circulating under the paper before you blew under it.

Comparing

What do you know about the air pressure under the paper—when you blow under the paper—as compared with the air pressure exerted on top of the paper?

Part II

Hypothesizing

What do you think will happen to a wad of paper placed in the opening of a pop bottle if you blow across the bottle opening?

1. Wad a small piece of paper so it is about the size of a pea (¼-in or ½-cm diameter).
2. Lay the pop bottle on its side.
3. Place the small wad of paper in the opening of the bottle, next to the edge of the opening. (See diagram.)
4. Blow across the opening in front of the bottle. Make sure you bend down so that you are level with the bottle.

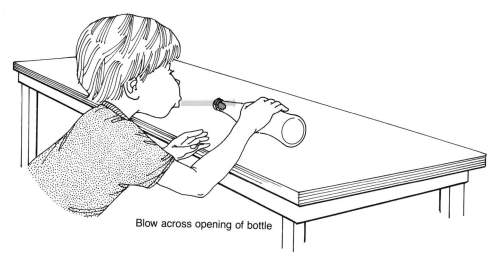

Blow across opening of bottle

Observing	*What happens to the wad of paper?*
Inferring	*Why is the wad of paper forced to do that?*
Comparing	*What do you know about the air pressure in the bottle and the air pressure at the opening of the bottle when you blow across it?*
Hypothesizing	*What do you think will happen if you place a wad of paper in the opening of a pop bottle (as before) and blow directly into the bottle?*

5. Blow hard directly into the bottle as shown.

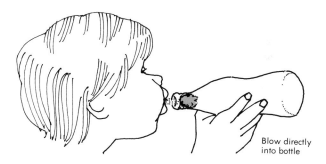

Blow directly
into bottle

Observing	6. Record your observations.
Inferring	*What do you conclude from your observations?*

Part III

Hypothesizing

If a pin with a head is inserted through the center of a card and then into a spool, what will happen when you blow through the other end of the spool?

1. Place the pin in the center of the index card so that the head is under the card. (See diagram.)

2. Put the thread spool over the pin.
3. Hold the card with one hand and the spool with your other hand.
4. While blowing, let go of the card. *Warning:* Instruct students *never to suck in* on the spool.

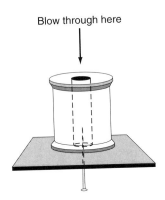

Blow through here

Observing	*What happened to the card while you blew through the spool?*
	What happened when you stopped blowing through the spool?
Inferring	*Why do you think this happened?*
Inferring	*What is holding up the card?*
Inferring	*Why does the air you blow through the hole not make the card fall?*
Inferring	*Why do you need the pin in the middle of the card?*

What Must I Know?   Two variables may affect the outcome: (1) The bottom of the spool must be very smooth (sandpaper it if necessary), and (2) the student must take a deep breath and sustain a long, steady air column down the spool.

Part IV

Hypothesizing   *What will happen to a Ping-Pong ball if it is placed in the large end of a thistle tube or funnel, and you blow through the small end of the thistle tube or funnel?*

1. Hold the Ping-Pong ball in the wide, larger opening of the thistle tube or funnel, put your mouth on the other end, and blow with a long, steady breath. (See diagram.) *Hint:* Get a deep breath before you put your mouth on the tube end to blow. *Caution:* After each person blows through the tube, wash the funnel thoroughly with soap and water and an alcohol wipe, if possible.

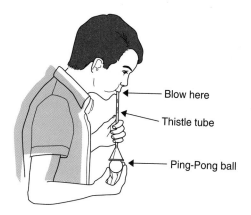

Blow here

Thistle tube

Ping-Pong ball

2. While blowing hard and steady through the tube end of the funnel, let go of the Ping-Pong ball.

Observing
Inferring

Record your observations.
Why does the ball do what it does?
Why does the ball spin around in the thistle tube or funnel?

Part V

Hypothesizing

If you were to hold a piece of paper by each corner and blow across the top of the paper, what would happen to the paper?

1. Hold the lower left corner of a piece of notebook paper with your left hand and the lower right corner with your right hand.
2. Blow hard across the top of the paper. (See diagram.)

Blow across top of paper

Observing

Inferring

What happens to the paper while you are blowing across it?
Why does the paper move in this direction?

How Will Students Use or Apply What They Discover?

1. *Why is it unwise to stand close to the edge of a platform as a moving train is coming?*
2. *When you rapidly pass by another student's desk that has a sheet of paper on it, what happens to the paper? Why?*
3. *How would this principle of air pressure work when you fly a kite?*
4. *What happens to a girl's skirt if a car speeds close by her?*
5. *What would happen if a plane stopped moving in the air? How could this happen?*

What Must I Know?/Where Do I Find It?

If a plane is moving fast enough, the upward pressure on the wings is enough to overcome gravity. The plane must keep moving to stay aloft. If it stopped in midair, it would glide down immediately.

6. *In the following drawing of the airplane wing, is the air moving faster at A or B? Why?*

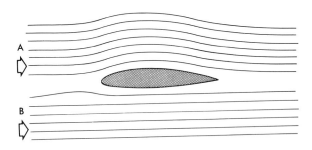

7. *How do wing slopes vary and why?*

Reference Books—Air Pressure

Teacher: Wayne Hoskings, *Flights of Imagination: An Introduction to Aerodynamics* (Washington, D.C.: National Science Teachers Association, 1987).
Students: Arthur Dorros, *Feel The Wind* (New York: Crowell, 1990).

SOUND ENERGY

QUICKIE STARTERS

What Makes a Drum Louder?

Materials

Cylindrical oatmeal container, puffed rice or wheat cereal, large balloon or sheet rubber, strong rubber band

Opening Question

How can you make a drum sound louder?

Some Possible
Activities

Stretch the large balloon or piece of sheet rubber over the open end of the oatmeal container and place a strong rubber band around that end to hold the rubber securely in place. This makes a simple drum. Sprinkle puffed rice or wheat cereal on the drum head. Tap the drum head softly and observe what happens. Now hit it harder. Ask:
What differences did you notice when you hit the drum softly and when you hit it harder?

Help students to see the patterns formed by the puffed cereal when the drum head is struck softly, and how the pattern changes when the drum head is struck harder. Also notice how much higher the cereal moves above the drum head when it is hit harder. Relate more energy (hitting the drum harder) with louder sound from the drum.

How Can You Make Sounds Less Noisy?

Materials

Two small battery-operated radios; several different-sized boxes, each of which can fit over one or more of the others and over the radio; cloth; paper; insulating material; cotton balls

Opening Question

How can we deaden the sound of this radio by using these materials?

Some Possible
Activities

Invite two groups of students to have a "deadening the sound" race, each using a radio with the same volume level and the listed materials. Give the groups a definite time (30–60 minutes) to brainstorm how they can deaden the sound of the radio, set up an experiment, and collect data. Later, discuss how sound can go through objects and what kinds of things deaden sound well. Then ask:

How can what you found in your "deadening the sound" race help to reduce sound in our classroom and make it more comfortable to our ears?

GUIDED DISCOVERY MINDS-ON/HANDS-ON ACTIVITIES

What Is Sound and How Is It Produced and Conducted? (K–6)

What Concepts Might Students Discover or Construct?

When an object vibrates, sound may be produced.
Sound may be made by vibrating a number of different objects.
Sound may be conducted by a number of different objects.

What Will We Need?

As many of the following things as possible should be placed at work stations for groups of four or more students:

Rubber band	Alarm clock	Bell
Fork and spoon	4 feet of string	Aluminum pie pan
6 empty pop bottles	Aluminum foil	Toothpicks
	Cotton	

What Will We Discuss?

How could you make a sound with a rubber band?

What Will Students Do?

Designing an Investigation

1. *How could you make a rubber band produce a sound? How is the sound produced?*

What Must I Know?

The students should stretch a rubber band and cause it to vibrate. They should get the idea that the vibration causes the sound. *Caution:* Point out that students must be careful not to let the stretched rubber bands pop off their hands and that they must not try to snap each other with the rubber bands.

Hypothesizing

Can you hear sound by placing your ear against different objects while causing them to make a sound?

2. Try making sounds with the different objects.

Hypothesizing

What can you do to stop the sound once it has started?

3. Test your ideas.

Observing

4. Determine which materials are better than others for producing sound.

Comparing

In what ways are these materials the same or different?

How Will Students Use or Apply What They Discover?

1. *How would you produce a loud sound?*
2. *What would you do to make our classroom less noisy?*
3. *Why do drapes in a room make sounds softer?*

How Does the Length of an Air Column Affect Sound? (K–6)

What Concepts Might Students Discover or Construct?

The higher the pitch of a note, the more rapid the vibrations of the producing body.

Pitch can be varied by adjusting the length of an air column.

The higher the water level in a bottle, the shorter the air column, and the higher the pitch (when blowing across the top of the bottle).

What Will We Need?

8 identical pop bottles
Medium-sized beaker
Soda straws (waxed paper straws work better than plastic)
Scissors

What Will We Discuss?

What might happen if you blew across the openings of pop bottles filled with varying amounts of water?
Would a sound be produced?
If sounds were produced, would they all be the same? If not, which would be the highest? The lowest?

PROCESSES

Part I

What Will Students Do?

1. Fill eight identical pop bottles with varying amounts of water.

Hypothesizing

What might happen if you blow across the lips of the bottles?
2. Blow across the bottles.

Observing — *Do all bottles give off the same sound?*
Observing — *Which bottle gives off the highest note? The lowest note?*
Hypothesizing — *How could you make a musical scale out of the pop bottles?*
3. Arrange the bottles to make a musical scale.
4. After you have made the musical scale, try to make a harmonizing chord.
   If you number the lowest note "1" and the highest note "8," what are the numbers of the bottles you used for your chords?
Inferring
5. *What conclusions can you draw concerning the length of an air column and the sound produced?*

Hypothesizing   *What is the relationship between the length of an air column and a note produced by an open tube?*

Part II

1. Give each student a soda straw and a pair of scissors.
2. Have students cut and pinch the straw to form a reed like the one shown.

Pinch here

Side view

Cut a V

Top view

Hypothesizing   *Why do we cut and pinch the straw?*

3. Have students blow on the "V" cut into straw. (*Note:* They will need to experiment to get the proper lip vibration.)
4. Now cut the soda straws into different lengths to get different pitches.

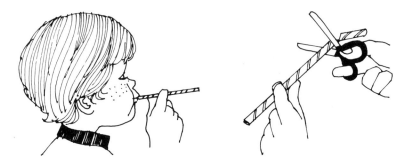

Inferring   *What is the relationship between the length of a straw and the sound it produced?*

Hypothesizing   *How can the soda straws be used to play songs?*

How Will Students Use or Apply What They Discover?

1. *How would the results vary if you put equal amounts of water in bottles of varying sizes?*
2. *Does the thickness of the glass in the pop bottle affect the tone produced?*
3. *Could you produce the same results using test tubes?*
4. *Does the pitch differ when hitting bottles with a spoon or ruler and when blowing over the top of the bottles? Test it.*
5. *How can the soda straws be used to play songs? Experiment to get the straws calibrated in lengths in relation to octave. Then have students play simple songs like "Mary Had a Little Lamb."*

What Must I Know?/Where Do I Find It?

Once a scale is achieved, drop oil from a medicine dropper onto the top of the water in each bottle, just enough to cover the top. This will prevent evaporation and a change in pitch.

How Do Solids and Liquids Conduct Sounds? (4–6)

What Concepts Might Students Discover or Construct?

Sound can travel through solid substances.
Sound can travel through liquid substances.
Sound can travel through gaseous substances.

What Will We Need?

2 paper cups	Wooden ruler
20 feet of strong cord or nylon fishing line	Bucket
20 feet of steel wire	Water
20 feet of copper wire	2 rocks
1 board about $12 \times 4 \times 1$ in	Buttons

What Will We Discuss?

Have you ever heard people talking when you were in one room and they were in another room next to yours?
How do you suppose you could hear them through the wall and the air? You know that sound travels, but what substances will sound travel through?

PROCESSES

What Will Students Do?

G

Part I

1. Get two paper cups and 20 feet of string or nylon fishing line.
2. With a pencil, punch a very small hole in the bottom of the paper cups just large enough to stick the string through.
3. Stick the ends of the string through each one of the paper cups. Tie a button to the ends of the string ending inside the cups so the string will not be easily pulled from the cups. (See diagram.)

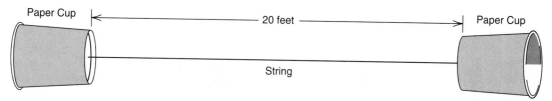

Paper Cup |◄———————— 20 feet ————————►| Paper Cup

String

Hypothesizing

When you talk into one of the cups, what will happen to the other cup? Why?

4. Talk into one cup while another student holds the other cup to his or her ear and listens.

Designing an Investigation

How can sound best be transferred from one cup to the other? Hint: Make sure the cord is stretched very tightly and that nothing is touching the string. Why?

Observing

Record what you did to best transmit the sound.

Hypothesizing

5. *How will the sound be conducted if you use copper or steel wire? Try it.*

Observing

What happens when you use copper wire?

Inferring and Comparing

Is the sound carried better through copper wire than through string? Why or why not?

Hypothesizing   6. *Why is it important for the string to be tight and not touching anything?*

Part II

G

Observing
1. Obtain a small board or meter- or yardstick and a pencil.
2. Hold a board or meterstick to your ear. Scratch the other end of the stick with a pencil. What happens?
3. Hold the stick away from your ear and repeat the activity.

Applying   *Does sound travel better through a solid or through the air?*

Part III

G

1. With one hand, hold a wooden ruler or meterstick firmly against a desk. With the other hand, pluck the overhanging part of the ruler, causing it to vibrate.

Hypothesizing
Designing an
Investigation
2. *What causes the sound to be produced?*
   Produce a high-pitched sound by vibrating the stick.
   Produce a low-pitched sound by vibrating the stick.

Part IV

Hypothesizing
Designing an
Investigation

How is sound carried in liquids?
How would you find out?

1. Obtain a large bucket full of water. Take two pieces of metal or two rocks and hit them together under water.

Inferring

2. *Did you hear a sound when you hit the objects together? Why? What is your conclusion about the ability of a liquid to carry sound?*

How Will Students Use or Apply What They Discover?

1. *How far do you think sounds would travel between phones using copper wire, string, and steel wire?*
   Design an experiment to see which conducts sound farther.
2. *How would you use eight rulers to make a musical scale?*
   Think about what you did to get a low pitch and a high pitch.
3. *What is the purpose of making musical instruments out of wood?*
4. *How well do you think liquids other than water conduct sounds?*

Reference Books—Sound

Teacher: Peter Riley, *Light and Sound* (New York: David and Charles, 1987).
Students: Melvin Berger, *The Science of Music* (New York: Crowell, 1989).

SIMPLE MACHINES (MECHANICS)

QUICKIE STARTERS

How Can You Make Balls Roll Faster?

Materials

Balls of different sizes, including Ping-Pong, golf, tennis, and larger ones; straws; boards to make inclined planes

Opening Question

What things can you do with these balls?

Some Possible Activities

Find out which balls roll easiest across the floor, what happens when they are kicked, and which ones will roll the farthest after rolling down an inclined plane. Find out which balls balance best. Throw the balls against the wall at different angles and find out how they bounce off the wall. For example, how should you throw the ball so it will come back to you? Float the balls in water and find out which ones float and which do not. Also, notice how deep they sink in the water. Line up the balls in a vertical line leading from an inclined plane. Roll a ball down the inclined plane so it hits the end of the line. Then roll two balls down so they hit the line one after another. Place all but one of the balls in a close group. Roll another ball into the group and see how the balls scatter. Play croquet with different balls. Construct a tetherball.

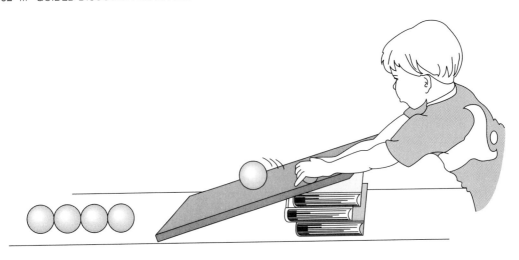

How Do Wheels Help Toys Move?

Materials

Rollers, small round wheels, buttons, toy cars, small round rocks, or-anges, apples, thimbles, boards to make inclined planes, disks cut from poster board, thumb tacks, match boxes

Opening Questions

What can you do with these things?
What kinds of games can you play?
How can you make a toy car using the match boxes and other things?
Which of the things you see are wheels? Which are not wheels?
How are wheels different from the other things?

Some Possible Activities

The students could try seeing how far different things would roll on the floor after rolling down an inclined plane. They could also make toy cars with the match boxes by tacking the bottle caps or buttons to the sides. The students may also be invited to make toy cars out of a square, small board where axles are made from clothes hangers. These are stapled to the board and then bent at the ends after the button or bottle cap wheels are attached.

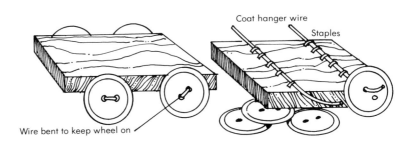

Coat hanger wire
Staples
Wire bent to keep wheel on

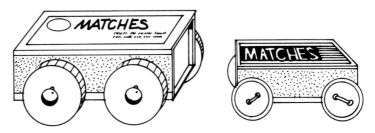

GUIDED DISCOVERY MINDS-ON/HANDS-ON ACTIVITIES

What Is an Inclined Plane and How Can You Use It? (K–8)

What Concepts Might Students Discover or Construct?

Inclined planes are used for moving objects that are too heavy to lift directly. The work done by moving an object up an inclined plane is equal to the weight of the object times the height of the plane.

Resistance × height of plane = Effort × length of plane

An **inclined plane** is one example of a **simple machine.**

What Will We Need?

Smooth board 4 ft × 6 in
Support block 4 × 8 in
Spring scale
Block with screw eye in one end or a rubber band wrapped around it to be pulled by a scale

What Will We Discuss?

What is an inclined plane?
Why use an inclined plane?
Where are there inclined planes on the school grounds?

PROCESSES

What Will Students Do?

Hypothesizing

1. Take the 4-foot board and place the 4 × 8-inch block under one end so that end of the board is raised 4 inches. Place the block with the screw eye in it on the inclined board as shown in the diagram. Slip the hook of the spring scale through the eye of the block.

   What force do you think will be required to pull the block?
   Will it be greater, equal to, or less than the weight of the block? Why?

2. Slowly and evenly pull the scale and block up the board.

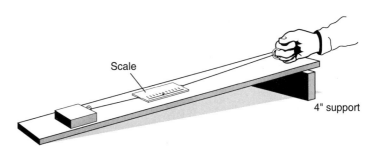

Scale

4" support

Measuring   3. Record the amount of force needed to pull the block up the board. Do this several times, and record your observations.
Using the data obtained, determine the average force required to pull the weight.
4. Repeat the activity, but this time make the inclined plane steeper by changing the support block so its 8-inch dimension is under the end of the board.

Measuring   5. Again, find the average force needed to pull the weight up the board.
Comparing   *How do the two forces compare?*
Applying   6. Lift the block straight up, as shown in the diagram. Repeat this several times and find the average reading on the scale.

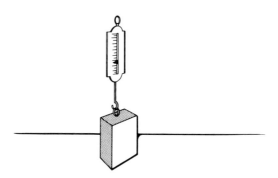

7. The following formula is used to calculate the force needed to move a weight up an inclined plane:

Resistance × resistance distance = Effort × effort distance

Inferring   Use this formula to calculate the force that should have been necessary to move the weight up the inclined plane.
Inferring   *Why do the experimental results and the calculated results not agree exactly?*
Hypothesizing *What can you say about the amount of force required as an inclined plane becomes steeper?*
Hypothesizing *What is the advantage of having a long inclined plane rather than a short inclined plane if both planes are the same height?*

How Will Students Use or Apply What They Discover?
1. *Why do roads not go straight up and down mountains?*
2. *Which of the following examples is an inclined plane?*
   a. ramp   d. stairway
   b. hill   e. wedge
   c. gangplank   f. head of an axe
3. A person moved a 100-pound safe up an inclined plane 20 feet long and 2 feet high.
   How much effort did the person have to use to move the safe?

What Is the Advantage of Using a Wheel and Axle? (K–8)

What Concepts Might Students Discover or Construct?

A **wheel** is a simple machine that aids in moving an object.

Every wheel has an axle. The wheel is used to turn the axle or the axle is used to turn the wheel.

The work obtained from a simple machine is equal to the work put into it minus the work used in overcoming friction.

A small effort applied to a large wheel can be used to overcome a large resistance on a small wheel.

A **wheel and axle** machine usually consists of a large wheel to which a small axle is firmly attached.

The mechanical advantage is equal to the radius of the wheel divided by the radius of the axle.

What Will We Need?

1 bicycle per class
Board
Hammer
Screw hook
Nail
Rubber bands

Balance weight
4 spools from thread
5 or 6 round pencils
1 of the following: can opener, egg beater, or meat grinder

PROCESSES

What Will Students Do?

Hypothesizing

Measuring
Observing

Observing

Part I

1. *In what way does the wheel help to move objects?*
2. Turn the screw hook into the end of a block of wood. Attach a rubber band to the hook (a spring balance can be used instead) and measure the stretch of the rubber band as you drag the block on the table. Use a wooden ruler to make a measurement just before and after the block begins to move.
   Record all of your measurements.
3. With the rubber band on your finger, lift the block into the air and measure the stretch.
4. *What change is made in the stretch of the rubber band?*
5. Now place two round pencils underneath the block and measure the stretch of the rubber band just before and after the block begins to move.

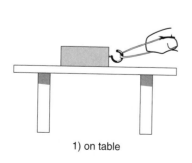

1) on table

2) lift up

3) on pencils

Observing

6. *What happens to the stretch of the rubber band this time?*

Comparing

7. *What difference do the pencils make underneath the wood as you try to move it?*

Comparing

8. *How does your measurement change?*

Inferring

9. *What do you suppose is the purpose of measuring the movement of the block of wood?*

10. Try the experiment again, only this time use four spools for the wheels and round pencils for the axles. Place the wood on the axle.

Observing

Observe what happens as you push the block of wood very gently.

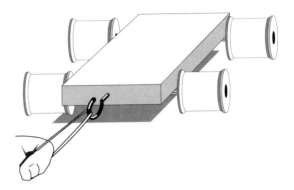

Measuring

11. Measure the stretch of the rubber band as you pull the block of wood.

Comparing

What difference is there in the stretch of the rubber band this time compared to moving the board without wheels?

Part II

1. Obtain a small winch or use a pencil sharpener, meat grinder, or can opener.

Hypothesizing

What is the advantage of using a winch?

2. Hook a weight to the axle as shown in the diagram.

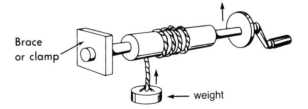

Hypothesizing

What do you think will be gained if a large wheel is turned to move a small axle?

3. Turn the large wheel.

4. Count the number of turns you make to raise the weight 2 inches.

What Must I Know?

A small force applied to a large wheel can be used to move a large resistance attached to the axle. This is done, however, at the expense of distance, since the large wheel has to be moved a great distance to raise the resistance a short way.

Part III

Inferring

1. Observe a bicycle.

   Where on a bicycle is friction used to advantage?
   How is the bicycle wheel constructed to help reduce friction?

What Must I Know?

The wheel produces less friction because there is less surface area coming in contact with pavement than if a weight such as a person were pulled along a surface.

Observing

2. *Where are the wheels and axles on a bicycle?*
   When you ride a bicycle, where do you apply the force?

Inferring

   Why do you apply the force to the small wheel?

What Must I Know?

The effort is applied to the small wheel to gain speed. Using a great force, you move the small sprocket a short distance, and it, in turn, moves the large wheel a greater distance but with less force. Look at the diagrams of the following objects and decide whether they increase the ability to move heavier objects or increase the speed.

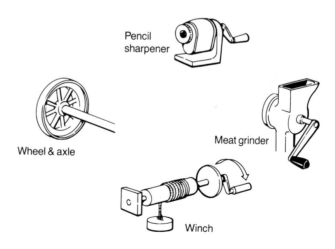

Pencil sharpener

Wheel & axle

Meat grinder

Winch

How Will Students Use or Apply What They Discover?

1. Pulling an object across the table produced a force.
   How can you tell which required a greater amount of force to pull: the board without pencils under it or the board that had the pencils as axles?

What Must I Know?

A spring scale can be substituted for the rubber band. If you have a balance, you can determine how many pounds of force you need to pull the board across the table. If you use a rubber band you must calculate how far the rubber band stretches. The rubber band will not stretch as much the first time.

2. *How are roller bearings and ball bearings used?*
3. A girl wants to move a heavy desk drawer across her room to another shelf.
   How can she go about doing this with the least amount of effort and the greatest amount of speed?

What Is a Jack and How Is It Used? (4–8)

What Concepts Might Students Discover or Construct?

A **screw** is an inclined plane wrapped around a rod.
As with an inclined plane, force is gained at the expense of distance. A large weight can be moved by a small force if the smaller force is applied over a greater distance.

What Will We Need?

Triangular pieces of paper	Model of a hill
Pencil	Board
Ring clamp	Nail
Hammer	Several screws
Screwdriver	Colored pencil or crayon
Tape measure	

What Will We Discuss?

Show the class several examples of screws and ask the following questions:
What are these called?
What purpose do they serve?
Where are they in the classroom?
What advantage do they have over nails?
What type of machine studied thus far resembles a screw?

What Must I Know?

A screw is a circular, inclined plane.

PROCESSES

What Will Students Do?

1. Obtain a small piece of paper and cut it in the shape of a triangle as shown in the diagram. Color the edge of the paper so you can see it, then wind the paper around the pencil.

Paper

Pencil

Paper wrapped around pencil

Observing

What kind of machine did the paper represent before you rolled it around the pencil?

Observing   *What kind of machine did the paper represent after you rolled it around the pencil?*

Comparing   *How are the screw and the inclined plane related?*

2. Obtain a C-clamp and insert a pencil as shown in the diagram.

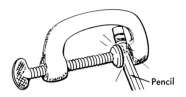

Pencil

Hypothesizing   *What do you think will happen to the pencil when you move the screw inward?*

Hypothesizing   *How much effort will have to be applied to break the pencil?*

3. Look at the diagram of the jack.

Jack

Communicating   Describe how the jack works.

Comparing   *How is the jack similar to a screw?*

Inferring   *What is the purpose of using a jack on a car?*

Inferring   *How is it possible for a person who weighs 150 pounds to lift a car weighing 3,000 pounds by using a jack?*

How Will Students Use or Apply What They Discover?

1. When were jacks used in old barber shops?
2. Where else are jacks used?
3. *How many seconds would a person have to exert a force to raise a car a small distance?*
4. What machine is involved in a spiral notebook?
5. *If you were asked to push a heavy rock to the top of a hill, how would you move it up the hill?*

What Is a Movable Pulley and How Can You Use It? (4–8)

What Concepts Might Students Discover or Construct?

Pulleys that move with the resistance are called **movable pulleys.** Movable pulley systems have a mechanical advantage greater than one. The mechanical advantage of a movable pulley system is equal to the number of stands holding up the resistance.

What Will We Need?	Ring stand for attaching pulleys Pull-type scale 50-g weight String or nylon fishing line 2 single pulleys 100-g weight Yard- or meterstick

PROCESSES

What Will Students Do?

1. Obtain a ring stand and a clamp for attaching a pulley, a single pulley, a pull-type scale, and a 100-gram weight. Assemble your equipment as shown in the diagram.

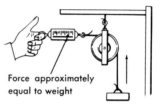

Force approximately equal to weight

Hypothesizing

How much do you think you will have to pull on the scale to raise the 100-gram weight?

2. Pull on the scale and raise the weight.

Observing
How is the scale affected when you raise the weight?

Measuring
3. Repeat this activity several times and record each measurement.

Hypothesizing
What do you think will happen when you use two pulleys to raise the 100-gram weight?

4. In addition to the equipment you have, obtain a single fixed pulley and a 50-gram weight. Assemble your equipment as shown in the diagram.

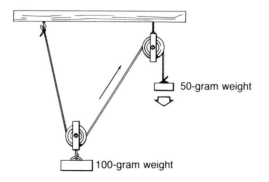

50-gram weight

100-gram weight

Observing
5. Pull the 50-gram weight and record your observations.

6. Remove the 50-gram weight and attach the scale.

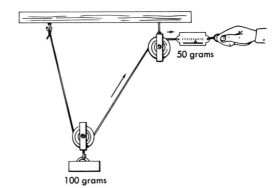

50 grams

100 grams

Hypothesizing	*How will the scale be affected when you raise the 100-gram weight?*
	7. Raise the weight by pulling on the scale.
Observing	*What happens to the scale when you raise the weight?*
Measuring	8. Repeat the activity several times and record each measurement.
	Why is there an advantage in using this type of pulley system?
	9. Remove the scale and once again attach the 50-gram weight.
Hypothesizing	*How far do you think the 50-gram weight will move when it raises the 100-gram weight?*
Hypothesizing	*How far do you think the 100-gram weight will move when it is raised by the 50-gram weight?*
	10. Obtain a yard- or meterstick.
Observing	11. Move the 50-gram weight and measure how far both the weights move.
Measuring	12. Repeat this part of the activity several times and record your measurements.
Summarizing	*What can you say about pulleys from the measurements you just recorded?*
	13. Look at the measurements you recorded when one pulley was used and those you recorded when two pulleys were used.
	What does the information tell you about pulleys?
How Will Students Use or Apply What They Discover?	*What kind of pulley system would be needed to raise a piano weighing 300 pounds?* Draw a sketch of that pulley system.

What Is a Lever and How Can You Use It? (4–8)

What Concepts Might Students Discover or Construct?	A **lever** is a simple machine. A lever cannot work alone. A lever consists of a bar that is free to turn on a pivot called the **fulcrum.**

By using a first-class lever, it is possible to increase a person's ability to lift heavier objects. This is called the **mechanical advantage.** The mechanical advantage of a lever is determined by the formula

$$\text{Mechanical advantage} = \frac{\text{Effort arm}}{\text{resistance arm}}$$

The weight times the distance on one side of the fulcrum must equal the weight times the distance on the other side if the lever is balanced. A first-class lever has the fulcrum between the resistance and the effort.

What Will We Need?

Meter- or yardstick
100-g weight
20-g weight
Roll of heavy string or nylon fishing line
Assorted weights of various sizes
Platform with an arm for suspending objects

What Must I Know?

Define resistance, force, and fulcrum before beginning the activity.

PROCESSES

What Will Students Do?

1. Using some heavy string, a yardstick, a 100-gram weight, a 20-gram weight, a ring stand, and a ring clamp, assemble the apparatus as shown in the diagram.

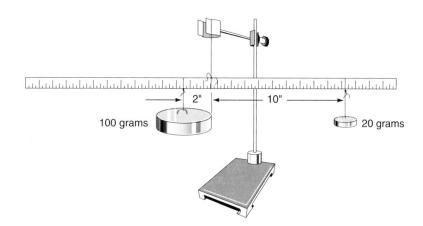

Hypothesizing

Where do you think you should attach the 100-gram weight and the 20-gram weight so the yardstick will balance?

2. Attach the weights so the yardstick is balanced.

Observing

How far is the 100-gram weight from the end of the yardstick?

Observing

How far is the 20-gram weight from the end of the yardstick?

3. Look at these three things: the string, which is suspending the yard-stick, the 20-gram weight, and the 100-gram weight.

Inferring   *What is the relationship between the weight and distance on each side of the fulcrum?*

Inferring   *What are the advantages of using a first-class lever of this type?*

4. Use the following formula to calculate the mechanical advantage (M.A.) of the lever.

$$M.A. = \frac{Effort\ arm}{resistance\ arm}$$

What Must I Know?/Where Do I Find It?

At the completion of the activity, explain to the class that a **first-class lever** consists of a bar that is free to turn on a pivot point called the **fulcrum**. The weight moved is called the **resistance**. The force exerted on the other end of the lever is called the **effort**. Draw the diagram on the board to illustrate this point. State that in a first-class lever, the fulcrum is always between the resistance and the effort. Have students do some different problems using the formula given in Step 4. Use metric measurements, if possible.

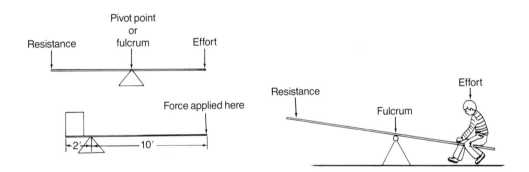

How Will Students Use or Apply What They Discover?

1. *How is the M.A. affected when different weights are used?*
2. *What does an M.A. of 4 mean?*
3. *Where are first-class levers used?*

Reference Books—Simple Machines

Teacher: Harvey Weiss, *Machines and How They Work* (New York: Harper and Row, 1983).

Students: Rose Wyler, *Science Fun With Toy Cars and Trucks* (Englewood Cliffs, NJ: Messner, 1988).

MAGNETIC AND ELECTRICAL ENERGIES AND INTERACTIONS

QUICKIE STARTERS

What Can Magnets Do?

Materials

Several strong magnets, steel ball

Opening Question

What might happen if you bring a magnet next to a steel ball or another magnet?

Some Possible Activities

Put a magnet on a table and hold a steel ball 1 inch (2–3 cm) away from the magnet's end.
What happens when you let go of the steel ball?
Try it again.
Why do you think this happens?

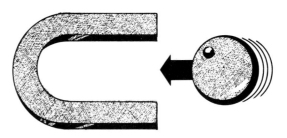

Now try the same thing using two magnets.
What happens to the magnets?

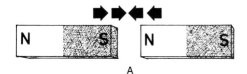

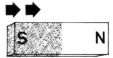

A   B

Try the same thing again, but turn one magnet around so its opposite end faces the first magnet.
What happens now? Why do you think this happens?
What other things might you be able to move with magnets?
How could you find out?

What Are the Shapes and Names of Magnets?

Materials

Large assortment of magnets of different sizes, shapes, colors, and materials (lodestone, bar, U-shaped, horseshoe, cylindrical, disk, doughnut-shaped); variety of items attracted to magnets (paper clips, iron or steel washers and nails); variety of objects not attracted to magnets (rubber bands, paper, plastic chips, bits of wood); 2 shoe boxes, one labeled "Magnets Pick Up" and one labeled "Magnets Do Not Pick Up."

Opening Questions

How are all these things [magnets] the same?
What are they called?

Some Possible
Activities

I **G**

Touch one magnet at a time to the piles of paper clips, iron or steel washers, and nails.
What happens to the paper clips and other things?
Try the same thing with the other objects.
What happens? Why do you think the paper clips, the iron or steel washers, and the nails were pulled to and stuck to the magnets?
Put those objects that were picked up by the magnets into the box marked "Magnets Pick Up" and those objects that were not picked up by the magnet into the box marked "Magnets Do Not Pick Up." Objects that pull and hold iron and steel things are called **magnets,** and their exact names are descriptive of their shapes, such as lodestone, bar magnet, U-shaped magnet, cylindrical magnet, and doughnut-shaped magnet.
What other shapes might magnets have?
Bring in magnets you have at home.
Where are the magnets used?

GUIDED DISCOVERY MINDS-ON/HANDS-ON ACTIVITIES

What Is a Magnet? (K–6)

What Concepts
  Might Students
  Discover or
  Construct?

The place on the magnet where it picks up iron or steel objects is called the **pole.** A magnet has two poles, one called the north, and the other called the south.
The same or like poles push apart or repel. Different or unlike poles pull together or attract.
Around every magnet is an area called the **magnetic field,** which is made up of invisible magnetic lines of force.

What Will We Need?

2 cylindrical bar magnets
Steel needle
Glass or plastic pan
2 rectangular bar magnets

String
⅛-in slice of cork
Water

What Must I Know?

The materials listed are for a group of two or three students. Set up stations and equip each group with a set of materials.

What Will We
  Discuss?

Display a cylindrical bar magnet for the class.
What is this called?
What is it made of?
How can it be used?
What are the properties or characteristics of a magnet?
What things can a magnet do?
What do you think will happen if two cylindrical bar magnets are placed side by side?
How could you find out?

PROCESSES

What Will Students Do?

Observing

Observing

Part I

1. Place one cylindrical bar magnet on the table and bring the second magnet near it.
   Observe what happens.

2. Reverse one of the magnets. Observe what happens.
   What happens when you put the second magnet beside the first one?
   What happens when you turn one magnet around?

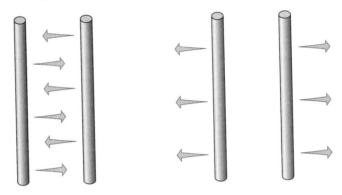

Why do you think one magnet rolls when the other comes near it?

What did you notice when the magnets pulled together?

What did you notice when the magnets pushed apart?

Inferring

How do you know from this activity that both ends of the magnet are not the same?

Inferring

What did you do to make the magnets push apart?

Inferring

What did you do to make the magnets pull together?

Part II

1. Using two rectangular or cylindrical bar magnets, tie a string around the middle of one of the magnets as shown in the diagram.

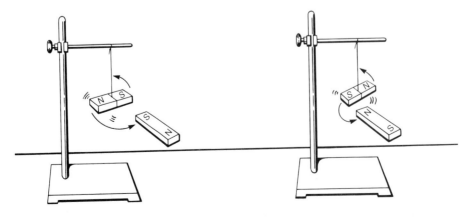

Hypothesizing

2. By holding the string, suspend the magnet in the air.
   What do you think will happen when another magnet is brought near the suspended one?

Inferring

Hypothesizing

3. Bring another magnet near the suspended one.
   Why do you think the magnet moves?
   What do you think will happen when you reverse the magnet in your hand?

Observing

Inferring

4. Reverse the magnet and bring it near the suspended one.
   Why does the suspended magnet react differently when you approach it with the other end of the magnet?

Inferring

Inferring

What causes the magnet to react in different ways?
   How do you know there is a force present even though it cannot be seen?

Explaining

What is a force?

What Must I Know?

Point out that a **force** is a push or pull. This can be shown by pushing or pulling a child who is seated in a chair.

Part III

Hypothesizing

How can you measure the force of attraction between certain objects and magnets?

What Will Students Do?

1. Get a meterstick without a metal edge, a large and a small bar magnet, a paper clip, a steel washer, a steel BB, and transparent tape.
2. Tape the meterstick to your desk top so it will not move. Put a paper clip at the end of the meterstick, and place the large bar magnet at the 6 cm line (as shown in the diagram).

3. Very slowly move the magnet along the meterstick's edge toward the paper clip. Stop exactly when the paper clip starts to move toward the magnet!

Observing

How many centimeters away was the magnet when the paper clip started to move?

Record your findings on the following chart.

Object	Distance From Clip to Magnet

4. Repeat this two more times, then average the three findings.

Hypothesizing   *Why average three observations?*

5. Do the same tests using the steel BB and the washer.

Inferring   *If the distances the objects moved were different, why do you think this is so?*

6. Repeat the tests using the small magnet with each object, three times each. Average the findings, and record the data on your chart.

Comparing   *Which of the two magnets was the stronger?*
Inferring   *How do you know from your findings?*
Inferring   *Why do you think the distances between the magnet and the paper clip, the BB, and the washer were different?*
Inferring   *What do these tests tell you about the strength of magnets and how different objects are affected?*
Communicating   Using the data from your charts, graph the results of these tests.

Part IV

1. Obtain a steel needle, a magnet, and a pan with an inch or two of water in it.

Hypothesizing   *What can you find out about the needle and the magnet?*

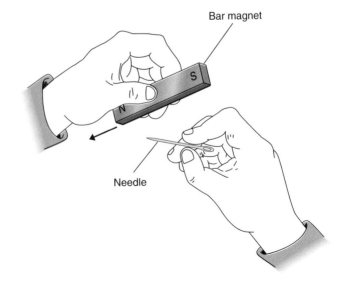

Bar magnet

S

N

Needle

2. Make a magnet of the needle (magnetize it) by holding a magnet in one hand and stroking a needle in one direction only several times. Lay the needle on the cork so the needle is in a horizontal position. Float the cork in the water you have placed in a pan as shown in the diagram. (*Hint:* Adding one drop of liquid dishwashing detergent to the water will enable the floating cork to turn much more easily as the needle responds to the magnet.)

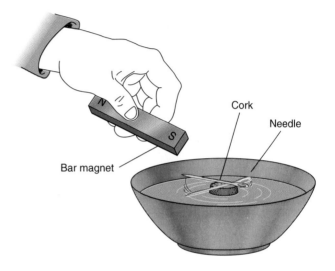

3. Bring a magnet near the needle on the cork.

Inferring   *Why do the cork and the needle move when you bring a magnet near them?*

Inferring   *What happens to the needle when it is stroked with the magnet?*

Summarizing   *What caused the cork and needle to move?*

How Will Students Use or Apply What They Discover?

1. *How does a compass work?*
2. *How could you use a magnet to make a compass?*

What Is Static Electricity? (4–8)

What Concepts Might Students Discover or Construct?

All bodies are capable of producing electrical charges.
Conductors allow electrons to move, but **insulators** do not allow electrons to move easily.
Like charges repel; unlike charges attract.

What Will We Need?

Lucite or resin rod or a hard rubber comb		Large piece of paper
		Balloon
Wool cloth	Flour	Tap water
Glass rod		Piece of silk about the size of a small handkerchief
Small pieces of paper		

What Will We
Discuss?

*What can you state about how poles of magnets react toward one
another?*
*What is the energy that we use to produce light and to operate many
machines and household appliances?*
What things can produce electricity?
How can you find out if all charges of electricity are the same?

PROCESSES

Part I

What Will Students
Do?

1. Obtain the following materials: a lucite or resin rod or a hard rubber
comb, wool, flour, a glass rod, small pieces of paper, a large piece
of paper, a balloon, tap water, and a piece of silk.
2. Take the resin rod (or hard rubber comb) and rub it with the wool
cloth.

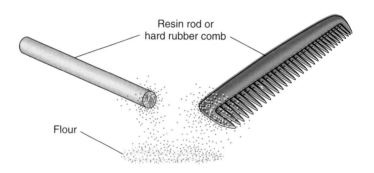

Hypothesizing

*What do you think will happen when the rod is touched to the
flour?*
3. Touch the rod to some flour.

Observing   *What happens to the flour?*
Hypothesizing   *Why do you think the flour is affected by the rod?*
4. Clean the rod, rub it again, and touch it to the small pieces of paper.
Observing   *What does the rod do to the paper?*

Part II

5. Rub the rod briskly with the wool cloth.
6. Turn on a water tap so a very slow stream of water comes out.
Hypothesizing   *What do you think will happen to the stream of water when the rod
is moved close to it?*
7. Move the rod close to the stream.
Observing   *What happens as the rod comes near?*
Inferring   *Why does the water react as it does?*
Inferring   *Why do you think it reacts as it does without being touched?*

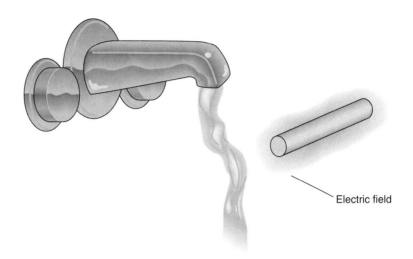

Electric field

What Must I Know?	The students should note how close they have to bring the rod before it affects the stream of water. Develop the concept that there is an invisible field of electrical force around the rod that either pushes or attracts the water. This force cannot be seen, but it must be there because it affects the stream of water. Define force as a push or pull. In this case, the water is pushed or pulled, without being touched, by moving the rod toward and away from the water.
Designing an Investigation	*How can you find out if rubbing the cloth on the rod causes the electrical force?*

8. Rub the rod again with the cloth.
9. Now rub your hand over the rod.

Hypothesizing   *What do you think will happen to the stream of water?*

10. Repeat the procedure by approaching the slow stream of water with the rod.

Observing   *What effect does the rod have on the water this time?*

Inferring   *Why does the rod not have the same effect?*

Inferring   *What happened to the charge that the wool cloth induced in the rod?*

Inferring   *Why do you think the charge failed to last?*

What Must I Know?   When the resin rod is rubbed with wool or fur, **electrons** are rubbed off these materials onto the rod. The rod, however, is an insulator, so the electron movement is slight. The rod becomes negatively charged since each electron produces a small amount of negative charge. When a hand is rubbed over the rod, the rod becomes discharged because the electrons leave the rod and enter the hand. The rod is then neutral. Explain the difference between a conductor and an insulator.

Part III

Summarizing

Inferring

1. *After your discussion concerning conductors and insulators, would you say the rod is a conductor or an insulator?*
   Why do you think so?
2. Obtain two balloons.
3. Inflate the balloons.
4. Tie a string to each balloon and suspend them from a bar or a coat hanger as shown in the diagram.

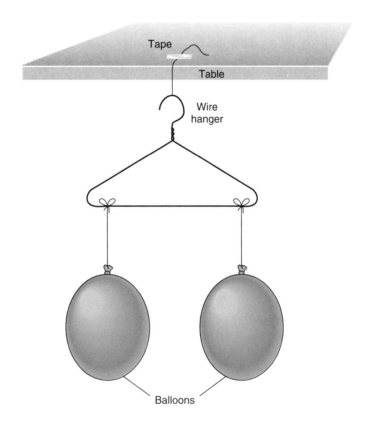

Tape

Table

Wire
hanger

Balloons

5. Rub each balloon with the wool cloth.

Observing   *What do the balloons do?*
Inferring   *Why do they repel each other?*
Summarizing   *Do you think the balloons are conductors or insulators?*
Hypothesizing   *What do you think will happen if a charged resin rod is brought near the balloons?*

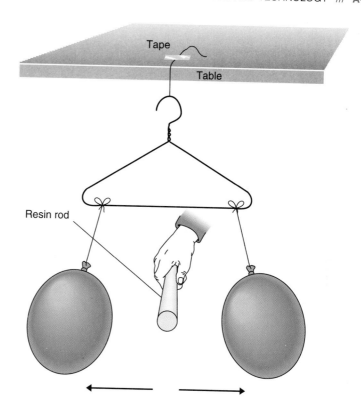

6. Rub the resin rod with wool and place it near the balloons.

Observing   *In which direction do the balloons move?*

Inferring   *Why do you think they were repelled by the rod?*

Assuming   *Do you think the balloons have a like or unlike charge? Why?*

Hypothesizing   *What do you think will happen to the balloons if you touch them with a glass rod?*

What Must I Know?

These balloons were charged in the same way; therefore, each must have the same charge. When they do have the same charge, they repel each other because like charges repel.

7. Rub the glass rod with the piece of silk.
8. Place it near the balloons.

Observing   *What happens as it comes near the balloons?*

Comparing   *How does the glass rod affect the balloons in comparison to the resin rod?*

Comparing   *What can you say about the charge on the resin rod compared to the glass rod?*

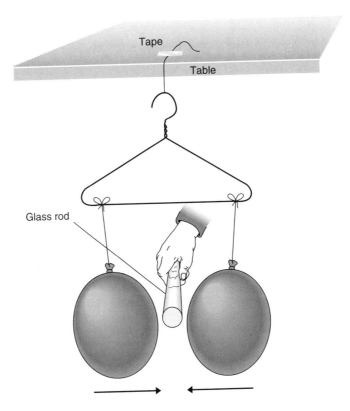

 Glass rod

What Must I Know?

The glass rod will have a positive charge since electrons were rubbed off the rod onto the silk. It will attract the balloons because they were negatively charged by the resin rod, and unlike charges attract.

Part IV

1. Vigorously rub one of the inflated balloons against the piece of wool.
2. Place the balloon on a wall. (See diagram.)

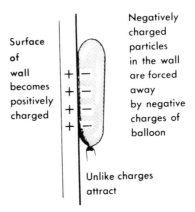

Surface of wall becomes positively charged

Negatively charged particles in the wall are forced away by negative charges of balloon

Unlike charges attract

Hypothesizing	*What do you think will happen to the balloon?*
Inferring	*Why does the balloon not fall?*
Inferring	*Is the force that pulls the balloon to the wall greater or less than the gravitational force pulling the balloon down to earth?*
Inferring	*What happened to the negatively charged particles in the wall when the balloon came near?*
Summarizing	*After following the previous steps, what can you say about charging matter?*
Summarizing	*What is a conductor?*
Summarizing	*What is an insulator?*

What Must I Know? When you rub the balloon with wool, it becomes negatively charged, because it got an excess of electrons from the wool. When the balloon is placed next to the wall, the balloon's negative charge forces the electrons in the wall away from the surface, leaving the surface positively charged. The balloon sticks because the unlike charges attract. The balloon is negative and the wall surface is positive, as is indicated in the diagram.

How Will Students Use or Apply What They Discover?
1. *What is electricity?*
2. *How can you use a magnet to make electricity?*
3. *Why might you get a shock after walking across a wool carpet and then touching a metal doorknob?*
4. *Why does your hair get attracted to your comb? Why is this most noticeable on very dry days?*
5. *Why do clothes stick together after being dried in a clothes dryer?*

How Can You Make Electricity by Using Magnetism? (4–8)

What Concepts Might Students Discover or Construct? Around a magnet there are magnetic lines of force.
If you break the magnetic lines of force, you can make electricity.
A force is defined as a push or a pull.

What Will We Need? Copper wire (about 3 yards)
Magnetic compass
Bar magnet

What Will We Discuss? *How is electricity used?*
How does electricity get to your home for you to use?
What is the area of force around a magnet called?
What is a force?
How can you use a magnet to produce electricity?

PROCESSES

What Will Students Do?

1. With a partner, obtain a length of wire (about 3 yards), a bar magnet, and a magnetic compass.
2. Take the wire and wrap it 20 to 30 times around the magnetic compass as indicated in the diagram.

3. Loop the other end of the wire into a coil as shown in the diagram.

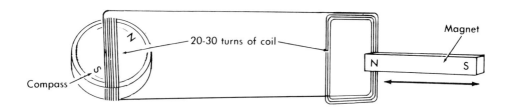

Inferring	*What happens when electricity goes through a wire?*
Inferring	*What do you think the area around the wire could be called?*
Inferring	*What has the electricity produced?*
Designing an Investigation	*How do you think magnetism could be used to produce electricity?*
Observing	4. Take the bar magnet and plunge it back and forth through the coil of wire. Instruct your partner to watch what happens to the compass.
Observing	*What happens to the compass?*
Inferring	*Why do you think the compass needle does what it does?*
Applying	*What attracts the compass needle?*
Hypothesizing	*What do you think causes the needle to be deflected?*
Hypothesizing	*Where do you think the magnetism was produced to cause the compass needle to move?*
Inferring or interpreting	*If there is magnetism produced in the wire around the compass, what do you think the plunging of the magnet through the coil of wire has to do with it?*
Inferring or interpreting	*When is electricity produced in the wire?*
Summarizing	*What is the force of a magnet called?*
Summarizing	*What does a magnet do to a magnetizable object?*
Summarizing	*What does a magnet do to a nonmagnetizable object?*
Summarizing	*Explain how magnetism can be used to produce an electrical current.*

What Must I Know?

Around every magnet there is an area that can push or pull susceptible objects such as iron filings. This area is thought to consist of lines of force. When these lines of force are broken by plunging the magnet back and forth through a coil of wire, electricity is made in the wire. **Electricity** is defined as a flow of electrons along the wire, producing an electrical current. Whenever there is an electrical current produced, there will be a magnetic field around the wire. This magnetic field causes the magnet (compass needle) in this activity to move. Using magnets to produce electricity is the principle involved in making electricity in a dynamo. Make certain that the compass is far enough away from the magnet to avoid direct magnetic influence.

How Will Students Use or Apply What They Discover?

How can you use electricity to make a magnet?

How Can You Make a Temporary (Electro) Magnet? (4–8)

What Concepts Might Students Discover or Construct?

When electricity passes along a wire, it produces a magnetic field around the wire that acts like a magnet.
A magnetic field can make iron temporarily magnetic.
The more electric current flows through a wire in a unit of time, the more magnetism is generated around the wire.
If a circuit is broken, electricity will not flow.

What Will We Need?

Insulated copper wire
Iron nail
Dry cell battery
Teaspoon of iron filings
Paper clips

What Will We Discuss?

How is magnetism made by electricity?
By using a wire that is carrying a current, how could you make a large magnetic field?
If you wanted to magnetize a nail, how would you do it?

What Must I Know?

The supplies listed under "What Will We Need?" are for two to four students.

PROCESSES

What Will Students Do?

1. Obtain a dry cell battery, an iron nail, a piece of insulated copper wire, some iron filings, and a paper clip.
2. Wrap the wire around the nail several times as shown in the diagram.
3. Scrape the insulation off two ends of the wire. Connect only *one* end of the wire to one terminal of the dry cell. When you do the activity, touch the other end of the wire to the other terminal of the dry cell for only a few seconds. *Caution:* Do not let the other wire and terminal remain in contact for more than a few seconds as intense heat builds up, and you could get a burn through the insulation.

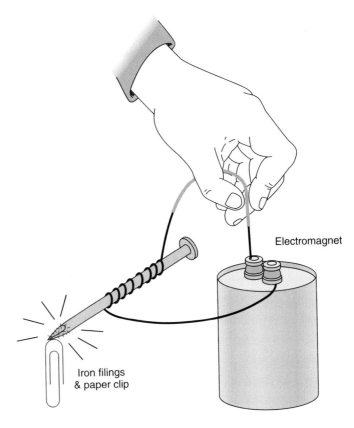

Electromagnet

Iron filings
& paper clip

CAUTION: DO NOT HOLD WIRE TO TERMINAL FOR MORE THAN 3 SECONDS!

Hypothesizing   *What do you think will happen to some iron filings if you place them near the nail and then touch the loose end of the wire to the terminal? Do this carefully, and release one end of wire from the terminal after a few seconds.*

4. Place a paper clip on the nail and repeat.

Observing   *What happens to the filings and paper clip while the loose end of the wire is touching the terminal?*

Inferring   *Why do the iron filings temporarily stay on the nail?*

Inferring   *What is temporarily produced around the wire when both ends of the wire are touching both terminals?*

Inferring   *What did the nail temporarily become?*

Observing   *What happened to the iron filings and nail when you removed the loose wire so that it no longer touched the terminal?*

Inferring   *Why do they fall when you disconnect the wire?*

Applying   *What must you do with the circuit to produce electricity?*

Summarizing	*What can you say about the production of magnetism around a wire when electricity goes through it?*
Summarizing	*What would you call the temporary magnet you made by passing electricity through a conductor?* (**electromagnet**).
Designing an Investigation	*How do you think you could increase the strength of the magnetism in the nail?*
Hypothesizing	*What do you think would happen if you wrapped more wire around the nail?*
Hypothesizing	*Will the magnetism increase or decrease? Why?*
Assuming	*Is the magnet you produced a temporary or a permanent magnet? Why?*
Inferring	*How do you know?*

How Will Students Use or Apply What They Discover?

1. Try an experiment where you test whether more turns of wire affect how many paper clips your electromagnet picks up.
2. Collect data and set up a graph like the one shown.

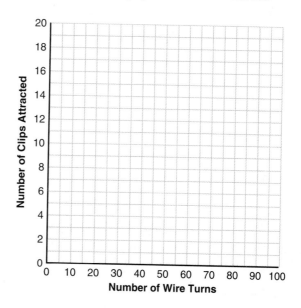

3. *By what other means could the magnetic field around the nail be increased? What do you think might happen if you used a bigger dry cell or more dry cells connected together?*

How Are Parallel and Series Circuits the Same and Different? (4–8)

What Concepts Might Students Discover?

For the electrons to move in a circuit, there must be a path that is unbroken to and from the source of electrical energy.
If one lamp burns out in a series circuit, the circuit is broken.

In a parallel circuit, one lamp can burn out, but the rest of the circuit will still function.

What Will We Need?

2 dry cells
4 small lamps
4 sockets

Connecting wires
2 switches

What Will We Discuss?

In what different ways can you use a dry cell and wire to make a circuit?
How could you make a parallel or series circuit?
What would happen if one light on a string of Christmas tree lights were unscrewed?
What would you do to find out?
Why is it that strings of Christmas tree lights do not all behave the same?

PROCESSES

What Will Students Do?

Hypothesizing

1. Connect a dry cell, two small lamps, a switch, two sockets, and connecting wires so the light works.
   What do you need to do to make the lights work?

What Must I Know?

The diagram of the series circuit is for your information. It should not be shown to the students until they have completed the activity.

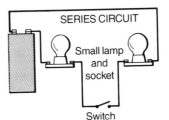

Hypothesizing
Hypothesizing

What purpose does the switch serve?
What do you think will happen when you unscrew one of the lights?

2. Unscrew one of the lights.

Inferring
Hypothesizing

Why did the other light go out?
What can you do to make the lights go on again?

3. Using the same equipment, rearrange the circuit so that if one light goes out, the other will still burn.

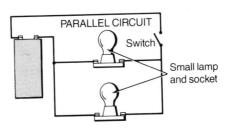

What Must We Know?

The diagram of a parallel circuit is available for your information. It should not be shown to the students until after they finish this activity.

4. Unscrew one of the lights. If you wired it differently than the first time, one of the lights should still burn even though you unscrewed the other.

Inferring

Why?

Comparing

What is the difference between the two types of circuits you have constructed?

What Must I Know?/Where Do I Find It?

In a **parallel circuit,** there may be more than two paths for the current to take to complete its circuit. If one of the circuits is broken, the current can still use the other circuit, as indicated in the preceding diagram.

How Will Students Use or Apply What They Discover?

1. *What kind of circuits do you have in your home?*
2. *How could you find out what kind of circuit a string of Christmas tree lights is?*
3. Examine a flashlight. *What kind of a circuit does it have?*

Reference Books—Magnetic and Electrical Energies and Interactions

Teacher: Martin J. Gutnik, *Electricity from Faraday to Solar Generators* (New York: Watts, 1986).

Students: Melvin Berger, *Switch On, Switch Off* (New York: Crowell, 1989).

LIGHT ENERGY, SHADOWS, LENSES, AND COLOR

QUICKIE STARTERS

How Does Light Move and Pass Through Some Things?

Materials

Flashlights, transparent materials (clear plastic food wrap, sandwich bags, and cups); translucent materials (waxed paper, cloudy plastic); opaque materials (oaktag or construction paper, thin pieces of wood and metal); printed page of directions

Opening Questions

Give each student a flashlight. Darken the room and write this statement on the chalkboard, "We cannot see without light." Ask: *Can you tell what I wrote on the chalkboard? Why not? How can you use your flashlights to find out what I wrote?* Turn the lights on and discuss why

light is needed for us to see things. (*Hint:* Take the flashlights away before the discussion.) Ask:
Does light move through all materials?

Some Possible Activities

Give each group of four students some samples of the transparent, translucent, and opaque materials, along with a page with print on it. Ask the students to place one kind of material at a time over the printed page you gave them. For each material, have students fill in a chart with one of these choices: (1) can see through it easily, (2) can see through it but it is very cloudy, (3) cannot see through it.

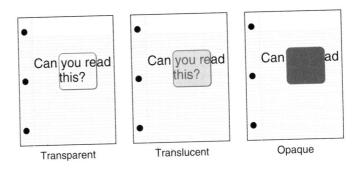

Transparent   Translucent   Opaque

How Can You Make A Shadow Theater?

Materials

Flashlight or filmstrip projector, waxed or rice paper, heavy cardboard or thin wood, puppets made from cardboard

Opening Questions

How are shadows made?
How can we use this information to make a Shadow Theater?

Some Possible Activities

Have students stand in front of a source of light (i.e., a flashlight or filmstrip projector). Turn off the classroom lights and turn on the flashlight. The students will see their shadows. Explain that the students are opaque and light cannot pass through them. Shadows, then, are the result of blocked light by opaque materials. Have students make puppets from cardboard. Make a screen out of a heavy cardboard or wood frame which holds waxed paper or rice paper. Shine a flashlight on the puppet that is between the flashlight and the screen, as shown in the diagram.

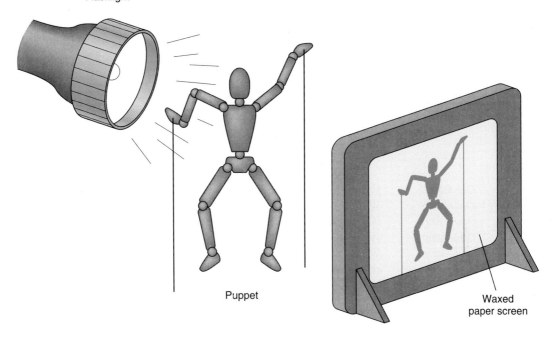

Flashlight

Puppet

Waxed
paper screen

How can the size of the shadows be changed?
How can you make the shadows darker or lighter?
How else can the shadows be changed?

GUIDED DISCOVERY MINDS-ON/HANDS-ON ACTIVITIES

What Does a Prism Do to White Light? (K–8)

What Concepts Might Students Discover or Construct?	White light, when passed through a prism, disperses to form a continuous **spectrum,** or a rainbow. White light is a mixture of many colors of light. Each color in the spectrum has a different wavelength.
What Will We Need?	A prism
What Will We Discuss?	*What is a prism?* *What does a prism do?*
What Must I Know?	This activity should be done in groups of two or more students.
PROCESSES	**Part I**
What Will Students Do?	1. Obtain a prism.

Hypothesizing   *What do you think will happen to the light rays after they pass through the prism?*

2. Place the prism in the path of a strong beam of light as indicated in the diagram.

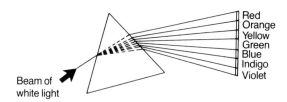

Observing   *What happens to the light rays when they pass through the prism?*
Observing   *What colors do you see?*
Observing   *Which color seems to have bent the most?*
Observing   *Which color seems to have bent the least?*
Inferring   *What do you know about the way the different colors of light are* **refracted** *(bent) by the prism?*
Inferring   *What is white light made of?*

What Must I Know?   The students should see that white light is produced by the combination of several wavelengths of light. Draw a prism on the board and have the students show how the spectrum is formed. Their drawing should be something like the previous diagram.

Part II

Hypothesizing   *What do you think will happen if you look through the prism at your partner?*

Experimenting   1. Look at your partner through the AB side of the prism.

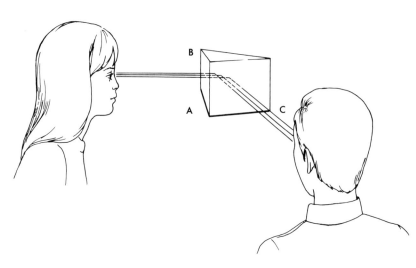

2. Record your observations.

Inferring

Why is it possible to see your partner without looking directly at him or her?

Inferring

What happens to the light entering the prism that makes it possible for you to see your partner?

Inferring

What does the prism do to the light rays?

Comparing

What is the difference between a prism and a mirror in the way that each affects light?

What Must I Know?

Prisms are used in expensive optical equipment instead of mirrors because prisms absorb less light. At the conclusion of this activity, place a diagram of a prism on the board and have the students draw how light passes through it. If they do not understand how a prism can be used in a periscope, draw and discuss the following diagram.

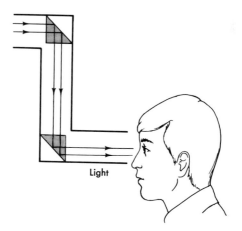

Light

How Will Students Use or Apply What They Discover?

1. *What happens to X-rays when they pass through a prism?*
2. *What would happen if you passed light through two prisms?*
3. *Why are prisms used in expensive optical equipment instead of mirrors?*

How Does Light Appear to Travel? (3–8)

What Concepts Might Students Discover or Construct?

Light appears to our eyes to travel in a straight line.

What Will We Need?

4 index cards (5 x 8 in)
Hole puncher or pointed object (pencil)
Flashlight or projector
Matches
Candle

Modeling clay
Round (oatmeal) box
Rubber band
Waxed paper
Pie tin

What Will We Discuss?

How does light appear to your eyes to travel?

What Must I Know?

You may conduct these simple activities, or students may do them by themselves, to assist them in seeing that light appears to our eyes to travel in a straight line. In a camera, due to light appearing to travel in a straight line, images appear upside down (inverted). Focusing—moving objects back and forth—is also a result of light appearing to travel in a straight line.

PROCESSES

What Will Students Do?

Part I

1. Holding all the index cards together, use a hole puncher or pointed object to punch a ¼-inch (7-mm) hole in the center of each card. Push each card into a lump of modeling clay and space the cards about 1 foot (30 cm) apart, making sure to line up the center holes as shown.

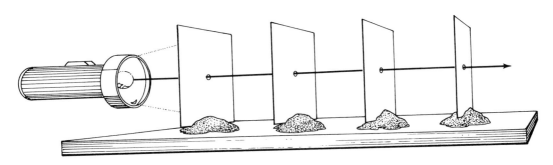

Hypothesizing

What do you think will happen if you shine the light through the first card?

2. Shine a light using the flashlight or projector through the first card's hole.

Observing

What do you notice about the path of the light?

Hypothesizing

3. *What will happen if you move the first card 1 inch (25mm) to one side?*

4. Move the first card 1 inch to the left or right.

Observing

What happens now?

Comparing

How is this different from what you observed in Step 2?

Inferring

What does this tell you about how light appears to travel?

Part II

What Must I Know?

You should demonstrate this activity for immature or unruly students. For older students, this activity should be done in groups of two. One student will perform the activity while the other observes and vice versa.

What Will We Discuss?

How does a camera use light?
What does it mean to focus a camera?

What Will Students Do?

1. Obtain a round oatmeal box, waxed paper, rubber band, candle, and matches. Puncture a very small hole in the end of the box with your pencil. Cover the open end of the box with waxed paper and secure the paper with a rubber band.
2. Place the candle (attached to the pie tin with melted wax) in front of the pin-hole end of the box and light the candle. Darken the room.
3. Move the small-holed end back and forth in front of the candle while your partner watches the waxed-papered end.

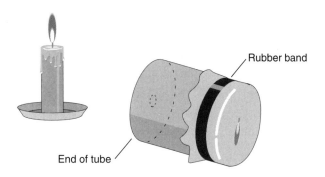

Rubber band

End of tube

Observing *What appears on the waxed-papered end of the box?*
Observing *What is different about the image on the waxed paper?*
Inferring *Why do you think the image appears this way?*
Hypothesizing *Why did you move the punctured end of the box back and forth?*
Inferring *From this activity, what would you conclude about how light appears to travel?*
Inferring *How do you think a picture of an object appears on the film in back of a camera?*

How Will Students Use or Apply What They Discover?

1. *What would happen to the image on the waxed paper if you moved the box 3 feet (or a meter) from the candle?*
2. *What would happen to the image if you blew the candle flame out? Why?*

What Must I Know?/Where Do I Find It?

After students have completed the previous activity, place the diagrams on the board and have students draw the image of the candle. They should draw something similar to what appears in the first diagram. Discuss how the light travels through the hole, as indicated by the second diagram, and results in an inverted image on the waxed-papered end.

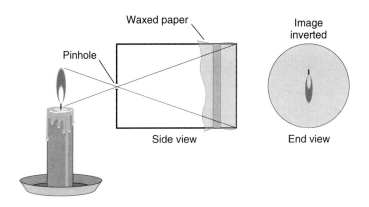

Waxed paper

Pinhole

Side view

Image inverted

End view

Reference Books—Light Energy, Lenses, Shadows, and Color
Teacher: Isaac Asimov, *How Did We Find Out About Lasers?* (New York: Walker, 1990).
Student: Cary Sneider and Cherly Hawthorne, *Color Analyzers* (Washington, D.C.: National Science Teachers Association, 1989).

Life Sciences and Technology

PLANT ANATOMY AND PHYSIOLOGY

QUICKIE STARTERS

How Can Some Plants Grow Without Seeds?

Materials
Small tumblers (preferably clear plastic); small sweet potatoes, white potatoes, and carrot tops (with some root); toothpicks; cuttings from coleus, philodendron, ivy, and other houseplants

Opening Questions
How can we get new plants to grow without planting seeds?
What is needed for new plants to grow?
How can we take good care of our new plants?

Some Possible Activities
Put three toothpicks each in a sweet potato, white potato, and carrot, as shown in the diagram. Place the plants in small tumblers of water. Take cuttings of houseplants and place them in small tumblers of water. Put all the tumblers in a well-lit place and make sure the water levels are maintained so that they always touch the plants. Have students observe and measure the changes in the plants, such as root development, height, number of leaves, etc.

Coleus and Philodendron

Toothpicks

Sweet potato

White potato

Carrot

What Kinds of Things Can We Do With Plants?

Hug and Feel a Tree

Have students hug a tree trunk, feel its surface, and describe how it feels. Encourage students to smell the bark. Have them draw and give a name to their favorite tree or they can cut pictures of trees out of magazines.

Press Plants

Invite students to collect parts of plants, such as leaves and flowers. *Caution:* Stress collecting fallen plant parts only. Do not allow students to pick from living things. Also, make sure students do not collect any parts from poisonous plants such as poison ivy. Have students press the plant parts between newspapers. Place some books or something heavy on the newspapers. After several days, remove the weights and newspapers. Discuss how drying helps to preserve the plants.

**Make Splatter
Pictures of Leaves**

Have students collect different types of leaves and bring them to class. Tell students to place the leaves on colored paper. Then show students how to dip brushes in poster paint and splatter paint over the leaves to make a picture outline. Have students compare the different types of leaves and what methods they had to use to make good splatter pictures. For example, ask how the thickness of the paint affected the quality of the picture.

GUIDED DISCOVERY MINDS-ON/HANDS-ON ACTIVITIES

What Are Seeds and How Do They Grow? (K–3)

**What Concepts
Might Students
Discover?**

Soaked bean seeds are different from dried beans.
A seed has different parts: the **embryo** (tiny plant), the **cotyledon(s)** (stored food), and a **seed coat** (skin). Each part is needed for the germination and growth of the plant.

Part I   What Are the Parts of a Seed?

What Will We Need?

1 lima bean seed soaked overnight
1 unsoaked lima bean seed
Piece of waxed paper
Hand lens

**What Will We
Discuss?**

*What is a seed and what parts does it have?
How can we find out?*

PROCESSES

**What Will Students
Do?**

Give each student the materials listed. Ask students to respond to the following questions, using their seeds as their sources of observation. List the responses on the board.

I

*Observing
Hypothesizing*

*How are soaked seeds different from dried seeds?
What do you think you will see when you open your seeds?*

Comparing   1. Open your soaked seed. *Hint:* Demonstrate for students how to do this.
How does what you see compare with your hypotheses (guesses)?

Labeling   2. Draw and label a picture of your open seed.

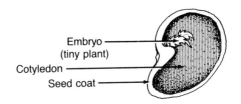

Embryo (tiny plant)
Cotyledon
Seed coat

Inferring   *Which part of the seed do you think might grow into a plant?*
Inferring   *What do you think might happen to the other parts of the seed?*
Inferring   *Which parts do you think are needed for the plant to grow?*
Designing an   *How could you set up an experiment to test your ideas about what*
Investigation   *seed parts are needed for the plant to grow?*

What Must I Know?   This activity is an important introduction to what a seed is, what its parts are, and the functions of those parts in producing a new plant. Activities that follow will investigate variables that affect seed germination.

Part II   Which Parts of a Seed Are Needed for It to Grow Into a Plant?[1]

What Will We Need?   1 plastic bag
1 paper towel
5 soaked lima beans
Paper clip
Stapler

What Will We Discuss?   *What parts of a seed are needed for it to grow into a plant?*

Designing an   *How can we test to see which seed parts are needed and which are not?*
Investigation   *Which parts of a soaked bean can you remove to see if they are needed for growth?*

PROCESSES

What Will Students Do?   1. Using a plastic bag, a paper towel, and a stapler, set up a "germination bag." (See diagram.)

[1]For greater details and expanded directions, see "From Seed to Plant," *Elementary Science Supplement to the Syllabus, Level I* (Albany, N.Y.: The State University of New York, The State Education Department, 1986), 39–54.

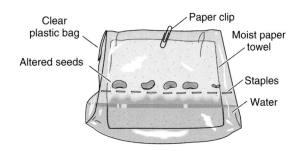

2. Prepare five soaked lima beans as follows and put them into the germination bag: a complete bean, a bean with the seed coat removed, a bean with one cotyledon removed, one cotyledon only, and the embryo only.

3. Put water in the germination bag as shown, close the bag with a paper clip, and attach it to a bulletin board, wall, or chalkboard.

4. Observe your germination bag for several days. *Note:* Open the bag daily for 15 minutes to prevent mold formation and add just enough water to keep the paper towel slightly moist.

Hypothesizing	*Which of the five seeds, if any, started to grow?*
Inferring	*Why do you think that is so?*
Observing	*How were all seeds in your germination bag treated the same?*
Observing	*Which seed or seed part grew best?*
Observing	*Which parts did not grow at all?*
Inferring	*Why do you think they did not grow?*
Observing	*Which seed parts are needed in order for a seed to grow?*
Observing	*From observing your germination bag, which seed part(s) do you think can be removed without stopping the seeds from growing?*
Inferring	*Why do you think this is so?*
Inferring	*Do all whole seeds grow? Why or why not?*

How Will Students Use or Apply What They Discover?

1. *Why might seeds die after they have sprouted if they are not planted in soil?*
2. *How long might sprouts live if not planted in soil?*
3. *Why do some kinds of sprouts live longer than others?*
4. *What might happen to seeds if they remain wet for a long time?*
5. *Why do seeds not germinate if the embryos are removed?*
6. *Why will seeds die if the cotyledons are removed?*

Part III   How Does Temperature Affect the Sprouting or Germination of Seeds?

What Will We Need?

8 lima bean seeds
8 radish seeds
2 clear plastic bags
2 paper towels

PROCESSES

What Will Students Do?

1. Place four lima bean seeds and four radish seeds in two separate plastic germination bags, adding a paper towel and water to each bag.

 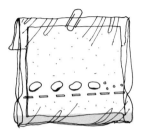

2. Put one germination bag in a cool place (i.e., the refrigerator in the teachers' room or cafeteria) and one near a sunny window, a heater, or a radiator.

Hypothesizing

How do you think the difference in temperature will affect the germination of the seeds?

Collecting and Recording Data

3. Observe your germination bags each day for one week. Record your observations. *Note:* Open the bags daily for 15 minutes to prevent the formation of mold and keep the paper towels just slightly moist.

4. At the end of the week, compare the seeds in the two germination bags.

Comparing

What differences do you notice?

Inferring

Why do you think these differences occurred?

What Are the Parts of a Plant? (K–8)

What Concepts Might Students Discover?

Plants have leaves, roots, stems, and flowers.
Not all plants have all four parts.
Leaves are able to make food.
The stems carry minerals and water from the roots to the leaves and flowers.
Flowers make seeds that can produce more of the same type of plant.
Some roots store food.

Part I   What Are the Parts of a Plant?

What Will We Need?

One complete plant such as a daisy, geranium, coleus, or petunia for the entire class

What Will We Discuss?

Pull up a complete plant out of its pot, remove the excess soil from its roots, and show the plant to the class. Ask:
How do you think roots are useful to this plant?

Expect and accept various ideas. Allow the students opportunities to propose and examine their ideas.

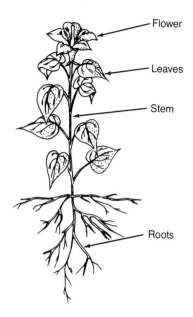

- Flower
- Leaves
- Stem
- Roots

Part II   How Do Roots Grow?

What Concepts Might Students Discover?

Roots grow around objects in the soil.
Seeds need water to grow.
Roots grow downward.

What Will We Need?

4 germinated bean seeds	Paper towels
4 small pebbles	2 pieces of glass or thick clear
2 tongue depressors or	plastic to place seeds between
applicator sticks	Tape

What Will We Discuss?

What do you think might happen to roots if they were planted facing up instead of down, or if something were in their way?

What Must I Know?

In the primary grades, this activity might have to be done as a demonstration because of the difficulty young children might have in manipulating the equipment. For older students, this activity should be done in groups of two to four students.

What Will Students Do?

1. Place four bean seeds (that have already been germinated) in between two moist paper towels. Put the paper towels with the seedlings between two pieces of glass or rigid clear plastic. Put small pebbles under each root, place the applicator sticks or tongue depressors between the pieces of glass or clear plastic, and tape as shown in the diagram.

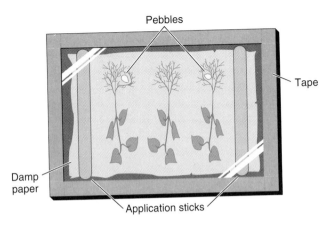

Pebbles

Tape

Damp paper

Application sticks

Hypothesizing

What is the reason for putting the tongue depressors between the pieces of glass or plastic? Why tape the sides?

2. Stand the glass so the roots point up and the stems point down.

Hypothesizing

What do you think might happen to the growth of the stems and roots?

Observing and Recording

3. Observe the plant growth for several days and record your observations.

Inferring

Was your hypothesis true or false? Does it need to be modified?

Designing an Investigation

If you were going to do this activity again, how would you change it to make it better or more interesting?

How Will Students Use or Apply What They Discover?

1. *How might the roots react if objects like cotton, a piece of wood, or a rock were placed in their way?*

2. *What would happen to the roots if the glass were rotated 90° in the same direction every day? Try it and keep records of your observations.*

Part III   How Does Water Get Into a Plant?

What Concepts ● Might Students Discover?

Roots absorb water through small root hairs.
Root hairs are damaged when a plant is transplanted or pulled.

What Will We Need?

Radish seeds   Pan or dish
Paper towels   Plastic wrap
Water   Hand lens

What Will We Discuss?

What could you do to determine what a root does for a plant (its function)?

What Will Students Do?

1. Obtain a paper towel, several radish seeds, and some plastic wrap. Soak the towel so it drips with water. Place the towel in a dish or pan. Place several radish seeds on the towel and cover the pan with plastic wrap.

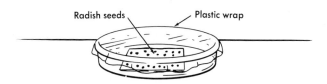

Radish seeds   Plastic wrap

Observing and
Recording
Observing

2. Observe for several days and record your observations. Use a hand lens.

What do you notice about the roots?

What are the small fuzzlike projections coming from each root called?

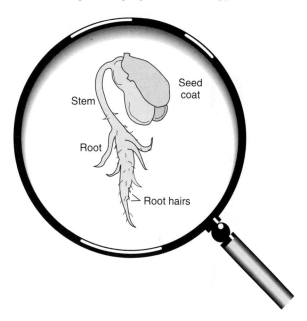

Stem

Seed coat

Root

Root hairs

Inferring

Why do you think the root has root hairs?

Hypothesizing

What could happen to the roots and root hairs of a plant when the plant is transplanted?

Hypothesizing

Why is some transplanting unsuccessful?

Designing an
Investigation

What would you do to determine what the function is of roots and root hairs?

Hypothesizing

What do you think might happen if you remove the root hairs from the root?

Hypothesizing

What do you think might happen if you expose the root hairs to air and sun?

How Will Students
Use or Apply
What They
Discover?

1. *Why are roots different shapes?*
2. *Why are some roots comparatively shallow and others deep?*
3. *How do people use the roots of plants?*
4. *What are the functions of the root, other than to absorb food materials?*

Part IV   How Are Roots Useful?

What Will We Need?

2 small, healthy coleus, geranium, or petunia plants
2 empty, clean milk cartons

What Will Students Do?

1. Obtain two similar pentunia, coleus, or geranium plants and remove all the roots from one plant. Obtain some soil and fill the bottom half of two milk cartons. Place the petunia without roots with its stem down, on top of the soil.

Observing
Inferring

What do you notice about the plant when you let go?
How do you think roots might have helped this plant?

2. Push the bottom part of the stem to a depth of almost two inches into the soil. Water the plant daily. Allow it to remain undisturbed for four or five days. As a control, plant the other petunia with roots as shown.

Hypothesizing
Observing
Summarizing

What do you think will happen to the plant without roots?

3. After 4 or 5 days, record what happens.
From your observations, how do you think roots might have helped the plant?

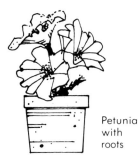

Petunia
with
roots

Petunia
without
roots

What Must I Know?

Some plants might develop new roots in this situation. If they do, remove the plant and discuss the function of the newly developed roots.

Part V   What Are the Purposes of a Stem?

What Concepts Might Students Discover?

Water must move from the roots to the leaves if a plant is to make food and live.
One of the main purposes of the stem of a plant is to carry water from the roots to the leaves.
There are small tubes, called **capillaries,** inside the stem that carry water to the leaves.
Water moves up the stem.

What Will We Need?

Geranium, coleus, or celery stem
Red food coloring or ink
Drinking glass or clear plastic cup

Blotter paper
Water

What Will We Discuss?

How does water get from the roots of a plant to the leaves?
How do you think a florist produces blue carnations?
If you wanted to change a white carnation into a blue carnation, what would you do?
How could you find out if your idea was correct?

What Will Students Do?

Hypothesizing

1. Obtain a geranium, celery, or coleus stem with leaves on it, some food coloring or red ink, some water, and a drinking glass. Put some water in the drinking glass and color it with the food coloring or ink. *Important:* If possible, provide a white flower (carnation) for this activity as well.
   Why do you think you added coloring to the water?
2. Cut a small slice off of the bottom of the stalk of your stem and set the stem into the glass of colored water. Allow it to sit in a sunny area for two hours.
3. At the end of this period, cut open the stem.

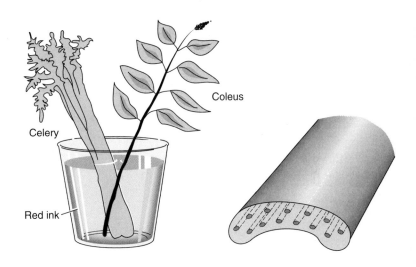

Observing   *What has happened to some of the colored water?*
Observing   *What parts of the stem appear to contain the colored water? How do you know?*
Describe these parts.
Inferring   *From this activity, what can you conclude about how a stem functions?*

How Will Students Use or Apply What They Discover?

1. *What effects might different temperatures have on how rapidly a solution moves up a stem?*
2. *What do you think might happen if you put half of a split stem in one color of water and the other half in another color of water?*

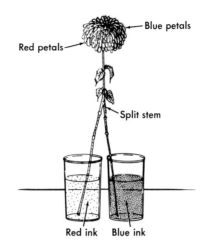

3. *What happens to the upward movement of water in a stem when the plant is in the dark or out of sunlight? How could you find out?*

Part VI Why Do Some Parts of Plants Grow Upward?

What Concepts Might Students Discover?

Light and gravity play a role in determining how plants grow.
Roots respond to gravity.
Stems are affected by light.

What Will We Need?

Shoe box with cover	Sunny window or light source
Clean milk carton	Germinated bean seeds
Germinated bean seeds between glass (from Part II activity)	Potting soil
	Ruler

What Will We Discuss?

What do you think might happen to a plant if its light source is very limited?
What do you think might happen to the stem of a plant if it is inverted (turned upside down)?
What effect does light have on the way a plant grows?
What might happen to the way a plant grows if it were placed near a window?
What effect does gravity have on the parts of sprouting seeds?
What could you do to find out?

What Must I Know?

The students should suggest arranging the sprouting seeds and apparatus as shown.

Seeds on soaked paper covered by glass or plastic wrap.

What do you think might happen to the stems if you rotate the seedlings every few days?

What Will Students Do?

Observing and Recording

1. Place the germinated bean seeds encased in taped glass or clear plastic sheets in bright light, but not in direct sunlight.

2. Keep a one-week record of your observation of how the stems and roots grow as you rotate the glass sheets 90° each day.

What Must I Know?

The roots will grow down (toward the earth) and the stems will grow up (away from the earth). The plant responses that cause this are called **tropisms. Geotropism** forces roots down as auxins (plant hormones) are concentrated by gravity along the bottom cells of stems and root tips. The bottom cells in the stem are stimulated by the hormones to grow faster than cells higher up; they get longer and curl upward. Root cells are more sensitive to these hormones than are stem cells, so the root cells inhibit cell growth. Root top cells elongate faster and root tips curve downward.

Communicating

3. Graph your findings or present them in another pictorial or visual way.
    Hint: How could you use your ruler in your observations?

Inferring   *What can you conclude from your data?*

Inferring

Hypothesizing   *What would you expect other plants and seeds to do under similar conditions?*

Hypothesizing   *What results would you expect if you used different or limited light sources? Try this.*

4. Plant four germinated bean seeds ¾″ to 1″ (2 cm) deep in moist soil in a clean milk carton.

5. Place the milk carton in a shoe box that has only a single, 1″ hole cut in the middle of one end, cover the box, and turn the opening toward bright sunlight or a strong lamp, as shown in the diagram.

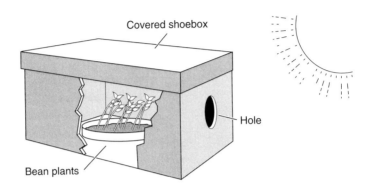

Covered shoebox

Hole

Bean plants

Observing 6. Lift the cover every two days and see how the beans are growing. Add water as needed.
What is happening to the stems and leaves?

Inferring *Why do you think they are growing as they are?*

Hypothesizing *What do you think might happen if you turned the milk carton with the seeds completely around?*
Try it and observe what happens in two days. Repeat this procedure.

What Must I Know? Students should see that the beans grow toward the opening in the shoe box, and when turned around, they reverse their direction of growth toward the opening again. Green plants need sunlight and are forced toward the light by **phototropism,** which causes the cells on one side of leaves to grow faster than the other. This causes the turning effect of the leaves toward the sunlight.

Applying *Of what value is this experiment to you?*

How Will Students Use or Apply What They Discover?
1. *What other living things are affected by light and gravity?*
2. *What are some other factors that affect the growth of plants?*
3. *Design an experiment to test some of these factors.*
4. *Knowing what you do about phototropism, why is it necessary to turn your plants at the windowsill every few days? What might happen if you do not turn them?*

What Is Variation? (K–8)

What Concepts Might Students Discover?
There is tremendous variation in nature.

What Will We Need?	A variety of fallen leaves collected Large bag of pea pods from home or school Paper plates Ruler
What Will We Discuss?	*How are leaves the same and different?* *How could you find out?*

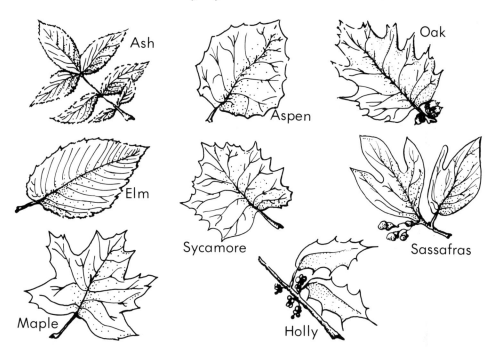

PROCESSES

Part I   How Are Leaves Alike and Different?

**What Will Students
  Do?**

1. Collect different kinds of leaves and obtain a ruler.

Comparing
Inferring

2. Place the leaves on your desk and compare them.
   What can you say about the shapes of the leaves? How do they differ in size?

Classifying

3. Place the leaves in groups according to properties, i.e., color, size, kind (maple, oak, etc.), number of points, arrangement of veins, etc.
   How many groups did you get?

Inferring

Why do you think leaves vary in size, shape, color, number of points, etc.?

What Must I Know?

Leaves may vary because of inheritance, or because of the environment in which they live. For example, the leaves of a particular species may be large if the environment in which the plant grows richly supplies the things needed by the plant.

Summarizing

Summarize how your leaves vary.

PROCESSES

**What Will Students
and Teacher Do?**

**How Will Students
Use or Apply
What They
Discover?**

Recording

Hypothesizing

Inferring

What Must I Know?

**How Will Students
Use or Apply
What They
Discover?**

**What Concepts
Might Students
Discover?**

What Will We Need?

Part II   How Do Seed Pods Vary?

1. Get two pea pods, open each pod, count the number of peas in each pod, and put peas and pods on your paper plate.

Ask who found the most peas in their pods and record this number on the chalkboard. Do the same for the least number of peas. Draw a horizontal line between the extreme numbers and divide the remaining space into equal spaces. For example, if the range is 2 to 10, mark the spaces 2, 3, 4, 5, 6, 7, 8, 9, 10.

Have students come to the chalkboard and place an X above the number that corresponds to the number of peas in their pods. This will provide a histogram or line plot like the one shown.

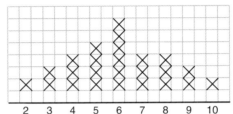

If you open another pea pod, what might be the most likely number of peas in it?

Is there a relationship between the number of peas in the pod and the pod's length?

You can substitute almost any fruit—string beans, melons, apples—for counting and making histograms or line plots. You can guide your students to observe that seeds from plants in the same family produce identical numerical seed patterns.

1. *What other things in nature vary?*
2. *How do dogs vary?*
3. *How do humans vary?*

How Is Sunlight Used by Growing Plants? (K–8)

Leaves produce gases and water vapor during photosynthesis.
Gas will expand when heated.
Because gases are lighter than water, they will go through water and escape.
Water vapor from leaves condenses on plastic film.
Leaves have little openings (called **stomata**) through which air enters or leaves the leaf.

One-gallon wide-mouthed jar	3 small identical geranium plants	Lamp or sunlight
Elodea water plants	2 large clear plastic bags	Wooden splint
Glass or plastic funnel	Plastic ties	Hand lens
Test tube	Warm water	Matches

**What Will We
Discuss?**

*What happens when your head is under water and you let some air out
of your mouth? What do you see? What do you think might happen to
a leaf if it were placed under water in sunlight?*

PROCESSES

**What Will Students
Do?**

Part I   What Comes Out of Leaves in Sunlight?

1. Put a water plant such as elodea in a one-gallon wide-mouthed
   jar.
2. Invert a glass or plastic funnel over the elodea and place a test tube
   completely full of water over the stem of the funnel, as shown in the
   diagram.

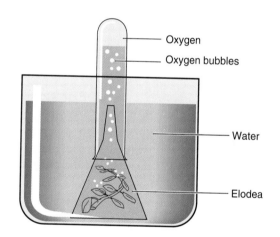

Oxygen
Oxygen bubbles
Water
Elodea

3. Place the jar in direct sunlight for three days.

Observing

*What do you see coming up from the elodea plant?
What happened to the level of water in the test tube?*

*Hypothesizing
Designing an
Experiment*

*What do you think might be in the test tube?
How might you set up an experiment to find out what is in the test
tube?*

The teacher or a responsible student should perform the following steps
if students are too young.

4. When most of the water in the test tube has been displaced, quickly
   remove the test tube and insert a glowing splint or lit match into the
   test tube, as shown in the diagram.

Observing
Inferring

What Must I Know?

What do you see happening to the wooden splint or lit match?
Why do you think this happened?

If students do not infer from this activity that the splint burned brightly because of oxygen given off from the elodea plant in sunlight, you can tell them. Students can be guided to see that oxygen is given off by plants during photosynthesis.

Leaves have small pores called stomata through which air enters and gases escape.

Have students use hand lenses to view stomata.

Part II What Else Comes Out of Leaves in Sunlight?

What Will Students Do?

1. Place a clear plastic bag over one geranium and tie the bag around the stem, just above the soil level.
2. Wave a second plastic bag through the air and tie it as well, as illustrated in the diagram.

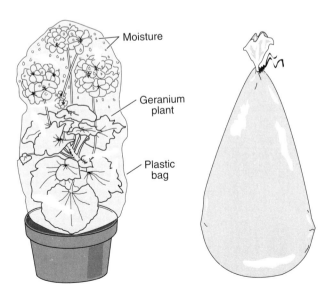

Moisture

Geranium plant

Plastic bag

3. Put both plastic bags in direct sunlight for at least three hours.

Observing — *After three hours, what do you see forming on the top of the plant in the plastic bag?*

Inferring — *What do you think they are?*

Inferring — *Where do you think they came from?*

Hypothesizing — *Why do you think the plastic was tied off above the soil line?*

Observing — *How is the plastic bag without the plant different after three hours?*

Inferring — *Why do you think this happened?*

Hypothesizing — *Why do you think the empty plastic bag was used in this activity?*
What is this called in an experiment? (Control)

What Must I Know? Moisture is formed in the plastic bag with the plant as a byproduct of photosynthesis in the leaves. The purpose of tying off the bag at the stem was to prevent moisture evaporating from the soil from entering the bag. The "empty" clear plastic bag is the control.

References—Plant Anatomy and Physiology
Teacher or older students: Linda Penn, *Plant Ecology* (New York: Watts, 1987).
Younger students: Carol Learner, *Plant Families* (New York: Morrow, 1989).

ANIMAL ANATOMY AND PHYSIOLOGY

QUICKIE STARTERS

What Are the Stages That Insects Go Through?

Materials Jars with covers (clear plastic, if possible), mealworms (from pet shop), bran or other cereal flakes, hand lenses, spoons, pictures of people and insects at different growing stages

Opening Questions *What are the stages insects, such as moths, butterflies, and mealworms, go through in their life cycles?*
What are the stages people go through as they grow?
How are the stages alike and different?

Some Possible Activities Using pictures of people and insects at different stages of growth, discuss how these living things grow. Introduce the mealworms and challenge students to hypothesize how the mealworms will grow and change in several stages. Using spoons, you or the students can transfer several mealworms and some bran or cereal flakes into a jar with a lid. Provide a jar for each student or group of two or three students. Punch several small holes in the lids for air. Have students observe the mealworms twice a week and record on a chart or log any observed changes in appearance (color, length, stage, etc.) or behavior. At the end of observations, help students make a chart comparing the stages of insects' lives with humans', like the one shown.[2]

Stages	
People	**Insects**
Child	Larva
Teenager	Pupa
Adult	Adult

In addition, make the following diagram with students and include photos or drawings to visualize the stages of mealworm (and other insect) metamorphosis.

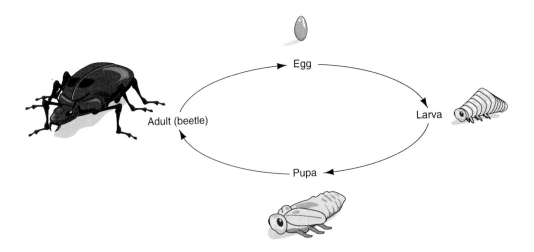

Make the same kind of diagram for stages of human life, i.e., infant, child, teenager, and adult.

---

[2]For additional information on insect stages and record keeping, you are urged to read *Elementary Science Supplement to the Syllabus, Level I* (Albany, NY: The University of the State of New York, The State Education Department, 1988): 62–64; and John Hall, "Creepie Crawlers," *Understanding the Healthy Body, CESI Sourcebook III,* ed. David R. Stronck (Columbus, OH: SEMAC Information Reference Center, 1983) 83–84.

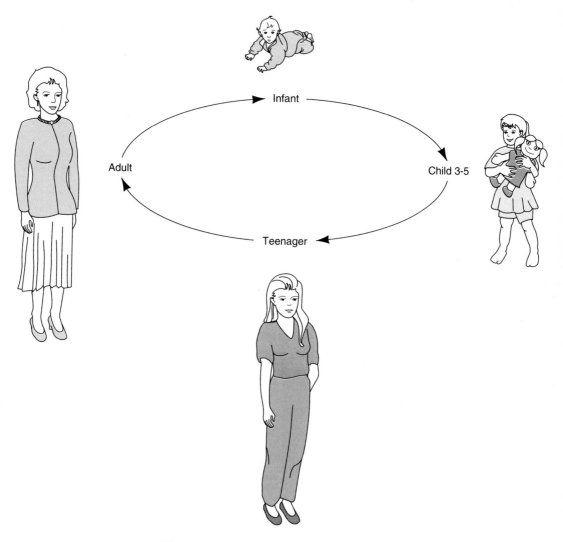

Infant

Child 3-5

Teenager

Adult

What Do Fish Need to Live?

Materials	Gallon (4-liter) glass or plastic container, seasoned water (tap water left to stand overnight to remove chlorine), gravel or sand, aquatic plants, 2 or 3 goldfish or guppies, dip net, live or dried fish food
Opening Questions	*What things do fish need to live?* *How can we learn to take care of our fish?* *What must we do to keep the fish healthy?*
Some Possible Activities	Refer to the index in this text to find the instructions for setting up and maintaining a freshwater aquarium, using the materials listed here. Help students set up the aquarium and establish routines for feeding, cleaning, and changing the water when it becomes smelly or cloudy.

Point out that guppies and goldfish can be raised at normal classroom temperatures. Discuss why the following elements are needed for the fish to live: water, plants, food, and light. Carefully remove any pregnant fish (usually identified by a swollen abdomen with a dark spot) with the dip net and place them in a separate aquarium. For older students, discuss the relationships among variables, parts of the aquarium, and the effects upon the lives of fish. For example: *How does the amount of light affect the algae in water? What is the number of fish one gallon of water will support, as observed by fish gulping at the top of the water? How do overfeeding and pollution of the water affect the fish?*

GUIDED DISCOVERY MINDS-ON/HANDS-ON ACTIVITIES

What Do You Know About the Birds Around You? (K–8)[3]

What Concepts Might Students Discover?

Birds vary in color and size.
Birds sing different songs.
Birds make different kinds of nests.
Birds eat different kinds of food.
The male bird may have a more colorful plumage than the female.
Some birds migrate.
Some birds change color with the season.
Birds care for their young.
Some birds prey on other birds.
Some birds dominate the eating of food.
Birds need trees and shrubs for protection from predators.

What Will We Need?

Bird food (bread, popcorn, commercial birdseed)
Bird feeders (commercial or made in class)
Plastic cups
Small pieces of cloth
Water trays
Bird book (showing local birds)
Pictures of birds

What Will We Discuss?

Carefully record on the board the responses of students to the following questions:
How might we attract birds to our school grounds so we can observe them?
What kinds of birds might we attract in our neighborhood?
How are birds alike and different?
Where do some birds go during the winter?
What kinds of homes do birds live in?
What are some behaviors that are unique to birds?
What kinds of foods do birds eat?

---

[3]For more specifics on bird behavior, food preferences, and relevant observational activities, see *Outdoor Biology Instructional Strategies: For the Birds Folio* (Berkeley, CA: The Regents of the University of California, 1980), published by Delta Education, Inc., P.O. Box 915, Hudson, NH 03051–0915.

Where would be the best place to set up a bird feeding/observation station on our school grounds?
What are the names of some local birds?
What do these birds look like?

What Must I Know?

If the natural environment lends itself to feeding and observing birds, have students observe birds on the way to and from school, or take a class field trip to a local area, park, or zoo. In a city, you will probably see sparrows or pigeons, jays in picnic areas, ducks in ponds, geese on golf courses, and seagulls at the seashore. In addition, you may want to provide pictures of different birds, nests, and eggs for students to handle, observe, and discuss.

What Will Students Do?

G

1. *As a result of our discussions, what would make a good bird feeding/observing area?* (Tree and shrub shelter that is free from predators and visible from the classroom) *How could we find out?*

Observing

Survey your school grounds and pick the best spot. Put up bird feeder(s) and a watering tray, after finding out what kinds of birds are common in your area, what their food preferences are, how they eat (on-ground or from feeders), and any other information that will make your feeding/observing most useful for birds.

Designing an Experiment

Once birds are attracted to your site, what kinds of experiments can you design to answer the following questions about birds?

A. What kinds of foods do different birds prefer?

Comparing

Try offering small equal amounts of two kinds of food (i.e., bread and birdseed) to the birds at the same time. *Caution:* Do *not* feed birds directly from your hand; instead, place food on the ground.

Observing

Which food do they prefer?

B. How can you get birds to come as close to you as possible?
(Offer food; be quiet and motionless)

C. Where do birds prefer their food to be put?
Put some food in such places as a birdfeeder on a tree limb or a pole, on the ground, in a plastic cup, under a piece of cloth, etc.

Observing   *Did different birds like different places?*
What was the most popular feeding spot?

D. Does one individual bird or kind of bird get the most food?

Observing   Try to find one bird or kind of bird that seems to get most of the food. *How does he do it?*
What happens when you try to give food to the other birds?

Hypothesizing   *Why do you think this happens?*

E. Do loud noises or sudden movements affect birds more?
While birds are gathered, make a really loud noise, but make sure to remain perfectly still.

Observing   *What happens to the birds?*
Now make a sudden dramatic movement, but be very quiet.

Observing   *What happens now?*

Comparing   *Did the loud noise or the sudden movement scare the birds more? How do you know?*

Hypothesizing   *Why do you think this is so?*

How Will Students Use or Apply What They Discover?

1. *How can you find out more about birds?*
2. *Why is it so important to continue feeding birds and supplying water once we begin?*
3. *Why is it so much fun to feed and observe birds?*
4. *How are these "wild birds" the same and different from domestic (pet) birds like parrots, canaries, etc.?*
5. *How do birds help people?*
6. *How might birds harm people?*
7. *What are some different ways birds in our neighborhood build their nests?*

What Must I Know?

The following types of questions can be asked about any of the local birds. These questions may have to be modified, however, depending on the kinds of birds that are found in your region.

Redheaded Woodpecker. (1) *Where does the woodpecker builds its nest?* (2) *How does it build its nest?* (3) *What kind of food does the woodpecker eat?* (4) *How does the woodpecker benefit and harm our environment?*

Hummingbird. (1) *How does the male hummingbird differ in color from the female?* (2) *Where do hummingbirds get their food?* (3) *Are hummingbirds as big as a cardinal or sparrow?* (4) *Why do you have difficulty finding their nests?* (5) *How do hummingbirds help in the pollination of plants?*

Starling. (1) *Why do many other birds prefer not to live near starlings?* (2) *What color is the starling?* (3) *How does the starling vary in color compared to the hummingbird and woodpecker?* (4) *Why do farmers dislike starlings during fruit harvesting season?*

How Do Ants Live? (K–8)

What Concepts Might Students Discover?

Ants are social insects.
All insects have three body parts: the head, thorax, and abdomen.
All insects have six legs.
Ants are beneficial because they help keep the forests and fields clean.

There are different kinds of ants in a colony.
These different ants do different kinds of work in the colony.

What Will We Need?

Large-mouth glass jar (commercial mayonnaise or pickle jar)
Screw-top jar with very small holes in the top
Soil to fill the jar two-thirds full
Small sponge
Pan large enough to hold the large-mouth glass jar
Sheet of black construction paper
Crumbs and bits of food: bread, cake, sugar, seeds
Colony of ants
Empty washed soup can

What Will We Discuss?

What do the different kinds of ants look like?
In what ways are the ants different?
How does the body of a worker ant compare to that of a queen ant?
How many pairs of legs do ants have?
What are the antennae on the head used for?
What does the egg of an ant look like?
Where do ants make their homes?
How do ants move?
How could you keep ants from leaving a jar?

What Must I Know?

You should become familiar with the life cycle and body parts of ants, such as shown in the diagram.

Ant eggs

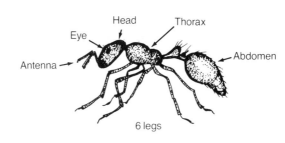

Head
Eye
Thorax
Antenna
Abdomen
6 legs

Mature ant

PROCESSES

What Will Students Do?

Designing an Investigation Hypothesizing

1. Obtain a large-mouth glass jar with a screw cover, a clean empty soup can, soil to fill the jar two-thirds full, a sponge, a large pan, a sheet of black construction paper, crumbs and bits of food (bread, cake, sugar, and seeds), and water.
   How could you arrange these materials to make a home for ants?

   What effect will a sheet of black paper placed around the jar have on the ants? (This simulates the dark underground so ants will tunnel close to the sides of the glass jar.)

Hypothesizing *Why place the soup can in the center of the jar with soil around it to the sides of the jar?* (So ants will not burrow into the center but will tunnel out to the jar's sides and be more visible.)
Where might you get ants? (Pet shop or home or school grounds)
What is the purpose of placing the jar in a pan of water? (So the ants cannot escape.)

Observing 2. Observe and record what the ants do.
Observing *How do the ants connect their homes in the jar?*
Hypothesizing *What might happen to the ants if they did not carry soil to the surface?*

Hypothesizing *What do you think might happen if there were no queen in the ant colony?*

Comparing *What changes have been made by the ants since they were first placed in the jar?*

How Will Students Use or Apply What They Discover?
1. *In what ways are ants useful to people?*
2. *What are some other insects that live and work together?*
3. *What are some living things that are sometimes mistaken for insects?*
4. *What might happen if the ant colony were placed in a light, warm place?*
5. *How are ants different from spiders?*
6. *What would be a good description of social insects?*

How Do Birds Differ from Mammals? (4–8)

What Concepts Might Students Discover?

Birds are the only animals that have feathers.
Both mammals and birds are warm-blooded.
Birds have two legs and two wings.
The female mammal has glands for nourishing her young with milk.
Mammals are more or less covered with hair.
Birds do not vary as much in structure as do mammals.
The bones of birds are somewhat hollow and light in weight.
Mammal bones are not hollow and are proportionately heavier.
Birds tend to eat approximately the amount of their weight in food each day.
Mammals do not eat as much per body weight as do birds.
Birds use considerable energy in flying and therefore need a great amount of food.
Female birds lay eggs.
Almost all female mammals give birth to live babies.
Only a few mammals, such as the platypus, lay eggs.

What Will We Need?

Live or stuffed specimens of birds and mammals or pictures of them.
Beef and chicken bones (one of each for every two students). If possible, these should be cut in half.
Wing bones of chickens (or any other bird).

What Will We Discuss?

Give as many common characteristics of birds as you can.
Give as many common characteristics of mammals as you can.
In what ways do birds differ from mammals?
What could you do to compare more closely the differences between birds and mammals?

What Must I Know?

The teacher should record on the board students' responses to the previous questions. Or allow students to divide into groups and discuss the questions. Each group could report its ideas to the class.

PROCESSES

What Will Students Do?

Do this activity in groups of two or more students. Encourage students to bring specimens, alive or stuffed, to school. Perhaps a pet day or an animal show might be arranged to make the most of this activity. Allow students to help furnish any of the other activity materials, such as beef and chicken bones. Encourage students to bring pictures of animals to class; place these on a bulletin board.

1. Obtain a cut chicken bone, a cut beef bone, and a wing bone of a chicken.

Classifying

How did you know which bone was from a chicken and which was from a steer?

Observing and Comparing

Examine the centers of the two bones and record how the structure of the beef bone differs from that of the chicken bone.

Comparing 2. Look at the chicken wing bone.
   How does its structure compare with the arm bones of a person?

Summarizing 3. Make a list of the characteristic ways birds and mammals differ.

Comparing 4. Compare your list with those made by other members of your class. Make any corrections or additions to your list that you think should be made, perhaps including the items that follow.

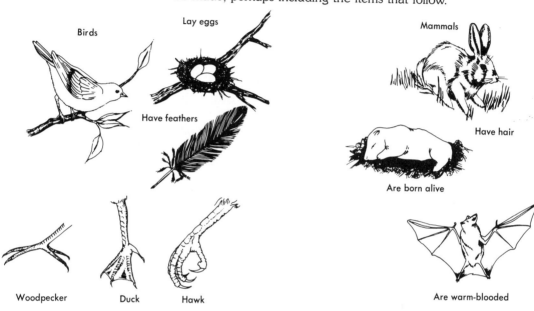

Birds

Lay eggs

Have feathers

Woodpecker   Duck   Hawk

Mammals

Have hair

Are born alive

Are warm-blooded

Other mammals: man, whales, bears, deer, etc.

How Will Students Use or Apply What They Discover?

1. *What are the main structural differences between birds and mammals?*
2. *How does the structure of a feather help a bird to fly?*
3. *How does the structure of a feather help keep birds warm in winter?*
4. *What do birds do to their feathers to make themselves warmer?*

How Does a Lack of Oxygen Affect Animals? (3–8)

What Concepts Might Students Discover?

Animals need oxygen to live.
Oxygen dissolves in water. Some animals need dissolved oxygen in water.
A gas will dissolve better in a cool liquid than in a hot liquid.
Fish breathe through gills.

What Will We Need?

2 pint bottles with caps
2 goldfish or other small freshwater fish in a small bottle
Burner and a stand or an electric hot plate on which to boil water
Matches
Pan large enough to boil a pint of water

**What Will We
Discuss?**

*What happens to the air dissolved in water when you boil the water?
What do you think might happen to fish if they were placed in water that
had been boiled and then cooled?
What would you do to find out?*

PROCESSES

**What Will Students
or Teacher Do?**

*Designing an
Experiment*

Hypothesizing

*Observing
Hypothesizing*

Observing

*Comparing
Inferring*

The teacher may choose to boil the water ahead of time for younger
students.

1. Obtain a jar with a fish, two pint-sized jars with caps, a burner or
   electric hot plate, and a large pan.
2. Heat the water to boiling and let it boil for several minutes.
3. While the water is being heated, label one jar "Boiled Water" and
   the other "Tap Water."
4. After the water has boiled, turn off the burner.
5. Carefully pour the boiled water into the jar labeled "Boiled Water,"
   cap the jar, and allow the water to cool to room temperature.
   What might happen if you place a fish in tap water?
   Place a fish in a jar filled with tap water and cap the jar.
6. Observe the fish's movements.
   *What might happen if you place a fish in the cooled boiled water and
   cap the jar?*
7. Place a fish in the jar of cooled boiled water and cap the jar.
   Observe the fish's movements. (*Caution:* If the fish turns on its side,
   take it out of the jar immediately, gently shake it in the air by the tail
   for a second, and place it into a jar of regular tap water.)
   How did the movements of the two fish vary?
   *Why did the fish in the cooled boiled water seem to vary in its
   movements compared to the other fish?*

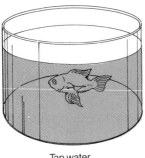

Tap water
A

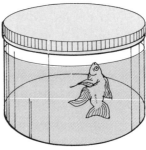

Cooled boiled water
B

What Must I Know?

When water is boiled, the air molecules dissolved in it move more
rapidly and escape into the air. The water lacks air as a result. Fish get
the oxygen they need from air dissolved in water. When the air passes

over the gills, the oxygen is absorbed by the blood passing through the gills. Fish are not able to survive in the boiled water because it contains little oxygen for the gills to absorb.

Inferring   *Why did you first heat the water and then cool it?*
Why was the lid put quickly over the heated water?

8. If you have not already done so, take the fish out of the jar of boiled water, gently shake it for a second or two by the tail, and place it in a jar of plain water.

Inferring   *Why is it necessary to shake the fish in the air for a few seconds?*

What Must I Know?   Shaking the fish causes air to pass over the gills so the fish gets oxygen from the air; the shaking also stimulates the circulation of the blood in the fish.

Inferring   *What do animals in the sea need to live?*
Inferring   *How do they get the oxygen they need?*

What Must I Know?   Explain to the class that air is composed of a mixture of gases and that it is the oxygen in the air that animals need to breathe.

How Will Students Use or Apply What They Discover?

1. *What experiment would you do to determine whether other animals require air (oxygen) to live?*
2. *How could you use the gill movement of fish to show that the boiled water does not contain oxygen?*
3. *Why might it be more difficult for fish to get oxygen from water containing a lot of algae than from clear water?*
4. *How might water pollution, like large amounts of detergents, affect fish breathing?*

References—Animal Anatomy and Physiology
Teacher or older students: Carol Hampton, Carolyn Hampton, and David Kramer, *Classroom Creature Culture: Algae to Anoles* (Washington, D.C.: National Science Teachers Association, 1986); and Ann Squire, *101 Questions and Answers about Pets and People* (New York: Fawcett, 1988).
Younger students: Arthur Dorros, *Ant Cities* (New York: Crowell, 1987); Ron Goor and Nancy Goor, *Insect Metamorphosis: From Egg to Adult* (New York: Atheneum, 1990); and Joanne Oppenheim, *Have You Seen Birds?* (New York: Scholastic, 1987).

HUMAN ANATOMY, PHYSIOLOGY, NUTRITION, AND HEALTH

QUICKIE STARTERS

How Big Are Your Lungs?

Materials   Dish pan, 2 ft (60 cm) of rubber or plastic tubing, ruler, measuring cup, water, gallon jug, drinking straws

Opening Questions

How much air do your lungs hold?
Do boys have bigger lungs than do girls?
Do smokers have more lung capacity than nonsmokers?
Do joggers' lungs hold more air than the lungs of people who do not jog?

Some Possible
Activities

Fill the dish pan about one-quarter full of water. Fill the jug to the very top with water. Put your hand tightly over the mouth of the jug and invert it in the dish pan, making sure not to let any air get into the jug. Put a clean straw into one end of the tubing and slip the other end into the mouth of the jug. With one continuous breath, keep blowing until you are completely out of air, as shown in diagram A.

When you cannot blow any more water out of the jug, slide your hand over the jug's mouth and turn it right side up. To measure how much air you exhaled, do this:

1. Pour measuring cups filled with water into the jug until you have refilled the jug, as shown in diagram B.
2. The amount of water you use to refill the jug is the amount of air you exhaled.

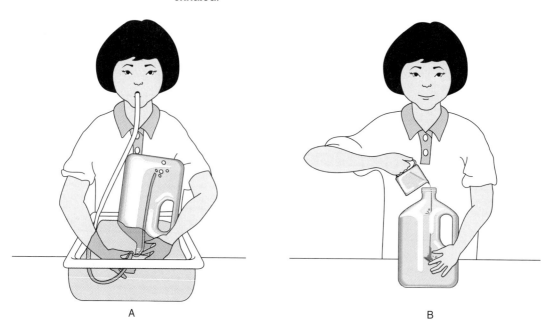

A   B

How Does Your Body Cool Itself?

Materials

2 old socks (wool or cotton are best) for each student, electric fan

Opening Questions

Why do you feel cool on a hot summer day when you come out of the water after swimming?

What parts of your body are at work to cool you down when you come out of the water?
Why does a fan cool us even on a hot day?

Some Possible Activities

Have students remove their shoes and socks and put a dry sock on one foot and wet sock on the other foot. Ask:
Which one feels cooler? Why?
To improve the cooling effect, use a fan to blow air over the students' feet. *Hint:* Suggest to students that they go to the bathroom before doing this activity.

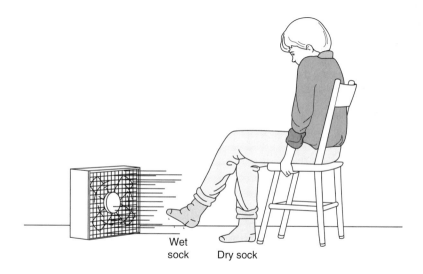

Wet
sock   Dry sock

GUIDED DISCOVERY MINDS-ON/HANDS-ON ACTIVITIES

How Do Humans Breathe? (K–8)

What Concepts Might Students Discover?

When a person exercises, breathing rate increases.
Breathing increases because more carbon dioxide is produced.
Carbon dioxide causes the diaphragm to involuntarily work more rapidly.
When the diaphragm moves up the rib cage, it forces air out of the lungs.
When the diaphragm moves down, air is pulled into the lungs.
Lung capacity varies from person to person and can be increased by aerobic training.
Gases and water vapor are exhaled from the lungs.

| What Will We Need? | Mirror (preferably metal)
Stopwatch
Tape measure
Scissors
2 plastic cups
Plastic drinking straws
½ c or 100 cc of limewater or
    calcium hydroxide (obtain
    from a drugstore) | Rubber bands
Small balloons
Model or chart of the chest
    cavity
Plastic sandwich bag
Water
Turkey baster |

What Will We Discuss?

What do you see when you breathe outside on a very cold day?
Why do you think that happens?
How might we find out?

PROCESSES

What Will Students Do?
Hypothesizing

Part I What Comes Out When You Breathe?

1. Obtain a mirror.

   When you breathe, what leaves your mouth?
   How might you find out?

2. Hold a mirror near your nose and mouth and exhale on it.

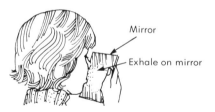

Mirror

Exhale on mirror

Observing   *What do you see on the mirror?*
Inferring   *Why does moisture collect on the mirror?*
Assuming   *Where does the moisture come from?*
Hypothesizing   *What kinds of gases do you think you exhale?*

What Must I Know?

Explain that exhaled air contains about 80 percent nitrogen, 17 percent oxygen, 0.03 percent carbon dioxide, and small percentages of other gases.

Inferring   *What happens to the nitrogen you inhale?*
Inferring   *What gas in the air do you need?*
Inferring   *What gas do you exhale more of than you inhale?*
How might we find out?

Part II How Can We Test Our Breath?

1. Obtain two clear plastic cups, a turkey baster, a straw, and 100 cc of limewater (or some calcium hydroxide). Mix half the limewater with regular water in each cup. Let the water settle.

Observing and Communicating

2. Put a straw in one cup and the turkey baster in the other. Describe how the limewater in the cups looks.
3. One of you blow through a straw into the limewater while the other pumps the bulb of the turkey baster into the limewater.

Observing

What happens to the limewater as you blow (exhale) through the straw into the water?

What do you notice at the bottom of the cup after a minute or two of blowing through the straw?

Inferring

Why does the water get "cloudy"?

What do you think is on the bottom of the cup?

Observing

What happens to the limewater when you squeeze the turkey baster into it?

Inferring

Why do you think the limewater did not change?

Hypothesizing

Why do you think the turkey baster part of the activity is important?

Inferring

What would the turkey baster part of the activity be called in an experiment?

What Must I Know?

When carbon dioxide is added to limewater, the water changes to a milky color because the carbon dioxide combines with calcium hydroxide to form a white precipitate. You can test the white powder that falls to the bottom with vinegar, which is a test for calcium or carbonate. The turkey baster was used to pump air into the limewater to show that air does not affect the limewater. This is our control. The variable being tested is carbon dioxide in breath.

How Will Students Use or Apply What They Discover?

1. *Why would an increase in carbon dioxide in the blood cause the heart to beat faster?*
2. *What does the following hypothesis mean: "A person needing oxygen naturally breathes faster"?*
3. *What other things would make you breathe faster? How could we find out?*

Part III   What Makes You Breathe Faster?

What Will We Discuss?

How many times a minute do you breathe?
How do you know?
How would you go about finding out?

What Must I Know?

This activity should be done in groups of three students: One does the activity, one is the timekeeper, and one is the recorder. At the completion of each activity, the students should rotate in their tasks until all have completed the activity. For exercise, students may run in place. For students unfamiliar with how to use a stopwatch, show them how it is used. Also explain that one breath is the exhale phase as a cloud forms on the mirror, and not both the exhale and inhale phases.

What Will Students Do?

1. Do the following with two other students: Using a stopwatch, one of you counts the number of times a second student normally breathes. Do this by counting the breaths on a mirror. Let the third student record the number of times the second student breathes. Do this three times, one minute apart.
2. Now do the same thing, but have the student being tested run in place for one minute.
3. Use this chart for recording your data.

TIME	AT REST	AFTER EXERCISE
One minute		
Two minutes		
Three minutes		

4. When you finish three "At Rest" and three "After Exercise" data collections, rotate the jobs until all three of you have breathed, counted breaths, and recorded data.

Comparing

What is the average number of times per minute a person breathes at rest?

Hypothesizing	*How would you figure that?*
Comparing	*What is the average number of times per minute a person breathes after exercise?*
Communicating	Graph your rest and exercise record on a diagram like the one shown.

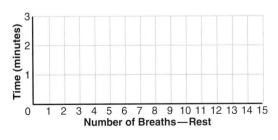

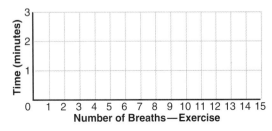

Hypothesizing	*What makes a person breathe faster?*
Inferring	*Why did you count the number of times a person breathes in three minutes rather than in just one?*
Hypothesizing	*What gas do you need from the air?*
Hypothesizing	*What do you breathe out or exhale?*
Designing an Investigation	*How can you prove that you exhale water?* (*Hint:* See the activity in Part I.)
Hypothesizing	*What gas do you breathe from the air that your body does not use?*

Part IV   Does Breathing Change Your Chest Size?

Designing an Investigation	*How does the size of your chest vary when you breathe? How might you find out?*

1. With a tape measure, check and record these measurements.

	Top of Chest	Lower Diaphragm
Inhale		
Exhale		

Interpreting

2. Construct a class graph to illustrate variations in measurement among students.
   Is there any observable correlation between inhale and exhale and chest measurements between boys and girls, tall and short, etc?

Part V   How Can We Make a Model of Lungs?

1. Obtain a plastic drinking straw, a small plastic bag, 2 rubber bands, a clear plastic cup, a small balloon, and scissors.
2. Cut the straw in half.

3. In the bottom of the cup, punch a hole the same width as the straw. (You or the teacher can use the heated tip of an ice pick.)
4. Stretch and blow up the balloon a few times.
5. Using a tightly wound rubber band, attach the balloon to the straw. Be sure the balloon does not come off when you blow into the straw.
6. Push the free end of the straw through the cup's hole and pull until the balloon is in the middle of the cup.
7. Place the open end of the cup into the small plastic bag and fold the bag around the cup, securing it tightly with a rubber band or masking tape if necessary. The plastic bag should be loose, not stretched taut, across the cup's opening.

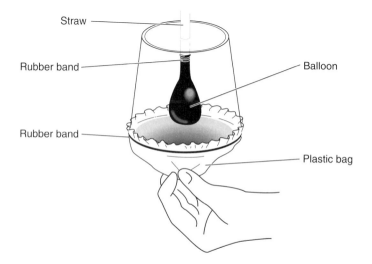

Hypothesizing   *What do you think might happen to the balloon if you pull down on the plastic bag at the bottom of the cup?*

Observing and Recording   8. Pull down on the plastic bag. Record your observation.

Hypothesizing   *What do you think might happen if you push up on the plastic bag?*

Observing and Recording   9. Push up on the plastic bag. Record your observation.

Inferring   *Why do you see these changes?*

Inferring   *Where in your body do you have something that works like this?*

What Must I Know?   Introduce the word diaphragm. Use a model or a chart of the chest cavity for reference.

Observing   *How do the diaphragm, lungs, and chest lie in relation to one another in the chest cavity?*

10. Diagram and label the parts of the body used in breathing, as shown in the diagram.

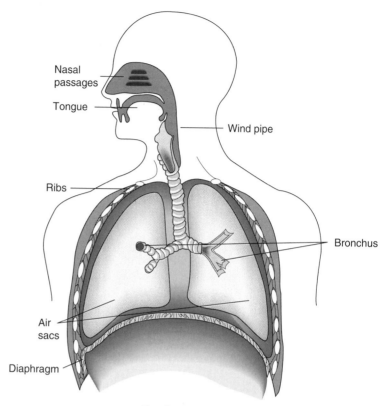

Respiratory system

How Does Our Skin Protect Us? (3–8)

What Concepts Might Students Discover?

The skin protects us from microorganisms that cause disease.
A cut or wound in the skin can let microorganisms enter the body.
Microorganisms sometimes cause infection and disease.
A cut or wound in the skin should be properly treated immediately to prevent microorganisms from causing infection.
Antiseptics kill microorganisms; thus, they can be used for the treatment of cuts or wounds.
Heat can kill microorganisms.

What Will We Need?

4 unblemished apples
3 sewing needles
Book of matches
Candle on a pie tin

Rotten apple
Small sample of soil
5 small pieces of cardboard for labels
Alcohol

What Will We Discuss?

How is the covering of an apple or an orange like your skin?
What are the advantages of the covering on apples, oranges, and other types of fruit?

How does the covering of your body, the skin, protect you?
What does it mean when a person says he or she wants to sterilize something?
In what ways might you sterilize something?

What Must I Know?

If open flame is not permitted in your school, or if you feel your students cannot handle it, you should sterilize the needles over open flame yourself. Otherwise, demonstrate to students how to safely do this.

PROCESSES

What Will Students Do?

G

1. Obtain five pieces of cardboard for labels, a candle in a pie tin, a match, three needles, and one rotten and four unblemished apples.
2. Put the labels *a, b, c,* and *d* on the four unblemished apples.
3. Sterilize three needles by heating them in the flame of a candle.
4. With a sterile needle, puncture apple *a* in three places. Apply alcohol over two of the punctures.
5. Push the second sterilized needle into the soil and then into three places in apple *b*.
6. Puncture apple *c* with the third sterile needle, but do not apply any alcohol to the three punctures.
7. Do nothing to apple *d* or to the rotten apple.
8. Place all four labeled apples in a warm place for several days.
   Why was apple d *not punctured?*

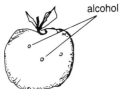

alcohol

(a) Three punctures with sterile needle; alcohol applied on two punctures

(b) Puncture with needle stuck in soil

(c) Puncture with needle but no alcohol

(d) Control (no holes)

Rotten

What Must I Know?

If necessary, point out that apple *d* is the control in the experiment. Be sure students understand the term *control.*

Hypothesizing
Comparing
Comparing

What do you think might happen if the apples stand for a few days?
In what ways do you think they will look alike?
How will they be different? Why?

9. Observe the apples daily. Every other day make a diagram or illustration of the changes taking place. Discuss these with your lab group.

Observing
Comparing
Comparing

What has happened to some of the apples?
How are the apples alike?
How are they different?

Inferring	*What do you think might have caused some of these changes?*
Comparing	*Which spots on the apples seem to be the most prominent? Why?*
Comparing	*Which other apple does apple c resemble most?*
Observing	*What has happened to apple d?*
Inferring	*What was apple d in your experiment?*

10. Cut all five apples in half. *Caution:* Do not eat the apples because the alcohol is poisonous.

Comparing	*Which apples seem to look most like the rotten apple?*
Inferring	*Why do you think so?*
Inferring	*Why did you apply alcohol over only two punctures in apple a?*
Observing	*What effect did the alcohol have? What about the third puncture?*

What Must I Know? Alcohol is an antiseptic. The alcohol destroyed most microorganisms present in the wound.

Inferring	*What happened to all the microorganisms on the needles after they had been heated?*
Comparing	*The skin of an apple is similar to what part of your body?*
Inferring	*Why did the rotten spots seem to grow a little larger each day?*

What Must I Know? Microorganisms have a fantastic growth rate. As long as there is a substantial amount of food present and space enough for growth, they will continue to reproduce.

Inferring	*What do you think might happen if your skin were punctured?*
Hypothesizing	*What might a person do to a wound or puncture if he or she did not want to get an infection?*

What Must I Know? The wound should be cleaned, an antiseptic applied, and the wound covered with a sterile bandage.

How Will Students Use or Apply What They Discover?

1. *How might you set up the previous experiment using oranges instead of apples? What do you think would happen?*
2. Conduct the same experiment, but this time place the apples in a cool place.
   What effect does temperature have on decay?
3. *In what other ways does your skin protect you?*

Why Does Your Body Need Food for Growth and Health?
(K–8)

What Concepts Might Students Discover?

Our bodies grow at different rates during different times in our lives. Students are constantly changing in height, weight, length of hair and nails, etc.
Food is needed for growth.
Food is needed for energy to do things in our everyday lives.
Foods contain nutrients necessary for energy, growth, and good health.
There are simple tests for identifying nutrients in foods.

What Will We Need?

Tape measures
Students' pictures of themselves
Pictures of malnourished children
Needle
Ringstand
Measuring cup

Scales for weighing students
Whole shelled walnuts
Cork
Celsius thermometer
Saucepan or Pyrex flask

Part I   Why Is Food Needed for Growth?

What Must I Know?

Before three years old, human growth is very rapid and then slows a bit. When a girl is ten or eleven, her cells begin to rapidly grow again. Boys at thirteen do the same. Our bodies grow by making new cells, and these cells need food, water, and oxygen.

What Will We Discuss?

Have you always been the size you are now?
Are you growing now? How do you know?
What helps you grow?
What could prevent you from growing?

PROCESSES

What Will Students Do?

1. Using information from your parents, fill in the following chart:

Recording

Age in Years	Height in Inches	Weight in Pounds	Photo
Birth			
1			
2			
3			
4			
5			
6			
7			
8			
9			
10			

Attach photos of you at each year to make a timeline that shows how you have grown.

Birth   1 year   2 year   3 year   4 year   5 year   6 year   7 year

Show pictures of malnourished or starving children and ask students to compare their pictures with these pictures.

Comparing

What differences do you see between these children and your pictures?

Inferring

Why do you think these children are so thin and sickly looking?

Measuring and Recording

2. Keep a weekly record of your current growth. Include your height and weight and any other characteristic you want.

3. Make a list of some of the activities you engage in each day, such as running, bike riding, etc.

Hypothesizing

How does food help you do these things?

Inferring

How might you find out?

Part II How Does Food Give Us Energy?

What Must I Know?

Since this activity uses open flame, use your discretion as to whether you do it or allow students to do it. Guide your students to see that the unit for measuring heat is the calorie, just as the unit for measuring temperature is the degree. The calorie is the amount of heat needed to raise 1 gram (about 1/2 a thimbleful or 1 M&M candy) of water 1 degree Celsius. *Note:* This calorie is known as the "small" calorie. The large Calorie in food calories is equal to 1000 small calories, and is spelled with a capital "C."

What Will Students or the Teacher Do?

1. Put a whole, unshelled walnut on the point of a needle and push the other end of the needle into a cork. Put the cork and walnut on the base of a ringstand with the walnut pointing up.

2. Put 1 liter of water into the saucepan and place the pan on the ringstand so that it is 1 inch above the walnut, as shown in the diagram.

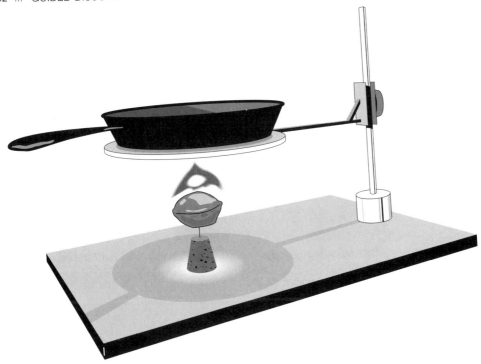

Measuring

3. Measure and record, in Celsius degrees, the temperature of the water.
4. With the match, light the walnut until the walnut is burning well.

Measuring and recording

5. As soon as the walnut stops burning, check and then record the temperature of the water.

Comparing

6. Subtract the water temperature before burning from the water temperature after the burning stopped.

Comparing

   What is the difference in temperatures?

What Must I Know?

You can introduce the concept that the difference in temperatures indicates the amount of energy (calories) released by the walnut when burned.

How Will Students Use or Apply What They Discover?

1. *Which of the following foods, in equal quantities, do you think will give more energy?*

   bread   celery   olive oil   sugar   apple

   How might you find out?
2. *How many Calories do you think your body "burns up" each day in activities? How might you find out?*
3. *If you eat more food Calories than you "burn up," what might happen to you?*
4. *If you eat fewer food Calories than you "burn up," what might happen to you?*

5. *Who probably "burns up" more food Calories: a professional basketball player or a "couch potato?" Why do you think so?*
6. *What other things does food give us besides energy? How can we find out?*

What Else Do We Need From Food and How Can We Test for It? (K–8)

What Concepts Might Students Discover?

Water is essential for life.

Six nutrients are needed to keep our bodies healthy and growing properly: carbohydrates (starch and sugar), fats, proteins, minerals, and vitamins.

We can test foods to see which nutrients and how much water they contain.

Because we are all different, we need different amounts of nutrients. People who study about nutrients (called **nutritionists**) suggest average amounts of nutrients. These amounts are called the Recommended Daily Allowances, or RDA.

Sometimes nutritionists recommend four basic food groups, such as meats and other proteins, fruits and vegetables, breads and cereals, and dairy products. However, there are people (called **vegetarians**) who are very healthy and yet never eat meat or dairy products. They get their needed nutrients from other foods.

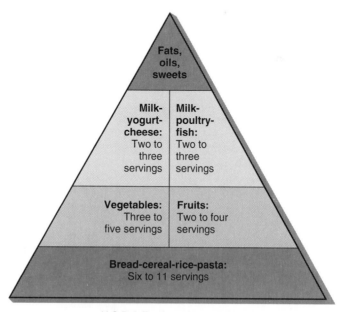

U.S.D.A Food-group pyramid

Part I Test for Water

What Must I Know?

Although water is not one of the basic nutrients, you must have it every day. You could not live without it. Besides getting water from the tap, here are some common foods and the percentages of water we get when we eat them.

lettuce	95%	carrots	90%
yogurt	90%	apple	85%
pizza	50%	bread	35%

What Will We Need?

Blunt plastic knives
Weighing scale or wire hanger balance
Box of paper clips
Apples, lettuce, tomatoes
Hand juicer

Paper plates
Small paper cups

Thick white bread
Bread toaster

What Will We Discuss?

How could we find out how much water is in certain foods?

PROCESSES

What Will Students Do?

Measuring and Recording

1. Using a weighing scale or the wire hanger balance shown in the diagram, weigh all foods and record their weights in the Before column of the chart.

2. Spread the lettuce leaves out on paper plates to dry overnight.

WATER CONTENT CHART		
	Weight in grams or paper clips	
Food	**Before**	**After**
lettuce		
tomato		
oranges		
apples		
bread		

Measuring and Recording

3. The next day, weigh and record the weight of the lettuce leaves left out overnight. Record your measurements in the After column of the chart.
   Did the leaves weigh more or less than before?
   Why do you think this happened?

Comparing
Inferring
Measuring

4. Weigh a tomato and record its weight in the Before column.
5. Using a hand juicer, squeeze out all the tomato juice.

Measuring and Recording

6. Weigh the tomato pulp (without the juice) and record this number in the After column.

Measuring

7. Using the orange and the apple, repeat steps 4, 5, and 6.

Measuring and Recording

8. Weigh the piece of thick white bread and record the weight in the Before column.

Recording

9. Toast the bread in the toaster, weigh it, and record the number in the After column.

How Will Students Use or Apply What They Discover?

1. *What foods can you think of that are eaten either naturally or dried?* (Grapes/raisins, apricots, plums/prunes, etc.)
2. *How does the shape of cut fruit pieces change when they dry out (shrink)? How might we find out?* (Cut up fruit pieces, trace their shapes with a marking pen, and compare the shapes when they dry.)

Part II   What Is Starch and How Do You Test for It?

What Concepts Might Students Discover?

Starch forms a large proportion of the nourishing parts of wheat, oats, corn, rye, potatoes, and rice.

Starch is part of a group of substances called **carbohydrates,** which all contain the same chemical elements: carbon, hydrogen, and oxygen. All ordinary plants are carbohydrates.

Starch turns blue-black in the presence of an iodine solution.

What Will We Need?	Paper plates Cornstarch
	Medicine dropper Iodine solution
	Thin slices of banana, apple, Granulated sugar
	    potato, white bread, cheese,
	    egg white, butter and cracker

What Will We Discuss?

Which of these foods contains starch?
How might we find out?
Iodine is a test for starch, but it is poisonous and must not be eaten. Always handle iodine carefully.

What Must I Know?

Iodine is used to test for starch. When iodine comes in contact with starch, the starch turns blue-black. *Caution:* Iodine solution is poisonous, may cause burns if it is too strong, and can stain clothing. For this reason, you may opt to dispense the iodine drops yourself if your students are too immature to safely do so themselves. In either case, point out the dangers to your students.

What Will Students or the Teacher Do?

1. On a paper plate, arrange and label each food sample as shown.

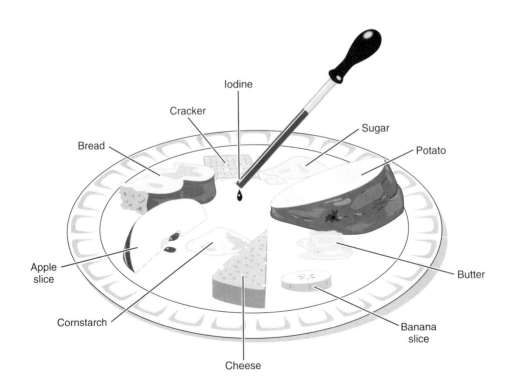

T G

Observing 2. Look at the colors of each food and record them on a chart.

3. Either the teacher or a student should place a drop of iodine solution on each sample of food.

Observing 4. Look at the color of each food where the iodine drop touched it.

Comparing 5. How have some of the food colors changed?

Classifying 6. Which foods have something in common after getting an iodine drop?

Inferring 7. If starch turns blue-black in iodine, which of your sample foods would you say contain starch?

Which do not have starch?

Important reminder: Because iodine is poisonous, do *not* eat any of the tested foods or give them to pets. Dispose of them properly.

Part III What Are Fats and How Do We Test for Them?

What Concepts Might Students Discover?

Some foods have a lot of fat and others have little or no fat.

Fats that are thick (solid) at room temperature usually come from animals like beef, pork, and lamb. These are called **saturated fats.**

Fats that are soft (semisolid) at room temperature usually are made from animals (i.e., lard and butter) or are man-made (i.e., margarine). Fats that are liquid at room temperature usually come from plants (i.e., peanut oil, olive oil, corn oil).

Fats are needed by our bodies, but too much fat can cause stomach and heart diseases.

Fats supply more than twice as much fuel and energy for the body as the same amount of starch, sugar, or protein.

Fats leave greasy spots, which is a simple test for identifying them.

What Will We Need?

Paper plates

Samples of common snack foods: peanuts, bread, butter, margarine, celery, carrot, mayonnaise, lettuce, bacon, corn and/or potato chips, pretzels, cheese, cookies, cake, apple, whole milk, etc.

Brown paper bags or brown paper towels cut into 2-in. squares (provide enough squares so that there is one for each food sample)

Source of light: sunlight or lamp

Medicine dropper

What Will We Discuss?

Why is it important to know which foods contain fats?

How much fat should we have in a healthy diet?

How are fats alike and different?

Are some fats "better" for the body than others?

What is cholesterol and what are the latest scientific findings about it and health?

How can we test some of our foods to see whether or not they contain fats?

What are some variables that we must control in our experiments?

What Will Students (and Teacher) Do?

Gather the class and ask:

How do you think we might test to see if foods contain fat?

List all suggestions, and then introduce this one if it was not suggested:

1. Put a drop of water on one square of brown paper. Next to it, smear butter the size of the water drop. (See diagram.)

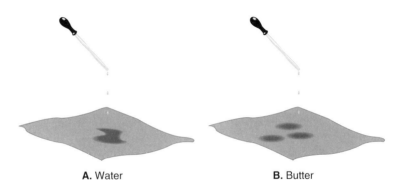

A. Water   **B.** Butter

Observing

How did the butter feel?

What Must I know?

Another test for fats is that they feel "slippery" when rubbed between the fingers.

Observing

Describe how both stains look.

Predicting

What do you think will happen to the two stains after 10 minutes? Write your guesses on the chalkboard.

Comparing

2. After 10 minutes, return to the paper and check.
   What happened to each stain?
   Where did the water drop go?
   Why is the butter drop still shiny?

What Must I Know?

The water evaporated but the butter stain remained shiny. This is the spot test for fats. Have groups of 2 to 4 students conduct their own spot tests using the samples of snack foods.

3. Get a paper plate containing samples of snack foods, 17 squares of brown paper, and a copy of the Fat Spot Test Lab Sheet shown in the diagram.

Predicting

4. Mark an X in the "Predicted Fat" column for foods you think contain fat.

Fat Spot Test Lab Sheet		
Food Samples	Predicted Fat	Contains Fat
Peanuts		
Bread		
Butter		
Margarine		
Celery		
Carrots		
Mayonnaise		
Lettuce		
Bacon		
Corn/Potato chips		
Pretzels		
Cheese		
Cookies		
Cake		
Apple		
Whole milk		
Yogurt		

5. Firmly rub each food sample 10 times on a separate square of brown paper, and label the paper with the food's name.
6. After 10 minutes, hold each paper square up to a source of light.

Comparing
Summarizing

7. Mark an X in the "Contains Fat" column of your chart for each food that left a greasy spot.
How did your predictions compare with your findings?
How would you summarize your test findings as to which foods contained the most fat?

What Must I Know?

Bring the following information to students' attention: Many scientists recommend that every day we should get no more than 30% of our Calories from fat, with no more than 10% of these Calories coming from saturated (animal) fat, and no more than 300 mg of cholesterol. Discuss how students might select foods with less fat and the importance of reading food labels for ingredients.

How Will Students Use or Apply What They Discover?

1. *What might happen to people if they eat too much fat, especially saturated or animal fats?*
2. *How could we have a party, serving good-tasting foods, and still cut down on the amount of fats we eat?*
3. *Why might it be healthier to eat such foods as skim milk, lowfat cottage cheese, and nonfat ice cream?*

Part IV What Is Protein and How Do We Test for It?

What Concepts Might Students Discover?

Protein is one group of food nutrients that the body uses for building tissues and repairing broken down cells.
Proteins are very vital for children's proper physical and mental growth and development.
Proteins are made of many amino acids, which are found in egg whites, milk curd, wheat gluten, the muscle fiber of meat, and beans and other vegetables.
Protein cannot be made by, or stored in, the body and must be eaten regularly to promote the repair of used body cells.

What Must I Know?

Tests for protein may be dangerous for some students, since they usually involve open flame or acids. Therefore, avoid the use of certain tests, do the tests as a teacher demonstration, or have more mature students (i.e., middle schoolers) do them after careful instruction and under close supervision.

What Will We Need?

Limewater
Water
Granulated sugar or cube
1-inch thin slices of cooked egg white, white bread, white turkey meat, cheese, mashed soybeans
Flour
Copper sulfate
Two medicine droppers
Paper plate

Feather
Candle in pie tin
Plastic cup
Clothespin
Matches

What Will We Discuss?

What is protein?
Why does our body need protein?
Which foods contain protein?
How can we test for protein?

What Will Students (and Teacher) Do?

1. Light the candle in the pie tin. Using a clothespin to hold a feather, put the feather in the flame.

Observing

How would you describe the smell of the burning feather?
That smell is the same as the one produced when protein is burned.

Designing an Experiment

How might we find out if burning proteins smell like burning feathers?

2. Using the clothespin as a holder, try burning bits of the sample foods.

Observing
Inferring

Which foods smell like burned feathers?
What do you think these foods are made of?
How else might we test for protein?

1. Dissolve as much copper sulfate as you can in 2 tablespoons of water in a cup. (*Caution:* Copper sulfate is a poison, so do not ingest.)
2. Arrange food samples on a paper plate as shown.

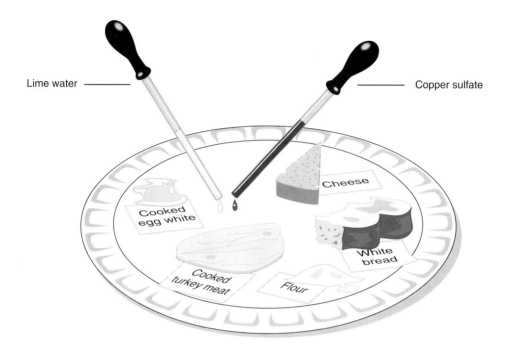

Lime water ——————

Copper sulfate

Cheese

Cooked egg white

White bread

Cooked turkey meat

Flour

3. Put a clean medicine dropper in the limewater and another one in the copper sulfate solution. *Caution:* After each use, make sure each medicine dropper is replaced in the proper solution. Do not mix the solutions.

4. For each food sample, do the following:
   A. Squeeze two drops of limewater on the sample.
   B. Squeeze two drops of copper sulfate solution in the same spot as the limewater on each food sample.

Observing
What color do you see on some food samples?

What Must I Know?
If the mixture of the limewater drops and the copper sulfate solution turns violet, the food contains protein. The darker the violet color, the greater the protein content.

Inferring   *Why do you think some of the foods turned violet?*
Inferring   *Why were some foods darker violet than others?*
Inferring   *Why did some foods not turn violet?*

How Will Students Use or Apply What They Discover?

1. Make a list of high-protein foods that you and your family eat.
2. *What do you think might happen to the quality of an incomplete protein if you mixed it with another incomplete protein, such as in dishes like macaroni and cheese, rice and beans, or bread and peanut butter? What other combinations might be tried?*

3. *Why do scientists caution us to eliminate, or drastically cut back on, animal proteins, even though they are complete proteins?*

Part V What Are Minerals and How Do We Test for Them?

What Concepts Might Students Discover?

Minerals make up a large part of our bones and teeth, which is why they are so important for children.

Although we need small amounts of many minerals (called trace elements), calcium is needed in larger quantities for bone and teeth formation.

Calcium is found in large quantities in milk and milk products and in smaller quantities in green leafy vegetables and oranges.

Vinegar (acetic acid) reacts with calcium and can be used as a test.

What Will We Need?

2 chicken leg bones stripped of all meat
2 covered jars large enough to hold the chicken bones
Soap
Water
Paper towels

What Will We Discuss?

What do bones do for our bodies?
Why must bones be strong and hard?
What might make bones strong and hard?
What might cause bones to get soft and weak?
How might we test for calcium?

What Must I Know?

Vinegar indicates the presence of calcium or a carbonate by fizzing and bubbling. Because vinegar is a mild acid, you and your students should wash their hands with soap and water after conducting the activity. After a few days, the chicken leg bone left in vinegar will get rubbery and very soft.

What Will Students (or the Teacher) Do?

Observing

1. Pass both chicken leg bones around the classroom and ask:

How do the bones feel? Are they hard or soft?
2. Place a chicken bone in each jar.
3. Pour vinegar in one jar only and water in the other, cover both jars, and let stand for several days.
4. Remove the bone from the jar of vinegar, rinse it thoroughly with water, and dry it well with a paper towel. Remove the other bone from its jar of water.
5. Pass both bones around classroom and ask:

Observing
Comparing
Inferring

Do both bones feel the same?
If not, how are they different?
Why do you think the bone that was in vinegar is soft and rubbery?

How Will Students Use or Apply What They Discover?

1. *Why do you think it is so important for students to eat a lot of milk products?*
2. *What might happen if you did not eat enough milk products?*
3. *Why would it be healthier to eat lowfat or nonfat milk products?*

Part VI   What Are Vitamins and How Do We Test for Them?

What Concepts Might Students Discover?

Scientists have discovered more than 25 vitamins our bodies need, but believe there are many more.

The lack of one vitamin could result in a vitamin deficiency disease such as rickets, scurvy, or pellagra.

Vitamin C is probably the best-known vitamin and is found in citrus fruits, tomatoes, raw cabbage, strawberries, and cantaloupe.

We can easily test for the presence of vitamin C.

What Will We Need?

Pan
Medicine dropper
6 clean baby food jars
Vitamin C indicator liquid
Variety of juices that are canned,
   frozen, or fresh: orange,
   apple, grape,
   pineapple, etc.

Empty plastic gallon jug
Teaspoon
Cornstarch
Measuring cup
Hot plate
Iodine
Ruler
6 wooden stirrers

What Must I Know?

A simple easy-to-make vitamin C indicator liquid can be made ahead of time and will keep for several days. You will know when it is time to dispose of it, because it will lighten from its optimum color of royal blue to a very pale blue. To make 1 gallon of vitamin C indicator:

1. Boil 1 1/2 teaspoons (6 mL) of cornstarch in 1 cup (250 mL) of water for two minutes.

2. Put 10 full droppers of the cornstarch mixture into a gallon jug of water, use a clean dropper to add 1 dropper full of iodine, cover the jug, and shake it until you have a uniform blue color.

When using the vitamin C indicator liquid, explain that the fewer drops of juice needed to make the blue color disappear, the more vitamin C it contains.

What Will Students Do?

1. Using your ruler to measure, pour 1 cm (1/2 in) of vitamin C indicator liquid into each of the six clean baby food jars. Label each jar with the name of the juice you will test for vitamin C.

Measuring and Recording

2. Using a clean medicine dropper for each juice, add one kind of juice to each jar of indicator liquid, one drop at a time, and record the number of drops. (See the diagram.) Stir the liquid indicator with a clean wooden stirrer as you add drops.

Canned orange juice	Fresh orange juice	Canned apple juice	Fresh apple juice	Canned grape juice	Frozen grape juice

Observing
Comparing

3. When the indicator is no longer blue, the test is finished.
   Which juice(s) caused the blue color to disappear with the least number of drops?

Comparing

   Which juice(s) caused the blue color to disappear with the most drops?

Summarizing

   From these tests, which juice(s) had the most vitamin C?

How Will Students Use or Apply What They Discover?

1. *How do you think the following conditions could affect the vitamin C content of foods: heat, sunlight, air, age of food, etc.? How could you design experiments to test these variables?*

2. *Which do you think is better for you—vitamins eaten in foods or vitamins taken in pills or supplements? How could you find out?*

3. *What might happen if you got too much of a vitamin?*

Part VII What Are Sugars and How Do You Test for Them?

What Concepts Might Students Discover?

Sugars are sweet substances made by green plants and are used mainly by humans for energy.

Sugars belong to a larger family of substances called saccharides or carbohydrates. These substances all contain carbon, hydrogen, and oxygen.

The chemical names of all saccharides ends in "ose." Fructose (found in ripe fruits) is called a simple sugar or monosaccharide; *mono-* means it is made up of one sugar molecule. If two sugar molecules combine, they form a disaccharide; *di-* means two. Sucrose, or table sugar, is a disaccharide of glucose and fructose, and is usually made from sugar cane or sugar beets.

An indicator for monosaccharides or simple sugars is TES-Tape™, used by diabetics to test for the presence of glucose in their urine.

The change in the yellow TES-Tape™ to a dark green characterizes a positive test for simple sugar.

Some common simple sugars are found in milk, honey, and ripe fruits, especially bananas. Starches broken down by chewing will also test positive for simple sugars.

What Must I Know?

Common table sugar will give a negative result on TES-Tape™, because sucrose is *not* a simple sugar. Other tests, such as ones using Benedict's solution or Fantastic™ cleaning solution, can test other sugars, but the teacher should demonstrate these because they require heat and the chemicals involved are poisonous. With proper instruction and careful supervision, responsible middle-school students could conduct these tests. Use your discretion.[4]

What Will We Need?

TES-Tape™ (get in drugstore)
Bananas (fairly ripe)
Milk
Different kinds of apples
   (Macintosh, Delicious, Rome)
Table sugar

Oranges
Maple syrup
Honey
Paper plates
Small paper cups

What Will Students Do?

Note: For efficiency in distribution, the teacher and/or designated students should prepare the following beforehand for each group of two to four students: paper plate containing cut samples of foods; separate small cups with very small samples of honey, milk, and maple syrup; 1″ TES-Tape™ strip for each food to be tested; data collection sheet.

[4]For ideas on how to perform other tests for sugars, see Robert C. Mebane and Thomas R. Rybott, *Adventures with Atoms and Molecules Book II: Chemistry Experiments for Young People and Adventures with Atoms* (Hillsdale, N.J.: Enslow Publishers, 1987); Mebane and Rybott, *Molecules Book III: Chemistry Experiments for Young People* (Hillsdale, N.J.: Enslow Publishers, 1991); and Jean Stangl, *The Tools of Science: Ideas and Activities for Guiding Young Scientists* (New York: Dodd, Mead and Co., 1987).

1. Get a paper plate that contains food samples, three cups, TES-Tape™ strips, and a data collection sheet.

Organizing

2. Assign one group member to each of the following tasks: tester, observer, and recorder.

3. *Tester:* Number each food, then write the numerals 1 through 10 on separate TES-Tape™ strips.

   Using the appropriately numbered strip that corresponds to the food being tested, touch ½″ of the TES-Tape™ to each food separately, until the strip is wet.

   Now hand the TES-Tape™ to the observer.

Observing

4. *Observer:* Look at the wet end of the TES-Tape™. *What color is the wet end?*

Communicating

Give the following information to your recorder:

A. The number of the sample TES-Tape™ strip

B. The name of the food sample

C. The color of the wet end of the TES-Tape™ strip

Repeat the preceding procedures with all of the food samples.

Communicating

5. *Recorder:* As each food is tested, record on the TES-Tape™ Data Collection Sheet the data that the observer gives you. Attach each TES-Tape™ strip in the appropriate place on the chart.

TES-Tape™ SUGAR TEST DATA COLLECTION SHEET		
Food samples	Tape color after test	Tape strip
Orange		
Banana, ripe		
Banana, green		
Maple syrup		
Milk		
Honey		
Mac apple		
Yellow Delicious		
Rome apple		
Table sugar		

Inferring   *From the data collected, which foods contain simple sugar?*

Inferring   *What evidence do you have to support this?*

Comparing   *From the changes in the TES-Tape™ color, which foods appear to have the most simple sugar? The least?*

Observing *Inferring*	*Which foods, if any, did not change the color of the TES-Tape™?* *Why do you think this happens?*

How Will Students
Use or Apply
What They
Discover?

1. Bring in labels from food packages, read the ingredients lists, and list all the forms of sugar each food contains, such as honey, brown sugar syrup, sweeteners, corn sugar, corn sweeteners, molasses, invert sugar, sucrose, fructose, dextrose, maltose, lactose, etc.
2. *What are some of the health problems that might develop if you eat too much sugar?*
3. Find out the amounts of sugar (both labeled and "hidden") in the common foods you eat, such as soft drinks—which contain about 6 teaspoons (25 g) per 12 ounces—or breakfast cereals—which contain about 2 1/2 teaspoons (10 g) of sugar plus 3 teaspoons (13 g) of other carbohydrates for a total of 5 1/2 teaspoons (23 g) per 1-ounce serving.
4. *What do you think might happen if you tested artificial sweeteners (saccharin, Aspartame, etc.) with TES-Tape™?*
5. *Why would it be healthier to eat fresh fruit as a snack rather than cakes, candy, and soft drinks, even though all of these contain sugar?*

How Does Your Body Change and Use Starch in the Foods You Eat? (4–8)

What Concepts
Might Students
Discover?

Large food particles must be broken down into smaller molecules before they can be absorbed into the body.
The breaking down of food by chemical means is called **digestion.**
Food must be dissolved before it can be used by the body.
Starch is a nutrient.
Starch must be changed to dissolved sugar for it to pass through the lining of the small intestine.

What Will We Need?

Cornstarch
Sugar
Iodine (a small bottle with an eye dropper)

Caution: Iodine is poisonous; do not allow students to handle it unsupervised. Also, iodine may stain skin, clothing, and other materials.

Spoon	3 clear plastic cups
Crackers (two per student)	Funnel
3 paper towels	4 cubes of sugar
Wooden stirrers	Water
2 jars with covers	TES-Tape™
4-in. squares of waxed paper	Iodine
Medicine droppers	

What Will We
Discuss?

How will the cracker be used by your body when you eat it?
What is going to happen to the cracker?

When will the cracker be ready to be used by your cells?
How will your body prepare this cracker for use?
If your body does not use every bit of the cracker, what is going to happen to that which is not used?
Where will your body digest this cracker?
What substances does your body contain to break down the cracker into usable substances?

PROCESSES

Observing
Observing

Part I   How Is a Starch Solution Different from a Sugar Solution?

1. Obtain a teaspoon of cornstarch, two clear plastic cups 3/4 full of water, and a teaspoon of sugar. Put the cornstarch into one cup of water and the sugar into the other. Stir each glass with a separate wooden stirrer.
How does the starch solution appear?
How does the sugar solution appear?

Water and sugar

Water and cornstarch

Inferring
Hypothesizing

Inferring

Which has dissolved? How do you know?
What do you think might happen if you let both glasses stand for a day?
How would the results of this experiment help to explain why starch has to be changed so your body can use it?
2. Stir the starch and water again until the starch is mixed with the water. Take a teaspoon of the starch and water mixture and put a drop of iodine into it to dilute the mixture to a straw color.

What Must I Know?

Observing

As pointed out in previous activities, iodine is used to test for starch. Starch in the presence of iodine turns blue-black.
What color does the mixture turn?
3. Rinse the spoon thoroughly and repeat Step 2, substituting sugar water for the starch and water mixture.

Comparing

Observing
Comparing

How does the result differ?
Put a drop of iodine on a cracker.
What is the result?
How does the color of the iodine on the cracker compare with the iodine in the starch and water solution?

Part II   How Does Molecule Size Affect the Ability to Pass Through a Filter?

1. Line a funnel with a piece of paper towel and set the funnel in an empty glass. Stir the starch in the glass of water again. Slowly pour some of the starch water into the funnel. After the water has run through the funnel, look at the inside of the paper.

Observing   *Is there any powder left inside the funnel?*

Hypothesizing   *How could you test to see if it is starch?*

Hypothesizing   *How could you test to see if there is any starch left in the water that passed through the filter?*

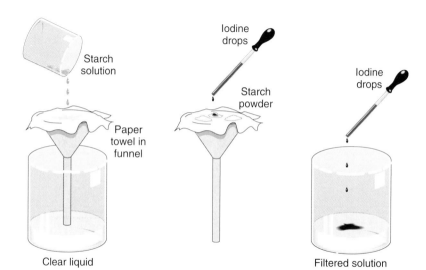

2. Perform the test for starch in water shown in the diagram.

Observing   *What color did the mixture turn?*

Inferring   *Is there starch present?*

Hypothesizing   *What do you think will happen if sugar water is poured through filter paper?*

Hypothesizing   *How could you tell if there was sugar in the water before and after you poured it through the funnel?*

Inferring   *Which do you think could go through the wall of your intestine better—starch or sugar? Why?*

Part III   How Does Saliva Affect the Digestion of Starch?

Hypothesizing   *How can we verify that saliva begins the process of digestion by changing starch to sugar?*

Observing

1. Test one cracker for starch by putting a few drops of iodine on it. *What color does the spot of iodine turn?*
2. Now test the same cracker for sugar by placing a few drops of water on it and then testing it with TES-Tape™.
3. Get another cracker, place it in your mouth, and chew it slowly for one to two minutes. Put a small amount of chewed cracker on a piece of waxed paper in two places.

Observing

4. Test one chewed cracker sample for starch using the iodine test. *What do you observe?*
5. Test the other chewed cracker sample for sugar using the TES-Tape™.

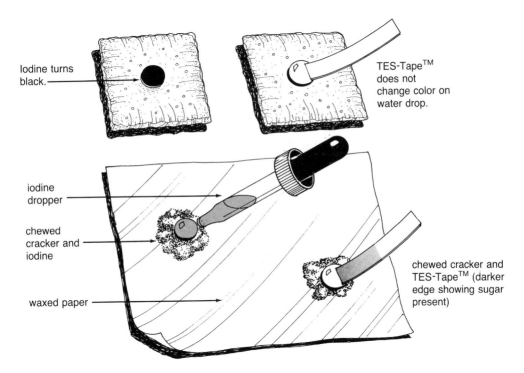

Iodine turns black.

TES-Tape™ does not change color on water drop.

iodine dropper

chewed cracker and iodine

chewed cracker and TES-Tape™ (darker edge showing sugar present)

waxed paper

Observing
Inferring

What change do you observe?
How has the saliva in your mouth changed the starch in the cracker?
Caution: Dispose of waxed paper and chewed cracker samples immediately. Do not touch other chewed cracker samples.

Part IV   How Can Large Molecules Be Broken Down?

1. Pour equal amounts of cold water into two jars. Place two cubes of sugar into each jar and screw the covers on tightly. Place one jar aside and let it stand still. Shake the other jar vigorously.

Observing

Compare the results occurring in the two jars.

No shaking   Shaking

Inferring	*Why did the sugar cubes break down and dissolve faster in one jar?*
Applying	*What does this activity tell us about chewing food before swallowing it?*

What Must I Know?

The more students chew their food, the more enzymes will be able to mix with the food to break it down chemically. Chewing also helps to break the food down into smaller particles so more of it comes in contact with the enzymes.

How Will Students Use or Apply What They Discover?

1. *How does saliva affect other foods such as poultry, fruits, and vegetables?*
2. *Why should diabetics control the amount of starchy foods they eat?*
3. Test other foods for starch content.
4. *How might heat affect the digestion of starch?*

Note: At the conclusion of your study of nutrients and health, a summary chart could be made using the mnemonic *Cats Wait For Mice Very Patiently.*

The Nutrient Chart			
	Nutrient	Bodily function	Food source
CATS	Carbohydrates (Starch & Sugar)	Energy	Grains; fruits; vegetables
WAIT	Water	Maintenance: carries nutrients in blood; maintains temperature	All
FOR	Fats	Energy/maintenance; carry some vitamins	All
MICE	Minerals	Maintenance: regulate and maintain body functions	Fruits/vegetables, dairy products
VERY	Vitamins	Maintenance: regulate and maintain body functions	Fruits/vegetables
PATIENTLY	Protein	Growth; tissue building/repair	Meats, legumes, dairy products

References—Human Anatomy and Physiology

Teacher or older students: Science Syllabus for Middle and Junior High Schools, Blocks A and B Living Systems: Human Systems (Albany, N.Y.: The University of the State of New York, The State Education Department, 1986).

Student: Philip Balestrino, *The Skeleton Inside You* (Scranton, Pa.: Harper, 1989); and Barbara Behm, *Ask About My Body* (Milwaukee, Wis.: Raintree, 1987).

Nutrition

Teacher or older students: Michael Jacobson, *The Fast Food Guide: What's Good, What's Bad and How to Tell the Differences* (New York: Workman Publishing, 1986).

Student: Ontario Science Center, *Food Works—Over 100 Science Activities and Fascinating Facts That Explore the Magic of Food* (Reading, Mass.: Addison-Wesley, 1987).

Health

Teacher or older students: Lynne Cherry, *Who's Sick Today?* (Bergenfield, N.J.: Dutton, 1986).

Student: Vicki Cobb, *Keeping Clean* (Scranton, Pa.: Harper, 1989).

SECTION 3

Earth, Ecology, and Environmental Sciences and Technology

ASTRONOMY (EARTH IN SPACE)

QUICKIE STARTERS

What Causes Shadows and How Can They Be Changed?

Materials — Flashlight, 2 pieces of white paper, scissors, paste, funnel, pencil or crayon

Opening Questions — *What are shadows and how are they formed?*
How can you make shadows larger or smaller?
What are some of the things (variables) that affect the size of shadows?
Why do shadows change shape and size during the day?

Some Possible Activities — Work with a partner. Put a funnel on a large sheet of white paper. One of you should shine the flashlight on the funnel while the other one traces and cuts the shadow out with scissors, in this sequence:

1. First, while holding the flashlight low, trace and cut out the shadow of the funnel.
2. Next, put a new piece of white paper under the funnel, hold the flashlight high, and then trace and cut out the shadow of the funnel.
3. Compare the size and shape of the two cut-out shadows.

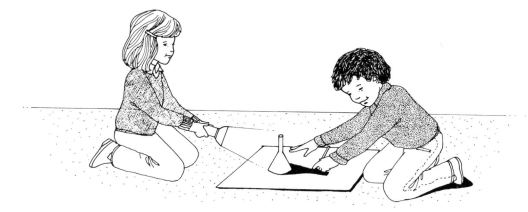

Why do you think the shadow was longer when the flashlight was held low?

During what part(s) of the day do shadows look this way outdoors?

How Can Shadows Help You Tell Time?

Materials

For each student or group of two to four students: Long nail, hammer, 8 1/2 × 11-inch pieces of white paper, square board big enough to hold the paper, pencil

Opening Questions

Do you think that shadows outdoors change during the day? How might we find out?

If shadows change, at what time will they be the shortest? The longest? Why do you think so?

Some Possible Activities

Put a piece of paper in the middle of the board and drive the nail into the board and paper as shown, making sure the nail will not easily come out of the board.

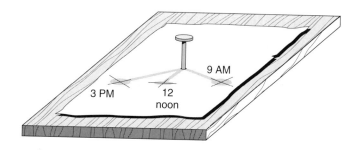

Place the board where it will get sunlight all day. Every hour, draw an X at the tip of the shadow cast by the nail. Write down the time you marked the X as well. Repeat this every school hour for one week, keeping the board in exactly the same spot. At the end of the week, assist students in answering these questions:

At what times during the day were the shadows the longest? The shortest? Were these times the same each day?

An instrument that is used to tell time by the position of the sun and its resulting shadows is called a **sundial.**

GUIDED DISCOVERY MINDS-ON/HANDS-ON ACTIVITIES

Why Is There Day and Night? (K–6)

What Concepts Might Students Discover?

The earth **rotates,** or turns around.
The earth rotates from west to east.
It takes 24 hours for the earth to make one complete turn or rotation. The rotation of the earth explains why part of the 24-hour period is night and part is day.
The sun is always shining, even when it is night and you cannot see the sun.

What Will We Need?

Strong flashlight or filmstrip projector
Knitting needle
Clay or styrofoam ball

What Will We Discuss?

When it is daytime here, where is it night?
When it is night here, where is it day?
What could you do to find out about daytime and nighttime on the earth?

What Will Students Do?

1. Make a clay ball as large as a baseball; use it as a model of the earth. A styrofoam ball may be used.
   In what way do you think the ball is like the earth?
2. Push the knitting needle through the clay or styrofoam globe. Darken the room. Let the flashlight or filmstrip projector, which represents the sun, shine on the ball.

Inferring
Inferring
Inferring

What side of the earth (ball) do you think is having night?
What side of the globe do you think is having day?
What tells you that the sun is always shining somewhere on the earth?

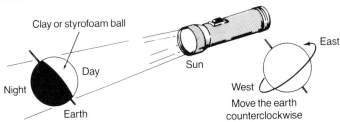

3. Stick a pin in the ball to represent the place where you live. Turn the ball slowly in a counterclockwise motion.

Hypothesizing	*Using the clay or styrofoam ball, how could you make night come to the place where you live?*
What Must I Know?	The ball, representing the earth, is turned slowly counterclockwise to show where night would begin to fall and where it would be midnight and sunrise.
Inferring	*What time of day is it when your pin is on the same side as the sun?*
Inferring	*When your pin is away from the sun, what time of day would it be?*
How Will Students Use or Apply What They Discover?	1. *What would happen if the earth did not turn?* 2. *If the earth did not turn, which side would you rather be on? Why?* 3. *Why is it inaccurate to say the sun "rises" in the east and "sets" in the west?* 4. *If it is 9 A.M. in New York City, what time will it be in San Francisco?*

Why Does the Moon Shine? (K–6)

What Concepts Might Students Discover?	Objects are seen when they give off their own light or when they reflect light from another source. The moon does not give off its own light. Its light is reflected light from the sun.
What Will We Need?	Flashlight Masking tape Large ball 1-inch-diameter ball of foil, with attached string 3-inches-diameter styrofoam ball, with attached string Box with tight-fitting lid (shoe box)
What Will We Discuss?	Darken the room, place a ball on the table, and ask: *What is on the table?* *What do you need to be able to see the object?* Turn on the lights. *Why do you see the ball now?* *Do you see it because it is giving off its own light or because it is reflecting light from some other source?* Look at the ceiling lights. *Why is it possible for you to see the lights? How is this light different from the light you see when you look at the ball?* Darken the room. *What are two reasons why you may not see any lights in the room?*

PROCESSES

What Will Students Do?	
Hypothesizing	*How do you think the moon shines?*
Inferring	*What is reflected light?*

1. Suspend the foil ball on a 1-inch string from inside the lid of the box, as shown in the diagram. Insert the flashlight in the end of the box and seal any space around it with masking tape. Make a small eye hole under the flashlight.

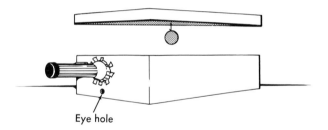

Eye hole

2. Put on the lid, and seal the edges around the lid.

Observing and
Inferring
What do you see when you look through the eye hole? Why?
3. Turn on the flashlight.

Observing and
Inferring
What do you see when you look through the eye hole? Why?

Inferring
Do you see the ball because it reflects light or because it gives off its own light?

Classifying
What two kinds of light do you see?

Inferring
What is the source of each kind of light?
4. Look out the window.

Inferring
Why are you able to see some objects?

Inferring
What is the source of light?

Inferring
Do the objects seen outside the window give off reflected light or light of their own?

Inferring
What does the sun give off?

Inferring
Why does the moon shine?
5. Obtain a styrofoam ball that has an attached string. Use your box, flashlight, and suspended foil ball, but add the larger styrofoam ball, suspending it 2 inches from the top, as shown in the diagram. Seal the edges of the box again. Then seal the old eye hole and make a new eye hole in the side of the box, as indicated in the drawing.

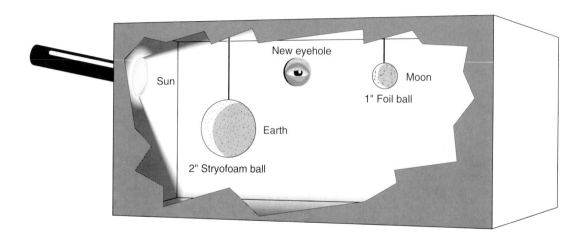

New eyehole

Sun

Moon

1" Foil ball

Earth

2" Stryofoam ball

Formulating a Model

If the small ball is the moon, what does the flashlight represent?

6. Turn on the flashlight and look through the new eye hole in the side of the box.

Inferring

What does the large ball represent?

7. Look at the ball representing the earth and tell which side is day and which side is night.

Inferring

On which side would you be if you could see the moon?

Inferring

How is it possible for you to see the moon if you are on the dark side of the earth?

Summarizing

Why does the moon shine?

How Will Students Use or Apply What They Discover?

1. *If you lived on another planet, would you be able to see earth?*
2. *What are the positions of the sun, moon, and earth (a) when it is night for you, and (b) when it is day for you, as shown in the diagram?*

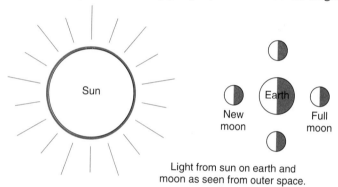

Light from sun on earth and moon as seen from outer space.

Why Does It Appear That There Are Phases of the Moon? (4–6)

What Concepts Might Students Discover?

Sometimes the moon appears fully round, appears to our eyes to change shape, or may appear to get smaller and smaller, or even larger and larger.

What Will We Need?

Black construction paper   Soft white chalk
Globe   Small ball
Basketball   Flashlight or filmstrip projector

What Must I Know?

Before the activity, consult the local newspaper to see when the moon's quarter will be visible.

What Will Students Do?

1. Take home a large sheet of black construction paper and some white chalk, and observe the moon for the next five days. Draw the shape of the moon as you see it each night. Note: Should the skies be overcast, making it impossible to observe the moon, use the local newspaper to get the information.

Observing

In what way does the moon's shape seem to change?

2. Using a globe, small ball, and a flashlight or filmstrip projector, make the following arrangement:

3. Place a pin on the night side of the earth as indicated in the diagram. The pin represents you.

Inferring

Draw how much of a moon you would see if you were where the pin is.

4. Move the moon around the earth to the day side.

Inferring

On which side of the earth is the moon when you cannot see it? Where is the moon when it is full?

5. Make diagrams to help you explain your answers to these questions.

6. Look at the following diagram which shows some positions of the moon in relation to the earth and the sun.

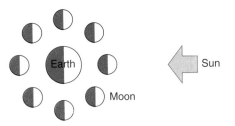

7. Choose two partners to help you. Using a basketball and flashlight, have one partner hold the flashlight and shine it on the basketball being held by your second partner, as he or she walks in a circle around you. See the diagram for how to do this.

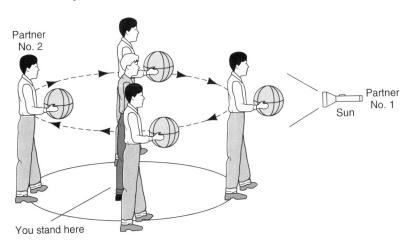

Inferring   8. As you observe the light on the ball in various positions, match the following moon phases with the appropriate eight moon positions shown in the diagram accompanying Step 6. What you see is what would be observed from the earth.

Phases of the Moon as Seen from the Earth

New moon	Waxing crescent	First quarter	Waxing (Gibbous)
Full moon	Waning (Gibbous)	Last quarter	Waning crescent

Inferring   *In what position is the basketball when it is covered by the shadow?*
Inferring   *Where would the moon have to be when it is covered by a shadow?*
Inferring   *When the basketball shows no shadow, what phase of the moon would this represent?*

Summarizing 9. Draw how the full moon looks from earth.
Summarizing   *What causes the phases of the moon?*

How Will Students Use or Apply What They Discover?

1. *If the moon is not out at night, on what side of the earth must it be located?*
2. *If the moon could remain motionless in the sky, how would it look every night?*

References—Astronomy (Earth in Space)
Teacher or older students: D. Louis and Mary Jane Finsand, *North Polar Constellations* (Washington, D.C.: National Science Teachers Association, 1991); and Fred Schaaf, *Seeing the Sky* (Washington, D.C.: National Science Teachers Association, 1990).
Younger students: Alan Harris and Paul Weissman, *The Great Voyager Adventure: A Guided Tour Through the Solar System* (Englewood Cliffs, N.J.: Messner, 1990); and Joseph W. Kelch, *Small Worlds: Exploring the 60 Moons of Our Solar System* (Englewood Cliffs, N.J.: Messner, 1990).

METEOROLOGY (WEATHER)

QUICKIE STARTERS

How Are Clouds and Fog Formed?

Materials

Ice cubes; 2 clear, narrow-mouthed bottles; hot and cold water

Opening Questions

What is a cloud and how is it formed?
What is fog and how is it formed?

Some Possible Activities

Fill a bottle with very hot water and let it sit for a few minutes. Now pour out most of the water, leaving about 2 cm (3/4 to 1 in) of water in the bottom of the bottle. For a control, set up an identical bottle with an equal amount of cold water. Place an ice cube in each bottle as shown in the figure. As your students observe the two bottles, ask:
What do you see happening in each bottle?
What do we call what you see in the hot-water bottle?

Why do you think clouds or fog formed in the bottle with hot water and not in the bottle with cold water?
How do clouds and fog form in nature?

What Is the Greenhouse Effect?

Materials

Large-mouthed jar with cover, 2 identical thermometers, 2 large cards, 2 rubber bands

Opening Questions

How does a greenhouse (where plants are grown) get so warm, even on a cold winter day?
During the summer, why is it hotter in an automobile when all the windows are shut tight rather than open? What is meant by "solar heating"?

Some Possible Activities

Get two thermometers that have identical readings and use rubber bands to attach them to large cards. Place one thermometer and card in a large-mouthed jar and screw on the cover. Set up a "heat trap" in a sunny window, as shown, to illustrate the principle of the greenhouse, cold frame, or solar house. Make sure each thermometer is shaded from the direct sunlight by the cards.

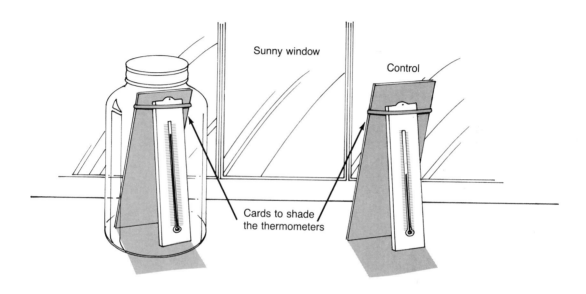

Take readings every half hour.
What differences do you observe on the two thermometers?
Why do you think the one in the jar is higher?
How is this knowledge used by architects and builders to make solar-heated houses?

GUIDED DISCOVERY MINDS-ON/HANDS-ON ACTIVITIES

How Can You Measure Temperature Changes?/What Is a Thermometer? (K–8)

What Concepts Might Students Discover?

Thermal energy (heat) gives increased energy to molecules, causing them to exert more pressure or expand.

Warm temperatures make things expand more than do cold temperatures.

An instrument that measures changes in temperature is called a **thermometer** (*thermo*—heat and *meter*—to measure).

What Will We Need? Clear, narrow plastic drinking straw
Scissors
Cold water or rubbing alcohol
Red food coloring
Small vial or medicine bottle
Modeling clay
3 × 5-inch index card
Tape

What Will We Discuss?
Where in this classroom might be the warmest places?
Where in this classroom might be the coolest places?
How could we find out the answers to these two questions?
What instrument(s) might we use in our investigation?

What Must I Know? This activity can be done individually or in groups of two to four students. Thermometers measure the temperature of matter, or how hot or cold something is. Mercury or colored alcohol is usually the liquid used in thermometers. When heated, the liquid expands and moves up the tube. We say the temperature goes up. Conversely, when cooled, the liquid contracts and moves down the tube. We say the temperature goes down. Thermometers are used in many scientific, as well as personal, aspects of life, such as in taking body temperatures, in measuring air or water temperatures, in cooking, etc.

PROCESSES

What Will Students Do?

Measuring

1. Put 2.5 cm (1 in) of cold water into the small vial or medicine bottle and add several drops of red food coloring. (*Note:* Rubbing alcohol responds more quickly to temperature changes and can be used instead of water, depending on the ages and maturity of your students.)

2. With scissors, cut the end of the drinking straw at a slight angle. (*Note:* Your results will be best if you use the narrowest straw you can. Also, changes in air pressure and evaporation may affect your thermometer. To prevent this, after setting up the thermometers, put a few drops of oil into the tops of the drinking straws, or seal the straws with modeling clay.)

3. Put the straw into the vial and completely seal the top of the vial with modeling clay, making sure it is airtight.

4. Tape a 3 × 5-inch index card to the drinking straw. As shown in the diagram, mark the level of the colored water in the straw.

Hypothesizing
What do you think might happen to the colored water in the drinking straw if you put your thermometer in a warmer spot?

Observing
5. Put your thermometer in a warmer spot or in a pan of warm water and observe what happens. On the card, mark the new height of the liquid in your drinking straw.

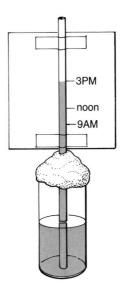

Recording Data	Draw a picture of what happened to the colored water in the drinking straw.
Inferring	*Why do you think the colored water moved up the drinking straw?*
Hypothesizing	*What do you think might happen now if you put your thermometer in a cooler spot?*
	6. Put your thermometer in a cooler spot or in a pan of cold water.
Recording Data	Draw a picture of what happened to the colored water in the drinking straw.
Inferring	*Why do you think the colored water moved down the drinking straw?*
What Must I Know?	Check each student's drawing to see if he or she observed that as the temperature goes up, so does the colored water in the straw. The colored-water level goes down when the temperature goes down. Discuss the interrelationship between expansion and contraction of molecules and temperature, or the amount of molecular motion.
How Will Students Use or Apply What They Discover?	1. Each day for a week, have students observe and record where the level of the liquid is in their thermometers at the opening, lunch, and closing time of school. Then have students answer these questions:
Comparing	*Of your three thermometer readings each day, which one was the highest and which one the lowest?*
Extrapolating	*During a week, which was the warmest morning, lunch, and afternoon?*
Hypothesizing	*Where do you predict tomorrow's levels will be for your three thermometer readings?*

Measuring/Comparing 2. Take thermometer readings and compare where the level of the colored water is in the coolest and warmest spots in your classroom.

Measuring 3. Using a commercial thermometer, measure the air temperature. Have students use this temperature to mark their drinking-straws cards with actual numerical readings. Have students take their daily readings on their thermometers for a week, with you giving them the actual numerical reading each time.

Predicting 4. After one week, ask your students to predict what the actual numerical temperature will be for the three daily readings.

Describing 5. Make a list of various jobs where people use thermometers. Describe how thermometers are used in each job.

How Can You Measure Air Pressure Changes?/What Is a Barometer? (K–8)

What Concepts Might Students Discover?

Air exerts pressure.
Air pressure changes.
Air pressure may indicate the type of weather.
Low air pressure usually indicates rainy or cloudy weather.
High air pressure usually indicates fair weather.

What Will We Need?

Can with plastic snap top (i.e., coffee can)
Large balloon
Straw
Glue
Straight pin
Index card

What Will We Discuss?

Have each student blow up a balloon. Ask:
What is in the balloon?
How do you know there is pressure exerted in the balloon?
How can you discover whether or not air has the same pressure at all times and in all places?
What is a barometer?
What is it used for?
How might location affect the readings of a barometer?

What Must I Know?

Room temperature will affect the barometer students make in this activity. This barometer does not, therefore, only measure air pressure differences. You may want to have some students keep their barometers outside class and then compare the readings from the different locations.

PROCESSES

What Will Students Do?

1. Obtain a can that has a plastic snap top, a straw, glue, a straight pin, and a card.

2. Cover the can with the plastic snap top, making certain the can is sealed completely. *Caution:* Often the plastic snap top will not suf-

ficiently seal the can. Using a piece of a large balloon and a tight rubber band to seal the can is a good alternative.

3. Place a small amount of glue in the center of the lid and attach a straw, as shown in the diagram. Place another drop of glue on the other end of the straw and attach the pin.

4. Mark an index card with lines that are the same distance apart. Tape the card on the wall as shown in the diagram.

Hypothesizing   *What might happen to the plastic snap top or balloon if the air pressure on it increases?*

Hypothesizing   *What might happen to the plastic snap top or balloon if the air pressure decreases?*

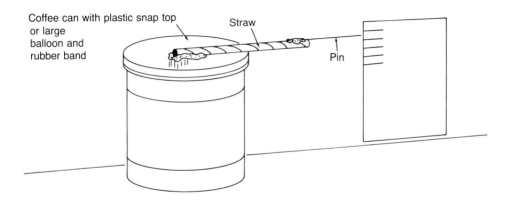

Coffee can with plastic snap top or large balloon and rubber band

Straw

Pin

What Must I Know?   When air pressure increases, it pushes down on the plastic lid or balloon, causing the straw to give a high reading. When the air pressure is low, the opposite will happen. A falling barometer may indicate that a storm is approaching.

5. Record the readings of the barometer three times a day for a week.

Comparing   *How do the readings of the barometer differ during the day?*

Comparing   *How do the readings differ from day to day?*

Inferring   *What might cause the readings to vary?*

6. Record the type of weather that exists at the time of each barometer reading.

Inferring   *What kind of air pressure generally existed during your fair-weather readings?*

Inferring   *What kind of air pressure generally existed during your stormy-weather readings?*

Inferring

7. Compare the readings of barometers in different locations. *What reasons can you give for your barometer readings?*

Applying

By using the readings of your barometer, predict what the weather will be.

How Will Students Use or Apply What They Discover?

1. *Does air travel from an area of higher pressure to an area of lower pressure, or from an area of lower pressure to an area of higher pressure? Why?*
2. *What could you do to improve your barometer?*
3. *What other materials could you use to make a barometer?*

How Can You Measure Humidity Changes?/What Is a Hygrometer? (4–8)

What Concepts Might Students Discover?

Air contains moisture.
Pressure and temperature affect the amount of moisture air can hold at any given time.
Relative humidity is the amount of water vapor actually contained in the atmosphere divided by the amount that could be contained in the same atmosphere.
Relative humidity can be measured.

What Will We Need?

2 thermometers
Small bottle or dish of water
Thread
Wide cotton shoelace
Empty milk carton

What Will We Discuss?

What instrument is used to measure the amount of water or humidity in the atmosphere?
How can this instrument be made and how does it work?

PROCESSES

What Will Students Do?

1. Obtain an empty milk container, two identical thermometers, a cotton shoelace, and some thread.
2. Cut a four-inch section from the cotton shoelace and slip the section over the bulb of one of the thermometers. Tie the shoelace section with thread above and below the bulb to hold the shoelace in place. Allow the other end of the four-inch section to rest in a small bottle or dish of water inside the milk carton.
3. Attach both thermometers to the milk carton as shown in the diagram.

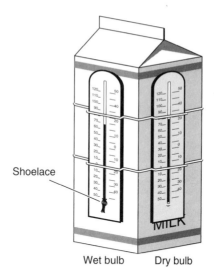

Shoelace

Wet bulb   Dry bulb

You now have a **hygrometer**—an instrument that measures the relative humidity in the atmosphere. *Caution:* The two thermometers should register the same temperature before the shoelace is placed over one of them; otherwise, the difference in readings must be considered a constant that is part of all computations.

4. When the shoelace is wet, fan it with a piece of cardboard for one minute.

Hypothesizing *What do you think might happen to the thermometer with the wet shoelace? Why do you think so?*

Observing 5. Check the temperature readings of the two thermometers.

Hypothesizing *How do you account for the difference in readings between the thermometer with the shoelace (called the "wet-bulb") and the one without the shoelace (called the "dry-bulb")?*

What Must I Know? When the shoelace is wet, the evaporation of the water results in a cooling of the wet-bulb thermometer while the dry-bulb thermometer will continue to read the temperature of the air around it. *Note:* This is the same phenomenon that occurred in a previous activity in Section 2, where students wore one dry wool or cotton sock and one wet wool or cotton sock to show the cooling effect of evaporation.

6. Compute the relative humidity by recording the temperature of the dry-bulb thermometer and the difference between the readings of the two thermometers, and applying these to the relative humidity table.

7. Take readings on your hygrometer every day for two weeks and record your findings. Also try readings in different places.

Inferring *What reasons can you give for different readings?*

FINDING RELATIVE HUMIDITY IN PERCENT

Difference in Degrees between Wet-Bulb and Dry-Bulb Thermometers

Air Temperature (Reading of Dry-Bulb Thermometer) in Degrees Fahrenheit

	1	2	3	4	5	6	7	8	9	10	11	12	13	14	15	16	17	18	19	20	21	22	23	24	25	26	27	28	29	30
30°	89	78	68	57	47	37	27	17	8																					
32°	90	79	69	60	50	41	31	22	13	4																				
34°	90	81	72	62	53	44	35	27	18	9	1																			
36°	91	82	73	65	56	48	39	31	23	14	6																			
38°	91	83	75	67	59	51	43	35	27	19	12	4																		
40°	92	84	76	68	61	53	46	38	31	23	16	9	2																	
42°	92	85	77	70	62	55	48	41	34	28	21	14	7																	
44°	93	85	78	71	64	57	51	44	37	31	24	18	12	5																
46°	93	86	79	72	65	59	53	46	40	34	28	22	16	10	4															
48°	93	87	80	73	67	60	54	48	42	36	31	25	19	14	8	3														
50°	93	87	81	74	68	62	56	50	44	39	33	28	22	17	12	7	2													
52°	94	88	81	75	69	63	58	52	46	41	36	30	25	20	15	10	6													
54°	94	88	82	76	70	65	59	54	48	43	38	33	28	23	18	14	9	5												
56°	94	88	82	77	71	66	61	55	50	45	40	35	31	26	21	17	12	8	4											
58°	94	89	83	77	72	67	62	57	52	47	42	38	33	28	24	20	15	11	7	3										
60°	94	89	84	78	73	68	63	58	53	49	44	40	35	31	27	22	18	14	10	6	2									
62°	94	89	84	79	74	69	64	60	55	50	46	41	37	33	29	25	21	17	13	9	6	2								
64°	95	90	85	79	75	70	66	61	56	52	48	43	39	35	31	27	23	20	16	12	9	5	2							
66°	95	90	85	80	76	71	66	62	58	53	49	45	41	37	33	29	26	22	18	15	11	8	5	1						
68°	95	90	85	81	76	72	67	63	59	55	51	47	43	39	35	31	28	24	21	17	14	11	8	4	1					
70°	95	90	86	81	77	72	68	64	60	56	52	48	44	40	37	33	30	26	23	20	17	13	10	7	4	1				
72°	95	91	86	82	78	73	69	65	61	57	53	49	46	42	39	35	32	28	25	22	19	16	13	10	7	4	1			
74°	95	91	86	82	78	74	70	66	62	58	54	51	47	44	40	37	34	30	27	24	21	18	15	12	9	7	4	1		
76°	96	91	87	83	78	74	70	67	63	59	55	52	48	45	42	38	35	32	29	26	23	20	17	14	12	9	6	4	1	
78°	96	91	87	83	79	75	71	67	64	60	57	53	50	46	43	40	37	34	31	28	25	22	19	16	14	11	9	6	4	1
80°	96	91	87	83	79	76	72	68	64	61	57	54	51	47	44	41	38	35	32	29	27	24	21	18	16	13	11	8	6	4
82°	96	91	87	83	79	76	72	69	65	62	58	55	52	49	46	43	40	37	34	31	28	25	23	20	18	15	13	10	8	6
84°	96	92	88	84	80	77	73	70	66	63	59	56	53	50	47	44	41	38	35	32	30	27	25	22	20	17	15	12	10	8
86°	96	92	88	84	80	77	73	70	66	63	60	57	54	51	48	45	42	39	37	34	31	29	26	24	21	19	17	14	12	10
88°	96	92	88	85	81	78	74	71	67	64	61	58	55	52	49	46	43	41	38	35	33	30	28	25	23	21	18	16	14	12
90°	96	92	88	85	81	78	74	71	68	64	61	58	56	53	50	47	44	42	39	37	34	32	29	27	24	22	20	18	16	14

Example:
Temperature of dry-bulb thermometer 76°
Temperature of wet-bulb thermometer 68°
The difference is 8°

Find 76° in the dry-bulb column and 8° in the difference column. Where these two columns meet, you read the relative humidity. In this case, it is 67 percent.

Applying

Using your hygrometer, can you predict which days are better for drying clothes outside?

How Will Students Use or Apply What They Discover?

1. *What other instruments can you find that will indicate or measure relative humidity?*
2. *How is relative humidity used by weather forecasters to predict weather?*
3. *Why were you asked to fan the wet-bulb thermometer?*
4. *How does relative humidity explain why you feel more uncomfortable on a humid 90-degree day than on a dry 90-degree day?*
5. *Why might you feel more comfortable in winter in a room that is 70 degrees with 65 percent relative humidity, than in a room that is 70 degrees but with only 30 percent relative humidity?*

How Can Solar Energy Be Used? (3–8)

What Concepts Might Students Discover?

Water in a saline solution absorbs the sun's energy and evaporates, leaving the salt behind. When cooled, water vapor condenses and changes into water droplets.

What Will We Need?

Salt	Large clear plastic bowl
Water	Plastic wrap
Tablespoon	Large rubber band
Small weight (rock)	Small glass custard cup
Large sheet of black construction paper	

What Will We Discuss?

In what ways can you make the sun do work for you?

What Must I Know?

This activity may be done individually or in groups of two to four.

PROCESSES

What Will Students Do?

Part I How Can You Make a Solar Still?

1. Pour 3 tablespoons of salt into the large clear plastic bowl, add 1" (2.5 cm) of water, and stir until all the salt is dissolved.
2. Place the small glass custard cup in the water in the center of the bowl.
3. Cover the large bowl with plastic wrap and fasten the wrap with a large rubber band.
4. Place a weight (small pebble) on top of the plastic wrap directly above the custard dish, as shown in the diagram.
   Caution: Make certain that the plastic wrap sticks tightly to the sides of the bowl and that the large rubber band keeps it sealed when the pebble is placed on the wrap.

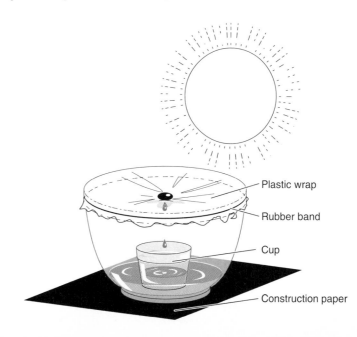

5. Carefully place the bowls in direct sunlight on a sheet of black construction paper, making sure the custard cup is directly under the weight pushing down on the plastic wrap.

Hypothesizing   *What do you think might happen to the salt water?*

Hypothesizing   *Why do you think you were told to cover the salt water with plastic wrap?*

Hypothesizing   *Why do you think you were told to put the bowl on black construction paper?*

Observing   6. Record your observations every day.

What Must I Know?

When there is only salt remaining in the large bowl and all the water is in the custard cup, Part II should be done by the group.

Part II   What Is Desalinated Water?

Take off the plastic wrap and taste the water in the custard cup.

Comparing   *How does the water taste?*

Inferring   *Where did the water in this dish come from?*

Inferring   *What happened to your salt solution?*

Inferring   *Where did the water go?*

Inferring   *Why did the water "disappear?"*

Applying   *How does the sun's energy (solar energy) benefit people?*

Applying   *How could this procedure be helpful to people who live near the ocean but do not have enough drinking water?*

How Will Students Use or Apply What They Discover?

1. *What are some other uses for this method of obtaining drinking water?*
2. *What are some other ways in which the sun's energy (solar energy) can be used to help people?*
3. *How does the pictured solar water heater work?*

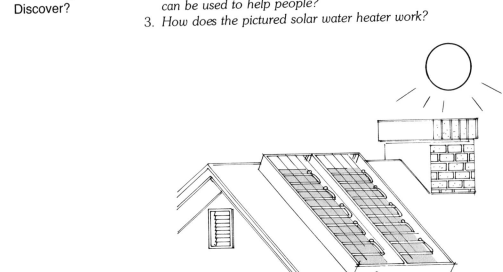

How Can You Measure Wind Direction and Speed? (K–8)

What Concepts Might Students Discover?

Wind, or moving air, brings about changing weather conditions.
A **wind vane** is an instrument that shows the direction from which the wind is blowing.
Winds are named for the direction from which they blow, i.e., a north wind is blowing from the north to the south.
An **anemometer** is an instrument that shows wind speed.

What Will We Need?

1 sq ft (1000 sq cm) corrugated cardboard
Empty thread spool
Soda straw
Construction paper
Ping-Pong ball
12″ (30 cm) monofilament nylon line
Protractor
Bubble level (hardware store)
Pencil with eraser
Glue
Scissors
Glass bead
Red marking pen
Tongue depressor
Long sewing needle
Straight pin

What Will We Discuss?

How can you tell the direction the wind is blowing?
How does knowing wind direction help us understand weather and weather prediction?
What instruments can be used to find wind direction and speed?
How can we make and use these instruments?

PROCESSES

What Will Students Do?

Part I What Is a Wind Vane and How Do We Make One?

1. Cut, from construction paper, an arrow-shaped point and tail fin, as shown in the diagram.
2. Attach the point and tail fin to the straw by cutting notches in both ends of the straw and gluing the cut-outs in place.
3. Attach the straw to a pencil by sticking the straight pin through the middle of the straw, through a glass bead, and into the pencil eraser. Make sure the straw can swing easily in all directions.
4. Glue the empty thread spool to the center of the corrugated cardboard and mark North, South, East, and West on the cardboard as shown in the diagram.
5. When the glue has dried, push the pencil into the hole of the spool and check to see that the straw moves easily. You now have a wind vane.

6. Carefully take your wind vane outdoors and line up the north label on your wind vane with the north on a magnetic compass.

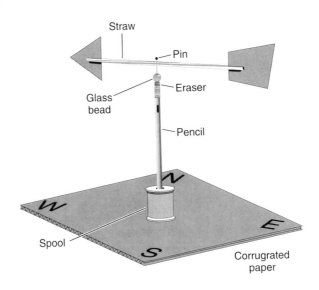

Observing	*What do you see happening to the arrow?*
Observing	*From which direction is the wind blowing? How do you know?*
Applying	*How would you name this wind?*

What Must I Know?

The arrow will swing around until the point faces the direction from which the wind is blowing. This direction then becomes the wind's name.

How Will Students Use or Apply What They Discover?

1. *Does the wind always blow from the same direction? How could we find out?*
2. Keep a record of wind observations three times a day for one week. Make sure to record the following data on a chart:

   Date
   Observation time
   Location
   Wind direction
   Any changes

3. *After one week, do you see*
   A. *any pattern of winds during the day?*
   B. *any pattern of winds from day to day?*
   C. *any prevailing or consistent direction from which the wind blows?*
   D. *any correlation between wind direction and weather conditions, i.e., temperatures, humidity, clouds, etc.?*

Part II How Can You Measure How Fast the Wind Blows?[1]

1. Thread a sewing needle with a 12″ monofilament line, push the needle through the Ping-Pong ball, and knot and glue the end of the line to the Ping-Pong ball. Glue the other end of the line to the center of a protractor. With the marking pen, color the line red.
2. Glue a bubble level to the protractor as shown in the diagram.
3. Glue a tongue depressor to the protractor as a handle. You now have an anemometer to measure wind speed.
4. When the glue is dry, carefully take your anemometer outside to test it in the wind.

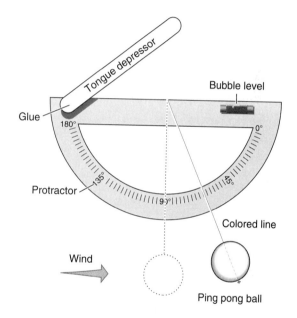

5. To take readings of the wind's speed, follow these directions:
   A. In the wind, hold the protractor level using the tongue depressor handle.
   B. Keep the protractor level by making sure the bubble is centered in the bubble level.

[1]The author highly recommends the following packet of activities for making and using weather instruments: *Science Activities in Energy*, *DOE/CA—0006* (P.O. Box 117, Oak Ridge, Tenn. 37830: American Museum of Science and Energy/Oak Ridge Associated Universities).

C. Observe any swing of the Ping-Pong ball and string and see what angle the string makes on the protractor. For instance, in the diagram the string moved to approximately 50 degrees.

How Will Students Use or Apply What They Discover?

1. Use your anemometer in various spots on your school grounds, then use the following chart to calibrate the wind speed.

PROTRACTOR ANEMOMETER WIND SPEEDS

String Angle	Wind Speed (Miles Per Hour)	String Angle	Wind Speed (Miles Per Hour)
90	0	50	18.0
85	5.8	45	19.6
80	8.2	40	21.9
75	10.1	35	23.4
70	11.8	30	25.8
65	13.4	25	28.7
60	14.9	20	32.5
55	16.4		

2. After you have tested the wind speed in different places on your school grounds, record the following data on a chart.

    Date
    Time
    Protractor angle
    Wind speed
    Wind direction

3. *Where does the wind blow the fastest on your school grounds?*
4. *Does wind blow faster at ground level or at higher levels?*
5. *Is there a place where wind blows faster, such as between two buildings or at a corner of two wings of a building?*

References—Meteorology (Weather)
Teacher or older students: H. Michael Mogil, *Weather Study Under a Newspaper Umbrella* (Washington, D.C.: National Science Teachers Association, 1989); and Peter Seymour, *How the Weather Works* (New York: Macmillan, 1985).
Younger students: Gail Gibbons, *Weather Forecasting* (New York: Macmillan, 1987); and Claire Martin, *I Can Be a Weather Forecaster* (New York: Watts, 1987).

GEOLOGY (EARTH'S CHANGING SURFACE)

QUICKIE STARTERS

How Can You Build Stalactites and Stalagmites?

Materials

Paper towel, Epsom salts, water, spoon, 30 cm (1 ft) of thick string, large tin can, 2 small jars or clear plastic cups, 2 heavy washers

Opening Questions

How are some rocks formed in caves?
What is a stalactite and how is it formed?
What is a stalagmite and how is it formed?
Where else are stalactites and stalagmites formed?

Some Possible Activities

Fill the large tin can about three quarters full of water. Add Epsom salts, one spoonful at a time, stirring vigorously after each addition, until no more Epsom salts will dissolve. (*Note:* Epsom salt crystals will fall to the bottom of the can when no more will dissolve.) Fill the two small jars or plastic cups with the Epsom salt solution and place the containers 5 cm (2 in) apart on the paper towel. Tie a heavy washer to each end of the string. Place one washer in each of the small jars or paper cups. *Note:* Arrange the string in the cups so that you have at least 5 cm (2 in) between the string and the paper towel.

After several days, mineral deposits will form on the paper towel and string as shown.

Note: Help students learn the difference between stalactites and stalagmites. Point out that the deposits that hang down are called **stalactites,** (C for ceiling), while those that point up are called **stalagmites** (G for ground).

How Are Rocks Broken Up?

Materials

2 plastic vials or medicine bottles with snap lids, dry bean seeds, water

Opening Questions

How can seeds break up rocks and soil?
How can we set up an experiment to test if seeds can break up rocks and soil?

Some Possible
Activities

Fill both vials or medicine bottles with as many dry beans as will fit. Add as much water as you can to one vial of beans. Snap the lids on tightly to both vials.

A Water   **B** No water

Ask students what they think might happen to the two vials. Observe both vials the next day. In the one with the water, the beans will have expanded and lifted the lid off. In the vial without water (called the control), there will be no observable change. Help students infer that swelling and growing plants change the land by breaking up rocks and soil just as the swelling beans lifted the vial's lid off.

GUIDED DISCOVERY MINDS-ON/HANDS-ON ACTIVITIES

How Are Crystals Formed? (K–6)

What Concepts
Might Students
Discover?

Crystals are nonlivng substances that form into rocklike bodies of various shapes.
Crystals grow in size when more layers of the same substance are added on; the same basic crystal shape, however, remains the same.
Crystal size is determined by differences in the rate of crystallization.
If crystals are disturbed in the forming process, they will break apart into hundreds of microscopic pieces.
True solids are crystalline in form.
Crystalline form is important in determining some of the properties of substances.

What Will We Need?

Tablespoon	2 jars with lids	Salt	Water
2 small glasses		Sugar	
2 pieces of clear silk thread		Copper sulfate	
2 pencils		Magnifying glass or hand lens	
Plastic wrap		White distilled vinegar	
Popcorn Rock™2		Food coloring	
Clear glass bowl			

[2]Inexpensive materials and directions for growing "Popcorn Rock" can be obtained from your local Popcorn Rock Dealer or from R. D. Barnes, 389 West 100 South, Bountiful, Utah 84010 (801)295-5762.

What Will We Discuss?	*What are crystals?* *How could you "grow" a crystal?* *What happens when a crystal is "growing?"* *Why is a study of crystals important?*
What Must I Know?	These activities can be done by individual students or by groups of two to four people.

PROCESSES

What Will Students Do?

Part I Growing Salt Crystals by Evaporation

Observing

1. Obtain a tablespoon of salt, a jar lid, and a small glass of water. Mix the salt into the glass of water. Stir the water well. Let the solution stand for a few minutes until it becomes clear.
   What happens to the salt?

Hypothesizing

2. Very gently pour some of the salt solution into the jar lid. Let the solution stand for several days where the lid will not be disturbed.
   What do you think might happen to the salt solution?

3. After several days have passed, use your magnifying glass to look at the materials in the lid.

Communicating
Comparing

4. Describe what you see.
   How are the materials in the lid different from your original salt solution?

Inferring
Hypothesizing

   Why do you now have a solid when you started out with a liquid?
   What name could you give to the formations in the lid?

What Must I Know?

The salt dissolved in the water. When the salt water stood for several days, the water evaporated, leaving behind salt crystals. Crystals are nonliving substances that are found in various geometrical shapes.

Salt crystals

Part II Growing Sugar Crystals by Evaporation

What Will Students Do?

1. Obtain a tablespoon of sugar, a jar lid, and a small glass of water. Be sure the tablespoon is clean. Mix a tablespoon of sugar into the glass of water. Stir the water well. Let the solution stand for a few minutes until it becomes clear.

Observing

   What happens to the sugar?

Comparing

   How is the sugar solution similar in appearance to the salt solution?

2. Very gently pour some of the sugar solution into the lid and let the solution stand undisturbed for several days.

Hypothesizing
What do you think might happen to the sugar solution?

Observing
3. After several days have passed, use your magnifying glass to look at the materials in your lid.

Sugar crystals

Communicating
4. Describe what you see.

Comparing
How are the materials in this lid different from the salt crystals? How are they alike?

Inferring
What happened to the sugar solution?

What Must I Know?
When the sugar water stood for several days, the water evaporated, leaving behind sugar crystals.

Part III   How Does the Rate of Evaporation Affect Crystal Size Formation?

Caution: Copper sulfate is poisonous; therefore, Part III should be done by the teacher as a demonstration for students to observe.

1. Wash your hands carefully. Obtain two pieces of clear silk thread, two jars, copper sulfate, two pencils, plastic wrap, and water.
2. Fill the jars three-fourths full of hot water. Add the copper sulfate to the water until the water is saturated with it. Make sure you stir the water constantly while adding the copper sulfate.
3. Prepare seed crystals of copper sulfate. These crystals can be formed in the same way as the salt or sugar crystals were. Obtain two seed crystals of copper sulfate that are about 1/8″ to 1/4″ in length. Tie each crystal to one end of separate pieces of silk thread. Tie the free end of each piece of thread to separate pencils. Rest each pencil on a separate jar, allowing the crystals to fall into the copper sulfate solution. Place the jars where they will not be disturbed.

Hypothesizing
Why was it necessary for me to wash my hands?

Hypothesizing
What do you think the copper sulfate solution will do to the crystals?

4. Watch the crystals carefully for several days.

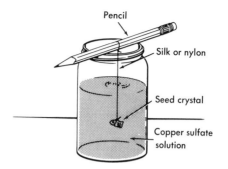

Pencil

Silk or nylon

Seed crystal

Copper sulfate solution

Observing 5. Record what happens to the crystals.

What Must I Know?   The copper sulfate solution causes the seed crystals to increase in size. Crystals "grow" as more layers of the same substance are added. The basic shape of the crystal remains the same.

Hypothesizing   *How could larger crystals be made?*

What Must I Know?   The slower crystals increase in size, the larger they become.
Hypothesizing   *How could the "growing" process of the crystals be slowed down?*

What Must I Know?   Reducing the rate of evaporation will cause the crystals to "grow" at a slower rate.

Hypothesizing   *How could the rate of evaporation of the copper sulfate solution be slowed down?*

6. Remove one of the pencils. Obtain some plastic wrap, and cover the top of the jar from which you removed the pencil. Pierce a hole in the plastic wrap large enough for the suspended crystals to pass through, then return the pencil to the top of the jar.

Comparing 7. Compare both jars closely for several days.
Observing   *How do the crystals formed in the two jars differ?*
Inferring   Explain why the crystals are different.

What Must I Know?   The crystal in the closed jar will be larger since the plastic wrap slowed down the rate of evaporation, causing the crystal to "grow" at a slower rate. The open jar will have a smaller crystal since the faster rate of evaporation did not allow as much time for the crystal to increase its size.

Hypothesizing   *After the third day, what do you think might happen if the crystals were disturbed during their periods of crystallization?*

Observing 8. Gently shake the jar without the plastic wrap and explain what happens.

What Must I Know?   If crystals are disturbed in the crystallization process, they will break apart into hundreds of microscopic pieces.

Inferring   *Where are crystals found in nature?*
Summarizing   *How do crystals form?*

Classifying   Explain why crystalline form is important in determining the properties of a substance.

Hypothesizing   *Why do some rocks have large crystals and some have small crystals?*

What Must I Know?   True solids are crystalline in form. Crystalline form is important in determining some of the properties of substances. Differences in the rate of crystallization determine differences in crystal size.

How Will Students Use or Apply What They Discover?
1. *How are crystals used in industry?*
2. *If there were no crystals on earth, how would people's way of living be affected?*
3. *How might you "grow" very large crystals?*

Part IV   How Can You Make "Popcorn Rock" Stalagmites?

What Must I Know?   "Popcorn Rock" is the trade name for a naturally occurring mineral found in the western United States. It is called Popcorn Rock because popcorn-like aragonite crystals (calcium carbonate) can form on the rock, in the same way that limestone formations are occurring in Carlsbad Caverns National Park, New Mexico.[3]

It is recommended that the Popcorn Rock Experiment begin on Thursday, as early in the morning as possible. Then allow seven days for the Popcorn Rock crystals to form, be observed, and discussed.

What Will Students Do?   *Day 1 (Thursday).*   Place the Popcorn Rock in a clear glass bowl and add just enough white distilled vinegar to cover the rock completely. Place the bowl in a place where it will not be disturbed.

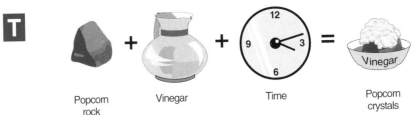

Popcorn   Vinegar   Time   Popcorn
rock   crystals

Hypothesizing   *What might happen to the rock in the vinegar?*
Observing and   Observe your rock three times a day and record any changes you see.
Recording

Observing   *Day 2 (Friday).*   *What do you see forming on the highest ridges of the rock late in the afternoon?*
Let the Popcorn Rock remain undisturbed over the weekend.

Observing   *Day 5 (Monday).*   *What do you see about 1/4 inch above the evaporating white vinegar?*

[3]The author is indebted to the following publication for excellent lessons using Popcorn Rock. The publication is available from its author: Richard David Barnes, *Popcorn Rock—An Experiment in Crystal Science* (Bountiful, Utah: PR NEWS, 1989).

Comparing	*What do the crystals look like?*
Inferring	*What do you think those crystals are?*
Hypothesizing	*Day 6 (Tuesday). Do you think the Popcorn Rock "grows" from the bottom (like hair) or does it "grow" from the tips of the crystals (like tree branches)?*

What Must I Know?   Bleached-blonde hair has new, dark-colored hair below the older, light-colored hair. Names carved in tree bark remain at the same level, even as the tree grows taller.

Devising an   *How might we devise experiments to resolve this?*
Experiment

Hypothesizing   *Day 7 (Wednesday).   How might putting a very small amount of food coloring in the vinegar help us resolve whether Popcorn Rock "grows" from the bottom or from the tips of the crystals?*
Try it.

What Must I Know?   Capillary action, similar to osmosis in trees, pulls the vinegar, calcium carbonate, and food coloring up from the bottom. If the aragonite crystals are "growing" from the bottom, the food coloring will remain in the lower crystals, formed after the vinegar was added. Popcorn Rock "grows" from the bottom, making it a stalagmite. Let the Popcorn Rock crystals form until all the vinegar has evaporated. If crystals get broken, put the rock back in the vinegar and start over.

How Will Students Use or Apply What They Discover?

1. Some students may have noticed that bubbles formed in the vinegar. *What caused the bubbles and how might we find out what the bubbles are?*
2. *What might happen if you allowed your Popcorn Rock crystals to form in a sealed plastic bag?*
3. *Why do you think vinegar was used to form the Popcorn Rock crystals? Would the same thing happen if a different liquid were used? Which liquid(s) would you suggest?*
4. *How might we test your hypotheses?*

How Are Rocks Alike and Different and How Do We Use Rocks? (K–6)

What Concepts Might Students Discover?   Rocks exhibit eight major properties or characteristics that are used to identify and classify them: hardness, texture, color, streak, cleavage, density, chemical, and luster. Simple tests can help us identify and classify rocks by their properties. Rocks are used in many forms in our everyday lives.

What Will We Need?

Large steel nail	Penny
Glass baby food jar	Newspaper
Hammer	Cloth sack
Magnifying glass	Rock samples
Safety goggles	

What Will We
Discuss?

Where could you find different kinds of rocks on our school grounds, at home, or on the way to school?
How are rocks the same and different?
When you feel rocks, how might they differ?
How might we test rocks to see if they are hard or soft, heavy or light, dark or light, etc.?

What Must I Know?

This activity should be done in groups of two to four students. *Cautions:* 1) In hardness tests, the use of a knife is recommended, but a steel nail is substituted here for safety reasons. 2) Safety goggles should be used when hammering rocks, and *always* put rocks in a cloth sack when hammering.

    You and designated students should assemble the following items in a cloth sack before the activity begins: a large steel nail, a penny, a glass baby food jar, a newspaper, a hammer, a magnifying glass, and six samples of different rocks.

What Will Students
Do?

Observing

Comparing

Comparing

Comparing

Comparing

Inferring

Inferring

Classifying

Communicating

Designing an Investigation

1. Open your cloth sack and place your materials on the newspaper.

2. Observe the rocks closely.
   In what ways are the rocks alike?
   In what ways do the rocks look different?
   When you feel the rocks, how do they differ?
   Compare two rocks of the same size.
   How does their weight compare? Is one heavier than the other?
   Why do you think some rocks are rough and jagged?
   What do you think has happened to the rocks that are smooth and rounded?

3. Place your rocks in groups (classifying them by properties).
   How did you group your rocks? In what other ways might you group your rocks?
   How do you think you could tell the hardness or softness of a rock?
   (Scratch with steel nail, penny, fingernail, and so on.)

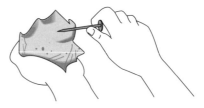

What Must I Know?

The Mohs' hardness scale ranks rocks from 1 to 10, with talc being softest at 1 and diamond hardest at 10. Here are some common materials that students can test and approximate their hardness.[4]

---

[4]For an expanded Scale of Hardness chart, see Alfred E. Friedl, *Teaching Science to Children—An Integrated Approach* (New York: Random House, 1986), 194.

Hardness Number	Common Materials	How to Test Hardness
1	Soft lead pencil	Greasy flakes on fingers
2	Chalk	Scratched by fingernail
3	Marble	Scratched by copper penny
4	Yellow brass	Scratched by nail
5	Glass bottle	Scratched by nail
6	Window glass	Scratched by file
7	Sandpaper	Scratches glass easily

Note: Materials above 8 are extremely hard and are not easy to test.

Hypothesizing

4. Try some of your ideas for testing other properties of rocks. *If two rocks were the same size, how could you find out which rock was heavier (denser)?*

What Must I Know?   The following is a simple test to find density.

1. Weigh the rock in air and record its weight.
2. Immerse the rock in water, weigh the rock, and record its weight.

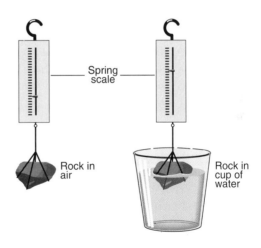

3. Subtract the difference in the weights.
4. Divide the "air weight" by the difference to get the specific gravity of the rock.

Note: Another way to show students that two objects with the same volume can be different weights due to their specific gravities involves the following activity.

1. Put a can of diet cola in a bowl of water and a same-size can of regular cola in another bowl of water.

2. The can of diet cola will float (because it is lighter in weight for its volume), while the regular cola will sink (because the sugar in it makes it heavier for the same volume).

Diet cola floats

Regular cola sinks

Designing an Investigation   *How could you tell whether a rock looked the same on the inside as it did on the outside?* (Place a rock in a cloth sack and cover the sack with newspaper. Wear safety goggles and hit the rock with a hammer.)

Designing an Investigation   *How would you find out how rocks become smooth and rounded?* (Place rocks in a *plastic* jar of water and shake the jar vigorously.)

Inferring   *Why are some rocks made of many smaller rocks or pieces?*

Observing   *Are the pieces of the rock rounded or jagged?*

Observing   *Are the pieces dull or shiny in the rock?*

Hypothesizing   *Why do you think they are like that?*

How Will Students Use or Apply What They Discover?

1. *In what ways are soft rocks used?*
2. *In what ways are hard rocks used?*
3. Survey your school, home, and community and make a chart of where rocks or rock materials are used daily. Use the following chart as an example.[5]

Everyday object	Product made from rock	Rock or mineral
Window	Glass	Sand
Wire or old penny	Copper	Copper ore
Fishing weights	Lead	Galena
Toothpaste	Fluoride	Fluoride crystal
Pretzel	Table salt	Salt crystal
Tooth filling	Gold	Gold nugget
Food can or foil	Aluminum	Bauxite ore

4. *What is concrete, how is it made, and how is it used?*

[5]For an expanded chart, see Richard David Barnes, *Popcorn Rock—An Experiment in Crystal Science* (Bountiful, Utah: PR NEWS, 1989), 15.

What Is a Fault and How Does It Change the Earth's Surface? (4–8)

What Concepts Might Students Discover?

Some land has been formed by sedimentation, causing layering.
When too much force is applied to the earth's layers, they crack.
The line where the earth's crust cracks and moves is called a fault.
A normal fault is where the earth's crust drops.
A thrust fault is where the earth's crust rises over an adjacent part of the earth.
Earthquakes may be caused by the earth's crust sliding along a fault.

What Will We Need?

2 quart jars	Water	Balance
Sand	2 plastic cups	Knife

Several types of soil—loamy, sandy, and clay
2 cigar-box molds filled with layers of colored plaster of paris
2 × 4 × 6-inch piece of wood cut along a sloping line

What Will We Discuss?

If great force is applied to a rock or parts of the earth's structure, what will happen to the rock or the structure?
What is an earthquake?
What causes an earthquake?

What Must I Know?

This activity should be done in groups of two to four students. The molds should be made ahead of time, by you and/or designated students, by mixing two or three *separate* pints of plaster of paris with different colors of food coloring. The wet plaster of paris should be layered in the cigar boxes and allowed to partially dry before cutting it as indicated in the following steps. *Caution:* Do not let the plaster of paris become too dry or it will be too hard to cut.

PROCESSES

What Will Students Do?

Observing
Hypothesizing

Comparing
Inferring
Hypothesizing

Hypothesizing
Observing and Recording

Part I How Does the Earth's Surface Form Layers?

1. Obtain a quart jar, some sand, and several types of soil. Half fill the quart jar with water. Add sand to the jar until the sand is 1 inch thick in the bottom of the jar.
   What happens to the sand?
   What will happen if you pour soil onto part of the sand?
2. Try it. Add several other types of soil to the jar and observe.
   How do the materials in the jar resemble parts of our earth?
   Explain how you think parts of our earth have become layered.
   What do you think might happen if you shake the jar of water, sand, and soils?
   What might happen if you let the jar stand for several days?
   Try it and record what you see in a few days.

Soil + sand + water,   After several days
shaken

Part II How Is a Fault Caused by Water Evaporating?

What Will Students Do?

Hypothesizing

1. Obtain a balance, a plastic cup half filled with water, and another cup half filled with sand. Place the cup of sand on one side of the balance and the cup of water on the other side.
   In what ways can you balance the sand and water?

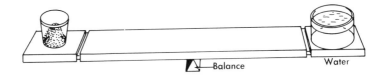

Hypothesizing

2. Use one of your methods to balance the sand and water.
   Now that these are balanced, what might happen if you take some sand from one side of the balance and place it on the other side by the cup of water?

Observing
Inferring

3. Do this and observe.
   How is what you did with the balance similar to some of the things that happen in the earth's crust? Materials shift on the surface of the earth.)

What Must I Know?

The land surface of the continents is always being worn away. The particles formed from this wearing away (**erosion**) often flow into streams and are carried to the sea. When the material gets to the ocean floor, it causes that part of the floor to become heavier and may cause the crust of the earth and the layers to bend. If they bend far enough, faults may appear. This is an explanation for one type of fault, although it is a rare type.

4. Rebalance the sand and water and let it stand undisturbed for several days.
   Why does the sand side go down?

Inferring

Part III   How Do Normal and Thrust Faults Change the Earth's Surface?

What Will Students Do?

Comparing

Summarizing

1. Obtain a cigar box mold from your teacher and remove the plaster block. Your teacher has cut the block in two. Raise one of these blocks above the other as indicated in the diagram.

   A place where the earth's crust and layers have broken similar to the one in your model, is called a **fault.**

   How is the appearance of the block similar to the appearance of the earth in some places you have seen?

   Explain how you think a rock structure could reach a condition similar to the one you have arranged in your model.

What Must I Know?

The rock structure could have formed a fault owing to stresses within the earth that drew the sections of rock apart. This stress could have caused one section to fall. This kind of fault is called a **normal fault** and is represented in the diagram.

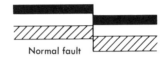

Normal fault

2. Obtain a 2 × 4 × 6-inch piece of wood that has been cut in two along a sloping line.

Comparing

   How is this model fault different from the normal fault? What would you call this type of fault?

What Must I Know?

Explain that this type of fault is called a thrust fault. The **thrust fault** occurs when compression pushes sections of rock closer together, forcing one section of rock to move or slide up, as shown in the diagram.

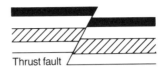

Thrust fault

Inferring

Summarizing

How could this structure have been formed in nature?

How would you define a thrust fault and explain how it works?

What Must I Know?

Other faults, such as the one that caused the San Francisco earthquake of 1989, may be caused mainly by horizontal movement of the earth. The San Andreas fault in California is of this type.

Hypothesizing

What connection is there between an earthquake and a fault?

What Must I Know?

Explain that earthquakes may be caused by the earth's crust sliding along a fault or by the forming of a fault.

How Will Students Use or Apply What They Discover?

1. *What effects do faults have on our earth?*
2. *Could faults be prevented? How?*
3. *How would you feel living in an area that has faults?*

References—Geology (Earth's Changing Surface)

Teacher and older students: Earthquakes (Washington, D. C.: National Science Teachers Association, 1989); Jonathan Ruthland, *The Violent Earth* (New York: Random House, 1987); and LeeAnn Srogi, *Start Collecting Rocks and Minerals* (Philadelphia, Pa.: Running Press, 1989).

Younger students: Paul Sipler, *I Can Be a Geologist* (Chicago, Ill.: 1986); and Rose Wyler, *Science Fun with Dirt and Mud* (Englewood Cliffs, N.J.: Messner, 1987).

ECOLOGY AND THE ENVIRONMENT

QUICKIE STARTERS

How Clean Is the Air You Breathe?

Materials

For each group of two to four students: four 10-cm square pieces of waxed paper, four 12-cm square pieces of wood, petroleum jelly, 16 thumb tacks, hand lens

Opening Questions

How can we find out if air in some areas has more particles in it than air in other areas?
Where do you think we might find these areas?
What might account for air in some areas having more particles in it than does air in other areas?
Where could the particles in the air have come from?
What effect could dirty air have on your health?

Some Possible Activities

With thumb tacks, attach squares of waxed paper to wood blocks and coat the waxed paper with a thin coating of petroleum jelly, as shown in the diagram.

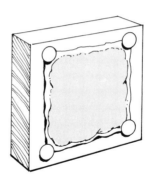

Put the wood blocks—"Particle Collectors"—outside in places where you think the air is "dirty," such as where there is a lot of bus and car travel, near airports, next to factories, etc. Also, put some in wooded areas, such as parks, and some indoors at home or at school. Make sure no one disturbs your collectors. Write down the place you put each collector and the date.

After four or five days, bring the collectors back to class, making sure you do not touch the sticky side of each collector. Look at the waxed paper with a hand lens.

Which collectors (places) had the most particles? Why?
Which collectors (places) had the fewest particles? Why?

Which Materials Break Down (Decompose) Easily?

Materials

For each group of two to four students, supply a plastic storage bag with a zip-lock seal that is about $10 \frac{1}{2} \times 11$ inches (268 mm $\times$ 279 mm), garden soil (not packaged fertilized potting soil), solid wastes, water, and earthworms.[6]

Opening Questions

What happens to our garbage after it is picked up by the garbage collectors?
Where is it taken?
Do some things break down (decompose) better than others?
What are they made of?
Do some things resist decomposing?
What are they made of?

Some Possible Activities

Put about 5 inches (12 cm) of garden soil in the bottom of the plastic bag. (Do not use packaged, sterilized soil, since you want bacteria and insects if possible.) Add ½ inch (1 cm) of thin pieces of solid wastes from the garbage or from the environment, such as leafy vegetables, fruits, aluminum foil, rubber bands, wooden toothpicks, different kinds of cloth and paper, styrofoam, and other plastic items. *Caution:* Do not put meat scraps or fats into your bag. Slightly moisten the soil, add three or four earthworms, seal the bag securely, and leave it at room temperature or near a radiator or heat source. Gently shake the bag daily. Observe and record what you see each week for four to six weeks, then go back and answer the opening questions.

[6]If you cannot get earthworms from local gardens or pet shops, send for *red worms* from Flowerfield Enterprises, 10332 Shaver Road, Kalamazoo, Mich. 49002 (616)327-0108; B & P, Box 398, Olathe, Colo. 81425 (303)323-6550; or the Cape Cod Worm Farm, 30 Center Avenue, Buzzards Bay, Mass. 02532 (508)759-5664.

GUIDED DISCOVERY MINDS-ON/HANDS-ON ACTIVITIES

How Does the Environment Affect Living Things? (K–8)

What Concepts Might Students Discover?

All living things have certain requirements that must be met by their environments.

A **habitat** is a place where an animal or plant naturally lives or grows.

An **environment** includes all the conditions in which an organism (plant or animal) lives, i.e., food, water, air, temperature, etc.

Certain environmental factors determine community types. Different environments are needed to sustain different types of life.

A **community** is a collection of living organisms that have mutual relationships among themselves and with their environment. Some types of communities are on land and some are in water.

Land communities can be subdivided into forests, bogs, swamps, deserts, and others.

Regions with similar geography, climate, vegetation, and animal life are called **biomes.**

Ecology is a branch of science that investigates the interrelationships of organisms and their environments and looks at how all living things are connected to each other and to their environments.

Natural phenomena can change an environment, but humans are one of the most powerful change agents.

What Will We Need?

3 large, wide-mouthed, commercial-sized mayonnaise jars with lids in good condition (try fast food restaurants)

Cup of coarse-grained gravel

4 cups of washed beach sand

5 small aquatic plants (approximately 3 to 4 inches or 10 cm in height)

Freshwater fantailed guppy
2 water snails
5-in or 12-cm square of fine-mesh screening material
Soda bottle cap
2 small cactus plants (approximately 3 or 4 inches or 10 cm in height)
Chameleon, lizard, skink, horned toad, or colored lizard
2 small dried twigs (no longer than three-fourths of the length of the mayonnaise jars)
Small water turtle or frog
Several small ferns, mosses, lichens, or liverworts

What Will We Discuss?

What does environment mean to you?
What are some things that live around you?
What are some environments that you know about?
What is ecology and why is it important for us to know about it?
What is an aquarium?
What is a terrarium?

What Must I Know?

All environments contain geological features, weather, climate, and living things (plants and animals), and all interrelate and affect each other. This is what the study of ecology is all about.

Students should learn how to set up and closely observe an aquarium—a water home for plants and animals—and different kinds of terrariums—land homes for plants and animals.

The following activities help students set up and observe three habitats closely for an extended period of time, and allow them to study the ecology of each environment.

PROCESSES

Part I   What Are the Parts of a Water Habitat (Aquarium) and How Do They Interrelate With Each Other?

What Will Students Do?

This activity is to be done in groups of four students. Each group might be responsible for only one habitat.

1. Obtain the materials listed.
2. Clean the mayonnaise jar thoroughly with soap and water and rinse it well.
3. Wash two cups of sand to be placed in the jar. Spread this over the bottom of the jar.
4. Fill the jar with water and let it stand for several days before adding plants and fish.
5. Place the aquatic plants as suggested by the pet shop owner.
6. Place the guppy and snails in the jar.
7. Now cover the jar with the screening material.

Food jar aquarium   Soda bottle aquarium

A simpler soda bottle aquarium[7] can be made as an alternative. This type of aquarium is also pictured in the diagram.

Inferring	*Why do you think it is necessary to clean the jar before using it?*
Inferring	*Why should the sand be washed before putting it in the jar?*
Inferring	*What would dirty water do to the gills of the fish?*
Inferring	*Why must the gills of the fish be kept clean?*
Inferring	*How do fish breathe?*
Hypothesizing	*How could you find out?*
Inferring	*Why do you think the water was allowed to stand for several days before the fish were placed in the aquarium?*
Inferring	*What does our health department add to water that might be injurious to fish?*
Inferring	*Why were the snails added to the water?*

What Must I Know?   The snails will eat the small green algae (the slimy plants that collect on the sides of the tank).

Hypothesizing	*Why were plants added to the aquarium?*
Inferring	*What would the fish eat in nature?*
	Would your guppy live if it did not feed on anything? Why?
Inferring	*What do plants make that the fish can use?*
Inferring	*What does the fish make that the plants can use?*

What Must I Know?   Plants make oxygen and food, and the fish produce carbon dioxide and waste products. The aquarium is not perfectly balanced, so food must be added from time to time for the fish.

[7]For free excellent directions on how to make simple aquariums and terrariums from empty soda bottles, send your request to Bottle Biology Project, University of Wisconsin-Madison, 1630 Linden Drive, Madison, Wis. 53706 (608)263-5645.

Part II What Are the Parts of a Dry-land Habitat (Desert Terrarium) and How Do They Interrelate With Each Other?

1. Obtain one of the large, commercial-sized mayonnaise jars.
2. Clean the mayonnaise jar and lid with soap and water and rinse them well.
3. Dry off the jar and screw the lid on.
4. With the jar on the floor, pound holes into the lid by using a hammer to nail through the lid.
5. Place the jar on its side.
6. Spread the remaining two cups of sand onto the bottom of the jar.
7. Place the small bottle cap filled with water, the cactus, and one twig into the jar.
8. Place a lizard, skink, chameleon, or horned toad in the jar.
9. Cover the jar with the punctured lid.
10. Water the terrarium once every two to three weeks only if dry. Place the jar so that it receives direct sun every day.

Note: Tape two pencils to the sides of the terrarium, as shown in the diagram, to keep the jar from rolling. A simple terrarium can also be made from an empty soda bottle, as shown in the diagram.

Food jar terrarium

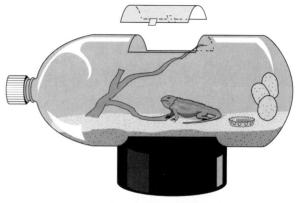

Soda bottle desert terrarium

11. Feed the animals live mealworms. These can be obtained from a local pet shop.
12. Keep the bottle cap filled with water.

Part III   What Are the Parts of a Wet-land (Bog) Terrarium and How Do They Interrelate With Each Other?

1. Clean one of the mayonnaise jars and its lid with soap and water and rinse them well.
2. Dry off the jar and screw the lid on.
3. With the jar on the floor, pound holes into the lid by using a hammer to drive a nail through the lid.
4. Place the jar on its side and tape wood strips to the bottom to keep the jar from rolling.

Lid

Gravel

Tape wood strips

Bog terrarium

5. Spread the gravel out on the bottom of the jar so it will be concentrated toward the back of the jar, as shown in the diagram.
6. Place the ferns, mosses, lichens, and liverworts over the gravel.
7. Pour some water in the jar. (Do not put in so much that it covers the back portion of the arrangement.)
8. Place a dried twig in the jar.
9. Place a small turtle or frog in the jar.
10. Cover the jar with the punctured lid.
11. Feed the turtle or frog insects or turtle food every other day.
12. Place the terrarium in an area where light is weak.

Comparing and Observing

How does the life found in the aquarium differ from that found in the desert and/or bog terrariums?

Observing

What kinds of conditions do the fish, turtle, frog, or lizard have to have to survive in their particular habitats?

Observing   *What kinds of conditions do the bog plants require to grow well?*

Observing   *What kinds of food do the fish, the lizards, or the turtle eat?*

Hypothesizing   *What do you think would happen to the turtle if you left it in the desert habitat, or to the lizard if you put it in the bog habitat?*

How Will Students Use or Apply What They Discover?

1. *What other kinds of environments or habitats could you make through the use of mayonnaise jars or soda bottles?*
2. *What does the "environment" have to do with the kinds of organisms found in it?*
3. *What are some organisms that are able to live in many different environments?*
4. *What might happen to a fern plant if it were transplanted to a desert region?*
5. *What might happen to a penguin if it were taken to live in a desert?*
6. *What might happen to a human being if he or she were suddenly moved into an arctic region?*
7. *What statements can you make about the effect of environment on a living thing?*
8. Complete the following chart for the aquarium or terrarium habitat you constructed, describing the food, water, shelter, etc., you provided for the organisms living there.

Name of Habitat:

Habitat living conditions	Description
Food	
Shelter	
Air	
Temperature	
Climate	
Water	
Others	

How Do Animals and Humans Affect Their Water Environments? (Water Pollution) (3–8)

What Concepts Might Students Discover?

All living things need water, and a steady supply of clean water is vital. People make their water impure or unclean (pollute) by adding such human and factory wastes as human sewage, nitrates from overuse of chemical fertilizers, pesticides and herbicides, phosphates from detergents, etc.

Because of the interrelationships between all parts of a habitat or environment, water pollution affects all living things.

What Will We Need?   See each individual activity for needed materials. *Note:* Some items may be used from previous activities.

Part I   What Are Some Effects of Water Pollution?

What Must I Know?   Humans often do things, sometimes unknowingly, that result in water pollution. This water pollution can affect water environments in ways that are extremely detrimental to the organisms that inhabit the water.

You can do this activity as a teacher demonstration or group activity. For each group of four students, four jars should be set up, by you and/or by designated student helpers, two weeks in advance of conducting this activity.

1. Fill four containers (see "What Will We Need" that follows) ⅓ full with aged tap water, ½" (4 cm) full of pond soil or aquarium gravel, and then fill the rest of the jar with pond water and algae.
2. Add 1 teaspoon of plant fertilizer to each jar, stir well, and loosely screw on the jar covers.
3. Put the jars near the window in good, indirect light, or under a strong artificial light.
4. Label the jars A, B, C, D.

What Will We Need?   4 quart or 2-liter clear containers (plastic soda bottles, food jars with covers, etc.)

Tap water aged for 3 to 4 days

Water with algae and other aquatic microorganisms from a freshwater aquarium or a pond

Soil and/or gravel from an aquarium or pond

Measuring cup and spoon

Plant fertilizer

Liquid laundry detergent (not green)

Motor oil

Vinegar

Hand lens

PROCESSES

What Will Students Do?

1. Each group has four jars that were set up two weeks ago. They contain pond water, algae, pond soil or aquarium gravel, and fertilizer.

Observing and Recording   On your recording sheet, describe how each jar looks. Make sure to use your hand lens.

Recording Observations

T G

Date	Observers/Recorders Names_____	
Jar	Observation before additive	Observation after additive
A		
B		
C		
D		

Hypothesizing   *Why do you think pond water, pond soil, and fertilizer were put into the jars?*

Hypothesizing   *Why do you think the jars were given a lot of indirect light?*

2. Add 2 tablespoons of detergent to jar A; enough motor oil to cover the surface of jar B; and ¼ to ½ cup (250 mL) of vinegar to jar C. Jar D will not have any additive and will be the "control." See the following diagram.

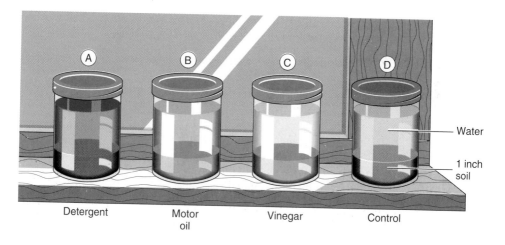

Hypothesizing

3. Loosely recover the jars and return them to the light as before. *What do you think might happen in each of the jars?*

Observing and Recording   Observe and record your observations two to three times a week.

Summarizing   After four weeks, summarize your observations.

Inferring   *Why do you think jars A, B, and C went through such changes?*

How Will Students Use or Apply What They Discover?	1. *How might you set up activities to try to reverse the effects of the pollutants used in jars A, B, and C?* 2. *Where in everyday life do we see the effects of water pollution like in jars A, B, and C?* 3. *How could they be prevented?*

Part II   How Can We Try to Reverse the Effects of an Oil Spill?

What Will We Need?

Feathers	Pan
Water	Motor oil
4 hard-boiled eggs	Dishwashing liquid
Paper towel	Turkey baster
Very large rubber band	Paper plate

What Will We Discuss?

How difficult do you think it is to clean up an oil spill?
How do you think it could be done?
What is the most effective way(s) to clean up an oil spill?
What devastating effects does an oil spill have on the environment?

What Must I Know?

Oil spills adversely affect land and water plants and animals directly by coating them with oil, often leading to their deaths. In addition, an oil spill affects future plant and animal life by destroying eggs and interfering with plant reproduction.

   Sometimes, the procedures used to reverse oil spills can interfere with environmental interrelationships, especially when chemicals are used.

What Will Students Do?

Fill a pan half full of water, cover the water surface with motor oil, and use it for the following parts of the activity.

Feathers in Oil/Water

1. Leave feathers in the oil/water mix for several minutes.
2. Remove the feathers.

Hypothesizing

How do you think we might remove oil from the feathers?
Try wiping the feathers with paper towels.

Observing

Did wiping with towels remove all the oil?
Try cleaning the feathers with dishwashing liquid.

Comparing
Designing an Investigation

Which method of cleaning the oil off the feathers was better?
What other ways might we try to remove the oil from feathers? Try them.

Eggs in Oil/Water

1. Put four hard-boiled eggs (with shells on) into the oil/water mix and then remove one egg at a time after each of these intervals: 15 minutes, 30 minutes, 60 minutes, 120 minutes.

Observing What happens to the eggs?

2. Try removing the oil from the eggs with the methods you used for the feathers.

3. After cleaning the oil off the eggs, crack and remove the shells.

Observing *Did the oil get into the inside of the egg that was in the oil for 15 minutes? The one for 30 minutes? The one for 60 minutes? The one for 120 minutes?*

Recording Record your findings.

If oil did get into the insides of the egg, can it be removed?

Removing or Containing Oil

Hypothesizing *Using the following materials, how might you remove or keep the oil from spreading: paper towel, diswashing liquid, turkey baster, large rubber band?*

1. Lay a paper towel on the surface of the oil and let it stay for 3 minutes. Remove the paper towel and put it on the paper plate.

Observing *What do you see happening to the paper towel and oil?*

2. Add more motor oil, if needed, and spread a very large rubber band on the top of the oil.

Observing *What happens to the oil?*

3. Using the turkey baster, try to suck up the oil.

Observing *What happens to the oil?*

4. Squeeze the oil back into the pan of water. Add several drops of dishwashing liquid.

Observing *What happens to the oil?*

Inferring *Which method was best for removing the oil?*

Inferring *Which method was best for keeping the oil together in one place?*

A Paper towel soaking up oil

B Rubber band containing oil

C Turkey baster removing oil

D Dishwasher liquid breaking up oil

How Will Students Use or Apply What They Discover?	1. *What possible problems and adverse effects might result when chemicals are used to remove oil from animals in a real oil spill?* 2. *How might an oil spill way up in Alaska affect people in the continental United States?* 3. Sometimes oil spills are purposely set on fire. *What adverse effects might this have on the environment?*

Part III   How Might We Reverse the Effects of Water Polluted by Phosphates?

What Concepts Might Students Discover?	Phosphates, from fertilizers and certain detergents, run off the land and pollute water ecosystems.
What Must I Know?	Phosphates can cause an overgrowth of algae, which may kill other living things by depleting the amount of oxygen in the water and adding too much carbon dioxide. These phosphate pollutants can be cleaned using calcium.
What Will We Need?	Jar A from Part I containing pond water, algae, fertilizer, and dishwashing detergent. 2 clear jars Spoon Lime (from plant nursery)
What Will We Discuss?	Refresh students about how the pond water with algae was altered by adding fertilizer and dishwashing liquid. The chemicals overstimulated algae growth. Now ask: *How do the adverse effects of too much fertilizer and detergents affect water environments?* *Can phosphate pollution of water be reversed?* *How might we do this?*
What Will Students Do? *Observing* *Hypothesizing*	1. Divide the pond water from jar A equally into two jars marked 1 and 2. 2. In jar 1, add 1 teaspoon of lime, stir well, and mark it 1—Lime Added. Mark the other jar 2—Control, and do nothing to it. *What change do you see in either jar?* *What do you think the white substance might be on the bottom of jar 1?*
How Will Students Use or Apply What They Discover?	1. *If overfertilization can cause phosphate pollution, how can we safely fertilize our lawns and gardens?* 2. *How might composting food and organic scraps (like grass clippings and leaves) help with both waste and fertilizing problems?* 3. *How might we wisely use detergents to prevent phosphate pollution?*

What Is Air Pollution, What Causes It, How Does It Affect the Environment, and How Might It Be Prevented and Reversed? (K–8)

What Concepts Might Students Discover?

Fuels made from things that were once living (wood, coal, oil, etc.) are called **fossil fuels.**

When fossil fuels burn, they give off a sooty material called carbon, as well as several invisible chemicals.

Particles and chemicals in the air are called **pollutants,** and they can cause health and other environmental problems.

When smoke particles and the moisture in the air are trapped near the earth's surface, they combine to form **smog** (*smoke* + *fog*).

Statutes, monuments, buildings, and other things in our outdoor environment are slowly being destroyed by pollution in our atmosphere.

We can sample our air to find air pollutants.

Cigarette and cigar smoking are dangerous for the smoker and pollute the air for others.

Gas wastes from automobiles and factories react with water in the air to form acids. These acids fall to earth in some form of precipitation (snow, rain, hail, sleet, mist, or fog) and in this form are called **acid rain.**

Acid rain is harmful to plants, animals, physical features of the environment, and people.

There are things that can be done to prevent and reverse air pollution.

What Will We Need?

See each individual activity for needed materials. *Note:* Some items may be used from previous activities.

Part I   What Are Air Pollutants and How Are They Formed?

What Will We Need?

Paraffin candle	Clothespin
Aluminum foil pan	Masking tape
Matches	

What Must I Know?

If students are too young or not yet responsible enough to use open flame, you should perform this activity.

PROCESSES

What Will Students (or Teacher) Do?
Hypothesizing
Observing

1. Light a candle. Tell students you are going to use a clothespin to hold the pan over the candle for 20 seconds.
   What do you think might happen to the pan?
   What do you see on the underside of the pan?

2. Rub the black substance with the sticky side of a piece of masking tape.

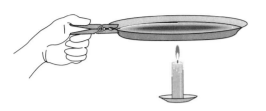

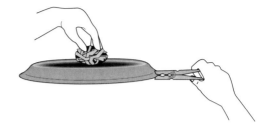

Inferring
Comparing

What do you think the black substance is?
Where have you seen material like this before?
Where might we find evidences of burned materials in our environment?

Part II   How Can We Find Air Pollutants in Our Environment?

What Will We Need?

Funnels	Jars
While filter paper	Hand lens
Litmus or hydrion paper	

What Must I Know?

This activity works best on a rainy day.

What Will Students Do?

G

1. Put a funnel in a jar and line the funnel with white filter paper.
2. On a rainy day, place several jars with funnels in different spots on your school grounds.
3. When the rain stops, collect the jars and remove the filter papers.
4. Open the filter papers and allow them to dry.
5. While the filter papers dry, test the rain water in each jar with litmus or hydrion paper.

Hypothesizing Why do you think we are going to test the water with litmus or hydrion paper? What do you think we are looking for?

Inferring If the pH of the rain water tested is above 7, what might that mean?

Communicating Make a list of all the other pH values obtained by other members of the class.

Comparing Compare the findings.

Inferring If differences are found, how might they be explained?

Hypothesizing How might findings differ if samples were gathered from different places in your community such as bus stops, an airport, factories, etc.?

6. Now that the filter paper has dried, use a hand lens to look at it.

pH paper

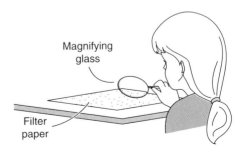

Magnifying
glass

Filter
paper

Observing   *What do you see on the filter paper?*
Inferring   *Where do you think the residue came from?*
Hypothesizing *If you repeat this activity on a dry day, do you think you might collect more or less particles than on a rainy day? Why?*
Try it and compare.

Part III   How Can We Find Out If Vehicles Pollute the Air?

What Must I Know?

Safety is a prime factor in this activity. You, a parent, and/or your school custodian should work together with students to conduct this activity. When doing the actual data collection, have the driver start the vehicle with the car in park and with the hand brake on. A second adult should stay with students to make sure they are away from the vehicle at all times!

What Will We Need?

Yard- or meterstick	Index cards
Jar of petroleum jelly	Thumbtacks
Hand lens	Cars, school buses

What Will Students (and Adults) Do?

1. Make a chart on the back of each index card that contains the following information:

   Date of testing
   Vehicle manufacturer
   Model
   Year of vehicle
   Last tune-up date
   Name of tester

2. Fill in this information *before* testing each vehicle.
3. Then lightly smear petroleum jelly on each card to be used.
4. With thumbtacks, attach the card, petroleum jelly side up, to a yard- or meterstick as shown in the diagram.
5. Go outside, accompanied by adults, to a parking lot. While one adult starts a vehicle, you and a second adult hold the yardstick 6″ (15 cm) from the vehicle's exhaust pipe for 1 minute. *Caution:* Stay as far away from the vehicle as possible while still holding the card 6″ from the exhaust.
6. Return to the classroom and use a hand lens to examine the index cards.

Observing   *What kinds of solid particles did you find?*
Inferring   *Do you think there might be pollutants you cannot see?*
Hypothesizing *How might a Vehicle Inspection Station give you additional information about vehicle pollutants?*
Hypothesizing *Which vehicles might give off more pollutants than others?*
Hypothesizing *Why is it important to have vehicles inspected and tuned-up regularly?*

Inferring   After you and your classmates have tested many buses and cars, try to answer these questions:

Does the age of the car affect the amount of pollutants it emits?
Does the size of the car and engine make any difference?
Does the kind of gasoline used (regular leaded, regular unleaded, high-test unleaded, etc.) affect the amount of pollutants?
Does the brand of gasoline make any difference?

Part IV   What Is Smog and How Is It Formed?

What Must I Know? Because of the use of matches and open flame, decide if you or your students will conduct the following activity.

What Will We Need?

Large clear jar or bowl	Aluminum foil
5 to 6 ice cubes	Rope
Matches	Warm water

What Will Students (or Teacher) Do?

1. Put some warm water in a jar or bowl, swish it around, and pour it out, but leave some water droplets inside to make the air moist in the bowl.
2. With a match, light a piece of rope and drop it into the jar or bowl.
3. *Quickly* cover the top of the bowl tightly with aluminum foil.
4. Place ice cubes on top of foil as shown in the diagram.

Observing   *What happens to the air inside the bowl when the temperature drops because of the ice cubes?*

Observing   *How do you know?* (Smoke rises.)

Inferring   *Why is this phenomenon called* smog? (smoke + fog)

Inferring   *In real life, what things are like the burning rope* (vehicle and factory emissions), *ice cubes* (cold air inversion), *and warm water* (water vapor in the air) *that contribute to atmospheric smog?*

Part V   How Does Cigarette and Cigar Smoking Add to Our Pollution?

What Must I Know? This activity should be conducted by you, and preferably done outdoors.

What Will We Need?

Cotton	Turkey baster
Cigarette	Matches

**What Will the
Teacher Do?**

1. Put a piece of cotton into the glass part of the turkey baster.
2. Light a cigarette and insert the unlit end into the baster's spout, as shown in the diagram.
3. Compress and release the rubber bulb until the cigarette is completely finished smoking.

Observing

    What did you notice coming out of the cigarette?

4. Remove the cotton from the baster.

Observing

    What do you see on the cotton?

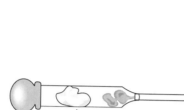

Cotton

Stained
cotton

Hypothesizing

If we did this activity with a filtered cigarette, would the results be any different?

*Designing an
Investigation*

How would you go about testing your ideas?

How would you test to see if pollutants go into the air as well as into the cotton?

Inferring

Do smokers pollute the air as well as harm themselves?

Part VI   How Do Smokers Pollute the Air?

What Will We Need:

Index cards   Petroleum jelly
Twine

**What Will Students
Do?**

1. Prepare several index cards by covering them with a thin layer of petroleum jelly as you did for Part III.
2. Hang a card by a string from the ceiling in a room where:
   A. people frequently smoke cigarettes.
   B. people rarely smoke cigarettes.
   C. people never smoke cigarettes.
3. Make sure that the kind of room is written on the back of each card.
4. After 1 week, collect all the cards and bring them back to the classroom.

Observing
Comparing

Using a hand lens, what do you see on each card?

What differences do you see between cards from smoking and non-smoking rooms?

Inferring
Inferring

What do you think might cause the difference?

What does this activity tell you about how smoking cigarettes might affect others as well as smokers themselves?

Part VII How Does Air Pollution Affect the Physical Things in an Environment?

What Will We Need?

Small squares of wood   2 plastic garbage bags
Various colors and types of paint (water-based, oil-based, acrylic, etc.)

What Must I Know?

After the garbage bags are filled full of painted squares, ask one of the school bus drivers to fill the bags with bus exhaust.

What Will Students (and Bus Driver) Do?

1. Paint the small wooden squares with a variety of paints and colors.
2. After the squares are dry, on the back of each square record the colors and types of paint used.
3. Place half of the squares of wood inside one large plastic garbage bag and half in a second garbage bag.
4. Have the school bus driver fill the garbage bags with bus exhaust and fasten the bags quickly and tightly to retain the fumes.
5. At the end of one week, check the pieces of wood in one garbage bag.

Observing
What changes, if any, do you see?

6. At the end of two weeks, check the pieces of wood in the other garbage bag.

Observing
What changes, if any, do you see?

Comparing
How do the pieces of wood that were in the bag for one week compare to those that were in for two weeks?
What were the changes?

Inferring
What caused this to happen?

Applying
Based on your observations in this activity, why do you think we have to paint our buildings so often?

Part VIII How Might Pollutants in the Air Affect the Growth of Plants?

What Will We Need?

2 spray bottles   Water
Vinegar   Bean seedlings
Soil   Clean milk cartons

What Must I Know?

Either use bean seedlings from previous activities, or plant new ones a week or two before this activity.

What Will Students Do?

1. Get two clean milk cartons, punch small holes in the bottom, fill the cartons with potting soil, and put four to six bean seedlings in each carton.
2. Label one milk carton "Water," and the other one "Vinegar."
3. Fill one spray bottle with water and label it "Water." Fill the other bottle with vinegar and label it "Vinegar."
4. Put both milk cartons in direct sunlight. Spray the "Water" milk carton with water and the "Vinegar" milk carton with vinegar.
5. Repeat step 4 daily for 1 week, making sure to spray each milk carton with its corresponding sprayer, as shown in the diagram.

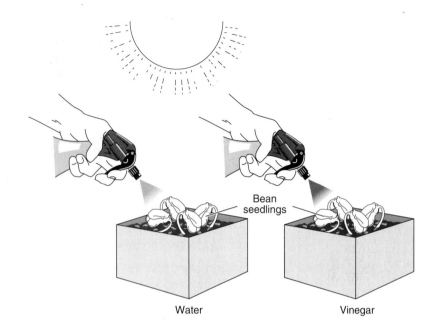

Water   Vinegar

Observing   What happened to the bean seedlings in the milk carton sprayed with water?

Observing   What happened to the bean seedlings in the milk carton sprayed with vinegar?

Hypothesizing   From your experiences with previous activities, how could you find out the pH of the soils?

Inferring   How is this activity related to the effects of acid rain on plants?

Part IX   What Are Some Ways to Clean Polluted Air?

What Will We Need?   Large metal bucket   Plant sprayer with water
Disposable vacuum bag full of dust

What Must I Know?   Discuss how some industries have soot and dust rising from them all the time. Some industries burn garbage too. They must use pollution-control devices to clean the air in their smokestacks. One of these devices is the **scrubber,** which removes dirt particles and most of the poisonous sulfur and nitrogen oxides from the soot. A scrubber sprays a liquid on the pollutants, trapping them, then carries the pollutants away before they can go out of the smokestack. The liquid and pollutants form a thick liquid or paste known as **sludge.** This is then treated with a chemical and made into non-polluting cakes. Researchers are trying to turn these cakes into building materials to recycle them.

Do this activity yourself, outdoors, and make sure students are up-wind to avoid the dust.

What Will the Teacher Do?

1. Go out to a spot on the playground that is far away from the school building.
2. Slowly pour dust from the vacuum bag into the bucket. As the dust falls, squirt it with water.

Observing   *What happens to the dust?*

Inferring   *How is the wet dust, called sludge, now less polluting than when it was dry?*

Hypothesizing   *How do you think this process is used to keep soot and dust from escaping factory smokestacks?*

Hypothesizing   *What do you think can be done with the dried sludge?*

Part X   What Can We Do to Control Air Pollution in Our Environment?

What Will We Need?   Low-level light houseplants: spider plants, golden pothos, azaleas, mums, Dracaenas, bamboo, Fiscus

What Must I Know?   NASA and other scientific groups have found that houseplants are excellent filters of indoor pollution because they take in pollutants and trap them in the soil. The plants listed in What Will We Need are especially suited for this purpose and are ideal for schools. They tolerate low light conditions, dryness, and periods of neglect, such as vacation periods. For a free fact sheet about plants that have proved to be effective air cleaners, send a self-addressed stamped envelope to The Foliage for Clean Air Council, 4405 N. Washington St., Falls Church, Va. 22046.

What Will Students Do?

What are some ways we could clean the air in our classroom?

1. Discuss ways of cutting indoor air pollution and recommend growing plants if students do not suggest it.
2. *How can we find out which plants are best for cleaning indoor air and how to care for these plants?*
3. Make a list of the most desirable air-cleaning plants and collect as many as you can by buying them, asking students to bring in their own from home, asking local plant nurseries to donate plants and/or cuttings, etc.
4. Find the best places in the classroom for each particular plant.

How Will Students Use or Apply What They Discover?

1. *If a minimum of one 12"-tall plant is recommended for every 100 square feet of floor surface, how many air-cleaning plants should we have in our classroom?*
2. *What other kinds of air-cleaning plants might we consider for our classroom?*
3. *Why would mixing fish-tank-filter charcoal with the soil in our air-cleaning plants help filter out air pollutants?*
4. *Why is NASA so interested in researching plants that filter air pollutants?*

References—Ecology and Environment

Teacher and older students: Philip Neal, *Acid Rain—Considering Conservation* (London: B. T. Batsford, 1991, distributed by Trafalgar Square, North Pumfret, Vermont 05053); Linda Penn, *Plant Ecology* (New York: Watts, 1987); and Michael Bright, *Pollution and Wildlife* (New York: Watts, 1987).

Younger students: Tilde Michaels, *At the Frog Pond* (Philadelphia, Pa.: 1989); Adrian Forsyth, *Journey Through a Tropical Jungle* (New York: Simon and Schuster, 1989); and Thomas Wiewandt, *The Hidden Life of the Desert* (New York: Crown, 1990).

SECTION 4

Guided Discovery Science Activities for Special Needs Students

The activities in this section are designed for special needs students. You either have, or soon will have, such students in your classroom. There are over 8 million youngsters in schools today (1 in 10) with some form of special need. Public Law 94-142 calls for mainstreaming special needs students into the regular classroom whenever practical. Whether the special need is a sensory, mental, emotional, or social one, it is important for you to find ways to include students having special needs into your class.

Guided discovery science activities can provide a sense of achievement to special needs students who seldom enjoy such success in school. It is not easy to accomplish the task of providing individualized science activities; however, by becoming aware of your students' special qualities and the possible ways of helping each student best function within his or her limitations, you will begin to individualize your science program.

Labels often get in the way of looking at individuals. "Special" individuals differ signifi-

cantly in what they need to succeed in the world. They have, as Norris Haring says, "special needs, a phrase that is becoming more and more popular as a description of these members of our society."[1]

Guided discovery science activities are presented for students with the following special needs:

1. Sensory challenged
2. Developmentally delayed (previously referred to as educable mentally handicapped)
3. Visual perception problems
4. Emotional special needs
5. Deaf or hearing impaired

Although other special needs and disabilities are prevalent and important, the activities in this section are limited to these five categories of students, because they are the most frequently encountered by classroom teachers.

[1]Norris G. Haring and Linda McCormick, eds., *Exceptional Children and Youth,* 5th ed. (Columbus, Ohio: Merrill Publishing Co., 1990), 1.

These activities are not meant to be exhaustive, but are suggestions of ways to meet the special needs of your students in science. As you practice using the activities, you will get to know your students better and will be able to find more ways to provide successful science/learning activities for them. You can modify the guided discovery science activities in Section 5 for this purpose, as well. Learning to be more sensitive to students with special needs will help you respond more sensitively to all of your students. The unexpected gain to you of focusing upon "special needs" students will be to see all your students as special.

The format used in this section is the Quickie Starter format used in Sections 1 through 3. This less formal format was selected because special needs students generally respond better when activities are hands-on, concrete, and more open-ended. This format also allows the teacher to have more flexibility in modifying the activities to meet the special needs of individual students. As you become more confident with science activities for special needs students, you will be able to modify some of the activities in Sections 1 through 3, as well.

STUDENTS WITH SPECIAL SENSORY NEEDS

How Can Blind or Visually Impaired Children Learn about Magnets? (K–8)

Materials
           Assorted magnets, common objects attracted and not attracted by magnets (paper clips, rubber bands, plastic and metal zippers, pencils, paper, wire, and so on, 2 shallow boxes (*Note*: Avoid sharp or pointed objects.)

Opening
Questions
           What are magnets?
           What things do they pick up?

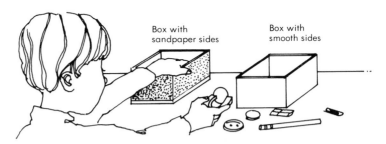

Box with sandpaper sides

Box with smooth sides

Some Possible
Activities
           Have students handle the magnets and describe their shapes (bar, disc-shaped, horseshoe, U-shaped, cylindrical, and so on). Ask:
           How will you know if a magnet picks up (attracts) an object?
           Students will readily discern by touching the magnet that something was attracted to it if an object "sticks" to the magnet. Ask students to name the objects on the table and then test to find out which objects are

attracted by the magnet. They can sort objects tested by the magnet into two shallow boxes. One box with smooth sides can be for objects attracted by magnets. Sandpaper glued to another box for objects not attracted by magnets can facilitate tactile sorting. Once students understand the sorting system, they can verify the contents of both boxes by themselves and even test new objects.

In What Ways Can the Blind or Visually Impaired Identify Objects in the Environment? (K–8)

Materials

Masks to cover eyes, pairs of noisemakers (rattles, party horns, "clickers," and so on)

Opening Question

Can you find your partner if you cannot see him or her? How?

Some Possible Activities

Take a group of sighted and blind or visually impaired students outside your classroom to a relatively open (free of trees, shrubs, or other obstacles) lawn area. Have other students or adults keep students from moving outside the area as they engage in this activity. Play a game in which students assume the roles of limited-vision animals. Have students pair up. Instruct sighted students to wear masks over their eyes. Have one student in each pair be a predator, the other prey. Give each prey one of a variety of noisemakers (clickers, party horns, and so on). At a signal from you, prey try to find the other prey who have the same noisemakers. Predators, in the meantime, try to capture the noisy prey.

After the game, have students all sit quietly and listen to the environmental sounds. Ask:
Which sounds can you identify?
Which sounds are made by the same source?
In which direction do you hear the various sounds?
Which sound do you like the best? Why?
Which sound do you like the least? Why?
How do you think a particular sound was made?

For more information about this and other life science activities for the visually impaired student, see Larry Malone and Linda DeLucchi, "Life Science for Visually Impaired Students," *Science and Children* 16, no. 5 (February 1979): 29–31.

What Are Some Ways for Blind or Visually Impaired Students to Find Out About Their Bodies? (K–8)

Materials

Stethoscopes, braille-faced clocks

Opening Question

Does your heart beat faster when you lie down, stand up, or run?

Some Possible Activities

After raising the question with blind or visually impaired students, give simple instructions on how to use the equipment and carry out the activity. Introduce the term *variable* and explain that the variable they will investigate is body position and how it affects their heart rate. Have students learn to use the stethoscope to listen to their heartbeats while counting the beats per minute on the braille-faced clock. An adult or older student can help younger students with the numbers. After students have taken and recorded their heart rates in lying, standing, and running situations, discuss the results. Help them to see the effect of body position on heart rate. You can extend the activity by asking further questions. Ask:

What other variables could be investigated in this activity?

What effect would the following things have on heart rate: age, amount of movement, time of day, drinking soda pop, smoking, and so on?

Encourage students to explore the variables without giving them specific directions on how to do it.

How Can Blind Students "See" and Compare Polluted Water? (4–8)

Materials

4 jars of water containing different pollutants, light sensor (available on Federal Quota from the American Printing House for the Blind, P. O. Box 6085, Louisville, Ky. 40206), light source (sunlight, filmstrip projector, and so on)

Opening Question

How can you use your sense of hearing to find out which jars contain the most polluted water?

Some Possible Activities

Prepare four jars of water with varying amounts of pollutants (soil, debris, egg shells, and so on). Introduce and demonstrate to the students the light sensor device. This device produces an auditory signal of varying pitch and volume as a result of its exposure to different intensities of light. Set up the four jars of various pollutants with a light source behind them, as shown in the diagram.

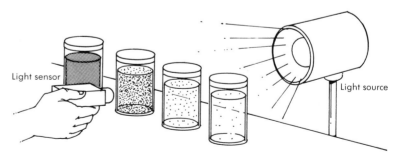

Light sensor

Light source

At close range, have students point the light sensor directly at each jar, as shown in the diagram. A beeping sound will be emitted; the greater the amount of light coming into the sensor, the higher and more frequent the beeping. Students will discover that the fewer pollutants in each jar, the greater the amount of light coming through the jar, and, therefore, the more shrill and rapid the beep from the sensor. More pollutants result in much less light coming through the jar to the sensor, and thus a slower and lower pitched beep occurs. *Note*: For an excellent expanded description of using the light sensor with blind students, see Frank L. Franks and LaRhea Sanford, "Using the Light Sensor to Introduce Laboratory Science," *Science and Children* 13, no. 6 (March 1976): 48–49.

STUDENTS WITH DEVELOPMENTAL DELAYS

How Can Students With Developmental Delays Learn to Develop a Thermic Sense (Sense of Temperature)? (K–8)

Materials
Several metal bowls, water of varying temperatures

Opening Questions
How do hot things feel?
How do cold things feel?

Some Possible Activities
Fill several metal bowls with varying temperatures of water, from ice cold to very warm. *Caution*: Do not use water hot enough to scald or injure any student. Let the water sit in the bowls for a few minutes, then have the students feel the *outside* of the bowls. Ask:
Which bowl feels cold?
Which one feels warm?
Which one feels hot?
If a student does not know the difference, try the following procedure. Say:
This bowl feels cold.
Does it make your hand cold?
This bowl is hot.
Is your hand hot?
Where else have you felt hot and cold things?
Relate this activity to everyday experiences by comparing it to holding a glass of iced drink, a cup of hot soup, and so on.

Hot

Cold

Point out the dangers of hot and cold. Ask:
Why should we use a potholder if we are holding something hot from the oven or stove?
Why should you wear a coat and gloves when it is very cold outside?
Where are very hot things in our homes and school?
Have pictures of ovens, stoves, radiators, etc. Ask:
Which things are very cold in our school?
Take students to the cafeteria and have them show you (or you show them) the refrigerator or freezer.

How Can Students With Developmental Delays Learn the Concept of Weight? (K–8)

Materials

Small blocks of wood of the same size, but made of different kinds of woods, such as balsa (model airplane wood), oak, pine, or mahogany

Opening Question

Which of these blocks do you think would be the heaviest? Lightest?

Some Possible Activities

Ask students to explain what it means when people say something is heavy. Have them use whatever words will help them to develop the concept, as long as the words do not connote misconceptions. They might say, "It's harder to lift." If they have difficulty with the concept of heavy and light, help them to develop it. Now give them the blocks. Ask:
Do you think they all weigh the same?
Which one seems the heaviest? Lightest?
Have students feel the blocks and place them in order from heaviest to lightest. Label the heaviest block with an *H* and use an *L* for the lightest one. Ask students what things in the classroom are heavy and light. Place an H and L on the objects selected (Some examples of heavy might be: desks, cabinets, people; examples of light: paper, pencils, paper clips; and so on.) Explain why it is dangerous to lift very heavy things.

How Can Students With Developmental Delays Learn to Discriminate Tastes? (K–8)

Materials

Box of cotton swabs; bottles of solutions of common liquids that are salty, sweet, sour, bitter, acid, and neutral

Opening Questions

How many of you would like to play a game?
Are you a good detective?

Some Possible Activities

Tell students they are going to play a detective game to try to find out what is in the bottles you have. Caution them never to taste anything they do not know about. Ask why they should not do this, and explain the dangers of poisons. Tell students that none of the things in the bottles is poisonous and that they are things they taste every day.

Give each student his or her own swab and explain why this is necessary (to prevent spreading germs, colds, other diseases, and so on). Give all students a sample of something sweet, such as syrup. Ask: *What kind of taste is this?*

Have them agree that it is sweet and, if possible, have them identify the source. Throw the cotton swabs away and give each student a second one. This time use a sour solution. Repeat the identification procedure and orally introduce the word *sour;* if appropriate for the group, write the word on the chalkboard. Repeat this procedure for all of the solutions.

Ask students what kinds of foods they eat that are salty, sweet, sour, bitter, acid, or neutral. Have them cut out pictures from magazines for each category. Discuss their lunch in school and visit the cafeteria to observe some foods. Have students note which category each food is in.

Note: For older or less developmentally delayed students, you can show them that different places on the tongue react more strongly to certain tastes. Touch solutions to these four sensation areas of the tongue.

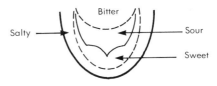

How Can Students With Developmental Delays Learn to Recognize Common Odors? (K–8)

Materials

Common strong-smelling substances in jars, such as onion, perfume, alcohol, pepper, cinnamon, peppermint, and so on

Opening Question

Who can tell us what this odor (smell) is?

Some Possible Activities

Have students smell a familiar substance (peppermint) by holding the appropriate jar at least one foot from their noses and fanning the odor towards them. (This avoids overwhelming the student with the odor and teaches him or her a safe way to smell unknown substances that might injure the student's sensitive nose.) *Note:* At first, to help students learn to recognize various odors, present the smell in the appropriately labeled jar, allowing students to see the material. Then ask students to discriminate among various odors while blindfolded.

For students who are more advanced, wait to label the jars after students identify the odors. Use both oral and written words for the names of odors, as appropriate. Have students identify odors in their homes, school, and outdoors. Have them cut pictures from magazines of common strong-smelling substances and label them, such as gasoline, flowers, paint, smoke, etc. Have students identify odors they like and dislike. Stress that some odors are dangerous, such as gas and smoke.

STUDENTS WITH VISUAL PERCEPTION PROBLEMS[2]

Observing Properties of Leaves (K–3)

Materials	Variety of leaves (maple, oak, elm, birch, etc.)
Opening Question	*What do you notice about the shape of this leaf?*
Some Possible Activities	Have each student look at a maple leaf. Ask:
	What is this?
	Where do you think it came from?
	How many points does it have?
	What color is it?
	How many large lines (veins) are there coming from the stem?

[2]The author is indebted to the following article and others in the *Science and Children* issue devoted to Science for the Handicapped: Marlene Thier, "Utilizing Science Experiences for Developing Perception Skills," *Science and Children* 13, no. 6 (March 1976): 39–40.

Let the student experience the leaf through sensory activities, that is, feeling it with the hand, rubbing it against the cheek, smelling it, and crushing it.

What does the smell make you think of?

How else would you describe the leaf?

Ask students to think of other properties. Introduce the word *property* for students to use when referring to the leaf's attributes. Introduce other species of leaves. Ask:

How are the leaves alike? Different?

What properties are the same?

What properties are different?

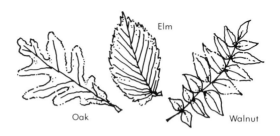

Comparing Properties of Shells or Buttons and Classifying Them (K–3)

Materials	Assortment of shells or buttons
Some Possible Activities	Give each student a handful of shells or buttons. Ask: *How are these things alike?* *How are they different?* Group them together by the same property. *Which properties might you use?*

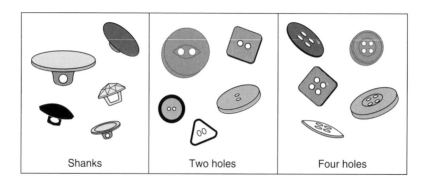

Allow students to group the objects. Ask:
How can you group the buttons according to a different property?
Note: In this activity, students not only make visual discriminations, but also act upon them.

Using Plants to Teach Visual Sequencing (K–3)

Materials

Milk cartons, soil, pea seeds, chart paper

Some Possible Activities

Have each student plant a pea seed in a milk carton. Make certain students keep the soil moist and that they have a certain time each day for observing the plant and recording their observations. As soon as germination takes place and plants break through the soil, set up a chart for students to use to record the growth of each of their plants. Have them mark on the chart any changes that take place each day. They can measure plant height by using gummed paper to show the various stages of growth over a six-week period, as shown in the diagram.

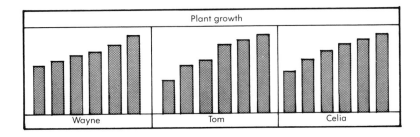

When working with younger children, plant an additional seed each week so students can see plants ranging in growth from one to six weeks. This will help them with visual sequencing. They begin by observing a natural phenomenon, then learn to record small changes over a period of time and in a sequenced progression—something they need to know.

Learning Relative Position and Motion (K–6)[3]

Materials

Mr. O for each student, white pipe cleaners, gummed white dots, blocks

Some Possible Activities

Students with perceptual problems usually have poor directionality concepts. "Mr. O," from the SCIS Relative Position and Motion unit, can help these students to learn position in space, relative position in the environment, directionality, and figure-ground relationships.

[3]For a detailed description of Mr. O, see Robert Karplus et. al., *Relative Position and Motion* (Level 4), Teacher's Guide SCIS (Chicago: Rand McNally & Co., 1978), pp. 29–39.

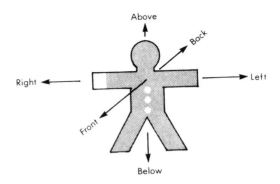

Show students Mr. O. Tell them that he sees things only from his point of view. Cut out a Mr. O for each student. For younger children, after introducing Mr. O, play a game to familiarize them with his parts and to introduce words for directions in relation to him, as shown on the Mr. O sketch. Younger children can also hang Mr. O around their necks while you point out the following things:

Mr. O's right hand is white.

Put a white pipe cleaner around your right hand.

Mr. O has three white buttons on the front of him.

Put three white gummed paper dots on the front of you.

Now ask the students to place a block to the right of Mr. O. Ask:

Where is the block in relation to Mr. O?

Where is the block in relation to you?

Is it near or far?

Do the same with the left side, in front of, in back of, above, and below, using only one variable at a time. Gradually build to more than one variable.

Once the student begins to understand this use of Mr. O, take Mr. O from around the child's neck and turn Mr. O to face him or her. Ask:

Where is Mr. O's hand now in relation to yours?

Place the block to the right, left, front, and back of Mr. O, and ask the student to report the position, relative first to Mr. O, and then to himself or herself.

Note: Students become aware of needed changes in describing directionality from a non-ego-centered frame. They begin to develop direction-giving capabilities through awareness of relative position in space and figure-ground relationships. Students with visual perception problems have great difficulty with this task and need the systematic help shown here.

Outside-the-Classroom Walk to Develop Visual Scrutiny and Analysis (K–6)

Materials   Small envelopes or plastic bags, paper, pencils

Some Possible Activities

Select a site outside your classroom where you and your students can take a walk. Before going, instruct students to observe, record, or collect the following:

■ Task cards (3″ × 5″ index cards can be used to write down what the students will look for.)
■ Samples of five different-colored natural objects that have fallen to the ground (Caution students not to pick anything from living organisms.)
■ Places (to be listed on their recording sheets) where they saw
  a. three different colors on the same plant
  b. five different shades of any one color (green, for instance) along the path
  c. six different textures on living organisms
  d. as many different colors as they can find
■ Samples of evidence that animals have inhabited the environment
■ Samples of dead insects
■ Samples of evidence that people have been in the area
■ Samples of different kinds of seeds in the area
■ Other samples that are applicable to your outdoor site

Have the students place their samples in small envelopes, plastic bags, or other suitable containers. With younger children or children who have severe visual perception problems, it is best to use one of the activities at a time, so they focus on one variable in their environment and filter out distractions. The activities also are progressive, moving from observing many different plants (looking at plants and finding colors) to finding the same variable on only one plant (how many different colors on one plant). Later, in the classroom discussions, help students describe their samples and share them with their classmates. Further activities in pasting samples on paper, writing descriptive words for each object, and talking about their findings aid students who have visual perception problems in developing needed skills for further exploration of their environments and for reading, writing, and spelling.

EMOTIONALLY HANDICAPPED CHILDREN

Learning About Our Environment by Touching (K–6)

Materials

Paper, crayons, chalk, soft pencils, aluminum foil

Opening Question

How can our fingertips give us different kinds of information than can our eyes?

Some Possible Activities

Direct contact with and the understanding and mastery of everyday living experiences under a sensitive teacher's guidance can produce an extensive and exciting learning environment for the emotionally handicapped child. One such activity can be a tactile experience. Take your students (with assistance from parents) on a walk around the school. Have students select surfaces and use the suggested materials to do rubbings of those surfaces. In urban areas, they can do rubbings of sidewalks, manhole covers, grates, signs, and fences. The rubbings can be used to create texture panels and are also effective when they are individually matted and mounted. You might also attempt to get your students to talk about how the objects felt, whether they were rough, smooth, soft, hard, wet, or dry.

You can find many more activities for emotionally handicapped children in the following practical book: "An Outdoor Education Guide for Urban Teachers of the Emotionally Handicapped," Proceedings presented by the State University of New York State Education Department Division for Handicapped Children, and the Division of Health, Physical Education and Recreation, in co-sponsorship with State University College of Arts and Science at Plattsburgh and Clinton, Essex, Warren, and Washington Counties BOCES, Special Study Institute, funded through PL 91-230 (June 1974).

Learning About Our Environment by Listening and Moving (K–6)

Materials

A walking trip in the community

Opening Questions

What people-made sights and sounds can you identify?
How can you use your body to reproduce these sights and sounds?

Some Possible Activities

Sitting or working in a confined space for long periods of time (a desk and chair, for instance) creates static learning experiences. This is especially true for emotionally handicapped children. They need to stretch and expand their bodies and minds, probably more than other children. These students can also begin to feel the same freedom of movement outside as they would experience in a gymnasium. Take students into the community and ask them to identify the following people-made sights and sounds.

Taxi cabs   Cars
Fire alarms   Buses
Airplanes   Helicopters
Ambulances   Fire engines
Construction machines Trucks
Motorcycles   Air hammers

Ask:
What are the sounds of each vehicle?
How can you use your body to show the intensity and rhythm of each vehicle?
How is the fire engine sound different from the ambulance sound?
Show the differences with your movements.
Would you move in a fast, slow, or jerky way if you sounded like an airplane? A dump truck?
How are car horn sounds different? Make the sounds.
How do various sounds make you feel? Happy? Sad?
Show how you feel by your movements.
Imitate with your body a vehicle starting and stopping.

DEAF AND HEARING IMPAIRED CHILDREN

There are many benefits for hearing impaired students in the regular classroom; however, they should be about the same chronological and mental age, and there must be an attempt to individualize instruction.

All of the guided discovery science activities described for other special needs students are applicable for the deaf and hearing impaired, as are the guided discovery activities in Sections 1 through 3, when you use the following minimal adaptations of your regular classroom procedure.

1. Seat students where they can see your lip movements easily. Avoid having them face bright lights or windows.

2. Speak naturally, in complete grammatical sentences. Do not over-emphasize lip movements or slow your rate of speech. Do not speak too loudly, especially if the student is wearing a hearing aid.

3. Avoid visual distractions such as excessive make-up, jewelry, or clothes that might draw attention away from your lips.

4. Do not stand with your back to a window or bright light source. This throws your face in a shadow and makes speech reading difficult.

5. Try not to move around the room while speaking, or to talk while writing on the board. If possible, use an overhead projector, which allows you to speak and write while still maintaining eye contact with students.

6. During class discussions, encourage deaf and hearing impaired students to face the speaker. Allow them to move around the room, if necessary, to get a better view.

7. In some cases, a manual interpreter might be assigned to a student. Allow the interpreter and student to select the most favorable seating arrangements. The manual interpreter should interpret everything said in the classroom as precisely as possible. The interpreter may also be asked to interpret the student's oral or signed responses to the teacher and class. Interpreters are not tutors or classroom aides, but rather professional personnel who facilitate classroom communication.

8. When possible, write assignments and directions on the chalkboard or distribute photocopied directions to the class. If assignments are given orally, you might ask a hearing student to take notes for a deaf or hearing impaired student.

9. Ask deaf or hearing impaired students to repeat or explain class material to make sure they have understood it. Embarrassed by their special needs, deaf or hearing impaired students might learn to nod affirmatively when asked if they understood, even though they may not have understood the instructions at all.

10. If a student has a hearing aid, familiarize yourself with its operation and ask the student or the student's special teacher to demonstrate it to the class. The student should assume responsibility for the care of the aid.

11. Maintain close contact with the other professional personnel who have responsibility for the student's education. If possible, regularly exchange visits with the special class teacher or therapist to observe the student in other educational settings.[4]

[4]Adapted from Haring and McCormick, *Exceptional Children and Youth*, 318–319.

SECTION 5

Piagetian Types of Guided Discovery Activities

Outlined in this section are a few special Piagetian types of activities to help you see how Piaget's theory may be applied to different elementary-school levels. These activities are given headings of specific operational cognitive abilities, such as classification and conservation, to show you how to take an operation and devise activities to involve students in these processes. Many of the other activities in this section are also Piagetian in design, but are not organized around specific operations as are these Piagetian activities.

In conducting these activities, you should realize that perhaps one-half or more of your students may not perform the tasks correctly. If this happens, the students who did not achieve these specified goals need further involvement with similar experiences. By no means should these students be told that they failed. Piaget stated that the students themselves will know when they perform the tasks correctly. He believed, for example, that appropriate reinforcements for physical knowledge can come only from the objects themselves.

These activities are not included specifically to teach a particular operation, but to demonstrate how students might be involved in physical experiences relative to their approximate development. Each student will get out of the activity what he or she is cognitively ready to assimilate. The activity questions are provided to illustrate how you might interact with students to determine what they are focusing on and how they reason. Practice in the use of these activities should sensitize you to students, listening closely to them and learning how to intervene with questions to cause them to think about what they are doing. Learning this style of teaching should help you better develop students' thinking processes and science knowledge.

Class Inclusion: Do Children Know That Subclasses Are Included in a Major Class? (Ages 6–7)

1. Show several pictures of plants and animals. Ask:
   How many plants are there?
   How many animals are there?
   Are there more animals than plants?
   Are there more living things than just the animals?
2. Invite students to collect pictures of animals that move fast and slow, for example, a fly or a rabbit and a turtle or a snail. Try to get more examples of fast animals than of slow ones. Place the pictures of the animals on the tackboard. Ask:

Which moves faster?

What are all the pictures of?
How many slow animals are there?
Are there more fast animals than slow animals?

Discussion

Class inclusion is a very important operational ability. It is a good indicator that a student is developing representational thought, which is essential in using such symbols as letters of the alphabet. A student who has difficulty with class inclusion probably has problems with reading.

Spatial Relations (Ages 6–7)

1. Give students pieces of straw and ask them to construct a diamond shape as best they can. Their construction should be accurate, with the points at the top and bottom.

2. Ask students to duplicate the following designs:

Discussion

If students cannot duplicate the correct shape or size of an object, they do not have good geometrical spatial conceptualization.

Try having students read words with letter combinations (words) such as "park," "bath," "dad," "quick," "man," and "woman." If students do not perform well on the spatial tasks and the letter discrimination, involve them with activities found in the Elementary Science Unit: Attribute Games and Problems, Webster Division, McGraw-Hill, 1974, or Material Objects Unit SCIS II, Rand McNally, 1976. Both of these units contain activities to help students discriminate better and develop class inclusion concepts.

Ordering: Placing Objects in Order (Ages 6–8)

Give students 10 cards showing different animals. Each drawing should be larger than the previous one. Tell them: "Place the animals in order, starting with the smallest. Number the animals in order." Have students check their answers with those of other students. Note if they seem to put things in order mainly by trial and error, or if they have some organized procedure for ordering. If students do this task well, you may want to give them 4 more pictures that fit in between the 10 original animal sizes. Have students place these four pictures where they think they belong.

Discussion

If students perform this task well, they probably are capable of performing similar ordering tasks relatively well.

Associativity: Realize That It Does Not Matter How You Arrange Things, the Number or Area Will Remain the Same (Ages 6–8)

1. Place 10 counters, blocks, or buttons in a straight line and have students count them. Then move the counters to form a circle. Ask: *Are there more, fewer, or the same number of counters now as there were when they were in a straight line?*
   How would you prove you are right?
   Note that this activity is also related to conservation of substance and number, but here you are trying to find out if students know that reorganizing the counters does not change their number.
2. Invite students to count counters in two directions—for example, from left to right and then right to left—to see if they get the same number. Have them count two groups of objects, for example, a group of three and a group of two, and then count all of the objects together to see what number they get. Then have them count first

the group of two and then the group of three to see what number they get.

Discussion

If students have mastered associativity, they will realize that three and two equals five objects, and that two and three equals five objects as well.

One-to-One Correspondence (Ages 6–8)

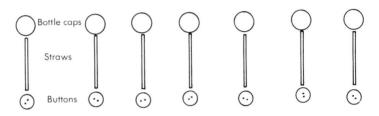

Bottle caps

Straws

Buttons

Obtain five bottles caps, buttons, straws, or any other type of marker that you want to use. Have students line up the buttons in a row, then ask them to line up the bottle caps directly across from the buttons. Ask:
Are there more, fewer, or the same number of buttons as bottle caps?
Then move the buttons so they are spread out, but do not move the bottle caps. Ask:
Are there now more, fewer, or the same number of buttons as bottle caps? Why?
If students think there are more buttons than bottle caps, ask:
Please count them. Now what do you think?
If they still do not realize that each button corresponds with each bottle cap, have them connect each pair by placing a straw between them. Ask:
Are there more, fewer, or the same number of buttons as bottle caps now?

Discussion

If students still cannot conceptualize one-to-one correspondence, have them place the materials in a box to be collected. Repeat this activity several times, using different markers, until the students do correspond.

Coordinating Systems—Horizontal and Vertical (Ages 6–12)

This is an exercise in reproducing and estimating the length of a line. Give students a meterstick, compass, string, small triangle that has a right angle, rulers, and paper strips. Ask:

What is the length of each line?
Can you draw a picture just like this one?

Remove the picture from students' vision. Tell them that they may refer to it again if necessary.

Discussion
Children of ages 6 to 7 usually use no measurement.
Ages 7 to 8 measure the length of the lines.
Ages 9 to 10 superimpose the right-angled triangle to measure angle.
Ages 10 to 12 begin to use measurement to accurately reproduce the angle.

Students unable to coordinate the horizontal and vertical as presented here may have problems in geometry and in understanding certain science concepts, particularly geology and astronomy.

Conservation by Length (Ages 7–8)

Take two strips of paper of the same length. Ask:
Is this strip just as long as the other?
Cut up one of the strips and combine the pieces as shown on the right side of the diagram. Tell the students that you have a rabbit that is going to move along the two paper paths. Ask:
Would the rabbit make just as many hops on each path, or would it make more or less hops on one of the paths?
Why do you think so?
If students think the uncut paper is longer, they do not conserve length and will have difficulty understanding units and measurement.

Conservation of Length (Ages 7–8)

Draw the following diagrams of the snakes. Ask:

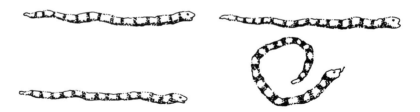

What do you notice about the lengths of the snakes on the left?
In the diagram on the right, is the coiled snake longer, shorter, or the same length as the other snake?
Take a rope and lay it out flat. Then coil it. Ask:

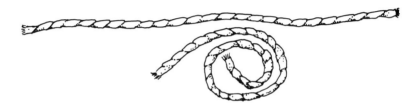

Is the rope now longer, shorter, or the same length as when it was straight?

Discussion
Ask students to measure the rope. Even if students measure the rope, however, if they do not conserve length, they will still think the curled rope is shorter.

Conservation of Area (Ages 7–8)

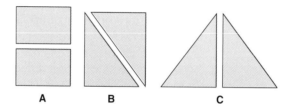

Cut a full piece of paper into two rectangles (A). Ask:
Do these two pieces of paper cover the same amount of table?
Cut another full piece of paper diagonally, as shown in B, and arrange the pieces as shown in C. Ask:

Do the cut pieces of paper in C cover as much area as the paper in A?
Why do you think your answer is correct?
How could you prove your answer is right?

Discussion

If students suggest that C covers as much as A, this indicates they conserve area. They should then suggest that if the two pieces of paper in C were combined together as in A, they would be the same. This indicates that students are capable of reversing and establishing logical necessity. This also means that they reason; since nothing has been taken away, the paper covers as much. Reversibility and logical necessity are intrinsically involved in conservation tasks.

Ascending a Class Hierarchy (Ages 7–8)

Prepare 10 pictures of animals. Include some birds, fish, and mammals. Ask:

Please group these animals any way you want. How did you group them? Why did you group them that way?
Which of these groups were fish?
Which of these groups were birds?
Which of these groups were mammals?
Is there some way we can place all of the pictures in one group?
What would the group be? Why?
Are birds animals?
Are fish animals?
Are hairy animals (mammals) animals?

Discussion

If students realize on their own that all of these things are animals, and that the subgroups of birds, fish, and mammals can be grouped under animals, they are able to ascend a classification hierarchy.

Time—Understanding Sequence and Duration (Ages 7–8)

Time requires the coordination of motions. Set up the apparatus shown in the diagram.

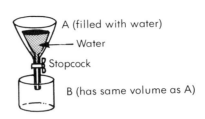

A (filled with water)
— Water
Stopcock
B (has same volume as A)

Give students a sheet with several sketches of the apparatus, but show no water in either the top or bottom container. Have students note, during your demonstration of the apparatus, the water level in A. Let a little water flow from A to B. Ask:
Please draw where the water is now in A and B.
Repeat this six or seven times, varying the amount of water you let through the stopcock. Ask:
Please number your drawings in order in the margin.
You determine whether the order is correct. Ask:
Please cut off the numbers indicating the order.
Now cut the paper into strips so that each separate drawing is on its own strip.
Shuffle the drawings and then arrange them in their proper order.
When water A was at (pick a certain level), where was the level of B?
In which drawing did the amount in B equal the amount in A?
Did the time it took for the water to leave A equal the time it took to fill B?
Does the liquid take as much time to go from this level of A to this (point to one level change) as it does to go from here to here in B?

Discussion

Time is a relatively complex thing for primary school children to learn. To comprehend it, they have to understand that motion is involved with time. They also have to understand that in time, things follow a sequence, have a duration, occur in a succession, and are simultaneous. When water goes from A to B, all of these things occur.

Furthermore, to read time on a clock, children must be able to order, know numbers, and know what units are. They also must understand that numbers and units may be repetitive and follow in succession in linear as well as a circular manner, as in seconds, minutes, and hours on a clock. Teachers may be fooled into thinking some young children understand time if they can read a digital clock. This may not be the case. All the children may be doing is mouthing a sequence of numbers without really understanding their relationship to the duration of time. After all, 4:30 has quite a different meaning from 430, although the same numbers are used.

Spatial Relations (Ages 7–8)

Ask students to draw a mountain and place trees on it.

Discussion

If they have good spatial relations, students will draw the trees perpendicular to the mountain.

Constructing a Set Containing a Single Element (Ages 7–9)

Show six triangles. Let five triangles be all red and the sixth one yellow. On the back of the yellow one, make an X. Show the students both sides of the triangles. Then place all of the triangles color side up with no markings. Ask:

Which one of these objects is entirely different from the others?
What makes it different?
How could we group all of these objects?

Discussion

If students can identify the triangle with the X on the back as being different, they are able to establish a set as having a single element.

Making All-and-Some Relationships: Realize That Some Objects (Those in the Subset) Are Also Included in the Group Referring to All of Them (the Set) (Ages 7–9)

Cut triangular, circular, and rectangular shapes out of colored paper. Ask:
Are all of the squares red?
What color are all of the circles?
What color are the triangles?
Are all of the triangles red triangles?
Invite students to group all of the triangles together. Ask:
Are all of these things triangles?
Are some of these triangles green?
Are all of these triangles green?

Discussion

Some students in this age group have difficulty differentiating between *some* and *all* because they do not class-include well. The advent of this ability indicates that the students are beginning to develop the class-inclusion operation. They still may not, however, understand that all dogs are also animals, for example.

Reordering (Ages 8–10)

Cut 10 straws so they vary from short to tall. Prepare 10 pictures of trees ordered in a similar way. Ask students to order the straws from short to tall and place the trees in the opposite order (tall to short) next to them. One study found that only about 10 percent of second graders can do this.

Discussion
Reordering means the ability to order in different ways, foward as well as backward. This activity requires students to order in each way, as well as to do one-to-one correspondence. For example, for every large tree, there is a small straw.

Spatial Reasoning (Ages 8–10)

Show a tipped jar and tell students the jar is supposed to be one-half filled with water. Ask:
Please draw how you think the water will look in the jar.
After they have finished their drawings, take a jar and fill it one-half full of water. Have students check their drawings with what they see.

Discussion
Most students in this age group do not have a good concept of coordinates. Therefore, they will draw the water oriented to the sides or bottom of the jar rather than to the table it is sitting on.

Unit Repetition or Iteration (Ages 7–10)

In this exercise, students measure a large area by using a small unit over and over again. Cut a rectangle as shown in A. Then cut a smaller triangle as shown in B, with one side 2 cm long. Ask:

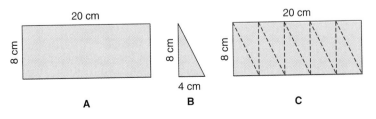

How would you use triangle B to determine the area in A?
Why do you think your response is correct?

Discussion
If students achieve the task, this shows they can use units to determine area by superimposition. In this case, they superimpose the small triangle on the larger rectangle and then total the number of triangles used. More advanced students may be able to determine the area mathematically.

Ordering by Weight (Ages 9–10)

Soil   Salt   Sand   Water   Baking soda   Rice   Flour

Obtain several (six or more) different metal containers of the same volume, or use medicine vials or empty 35-mm film containers of the same volume, and fill them with different kinds of materials, such as salt, sand, soil, water, baking soda, rice, flour, and so on. Ask:
Please place these things in order by weight.
Now weigh the containers and order them. Ask:
How good were your estimations?

Discussion
Students may have difficulty ordering by weight for as long as two years after they are able to order by length or height.

Concept of a Null Class (Ages 9–11)

Cut 12 triangular, circular, and rectangular shapes from colored paper. Draw and paste pictures of plants, animals, or houses on 9 of them. Leave the other 3 papers blank. Ask:
Please group these things any way you wish.
Now place the objects in only two groups: blank and non-blank.

Discussion
Students up to about age 11 have difficulty realizing the existence of a null set. This may be attributed to their concrete thinking; a null set requires abstract reasoning.

Descending a Classification Hierarchy (Ages 9–11)

Ensure that students know the characteristics of mammals. Prepare 10 pictures of mammals, birds, and other animals. Include several dogs, as well as other mammals, and ducks, as well as other birds. Ask:

Please group these animals any way you like. What groups did you form?
How many mammals did you get?
How many birds did you get?
Is there any way you can divide your mammal group? How?
Is there any way you can change your bird group?
What group of animals do dogs belong to?
What group of animals do ducks belong to?
What group do mammals belong to?
What group do birds belong to?
Ask the students to mix together all of the pictures again, make a few groups, and then use these groups to make some subgroups. Ask:
How did you group your animals?
Why did you group them that way?

Discussion
If students go from animals, to mammals and birds, and then to dogs and ducks, they have indicated they can descend a classification hierarchy.

Conservation of Weight (Ages 9–12)

Obtain some clay. Have students prepare two round balls that weigh the same. They can check the weight of the balls by using a balance. Ask:

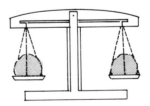

Please make one of your clay balls into a hamburger shape. Will this piece of clay now weigh more, less, or the same amount as before?
How can you tell?
Have students weigh the clay and find out. Ask:
What did you find out?
Why do you think it weighs the same?
Is there some rule you can give about changing the shapes of things and what happens to their weight?

Discussion

If students state that spreading things out changes the thickness but also increases the area covered, and that there is no loss in weight, they are giving a compensation type of justification. This means that the weight of the increased area compensates for the loss in weight in the thick area. If they state that when you roll the ball up again, it will weigh the same, they are demonstrating reversibility. This means they can reverse their thought processes. Both reversibility and compensatory reasoning characterize concrete-operational thought.

Conservation of Displacement Volume (Ages 11 and older)

Obtain a graduated cylinder or use a jar. Fill it three-fourths full of water. Take a cube of clay and wrap a string around it so it can be lowered into the water. Have students place a rubber band around the container to estimate where the water will be when the clay is lowered into it. Lower the clay very slowly. Ask:

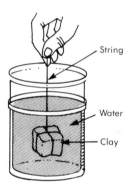

String

Water

Clay

How good was your estimate?
Move your rubber band so the top of it marks where the water is. Now take your clay out of the water. Cut the clay in half. Tie each half with string. Estimate where you think the water will be now when you lower these two halves into the water. Use a marking pencil to mark where you think it will be. Do not move your rubber band. Slowly lower your two pieces of clay into the water. Ask:
What did you discover?
Can you give a rule for what you discovered?

Discussion

If students explain that the volume of the two halves of clay is the same as the volume of the whole piece and that they displace the same amount of water, they are conserving displacement volume. Here it is the volume, and what it displaces, that is important, not the weight.

Law of Buoyancy—Flotation (Ages 11 and older)

An object will float if its weight is less than that of an equal volume of water. The object will float above the water line when its weight displaces an equal amount of weight in water.

Tell students that 1 mL of pure water weighs 1 gram. Have them make a small clay boat, or make one out of a small milk carton, and then weigh the boat. Tell students you have a rectangular barge that weighs 500 grams and has a volume of 1000 mL. Ask:
How much water would the barge displace?
How far would it sink into the water? Why?

Discussion

If they suggest that it would sink about halfway in the water, they probably understand the concept of buoyancy and flotation. A further check would be to give them problems where odd numbers of weights and volumes are used for the barge. They should then estimate how many grams and milliliters of water their boat will displace. Have them obtain a large graduated cylinder or calibrated beaker and fill it three-fourths full of water, record the amount of water in the container, and then place the boat they made into the water. Ask:
How far does the ship sink in the water?
Add a 10-gram weight and determine how high the water moves. Ask:
How high would it move with a 20-gram weight? Why?

Conservation of Internal Volume (Ages 10–12)

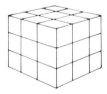

Present students with 27 small cubes arranged to form a large cube. Tell the students that each cube represents a hollow room and all of the cubes have open doors between them. Inside the hollow rooms is a butterfly that flies from room to room. These modular rooms can be rearranged by the owner.

One day the owner has to move the modules to a different lot. She has to arrange the modules in a different way. Ask:

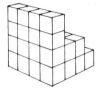

Is there just as much, more, or less space inside now for the butterfly to fly? Why?
How would you prove it?
How could you use mathematics to prove it?

Discussion
If students indicate that no rooms have been taken away or added, so there is the same amount of interior, they are using logical necessity to justify their answer. A more sophisticated response showing higher cognitive abilities would be to demonstrate that the number of rooms is the same.

Spatial Relations (Ages 11–12)

This activity is meant to discover if the student realizes that the angle at which light or an object hits a surface or another object will be reflected back at the same angle. In scientific terms, the angle of incidence equals the angle of reflection.

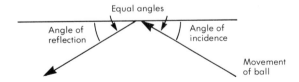

Give students a marble or Ping-Pong ball. Invite them to hit it against a wall. Ask:
What kind of rule can you discover about how the ball bounces back?

Discussion
If they come up with an explanation that the ball seems to bounce from the wall as it goes in, they probably understand the rule.

Continuous Divisibility (Related to Concept of Infinity) (Ages 11–12)

Ask students to divide a circle through its center as many times as possible, and see how long students keep at it. Ask:
How long could you keep on dividing the circle?

Discussion

If they come up with the idea that this could go on and on and on, they have grasped the basic concept of infinity and realize that some things, as in nature, can be continuously divided; for example, the measurement of temperature, time, motion, and change are infinitely divisible. Consider whether students understand the continuous possibility of divisibility. Ask:

How long could you go on dividing a rod or line?

Spatial Relations (Ages 11 and older)

Show one surface of a cube. Ask:

How many edges cannot be seen?

Discussion

Most students have difficulty perceiving an object from different viewpoints. Many adults have difficulty with this problem, too, and suggest numbers other than eight.

LIST OF APPENDICES

FIFTY YEARS OF ELEMENTARY-SCHOOL SCIENCE: A GUIDED TOUR

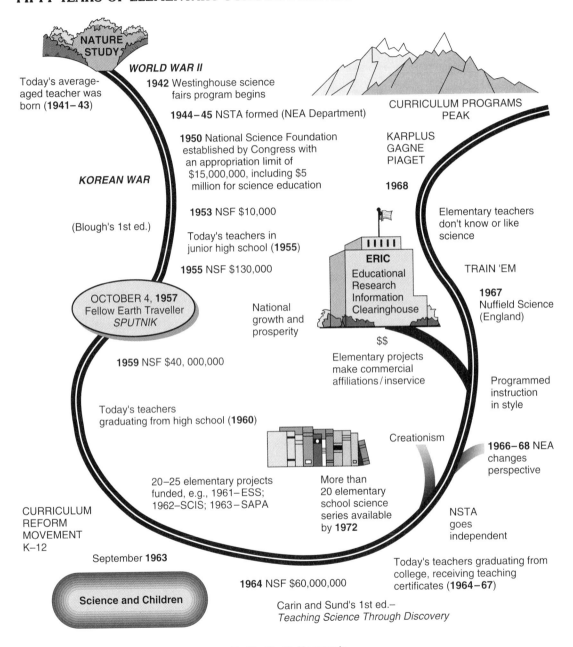

NATURE STUDY

WORLD WAR II

Today's average-aged teacher was born (**1941–43**)

1942 Westinghouse science fairs program begins

1944–45 NSTA formed (NEA Department)

CURRICULUM PROGRAMS PEAK

1950 National Science Foundation established by Congress with an appropriation limit of $15,000,000, including $5 million for science education

KARPLUS
GAGNE
PIAGET

1968

KOREAN WAR

(Blough's 1st ed.)

1953 NSF $10,000

Today's teachers in junior high school (**1955**)

1955 NSF $130,000

Elementary teachers don't know or like science

TRAIN 'EM

OCTOBER 4, **1957**
Fellow Earth Traveller
SPUTNIK

National growth and prosperity

ERIC
Educational Research Information Clearinghouse

1967
Nuffield Science (England)

$$

1959 NSF $40, 000,000

Elementary projects make commercial affiliations / inservice

Programmed instruction in style

Today's teachers graduating from high school (**1960**)

Creationism

1966–68 NEA changes perspective

CURRICULUM REFORM MOVEMENT K–12

20–25 elementary projects funded, e.g., 1961–ESS; 1962–SCIS; 1963–SAPA

More than 20 elementary school science series available by **1972**

NSTA goes independent

September **1963**

Today's teachers graduating from college, receiving teaching certificates (**1964–67**)

Science and Children

1964 NSF $60,000,000

Carin and Sund's 1st ed.–
Teaching Science Through Discovery

By Phyllis R. Marcuccio

Source: Modified from Phyllis R. Marcuccio, "Forty-Five Years of Elementary School Science: A Guided Tour." Reproduced with permission by *Science and Children* 24, no. 4 (January 1987): 12–14. Copyright 1987 by the National Science Teachers Association, 1742 Connecticut Avenue, N.W., Washington, DC 20009.

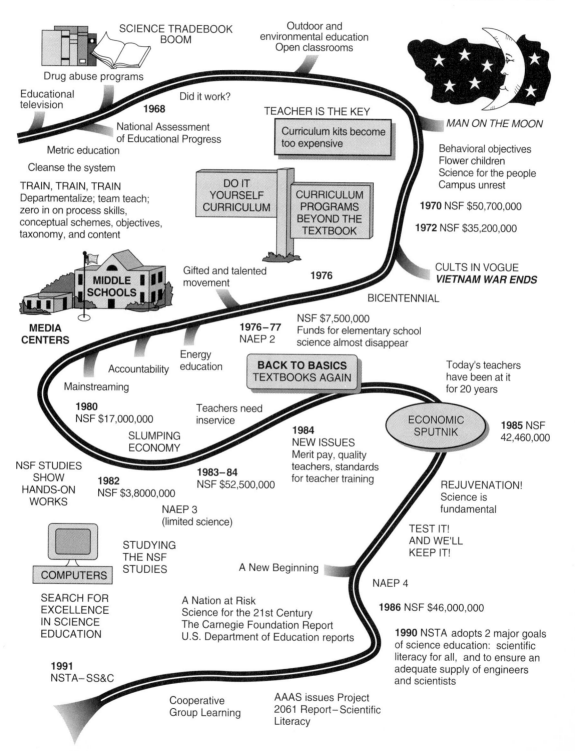

SCIENCE TRADEBOOK BOOM

Outdoor and environmental education
Open classrooms

Drug abuse programs

Educational television

Did it work?

1968

MAN ON THE MOON

National Assessment of Educational Progress

Metric education

Cleanse the system

TRAIN, TRAIN, TRAIN
Departmentalize; team teach; zero in on process skills, conceptual schemes, objectives, taxonomy, and content

TEACHER IS THE KEY

Curriculum kits become too expensive

Behavioral objectives
Flower children
Science for the people
Campus unrest

1970 NSF $50,700,000

1972 NSF $35,200,000

DO IT YOURSELF CURRICULUM

CURRICULUM PROGRAMS BEYOND THE TEXTBOOK

MIDDLE SCHOOLS

Gifted and talented movement

1976

CULTS IN VOGUE
VIETNAM WAR ENDS

BICENTENNIAL

MEDIA CENTERS

Accountability

Energy education

Mainstreaming

NSF $7,500,000
Funds for elementary school science almost disappear

1976–77
NAEP 2

BACK TO BASICS
TEXTBOOKS AGAIN

Today's teachers have been at it for 20 years

1980
NSF $17,000,000

Teachers need inservice

SLUMPING ECONOMY

1984
NEW ISSUES
Merit pay, quality teachers, standards for teacher training

ECONOMIC SPUTNIK

1985 NSF 42,460,000

NSF STUDIES SHOW HANDS-ON WORKS

1982
NSF $3,8000,000

1983–84
NSF $52,500,000

REJUVENATION!
Science is fundamental

NAEP 3
(limited science)

TEST IT!
AND WE'LL KEEP IT!

COMPUTERS

STUDYING THE NSF STUDIES

A New Beginning

NAEP 4

SEARCH FOR EXCELLENCE IN SCIENCE EDUCATION

A Nation at Risk
Science for the 21st Century
The Carnegie Foundation Report
U.S. Department of Education reports

1986 NSF $46,000,000

1991
NSTA–SS&C

1990 NSTA adopts 2 major goals of science education: scientific literacy for all, and to ensure an adequate supply of engineers and scientists

Cooperative Group Learning

AAAS issues Project 2061 Report–Scientific Literacy

/// NOTES ON THE GUIDED TOUR

Notable achievements

- Elementary-school science now has a niche in elementary schools: it is accepted as important for all students; it is integrated with other subjects in the curriculum; and it is supported by principals and other administrators.
- There is a new breed of elementary science specialists.
- Hands-on teaching is giving rise to new ideas and techniques and is fostering creativity, intuition, and problem-solving skills. (Hands-on teachers are "guides" rather than "tellers.") The popularity of hands-on teaching is also creating a need for more inservice training and for more science centers and labs.
- Nonschool settings, such as outdoor education centers and museums, have increased their support, often introducing subject matter that includes issues of social concern like pollution, ecology, and energy education.
- Teaching tools—books, software, television, and other audiovisual equipment—have become better in a number of ways: they are more accurate, attractive in format, and sensitive to social issues like affirmative action.
- Up-to-date research in science education is readily available through ERIC (Educational Research Information Clearinghouse).
- Recent and projected certification programs subject teachers to more rigorous standards.
- Studies and testing, forums and conferences exist to deal specifically with the concerns of elementary science.
- Teacher education institutions now train for junior high certification, and they have redesigned the way in which preservice teachers are taught to teach elementary science.
- The business and industry communities, concerned about the interrelationships among science, technology, and society, have sought a role in science education. Organizations like the American Chemical Society, the National Acad-

emy of Science, and the American Association for the Advancement of Science have also cooperated to forward the cause of science education.
- SI metric measure has been generally adopted.
- A teamwork approach to curriculum building now exists among teachers, scientists, administrators, community, and government.
- There are established pockets of commitment to science, and programs have been developed to point out excellent science teaching throughout the country.

Familiar road signs

- Surges in National Science Foundation funding
- Efforts following crisis situations
- The continuing presence of textbooks
- National Assessment of Educational Progress reports
- Calls for new curricula
- Calls for inservice programs

Some remaining problems

- Teachers continue to be educated in the same way.
- No comprehensive, agreed-on scope and sequence has been established.
- Progress depends on funds from the National Science Foundation.
- The pool of students interested in science is shrinking—nearly half the current ninth-grade class in urban high schools will not even graduate, let alone seek science-related careers.
- Despite millions of dollars spent on curriculum studies, teachers still depend on textbooks.
- The United States continues to lag behind other countries in the amount of science being taught to children.
- The best science students are not attracted to science teaching careers.
- Average Americans care more for pseudoscience than science.
- Teachers do not apply educational research.

APPENDIX B

SCIENCE SUPPLIES, EQUIPMENT, AND MATERIALS OBTAINABLE FROM COMMUNITY SOURCES

This is only a partial list of places in the community that are possible sources of items for a science program in elementary and middle schools. Other sources that should not be overlooked include local factories, the janitor or custodian of the school, the school cafeteria, radio and television repair shops, florists' shops, other teachers in the school, junior and senior high-school science teachers, and so on. The materials are there; it just takes a little looking.

There are times, though, when in spite of the most careful searching, certain pieces of equipment or supplies are not obtainable from local sources; there are also many things that schools should buy from scientific supply houses. A partial list of some selected, reliable scientific supply houses is given in Appendix D.

Dime Store or Department Store

balloons
balls
candles
compasses (magnetic)
cotton (absorbent)
flashlights
food coloring
glues and paste
inks
magnifying glasses
marbles
mechanical toys
mirrors
mousetraps
paperbook matches
scissors
sponges
thermometers

Drugstore

adhesive tape
alcohol (rubbing)
bottles
cigar boxes
cold cream
corks
cotton
dilute acids, preferably 1–5%
dilute H_2O_2 (1 1/2%)
forceps
heat-resistant nursing bottles
limewater
medicine droppers
pipe cleaners

rubber stoppers
soda bicarbonate
spatulas
straws
sulfur
TES-tape™
tincture of iodine, diluted to straw color

Electrical Appliance Shop

bell wire
burned-out fuses and light bulbs
dry cells
electric fans
electric hot plates
flashlight bulbs
flashlights
friction tape
magnets (from old appliances)
soldering iron

Fabric Shop

cardboard tubes
cheesecloth
flannel
knitting needles
leather
needles
netting
scraps of different kinds of fabrics
silk thread
spools

Farm or Dairy

birds' nests
bottles

clay
containers
gravel
hay or straw
humus
insects
leaves
loam
lodestone
rocks
sand
seeds

Fire Department

Samples of materials used to extinguish various types of fires
water pumping equipment

Garden Supply Store

bulbs (tulips, etc.)
fertilizers
flowerpots
garden hose
garden twine
growing plants
labels
lime
seed catalogs
seeds
spray guns
sprinkling cans
trowels and other garden tools

Gas Station

ball bearings
cans

copper tubing
gears
gear transmissions
grease
inner tubes
jacks
maps
pulleys
tools
valves from tires
wheels

Grocery Store

aluminum foil
ammonia
baking soda
borax
candles
cellophane
clothespins
cornstarch
corrugated cardboard boxes
fruits
paper bags
paraffin
plastic wrap
salt
sponges
sugar
vegetables
vinegar
wax
waxed paper

Hardware Store

brace and bits
cement
chisels
clocks
dry-cell batteries
electric push buttons, lamps, and
    sockets
extension cords
files
flashlights
fruit jars

glass cutters
glass friction rods
glass funnels
glass tubing
hammers
hard rubber rods
insulated copper wire
lamp chimneys
metal and metal scraps
nails
nuts and bolts
paints and varnishes
plaster of paris
pulleys
sandpaper
saws
scales
scrap lumber
screening
screwdrivers
screws
steel wool
thermometers (indoor and
    outdoor)
3–6 volt toy electric motors
tin snips
turpentine
wheelbarrow
window glass (broken pieces will do)
wire
yardsticks

Machine Shop

ball bearings
iron filings
iron rods
magnets
nuts and bolts
scrap metals
screws
wire

Medical and Dental Offices and Hospitals

corks
flasks
funnels

glass tubing
hard lenses
litmus paper
microscopes
models, such as teeth
rubber sheeting
rubber stoppers
rubber tubing
test tube holders
test tubes
thermometers
tongue depressors

Music Shop

broken string and drum heads
musical instruments
pitch pipes
tuning forks

Pet shop

air pumps
animal cages
ant houses
aquariums
cages
fish
insects
nets (butterfly, fish, etc.)
plastic tubing
strainers
terrariums

Restaurant, Diner, or Fast-Food Outlet

beverage stirrers
bones (chicken, etc.)
bottles
cans (coffee, 5-gallon size)
drums (ice cream)
five-gallon cans (oil)
food coloring
gallon jars (wide-mouthed, pickles,
    mayonnaise, etc.)
gallon jugs (vinegar)
pie tins
plastic spoons
plastic trays
soda straws

For additional sources of common, easily obtained supplies and apparatus suitable for your elementary- or middle-school science program, see Alfred DeVito and Gerald H. Krockover, "Gear to Gather for the Well-Appointed Science Classroom," in NSTA *Directory of Science Education Suppliers* (Washington, DC: National Science Teachers Association, 1983), 11–12.

APPENDIX C

FREE AND INEXPENSIVE MATERIALS FOR USE IN THE ELEMENTARY SCIENCE CLASSROOM[1]

To ensure maximum returns for your efforts to get free and inexpensive materials, follow these suggestions:

- Addresses (and any prices) may change, so check the sources in libraries or post offices for up-to-date information before mailing.
- Check to see if the source has an 800 toll-free number for faster service.
- Always use school stationery for written requests; include a self-addressed, stamped envelope; be as specific as possible as to what you need; do not ask for large amounts of materials and thank them in advance.
- A thank-you note after receiving materials is always appreciated.

1. "**Ad-vailables.**" *Science and Children* magazine. The National Science Teachers Association, 1742 Connecticut Ave., NW, Washington, DC 20009. $20/8 issues.
   Regular column describes free or low-cost supplementary materials, publications, and events of interest to elementary-school, middle-school, and junior high-school science teachers.
2. **Educators Guide to Free Audio and Visual Materials.** James L. Berger and Walter A. Wittich, eds. Educators Progress Service, 214 Center St., Randolph, WI 53956. 1980. $13.50.
   Subjects, titles, and distributors are included in this annotated listing of videotapes, audiotapes, scripts, and audiodiscs. (Revised yearly.)
3. **Free Stuff for Kids.** Meadowbrook Press, 18318 Minnetonka Blvd., Deephaven, MN 55391.
   Materials on many topics, including science. Single copy free. (Revised yearly.)
4. **Consumer Information Catalog.** Consumer Information Center, Pueblo, CO 81009.

[1]Modified from Paula J. Zsiray and Stephen W. Zsiray, Jr., "Utilizing Free and Inexpensive Materials in the Science Classroom," *Science and Children* 19, no. 5 (February 1982): 20–21.

Describes selected federal publications. Most are free or under $3. (Published quarterly.)
5. **Free for the Taking.** Joseph R. Cooke. Fleming H. Revell Co., 184 Central Ave., Old Tappan, NJ 07675. $7.95.
   Lists free materials on many science subjects.
6. **Educators Guide to Free Films.** John C. Diffor and Mary F. Horkheimer, eds. Educators Progress Service, 214 Center St., Randolph, WI 53956. $17.75.
   Describes films for educational and recreational use. Listed by subject, title, and distributor. (Revised yearly.)
7. **Educators Guide to Free Filmstrips.** John C. Diffor and Mary F. Horkheimer, eds. Educators Progress Service, 214 Center St., Randolph, WI 53956. $13.
   Comprehensive listing of filmstrips, slides, and transparencies. Listed by subject, title, and distributor. (Revised yearly.)
8. **Educational Media Yearbook.** Libraries Unlimited, Inc., P.O. Box 263, Littleton, CO 80160. $20.
   Contains a multimedia information section with an annotated listing of free materials. (Published alternate years.)
9. **FAA Film Catalog.** Federal Aviation Administration, 800 Independence Ave., SW, Washington, DC 20003. 1976.
   Lists over 75 films, filmstrips, and slides. Description, length, and date of film are included.
10. **Forest Service Films Available on Loan.** Contact your local U.S. Forest Service office. 1973.
    Provides a variety of color/sound films on many topics prepared by the U.S. Forest Service.
11. **Free and Inexpensive Learning Experiences.** 1220 Maple Ave., Los Angeles, CA 90015. $24 per year.
    Lists materials on a variety of topics, including the environment and science.
12. **Free and Inexpensive Learning Materials.** Incentive Publications, P.O. Box 12522, Nashville, TN 37212. 1979. $4.95 plus $1 postage.

Excellent coverage of free and inexpensive materials, including science.

13. **Free! The Newsletter of Free Materials and Services.** Ken Haycock, ed. Dyad Services, London, Ontario, Canada. $10 per year. Annotated list of materials evaluated and recommended by teachers and librarians. (Bimonthly.)

14. **Freebies: The Magazine with Something for Nothing.** P.O. Box 5797, Santa Barbara, CA 93108. $6/9 issues. Contains information on how to utilize free and inexpensive materials and where to get them.

15. **Free Magazines for Teachers and Libraries.** Ken Haycock. Ontario Library Association, 2397 Bloor W. Toronto, Ontario, Canada. 1977. International sources of free magazines indexed by subject and title.

16. **Index to Free Educational Materials/Multimedia.** National Information Center for Educational Media, University of Southern California, Los Angeles, CA 90007. 1977. $26.50. More than 20,000 titles indexed by subject and producer/distributor.

17. **Educators Index of Free Materials.** Linda Keenen and Wayne J. Krepel, eds. Educators Progress Service, 214 Center St., Randolph, WI 53956. 1980. $39.50. Annotated listing of free materials, including science topics. (Revised yearly.)

18. **Bibliography of Materials for Environmental Education.** Wisconsin Vocational Studies Center, University of Wisconsin, 1025 West Johnson St., Madison, WI 53706. Bibliography of environmental education materials. Free loan materials included.

19. **"Materials/Information Center."** *Instructor* magazine, 757 Third Ave., New York, NY 10017. $16. Lists catalogs and other resources offered by advertisers in the current issue.

20. **NWF Conservation Education Catalog.** National Wildlife Federation, 1412 Sixteenth St., NW, Washington, DC 20036. 1981. Free.

Lists materials available on conservation of natural resources.

21. **Free and Inexpensive Materials in Environmental Science and Related Disciplines.** Ann Hope Ruzow. Vance Bibliographies, P.O. Box 229, Monticello, IL 61856. 1978. $2.50. Tabulates sources of materials in environmental sciences.

22. **Educators Guide to Free Science Materials.** Mary H. Saterstrom and John W. Renner, eds. Educators Progress Service, 214 Center St., Randolph, WI 53956. 1980. $15.50. Annotated listing of audiovisual and science curriculum enrichment aids. (Revised yearly.)

23. **Science and Technology Programs.** Available from any local Bell Telephone Company. 1980. Lists free science films available from Bell Telephone Co.

24. **Selected U.S. Government Publications.** Superintendent of Documents, U.S. Government Printing Office, Washington, DC 20402. Lists selected government publications, many of which apply to science. (Monthly.)

25. **Free Magazines for Libraries.** Adeline Mercer Smith. McFarland and Co., Inc., P.O. Box 611, Jefferson, NC 28640. 1980. $16.95. Sources of free magazines, many of which deal with science subjects.

26. **Guide to Government Loan Films.** Daniel Sprecher, ed. Serina Press, 70 Kennedy St., Alexandria, VA 22305. 1978. $12.95. Describes more than 3,000 16-mm films available on loan in the U.S.

27. **Guide to Government Loan Films, Vol. 2.** Daniel Sprecher, ed. Serina Press, 70 Kennedy St., Alexandria, VA 22305. 1976. $9.95. Lists films, filmstrips, and slides available on free loan from federal agencies.

28. **The Book of Free Books.** W. M. Tevarrow. Contemporary Books, Inc., 180 North Michigan Ave., Chicago, IL 60601. 1979. Annotated selection of books on a variety of subjects, including science. Book is out of print, but can be found in many university libraries.

APPENDIX D

SELECTED SOURCES OF SCIENTIFIC SUPPLIES, MODELS, LIVING THINGS, KITS, COMPUTERS, AND COLLECTIONS[2]

Accent Science
P. O. Box 1444
Saginaw, MI 48605
(517) 799-8103

American Geological Institute
4220 King St.
Alexandria, VA 22302
(703) 379-2480

American Science and Surplus
601 Linden Pl.
Evanston, IL 60202
(708) 475-8440

Apple Computer, Inc.
20525 Mariani Ave.
Cupertino, CA 95014
(408) 996-1010

Bausch & Lomb
42 East Ave.
Rochester, NY 14603
(716) 338-6000

Bel-Art Products
6 Industrial Rd.
Pequannock, NJ 07440
(201) 694-0500

Carolina Biological Supply Co.
2700 York Road
Burlington, NC 27215
(919) 584-0381

[2]For an extensive 114-page compilation of sources for science equipment/supplies, computer software, educational services, media producers, and publishers, see Phyllis Marcuccio, compiler, *Science Education Suppliers 1991* (Washington, D. C.: National Science Teachers Association, 1991).

Center for Multisensory Learning
Lawrence Hall of Science
University of California
Berkeley, CA 94720
(415) 642-8941

Central Scientific Co. (CENCO)
11222 Melrose Ave.
Franklin Park, IL 60131
(800) 262-3626

Chem Scientific, Inc.
67 Chapel St.
Newton, MA 02158
(617) 527-6626

Connecticut Valley Biological Supply Co., Inc.
62 Valley Rd.
Southampton, MA 01073
(800) 628-7748

Delta Education, Inc.
P. O. Box 915
Hudson, NH 03051-0915
(800) 258-1302

Edmund Scientific Co.
101 E. Gloucester Pike
Barrington, NJ 08007
(609) 573-6240

Educational Activities, Inc.
P. O. Box 392
Freeport, NY 11520
(800) 645-3739

Education Development Center
55 Chapel St.
Newton, MA 02160
(617) 969-7100

Fisher Scientific Co., Educ. Div.
4901 W. Le Moyne Street
Chicago, IL 60651
(800) 955-1177

Frey Scientific Co.
905 Hickory Lane
Mansfield, OH 44905
(419) 589-1900

Hubbard Scientific
1946 Raymond Dr.
Northbrook, IL 60062
(800) 323-8368

Ideal School Supply Co.
11000 S. Lavergne Avenue
Oak Lawn, IL 60453
(800) 323-5131

Lab-Aids, Inc.
249 Trade Zone Dr.
Ronkonkoma, NY 11779
(516) 737-1133

LaPine Scientific Co.
13636 Western Ave.
Blue Island, IL 60406
(708) 388-4030

McKilligan Supply Corporation
435 Main Street
Johnson City, NJ 13790
(607) 798-9335

NASCO
901 Janesville Avenue
Fort Atkinson, WI 53538
(414) 563-2446

Nasco West Inc.
P. O. Box 3837
Modesto, CA 95352
(209) 529-6957

Sargent-Welch Scientific Co.
7300 N. Linder Avenue
Skokie, IL 60077
(800) SARGENT

**Science Kit and Boreal
Laboratories**
777 E. Park Drive
Tonawanda, NY 14150
(800) 828-7777

**Ward's Natural Science
Establishment, Inc.**
5100 West Henrietta Rd.
P. O. Box 92912
Rochester, NY 14692-9012
(800) 962-2660

Wilkens-Anderson Co.
4525 W. Division St.
Chicago, IL 60651
(312) 384-4433

APPENDIX E

NONCOMMERCIAL SOURCES AND CONTAINERS FOR LIVING THINGS

Organisms	Noncommercial Source	Culture Containers
POND SNAILS	Freshwater ponds, creeks	Aquaria, large battery jars, gallon glass jars
LAND SNAILS	Mature hardwood forests: on rocks, fallen logs, damp foliage	Terraria, large battery jars
DAPHNIA	Freshwater ponds: at water's edge, and associated with algae	Gallon glass or plastic jars
ISOPODS AND CRICKETS	Under rocks, bricks, and boards that have lain on the ground for some time; between grass and base of brick buildings	Glass or plastic terraria, plastic sweater boxes (Provide vents in cover.)
MEALWORM BEE-TLES	Corn cribs, around granaries	Gallon glass jars with cheese cloth
FRUIT FLIES	Trap with bananas or apple slices. (Place fruit in a jar with a funnel for a top.)	Tall baby food jars, plastic vials (Punch hole in jar lids, cover with masking tape, and then prick tiny holes in tape with a pin.)
WINGLESS PEA APHIDS*	Search on garden vegetables, e.g., English peas	On pea plants potted in plastic pots, milk cartons (Keep aphids in a large terrarium so they cannot wander to other plants in the school.)
GUPPIES	Obtain free from persons who raise guppies as a hobby. (They are usu-ally glad to reduce the population when they clean tanks.)	Aquaria, large battery jars
CHAMELEONS*	Dense foliage along river banks or railroad tracks (Catch with net or large tea strainer.)	Prepare a cage using a broken aquarium. (Broken glass can be replaced by taping cloth screening along sides.)
FROGS*	Along edges of ponds, ditches, creeks (Catch with large scoop net.)	Large plastic ice chest (Set near a sink so a constant water supply can be provided.)
CHLAMYDOMONAS AND EUGLENA	Freshwater pond	Gallon glass jars, aquaria, battery jars

Organisms	Noncommercial Source	Culture Containers
ELODEA (ANAR-CHARIS)*	Ponds, creeks: usually along edge or in shallows	Aquaria, large battery jars
EELGRASS*	Wading zone of brackish water	Aquaria, large battery jars
DUCKWEED	Edge of ponds or freshwater swamps	Aquaria, large battery jars
COLEUS AND GE-RANIUM	Persons who raise them (Start by rooting cuttings in 1 part sand, 1 part vermiculite, in plastic bags; keep moist.)	Clay pots, milk cartons, tin cans

*These species are difficult to obtain from their natural habitats. Unless you have a convenient source, it is better to buy them commercially. Try a local aquarium or pet shop.

Source: Carolyn H. Hampton and Carol D. Hampton, "The Establishment of a Life Science Center." Reproduced with permission by *Science and Children* 15, no. 7 (April 1978): 9. Copyright 1978 by The National Science Teachers Association, 1742 Connecticut Avenue, N. W., Washington, DC, 20009.

For additional excellent articles on raising and using living things in elementary-school classrooms, see Carolyn H. Hampton, et al., *Classroom Creature Culture: Algae to Anoles. A Collection from the Columns of Science and Children* (Washington, DC: National Science Teachers Association, 1986).

FOOD REQUIREMENTS FOR VARIOUS ANIMALS

Food and Water	Rabbits	Guinea Pigs	Hamsters	Mice	Rats
Daily					
pellets or grain	rabbit pellets: keep dish half full	corn, wheat, or oats	large dog pellets: one or two		canary seeds or oats
green or leafy vegetables, lettuce, cabbage, and celery tops or	keep dish half full 4–5 leaves	2 leaves	1½ tablespoon 1 leaf	2 teaspoons ⅛–¼ leaf	3–4 teaspoons ¼ leaf
grass, plantain, lambs' quarters, clover, alfalfa or	2 handfuls	1 handful	½ handful	—	—
hay, if water is also given					
carrots	2 medium	1 medium			
Twice a week					
apple (medium)	½ apple or salt block	¼ apple	⅛ apple	½ core and seeds	1 core
iodized salt (if not contained in pellets)		sprinkle over lettuce or greens			
corn, canned or fresh, once or twice a week	1/2 ear	1/4 ear	1 tablespoon or ⅓ ear	¼ tablespoon or end of ear	1/2 tablespoon or end of ear
water	should always be available		necessary only if lettuce or greens are not provided		

APPENDIX F
FOOD REQUIREMENTS FOR VARIOUS ANIMALS, *Continued*

Food and Water	Water Turtles	Land Turtles	Small Turtles
Daily			
worms or night crawlers	1 or 2	1 or 2	1/4 inch of tiny earthworm
or			
tubifex or blood worms and/or			enough to cover 1/2 area of a dime
raw chopped beef or meat and fish-flavored dog or cat food	1/2 teaspoon	1/2 teaspoon	
fresh fruit and vegetables		1/4 leaf lettuce or 6–10 berries or 1–2 slices peach, apple, tomato, melon or 1 tablespoon corn, peas, beans	
dry ant eggs, insects, or other commercial turtle food			1 small pinch
water	3/4 of container	always available at room temperature; should be ample for swimming and submersion; large enough for shell	half to 3/4 of container

Food and Water Plants (for Fish)	Goldfish	Guppies
Daily		
dry commercial food	1 small pinch	1 very small pinch; medium-size food for adults; fine-size food for babies
Twice a week		
shrimp—dry—or another kind of dry fish food	4 shrimp pellets or 1 small pinch	dry shrimp food or other dry food: 1 very small pinch
Two or three times a week		
tubifex worms	enough to cover 1/2 area of a dime	enough to cover 1/8 area of a dime
Add enough "conditioned" water to keep tank at required level	allow one gallon per inch of fish; add water of same temperature as that in tank —at least 65° F	all 1/4 – 1/2 gallon per adult fish; add water of same temperature as that in tank —70°–80° F
Plants: cabomba, anarcharis, etc.	should always be available	

Food and Water	Newts	Frogs
Daily		
small earthworms or mealworms or tubifex worms or raw chopped beef	1–2 worms	2–3 worms
	enough to cover 1/2 area of a dime	enough to cover 3/4 area of a dime
water	enough to cover a dime	enough to cover a dime
	should always be available at same temperature as that in tank or at room temperature	

Source: Grace K. Pratt, *How to . . . Care for Living Things in the Classroom* (Washington, DC: National Science Teachers Association, 1978), 11.

APPENDIX G

PLANNING A LEARNING CENTER

State Purpose

The purpose of a learning center should be clear, both to the teacher and the students, and should be stated as a part of the center, e.g., "At this center you will examine some seeds. You will compare sizes, weights, volumes, and shapes of the seeds."

Consider Student Levels

The center must be appropriate for the students who will be using it. The backgrounds and experiences, cognitive levels of operation, socioeconomic levels, maturity levels and levels of independence, and psychomotor levels of students must be defined and used as the basis for planning the activities and expected learning outcomes of the center.

Define Concepts and Skills to Be Developed

A clear statement of the concepts, subconcepts, and skills to be developed by the students using the center is necessary if the center is to be a true teaching/learning situation. Fulfilling this criterion is the point where many centers break down into "busy work."

Outline Expected Learning Outcomes

These statements can be in the form of performance—or behavioral—objectives. Here, a concise statement of what the student is expected to learn as a result of using the center can also serve as a guideline for evaluating student success.

Select Appropriate Activities and Methods

These must be carefully selected to harmonize with the criteria previously mentioned. The activities must serve the purpose of the center and be appropriate to the students using it. They must be designed to assist students in reaching the expected goals. The directions must be clearly within the abilities of students and presented so that students can follow them independently. The materials must be readily available.

Do Evaluations

Use the objectives for the center as a base to determine whether the student has attained the expected learnings, concepts, and skills stated. The center and its materials may need periodic servicing.

Implement Change As Needed

Student performance will provide insight into how each center can be improved or changed to meet the needs of the students it serves, the curriculum, and the objectives and goals stated for the center.

APPENDIX H

SELECTED PROFESSIONAL REFERENCES FOR THE TEACHER OR SCHOOL LIBRARY

Professional Books in Elementary-School Science

Abruscato, Joseph. *Teaching Children Science.* Englewood Cliffs, NJ: Prentice-Hall, 1988.

———, and Hassard, Jack. *Loving and Beyond: Science Teaching for the Humanistic Classroom.* Pacific Palisades, CA: Goodyear Publishing Co., 1976.

Blough, Glenn O., and Schwartz, Julius. *Elementary School Science and How to Teach It,* 7th ed. New York: Holt, Rinehart & Winston, 1984.

Cain, Sandra E. *Sciencing: An Involvement Approach to Elementary Science Methods,* 3rd ed. New York: Merrill/Macmillan, 1990.

Esler, William K., and Esler, Mary K. *Teaching Elementary Science,* 5th ed. Belmont, CA: Wadsworth, 1989.

Friedl, Alfred E. *Teaching Science to Children: An Integrated Approach.* Westminster, MD: Random House, 1986.

Gabel, Dorothy. *Introductory Science Skills.* Prospect Heights, IL: Waveland Press, 1984.

Gega, Peter C. *Science in Elementary Education,* 6th ed. New York: Macmillan, 1990.

Harlan, Jean. *Science Experiences for the Early Childhood Years,* 4th ed. New York: Merrill/Macmillan, 1988.

Harlen, Wynne. *Teaching and Learning Primary Science.* New York: Teachers College Press, 1985.

———, ed. *Primary Science: Taking the Plunge.* London: Heinemann Educational Books, 1986.

Henson, Kenneth T., and Janke, Delmar. *Elementary Science Methods.* New York: McGraw-Hill, 1984.

Jacobson, Willard J., and Begman, Abby Barry. *Science for Children,* 2nd ed. Englewood Cliffs, NJ: Prentice-Hall, 1991.

Kauchak, Donald, and Eggen, Paul. *Exploring Science in Elementary Schools.* Chicago: Rand McNally, 1980.

Lerner, Marjorie E. *Readings in Science Education for the Elementary School.* New York: Macmillan, 1985.

Lorbeer, George C., and Nelson, Leslie W. *Science Activities for Children,* 9th ed. Dubuque, IA: Wm. C. Brown Publishers, 1992.

Lowery, Lawrence, and Verbeeck, Carol. *Explorations in Physical Science.* Belmont, CA: D. S. Lake Publishers, 1987.

McIntyre, Margaret. *Early Childhood and Science.* Washington, DC: National Science Teachers Association, 1984.

Peterson, Rita; Bowyer, Hane; Butts, David; and Bybee, Rodger. *Science and Society: A Sourcebook for Elementary and Junior High School Teachers.* New York: Merrill/Macmillan, 1984.

Renner, John W., and Marek, Edmund A. *The Learning Cycle and Elementary Science Teaching.* Portsmouth, NH: Heinemann, 1988.

Sprung, Barbara, et al. *What Will Happen If . . . Young Children and the Scientific Mind.* New York: Educational Equity Concepts, 1986.

Tolman, Marvin N., and Morton, James O. *Science Curriculum Activities Library Series: Physical Science Activities for Grades 2–8, Earth Science Activities for Grades 2–8, Life Science Activities for Grades 2–8.* West Nyack, NY: Parker Publishing Co., 1986.

Victor, Edward. *Science for the Elementary School,* 6th ed. New York: Macmillan, 1989.

Wasserman, Selma, and Ivany, J. W. George. *Teaching Elementary Science: Who's Afraid of Spiders?* New York: Harper and Row, 1988.

Wolfinger, Donna M. *Teaching Science in the Elementary School.* Boston: Little, Brown, 1984.

Zeitler, William R., and Barufaldi, James P. *Elementary School Science: A Perspective for Teachers.* New York: Longman, 1988.

Science Education Periodicals for Teachers and Children

Children and teachers can keep abreast of the rapid development in science research and science education by referring to the following periodicals. They provide the most information and are an invaluable supplement to science textbooks.

(T) teacher oriented
(C) child oriented

American Biology Teacher. The National Association of Biology Teachers, 19 S. Jackson St., Danville, IL 61832 (Monthly) (T)

American Forests. The American Forestry Association, 919 17th St., N.W., Washington, DC 20006 (Monthly) (T)

The American Journal of Physics. American Association of Physics Teachers, 57 E. 55th St., New York, NY 10022 (Monthly) (T)

The Aquarium. Innes Publishing Co., Philadelphia, PA 19107 (Monthly) (C & T)

Audubon Magazine. The National Audubon Society, 1130 Fifth Ave., New York, NY 10028 (Bimonthly) (C & T)

Biology & General Science Digest. W. M. Welch Co., 1515 Sedgwick St., Chicago, IL 60610 (Free) (T)

Chemistry. Science Service, 1719 16th St. N.W., Washington, DC 20009 (Monthly) (T)

Cornell Rural School Leaflets. New York State College of Agriculture, Ithaca, NY 14850 (Quarterly) (T)

Current Science and Aviation. American Education Publications, Discover, Time Inc., 3435 Wilshire Blvd., Los Angeles, CA 90010 (C & T)

Enter. Enter, One Disk Dr., P. O. Box 2686, Boulder, CO 80322 (10 issues a year) (C)

Geotimes. American Geological Institute, 1515 Massachusetts Ave., N.W., Washington, DC 20025 (Monthly) (T)

Grade Teacher. Educational Publishing Co., Darien, CT 06820 (Monthly Sept.–June) (T)

Journal of Research in Science Teaching. John Wiley & Sons, 605 Third Ave., New York, NY 10016 (T)

Junior Astronomer. Benjamin Adelman, 4211 Colie Dr., Silver Springs, MD 20906 (C & T)

Junior Natural History. American Museum of Natural History, New York, NY 10024 (Monthly) (C & T)

Monthly Evening Sky Map. Box 213, Clayton, MO 63105 (Monthly) (C & T)

My Weekly Reader. American Education Publications, Education Center, Columbus, OH 43216 (Weekly during the school year) (C)

National Geographic. National Geographic Society, 1146 Sixteenth St., N.W., Washington, DC 20036 (Monthly) (C & T)

Natural History. American Museum of Natural History, 79th St. and Central Park West, New York, NY 10024 (Monthly) (C & T)

Nature Magazine. American Nature Association, 1214 15th St., N.W., Washington, DC (Monthly Oct. to May and bimonthly June to Sept.) (C & T)

Our Dumb Animals. Massachusetts Society for the Prevention of Cruelty to Animals, Boston, MA 02115 (Monthly) (C & T)

Outdoors Illustrated. National Audubon Society, 1000 Fifth Ave., New York, NY 10028 (Monthly) (C & T)

Physics and Chemistry Digest. W. M. Welch Co., 1515 Sedwick St., Chicago, IL 60610 (Free) (T)

Popular Science Monthly. Popular Science Publishing Co., 335 Lexington Ave., New York, NY 10016 (Monthly) (C & T)

Readers Guide to Oceanography. Woods Hole Oceanographic Institute, Woods Hole, MA 02543 (Monthly) (T)

School Science and Mathematics. Central Association Science and Mathematics Teachers, P. O. Box 48, Oak Park, IL 60305 (Monthly 9 times a year) (T)

Science. American Association for the Advancement of Science, 1515 Massachusetts Ave., N.W., Washington, DC 20025 (T)

Science and Children. National Science Teachers Association, Washington, DC 20036 (Monthly 8 times a year) (C & T)

Science Digest. 959 8th Ave., New York, NY 10019 (Monthly) (T)

Science Education. Science Education Inc., C. M. Pruitt, University of Tampa, Tampa, FL 33606 (5 times yearly) (T)

Science Newsletter. Science Service, Inc., 1719 N. Street, N.W., Washington, DC 20036 (Weekly) (T)

Science Teacher. National Science Teachers Association, National Education Association, 1742 Connecticut Ave., N.W., Washington, DC 20036 (Monthly—Sept.–May) (T)

Science World. Scholastic Magazines, Inc., 50 W. 44 St., New York, NY 10036 (T & C)

Scientific American. 415 Madison Ave., New York, NY 10017 (Monthly) (T)

Scientific Monthly. The American Association for the Advancement of Science, 1515 Massachusetts Ave., Washington, DC 20025 (Monthly) (T)

Sky and Telescope. Sky Publishing Corp., Harvard College Observatory, Cambridge, MA 02138 (Monthly) (C & T)

Space Science. Benjamin Adelman, 4211 Colie Dr., Silver Springs, MD 20906 (Monthly—during school year) (Formerly *Junior Astronomer*) (C & T)

3-2-1 Contact. Children's Television Workshop, P. O. Box 2933, Boulder, CO 80322 (10 issues per year) (C & T)

Tomorrow's Scientists. National Science Teachers Association, Washington, DC 20036 (8 issues per year) (T)

Weatherwise. American Meteorological Society, 3 Joy St., Boston, MA 02108 (Monthly) (T)

APPENDIX I

PROFESSIONAL SOCIETIES FOR SCIENCE TEACHERS AND SUPERVISORS

American Association for the Advancement of Science
1515 Massachusetts Ave., N.W.
Washington, DC 20005

American Association of Physics Teachers
335 E. 45th St.
New York, NY 10017

American Chemical Society
Chemical Education Division
1155 Sixteenth St., N.W.
Washington, DC 20036

Association for Supervision and Curriculum Development
1201 Sixteenth St., N.W.
Washington, DC 20036

Central Association of Science and Mathematics Teachers
(No permanent headquarters.
Current officers listed in *School Science and Mathematics*.)

Council for Elementary Science International
1742 Connecticut Ave., N.W.
Washington, DC 20036

National Association of Biology Teachers
1420 N. Street, N.W.
Washington, DC 20005

National Association for Research in Science Teaching
(No permanent headquarters.)

National Association of Geology Teachers
(No permanent headquarters.
Current officers listed in *Journal of Geological Education*.)

National Science Teachers Association
1742 Connecticut Ave., N.W.
Washington, DC 20036

APPENDIX J

SAFETY SUGGESTIONS FOR MINDS-ON/HANDS-ON ACTIVITIES

1. Do not permit students to handle science supplies, chemicals, or equipment in the classroom until they have been given specific instructions in their use.

2. Instruct students to report immediately to the teacher
   - any equipment in the classroom that appears to be in an unusual or improper condition,
   - any chemical reactions that appear to be proceeding in an abnormal fashion,
   - any personal injury or damage to clothing caused by a science activity, no matter how trivial it may appear.

3. Prevent loose clothing and hair from coming into contact with any science supplies, chemicals, equipment, or sources of heat or flame.

4. Do not allow science materials, such as chemicals, to be transported through hallways by unsupervised students or during a time when other students are moving through the hallways.

5. Instruct students in the proper use of sharp instruments, such as pins, knives, and scissors, before they use such objects.

6. Instruct students never to touch, taste, or inhale unknown chemicals.

7. Instruct students never to pour chemicals (reagents) back into stock bottles, and never to exchange stoppers or caps on bottles.

8. Warn students of the dangers in handling hot glassware or other equipment. Be sure proper devices for handling hot objects are available.

9. Check electrical wiring on science equipment for frayed insulation, exposed wires, and loose connections.

10. Instruct students in the proper use of eye-protection devices before they do activities in which there is a potential risk to eye safety.

11. Give appropriate, specific safety instructions prior to conducting any activity in which there is a potential risk to student safety, and provide appropriate reminders during the activity.

12. Instruct students in the location and use of specialized safety equipment, such as fire extinguishers, fire blankets, or eye baths, when that equipment might be required by the science activity.

13. Instruct students in the proper care and handling of classroom pets, fish, plants, or other live organisms used as part of science activities.

14. Have sufficient lighting to ensure that activities can be conducted safely.

15. For students with handicapping conditions or special needs, ensure safe access to the facility, equipment, and materials. Consider:
    - access to laboratories and equipment, placement of chemicals, distances required for reaching, and height and arrangement of tables.
    - physical accessibility to equipment needed in cases of emergency.

16. Provide practice sessions for safety procedures.

Source: *Elementary Science Syllabus* 49.

A P P E N D I X K   MODEL FOR PROBLEM SOLVING (SAMPLE)

Steps	Focus questions/question stems

Planning	1. What is the problem?
	2. What background information do I already have?
	   ■ What do I already know about . . . ?
	3. What new information do I need?
	4. What procedure or sequence of actions do I need to follow?
	   ■ How can I find what I need to know about . . . ?
	5. How will I know when I have solved the problem?

Obtaining Data	What information is needed? ■ What are the properties of . . . ? ■ What are the names of . . . ? ■ What kinds of . . . ? ■ How long, wide, big . . . is it? ■ How much does it weigh? ■ What color is it? ■ How hot is . . . ?
Organizing Data	In what useful way(s) can the information be organized? ■ Which ones belong to this group? ■ In what order do these . . . belong? ■ What categories are there? ■ How can this be graphed? ■ What is the result of this . . . calculation?
Analyzing Data	What useful analyses can be made of the organized information? ■ In what ways does . . . compare/contrast with . . . ? ■ What seemed to be the effect of . . . ? ■ What seemed to cause . . . ? ■ What must have been the pattern (sequence) of events? ■ What factors (variables) are involved? ■ What assumptions were made?
Generalizing and/or Synthesizing from Data	What can be drawn from the analyses of information? ■ How can I explain . . . ? ■ How can I show I need to . . . ? ■ What is the principle of . . . ? ■ If this continues, then what is likely to happen? ■ What can I predict? ■ What might happen if I . . . ? ■ What model shows what we know about . . . ? ■ What new problems does this suggest? ■ How does . . . apply to . . . ?
Decision Making	1. What decision needs to be made? 2. What are the alternative choices and the reasons for each? 3. What are the consequences of each alternative? 4. Who will be affected by each possible choice and in what way? 5. What values are directly related to each choice, and how do they relate to it? 6. Which choice is the best choice?

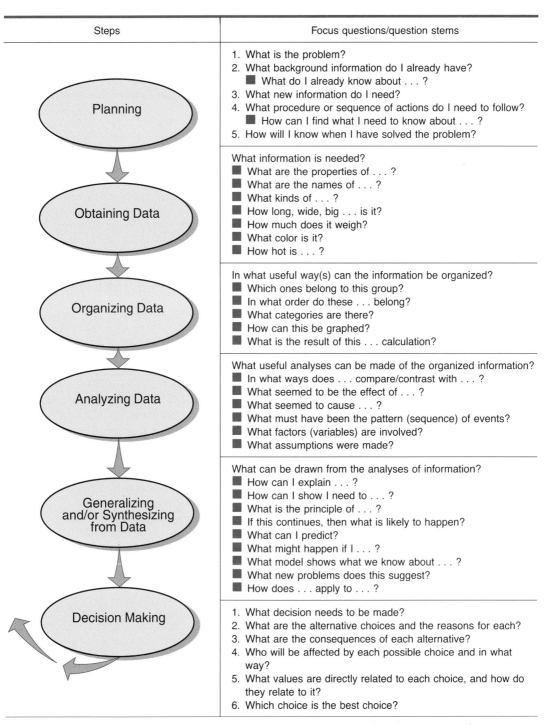

Source: *Elementary Science Syllabus,* 18–19. Reproduced with permission by the University of the State of New York. Copyright 1985 by The University of the State of New York, The State Education Department, Division of Program Development, Albany, NY 12234.

Skills	Products
■ Communicating information ■ Creating models ■ Formulating hypotheses ■ Manipulating ideas ■ Predicting ■ Questioning ■ Recording data ■ Using cues	1. A statement of the problem 2. List of facts (background information) 3. List of questions (related to later steps in the process) 4. Sequential plan (a list of tasks, student assignments, and times for completion) 5. Sketch or description of the expected (predicted) final product
■ Acquiring information ■ Developing vocabulary ■ Manipulating materials ■ Measuring ■ Observing ■ Recording data ■ Using cues ■ Using numbers	■ Collections ■ Counts ■ Definitions ■ Lists ■ Photographs ■ Sketches ■ Tape recordings
■ Classifying ■ Communicating information ■ Creating models ■ Manipulating ideas ■ Manipulating materials ■ Replicating ■ Using numbers	■ Calculations or computations ■ Charts, tables ■ Diagrams, scale drawings ■ Graphs ■ Groups, categories of information ■ Outline ■ Sorted objects
■ Identifying variables ■ Inferring ■ Interpreting data ■ Manipulating ideas ■ Using cues	■ Description of a pattern or sequence ■ List of variables ■ Statements of cause and effect relationships ■ Statements of similarities and differences ■ Summary
■ Acquiring information ■ Communicating information ■ Creating models ■ Formulating hypotheses ■ Generalizing ■ Manipulating ideas ■ Predicting ■ Questioning	■ A model or simulation ■ A new hypothesis ■ A new prediction, problem, theory ■ Applications to new situations ■ Statements of principles ■ Statements which accept or reject hypotheses ■ Statements which confirm or do not confirm predictions ■ Written report
■ Acquiring information ■ Communicating information ■ Making decisions ■ Manipulating ideas ■ Questioning	1. Statement of the decision to be made 2. List of alternative choices, supported by reasons 3. List of consequences of each alternative 4. List of persons directly affected by each choice and the way each is affected 5. List of values related to each choice supported by statements of how the values relate 6. A personal choice, supported by defendable reasons for the choice

APPENDIX L

CONSTRUCTING STORAGE AREAS FOR SUPPLIES AND HOUSES FOR LIVING THINGS

Your classroom has unused space that can be used for storage, such as spaces below window ledges, countertops, sinks, above and around heating units (radiators), and even under student desks.

You can purchase excellent commercially made cabinets that fit any of these spaces, or your students and/or your custodian and you can construct them. With some creativity, you and your students can arrange these cabinets in a variety of ways.

Small Items Storage. With a guided discovery activities science program, you will constantly need to store many small items. Shoe, corrugated cardboard, cigar, and other small boxes provide space for collecting, organizing, and storing small, readily available materials for particular science areas. The following diagrams illustrate how to construct and store shoe boxes for small science items. Cardboard

or clear plastic shoe boxes may be used. You may also use large cardboard boxes for storage, placing them in easily obtained wood or steel shelving units especially designed for this purpose. Your custodian can help with this.

SHOE BOX COLLECTION

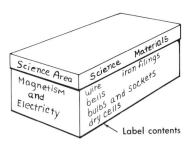

Label contents

STORAGE OF SHOE BOX COLLECTIONS

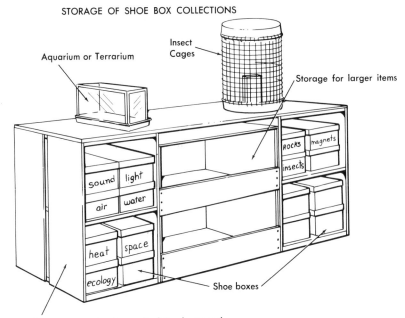

Four orange crates, two vertical, two horizontal

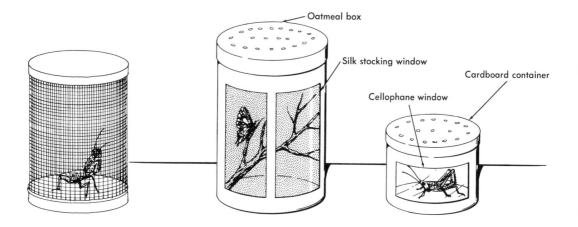

- Oatmeal box
- Silk stocking window
- Cellophane window
- Cardboard container

Living Things Storage

Encourage your students to bring small animals (including insects) and plants into your classroom. To be well-prepared, have the following kinds of containers available:

- Insect cages
- Small animal cages
- Aquariums
- Terrariums

Insect Cages. Use small cake pans, coffee can lids, or covers from ice cream cartons for the cage cover and base. Roll wire screening into a cylinder to fit the base, then lace the screening together with a strand of wire.

You can cut windows in a paper coffee container, oatmeal box, or another suitable cardboard or styrofoam container. Cut out the window and glue clear plastic wrap, cellophane, silk, a nylon stocking or some other thin cloth over the opening as shown.

Another home for insects such as ants that live in the soil can be made by filling a wide-mouthed quart or gallon pickle or mayonnaise jar with soil up to two inches from the top. Cover the jar with a nylon stocking and place it in a pan of water. Put the insects in and cover the jar with black construction paper to simulate the darkness of being underground.

Small Animal Cages. You can also use some of the insect cages for other small animals. Larger animals can be housed in cages that you and your students construct from window screening. Cut and fold the screening as shown in the diagram. Use nylon screening or be very careful of the sharp edges of wire screening. Tack or staple three sides of the screening to a wooden base and hook the other side for a door.

For housing *nongnawing* animals, you will need a wooden box and sleeping materials such as wood shavings. *Gnawing* animals need a wire cage. A bottle with a one-hole stopper and tubing hung on the

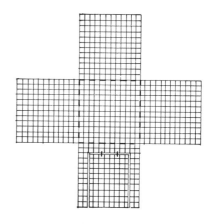

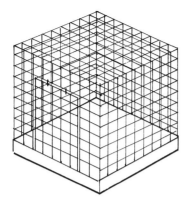

side of the cage will supply water. Before proceeding, consult publications such as *Science and Children* and read some of the articles on the care and maintenance of various animals.

Terrariums. The word *terrarium* means "little world." In setting up a terrarium for any animal, you should try to duplicate in miniature the environment in which the animal originally lived. You can make a terrarium with five pieces of glass (four sides and bottom) taped together. The top should be made of glass as well, but should have a section cut out to allow access to the terrarium. Place the finished glass terrarium in a large cookie or cake pan. Commercially made terrariums are also available.

Another simple terrarium can be made from a two-liter, plastic soda pop bottle, charcoal, pebbles, topsoil, small plants, and scissors (see the diagram).

Suggestions for caring for plants and animals and for setting up different kinds of terrariums can be obtained from

■ Biological Supply House, Inc., 8200 South Hoyne Avenue, Chicago, IL 60620. Free by writing on school stationery for Turtox Service Leaflets, especially: No. 10 —*The School Terrarium* and No. 25 —*Feeding Aquarium and Terrarium Animals.*

■ NSTA Publications, 1742 Connecticut Avenue, N. W., Washington, D. C. 20009. Send $1.50 for How to Do It Pamphlets, especially: *How to Care for Living Things in the Classroom,* by Grace K. Pratt (Stock No. PB 38/4).

Soak the bottle in warm water to remove labels and glue. Carefully pry the bottom (a) from the bottle (b) so the bottom remains intact. Turn the bottle on its side. Rub your hand over it to find the ridge. With scissors, make a slit about 1.5 cm above the ridge. Cut all the way around the bottle at that level, staying above the ridge. Discard the top of the bottle and the cap.

Put layers of charcoal, pebbles, and topsoil into part a. Select and arrange the plants in the soil. You can add moss, bark, or small ornaments to your terrarium. Moisten, but do not saturate, the soil. Invert bottle (b) upside down into a. Push down gently to seal. Your terrarium is ready!

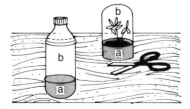

Constructing a soda pop bottle terrarium

Source: Virginia Gilmore, "Helpful Hints—Coca-Cola© Bottle Terrarium." Reproduced with permission by *Science and Children* 16, no. 7 (April 1979): 47. Copyright 1979 by the National Science Teachers Association, 1742 Connecticut Avenue, N. W., Washington, D. C. 20009.

Computer and Telecommunications Glossary

For those with little or no experience with computers or telecommunications, here is a beginner's list of common terms and definitions.

Address A number or name that tells where to find a place in a computer's memory.

Authoring Language A Computer program which helps a person write lessons or other programs for a computer.

BASIC Stands for **B**eginners **A**ll-Purpose **S**ymbolic **I**nstruction **C**ode, which is an easily learned language that all microcomputers use.

Baud Rate The speed at which telecommuted data are transmitted, measured in bits per second. Common baud rates are 300 and 1200.

Binary Code A code for writing information for a computer using 1s and 0s to stand for numbers and letters.

Bit Stands for **BI**nary digi**T**, the basic unit for computer memory.

Boot The start-up program used when the computer is turned on, and referred to as in "boot the disk."

Bug A mistake in a computer program or a problem with the hardware. To get rid of a "bug," you "debug" the program.

Bulletin Board System A computerized system on which messages are left for others to read; BBS for short.

Byte A group of bits: one byte is eight bits. It takes one byte to store each unit of information. For instance, the word *love* requires four bytes.

CAI Teaching by computer or **C**omputer-**A**ssisted (Aided) **I**nstruction.

Cathode Ray Tube (CRT) A technical name for the computer's monitor or TV screen that visually shows its stored electronic data.

Central Processing Unit (CPU) The heart of the computer dealing with information.

Chip A very tiny piece of silicon that carries many electrical signals.

COBOL Stands for **CO**mmon **B**usiness **O**riented **L**anguage, and is another computer language used mostly for business applications.

Communication Satellite A satellite used to facilitate telecommunications.

Dedicated Phone Line A telephone line which is used only for modem telecommunications in order to eliminate the possibility of interruption, which can garble the transmission.

Download To transfer information (files) from one computer from another.

Electronic Mail Personal messages sent electronically and called E-mail for short. To send or receive a message requires an I. D. number and password.

Information Utility A company from which you can access information via computer. Examples are CompuServe and THE SOURCE.

Keyboard Similar to a typewriter keyboard and used to type information into a computer.

K An abbreviation for **K**ilo, which means 1,000, and is the unit of computer memory. 64K of memory equals 64,000 bytes. The larger the K your computer has, the more memory or amount of data it can store.

Log-In To sign in on a computer.

LOGO Another computer language used widely in education. It includes a graphic system called "turtle graphics." LOGO is a very interactive language.

Menu A display shown on the monitor or TV screen that gives a list of options—like a table of contents in a book.

Modem Stands for **MOD**ulator-**DEM**odulator. This is a hardware unit that allows a computer to transmit or receive data over a telephone line. The modem may be external or internal to the computer.

On-Line Being electronically connected to another computer.

Output The information a computer sends out. To see this information, an output device is needed, such as a monitor or TV screen or printer.

PASCAL A high-level computer language named for the French mathematician, Blaise Pascal.

Peripheral Any piece of equipment connected to a computer, such as a monitor, modem, or printer.

PILOT Stands for **P**rogrammed **I**nquiry **L**earning **O**n **T**eaching and is an easy language used primarily by educators to create CAI programs.

Print Out A paper copy of electronically stored information from a computer produced by a computer-connected printer. Often called "hard copy."

Program A set of instructions that tells the computer what to do and how to do it. See the many programming languages listed previously in this glossary.

RAM Stands for **R**andom **A**ccess **M**emory. While the computer is on, it stores information for a short period of time.

ROM Stands for **R**ead **O**nly **M**emory. This information can only be "read" by the computer, cannot be changed, and is not erased when the machine is turned off.

Software The programs and data used to control the computer. Programmers write software for microcomputers.

Telecommunications The transmission of signals from one computer to another over long distances, using telephone lines, microwaves, and/or satellites.

Teleconferencing A number of computer users can link up and hold a conversation, just like a "conference call" by telephone.

Upload To transfer information (files) from your computer to another.

Word Processing A way of making written communication more creative by allowing the user to change words, rearrange paragraphs, correct spelling and grammar, and perform other editing functions. When writing is completed electronically, hard copies are secured from the computer-attached printer.

Piagetian Glossary

Abstraction   Mental activity or feedback involving the performing of operations.

Accommodation   The modification or fabrication of schemata (mental structures that adapt and change with cognitive development). The application of an existing structure to a new situation in the environment.

Adaptation   A cognitive, continuous process consisting of assimilation and accommodation.

Affectivity   Behavior involving feelings, interest, values, attitudes, maturation.

Assimilation   The process of integrating new perceptual stimuli into behavioral patterns or schemata.

Associativity   The process of putting together elements in different ways to get the same result, or the process of reaching the same goal by different paths.

Centration   The tendency of an organism to focus only on one part of a stimulus, e.g., on the length of a candy bar rather than the length and width together.

Cognitive Process   Mental process, involving reasoning, perceiving, memorizing, imagining, abstracting, etc.

Concrete Operation   A stage of mental development involving the individual's performing such logical operations as adding, subtracting, seriating, classifying, numbering, and reversing.

Conservation   The realization that changing an object physically, e.g., by shape, length, direction, or position, does not alter the amount present.

Egocentricity   The tendency of an individual to perceive others as though they have his identical schemata or believe that the way he sees something is the only way it can be interpreted.

Epistemology   The branch of philosophy concerned with the nature of knowledge. To Piaget it was open to psychological investigation, i.e., what knowledge or mental operations are learned before others, what is the sequence of mental abilities?

Equilibration   The regulating process by which the individual continuously changes and develops.

Formal Operation   A stage of mental development involving an individual's performing hypothetical, propositional, and reflexive thinking.

Identity   The operation of comparing, contrasting, or giving an example of a concept. The mind compares two sets (one-to-one correspondence) to see if they are equal.

Intelligence   All the mental processes and coordinations of these that structure the behavior of the individual. To Piaget, intelligence was not fixed; it grows.

Internalization   The process of making symbols, language, memories, and images a part of the mind.

Intuitive   A tendency to make judgments without using the mind to reason about them.

Knowledge   All that has been perceived and grasped by the mind.

Learning   The process of assimilating or accommodating.

Measurement   The ability to number, order, or perform seriation.

Memory The act of using mental images to reconstitute the past through recognition, evocation, etc. It differs from perception by not being dependent upon the present and from intelligence by not being concerned with solving problems.

Object Permanence The realization that an object continues to exist when not present in the perceptual field.

Operation A mental action, e.g., multiplying, combining, classifying, etc. It can be reversible.

Ordering or Seriating Placing objects in order in a series.

Perception The process of being aware of something through the senses.

Preoperational A stage after the sensorimotor, but prior to the concrete-operational period, in which children learn symbols, names, and language, but cannot yet perform operations.

Reversibility The process of reversing a mental operation.

Sensorimotor The first stage of mental development in which the knowledge the child learns is related to sensory inputs and her motor or muscular responses.

Stages A period of development or intelligence characterized by certain general mental structures.

Structure Mental organization or coordination in systematizing information. It may involve the interrelating parts or schemata.

Transformation The process of something constantly changing in appearance.

Transitivity The process of being able to perform the following type of mental operation: A>B, B>C, therefore A>C.

INDEX